HEIDEGGER AND THE QUESTION OF NATIONAL SOCIALISM:
DISCLOSURE AND GESTALT

NEW STUDIES IN PHENOMENOLOGY AND HERMENEUTICS

Kenneth Maly, General Editor

New Studies in Phenomenology and Hermeneutics aims to open up new approaches to classical issues in phenomenology and hermeneutics. Thus its intentions are the following: to further the work of Edmund Husserl, Maurice Merleau-Ponty, and Martin Heidegger – as well as that of Paul Ricoeur, Hans-Georg Gadamer, and Emmanuel Levinas; to enhance phenomenological thinking today by means of insightful interpretations of texts in phenomenology as they inform current issues in philosophical study; to inquire into the role of interpretation in phenomenological thinking: to take seriously Husserl's term *phenomenology* as 'a science which is intended to supply the basic instrument for a rigorously scientific philosophy and, in its consequent application, to make possible a methodical reform of all the sciences'; to take up Heidegger's claim that 'what is own to phenomenology, as a philosophical "direction," does not rest in being *real*. Higher than reality stands *possibility*. Understanding phenomenology consists solely in grasping it as possibility'; to practice *phenomenology* as 'underway,' as 'the *praxis* of the self-showing of the matter for thinking,' as 'entering into the movement of enactment-thinking.'

The commitment of this book series is also to provide English translations of significant works from other languages. In summary, **New Studies in Phenomenology and Hermeneutics** intends to provide a forum for a full and fresh thinking and rethinking of the way of phenomenology and interpretive phenomenology, that is, hermeneutics.

BERNHARD RADLOFF

Heidegger and the Question of National Socialism

Disclosure and Gestalt

UNIVERSITY OF TORONTO PRESS
Toronto Buffalo London

ISBN 978-0-8020-9315-8

Printed on acid-free paper

Library and Archives Canadian Cataloguing in Publication

Radloff, Bernhard, 1952–
    Heidegger and the question of National Socialism : disclosure
    and gestalt / Bernhard Radloff.

    (New studies in phenomenology and hermeneutics)
    Includes bibliographical references and index.
    ISBN 978-0-8020-9315-8

    1. Heidegger, Martin, 1889–1976 – Political and social views.
    I. Title.   II. Series: New studies in phenomenology and hermeneutics
    (Toronto, Ont.)

    B3279.H49R32 2007   193   C2007-903463-2

This book has been published with the help of a grant from the Canadian
Federation for the Humanities and Social Sciences, through the Aid to
Scholarly Publications Program, using funds provided by the Social Sciences
and Humanities Research Council of Canada.

University of Toronto Press acknowledges the financial assistance to its
publishing program of the Canada Council for the Arts and the Ontario Arts
Council.

University of Toronto Press acknowledges the financial support for its
publishing activities of the Government of Canada through the Book
Publishing Industry Development Program (BPIDP).

040208-p8

Contents

Acknowledgments

Work on this project was supported by the Faculty of Arts, University of Ottawa, in the form of research grants enabling archival research in Germany. Publication was supported by the Research and Publications Committee, Faculty of Arts, University of Ottawa.

Earlier versions of parts of this book have appeared as follows:
Chapter 2 first appeared as 'Heidegger and the Question of Rhetoric,' *Existentia* (Budapest) 11 (Fall 2001): 437–456. Chapter 4 first appeared as 'Volk, Work, and Historicity in Heidegger's *Logik* of 1934,' *Existentia* 12 (2002): 317–44. Section 3 of chapter 7 first appeared as 'An Ontology of Limit: Heidegger's Retrieval of Aristotle, the Work of Art, and the Possibility of the Political,' *Existentia* 12 (2003): 249–74. Finally, the first version of the Conclusion appeared as 'Heidegger's Critique of Imperial Truth,' *Existentia* 10 (Fall 2000): 51–68. My thanks to Gábor Ferge, editor-in-chief of *Existentia,* and the Societas Philosophia Classica for permission to republish.

Chapter 6 first appeared in two parts: 'Heidegger and Carl Schmitt: The Historicity of the Political' (Part One), *Heidegger Studies* 20 (2004): 83–99, and 'Heidegger and Carl Schmitt: The Historicity of the Political' (Part Two), *Heidegger Studies* 21 (2005): 75–94; reprinted here by permission of Duncker and Humblot (Berlin).

Part of chapter 3, originally published as 'Heidegger's Retrieval of Aristotle and the Relation of Volk and Science in the Rector's Address of 1933,' *Philosophy Today* 47:1 (Spring 2003): 3–22, is reprinted by permission of DePaul University. Another part of chapter 3, first published as 'Heidegger and the Question of the Fundamental Attunement of Science in the Political Situation of 1933–1934,' *International Studies in Philosophy* 37, no. 4 (2005): 51–70, is reprinted here by permission.

My thanks also to Len Husband and to Richard Ratzlaff of the University of Toronto Press for their guidance and support in the publication process, and to James Thomas for his fine work copy-editing the typescript for the Press. I am also grateful to the anonymous reviewers of this book for their helpful and insightful comments.

Many of the ideas which came to form this book first emerged in a graduate seminar on Heidegger and Derrida held at the University of Ottawa in 1996. I would like to thank the members of that seminar, and especially Dean Lauer, David Hindman, James Parsons, Omid Payrow Shabani, and Timothy Wilson.

This book has been published with the help of a grant from the Canadian Federation for the Humanities and Social Sciences, through the Aid to Scholarly Publications Program, using funds provided by the Social Sciences and Humanities Research Council of Canada.

Abbreviations

Page references to the original text will be followed by the solidus (/) and page references to the translation, where applicable. The translation of *Sein and Zeit* (*Being and Time*) by Joan Stambaugh is indicated by SZ; in those cases where the translation by Macquarrie and Robinson is used this will be indicated by SZ-MR.

GA16, no. 121	– 'Das Geleitwort der Universität'
GA16, no. 124	– 'Zur Eröffnung der Schulungskurse für die Notstandsarbeiter der Stadt an der Universität'
GA16, no. 125	– 'Der Ruf zum Arbeitsdienst'
GA16, no. 126	– 'Das unverbrauchte Alemannentum'
GA16, no. 154	– '25 Jahre nach unserem Abiturium'
GA16, no. 155	– 'Die deutsche Universität'
GA16, no. 156	– 'Zur Einrichtung der Dozentenschule'
GA16, no. 158	– 'Die gegenwärtige Lage und die künftige Aufgabe der deutschen Philosophie'
GA16, no. 184	– 'Erläuterungen und Grundsätzliches'
GA16, no. 285	– 'Gedenkworte zu Schlageter'
GA18	– *Grundbegriffe der Aristotelischen Philosophie*
GA19	– *Platon: Sophistes*
GA20	– *Prolegomena zur Geschichte des Zeitbegriffs*
GA22	– *Die Grundbegriffe der Antiken Philosophie*
GA 24	– *Die Grundbegriffe der Phänomenologie*
GA25	– *Phänomenologische Interpretation von Kants* Kritik der reinen Vernunft
GA26	– *Metaphysische Anfangsgründe der Logik im Ausgang von Leibniz*
GA27	– *Einleitung in die Philosophie*
GA29/30	– *Die Grundbegriffe der Metaphysik*
GA31	– *Vom Wesen der menschlichen Freiheit*
GA33	– *Aristoteles, Metaphysik Theta 1–3*
GA34	– *Vom Wesen der Wahrheit*
GA36/37	– *Sein und Wahrheit*
GA38	– *Logik als Frage nach dem Wesen der Sprache*
GA39	– *Hölderlins* Germanien *und* Der Rhein
GA40	– *Einführung in die Metaphysik*
GA42	– *Schelling*
GA43	– *Nietzsche: Der Wille zur Macht als Kunst*
GA45	– *Grundfragen der Philosophie*
GA51	– *Grundbegriffe*
GA53	– *Hölderlins Hymne 'Der Ister'*
GA54	– *Parmenides*
GA55	– *Heraklit*
GA56/57	– *Zur Bestimmung der Philosophie*
GA58	– *Grundprobleme der Phänomenologie*
GA61	– *Phänomenologische Interpretationen zu Aristoteles*

GA63	– *Ontologie*
GA65	– *Beiträge zur Philosophie (Vom Ereignis)*
GA69	– *Die Geschichte des Seyns*
GA90	– *Zu Ernst Jünger*
LTH	Schmitt, *Der Leviathan in der Staatslehre Thomas Hobbes*
NI	Heidegger, *Nietzsche*, vol. 1
NII	– *Nietzsche*, vol. 2
PE	Baeumler, *Politik und Erziehung*
PL	Heidegger, 'Platons Lehre von der Wahrheit'
PR	Schmitt, *Politische Romantik*
PT	– *Politische Theologie*
RK	– *Römischer Katholizismus und politische Form*
SBV	– *Staat, Bewegung, Volk*
SU	Heidegger, 'Die Selbstbehauptung der deutschen Universität'
SW	Jünger, *Sämtliche Werke*
SZ	Heidegger, *Sein und Zeit* (*Being and Time*, trans. Stambaugh)
SZ-MR	– *Being and Time* (Macquarrie and Robinson, trans.)
UAR	Schmitt, *Über die drei Arten des rechtswissenschaftlichen Denkens*
UK	Heidegger, 'Der Ursprung des Kunstwerkes'
UK-HS	– 'Vom Ursprung des Kunstwerkes: Erste Ausarbeitung'
UL	Jünger, 'Über die Linie'
UM	Heidegger, 'Überwindung der Metaphysik'
VGE	Krieck, *Völkischer Gesamtstaat und nationale Erziehung*
VL	Schmitt, *Verfassungslehre*
WG	Heidegger, 'Vom Wesen des Grundes'
WM	– 'Was ist Metaphysik?'
WP	– 'Die Zeit des Weltbildes'
WW	– 'Vom Wesen der Wahrheit'
WWH	Krieck, *Wissenschaft Weltanschauung Hochschulreform*
ZS	Heidegger, 'Zur Seinsfrage'

HEIDEGGER AND THE QUESTION OF NATIONAL SOCIALISM:
DISCLOSURE AND GESTALT

Introduction

The Problem of Formlessness

The object of this book is to investigate the philosophical foundations and cultural context of Martin Heidegger's political and aesthetic thought in relation to the question of being, the question which determined the course of the philosopher's thought. In particular, I will focus on the question of 'form,' in the sense of *gestalt*, as the guiding thread which determined not only Heidegger's understanding of the being of beings in the 1930s, but also German conservative thought in the arts, technology, and political science. The question of gestalt signifies the necessity of giving form to an existence impacted by the threat of formlessness emerging from technology and social upheaval. According to Heidegger, however, the cultural critique of the conservatives failed to grasp the roots of formlessness in the very metaphysical destiny of the West. Consequently a concept of form, as gestalt, has to be won from the deconstruction of metaphysics as realized in technology.

Heidegger's understanding of gestalt offers entrance into the meaning of being as he unfolds it after 1933. It is my argument that Heidegger understands being as *differentiated presencing in beings*, and that being, consequently, is always to be conceived as in-corporated, finite, temporal, and historically sited in beings. The metaphysical concept of being as Idea, abiding presence, the transcendental, and the most general and abstract category of beings is shown to be derivative of the historicity of being.

Since the publication of Victor Farias's *Heidegger and Nazism*, the question of the relation 'Heidegger's politics' to his thought has been posed in numerous publications.[1] The most significant of these no longer dispute that this relation is essential to the understanding of Heidegger's philosophy. The works of Derrida, Lacoue-Labarthe, Thiele, Rickey, Ward, Schürmann, and Zimmerman may be mentioned as contributions to this discussion.[2] Other works, such as Hans Sluga's, offer a precise historical account of aspects of German politics in the 1930s; Herf's sociology of conservative German thought in the 1920s and 1930s renders much useful information, but, like Ott's biography of Heidegger, it is philosophically uninformed.[3] Although there are, moreover, many substantial historical works dealing with the Weimar period and the 'conservative revolution' leading to 1933, Heidegger's thought is ignored or not given the significance it deserves.[4] Conversely, a number of works on Heidegger's understanding of being show an appreciation of the historicity of being, but fail to relate the question of the differentiated presencing of being to Heidegger's political engagement in a convincing way, or neglect to do so at all.[5] In these philosophical works, moreover, one misses a sense of the dense and often contradictory texture of the period to which Heidegger belonged. Consequently the need remains for a thorough treatment of the political philosophy of Heidegger in terms of his key question – the question of being – and of Heidegger's understanding of being as a response to the cultural crisis of interwar Germany. This crisis, I argue, was essentially a crisis of threatened formlessness. And precisely as such, it was also a crisis of the meaning of being as that which grants to each entity the singularity of its presence. The approach I undertake here, in terms of the differentiated presencing of being as gestalt, attempts to show that Heidegger's work, at least in one, essential respect, is a response to this dual crisis. My object is to establish the systematic and historical unity of the question of being and to show the impact of this question on the idea of the political in Heidegger's thought. Precisely because the question of being arises out of the history of being it is not, as often claimed, detached from concrete historical existence. While Heidegger was undoubtedly mistaken regarding the character of National Socialism, this movement, as well as the conservative revolution itself, was, at least initially, sufficiently complex and internally contradictory to allow Heidegger to read them as the beginning of a new founding, or gestalt-giving, of the *Volk* and its state. And only what has gestalt, in Heidegger's understanding of the tradition, has being, and has a future. The present work consequently offers itself not only as a contribution to Heidegger studies, but also, taking Heidegger's political philosophy seriously, as a reflection on the politics of gestalt.

In chapter 1, I argue that Heidegger's destruction of the history of metaphysics offers a challenge to planetary, cosmopolitan thinking. The concept of the planetary, understood as the representational space of subjectivity, is opposed to that of the earth; the earth is conceived in its historicity as the homeland of its peoples. To think the earth, in turn, leads to the site opened up by the historicity of Dasein, and to the articulation of this site in works, rites, acts, and thought. As my commentary on three short texts from Heidegger's late work shows, a work of art, as image, for example, is one way in which this site is articulated and 'incorporated.' What is given in the image in this way is no longer conceived aesthetically, as grounded in the metaphysics of imitation.

Heidegger understands the site of the historicity of Da-sein as the site of the differentiation of being (*Seyn*). The second part of chapter 1 lays out the hermeneutic situation of Heidegger's *Contributions to Philosophy* (GA65) in the consummation of metaphysics as nihilism, and the sense of crisis and the need for decision this implies. The distinction between beingness (*Seiendheit*), as conceived by metaphysics, and being (*Seyn*), which the *Contributions* map out, is essential to our understanding of the differentiation of being in beings. This, in turn, allows us entrance into the question of the historicity of being as articulated in beings, and into the necessity of founding being in beings in response to nihilism. Nihilism is understood as the abandonment of beings to their mere calculability and functionality. The founding of the site of Da-sein, its articulation through works, labour, leadership, and thought is to be conceived as a direct response to the crisis of nihilism. Consequently it is my thesis that the history of being, and the historicity of Da-sein, are conjoined, and that this juncture leads directly to reflection on the founding of being in art and in the constitution of the political.

There is considerable discussion in the secondary criticism as to whether or not Heidegger offers, in *Being and Time* or elsewhere, grounds for a social philosophy and thus for political philosophy. In chapter 2, which is based primarily on *Being and Time*, I approach this problem through Heidegger's understanding of *Mitsein* in relation to the disclosive power and political function of authentic rhetoric as a mode of disclosure. Consequently I argue that Heidegger does allow for a positive concept of the political, or public, sphere, grounded in the historicity of *Dasein* as *Mitsein*. This creates the philosophical conditions for Heidegger's own 'political activism' in 1933–4 (particularly in the area of university reform), an engagement which is consequently not to be viewed as an aberration or an opportunistic concession to the new regime, but as following from the fundamental theses of *Being and Time* itself.

In chapter 3, I examine the meanings of the concept of 'gestalt' in the cultural critique of Weimar Germany and the early Nazi period, with particular reference to the writers of the Conservative Revolution. Given the special significance of the work of Carl Schmitt and Ernst Jünger I will examine their work separately, in chapters 6 and 7, respectively. I take my point of departure from the Rector's Address of 1933, with the intention of elucidating its fundamental philosophical theses in the context of contemporary political ideologies and realities. As Heidegger's brief engagement for National Socialism in the Rector's address of 1933 makes evident, Heidegger's sense of *Heimat, Volk,* and State entered into dangerous liaison, at least for a time, with the new regime.

Heidegger's confrontation with the discourses of 1933 implicates above all his attempt to free the concept of Volk from racial interpretations, and at the same time to bring it into fruitful relation to the State and to the 'earth' as the historical native soil of a people. The concept of gestalt, in turn, has to be freed of formalist and Platonic implications. To establish the common ground of Heidegger's thought and the 'revolution' of 1933, I examine the discourse of 'style' and gestalt to refine our sense of Heidegger's appropriation and critique of contemporary ideologies. Consequently, it becomes necessary to examine the writings of Weimar cultural critics and National Socialist ideologues dealing with the formation of national character as determined by history, 'race,' Volk, and education. The question of 'national aestheticism,' understood as the concept of the re-formation of national character by reference to an ideal, finds its proper place here. The thesis of national aestheticism, which has gained wide currency in the secondary literature, itself requires revision. It will become evident that the 'gestalt' of the Volk is to be conceived less as the imitation of an ideal form than as the cultural and historical 'rhythm' of a people. The concept of 'rhythm,' understood as the defining, embodied historicity of the Volk, as articulated in the work of conservative revolutionaries and writers of the National Socialist period, cannot be reduced to a discourse of 'race' or a national aestheticism of race. We shall see that Heidegger's deconstructed concept of 'form' implicates an understanding of gestalt as rhythm, and that this allows – at least to some degree – a common point of departure with conservative discourses.

One of the abiding themes of conservative cultural critics was the alienating power of contemporary science and technology, and Heidegger evidently had some sympathy for this view, although on his own philosophical grounds. Yet critics of technology also explicitly pose the question of the possible integration of technology into the historical tradition of a people. In fact, for many of these critics, technology is to be given a new gestalt through its fusion with tradition. The position Jünger takes, that technology dissolves all existing, traditional forms of culture, is challenged by conservative writers such as Hardensett in favour of the view that a new synthesis of technology and tradition is possible.[6] This raises the question of the leadership role of the State, and the possibility of overcoming the primacy of economic and technological imperatives by a politics of the Volk, and of science in service of the Volk. This position is echoed in the Rector's Address, and in Heidegger's political speeches of 1933–4, as well as in his *Logik* of 1934 (GA38).

A central, common theme of the discourses of 1933 is that the Volk is to be brought into a new, 'authentic' relation to its own 'native soil.' Karl Haushofer, the 'founder' of geopolitics, editor of the periodical *Zeitschrift für Geopolitik* (1924–44), and the director of an institute devoted to the study of geopolitical questions under the National Socialist regime, offers insight into the relation between Volk and earth in the ideological perspective of the extreme right. Haushofer's work has serious philosophical and political content, as recent research has shown.[7] Much of Haushofer's work, for example, deals with the geopolitical concepts of limit and border (*Grenze*) as determinations of *Heimat, Reich*, and State. Reference to Haushofer's contribution and those of other conservative revolutionaries will allow for a more precise circumscription of Heidegger's reflection on the essence of the political as founded in the internal self-limitation of the polity. Other Nazi ideologues, such as Walther Darré and Walther Schoeneichen, propose analogous concepts of 'limit.'[8] Darré was the pre-eminent representative of agrarian ideology in interwar Germany and sometime minister for agrarian affairs under Hitler. His works implicate concepts of *Heimat*, historical rootedness, and limit, which I propose to differentiate from those of Heidegger, thereby to clarify more precisely the character of Heidegger's early engagement for the new regime. Schoeneichen, as Luc Ferry has shown, wrote the most significant German works on ecology during the period of the Third Reich.[9] Schoeneichen, and more generally, the ecological ideology and legislation of the National Socialists, articulate concepts of nature and of the ecologically founded determination of mankind which call for critical commentary. Again, my object is to determine to what extent Heidegger was liable, given his understanding of being, to recognize in these ideas reflections of his own expectations of a new beginning after 1933.

In the works of these authors, supplemented by readings of less-known writers publishing in significant journals of the period, we may expect to find an articulation of key political concepts, thus allowing one to distinguish, for example, between *Volk, Heimat, Staat, Reich, Nation, Rasse,* and *Bewegung* (people, homeland, state, *Reich,* nation, race, movement) as terms of political discourse. Despite the wealth of material devoted to Heidegger's politics, these distinctions have for the most part not been made in discussion of the philosopher's work. It is necessary to establish these distinctions, and others, and their concrete historical context, as the first step toward determining the universe of discourse out of which Heidegger's engagement for National Socialism emerged.

To think being as articulated, as gestalt, implies a philosophical and historical treatment of Heidegger's understanding of the differentiated incorporation of being in concrete historical existence. Heidegger's concept of being, in effect, constitutes not only the ground of his turn toward the new regime in 1933, but also determines his understanding of the relation of nation, labour, and historicity. In chapter 4, I focus in detail on Heidegger's *Logik* of 1934 to explicate his understanding of labour, or work, as grounded in the historicity of Dasein. Heidegger, in effect, did not commit himself to the new regime in 1933 out of opportunism, but evidently anticipated a genuine revolution, and thus the founding of a 'third way' between liberal capitalism and Soviet communism. The *Logik* explicates 'work' as a structure of temporalization founded in the Care structure of the existential analytic and the historicity of Volk. Work as being-open, or ex-posed, positioned in the midst of beings and under the necessity of bringing them to an ordered stand is the truth within which Dasein stands and into which it is thrown.

Chapter 5 focuses on *An Introduction to Metaphysics* (GA40) (1935). Analysis of the explicitly political statements of the lectures (which have aroused considerable controversy) has to be integrated into an explication of the movement of the text as a whole and its fundamental philosophical theses. Chapter 3 already examines the critique of 'intellectualism' in Baeumler and Krieck, among others. In his own way, Heidegger shares this critique. The problem of intellectualism is especially significant to the question of university reform and the task of developing a new sense of *Bildung* to replace the humanistic ideal of education. Baeumler's appropriation of Nietzsche is of significance here, as it clearly also was for Heidegger. The critique of intellectualism implicates an attack on the perceived formlessness of liberal culture and more fundamentally, a deconstruction of the primacy of conceptual schemata over lived and historically rooted existence. It is evident from key works of this period that the term *Geist* (spirit), for example, often signifies the operation of an intellect alienated from and hostile to the 'life' and 'soul' of a people (Klages, for example). In chapter 5, my first object will be to differentiate the critique of intellectualism carried out from the ideological position of the Conservative Revolution and National Socialist writers from Heidegger's often allied but fundamentally distinct deconstruction of objectifying thinking. Heidegger's understanding of the problem of 'intellectualism' in effect calls for a destruction of the metaphysical *chorismos* of being and beings opened up by Plato's thought. Being (*ousia*) is retrieved as the event of presencing in its coming to a stand in a being, thus to presence out of the limit proper to it. What presences in this way, out of the limit (*peras*), has gestalt, is *morphe.* What this implies for Heidegger's understanding of the political is that the differentiation of being, its dispersal in beings, must be given a site: this, in turn, raises the question of the relation of Volk and artwork and homeland to the differentiation of being in beings. I argue the thesis that the political, in Heidegger's sense, signifies the institution of the differentiation of being in the works and rites of an historical people.

To determine the extent of the affinity between the concept of Volk and state which Heidegger implicitly holds, and the concept held by the Conservative Revolution, I examine key works of Carl Schmitt, author of *The Concept of the Political.* This often discussed, and often misunderstood text defines the state as a self-delimited historically rooted form of existence. The charge of 'decisionism,' as directed against Heidegger, as well as Schmitt, has become common currency in the critical literature. I argue that this interpretation is fundamentally misconceived as directed against Heidegger, and can be brought against Schmitt himself only in a very qualified sense. Schmitt's political thought rather exhibits a kinship to Heidegger's insistence that being differentiates itself in the historically founded. Heidegger shares with Schmitt a critique of liberalism. The two thinkers are divided, however, by fundamental differences which I propose to work out in detail in chapter 6.

Chapter 7 offers five studies of the *Contributions,* focusing on the related questions of the artwork, the political, Volk, and technology in Heidegger's destruction of metaphysics. The possibility of founding the differentiation of being (*Seyn*) in beings is the key issue in question. My central argument is that being differentiates itself and founds itself in beings through the site opened up by the historicity of Dasein as Volk.

The interpretation of Heidegger's concept of Volk has long been a crucial point of contention in the secondary literature, and evidently is central to any interpretation of his 'political philosophy.' In 'Volk, Differentiation, Founding,' the first section of chapter 7, I show that Heidegger explicitly rejects the National Socialist misinterpretation of Volk because it merely reinstates a discourse of collective subjectivity and hence remains entangled in metaphysics. Heidegger holds that Volk is not a collective subject, but the site of the differentiation and gathering of being as founded in beings. The political implications of Heidegger's critique of collective subjectivity, however, also encompass liberalism and the technological imperatives of capitalism. Thus Heidegger's critique of the sciences – including the historical disciplines, in section 76 of the *Contributions* – denies them a founding power, such as could give gestalt to the historical existence of a people. Inasmuch as socio-historical discourses are rather governed by a logic of transparency and control, they follow the logic of technicity of modern society. Heidegger conceives of Volk as a counter-movement to socio-technical transparency and the dictates of production and consumption.

I argue that Heidegger understands Volk as the site of the founding of the differentiation of being in ritual, art, labour, leadership. Heidegger anticipates this site as the possibility of bringing beings into the shelter (*Bergung*) of their proper gestalt, that is, into the mode of being proper to each. Inasmuch as the Volk opens up this site, it institutes the historically specific differentiation of being in beings in response to the challenge of technicity and the reduction of the earth to the destructive uniformity of a storehouse of raw materials. The question of Volk, of being, and of human responsibility to other beings and the earth itself are intimately conjoined as responses to the challenge of the in-differentiation of all entities that the essence of technology inaugurates.

The *Contributions* allows us to determine the historical and systematic place of the 'Origin of the Work of Art' in Heidegger's thinking. Truth – the disclosure of the event of being – must be founded, that is, brought to a stand in a being. What takes a stand to give a stand to the event of truth is *morphe*, which Heidegger explicitly glosses as Gestalt in the artwork essay. The work of art, therefore, is one way in which the truth of being is founded in a being. In the second section of chapter 7, 'The Artwork and the Site of the Political in the *Beiträge*,' I work from the context established by the *Contributions* – especially part V of that work, 'The Founding' – to interpret the artwork essay. This leads us directly to some of the central questions of Heidegger's later thought: the relation of Dasein and *Seyn*, the dispersal and differentiation of *Seyn*, the founding of the truth of being in beings, and the possibility of the Volk as the site of this founding. The work of art allows the event of disclosure to happen in the strife of earth and world, in such a way that truth is sheltered in the work. The movement of withdrawal (*lethe*) at the heart of truth (*aletheia*) is preserved. The artwork does not represent, it establishes truth by setting it into the work. This event allows the possibility of a community (*Da-sein* as *Mitsein*) no longer defined by socio-technical discourses of representation founded in modern subjectivity. The work of art, therefore, is one way in which the possibility of a postmetaphysical polity is opened up.

In the next section of chapter 7, 'Limit and Gestalt,' I undertake to show – by reference to Heidegger's retrieval of Aristotle's concept of being (*ousia, energeia*), particularly in 'On the Being and Conception of *Phusis* in Aristotle, *Physics* B, 1' – the basis of Heidegger's deconstruction of the aesthetics of 'form' and 'content' in his 'The Origin of the Work of Art.' Heidegger in fact re-interprets *ousia* as gestalt; a being has gestalt (hence being) in as much as it has the *arche* (or 'origin') and *telos* of its temporal unfolding in itself, thus to come to presence in its delimited specificity. Gestalt is understood as the singular rhythm of a being's unfolding and withdrawal according to the measure of its own inherent limit (*peras*). The gestalt of the artwork which emerges by way of the retrieval of Aristotle cannot be read as the imitation of a model in the tradition of aesthetics. The artwork is rather conceived as an event of disclosure which has the possibility of founding a community. The artwork founds the differentiation of being (*Seyn*) in a being. Therefore the artwork is implicated in the founding of political being in the postmetaphysical sense that the community, and the identity proper to it, no longer derive from collective subjectivity.

With the exception of Palmier's monograph, the literature gives little serious attention to Heidegger's relation to Jünger's thought.[10] In the following section of chapter 7, 'Style and the Gestalt of Global Technology,' I interrogate Heidegger's understanding of gestalt in relation to Jünger, and in particular I focus on his *Der Arbeiter*, which had a considerable impact on Heidegger's concept of technology. The recently published (2004) volume on Jünger in the complete edition (GA90) provides an additional source for Heidegger's interrogation of the metaphysical concept of 'gestalt,' and raises the question of how the essential difference of this metaphysical concept and the non-metaphysical 'gestalt' of beings is to be determined. Jünger's concept of the 'total mobilization' of all resources, human and non-human, under the

regime of technology, gave a decisive impetus to Heidegger's own reflections on the essence of technology, the dis-integration of beings, and the
possibility of the sheltering of beings in the site opened up by Da-sein as
the site of *Seyn*. This discussion of the *Contributions* as a reflection on the
incorporation of being in the gestalt of beings focuses on the question of
'style.' Heidegger understands 'style' as the law of the disclosure (truth)
of the historicity of being as founded in beings. Dasein itself has a style of
attunement, or openness, to being, which determines the How of the
manifestation of beings.

What Jünger calls the gestalt of the Worker also implicates a style of
making-manifest of the being of beings. In Jünger's terms, 'work' signifies
the dissolution of the rank-differentiation of entities to facilitate their
total mobilization in the service of technicity as represented by the gestalt
of the Worker. For Heidegger the question arises whether this movement
of in-differentiation still allows a people, insofar as it is rooted in the specificity of their historical tradition, the possibility of unfolding its own style
of existence, or gestalt. Volk signifies a counter-movement to in-differentiation, and the reduction of all beings to the availability of stock-on-call.
The related question, whether *technology* can be given a style commensurate with the historical specificity of a people, is raised by Heidegger
without being answered. Although it would seem that Heidegger does
not grant technology this measure of history-founding power, rather reserving it for the work of art, the *Contributions* is not conclusive on this
subject. In the final section of chapter 7, I offer a brief reflection on the
question of *freedom* as it relates to the project of the *Contributions*.

In my Conclusion, I raise the question of the relation between Heidegger's understanding of truth, modern subjectivity, and imperialism. This
discussion, which focuses on the *Parmenides* (GA54), examines Heidegger's reflection on the fanaticism of the modern state and imperial
politics, as founded in an 'imperial' (representational or objectifying)
concept of truth. In these lectures, as well as in the lectures on Hölderlin,
Heidegger intimates the postmetaphysical concepts of *Heimat*, the *Volk*,
and the state. He argues that the modern state is founded in the representational 'staging' of reality by the collective subject of modernity, as
codified in normative thought and socio-technical discourse. Whereas
imperial or representational truth is the condition of the planetary space
of globalization, Heidegger's thought of *Heimat* articulates the bounded
horizon of the historicity of being as concretely incorporated and instituted in the existence of a people. This implies a direct challenge to the

politics of globalization and its philosophical premises. Heidegger's political thought is conceived in response to the *differentiation of being* (*Seyn*) as it is constituted in the concretely realized historicity of a people, and in-corporated in the locality and gestalt of beings. Far from being a transcendental signified beyond and above human existence, darkly hovering over mankind to determine the course of human history, *Seyn* concretely articulates itself in the Dasein of a people as the site of the disclosure of what is. For this reason, Heidegger's political thought stands opposed to the universalist claims of the socio-technical organization of the planet, and, in an age of the limitless, his 'politics of being' articulates the necessity of an inherent limit that gives to each its own.

Heidegger's Transformation of *Gestalt* Discourse

Yet what thus comes up and becomes intrinsically stable, encounters, freely and spontaneously, the necessity of limit, *peras* ... That which places itself in its limit, completing it, and so stands, has form [Gestalt], *morphe*. (GA40, 64–5/60)

Limit and end are that wherewith the essent begins to *be*. It is on this basis that we must understand the supreme term that Aristotle used for being, *entelecheia* – the holding (preserving)-itself-in-the-ending (limit). (GA40, 64/60)

Form, *forma*, corresponds to the Greek *morphe*, the circumscribing limit [Grenze] and delimitation which forces and sets a being in that which it is, so that it stands in itself: the gestalt [Gestalt]. (GA43, 138)

The strife that is brought into the rift and thus set back into the earth and thus fixed in place is the *figure* [*Gestalt*]. Createdness of the work means truth's being fixed in place in the figure ... What is here called figure [Gestalt] is always to be thought in terms of the particular placing [Stellen] and enframing [Gestell] as which the work occurs when it sets itself up and sets itself forth. ('Origin of the Work of Art,' UK 50/189)

Because Goethe's understanding of gestalt pre-figures later developments of 'organicist' discourse, including the discourse of radical conservatism in the Weimar Republic, a brief consideration of his idea of 'morphology' is useful here. By the end of the nineteenth century,

Goethe's idea of the 'self-actualizing wholeness of organic forms'[11] would inspire many divergent reactions to positivism and to the disintegrating tendencies of scientific analysis, as well to modern industrial society in general.[12] The idea of gestalt would be taken up as a scientific thesis about perception by gestalt theory (Christian von Ehrenfels, Wertheimer) and as an historical and cultural-morphological thesis by racialist ideologues such as Chamberlain and Rosenberg. As Mitchell G. Ash has shown, pre-war Austro-German, and later, Weimar, culture, saw widespread appeal made to the idea of a unifying gestalt in various disciplines, from philosophy and experimental psychology (Dilthey, Husserl, Jaspers), to biology (Hans Driesch, von Uexküll) and political economy (Othmar Spann), and this across the entire political spectrum, from the radical Right to the liberalism of Wertheimer.[13] Weimar especially, politically and economically fractured as it was, sought cultural renewal in new concepts of wholeness. After a brief consideration of Goethe's morphology, I will sketch some of the key theses of *Gestalt* theory. My intention in both cases is the very limited one of mapping out the terms of discourse, if only in a preliminary way, to which the conservative discourse of gestalt responds and reacts. This will prepare us, in turn, for a confrontation with the question of gestalt in Heidegger's thinking.

In reaction against the analytic tendency of empiricism, and against Hegel, who insisted on the primacy of the concept (*Begriff*) in the constitution of knowledge, Goethe attempted to found knowing in the concretely embodied universal. This implicates the correlation of *Gestalt* and *Bildung*: in the first instance, Goethe defines the gestalt of an entity as that which gives it a specific identity, or character. *Bildung* refers to the process of formation which generates a determinate entity.[14] Consequently, gestalt, in its complete sense, signifies the being of an entity conceived in terms of its entelechetic unfolding toward its immanent limit and completeness. The gestalt is the *Urphänomen* – the intrinsic form. The identity of the thing is not given by an atemporal Platonic universal, but by 'the unique, distinguishing patterns of individual organisms.'[15] The concepts of gestalt and *Bildung*, in their description of an entity, signify the union of the ontological (being) and of the genetic (becoming).

The object of Goethe's morphological studies in botany 'is not to unveil [to go behind the phenomenon, thus to analytically decompose it], but to hold in contemplation [schauen] the self-regulation at work in nature, by means of experimental re-enactment and symbolic representation.' Thus the comparison of morphological features allows us to distinguish a type (*Typus*), understood as a constant, or shared, element.

The type is the common element of a synchronic comparison.[16] It signifies the unity of *Bild* and *Begriff*, which does not exist as such in any given entity, but nonetheless – as the *Naturgesetz* or *Bauplan* of a particular species – gives the particulars their order and gives order to our perceptions. The diachronic comparison of stages of growth, in turn, renders 'a kind of ideal whole' called the *Idee*.[17] The combination of these two ways of seeing (diachronic and synchronic) renders the *Urform*, which in its singular instantiation makes manifest the *Urphänomen* (*Gestalt*) as a concretely embodied universal.[18] Gestalt signifies the self-manifestation of the phenomenon. The object of Goethe's 'scientific method' is to bring the gestalt to light, thus to allow phenomena to show themselves in the relation of figure and ground, of gestalt and world, or horizon of perception. This notion would be taken up by gestalt theory at the close of the nineteenth century.

The gestalt psychologists (especially von Ehrenfels, Koffka, Köhler, and Wertheimer) show that what we encounter in primordial experience is neither (*i*) atoms of sensation, as postulated by empirical psychology, nor (*ii*) unequivocal objects presumed by common sense; but rather (*iii*) each moment or thing presenting itself as part of a meaningful totality or perceptual field, part of a dynamic whole given by an intentional totality.[19] Since perception presents us with 'actual things and events,' rather than 'sensory elements,' as Kurt Lewin writes, 'the stimulus to perception ... must be assessed not according to its physical intensity but according to its psychological reality.'[20] In his 'On "Gestalt Qualities"' (1890), Christian von Ehrenfels, student of Franz Brentano, raises the question whether a melody, for example, is the mere sum of its parts, or something – a whole – distinguishable from the sum.[21] He argues that the 'Gestalt quality' is more than the sum of its parts, although a complex of elements given to sensation is the foundation (*Grundlage*) 'necessary for the existence of a given Gestalt quality.'[22] The quality is a presentational content which is nonetheless distinguishable from the *Grundlage*. 'Certain groups of objects,' Gurwitsch comments, 'especially homogeneous ones, are given to perception with an immediate character of grouping and unity. This character appears as an autonomous sensory fact.'[23] The equivocal character of a visual figure (Do we see opposed profiles or the outline of a vase?) 'must be due to production' by the mind, for there is no change in the stimuli. 'Gestalt theory gives an absolute primacy to immediate observation, as opposed to every theoretical consideration.'[24] It should be noted that whereas Ehrenfels conceives the 'gestalt quality' as an *attribute* of phenomenal wholes, the Berlin school of Carl Stumpf, to which Köhler belonged, takes a gestalt *to be* a 'special kind of whole' in the sense that the quality is intrinsic to the gestalt, not separable from the supposed fundamenta.[25]

The question arises whether gestalt qualities, or, a gestalt, is inherent in the object or dependant on an act of consciousness. Ehrenfels had initially left this open, although he intimates that our concepts are founded in the self-presentation of the gestalt.[26] Evidence for this, Ehrenfels holds, is given by the 'intimate unity in which we combine presentational contents of physical and psychical occurrences – contents of the most conceivably different kinds – into integral concepts.' Consequently, 'gestalt qualities comprise the greater part of the concepts with which we operate.'[27] Koffka also held that 'to apply the gestalt category means to find out which parts of nature belong as parts to functional wholes.'[28]

In the first instance, gestalt qualities are referred to sensation and perception; as such they can be temporal (a melody) or nontemporal (visual, tactile). This does not exhaust the extension of the idea of gestalt, however, for 'changes such as the waxing or waning of a desire, a pain, an expectation, if they become the objects of an inner presentation are peculiar temporal gestalt qualities.' Ehrenfels adds that it is 'clearly Gestalt qualities of this kind that serve to a large extent as the basis of aesthetic effects and poetic creations.' The stylistic affinity of artworks also rests on gestalt qualities.[29] Gestalt qualities are produced by the imagination in art, architecture, music.[30] Moreover, he argues that the common comportment, or *habitus*, exemplified by relatives of a family shows 'a resemblance manifested in their whole physical nature and bearing, a resemblance which often resists analysis into relations of identity between individual constituent parts.'[31] Koffka likewise recognized that 'there are Gestalt processes also in the realm of human action, above all in motor actions, speaking, writing, singing, sketching.'[32] Wertheimer applied the notion of gestalt to the unity of body and mind as expressed in the physiognomy, action, movement, and thought of a person.[33] Köhler, similarly, maintained that 'the processes of learning, of reproduction, of striving, of emotional attitude, of thinking, acting, and so forth, may be included as subject-matter of gestalt-theory insofar as they do not consist of independent elements, but are determined in a situation as a whole.'[34] The unity of action and behaviour generates a certain style of comportment and is in this sense a unified whole. Higher-level gestalten, Barry Smith argues, constitute an historical paradigm: 'wholes may come to manifest a high degree of inter-partial unity because their parts have grown together, for example as a result of sharing historically a common fate.'[35] A tradition constitutes a temporal gestalt of this kind.

A gestalt, moreover, is defined by degrees, or 'levels,' of perfection, and by its relative 'purity.' In 'Gestalt Level and Gestalt Purity,' Ehrenfels argues that levels of gestalt are determined by the relative unity of part and whole.[36] Higher levels reflect an ascent in the degree of formedness, and this is a value for human feeling, and a value in itself. Gestalt purity, in turn, is manifested by ideal forms such as the sphere. The degree of purity of the sphere cannot be logically surpassed, although the level is not a high one. Thus a rose, for example, has a higher level of gestalt than a sphere, but a lower degree of purity.[37] In aesthetic terms, the 'lawfulness' of a given phenomenon signifies the consummate realization of a given type.[38] Wertheimer's notion of '*Prägnanz*' signifies 'the tendencies toward certain kinds of order' in 'perceptual and memory phenomena.'[39] As Smith notes, Edwin Rausch explicates *Prägnanz* as the lawfulness, originality, integrity, simplicity, meaningfulness, and expressivity of a phenomenon. The inclusion of meaningfulness and expressivity signifies that the object appears within an historical, cultural horizon. Therefore, *Prägnanz* is not merely a formal determination of objects.[40] According to Gurwitsch, the purity of an optimum gestalt means, 'phenomenally, a maximum of stability, clarity, and good arrangement, and physiologically, a minimum of expense of energy in the corresponding processes of mental excitation.'[41] Kurt Goldstein, the teacher of Gurwitsch,[42] had come to similar conclusions: 'it follows that preferred behavior, good Gestalt, or whatever one chooses to call it, represents a very definite *form of coming to terms of the organism with the world, that form in which the organism actualizes itself, according to its nature, in the best way ...* Tendency toward preferred behavior means self-organization of the system.'[43] The 'field theory' of Kurt Lewin (of the Berlin school) also insists that '*only by the concrete whole which comprises the object and the situation are the vectors which determine the dynamics of the event defined.*' Consequently, in a way which has evident similarities to Heidegger's concept of being-in-the-world, the 'dynamics of sensory psychology,' for example, depend on 'the structure of the whole surrounding field.'[44]

The philosophically most fruitful development of gestalt theory emerged from the phenomenology of Gurwitsch and Merleau-Ponty, which Husserl himself anticipates. In 'The Limit of the Concept of Gestalt,' Gurwitsch holds that Husserl postulated two kinds of unity of a multiplicity: (*i*) conceptual or categorical unity; and (*ii*) a unity 'immediately experienced and given alongside and at once with the sensory data.'[45] The latter is not constituted but given. In his 'Phenomenology of Thematics and of the Pure Ego: Studies of the Relation between Gestalt Theory and Phenomenology' (1929), Gurwitsch notes that Husserl's 'figural factors,' as postulated in chapter 11 of *The Philosophy of Arithmetic*, mean 'hardly anything different from Ehrenfels' "Gestalt-qualities."'[46] This is supported by Husserl's comment to this effect in the *Logical Investigations* of 1900–1.[47] According to Husserl, a collection, such as a swarm of birds, is grasped in a 'unitary total intuition.' 'When we set into relief a specific collection in intuitive unity, that figural moment steps forth which exerts the strongest stimulus on our grasping.'[48]

Against the Berlin school of gestalt psychology, however, Husserl maintains that a gestalt quality – e.g., a tone – is not synthesized from sound waves on the neurological level, but constituted by the intentionality of consciousness.[49] Both Gurwitsch and Merleau-Ponty would also critique the naturalistic basis of the gestalt theory of Köhler and Koffka, for 'they postulated the material world as the only real world' and held that gestalt perception is neurologically founded.[50] Toward the end of the 1920s Husserl again castigated gestalt theory for its naturalism, the causal explanation of the gestalt experience, and the failure to consider the genetic constitution of the gestalt.[51] Husserl, nonetheless, like Ehrenfels, still posited a dualism of substratum (sensuous elements) and the gestalt or figuration. In the *Ideen I* (sec. 85) this dualism is articulated as the dualism of sensuous *hyle* and intentional *morphe*.[52] Gurwitsch rejects this dualistic thesis to develop what is in his view a more consistent theory of gestalt, founded in Husserl's phenomenology, while supplementing it. In *Studies in Phenomenology and Psychology*, Gurwitsch focuses on the epistemenological problems of gestalt theory: following Husserl's *Ideen*, Gurwitsch's essay 'begins with pure consciousness in the form of the *cogito*: something is given to me – something objective.' Consequently he accepts the *epoché*, and focuses on the object only as given to consciousness (i.e., as 'theme', sense). Consciousness is characterized by the intentionality of being-perception, wishing, and so on, and the ego lives in such acts of intentionality.[53] The world of stimuli – and the world of 'real things' – falls away in favour of what is present to consciousness. The fundamental problem posed is that of the relation of part to whole: 'The curved line is not a content with properties of its own. Instead it is defined and determined by the configuration to which it belongs and the role it plays in the configuration.' 'What a "part" – better stated, constituent – of a certain Gestalt is, how it stands in it, is determined by the structure of the Gestalt.'[54]

Therefore Gurwitsch rejects the empirical thesis that atomic stimuli (sense data) constitute an objective world which is then composed into wholes by mind or brain. Gestalt theory of knowledge 'takes its departure from the original orderedness, structuredness, and organization of the immediately given, the primal phenomenological material.'[55] Gestalt features of experience, including qualities such as 'close by,' 'next to,' and so on, are immediately, phenomenologically given. What is given is always a theme ('object') standing in a field – it never stands alone; relations of temporal or local proximity, of qualitative similarity, establish a 'Gestalt connection.' The ground (thematic field) is organized around the figure ('theme').[56] Gurwitsch in effect postulates two types of 'gestalt connection': (i) that of the theme as the total system of its constituents (as opposed to a mere sum); and (ii) the union of theme and the thematic field; the theme is an independent whole, but the field is mere background.[57] The figure has thing-character; the ground has stuff-character. 'The primary distinction of the theme consists in its peculiar independence with regard to whatever else belongs to the thematic field. Self-sufficient, unitary, and delimited, resting entirely on itself, it stands in the thematic field which fades into the indefinite in several directions.'[58] Despite Gurwitsch's attempt to establish the 'self-sufficiency' of the theme, however, the criticism can be brought that his theory of gestalt still entails transcendental idealism, for it 'locates phenomena within the sphere of immanence' to establish themes as atemporal, self-same units of meaning. This contradicts his intention to grant the stream of experience its own autochthonous structure.[59]

In response to difficulties associated with the residual Cartesianism of Husserl, Merleau-Ponty drew extensively on gestalt theory to formulate his own philosophical position. He could overcome the form, matter dualism of Husserl, because, having abandoned Husserl's theory of the atemporality of meaning, Merleau-Ponty holds that meaning and signs, the 'form and the matter of perception ... are related from the beginning.'[60] His revision of gestalt theory is interesting to us insofar as he pays particular attention to the 'embodiment' of the gestalt as a condition of experience, for this concept has evident similarities to discourses on gestalt in Germany, which we shall examine to establish the cultural context of Heidegger's thinking. Merleau-Ponty develops the gestalt theorists' notion that 'the synthesizing forms of our experience are not ideas but corporeal a prioris. These givens of the body, physiological forms which establish the general horizons of the world of our experience, prepare the possibility of intellectual knowledge but are effective prior to it and as its ground; they are themselves moments of Being.'[61] The 'sensory units' – or gestalten – which are the 'basis for our perception of the world' are the 'result of a natural or spontaneous organization on the part of the organism.'[62] The gestalt does not go beyond experience, nor is it a condition of experience. 'Gestalt forms are, so to speak, constantly at work, organizing and delineating our immediate bodily experience.'[63] 'Matter,' Merleau-Ponty writes, 'is "pregnant" with its form, which is to say that in the final analysis every perception takes place within a certain horizon and ultimately in the "world."'[64] This implies, in M.C. Dillon's words, that Merleau-Ponty 'recognizes the Gestalt as a dynamic and emergent (rather than static) unity: the meaning of the theme is taken to be diachronic, unfolding through time.'[65]

As we have already noted, moreover, forms of behaviour, or of comportment, also take typical gestalten. The world takes shape in typical forms of embodiment: 'I experience the unity of the world,' Merleau-Ponty writes, in *The Phenomenology of Perception*, 'as I recognize a style,' that is, as a certain way or manner of being.[66] 'As Gestalt psychology has shown,' Merleau-Ponty writes, 'structure, Gestalt, meaning, are no less visible in objectively observable behaviour than in ourselves.'[67] This would implicate, he continues, the possibility of a science 'based on the description of typical behaviours.' The question of style arises in response to the problem of identity within temporal flux; it is necessary to postulate an identity without recurring to the identity given by atemporal meaning as constituted by consciousness. 'Style' signifies a manner or way of being, not an invariant quality. The theme (object, event, person) has a stylistic identity within the horizon established by a world as a context of meaning.[68] 'Stylistic identity' signifies the identity of a certain rhythm, a certain regularity of the unfolding of time within the temporalization of a world; it is a concept we will encounter again – in conservative and nationalist discourse, no less than in Jünger and Heidegger.

Two questions arise at this point: (*i*) To what extent is the conception of gestalt in conservative and nationalist discourse of the 1920s and 1930s comparable to the idea of gestalt in the tradition of gestalt theory, and gestalt phenomenology? The answer to this question would allow us to anticipate more clearly the field of discourse out of which Heidegger's work emerges. (*ii*) To what extent would Heidegger implicitly or explicitly draw on a concept of gestalt, retrieved from the metaphysical tradition, to unfold his own understanding of being in the course of the 1920s and 1930s? This question will only be answered in a preliminary, schematic way, in preparation of the body of this text.

In chapter 3, I will examine the literature of the Conservative Revolution in detail to determine its understanding of gestalt. At this point, the theses of gestalt theory and gestalt phenomenology, which conservative discourse also held, may be summarized as follows. This is not to say that these theses derive from the same premises, or lead to the same conclusions. My object is simply to establish a formal and historical framework for our subsequent discussion: (*i*) Formal gestalt theory and conservative discourse both insist on the unity of part and whole, the whole being more than the sum of its parts; the whole which thus emerges manifests its own being and character, such as cannot be grasped by an analytical decomposition of phenomena. (*ii*) Conservative revolutionaries also affirmed the concept of optimum form, exemplified in the 'good' gestalt of maximum purity. Gestalt in this sense, as resting independently in itself and distinct from its horizon, serves conservative discourse as an ideal of order, whereas (*iii*) the naturalism of the Berlin school, inasmuch as it sought a physiological basis for experience, was rejected by conservatives; the unity of body and mind (or soul) is affirmed. This unity supposedly articulates itself as the stylistic unity of body and mind.

Furthermore, (*iv*) although the gestalten are affirmed by conservatives as belonging to nature itself, there is a tendency to affirm equally the constitution and transformation of these forms by the collective subjectivity of a particular culture. This leads to a notion of cultural morphology, of typical national characteristics. Moreover, (*v*) conservative discourse accords with gestalt theory to affirm the concept of higher-order gestalten. These regulate (*a*) the style of *artistic production* in a particular period and culture; (*b*) the typical *comportment and character* of individuals of a particular culture (or 'race'); (*c*) the style of a culture's *institutions*; and (*d*) the way of unfolding of a people's *tradition* itself. These four aspects are in each case grounded in an historically specific rhythm, that is, a specific way of temporalization, understood as the unfolding of a potential into its proper limit. The specificity of a way of temporalization grants a style of work, of the artwork, of production, comportment, and of the institutions of a tradition, an ownness which is not inevitably identical with a concept of atemporal essence. Jünger, as we shall see, appeals to a discourse of type and gestalt in related senses. The extent to which these theses nonetheless depend on metaphysical concepts of the distinction of form and matter, on the primacy of the atemporal Idea (Plato), on the actualization of a perspective (Nietzsche), or on a naturalistic concept of racial substance can only be clarified as we proceed. We may anticipate that the primary distinction to be found between conservative discourse and National Socialist ideology will be that the latter valorizes a concept of racial gestalt more consistently and radically.

The significance of the idea of gestalt for Heidegger's thinking in the 1930s has to be won from his confrontation with the philosophical tradition, and particularly from his reading of Aristotle. This involves the deconstruction of fundamental metaphysical concepts – such as *morphe, arche, telos, peras,* and *entelecheia* – to win a non-metaphysical concept of wholeness and differentiated unity as gestalt. Heidegger's retrieval of these metaphysical concepts distinguishes his understanding of gestalt not only from the Platonic, or conversely, Nietzschean tendency of many conservatives, but also from the gestalt theorists, as well as from earlier phenomenological developments.

Let us briefly consider what Heidegger knew of gestalt theory in the narrower sense. His letters offer us some clues. The following testimonies are valuable not only as an insight into Heidegger's intellectual biography, but also prepare our subsequent elucidation of substantive issues. In this context, I will also refer briefly to Heidegger's lectures on biology, for they offer a philosophical commentary on 'organic unity,' which illuminates the issue of 'wholeness' in gestalt theory, the new biology, and Heidegger's own thinking.

Through the early writings of Husserl in particular, Heidegger will have been led to an acquaintance with the works of gestalt theorists. The Third Investigation of Husserl's *Logical Investigations* explicitly deals with the relation of part and whole, and the particular character of ontic and ontological wholes. Einar Øverenget has argued that in *Being and Time* 'Heidegger not only uses the terminology of parts and wholes, but he uses it in accordance with the conventions Husserl establishes in the Third Investigation' in his discussion of 'the structural make-up of Dasein,' as well as of the being of equipment.[69] The question of the distinction between a sum and a whole is, of course, central to gestalt theory. It is therefore likely that Husserl's discussion of this problem would have alerted Heidegger to contemporary work in gestalt theory. In fact, Heidegger would have learned of von Ehrenfels' work through a reading of Husserl's Sixth Investigation of the *Logical Investigations,* where von Ehrenfels' essay on gestalt qualites is explicitly referred to. Going by the evidence of a late letter (1960) to Imma von Bodmershof, Christian von Ehrenfels' daughter, we find that Heidegger praises von Ehrenfels as one who 'first brought to life again the idea of "gestalt" for modern thinking.'[70]

Evidently Heidegger was acquainted with the work of other gestalt theorists. In a letter of the 10th November 1926, to Elizabeth Blochmann, Heidegger somewhat cryptically remarks, that Wertheimer, in his '"psychology"' course, 'certainly offers the most modern of what can be heard in this field today.'[71] Wertheimer, Köhler, Koffka, and Kurt Lewin were all students of Carl Stumpf, himself the student of Franz Brentano. Equally significant is Heidegger's praise of Adhémar Gelb, an associate of Wertheimer and the neurologist Kurt Goldstein. In 1914, together with Goldstein, Gelb undertook research on brain-injured soldiers in an institute near Frankfurt. He would later, in 1929, join Wertheimer, Koffka, Goldstein, and Köhler on the editorial board of *Psychologische Forschung*, the chief organ of gestalt theory.[72] In February 1930, Heidegger recommended Gelb, or alternatively Kurt Lewin, for the chair in philosophy at the Friedrich-Wilhelms-Universität Breslau in Schlesia, showering both with praise. Gelb's research anticipates a new concept of psychology with fundamental implications for philosophy.[73] In May of 1932 Heidegger apparently encountered Gelb (now teaching in Halle) in Cologne, and again came away with a high opinion of him: 'I value him greatly and believe he will one day write the new psychology, which is growing out of the totally changed problematic of the new biology.'[74] Heidegger had in fact worked with Gelb since the winter of 1928–9 in the preparation of a posthumous edition of Max Scheler's philosophy.[75] In 'Analysis of a Case of Figural Blindness' (1918), Gelb and Goldstein show how the loss of the ability to see figures, or gestalten, due to traumatic brain injury is compensated for by neural plasticity.[76] Goldstein's and Gelb's research on brain injuries supported the conclusion that the organism compensates for the loss of particular capabilities by 'reorganizing sensory functioning at a lower level,' thus indicating that 'cortical "whole processing"' underlies sensory perception.[77] According to Goldstein, 'observation of patients with brain injury also teaches us that there is a tendency for the injured organism to maintain a performance capacity on the highest possible level, compared to its former capacity. When one performance field is disturbed, the most important performances of the field survive the longest, and tend to be most readily restored.'[78] The organism attempts to re-establish an ordered relation to its world; the unity of this relation constitutes a gestalt.

The question naturally arises as to what was significant to Heidegger in the research of Gelb and Goldstein. What does Heidegger mean, moreover, by his reference to 'the new biology'? These questions can be posed with greater precision by considering key theses of his lectures on biology in *Die Grundbegriffe der Metaphysik* of 1929–30 (GA29/30). Reference to Goldstein's *Der Aufbau des Organismus* (1934), which offers a systematic treatment of the underlying premises of the research Gelb and Goldstein had been conducting, can also illuminate both questions.

Heidegger's lectures on biology in the *Grundbegriffe* require a detailed treatment on their own terms, within the context of a paradigm shift initiated by Jakob von Uexküll and Hans Spemann, with which Heidegger was intimately acquainted. It is worth noting that von Uexküll has been reappropriated by the emerging field of 'biosemiosis,' and that Spemann's studies in embryology anticipated contemporary research in 'cloning'; Spemann, moreover, was a long-time colleague of Heidegger's at the University of Freiburg. As far as I know, such a study of 'Heidegger's biology' has not been undertaken. David Farell Krell's *Daimon Life* does not attempt to follow the movement of Heidegger's phenomenological method, and completely ignores the historical and theoretical context of the lectures.[79] What follows as a brief note is intended solely to advance the question of how Heidegger might have understood the concept of *Gestalt* as a particular kind of whole.

Admittedly Heidegger does not explicitly develop a non-metaphysical concept of gestalt until the 1930s, with the retrieval of *morphe* and *entelecheia* in a non-metaphysical sense. The *Grundprobleme* (GA24) of 1927 still uses the word *Gestalt* to translate the metaphysical concepts of *forma* and *essentia*, and makes no attempt to distinguish them from *morphe*, which is evidentially also thought according to its traditional, metaphysical determinations (GA24, 116–21). Yet the quality Heidegger ascribes to the wholeness of the organism – the movement of life back into its own *arche* – already anticipates the kind of wholeness which will later determine his understanding of gestalt. Not only is the organism a whole, rather than an aggregate of instrumental functions or parts – eyes for seeing, claws for grasping – but this whole has a kind of being-in-itself (*Eigentum*). 'Gestalt' will come to signify a way of being-in-itself, which is not merely the wholeness of a presentation composed of non-independent parts (*Momente* in Husserl's sense). What is crucial to Heidegger's sense of the gestalt of an entity is its movement of unfolding into its own inherent limit (*peras*) and its simultaneous movement of withdrawal back into its *arche* of movement. In a way commensurate with *a-letheia* (un-concealment) itself, limit and withdrawal shelter the entity in its own being.

Heidegger holds that contemporary biology had taken 'two decisive steps' away from the still-reigning 'mechanistic' view of life, which begins by dis-integrating the organic whole to begin with the cell as the putative fundamental element from which the organism is to be re-constructed.

Moreover, in a further act of analytic disintegration, the cell is defined bio-chemically by mechanistic biology. The first decisive step toward a new biology is made by Hans Driesch's 'holistic' interpretation of life: the 'organism is not a sum, constructed out of elements and parts, but rather the development and unfolding of the organism in each of its stages is guided by its own character of wholeness [Ganzheit]' (GA29/ 30, 379, 380). Driesch's experiments had shown that the determination of cells to their subsequent function 'takes place in relation to the whole and in consideration of this whole'; the cell is set on its own path of unfolding, but as a part of the whole. The decisive factor is the 'clear breakthrough of the idea of wholeness,' which excludes the interpretation of the unity of the organism as the consequent result of the relation of its parts. The idea of wholeness, Heidegger warns, should not mislead us, as it did Driesch, in the direction of neo-vitalism, consequently to posit a certain power, or entelechy, to explain the apparently inherent purposiveness of the organism (GA29/30, 381). Heidegger continues that Driesch's work is advanced and re-directed by Spemann to confirm a non-mechanistic account of organic wholeness. As Hamburger notes, Hans Spemann's own theoretical interpretation of his experiments rejects the neo-vitalistic approach to cell differentiation.[80]

The second decisive and equally important step is carried out by von Uexküll, especially in his *Umwelt und Innenwelt der Tiere* (1909), and in the *Theoretische Biologie* of 1928. As we shall see, von Uexküll shares with Goldstein the fundamental premise that an organism forms a unity with its environment. Heidegger no more accepts von Uexküll's theoretical interpretation of his observations than he does Driesch's neo-vitalism (GA29/30, 382–3). Again, what is decisive in von Uexküll's work, for Heidegger, is a fuller understanding of wholeness. Jakob Johann von Uexküll (1864–1944) argued that the structure of an organism, its development and relation to the environment, is informed by teleological principles. As opposed to mechanistic views of the organism as a primarily passive receptor of external stimuli, to which it merely reacts in reflex, von Uexküll holds that 'animals possessed extra-mechanistic properties of potentiality and self-directed activity.'[81] The organism forms a whole with its environment, a whole which is regulated by the interaction of the 'inner world' of the animal with its environing world. Goldstein also came to this conclusion: 'For each organism, not everything that occurs in the outer world belongs to its milieu. The only events which normally prove themselves as stimuli are those with which the organism can come to terms in a manner that its existence (i.e., the actualization of the performances which constitute its nature) is not essentially disturbed.'[82] In Heidegger's words, von Uexküll's investigations make possible a 'still more radical interpretation of the organism, inasmuch as its wholeness is not exhausted by the corporal wholeness of the animal, but rather, corporal wholeness is itself first understood on the basis of *that* primordial wholeness which has its limit in what we called the *ring of dis-inhibitions*' (GA29/30, 383). A brief explication of this 'ring' is in order, and this calls for a better understanding of the animal's wholeness.

Wholeness determines the kind of motion proper to the organism. This motion gathers the individual parts (the 'organs') into the whole, into the potential for being of the whole. Particular organs – e.g., the eye – are capabilities (*Fähigkeiten*) granted by a possibility inherent in the way of being of the organism. The mode of being of 'organization' signifies the ability to self-articulate itself in capabilities (GA29/30, 342). It is not that an organ has a capability, but that a particular capability articulates itself as this organ (GA29/30, 319–24). As capability-for, a capability is a kind of opening-up of a dimension, a movement-toward, but in this the capability presents itself, does not leave itself. It does not lose itself in the realization of a drive (*im Triebe*), but rather actualizes itself by holding itself in being in the drive. This leads Heidegger to claim that capability, as that which holds to itself, reveals the particular mode of the being-itself of the animal. The animal, as self-articulated capability, is self-generating, self-regulating, self-renewing: it has its own kind of property-in-itself (*Sich-zu-eigen-sein*), an ownness-in-itself (*Eigentum*) which determines its way of being, a way of being which is distinct from the selfhood of reflection, consciousness, personality (GA29/30, 339–40).

As one way of being-itself, the organism cannot be reduced to a mechanism or interlocking complex of mechanisms. The 'organ' is not a mechanism, but the articulation of a capability, and capability shows the mode of being-its-own-self proper to the animal. This Itself, phenomenologically disclosed by the holding to itself of capability, reveals that the wholeness of the organism maintains itself in and as a whole *by its movement of withdrawal* from being present-at-hand, from objectivity, from mere interaction-with and dissolution-in-the-world. This leads me to emphasize two essential points of Heidegger's discussion: (*i*) the animal has a kind of 'self' (*Eigentum*); and (*ii*) the self-ownness of the animal is granted by its movement of holding-to-itself in every motion-toward or capability-for. Capability implies the self-reserve of withdrawal from the mere being-present of instrumentality. In this sense the organism withdraws into its own *arche* of movement in the course of its unfolding or dis-inhibition.

As Roger Smith has shown, 'inhibition' became one of the fundamental concepts of modern biology, especially physiology, and of psychology, from the time of their inception in the nineteenth century.[83] Heidegger situates his analysis in this discourse without accepting its premises. The holding-to-itself of the animal does not encapsulate it in itself: equally primordial is its movement into a certain 'ring' of openness, the circle of its environment, which Heidegger refers to as the animal's 'ring of dis-inhibitions' (*Enthemmungsring*). Hence the other to which the animal relates is 'taken into the openness of the animal in a way we characterize as disinhibition (*Enthemmung*)' (GA29/30, 369). This corresponds to the thesis of von Uexküll that the organism forms a whole with its 'world.' The primordial unity (*Ganzheit*), and limit (*Grenze*), of the animal is granted not by its bodily form, but by its unity with the ring of dis-inhibitions which corresponds to its capability-for (GA29/30, 383). To interpret Heidegger's concept of organic unity in the related terms of Goldstein, this means that the reality of the organism and that of its environment mutually constitute each other: 'Reality means that something features in the adequate stimulus reaction of the whole organism, that such a reaction prevails which makes ordered behavior possible, and with it, the realization of the essential nature of the organism. In other words, a *thing is not real because of its stability; rather is stable because of its "reality."*'[84] According to Heidegger, the openness of the animal is given direction by its behaviour (*Benehmen*), which is sharply to be distinguished from the action (*Handeln*) of Dasein – it is a relatedness-to, but not a transcendence of what is related to its being (GA29/30, 369). The animal does not relate to an object (*Gegenstand*), but to such things as release its capabilities from being inhibited to being dis-inhibited; what dis-inhibits withdraws from the animal (things are never fixed in the stability of an object), and draws the animal into the 'ring' which limits and releases it (GA29/30, 372). Inhibition (*Hemmung*) holds the animal in itself; disinhibition (*Ent-hemmung*) signifies its actualization as a unity with its 'environment.' The unity of the organism with its environment constitutes its gestalt. According to Goldstein, 'what will turn out to be a gestalt for an organism depends predominantly on the organism's structure.'[85]

From the perspective of Heidegger's interpretation of Aristotle, which will concern us in detail in "Limit and Gestalt," the third section of chapter 7, this brief note on the biology lectures leads to the following conclusion: The unity of the 'self' of the animal, and its 'environment,' in one gestalt, is defined by its release into its own limit, *and* its withdrawal back into the *arche* of its unfolding. The following senses of withdrawal are implicated in the biology lectures: (*i*) the withdrawal of beings as beings, from the animal (this signifies, in a positive sense, the integration of an environment into the specific potentiality of an animal); (*ii*) the withdrawal of inhibition (*Ent-hemmung*) in the dis-inhibition of the animal; and (*iii*) the withdrawal of the animal back into itself (*Hemmung*): withdrawal as holding-to-itself holds it in its gestalt. Withdrawal (*steresis*) holds the animal in the gestalt of its being, in the unity of its potential (*dunamis*) and actualization (*entelecheia*). Only because it withdraws from total release into its *Umwelt*, in effect, from its own dis-integration (death), can it release itself into the environment and still remain itself. A potentiality of the animal actualizes itself only by continuing to be potentiality – it does not 'disappear' into the act. It is not an instrumental means to an end, but a way of being-itself. For this reason, Heidegger can speak of a kind of 'selfhood' (*Eigentum*) of the animal, as having a property in itself, whereas it would be senseless to speak of the 'self' of an instrument. The animal, therefore, is not a composition of a set of 'organs,' conceived instrumentally. The specific mode of temporalization of the living being grants a 'gestalt.' The implication, more generally, for Heidegger's understanding of gestalt is that a movement of self-reserving withdrawal from being-present – such as holds each in its own potentiality – defines beings in their being as gestalt.

A brief review of the senses of gestalt implicit in *Being and Time* is in order, to prepare for my discussion of Heidegger's work of the 1930s. Heidegger does not use the term *Gestalt* in *Sein und Zeit.* The reason for this, as I noted above, is evidently the metaphysical associations of the word, which he clearly indicates by using it to translate *forma, morphe,* and *eidos* in their metaphysical senses in the *Grundprobleme* of 1927 (GA24, 121). However, as the citations from the *Introduction to Metaphysics* and the Nietzsche lectures which head this section of my text indicate, Heidegger no longer ascribed a metaphysical sense to *morphe* by the mid-1930s. It is therefore necessary to ask if this retrieval of the Greek *morphe, eidos,* and *entelecheia,* in order to win a non-metaphysical sense of form as gestalt, is prefigured in *Being and Time,* and if so, in what way.

As a project of fundamental ontology taking its point of departure from the analytic of Dasein, *Sein und Zeit* founds 'sense perception' in the openness of Dasein to the being of beings. The truth of sensory perception is the truth – the disclosedness – of phenomena: seeing always discovers colours and contours; hearing, things-heard. We have ears because we hear – that is, because Dasein's transcendental constitution already is being-with the things themselves. Our being-in-the-world prefigures the possibilities of what is heard, what is seen. Consequently the thesis of

gestalt theory, that we do not perceive sense data, but particular, meaningful forms,[86] also follows for Heidegger, although on different premises (SZ 163–4/153). The epistemological thesis of gestalt theory,
which holds that we perceive forms, and that we tend to discover Closure,
Similarity, and so on, in the phenomena, demands an ontological foundation. Da-sein, as being-in-the-world, signifies that things are disclosed
in their specific being, as those entities which they are (which does not
exclude the possibility of misinterpretation). The tendency to see things
as unities, in terms of gestalt criteria, grounds itself in the being of the
things themselves. Husserl's theory of wholes in the *Logical Investigations*,
Third Investigation, would have directed Heidegger to the ways in which
the intentionality of consciousness grasps phenomenal wholes as wholes.
Heidegger's transformation of the question of intentionality, which
grounds it in being-in-the-world, in effect integrates the problem of
wholes into his analytic of Dasein's temporality and historicity. The call
of a bird, the approaching motorcycle, the glimpse of someone passing, is
already given as such by the hermeneutic As of understanding, by *Befindlichkeit*, and by Discourse (*Rede*), which together constitute Dasein in the
temporality of its being-in-the-world. What is 'perceived' in this way
already has gestalt in the sense that a determinate whole is grasped as
such in its local and temporal specificity, as having particular qualities,
and as standing-forth out of a context of significance (horizon, or 'background') in which it is embedded. In its being, Da-sein is always already
directed towards – it intends – the being of the thing (GA20, 40/31).
Moreover, since Heidegger explicitly defines historicity as a more concrete working-out of Dasein's temporality, the wholeness of entities
within the world is ultimately constituted by the interpretive horizon of
Dasein's historicity. The 'gestalt' of innerworldly beings is given by this
horizon, and this is one way the gestalt as whole is distinct from the formal concept of the whole explained in the *Logical Investigations*.

The act of working with a tool, which, as we recall, has the being of the
ready-to-hand, or handiness, grasps the tool in a pre-conceptual sense as
a 'figure' defined by its relation to its 'ground.' Even without being
grasped thematically, the hammer, for example, constitutes a figure, thus
to exemplify a certain wholeness in its mode of givenness, by the way in
which it 'fits the hand' and allows itself to be worked with. The interpretation which is already inherent in the use of a hammer (SZ 149, 157/
140, 147) pre-reflectively constitutes it as hammer, as being this kind of
entity. In this sense the hammer is 'figured,' takes gestalt as 'handy' to
the grip of one's hand. The How of our use of tools, furthermore, is

always given to us in concrete specificity by the historicity of Dasein, which makes possible the equipmental totality (*Zeugganzheit*) that defines the very being of tools (SZ 68/97).

Figure and ground together compose the unified gestalt of the equipmental context, from which work takes its sense and direction. To say that the equipmental context constitutes a gestalt inherent in the phenomena themselves means that it has a certain order, regularity, simplicity, as defined by the system of references of the work-place (SZ 102, 149/95, 139). Place has gestalt: place is not an abstracted space-point, but, in Calvin Schrag's words, it is 'the abode in which the world-experiencer lives and moves and searches for meaning.'[87] Defined by de-severance and directionality (SZ, sec. 23), the spatiality of being-in-the-world takes gestalt. The closeness, directionality, and so forth of equipment are inherent in our grasping of the 'perceptual field' (SZ 102, 110–11/95, 102–3). It is only with dissolution of the worldhood of the world, that circumspective 'space,' or place, is neutralized and reduced to pure dimension (SZ 112/103–4). And it is only by way of abstraction from the embodied historicity of Dasein that the gestalt of ways of being-with and working together is refigured into purely formal relations of dependency.

In summary, the senses of 'gestalt' implicit in *Being and Time* may be indicated as follows. All of the following senses are significant for Heidegger's understanding of the concept. However, because the gestalt of the work of art, and that of the cultural form and historicity of a people, including its political composition, will prove especially significant in determining Heidegger's relation to the radical conservatives, as well as for our understanding of the articulation of being (*Seyn*) in beings, these senses of gestalt will be the primary focus of this book. In the first instance, as we have seen, we can speak of the gestalt *of entities, that is, of the temporalization of the being of beings*. This sense pertains to nature, as the biology lectures attest, as well as to things produced, such as equipment or works of art. Evidently, the gestalt of these three kinds of entities would have to be determined differently in each case. In his essay on Aristotle's *Physics* B, 1 (1938), Heidegger's deconstruction and retrieval of the metaphysical concepts of *energeia* and *entelecheia* lead him to understand the being (*ousia*) of beings as gestalt (*morphe*). In the third section of chapter 7, 'Limit and Gestalt,' I will examine this essay in relation to 'The Origin of the Work of Art' in detail to unfold the gestalt of one, exemplary kind of entity – that of the artwork. Second, the gestalt of *the historicity of beings* (*world*). Entities within the world are historical in a secondary sense in their belonging to the historicity of Dasein as being-in-the-world (SZ, sec. 76). The gestalt is a whole grounded in historicity, in a way in which the concept of 'whole' of Husserl's Third Investigation is not. Moreover, we recall that Husserl still distinguishes between 'sensuous hule and intentional morphe': 'sense data give themselves as material for intentional formation or meaning [Sinngebungen].'[88] Heidegger does not make this distinction, for 'intentionality' is always already an attuned understanding, and as such being-with beings. Tools take gestalt out of the context of significance of the workshop, the workshop out of the world of Dasein. Tools, equipment, works of art, articulate the historicity of Dasein in different degrees and in different ways. We know that the artwork will be given exemplary status in terms of its power to 'in-corporate' and manifest the historicity of Dasein in a being. The ontological (existential) wholeness of the temporality of Dasein, its *Ganzsein,* is *the site of the disclosure of the gestalt of entities.*

As this site of disclosure, Dasein is always attuned to beings, and this attunement takes the existentiell or ontic form of moods (*Stimmungen, Gestimmtsein*) (SZ 134/172). According to *Sein und Zeit,* the Care-structure of Dasein grants it its wholeness, and articulates its temporalization. Thus the attunement, or *Befindlichkeit,* of Dasein, which always implicates a way of understanding (SZ, secs. 29, 31), determines the How of the manifestation of beings, together with discourse (*die Rede*), in Heidegger's analytic of the wholeness of Dasein. This existential, or ontological, structure is ontically articulated in moods and their attendant way of interpreting and articulating the world. As early as in the *Grundprobleme* of 1919 (GA58), Heidegger had argued that the How of experience is articulated by fundamental rhythms which order the significance of the What-is of entities and our own lives. This 'functional rhythm' gives the stream of living experience its form (GA58, 85). Dasein has the possibility, within certain limits, of freely shaping this rhythm to give order and stability to its own existence. In *Sein und Zeit,* this comes to word in the choices which Dasein makes, for example, in choosing the heros significant for its own concrete historical situation and its being-with others (SZ 385/437). In effect, the form of existence, in the *ontic sense of a structure of moodful understanding which orders the flow of experience, is the gestalt which Dasein gives to itself.* In Husserl's terms, mankind has the possibility of self-formation (*Selbsgestaltung*), which allows the formation of 'specific forms of life, or, types of humanity.' A human being can grasp his or her entire life with different degrees of clarity and evaluate its possibilities.[89]

According to Calvin Schrag, the dynamics and structure of experience are determined by the 'gestaltism of time and space': 'World experience, presented in the living present, is ever in the process of arriving from a past and moving into the future. Thus we come upon the retentional-presentational-protentional structure as the basic structure of temporalized world experience. This constitutes the gestaltism of time as horizon-form.'[90] While Heidegger, unlike Schrag, does not use the term *Gestalt* to characterize the existential structure of Dasein, the wholeness (*Ganzsein*) of Dasein evidently does articulate itself ontically in regulated rhythms of experience which prefigure the How of presentations, and which give Dasein a stability through the flux of experience. In the Aristotle lectures of 1931 (GA33), Heidegger interprets the Greek *bios* as 'the possibility of a freely chosen existence, which can be given gestalt [die Möglichkeit eines freigewählten und gestaltbaren Daseins], and which holds itself in what we call a way of comportment [Haltung]' (123). The gestalt which Dasein chooses for itself gives it its ontic stability, a stability which is ultimately grounded in the existential structure articulated by the analytic of Dasein. In this structure, being-toward-death, which throws Dasein back on its ownmost possibilities, is the very root of the stability of any comportment Dasein may concretely choose for itself.

The ontic forms of the historicity of Dasein take gestalt in ways of embodiment and enactment. Gesture, for example, is an embodiment of the historicity of gestalt. According to Schrag, 'gestures are movements of intentional experience in its expressive and communicative projection. It is not that gestures simply indicate or point to the intended contents of feeling, willing, and thinking; they are the concrete embodiment of these intentionalities ... My gestural embodiment reveals the structure and dynamics of my lived space as infused with meaning and value.'[91] This thesis, as we shall see, is anticipated by the conservative discourse of Weimar insofar as it attempts to describe the cultural specificity of ways of embodiment. Heidegger addresses the question of embodied gestalt in the attunement (*Befindlichkeit*) of Dasein: attunement signifies the invisible body of Dasein. It articulates itself ontically in gesture and comportment, as well as in forms of dance, sport, play, styles of music. This sense of gestalt will allow Heidegger, as we shall see, a significant point of contact with conservative discourse, which sought to propagate a national 'style' of embodiment in all its forms. Finally, the historicity of Dasein in this sense already implicates *the historicity of Volk*. The historicity of Dasein arises out of the ways it takes over its heritage, in the happening or 'historizing of a community, of a people (Volk)' (SZ 384/SZ-MR 436). This happening of a Volk, which Heidegger calls its 'destiny' (*Geschick*), is articulated ontically and concretely in the specific political institutions, forms of labour, art, and technology, as well in styles of leadership and thought of a people. Heidegger's reflections on labour, for example, in the *Logik* of 1934, is an explicit attempt to give labour in its relation to the state and the Volk a new ontic gestalt, or concrete articulation, in accordance with the historicity of Dasein.

In certain respects, Husserl's understanding of the forms of the life-world anticipates Heidegger. According to Husserl, cultural types of the formation of social-ethical life include, for example, the religious life: in such a culture, 'a consciously constituted idea of purposiveness [Zweck-idee] lives in a [form of] cultural humanity and, in [its] most conscious gestalt, in one of its social organs (in the priesthood).' This *Idee* is actualized in a will, 'which in an unmediated way belongs to the whole community and which is supported by the collective will of the community.' 'The idea of purposiveness is one of a universal and absolute regulation of the whole culture under the system of absolute norms derived from divine revelation.' Husserl continues, 'But in respect to the life of the community and the entirety of cultural development which takes place within it, we may say, that it has the peculiar form [Gestalt] of a [form of] life, of a development, which has in itself a unitary idea of purposiveness [Zweck-idee], which is constituted in the collective consciousness of the community, an idea of purposiveness which intentionally guides development.'[92] Later, in *The Crisis*, Husserl will recognize the objective a priori of the life-world.[93] Gestalt, however, is not only given in the a priori of a life-world – a new gestalt also can be produced, inducing a paradigm shift.[94]

The construction of a new gestalt of the community, based on its own anthropological premises (which are of course not to be confused with Husserl's thought) is a fundamental concern of the radical conservatives. And despite the clear distinctions between Heidegger's philosophy and the theses of the Conservative Revolution, we shall see that the re-constitution of a gestalt of the *Volk* is central to Heidegger's reflections of the early 1930s, just as it was to conservative discourse.

Finally, I will quote a passage from an interview with Max Müller (1985), a former student of Heidegger's. Müller offers this interpretation of Heidegger's thought:

> I believe that ... [Heidegger] saw the necessity of institutions ... very clearly. For everything turned for him on the [question of] *Gestalt*. Therefore the gestalt of leadership, or gestalt in Stefan George, or the gestalt of the worker, and also the form and gestalt of the community. Ernst Jünger had great influence on him. For ... [Heidegger], not abstract norms and values

were binding, but rather concrete gestalten, which one could follow and imitate. The gestalt, which a Volk has to win for itself, is the work. And this gestalt, on the one hand, has to be proper to it, and on the other, the opposition of objectivity and subjectivity disappears in it. It is our gestalt and yet an objective gestalt.[95]

Müller identifies the centrality of overcoming representational thinking in Heidegger's thought, and the necessity of ways and forms of being which can bind and obligate. The gestalt, understood as structure of temporalization, as 'embodied' historicity, discloses modes of being (whether the being of a thing or of an institution) that issue a call, and that call for a binding response. Undoubtedly the word *Gestalt* easily evokes misleading interpretations. Gottfried Schramm (who conducted this interview, along with Bernd Martin) glosses Müller's remark to mean that, for Heidegger, the problem of modern politics and its institutional structure is reduced to a fixation on charismatic leaders, and a mythical interpretation of institutions. I will show that this is a total misconception of the problem. To speak of *being and gestalt* in reference to Heidegger's thought, thus to think the differentiation of being in beings, is only possible in terms of the destruction of metaphysics.

As opposed to a tradition of interpretation which reads Heidegger's critique of modernity as evidence of his 'cultural pessimism' and disassociation from concrete historical realities (Habermas), postmodern thinkers such as Foucault, Baudrillard, and Paul Virilio have taken up Heidegger's phenomenology of the disintegration of the modern subject and the Enlightenment project in specific and fruitful interrogations of their own. What is most obviously at stake here, in these opposing responses to modernity, are two, very different senses of our hermeneutic situation.

The hermeneutic situation to which Heidegger responds, as he makes evident with considerable explicitness in both *An Introduction to Metaphysics* and the *Contributions to Philosophy*, is the dis-integration and functional integration of beings into the availability of stock-on-call. Heidegger's thesis is that this event consummates the history of metaphysics. This experience of the abandonment of beings (*Seinsverlassenheit*) to the objectivity of representation and the functionalization which follows from it creates the need to ask about being, to retrieve being from forgetfulness (*Seinsvergessenheit*). The question of being, however, does not lead away from beings, or from humanity, but seeks to overcome the *chorimos* between beings and being which constitutes the legacy of metaphysics.

To interrogate Dasein as the site of the disclosure of being, and to found being in beings, inaugurates the project of another beginning. Being 'is' nothing mystical, behind or above the phenomena, not the deterministic other of mankind. Nor is mankind, in its response to being conceived as wilful subject entangled in its own 'decisionism.' To say that Dasein is the 'site' of being signifies that Dasein is the project of the disclosure of being in beings. This implies a responsibility to beings as beings, to what is most proper to them. The functional determination of entities signifies a loss of being. In taking this experience as his point of departure in key works of the 1930s, Heidegger does not abandon the phenomenological method, but rather seeks to bring the structures of our contemporary experience to light by revealing their provenance in the history of the meaning of being. The project of Da-sein implicates the retrieval of another way of being, and another way of experiencing entities. To speak of the 'gestalt' of being as incorporated in beings, and as instituted in the communal institutions of Da-sein itself in its specificity and historicity, signifies an openness to possible modes of the temporalization of being that is more 'proper' to Dasein and to beings, if only in the sense of being less reductive than objectification and functional disintegration. The differentiation of being grants beings their singularity, their difference. The project of Da-sein in this sense, moreover, can only become binding insofar as it speaks to a possibility of our experience, as one retrieved from tradition, just as the thesis of the disintegration of beings has to be experienced as disclosive of the phenomena and our own contemporary world. The founding of Da-sein opens up a path to the historicity of *Seyn*, and the disclosure of *Seyn* through the site of Da-sein is given gestalt through the historicity of a people and in the emergence of entities into the light of historicity.

1 The Challenge of the Planetary

1.1 Earth and Site

The earth is not a planet. Heidegger's political thought emerges from the need to rethink the concept of the planet to which the discourses of science have given rise. For Heidegger, accordingly, the question of the essence of politics arises with the need to save the possibility of an earth which can still be the homeland of its peoples. The planet is an errant star which has thrust the earth, its sky, and attendant moon into forgetfulness. In a short essay of 1959 – 'Aufzeichnungen aus der Werkstatt' – Heidegger comments on the significance of space flight, inaugurated by the Soviet Union under Nikita Khrushchev's leadership in that year:

> What the rocket accomplishes is the technical realization of something, which, since centuries, ever more exclusively and decisively, is posed and represented as nature, and which is now put on call as a universal, interstellar reserve. (GA13, 152)

As an interstellar mass and resource on call the planet eclipses the earth, 'in the sense of the poetic dwelling of humanity on this earth' (152). The poetic dwelling of mankind on the earth is the grant of being as it sends itself in the non-representational saying and making manifest of the being of beings as given in the in-each-case-unique traditions of a people.

The technical organization and conquest of the world for space travel is founded on nothing merely technical, for it is in its own way sited in the historical essence of Western thought. Heidegger understands the essence of technology (*das Gestell*) as the historical destining of Western humanity, a destiny which has now become definitive for the entire

globe. To call the historical unfolding of technology a destiny and sending sent to the collective humanity of our time, as Heidegger proposes,
would seem to evoke a mythological way of thinking. Even without our
engaging this question here, it is noteworthy that the enthusiasts of space
exploration, for example, in their own way no less appeal to a sense of
the historical destiny of mankind to found their vision and to legitimate
the sacrifices it imposes. Thus Carl Sagan's *Pale Blue Dot,* for example,
evokes the mystique of emigration and homelessness: it is our destiny
never to be at home anywhere, to be driven by the fundamental unease
of a primordial rootlessness. The 'blue dot' of Sagan's title is already
indicative of the mathematical abstraction of the earth, and hence its
weightlessness on the scales of technological reason. The popular treatment which Sagan's book gives to a certain fundamental mood of
postmodern humanity is developed in contemporary thought in the
deconstruction of identity and the 'nomad' being of technological
humanity. The question which Heidegger raises, in turn, is whether the
earth as earth still holds a destiny in reserve, whether it is still capable of
calling mankind 'home.' What is this, and whence does it draw its power,
what we call – home? Perhaps Heidegger's entire political thought is
implicated in this question.

The planetary homelessness of mankind is itself a destiny, and the possible gateway of humanity's coming to be at home on the earth. According to Heidegger, everything depends on this turn – on the turn in – into
the truth of the essence of technology (GA13, 153). The 'truth' to which
Heidegger appeals here is the truth of arrival in sheltering unconcealment (*aletheia*), not the propositional truth of correspondence. This
implies that truth is rethought as the rhythm of a site to which an historically delimited humanity belongs, and from which it takes the truth – the
modes of the manifestation of being – which owns it. We are asked to
conceive the in-each-case-unique historical site governing the arrival and
departure of beings, a site which grants to each the unconcealment
and sheltering distance allowing them to be what they are. The propositional truth of representational thinking, conversely, aims at the proac-
tive calculation of the planet as a set of resources on call. It abstracts
from the uniqueness of the site in favour of the uniformity of the space-
time dimension. By representational thinking, according to 'The Age of
the World Picture,' Heidegger understands the re-presentation of entities for a subject. The subject is posited in advance as *subjectum,* as the
foundation of the manifestation of the being of beings. Planetary thinking is in essence representational, and the planet is the collective repre-

sentation of scientific-technical discourse. It is Heidegger's thesis that the truth of the site, which is nothing other than the openness of Dasein to being, is the condition of representational thinking, for things can only be represented to and for a subject insofar as subject and object come to encounter each other in the primordial openness of Dasein. Heidegger's political thought, understood as the pre-condition for a possible politics, centres on the question whether or not the consummation of the Greek experience of being in planetary technology also reserves the possibility of another founding, another beginning, which would be neither repetition nor emulation of the first, but something else entirely, and as such the unique historical moment of an historical people.

After 1945, what remained of Heidegger's belief in the historical mission of a people to found anew a site preserving the earth as earth? The conclusion of the essay quoted above appeals to the dual destiny of language: 'language on the racetrack of information, language on the way into the Saying of the event of appropriation' (*die Sage des Ereignisses*) (GA13, 154). Information – or the Saying of language: this intimates, Heidegger claims, the crossroads of a decision the technical masters of the planet cannot make, for planetary thinking merely consummates the decline from the first founding. Rather than deciding, planetary thinking institutes the regime of a planning and calculating which makes itself at home in the undecidability of mankind's technically conceived destiny. For 'decision' in Heidegger's usage of the 1930s means that what mankind is – is put up for decision. But insofar as representational-technical thinking has already decided in advance that humanity is to be defined as the collective subject of the will to power, and given that this subject itself serves the will to power, the being of humanity and the presencing (*Wesen*) of being are no longer open for questioning.

The language of 'information' – the discourse of the sciences and their technical offspring – is conceived as the crystallization of this mode of being. The form, or gestalt, of humanity to which technological discourse gives birth is planetary and cosmopolitan. Its City is everywhere, and nowhere. Technological discourse is a nexus of abstraction which deracinates even while creating the tantalizing simulacrum of a world.

To follow this path, therefore, is to race toward an end which has long since been decided. What of the other path? Heidegger speaks of the 'Sage des Ereignisses' (GA13, 154): the Saying of the event of appropriation. The thought of the *Ereignis* had been central to Heidegger's thought for more than twenty years before this essay of four pages was written. In a preliminary way, this much can be ventured: the *Ereignis* inti-

mates the event of the encounter of an historical humanity with its gods.
In the blink of an eye in which a glance is exchanged (*Er-äugnis*), a
human community and its gods are brought into the limits of what gives
each its own (*Er-eignis*). The community comes to be in the instant of the
glance, through the encounter with the gods. For this reason, given that
the *Ereignis* is conceived as a founded site, the Saying of *Ereignis* still calls,
even from the perspective of 1959, for a national community. Therefore
Heidegger's fundamental position of 1933–45, which insists that being
inscribes itself into a site founded in the historical life of a people, has
not changed, despite the much-remarked shift of emphasis from 'people' to 'language.' The 'decision' – which is to say, the differentiation
(*Ent-scheidung*) – *of being*, which delimits each from each and sends each
into the limit of its own being, calls for a site. Heidegger argues that the
planetary dimension does not permit this measure of decision, for all
that is has been determined in advance as a function of the uniform
space of technicity.

There is a fundamental difference, however, between Heidegger's estimation of the possibilities of political engagement, as expressed in
'Aufzeichnungen aus der Werkstatt,' and his decision for the new regime
of 1933. This difference is articulated by his reference to the 'reserves'
(*Reservationen*) to which thinking is relegated under the regime of planetary thinking: 'today authentic thinking, such as seeks out and responds
to the originary missive of being, lives only on "reservations"' (GA13,
152). Originary, or meditative, thinking (*das sinnende Denken*) is confined
to figurative reserves, thus to hold itself in reserve, and possibly to
reserve and prepare another experience of being in the planetary age.
But philosophy cannot directly intervene in politics, as Heidegger apparently thought in 1933, to help guide the transformation of the modern
university, and thus in some measure the state. In fact, as Heidegger's
reflections on the state of knowledge and the university in the *Beiträge* of
1936–8 already indicate, the university increasingly survives merely as the
technical construct of the organization of research and the transmission
of information. In the meantime, this view has become relatively well
established, as Lyotard's *The Postmodern Condition: A Report on Knowledge*
(1979), for example, testifies. Could the university serve the modest yet
necessary purpose of establishing reserves of thought? Given the pre-
eminence of the technical and information sciences in the organization
of the university, this too is increasingly doubtful.

The 'reservation,' moreover, is a signifier of an imperial history. It
declares the triumph of the unidimensionality of technical thought over

the rootedness of a people within the bounded sphere of their native soil and their gods. The reservation is what has been saved as 'native soil,' but which nonetheless remains circumscribed by the imperial system. Yet meditative thinking, in Heidegger's sense, also reserves the possibility of a withdrawal from the claims of conceptualization which posit the globe as one, undifferentiated dimension. This withdrawal and with it the possibility of the transformation of being can only unfold itself as reserving itself in language, as refusing to give itself as signifier and information.

The 'reservation' of thought reserves for thought a saying without immediate effect in the planetary epoch. The operational character of representational thought, conversely, will find its truth constantly affirmed by the technical success to which it gives rise. This mode of thought, which brings what is into the open to represent and fix it as a function of a system of operations, cannot attend to what is non-functional in beings, to that which withdraws from functionality to reserve its own truth. This realm of self-manifesting withdrawal from representation, in all modes of experience, is the domain of meditative thought (GA13, 152–3).

Art is one such essential mode. The question of art and that of the essence of the political are intimately related in Heidegger's thought. The node of this encounter is the site of being, which is to say, the place (*Ort*) where the presencing of being (*Wesung des Seins*) incorporates itself in the particular, historically de-termined and delimited forms of experience of a people. In Heidegger's estimation, the work of art, together with thinking, pre-eminently discloses being, and it does this by in-corporating presencing in the work.

Yet as a short text (dating from 1962 and published in the same volume) in praise of Stravinsky's music proposes, the work of art is no longer capable of founding the site (*Ort*) which would allow it to unfold its own truth (GA13, 181). The relation of dependence between the work and its world, hinted at here, is central to Heidegger's reflections of the 1930s. From the *Beiträge* it is apparent that Heidegger's political thought calls for the artwork to incorporate being; but these reflections on the essence of politics also attend a 'constitution' of being which would allow the work to found its own site. For although it is not within the power of the polity to grant a site, it is certainly within the means of the modern state, as well as civil society, to prevent the unfolding of a site. Liberalism, which reduces art to an object of consumption, and socialism, which restricts it to the re-presentation of a reality posited by conceptual thinking, are equally impotent, in Heidegger's estimation, to allow the artwork the space of its unfolding. From our own postmodern perspective, the system of the signifier, as Derrida develops it, in fact radicalizes both positions, thus to reduce the work (*ergon*) to a product of the conceptual system (*parergon*) which makes it manifest.[1] For this reason, at least according to Heidegger, it becomes necessary to conceive of the possibility of a third way. For the failure of liberalism and socialism, as exemplified by their respective cultural politics, is in each case indicative of essentially uprooted thought, which pursues deracination as the precondition of the planetary organization they in each case envision.

The advent of space travel has allowed us to see the image of our globe in the precise delimitation of its form against the backdrop of space, for the first time. And the contemplation of this image has sometimes, for some, evoked the awe of religious experience. But what is essential to the nature of the image? What is the place of the image, if it is to fully unfold its power? And what is the provenance of this power? Insofar as these questions circle around the issue of the sitedness of thought and image, particularly in the work of art, they are also questions concerning the essence of the political. The power of imaging media, which makes for a certain kind of politics, is self-evident. The dis-integration of place in the videoscape of television, of video, and of cyberspace technologies also allows for a precise technical fixation and stabilization of the 'face' of the planet. The face or aspect captured in this way consummates the *eidos* which is fixed in the 'idea' of Plato's philosophy. The reserve of images-on-call, in turn, opens a new space for politics, including the politics of art and the place which might still be granted to it within the global domain. As Jean Baudrillard argues in *Simulacra and Simulations*, the postmodern image is integrated into an imaging system which creates a simulacrum of the earth. The earth in the uniqueness of its multiplicity is pushed into forgetfulness. For the simulacrum announces the dimension of uniform availability that is the essence of the *Unwesen* of being. *Unwesen* is to be understood as the de-essentialization, as the withdrawal of the saving shelter of the site, and its surrender to uniform accessability. The information highway of the cyberworld puts the planet on call, but it cannot acknowledge earth-sitedness as a way of being. Insofar as the global image enters the repertoire of disembodied images-on-demand, it is liable to lose any force beyond that of a mere sentiment for the unity of the globe. While this sense may even be valuable in itself, this form of sentiment is not at all opposed to planetary thinking, and in fact furthers it by providing a justification for an ever more thorough rationalization of the planet for 'cosmopolitan' ends. The planetary image is infinitely removed from the image as the gateway to the manifestation of a particular communication of the divine.

In a short reflection, dating from 1955, on the *Sixtina* of Piacenza, Heidegger writes the following: 'But the image is not a copy nor a symbol only of the holy consecration. The image is the shining-forth of the play of the time-space of that site in which the offering of the Mass is celebrated' (GA13, 121). Neither copy (*Abbild*) nor symbol (*Sinnbild*), the image (*Bild*) is the arrival into presence (*Scheinen*) of the time-space of that particular site which the Mass consummates. And this also means that the image, as image, is not the representation of what is already established as reality but opens, through its own manifestation, the site (*Ort*) of its own, unique reality. Doubtless the image can be conceived as copy and as symbol. This understanding of the work is proper to aesthetics and its allied institutions, such as the museum; but the image loses the place proper to it in this domain because it cannot unfold its own site out of itself. As the form of the institutionalization of aesthetics, the museum constitutes a mode of representational thinking (*Vorstellen*) which 'levels everything into the uniformity of the "exhibition," which only offers positions in space [Stellen], but not sites [Orte]' (GA13, 120). The institution of aesthetics, in effect, is integral to planetary thinking. Aesthetics is the precondition of the establishment of a single, unitary dimension for art, and with it, of the effacement of the in-each-case-unique site of the work, such as the work itself founds. To establish the historical conditions of the work by reference to its socio-historical, psychological, and formal 'causes' is evidently central to aesthetic discourse and the neutral space it prepares for the work's manifestation. This neutral space, moreover, is entirely proper to a liberal politics of art, which precisely by these means – those of neutralization – prevents the work from unfolding its power, even as it integrates the image into the shadow 'world' of cyberspace.

But what, more precisely, does Heidegger understand by the 'time-space' to which he appeals as the site of the work? We have already noted that the time-space of the work is founded by the work itself – it is everything other than a prior dimension, whether of Newtonian or Einsteinian space and time, into which the work is placed. Heidegger notes that the *Sixtina*, for example, is a *Fenstergemälde*, according to the categorizations of art history. But what is a window?

Its frame delimits [grenzt] the openness of shining-through, in order to gather it, through the boundary, into released shining-forth. The window as admission of approaching shining is a prospect of arrival. (GA13, 120)

The nature of the time-space (*Zeit-Spiel-Raum*) of the site gains in clarity from this passage inasmuch as we are led to think the image by reference to the essential nature of the window. The image of the *Sixtina* is a 'window' precisely as passage and as the site of the gathering of this passage into the gestalt. Equally essential to the image-as-window is the delimitation of shining-forth by the frame, which is conceived here as the bourn through which the openness of illumination is liberated, concentrated, and gathered. The frame, as bourn, in this sense, has something essential in common with the meditation on *arche* and *peras*, which Heidegger develops elsewhere (in the essay of 1939 devoted to Aristotle's *Physics*, and in the Anaximander lectures [GA51] of 1941). The bourn of the image is the *arche* of its concentrated shining-forth. The unbounded, infinite, by contrast, is powerless to manifest itself as itself in its sited gatheredness – which may be why contemporary aesthetics, by way of a reflection on the unmanifest, gives such a central place to the aesthetics of the sublime. Derrida's reflection on Kant's *Critique of Judgement*, to be sure, gives considerable attention to the enframing of the work, or *ergon*, but with the explicit intention of de-constructing, or disassembling, the work as an autonomous manifestation of form (which it still is for Kant), in favour of the conditions which give rise to the *ergon*: the *parergon* as conceptual frame of, or condition of the possibility of, the manifestation of form.[2] The tendency of postmodern aesthetics, therefore, is to confirm the dissolution of the sited and finite disclosure of being into the system of simulations, understood as the digital modelling of a 'reality,' which is consequently produced as simulacrum. The image as simulacrum is at the furthest remove from the gestalt.

The work as image, therefore, demands that we bring together the gathering of the passage, the delimitation of the bourn, and the liberation of manifestation through the gestalt set off by the frame. In the liberation into appearance through the delimitation of the boundary, we may intimate the governing principle of an *arche*. The work, arising out of its own movement into manifestation (*arche*), brings itself into appearance within its proper limit. The gathering which the window *is* recalls Heidegger's interpretation of the *logos* in his *Heraklit* of the 1940s: *logos* pre-eminently means the gathering of the site to which thinking responds in saying, and out of which the being of being unfolds (GA55, 378–84). The image belongs to the time-space-play of the *logos*, and as such is a gathering of a site, understood as the historicity of the sending of tradition. The destiny coming to presence through the image is given a place, and opens a place for itself to found a site: 'the window as admission of approaching shining is a prospect of arrival' (GA13, 120). The image-as-window opens a site for the arrival of manifestation. Arrival, however, is not the presence of availability, but rather the reserve inherent in the approach of the distant, which remains distant even while approaching. The play (*Spiel*) of the time-space unfolds the play of near and far, of arrival and reserve, of the reserve and withdrawal from the representational thought of the mere copy (*Abbild*). For this reason, Heidegger writes that the image of the Madonna brings with it, in its sudden incalculable arrival into presence, 'the concealed, saving shelter of its provenance' (GA13, 120). In the unity of the bringing, the gathering, and the setting-into-the-work, the image is '*Gestalt*' (GA13, 121). The properly understood historicity of the image is its power to found a history by 'in-corporating' the rhythm of a particular time-space in a work. The withdrawal of the image from representational thinking (*das verborgen Bergende ihrer Herkunft*) is essential to the time-space of a site, for only insofar as the image is *geborgen* (saved, sheltered) in the distant approach of the unrepresented can it found a site. The representational dimension, conversely, dissolves the site into the uniformity of the planetary dimension.

The withdrawal from representational thinking and its calculations, in such a way as to found a site, is fundamental to the presencing of the image, and hence of the artwork. We have seen that the image presences in bringing the aspect of the Madonna to shine in and through the delimitation of the gestalt (GA13, 121). The word *Gestalt* is not used in a Platonic sense, hence it does not imply, in Heidegger's usage, the relation of copy and original, as has been claimed in respect to his use of the word in an aesthetic and political context. In fact, his usage of this word since the 1930s is free of this implication. It refers to the delimitation (*Grenze, Grenzgebung*) of presencing, which comes to a stand in the unique instance of the work. The root meanings of *Gestalt* we will find determining Heidegger's use of the word may be anticipated as follows: gestalt signifies (*i*) the proper, or self-determined, limit; (*ii*) the unfolding of the movement (*kinesis*) proper to an entity so as to bring it into its own *morphe*; hence (*iii*) the rhythm, the ownmost temporality of a being; therefore (*iv*) that which determines it in its ownness; where *ownness* designates (*v*) the historicity, or historically sited presencing, of the being of a being. In what follows, depending on the precise context, all of these senses will be in play.

The deconstruction of the relation of copy and original, which re-inscribes both as functions of an economy of signifiers, presupposes the universal and indifferent dimension of being-as-signifier. This dimension opens a system of co-ordinates but cannot allow the site as site, nor the image as the site of withdrawal from operational calculation. Heidegger understands the work-as-image as the event which gathers the time-space of a history to generate the site that consummates the construction of the church. This event is not available, on call. It only is in the instant of the exchange of a glance between the image and the communicant. 'Thus the image figures the site of the unconcealing saving shelter [of *aletheia*] as which the image, in unconcealing, presences [west]' (GA13, 121). In and through the delimitation of its gestalt, the image unfolds the site of a unique instance of arrival and saving withdrawal from manifestation. The truth (*aletheia*) appealed to here is thought as the event of the arrival into appearance in such a way as to save and shelter what is from mere availability to representational thinking and its conceptual formulae. The truth of representational thinking, in turn, decomposes the image into the discourses – historical-sociological, formal, and psychological – which 'cause,' or generate, the image. It is made to serve as a 'signifier,' meaning a certain quantum of productive energy of these discourses. What is developed in this respect in structuralism is only given a still more radical formulation in post-structuralism.

It is, therefore, Heidegger's argument that the truth of representational thinking and its discourses, which posit an object for subjectivity in order to re-present the object to and for subjectivity, is derivative of truth more primordially understood as unconcealment (*aletheia*). For in order for an object to appear over against a subject, there must already be an open space – the space of unconcealment – which makes the encounter possible. This open space is the site of being (hence Da-sein), from which the uniformity of the planetary dimension is an abstraction. The uniformity of Newtonian space and time abstracts from the multiplicity of sites. What is unique to the manifestation of beings in each case is 'forgotten.'

The forgetfulness of the unique measure of the presencing of being in and through beings is itself founded in the abandonment of beings to their mere objectivity and ultimately functionality: this is what Heidegger understands as *die Seinsverlassenheit*. Being as presencing withdraws from beings and allows them to pass over into the static schemata of their mere availability. Reflection on the abandonment of beings by being, and with it the occultation of the sitedness of the being of being, is central to Heidegger's thought in the thirties. The experience of *Seinsverlassenheit* is also crucial to the development of his political thought.

Heidegger's understanding of the *Unwesen* (de-essentialization) proper to the presencing of being itself demands that we rethink *Wesen* as 'presencing,' rather than as 'essence' in the metaphysical sense. Beings are forsaken to their *Unwesen* – they no longer presence. In Heidegger's usage of the *Beiträge* of 1936–8, they are *Unseiend* – non-beings; not nothing, but deprived of the 'aura' proper to their histori-cally sited self-manifestation and consequently reduced to the functions of an economy (GA65, 238/168). This abandonment of entities to their de-essentialization incites a shift in attunement to the whole of what is, and therefore calls for a decision regarding being. This decision will also be a 'political' decision – a determination of the con-stitution of the manifestation of beings in their differentiated, sited gatheredness.

This brief consideration of three late texts may serve to offer some pre-liminary insight into the premises of Heidegger's political thought. They also allow us to anticipate certain themes and questions central to those works, especially from the time of Heidegger's political engagement in the thirties, which I will consider below. I have suggested that the 'site' is crucial to Heidegger's understanding of being. If this is so, then the thought of being is the thought of the presencing of being in and through the delimitations of a particular historical site. Heidegger's phi-losophy is earth-sited thought: it emerges as a response to the abandon-ment of beings to the functional categories of conceptual thinking. The advent of being, its presencing, is always as sited. Heidegger's thought of being responds to the need to prepare a place, including the site of a polity, where being may be incorporated in the rhythms of the artwork – of dance, music, architecture – in the rituals of rule and sacrifice. Being in this sense means the embodied rituals and rhythms of a people histor-ically grounded in its own place. This interpretation of being is already decisive, as we shall see, for Heidegger's works of the thirties. Only within this horizon of thought are Heidegger's responses to, and expectations of, National Socialism at all comprehensible.

The sitedness of being in its in-each-case-unique space-time calls for a recovery of the finitude, or 'delimitation,' of being from the claim of transcendental categories of experience. These categories, as Heideg-ger's *Nietzsche* lectures argue, find their ultimate consummation in the de-limitation, or limitlessness, of the representational thinking of the will to will (NI 508–16/3: 32–38; NII 467). The gestalt of the work, which Heidegger interprets as the setting-into-the work of the unconcealment of being, is one way the presencing of being is founded. The sitedness of being means that the being of beings 'is' *Anwesen*: presencing in the gestalt. Heidegger's comments on *ousia* in the *Introduction to Metaphysics*, as well as his detailed unfolding of *ousia* in the Aristotle essay of 1939 (especially the reinterpretation of *ousia* as the differential boundedness of *morphe* and *en-ergon*) open and confirm the space for what is mapped out in the *Beiträge* and exemplified in 'The Origin of the Work of Art': to think being means to recover the ground whence the earth, in its delimited historical figurations, can unfold itself as 'native soil,' and in the multiplicity of sacred sites.

As the consummation of the original Greek founding, planetary thinking has its own – but limited – claim. In postmodern thinking, as represented by Derrida, for example, *ousia* is deconstructed in its metaphysical signification as substance in such a way as to found a functional system still derivative of metaphysical thinking. Precisely as planetary thinking it cannot recognize its own limitations. This way of thought understands the being of beings in terms of the objectivity and functionality, which is the precondition of the planet as planet – as an interstellar mass of resources on call. Planetary thinking implicates the large-scale organization and management of global resources, hence a high level of co-ordination of management structures, although not necessarily a centralization of command. The globe is perceived as a single uniform dimension, obedient to universal scientific laws and technical norms of productivity. The sole questions at issue for the incipient global order thus conceived is how to institute the most efficient global economy and the most flexible, pragmatic politics commensurate with the maximum, long-term, sustainable exploitation of the planet. The question of the being of the individual entity, its truth and uniqueness, cannot arise within the regime of the global mobilization of beings. This threefold Not may even be proclaimed as a value in itself, as a form of liberation from the 'metaphysical tradition.' The affirmation of this 'not,' which negates the sitedness of being in favour of the functional integration of beings into operational networks, reflects the fundamental dispositions of postmodern, planetary thinking. The Not affirms itself in the unease generated by deracination, in the boredom instigated by the mere simulacra of being, and in the enthusiasm of a will to master what is, was, and will be, thus to render it transparently available. Therefore, the planetary dimension is thoroughly ahistorical: because the historical world, like the earth itself, is perceived as a resource (a repertoire of concepts and images on call), planetary thinking must remain closed to the non-representational presencing of tradition, and to the possibility of the divine, which is, according to Heidegger, the root of history because it inaugurates the in-each-case-particular history of a people.

1.2 The Differentiation of Being and the Distinction of *Sein* and *Seyn*

The issues and questions arising out of the late texts we have considered are thoroughly developed for the first time in Heidegger's *Beiträge zur Philosophie (Vom Ereignis)*. In section 32 of that work, Heidegger formulates the task of philosophy as

> finding the simple aspects and homelike figures [Gestalten] to bring them into appearance, in which appearance the essential swaying [Wesung] of being is sheltered and lifted into the heart. (GA65, 72/50, modified)

The presencing of being, therefore, takes gestalt in beings. Heidegger refers to the forms (*Gestalten*) and aspects beings take in their historical specificity and singularity (*heimische Gestalten*). This already intimates that the presencing of being is always finite, and historically founding and founded. The presencing of being, in turn, implicates the distinction between *Seyn* and *Sein*, which has hitherto guided this account. *Seyn* is simply the archaic spelling for *Sein*; but the distinction that Heidegger intends by this variant spelling is crucial to his thought (GA65, 235/166). *Seyn* is not the highest and the emptiest category of what is, *Seyn* is not the ultimate cause of beings, nor the transcendental being of beings. This way of understanding being is proper to the ontotheology of metaphysics and pertains to the way being has been interpreted since the 'decay' of the first beginning – it pertains to *das Sein*. Being presences, unfolds, or holds sway (*west*) as the truth of beings. *Wesen* intimates the presencing of what has been reserved in the saying of *Seyn*: presencing gives itself to beings even as it withdraws from representational thought. The truth of beings is the site (the Da-) of the emergence of beings into the shelter of a gestalt, into the circumscribed limits of work, action, ritual, and rhythm. The presencing of *Seyn*, which withdraws beings from the objectivity and functionality of representational thinking, shelters and saves beings in the unrepresented. The metaphysical thought of being, by contrast, allows entities to be fixed in the representation schema of a 'transparency' and availability to calculation, wherein they become, strictly speaking, *Unseiend*. As I have noted, the non-being of the

Unseiend is not nothing, but rather evokes the reduction of being to the availability of stock-on-call (GA65, 238/168).

The distinction between *Sein* and *Seyn* unfolds itself pre-eminently in two aspects: (*i*) in the way the question of being is asked in the metaphysical tradition, as opposed to Heidegger's asking of the question; (*ii*) in the mode of being which the thought of *Seyn*, as opposed to *Sein*, in each case grants to beings. The metaphysical asking of the question throws being itself – or, more properly, its presencing (*die Wesung des Seyns*) – into forgetfulness. And insofar as presencing withdraws, beings are left to themselves, abandoned by *Seyn* to the 'reality' of conceptualization and the simulacra it brings forth.

Metaphysics asks about the being of beings. This is the guiding question (*die Leitfrage*) of metaphysics: 'Its most general form was formulated by Aristotle, as *ti to on*? What is a being, i.e., for Aristotle, what is *ousia* as the beingness of a being? Being here means *beingness*' (GA65, 75/52). The guiding thread of metaphysics, which determines how the being of beings is to be understood, is temporality. Being, or beingness (*die Seiendheit*), is conceived as the atemporal, the unchanging as opposed to the temporal nature of beings, which is conceived as a falling off from beingness. Hence the image is a falling off from the atemporality of the Idea, which is more in being precisely by being atemporal. Beingness, Heidegger continues, also signifies 'the *koinon*, what is common, and thus common for every being' (GA65, 75/52). Beingness is conceived as the emptiest of categories. Conversely, what Heidegger calls *die Grundfrage* establishes *das Seyn* as the ground of beings – not in the sense of the most general concept, or first cause of beings, but as the question which opens a ground, in effect, the Da- of a site allowing beings to manifest themselves in their uniqueness. The ground of beings as the time-space of presencing grounds itself in beings in the sense that the structure or rhythm of presencing is founded, and in each case founded differently, by the mode of manifestation of beings of a particular tradition and time. The *Wesung des Seyns* grounds beings by opening the site of their manifestation, wherein each can appear in the light of its own 'whiling,' its own time and specificity. Asking the *Grundfrage* implicates the project of opening up, in its concrete historicity, a ground which will allow thought to become rooted, hence to save and shelter what is in the rhythm proper to it. *Ereignis* is the name Heidegger gives to the rhythm of rhythms, the temporality of the opening-up and grounding of the site of Da-sein (GA65, 73–4/51).

Das Seiende and the reality of entities conceived and produced by the metaphysical thought of beingness are not identical (GA65, 74/52). Insofar as beings are totally circumscribed by the categories of metaphysics and denuded of the presencing of *Seyn*, they are ultimately given over to the abandonment of technicity and the purely producible. The abandonment of beings by being to the machinations of technicity is what Heidegger calls *die Seinsverlassenheit.* Heidegger judges the abandonment of beings by being to be the 'most profound mystery' of Western history (GA65, 219/153), as the secret of a destiny founded by Platonism and accentuated by Christianity. We may expect an understanding of this abandonment to also offer some insight into the more narrowly conceived political dimension of Heidegger's thought.

The second section of *Die Beiträge* is entitled 'Der Anklang' – 'The Echo.' The echo we are asked to hear is the 'echo of the essential swaying of be-ing [Wesung des Seyns] in the abandonment of the being' of beings (GA65, 107/75, modified); or still more precisely, 'the echo of be-ing [Seyn] as refusal in the abandonment of beings by being' (108/75). In the era of the consummation of metaphysics, under the regime of technicity, *Seyn* continues to presence precisely in withholding itself from beings, so as to give them over to the will to will. This will aims at what is producible and defines what is solely in terms of productivity and the product as a function of production values. The foundation of what has been called productionist metaphysics is the re-presentation of beings to and for the 'subject' as a function of the will to power. Under the regime of representational thinking, the triumph of the calculability of beings is the pre-eminent index of their abandonment by *Seyn.* Abandonment means that being no longer presences, or unfolds itself in and through beings, and that consequently the incalculability of presencing and hence the mystery of the being of beings withholds itself and is occluded in favour of their availability and transparency to representation. Not only this. For, mesmerized by the proliferation of entities as products of our own making, mankind grows blind to the incalculable presencing of being. The ever more precise manipulation of entities, which subjects them to the governance of technicity, goes hand in hand with the 'subjective' intensity of the experience of technicity, in all the possible forms of the acceleration and intensification of emotion. Intensification aims at the acceleration of the sense of being-alive, of living 'more' in ever shorter intervals of time. Heidegger fixes the kind of self-reflectivity which couples technicity and intensification in the term *Erlebnis* (GA65, 108/75). *Das Erlebnis* is the hyperreality of living, the hyperlife of the planetary 'individual,' plugged in and integrated into the hyperworld. Technicity unfolds as machination (*die Machenschaft*), which is not to be confused with the machinations of humans, but as the unfolding of the essence of technology (*das Gestell*) in all the modes of the pro-ductive securing and ordering of human and natural resources as available stock on call. Machination and intensification mutually condition each other to consummate the abandonment of being: human biochemistry must become thoroughly calculable, for example, to allow the chemical targeting of mental states, their modification and transformation. Understood as the condition of the experience of a 'world,' the biochemical manipulation and designer modification of moods intimate an integration of machination and intensification which is no longer founded on the 'subject,' but which rather disassembles the subject to integrate it into the interface of technicity and animality. This interface announces the consummation of metaphysics. It is nothing merely human.

According to Heidegger, not *Seinsvergessenheit*, but the abandonment of beings by being, or *Seinsverlassenheit*, is 'the most originary destining of the first beginning' (GA65, 115/80): metaphysics consummates itself in the withdrawal of being from beings, thus to allow the dis-integration of their proper limits and identities in favour of their integration into the economy of the interface. This event demands the attention of the phenomenological gaze to the dis-integration of the 'reality' (the being) of the things that are, which is indeed happening right before our eyes. Discussion of Heidegger's history of being has tended to focus on the forgetting, or oblivion, of being and its supposedly mystical overtones. But Heidegger pointedly insists that 'the *abandonment of the being of beings* is the ground of the forgottenness of being' (GA65, 114/80). It is the ground in the sense that beings are given-over to the mesmerizing spectacle of their availability and calculability and that this conceals the withdrawal of *Seyn* from them. Heidegger's development of this claim will concern us in greater detail in chapter 7, with specific reference to Heidegger's attempt to retrieve the being of *energeia* and *entelecheia* in the Aristotle essay of 1939. The abandonment of beings is the destiny which the disempowerment of *phusis* and the interpretation of being as idea inaugurate (GA65, 115/80). To say that *phusis* is disempowered, implicates, as Heidegger develops this question elsewhere, that *arche* is reinterpreted as principle or origin, as a metaphysically conceived ground of self-identical being-present, and no longer as the presencing (*Anwesen*) which illuminates the course of a being in its delimited specificity. Planetary thought heralds the differentiation of the non-differentiated: all differences defining entities are reduced to functional or operational differences, and the integration of these functions into the economy of production and consumption and the non-differentiated temporality proper to it consummates the planetary.

Anwesen, like the Greek ousia, can mean presence, and presence, in turn, may be interpreted as abiding, constant presence. This was the fate of the understanding of ousia in the decline of the Greek beginning (GA65, 223/156). But in ordinary language, as Heidegger points out in An Introduction to Metaphysics, Anwesen also refers to the bounded, well-defined gestalt of a being (a villa, for example), hence to the presencing of what becomes present out of the circumscription of its own limits. Ousia also has this sense of delimited presencing (GA40, 65/61). The de-limitation of being, conversely, which abiding presence implicates, degrades the entity itself (as this delimited gestalt) to the unbeing of the unabiding and inconstant: 'Beings continue to be what is present; and what actually is in being is the constantly present, which as such conditions every thing as thing, the un-conditioned, the ab-solute, ens entium, Deus, etc.' (GA65, 115/81). Conceived as the absolute and unlimited, the sitedness of being – hence the presencing, or holding sway (Wesung), of being (Seyn) in and through the temporality of the finite – is occluded and beings are relegated to the subsequentiality of what still is, but only as a copy is to an original, and thus without being fully in being (Unseiend). The being of beings is conceived as a falling-off from what truly is, as a decline from the Idea. The entities themselves become shadows of what is (GA65, 115, 222/81, 155). Postmodern thought, in turn, allows ousia as metaphysically thought substance to be deconstructed and posited anew as a functional system of signifiers. The withdrawal of being is fully consummated with the abandonment of beings to functionality. The absolute is now reconceived as the system of operational thinking, understood as the movement of the formal differentiation of beings insofar as they manifest themselves functions.

The nihilism of functionality is already prepared, according to Heidegger's account of the history of being, by Christianity: for entities are only insofar as they are made, and they could not remain in being for an instant were God to withhold being from them (GA65, 110–11/77–8). Christian theology offers the paradigmatic case of the explanation of the origin of beings: it offers a cause-effect schema which will be taken over and transformed by modern science. The ontotheology of metaphysics, therefore, establishes a gulf between the presencing of being and beings themselves, even as it constitutes the science of the being of beings and institutes the conditions, through the representation of entities, for the technical mastery of beings:

> Now beings are manifest *in this way* – they manifest themselves as object and as merely present, as if be-ing did not hold sway. Beings are what is indifferent and obtrusive at the same time, in the same undecidedness and randomness. (GA65, 115/81, modified)

Because the abandonment of beings gives them over to machination, and hence ultimately to the in-difference of being constituted functions of an operational economy, Heidegger calls *die Seynsverlassenheit* 'eine Ver-wesung des Seyns' (GA 65, 115/81). Insofar as *Seyn* withholds itself from entities, their residual functional being presences as the decay (*Verwesung*) of the arrival of a destiny (*Wesung*). Being is reduced to the emptiest of categories, and in the course of metaphysics, particularly in the train of Nietzsche, dissolves like a disappearing mist, overshadowed by the conceptual models of science and the hyper-reality these programs of simulation generate. The post-modern discourse of simulation and simulacra, as Baudrillard, for example, unfolds it, is a commentary on the consummation of metaphysics.

As such, the withdrawal of being from beings, thus to abandon them to the processes of simulation, 'must be experienced as the fundamental event of our history and be raised into knowing, as a formative and guiding power' (GA65, 112/78, modified). This demands, Heidegger continues, that the history of the abandonment of beings in the history of metaphysics be uncovered and be experienced as a distress which calls forth the necessity of a turn (*Not-wendigkeit*). Heidegger appeals to a formative, or gestalt-giving (*gestalterische*), knowledge (*Wissen*) rooted in the concern for the destiny of the West and therefore obligated to lead and capable of leading. The Rector's Address of 1933 appeals to *Wissen* in precisely this sense, and, as we shall see, it must be read in this light.

Let us briefly consider the sense of Heidegger's call for formative knowledge – that is to say, for a knowledge which gives form (gestalt). I have argued that the word *Gestalt* by no means necessarily implicates the Platonic metaphysics of original and copy. Nor is knowledge to be limited to the conceptual constructs of representational thinking. With this in mind, we can say one mode of formative knowledge would be the knowledge that gives gestalt by giving place and time to the presencing of the work of art. As opposed to the unsitedness of operational thinking, for which the planet itself is only the abstraction of economic and military planning, formative thinking responds to the holding sway of being: the work is itself the gestalt of the presencing of being through the limits of form. In terms of the project of the *Beiträge* as an essay in formative thought, 'The Origin of the Work of Art' is conceived as an attempt to open a place for the artwork. The work founds being by giving place to being in a being. Being differentiates and manifests itself in the presencing of the articulated limits of a being. Conversely, beingness (*die Seiendheit*) unfolds itself without limit in machination and the self-reflection of intensification. The distinction between the limit and the unlimited, which is founded in the difference between the being of metaphysics and the presencing of *Seyn*, is essential, for it in fact determines the difference between planetary and earth-sited thinking, including the politics proper to each. As the unity of the entire array of the interdependent applications of modern technology, from the social 'construction' of the individual to the determination of the human genome, machination presupposes a uniform dimension of operation. The surface of the globe is in principle conceived as one de-limited space by planetary thought. The earth as earth cannot arise. The appeal to the earth calls for recognition of a multiplicity of incomparable sites, as postmodern thought, in reaction to the metanarrative of modernity, has begun to recognize.

In the realm of historical reflection, machination names the order of 'generally calculable explainability, by which everything draws nearer to everything else equally and becomes completely alien to itself – yes, totally other than just alien. The relation of non-relationality' (GA65, 132/92). The relation of non-relation, which is the indifference of a purely functional differentiation of beings as signifiers, is unfolded in the post-structuralism of Derrida, as liberation from the determinations of presence and self-identity inscribed in entities by the metaphysical tradition.[3] In the economy of the movement of signification, the work of art, for example, is generated by its conditions of possibility (or *parerga*) as a set of signifiers. Once the work has been conceived in this way, deconstructive thought has already established the ground plan of comparison which would allow every work to be integrated into the uniform field of textuality. The work becomes a 'text' precisely in the sense that it surrenders its rhythm to the atemporal abstraction of the codes which govern and generate a text. The planetary world, as Baudrillard has developed this theme, is the world of codes – or simulation processes – which generate simulacra of the *réel*. Derrida's thinking exemplifies, perhaps better than any other, our own postmodern hermeneutic situation. It is significant that this situation is already anticipated by Heidegger's work of the

1930s, in ways that are only now becoming apparent. The 'relation of non-relation' increasingly defines our being in the era of globalization.

There is a relationship of sense between two notes audible to the ear, but the binary codes simulating these notes for the purposes of digitalization have no relation as music. This example illustrates the ends of planetary representation as the pre-emptive modelling of the earth. The relation of *relata* as signifying functions governed by codes disintegrates beings into the mutual in-difference of the same, hence into unrelatedness. The code, to be sure, which models a process is in being; but it has the being of beingness – or, more precisely, of a functionalized ideality – and not the being of the presencing of being. In the same way, information technology establishes a neutral dimension of proximity, actively excluding closeness, for closeness presupposes the distance of self-reserve. Self-reserve is governed by its own time, understood as the rhythm of the timely and untimely. In order for language, for example, to serve as 'information' it must already have submitted to the neutrality of a uniform temporal space. Poetry disintegrates into bytes of linguistic, rhetorical, and affective data from the instant it is sucked into the cybernet. The work as work cannot unfold its own rhythm under the conditions of the universal and indifferent availability of cyberworld 'access.' Technical processes such as these, which allow us a glimpse of what Heidegger understands by the relation of unrelatedness, intimate that machination implicates the thorough disintegration of tradition as the prelude to the institution of the planetary dimension. This dimension opens an order of the co-ordination of energies – including, of course, the psychosomatic energy of human resources – for the sake of a certain stability and long-term sustainable growth of the planetary economy.

As an articulation of the functionalization of entities, which reduces them to mere 'operators' within a global system of production and expenditure, the system of *l'écriture* in Derrida's thought offers an essential insight into the abandonment of beings. For the metaphysical foundation of the systematic exploitation of the earth, conceived as a single, uniform planetary dimension, is the dis-integration, or 'deconstruction,' in the Derridian sense, of the presence, proper identity, and being of beings. The deconstruction of the being of beings, in this sense, is the condition of the integration of beings into the global economy of the unlimited generation, substitution, and exchange of 'signifiers.'[4] The infinity of this play, which arises out of the ever more refined mobilization of what is, institutes what Heidegger calls 'the gigantic' (GA65, secs. 70–1). The movement of the differentiation of beings under the regime of the gigantic does not allow entities to rest in themselves, as governed by the self-reserve of their own being. Every measure of self-reserve impedes the circulation and exchange of signifiers. For this reason, because entities are delivered over in their entirety to exposure and transparency, the destitution of the being of beings is consummated in the gigantic. Yet the gigantic veils itself by manifesting itself in the guise of an intensification of life (*Erlebnis*). It masks the destitution of our abandonment to the non-being of functionality. Heidegger proposes that the self-concealment of the gigantic takes pre-eminently three forms, which are collectively encompassed by a fourth: the subjection of beings to calculation; their acceleration, in every sense, including the acceleration of information and every form of 'feedback'; and the rise of the power of the quantitative (GA65, sec. 58). The fourth, or the common dimension of these forms, is the publication and communication of any and every fundamental mood or attunement to being, such as rests in a self-reserved attentiveness to what is. The gigantic is at war with the self-reserved openness of simple attentiveness; it feeds on distraction. The triumph of publicity exposes every attunement to the calculations of the marketplace, to acceleration through the mass media, and to the quantification of a psychometrics of self-empowerment. In all these respects subjectivity joins forces with technicity to intensify the sensation of lived experience.

The *calculability* of what is: not only by means of number, but through the entire process of bureaucratization of human relations, as an ever more thorough-going organization of mankind and of nature. All beings are held to be calculable, in principle. Consequently, the incalculable is excluded because it is posited in advance as the not-yet-rationalized. *Acceleration,* conceived both as the process of the ever more precise and speedy unfolding of what is, as well as the unease of desire which hungers for new sensations, is allied to the calculability of beings, including the being of the observer who processes his own sensations with a view to intensifying them. The fundamental attunement of our contemporary humanity, Heidegger argues, arises out of our openness to the way the technologies of calculation and acceleration manifest what is. Our experience of an 'event' through the media, for example, is founded on an implosion of the real, as Baudrillard has shown. The 'rise of the masses,' as an historical and sociological phenomenon, is associated, certainly, with what Heidegger calls *quantification,* but this phenomenon is founded on the pre-eminence of an idea of the mathematical equality and in-difference of modern humanity, and thus on the incapacity to allow rank orders of being to arise. Quantification offers an insight into a levelling process which posits humanity as a whole as a single 'resource,' such as can be ultimately secured and improved by genetic mapping. Heidegger's reflections on quantification, therefore, should not be interpreted socio-historically and conflated with an opposition to social justice. According to Heidegger, the aspects of the gigantic are manifestations of the history of being, from which any sociology or historical critique also derives its claim as discipline: for the condition of 'critique' is the objectification of its subject of knowledge. Objectification, in turn, takes its condition of possibility from a specific understanding of being.

These modes of the unconcealment of being, through which Dasein is attuned to the governing whole, are gathered together, as I noted above, by a fourth characteristic of the consummation of metaphysics: the devaluation of attunement (*die Stimmung*) itself, in such a way as to conceal the power of attunement, and of the attuned word, to reveal what is. The nature of attunement – interpreted as mood or emotion or sentiment – is trivialized, manipulated, and over-exposed. The difference between inner and outer, between the social production of sentiment and the attunement of an individual, simply disappears (GA65, 122/85). And the erasure of this difference, we might add, is 'celebrated' by postmodernism as a triumph of the deconstruction of outmoded metaphysical categories. In all these respects the destitution of the being of beings is veiled, not simply by being concealed, but by the creation of a hyperworld of simulacra. The intensity of the cyberworld gives the sensation of a more liberated, freer life.

Heidegger's phenomenology of modernity, therefore, does not have a sociological critique of modern society as its end. The issue at stake is not the recovery of a distant past, nor is philosophy put in the service of the politics of reactionary, conservative modernism. The forces Heidegger reads as manifestations of the dis-integration of the being of beings have been celebrated, to be sure, as reflections of the democratization of society, and as evidence of the progressive character of technology. Yet this level of sociological analysis and political polemic neglects to ask the question of being: to argue, for example, that the modern media make for a more democratic dissemination of information (which may or may not be true) is not yet to engage the question of what language is, of whether it is essentially 'information,' or of whether the entity 'using language' is the master of language, and of its own being. Only if we ask ourselves these questions does the actual character of Heidegger's phenomenology of modernity emerge.

Calculation, acceleration, quantification, and publicity are not charac-
terizations of entities within the world, but a description of the *worldhood*
of modernity. They are modifications of the ontological-existential conditions of the presencing of entities within our world (cf. SZ, secs. 14–
18). The existential structure of Dasein, we recall, is articulated by State-
of-Mind or Situatedness (*Befindlichkeit*), along with Understanding and
Discourse. The masks of the destitution of the being of beings pre-eminently give expression to the Situatedness of Dasein, and therefore to
our throwness. This throwness, in turn, can only be experienced by way
of our moodful understanding of our being. Understanding, in turn, is
articulated by our experience of language. Heidegger's phenomenological descriptions of the being of beings under the regime of technology
are still methodologically founded in the analytic of Da-sein, and therefore serve the purpose of bringing to light the way beings become
present. And this calls for a description of the fundamental attunement
of our Situatedness. Only insofar as the fourfold dissimulation of our
throwness, and with it, our historically sited being-open to being,
becomes evident to us, Heidegger claims, will it be possible to experience the destitution of being and hence our need. Only this experience,
arising out of need, and an understanding founded in openness to the
possibilities which the tradition has reserved for the epoch of the consummation of metaphysics can prepare the ground for a turn toward
earth-sited thought.

The question therefore arises, whether and how the veils of the abandonment of being might come to be exposed as veils and fall away to
reveal the destitution of beings. What could bring about such a turn? Not
the acuteness of thought alone, if thought is not guided by the openness
of an attunement arising out of an understanding of the history of being.
For the dialectical ingenuity of thought can find a progressive impulse
in the convulsions of modernity. The possibility of a turn can be 'deconstructed' by way of an analytic of undecidability. What Heidegger
conceives as the project of a hermeneutic phenomenology can be histori-
cized as an ideological stance and rendered politically suspect. Insight
into what manifests itself as the destitution of the being of beings therefore presupposes the attunement proper to it and the epochal manifestation of beings. In section 76 of the *Beiträge*, 'Propositions Concerning
"Science,"' Heidegger argues that the concealed *telos* of science is a disposition of consummated boredom in the face of its own achievements.
Boredom arises out of an attunement to the whole which reveals the thorough-going in-difference of entities, thanks to the calculability of beings,

including the being we ourselves are (GA65, 157/109). In their non-being, as mere functions, the things themselves implode and enter into a kind of weightlessness. Processes of simulation 'stand in' for entities, which 'manifest' themselves only in the in-difference of signifiers on call. Can the in-difference of beings, which is the measure of their integration into the planetary economy, still give rise to a sense of horror at the loss of the being of beings? This attunement would be rooted in a knowledge of the first beginning of Western thought and its consummation (GA65, 158/109), and be guided by a glimpse of the possibility of the sitedness of being as a possibility the tradition has occluded but nonetheless reserved for the technological epoch.

As I intimated above, the necessity (*die Notwendigkeit*) of this turn toward the abandonment of beings, thus to see what is in the technological epoch, is rooted in a fundamental need or distress (*die Not*): 'all necessity is rooted in distress' (GA65, 45/32). It is need in its attuned exposure to the whole of what is which calls for a decision. Heidegger's commitment of 1933 can only become accessible to us in terms of his understanding of need, the nature of decision, and the issue at stake in decision. The need revealed by attunement to the whole of what is – the horror of the in-difference of beings – first brings us to ourselves in the midst of beings, and it thus opens up the possibility of founding a history which would be a response to the needfulness of beings, including our own. The deracination which the de-limitation of representational, planetary thinking brings in its train creates a need for forms of rootedness founded in the earth-sitedness of formative thinking. Distress is not to be conceived as a Not or negativity but as the index of the thrownness of a humanity, which responds to this distress by giving it gestalt, thus to found the site of an encounter with the whole of what is. The distress which arises with the recognition of the horror of the in-difference of beings sets Dasein back into the limit of its own historically sited and mortal being. In this sense Dasein reserves and founds itself and in reserving itself opens the site of attentiveness which allows what is to come to a stand and show itself in its own being.

It is Heidegger's claim that the fundamental attunement of self-reserved attentiveness (*die Verhaltenheit*) opens the site for the other beginning of the postmetaphysical era, just as wonder founded the Greek beginning (GA65, sec. 13). Dasein's self-reserved attentiveness to the being of beings responds to the withdrawal of entities from the determinations of their calculability, acceleration, and integration into a functional economy. In 'The Origin of the Work of Art,' the self-reserved

attentiveness of Dasein to being is set to work in the work of art and unfolded as the unconcealment of the presencing of being. For the work is
one essential way in which beings are made manifest in their being, thus
to show themselves out of the limit (*peras*) and gestalt proper to them.
The attunement of Dasein's self-reserve surrenders the representational
grasping of beings to let them shine and stand forth according to the
order of rank accorded by the work. The central significance of art for
Heidegger's thought already becomes evident. Art is conceived as a
countermovement to the in-differentiation of beings generated by the
movement of technological thinking. The experience of distress generates the fundamental attunement which necessitates a decision, understood as the founding of the distinctions of the orders of rank within the
whole sphere of the being of beings (GA65, 46/32–3). According to
Heidegger, the decision into which Dasein is called in the era of the consummation of metaphysics is fundamentally the following: either humanity will consummate and annul itself in the biotechnical interface of
metaphysical animality, or mankind will become Dasein, thus to go
under, as subject, to be reborn in the service of the gods and the earth.
The misguided political decision Heidegger made in 1933 has to be
understood in the light of this hermeneutic situation, as Heidegger himself saw it.

The decision of Dasein, moreover, as the response to the differentiation of being, is not to be confused with the decisions of a subject, and
hence with a concept of 'decisionism,' supposedly deriving from Carl
Schmidt, which Heidegger seemingly appropriated. The decision of
Dasein announces the openness of a response (*Ent-schlossenheit*) which
brings beings out of concealment to stand in the light of their own limits.
As such, decision institutes what Heidegger elsewhere, in both the *Introduction* and the Rector's Address, calls essential knowledge (*Wissen*, not
Wissenschaft). Attuned to the whole of what is, *Wissen* responds to the differentiation of being (*polemos, Auseinandersetzung*), and in responding,
'decides,' thus to bring beings to stand in the light of their own truth. In
the open site of decision beings can begin to be, each out of the limits of
their presencing. Through the openness opened up by the *question* of
being, de-cision inscribes the differentiation of being itself, thus to allow
the appropriation of beings, each to the delimitation out of which it
emerges into its own. The thought of decision is a retrieve of what
Heidegger had developed in *Being and Time* as the resoluteness (*die
Entschlossenheit*) of Dasein, but which proved liable to 'existentialist' misinterpretation. *Ent-schlossenheit* is dis-closure, hence the openness of the

play of the three dimensions of the temporal sitedness of Da-sein. Thought by way of the *Beiträge* and decision, it intimates the attuned openness of understanding to the presencing of being, out of which the differentiation of beings arises and in which presencing *Ent-schlossenheit* is founded. Attention to differentiation is already a response to the in-difference of beings as functions of a planetary economy. Given that dif-ferentiation is itself granted a 'value' (to formulate the question in the language of metaphysics), then this has evident consequences for very far-reaching, practical decision making on the global level – for example, in respect to species preservation, bio-diversity, bio-technology, and the singularity of peoples in the global order. The differentiation of being, and hence the requisite receptivity of thought which can grant it a site, is everything other than 'abstract' and removed from what most intimately touches mankind and the fate of the earth today. Decision, in Heideg-ger's sense, will determine whether being is to remain concealed in its presencing, by reduction to the most general and emptiest of categories, or 'come to word' to attune Dasein to the singularity of beings (GA65, sec. 44).

Given that this fundamental decision is also a political one, the ques-tion arises as to who makes it and how it will be made. Evidentially, at least in 1933, Heidegger himself decided for the 'people,' the Volk. Through the Volk, and the political state it gives itself, the differentiation of being is given gestalt in the rank order of entities, in technology and labour, in art, leadership, sacrifice, and thought. Whence the need for decision? The need arises out of the dis-shelter of the being of beings – their destitution, in the form of their reduction to the non-differentia-tion of the merely calculable. The need arises out of the fundamental deracination of being, which destroys tradition and devastates the earth. Need gives rise to necessity (GA65, sec. 17). The necessity, as Heidegger saw it, of founding the differentiation of being in beings is the root of his entanglement in National Socialism.

2 Rhetoric and the Public Sphere

2.1 Rhetoric, Truth, and the Public Sphere

As a result of the character and significance of Heidegger's Rector's Address of 1933, it has attracted great attention in recent years. Heidegger's attachment to some form of National Socialism can no longer be convincingly characterized as an aberration without essential relation to his thought. Considered as a political act the address has often been cited as evidence for Heidegger's commitment to National Socialism, even if to an unorthodox version purged of its racist elements. As such, the address is judged to reveal the hidden essence of Heidegger's philosophy and to betray its fundamental weakness. Alexander Schwan, for example, argues that Heidegger's understanding of the unity of the artwork, as well as his 'functional' conception of *Mitsein*, implicates a totalizing, authoritarian state of leaders and the led.[1] Heidegger's supposedly weak development of *Mitsein* in *Sein und Zeit* undermines, David Carr proposes, the possibility of an authentic social sphere, and thus the possibility of authentic politics.[2] Action, Löwith holds, is reduced to mere 'decisionism,' allied in thought to Carl Schmitt's theory of the authoritarian state.[3] The concept of authenticity, moreover, which guides action, is empty of content and consequently may be filled with any content whatsoever, including that of Nazism.[4] More dramatically, other commentators claim that Heidegger's concept of the historicity of being delivers Dasein over to a dark destiny which finally announces itself in Hitler.[5] Central to these reflections is the assumption that if Heidegger does not allow active, critical, and yet authentic participation in the public sphere – and he does not – then he must surrender Dasein, as a political being, to an authoritarian political order.[6]

At stake is the character of the public sphere (*die Öffentlichkeit*) of *Mit-sein*, and the possibilities of speech and action open to Dasein as a participant in the public realm. In what follows I shall argue that Heidegger's understanding of rhetoric implicates an authentic concept of *Mitsein* and therefore reveals a space for authentic participation in the public sphere. I propose that Heidegger conceives rhetoric as a positive possibility of the *logos* and of political life. It has as its goal the awakening of an attunement of Dasein as *Mitsein* to the concrete and authentic, and hence historically limited possibilities of existence, thus to bring Dasein to the actualization of its proper end in the polity. For reasons which I will specify below, I am construing 'rhetoric' more narrowly than Ernesto Grassi, for example, who takes his point of departure from Heidegger to identify rhetoric – understood as the originary power of language – with philosophy itself.[7] It is, rather, the implication of *Being and Time* that rhetoric should be distinguished from poetry as from philosophy, and that it has a special relation to our political being.

Heidegger's conception of the place of rhetoric in the polity allows us to understand the philosophical site of the Rector's Address as a political intervention. I shall argue, in agreement with S. Gebert, among others, that Heidegger's political engagement follows from the existential analytic of *Being and Time*, inasmuch as key concepts such as authenticity and resolve, as developed there, call for actualization 'in and with the community.'[8]

The *Rhetoric* of Aristotle, Heidegger maintains, in section 29 of *Being and Time*, should be considered as the 'first systematic hermeneutic of the everydayness of being-with-one-another' (SZ 138/130):

> Publicness as the kind of being of the they ... not only has its attunedness, it uses mood and 'makes' it for itself. The speaker speaks to it and from it. He needs the understanding of the possibility of mood in order to arouse and direct it in the right way.

Heidegger's particular concerns in this passage, devoted to the existential or 'ontological' condition of Dasein's moods (*Stimmungen*), are the *pathe* to which the second book of the *Rhetoric* is dedicated. We recall that the existential constitution of Dasein is equiprimordially structured by understanding (*Verstehen*), attunement (*Befindlichkeit*), and discourse (*Rede*). Attunement is the ontological condition of what we ontically experience as emotions or moods (*Stimmungen*). Heidegger appeals to the *Rhetoric* as a hermeneutic of moods, in particular, as a hermeneutic of the public sphere of *das Man*: the public One of everyday being-with. This sphere will always be governed by its own fundamental dispositions (*Gestimmtheit*). The orator who has learned to understand the possibilities of moods responds and speaks to these to 'awaken and guide' the dispositions of the public 'in the right way' (SZ 139/130).

The systematic place of this passage in *Being and Time* will concern us in detail below. A number of questions, however, come immediately to mind. Let me elucidate these, in the first instance, by recourse to Heidegger's Marburg lectures of 1924 (GA18) – *Grundbegriffe der aristotelischen Philosophie* – which comment explicitly on the *Rhetoric*, and by reference to the *Sophistes* of 1924–5, which considers the place of rhetoric in the philosophies of both Plato and Aristotle.

In the passage quoted above, everyday being-with constitutes the realm of the public sphere. This space of intelligibility is not only defined by governing dispositions, but itself generates them. The laying-bare of these dispositions calls for a 'hermeneutic' of the concrete, historically lived 'facticity' of everyday life. The facticity of Dasein refers to the 'how' of its engagement in the specificity of its situation (GA63, 7). To unfold modes of engagement, of being-in-a-world, is what Aristotle undertakes in the *Rhetoric*. The public sphere, therefore, is conceived as an open site of intelligibility structured by the common dispositions of an historical community. This site is unfolded in section 76 of *Being and Time* in terms of the historicity of Dasein. In this sense, even without explicit reference to the political, Heidegger's appeal to the *Rhetoric* implies that the public sphere in which the orator takes a stand is the open, dialogical space of the political, as constituted by *Mitsein* in speaking and listening to one another.

The implication that the *Rhetoric* is concerned not merely with the technique or art of persuasion, but should be conceived as a contribution to the proper constitution of the polity finds broad assent among commentators on Aristotle. According to Johnstone, the 'deliberative functions of rhetoric identify it as the instrument whereby individual moral visions are shared, modified, and fused into the communal moral principles that regulate our shared undertakings.'[9] Larry Arnhart enunciates this position more fully as follows: 'Perhaps, therefore,' because 'standards of nobility and justice are largely shaped by the laws, the nature of the regime is decisive for all three kinds of rhetoric. If it is, the architectonic supremacy of politics over rhetoric is confirmed.'[10] C.D.C. Reeve also holds, in reference to the *Nicomachean Ethics* (1094a1–b10), that *politike* is the 'architectonic science' controlling 'rhetoric as all the other crafts and sciences.'[11]

It remains to be determined in what sense 'politics' holds supremacy over rhetoric. Heidegger for his part takes his point of departure from the *pathe*, or governing dispositions to which the orator speaks. Do the *pathe* themselves, or perhaps the existential attunement to being to which they give expression, open up the space of intelligibility of a polity such as makes the formulation of laws possible? What is the relation, in Heidegger's terms, between the truth of fundamental attunement and the truth of statements as laid down in the legal constitution of a state? What, moreover, is the role of the orator, given his task is to 'awaken and guide' common dispositions in the 'right way'? Does rhetoric have an essential relation to the discovery of truth, and does this implicate a relation to the task of bringing about authentic *Mitsein*? If so, then the task of the orator would be to wrest possibilities of authentic being-with from the inauthenticity of the public self. The work of awakening and guiding the *pathe*, in turn, would itself be guided by an ideal of the polity and the truth proper to it.

Rhetoric, Heidegger holds in the Aristotle lectures of 1924, is not a merely formal discipline or technique of persuasion, but is an intimate possibility (*dunamis*) of the 'being with one another of mankind' ('Sein des Miteinanderseins des Menschen'). As such it belongs to the political realm (GA18, 114, 117). Through the *pathe* 'the possibilities of orienting-oneself about the world are essentially determined' ('die Möglichkeiten des Sichorientierns in der Welt [werden] wesentlich bestimmt'). Since rhetoric aims to awaken and guide the *pathe*, it must move the soul. The *pathe* are ways of being-moved, of being outside of oneself, with others and the things of the world (GA18, 242). The *pathe* themselves are ultimately determined by the movement of the soul toward its 'authentic' being. While this does not exclude the deceptiveness of the *pathe*, insofar as emotion can conceal and distort our being-in-the world (SZ 136/128), Heidegger implies that the soul's motion is governed by its *telos*, and that this *telos* brings the soul back to its inherent order of unfolding (*arche*). Movement toward 'authenticity' articulates the soul's movement back into its proper origin, out of which its authentic being arises. The implication is that the guidance of the *pathe* stands in intimate relation to the proper movement and *telos* of the soul. These passages already anticipate Heidegger's Aristotle lectures of 1931, *Aristoteles, Metaphysik Theta 1–3: Vom Wesen und Wirklichkeit der Kraft* (GA33, see 150–1).

This discussion of the soul's movement also anticipates Heidegger's understanding of *Befindlichkeit* in section 29 of *Being and Time*. The temporal sense of attunement, no less than that of understanding, consists in the finite transcendence or 'movement' of Dasein as thrown project.

Attunement in the first instance signifies the sitedness and historically specific thrownness of Dasein. Given that rhetoric has the *pathe* as its object, thus to awaken and guide them, rhetoric emerges as a way through which Dasein confronts its own thrownness to wrest from it the historically concrete possibilities of its being (GA18, 177–9).

The ways of speaking, in turn, which the *Rhetoric* examines, are nothing other than particular possibilities of saying and understanding already inscribed in the everydayness of Dasein (GA18, 110). The *pathe*, likewise, to which rhetoric speaks, are also already implicated in everyday Dasein. Our *Mitsein*, on Heidegger's account, is structured by the fundamental *pathe* which constitute Dasein's thrownness (*Geworfenheit* as *Gestimmtheit*). Since *Mitsein* is always understood as 'being in the *polis*' (*Sein-in-der-polis*) (GA18, 46), and the *polis* is the end which governs the orator, the orator will attempt to guide the *pathe* for the sake of our common *Mitsein* in the *polis*. This account, drawn from the Marburg lectures, also anticipates, as we shall see in detail below, the place implicitly given to the *pathe* in *Being and Time*. Moreover, given that the *pathe* are the expression of Dasein's attunement, and hence constitute a fundamental aspect of our being-in-the-world, the *pathe* will themselves lay out the essential pathways of attuned understanding, which are the condition of the generation of a state and its positive law.

The question now arises as to Heidegger's understanding of *telos* and the relation of *telos* to the movement (*kinesis*) and actualization (*energeia*) of the psyche. The practical life, Heidegger writes, is determined by Aristotle as the actualization of the soul (*puches energeia*): the soul actualizes itself in the *polis* and the *polis* is a way of being-human which arises out of *phusis* (GA18, 43–50). This account of the relation of the *polis*, *phusis*, and the soul substantially anticipates the Parmenides lectures of 1944 (GA54, 130–55). The saying of the orator will be determined by the end of public speech, and this end is realized in the actualization of the soul in its belonging-to the *polis*. The soul enters into its *telos* or consummation only as part of a community. Aristotle holds that the *polis* has the good of the community, not just of the individual, as its ultimate end. Politics is the art of communal and historically founded action for the sake of the community.[12] The end which is the subject of politics, moreover, encompasses every other end of being-with, for being-with has its end in the *polis*. In Heidegger's reading of Aristotle, therefore, the soul actualizes its *telos* as part of a community; the community delimits and consummates the soul's movement.

The end or *telos* of the *polis* itself is *eudaemonia* or 'happiness' (GA18,

43). With reference to the *Nicomachean Ethics* (A, 1–4), Heidegger argues that happiness is the good (*agathon*) which is its own end (GA18, 65–79). Heidegger insists that the end be determined as *peras*. Understood as the proper limit of a being's unfolding, *peras* designates not only the actualization of the possibilities of the psyche (GA18, 72–3), but also the proper limit (*agathon*) of a community. Dasein actualizes itself by unfolding itself according to its proper limits, within the concrete situation and according to the proper time (*kairos*). The *arete* of Dasein consists in this (GA18, 76, 188–91).[13] What is the end to which the orator speaks, in grasping the moment and appealing to the common dispositions which constitute *Mitsein*? This end can only be the *agathon* of the polity, which must be won from the sphere of the public space. For while the public realm, according to *Being and Time*, 'obscures everything' (SZ 127/119), this does not preclude but rather implicates the possibility of discovering the proper *telos* of the polity, hence the limit through which *Mitsein* can actualize itself. This is the proper work of the orator: to awaken and guide the fundamental dispositions of the public realm with a view to bringing the polity, and thus the being-with of Dasein, into the limits consistent with the actualization of their possibilities for being. *Rhetoric may consequently be defined as a mode of enactment of the essential limits of a community.*

Heidegger's *Sophistes* (GA19) devotes further discussion to the nature and place of rhetoric in the philosophy of Plato and Aristotle. With particular reference to the *Phaedrus* 271c10, Heidegger proposes to show that Plato, despite his negative judgment on rhetoric in the *Gorgias*, prepares the ground for Aristotle's *Rhetoric*. A brief review of key points can prepare our subsequent consideration of *Being and Time*. The interpretation Heidegger offers serves to grant rhetoric, as the *logos* of the public realm of being-with, a limited but legitimate place, subordinate to dialectic, in the guidance of the soul (GA19, 339). Rhetoric is not, unlike dialectic, motivated by the dis-covery of the 'idea of the constitution of being as such' (GA19, 350–1) – it is not directed explicitly toward *aletheia*, and thus is not an independent way of *aletheuein*, or un-concealment (GA19, 339). *Aletheuein* aims to discover the *arche* of beings (GA19, 37–8). Following Aristotle, *Nicomachean Ethics* VI, 3, the modes of *aletheuein* are five: *techne, episteme, phronesis, sophia,* and *nous*. Rhetoric is not one of these five. Nonetheless rhetoric is not without relation to *aletheuein*, and in particular to *phronesis*, insofar as rhetoric concerns the public sphere of practical reasoning.

This view finds collaboration in critical commentary on the *Rhetoric*.

Thus Halliwell, for example, refers to *Rhetoric* 1366b3–19 – which includes *phronesis* on the rhetorician's list of virtues – to argue that deliberative rhetoric is an exercise in *phronesis* (on the part of the speaker) and *sunesis* (on the part of the audience).[14] This would follow, as I noted above, from Aristotle's subordination of rhetoric to politics in the *Rhetoric* (1356a20–9). 'Aristotle's attitude,' Grimaldi argues, is that 'rhetoric *qua* rhetoric reaches out to truth.'[15] Also for this reason, because rhetoric is a derivative but legitimate mode of *aletheuein*, Heidegger can argue that Aristotle realized the positive idea of rhetoric which Plato anticipated by means of his dialectic (GA19, 338–9): the *logos* of rhetoric, while not theoretical, and while speaking to the *doxa* of everyday Dasein (GA19, 339), must nevertheless have an eye for the truth of beings, for the condition even of deception is the possibility of unconcealment (GA19, 319, 329). This does not mean that rhetoric, according to the *Phaedrus*, or the *Rhetoric* of Aristotle, necessarily aims at deception, but that its relation to truth is derivative of, or secondary to, the primary modes of *aletheuein*. Rhetoric is granted its 'independent right' (GA19, 339). And as opposed to Plato, Aristotle in fact gives it, Heidegger notes, separate but equal status (*antistrophos*) with his own, transformed idea of dialectic (*dialegesthai*) (GA19, 350).[16]

Insight 'into the right of everyday speaking with one another' can offer the 'motivation for the creation of a rhetoric' (GA19, 339). For this reason, moreover, Heidegger follows Aristotle, and rejects Plato's identification of the sophist and the orator (GA19, 219). The sophist attends to the words themselves, not to the matter at issue, which the *logos* of everyday speaking aims to reveal. The danger of taking the words themselves for the issue becomes especially acute in the written word, as the *Phaedrus* reminds us. The word becomes 'free-floating' (GA19, 340). As a result, it conceals, and concealing brings about forgetfulness (GA19, 341).[17]

Heidegger's interpretation of Plato's critique of writing in the *Phaedrus* emphasizes the distinction between the *logos*, whether written or spoken, as truth-revealing or as truth-concealing. The living *logos* points us back to the things themselves. The false (*eidolon*) *logos* manipulates the already-said and merely repeats it, resting without insight into the thing itself (GA19, 345).[18] This is the realm of the sophist. It is not, however, necessarily the realm of the orator. The sophist moves within the confines of *Gerede*, understood as the already-said. But the orator has the possibility of aiming at the things themselves, thus to wrest them from *Gerede* and common *doxa*. This possibility is founded, Heidegger implies, in the *logos* of everyday Dasein itself, for the *logos* of the public sphere, even understood as the realm of common opinion, is essentially founded on the finite transcendence and unconcealment of Dasein. The fact that the *Phaedrus* is structured by a tripartite discussion on eros, the soul, and discourse betrays a unitary reflection on the soul as transcendent. Rhetoric is a possibility of Dasein which, while belonging to the everyday, is grounded in the transcendental structure of Dasein (GA19, 314–15). This reflects the essential relation it bears to *aletheuein*, despite its derivative status as a mode of unconcealment.

At this point we can draw a number of preliminary conclusions. We have seen that rhetoric is subordinate to *phronesis* and hence to politics. The end of politics – the *eudaemonia* of the polity – is also the proper end, or actualization, of rhetoric. Heidegger not only rejects the identification of rhetoric and sophistry, but grants rhetoric the task of revealing the proper limits of the governing *pathe* of a community. Heidegger would therefore reject the view of Reeve that in 'an ideal city rhetoric has a minimal role to play, in a very corrupt one it has dressed itself up as politics and taken control.'[19] This conclusion is based on a mistaken view of the relation of rhetoric to the *logos* of everyday speech, and of the *logos* and the *endoxa* inscribed in it, to truth. For just as truth as unconcealment has an inherent tendency toward concealment, so the *endoxa* have a tendency toward truth. The more measured conclusion of Halliwell is closer to Heidegger's position. Aristotle's view of *phronesis* in the *Rhetoric*, Halliwell argues, is 'equivocal' regarding the 'functioning of popular morality in the context of civic deliberations.' The *phronesis* of the orator, responsive to the public, can be limited to a 'calculative and rational capacity not necessarily directed to ethical ends. Yet the rational, or 'expedient' (*sumpheron*), appeals of the orator are more correctly and broadly understood as 'choices aimed at the final end of *eudaemonia*.'[20] Consequently they are not at odds with the *phronesis* of *politike*. Halliwell concludes that 'the *Rhetoric* remains open to the possibility that the orator's engagement with public morality (*endoxa*) will sometimes, and not accidentally, succeed in contributing to the realization of the human good, and will do so in ways that embrace legitimate appeals to the criteria both of *phronesis* and to *sumpheron*.'[21] I judge this to be very close to Heidegger's own opinion, implicit in the passages we have considered, on the place of rhetoric in the polity. As I have noted, rhetoric is not a mere technique, nor morally neutral, but in the words of Markus Wörner a mode of 'unconcealment (*doloun*) of the true and the just.'[22] The particular mode of unconcealment in which rhetoric engages, as

noted above, involves a truth wrested from public morality or opinions –
in Heidegger's terms, as we shall see in greater detail below, from *Gerede*,
which inscribes the opinions of the public sphere in the already-said of
language.

This still leaves us unclear regarding the status of the *pathe* in relation
to the mode of truth the ideal conception of rhetoric implicates. Before
considering Heidegger's position as implicit in *Being and Time*, the basic
lines of argument in contemporary criticism may be mapped out as follows. Let us recall that the *Rhetoric* considers three modes of persuasion
(*pistis*): *ethos*, which pertains to human character in its various forms;
pathos, the 'emotion' or attunement of the audience; and the
'*enthymemes*,' or argument (1356a23–25). The translation of '*ta pathe*' in
Aristotle as 'emotion' should be construed broadly, Leighton argues, to
include sensation as well as the pleasures and pains of the body.[23] Desire,
or *orxesis*, is included on the evidence of *Nicomachean Ethics* 1105b21 and
Rhetoric 1378b4. *Orxesis* includes *thumos* (spiritedness), *boulesis* (wish),
and *epithumia* (appetite). It is evident that *ta pathe* involve both the body
and 'mental' and emotional 'states' – more precisely, ways of experiencing the world.

Considerable criticism concerns itself with the relation of the *pathe* to
the proofs expressed in the *enthymemes*, and the relative weight of each as
modes of generating belief. Engberg-Pedersen initially holds that the
pathe are peripheral to an 'accomplished rhetorical performance,' for
what counts 'is the argument, and the argument is about the facts of the
matter, the *pragma*.'[24] But this bold separation of the *pathe* and the
enthymemes remains doubtful, even on Engberg-Pedersen's own account,
for he admits that '*ethos*-proofs' are integral to the language game of
rhetoric as truth-finding. There is 'continuity' between the *endoxa* and
truth, thus an intrinsic connection between common beliefs and the
clarity of the judgments which are expressed in statements of proof.[25] It
follows that one might also see a correspondence between the *pathe*
and the *enthymemes*. For the common, and supposedly unclear, judgments of the *endoxa* are opinions structured by our attunement or emotional stance in the world. Certain opinions in effect already implicate
certain *pathe*. This would argue for 'continuity' between the ways of experiencing the world of the *pathe* and their explicit formulation in the form
of statements, or proofs, of the *enthymemes*. To formulate proofs, for
example, of the supposed guilt of a 'witch,' presupposes not only *endoxa*,
but also a certain attunement to our world. With reference to the *Rhetoric*
1377b30–1378a4, and especially 1388a26–29, Leighton concludes that

'emotions have certain judgements connected with them such that certain other emotions, their judgements, and other judgements too are excluded.'[26] Emotions structure our comportment in the world on the level of perception as well as on the epistic level in terms of their affect on 'beliefs and knowledge.'[27]

Emotions are 'forms of intentional awareness' 'directed at or about an object': belief may be held to be a constituent of emotion. If I experience something as fearful I will believe it to be threatening, and my comportment will change accordingly. Conversely, emotions are 'to some degree cognitive and based on beliefs.'[28] On Heidegger's view as presented in *Being and Time*, however, the attempt to ascribe priority to 'emotion' or to 'belief,' thus to determine which is the condition of which, mistakes the nature of the *pathe* as intentional ways of being. In this account, emotion is already, in itself, 'cognitive,' and beliefs in themselves attuned to one's being in the world.

The relation of *pathos* to *ethos* in the *Rhetoric* remains to be considered. Heidegger's argument may be given in preliminary outline as follows. Since the character of the speaker would be formed by his experiences, and these inscribe certain *pathe*, and the *pathe*, in turn, crystallize in an *ethos*, could it be that the two are founded in the fundamental unity of the attuned understanding of Dasein? And that this attuned understanding is itself founded in the historicity of Dasein? This reading of the relation of the *pathe* to *ethos*, which I hold to be implicit in Heidegger, is corroborated by Aristotle's discussion of the same relation. As Hellwig's account shows, the aim of arousing specific *pathe* presupposes knowledge of the *ethos* of the audience. This *ethos* is formed not only by the age, origin, and status of the listener, such as will influence the listener's *pathe*, but also by the 'values' of the polity to which the listener belongs, as the *Rhetoric* intimates (1366a6–12). 'For every constitution,' Hellwig concludes, 'has specific *ethe*,' which are constituted by the final goal of the polity. For this reason the orator must be sensitive to the 'collective' *pathos* – in effect, the *ethos* – of the orator's audience.[29] Aristotle consequently proposes in the *Rhetoric* (1365b24, 1366a6–12) that the orator should investigate the constitutions of polities to accommodate the orator's own *ethos* to that of the community the orator addresses. *Pathos* in the narrow sense of individual emotion is founded in the *ethos* of the polity.[30] The *ethos* reflects the *telos* and thus the collective attunement of a people, such as founds its understanding of a world and moves it to realize this understanding in concrete acts of decision.

The *ethos* of the orator can persuade only insofar as the orator's *pathos* is shared by the audience. The orator speaks out of and to the *pathe* which, as fundamental dispositions or *ethe*, govern and transfuse the *endoxa* of the public. Persuasion presupposes that both speaker and listeners stand within a shared light of unconcealment. Given the subordination, as we shall see in greater detail below, of the truth of judgments to the truth of unconcealment in *Being and Time*, Heidegger must hold that the unity of *pathe-ethe* is more fundamentally unconcealing (or 'truth-revealing') than arguments, and is the condition of their effectiveness. All three modes of *pistis* have a common ground in the *aletheuein* of *phronesis*, which is the potential (*dunamis*) the psyche of the orator realizes. Hence the status of the laws, as judgments based on the attuned understanding of *pathos* and *ethos*, is also clarified: although rhetoric as a mode of truth-finding is derivative of *phronesis*, and hence of *politike*, the positive laws of the polity, no less than the opinions of the public sphere, are founded in the historical *ethos* out of which and to which the orator speaks. We recall, for example, the place of the 'unease of desire' in the political economy of Locke, and the primacy of the fear of death in Hobbes's *Leviathan*. In each case, the polity and positive law are founded in a certain fundamental attunement to being. In Heidegger's terms, the promulgation of laws pertains to the ontic sphere of politics, and this realm is founded in the ontological structure of Dasein. To the extent of having engaged the fundamental, historically specific attunement of Dasein, the orator has the potential of shifting the foundations of the understanding of what 'laws' are, and thus of the nature and the specificity of their promulgation.

2.2 Rhetoric in *Sein und Zeit*

Our consideration of the place of rhetoric in *Sein und Zeit* presupposes that *Sein und Zeit* contains an implicit political philosophy, for rhetoric is subordinate to and takes its measure from politics. Thus we must in turn hold, in the words of Sigbert Gebert, that 'fundamental ontology, as an explication of the question of being, clarifies the condition of possibility of a philosophy of politics and consequently of political science.'[31] For only on this basis can the limited, but legitimate place of rhetoric in *Sein und Zeit* as a mode of truth-finding contributing to authentic *Mitsein* be established. In what follows I propose to unfold essential elements of the political philosophy of *Sein und Zeit* by way of the implicit place rhetoric is granted. Rhetoric offers us a guiding thread to Heidegger's concept of *Mitsein*, and *Mitsein*, in turn, allows us to bring the existential analytic to bear on the question of the political. The political philosophy of Heidegger arises out of his understanding of *Mitsein*, of the *action* proper to authentic *Mitsein*, and out of the concept of the finite *freedom* of *Mitsein* which he holds. The existential analytic opens a space for the political realm as founded in the *historicity* of Dasein as *Mitsein*; the call of conscience obligates Dasein to actualize its ownmost possibilities, hence *to act* to realize the concrete possibilities of its *Mitsein* and its historicity. Authentic action is founded in Dasein's resolute actualization of its finite *freedom* as constituted by its temporal structure and historicity. Although rhetoric is a derivative mode of *aletheuein*, it nonetheless stands in intimate and potentially creative relation to historicity, action, and Dasein's finite freedom. Appealing directly to the *pathe*, it has the power to awaken the authentic *ethos*, or historicity, of *Mitsein*. It does this insofar as it brings *Mitsein* back to itself from the self-concealment of *Gerede*, thus to bring about a turn in the attunedness (*Gestimmtheit*) of the public sphere. In this way it may wrest authentic possibilities of moodful understanding from the fallenness of the *endoxa*, or common attunedness of a historically sited humanity.

Rhetoric as an authentic possibility of being must be wrested from everyday *Mitsein*. Every possible form of authenticity – in acting and saying – is a '*modification*' of the fallenness of Dasein's historically sited and specific everydayness (SZ 130/122). The disclosedness of *Mitsein*'s everyday being is constituted by a certain pre-figuration of belief and conception (i.e., *endoxa*), as inscribed in the already-given of discourse (*Gerede*). The everyday selfhood of Dasein, as being-with-others (*Mitdasein*), is determined as *das Man*: this inauthentic 'they-self,' which is characterized by distantiality, averageness, and levelling down (SZ 128/120), constitutes 'what we know as "publicness"' (*die Öffentlichkeit*) (SZ 127/119). Inasmuch as the inauthenticity of the they-self belongs essentially to the existential (i.e., 'ontological') structure of Dasein, the impression arises that being-with-others, and thus also our political being, must inevitably be excluded from Dasein's authentic and highest possibilities for being. Yet

> *authentic being one's self* is not based on an exceptional state of the subject, a state detached from the they, *but is an existentiell modification of the they as an essential existential.* (SZ 130/122)

Given that Dasein, also the Dasein of authentic selfhood, is always essentially *Mitsein*, then the possibility of authentic *Mitsein*, as wrested from the inauthenticity of the they-self, must also belong essentially to the constitution of Dasein. The authentic selfhood of being-with-others would have to be won from everyday being-with 'by clearing away coverings and obscurities, by breaking up the disguises with which Da-sein cuts itself off from itself' (SZ 129/121; cf. GA63, 17). Heidegger's analytic of Dasein in fact implicates the possibility of authentic being-with-others, hence the possibility of an authentic 'public sphere.'

The first draft of 'The Origin of the Work of Art' refers to '*die Öffentlichkeit*,' in the positive sense of authentic being-with, as the communal site which the self-manifestation of the work opens up for itself (UK-HS 8).[32] Does rhetoric have an analogous role in the constitution of an authentic public sphere? We recall that the place of rhetoric in the structure of the existential analytic in the first instance consists in the awakening and guidance of the moods of the public realm (SZ 138/130). In speaking to the attunedness (*Gestimmtheit*) of the public, thus to awaken and guide, the orator seeks to uncover the things themselves, which the everyday public realm covers up (SZ 127/119). For we recall that rhetoric, in Heidegger's conception, is a mode of unconcealment, if only a derivative one, and therefore leads to the discovery of truth. Awakening and guiding presupposes the possibility of wresting authentic being-with from the they-world. The first step in this direction would consist in awakening the attunement (*Grundstimmung*) which fundamentally founds the attunedness (*Gestimmtheit*) which the inauthentic public realm 'makes' for itself, thus to conceal its own essential attunement from itself.

The condition of the ideal of rhetoric I have proposed as implicit in *Being and Time* is the possibility of authentic *Mitsein*. Heidegger claims that authenticity is 'ontologically' (i.e., existentially) fundamental to Dasein. Although everyday Dasein is characterized as inauthentic, 'inauthenticity has possible authenticity as its basis' (SZ 259/239). The condition of authentic *Mitsein*, however, is authentic being-oneself in the radical isolation of resolute being-toward-death: 'Da-sein *is authentically itself* in the mode of primordial individuation of reticent resolution that expects *Angst* of itself' (SZ 322/297). This 'self,' which the primordial mood of anxiety reveals, and which being-toward-death discloses, is not the isolated 'subject' of metaphysics, hence not an 'I'-self opposed to the other and to the 'we' of collectivity. Then wherein does the selfhood of the authentic self consist? How is it related to the 'we' of a community? 'Saying-I means the being that I always am as "I-am-in-a-world"' (SZ 321/295). Being-in-the-world constitutes a structure of finite possibilities for being. Authentic selfhood comes to be in the grasping of one's ownmost possibilities for being as revealed in the radical solitude of being-toward death.

> As the nonrelational possibility, death individualizes, but only, as the possibility not-to-be-bypassed, in order to make Da-sein as being-with understand the potentialities-of-being of the others. (SZ 264/244)

Consequently, inasmuch as authentic selfhood grasps itself in its finitude as possibility-for-being, hence as thrown project, it actualizes itself as *Mitsein* by taking up the possibilities granted by its heritage and being-with-others. Only out of the 'authentic being a self of resoluteness,' Heidegger writes, does 'authentic being-with-one-another' first arise (SZ 298/274).

In resolute being-toward-death, Dasein is brought before its ownmost, unique possibilities for being, hence delivered over to the possibility of its authentic selfhood. Heidegger's analysis of the call of conscience is intended to offer evidence for the claim that Dasein, which knows itself primarily in its inauthentic dispersal in the world of the 'they' and its concerns, does have an implicit awareness and understanding of the possibility of authentic selfhood (SZ 268–9/247–9). The call of conscience calls on Dasein to take up its own being as a finite, thrown possibility for being, thus to take responsibility for the inherent negativity of its being thrown and thereby to become its own 'ground' of being (284–7). 'Being its own thrown ground is the potentiality-of-being about which care is concerned' (SZ 284/262). To hear the call of conscience, hence to take up its thrownness, 'calls the self of Da-sein forth from its lostness in the they' (SZ 274/253). Hearing this call, Dasein is resolute (*entschlossen*) (SZ 297/273). Again, this does not signify Dasein's turn away from the 'world' and its being-with-others. Rather, resoluteness

> brings the self right into its being together with things at hand, actually taking care of them, and pushes it toward concerned being-with with the others ... Resolute Da-sein can become the 'conscience' of others. (SZ 298/274)

On what grounds can this discussion of authentic *Mitsein*, as incited by the call of conscience, be brought into explicit relation to the task of rhetoric? The orator 'turns' the attuned understanding of the auditors, prepares them for action, possibly incites them to act. The task of the orator is to arouse the conscience of the listeners, to let this aroused conscience bring Dasein before the necessity of decision. For to 'authentically hear the call' means 'to bring oneself to factical action' (SZ 294/271). Action (*Handeln*), the 'sober understanding of the basic factical possibilities of Da-sein' (SZ 310/286), should not be misunderstood as an exercise in practical reason as opposed to the theoretical (SZ 300/276–7). Yet isn't rhetoric explicitly practical, derivative of *phronesis*? Heidegger puts the distinction in question at issue (SZ 310/286). Given that the where-for of rhetoric is truth-finding and that this implicates a turn in mood no less than in understanding, this turn is already the actualization (*Vollzug*) of the self, and the condition of insight (*theoria*) and of 'action' in the narrow sense.

The call of conscience brings authentic *Mitsein* into actualization in the resolve of letting the other be:

> The resoluteness toward itself first brings Da-sein to the possibility of letting the others who are with it 'be' in their ownmost potentiality-of-being, and also discloses that potentiality in concern which leaps ahead and frees. (SZ 298/274)

Letting-be consists in active engagement for others. Resolve, however, such as actualizes itself in authentic *Fürsorge*, seizes on the possibilities for being given in the concrete Situation (SZ 299/275–6). The 'there' of the situation is not the already-given within which Dasein also happens to be, but is first opened up, as the site of existential possibilities, by the call of conscience and the resolve which responds to it: '*Resolution is precisely the disclosive projection and determination of the actual factical possibility*' (SZ 298/275). Subordinate to *phronesis*, and the public good, rhetoric responds precisely to these possibilities. This is only possible inasmuch as the orator and the orator's listeners are governed by the call of conscience and the demand, arising out of Dasein's radical solitude, of the authenticity it raises. Otherwise, the danger arises of mistaking the public 'conscience' of the they-self for the voice of authenticity (SZ 278/257). Resoluteness implies 'letting oneself be summoned out of one's lostness in the they' (SZ 299/275). Not, however, to flee society or to withdraw from its reality, but to grasp Dasein's ownmost possibilities as factically given 'in the They' (SZ 299/275). Therefore, rhetoric, the direct, politically engaged mode of the actualization of the call, begins its appeal from the common *doxa* which govern the concrete specificity of Dasein's sitedness: resolve seizes on its ownmost possibility for being as factically given.

Rhetoric is a way of transforming the specificity of *Mitsein*'s disclosedness, and thus its historically sited truth. We recall that central to *Being and Time* is the claim that truth is not a quality of statements, in the first instance, but of Dasein's being-open to being (SZ 155, 218/145, 201). Only with the 'disclosedness of Dasein is the *most primordial* phenomenon of truth attained' (SZ 220–1/203). Truth, moreover, as the disclosedness of Dasein and of the being of beings, is evidently not simply given but rather must constantly be wrung from the tendency inherent in the constitution of Dasein toward concealment and untruth. Therefore,

> Da-sein must explicitly and essentially appropriate what has also already been discovered, defend it *against* illusion and distortion, and ensure itself of its discoveredness again and again ... Truth (discoveredness) must always first be wrested from beings. (SZ 222/204)

The question arises as to the place and task of rhetoric within the economy of truth, understood as the strife of concealment and unconcealment. It is my thesis that rhetoric is one significant and specific way of the disclosure and of the transformation of Dasein. The specific task of rhetoric is to win the things themselves back from their concealment by the already-said. As a work of disclosure, rhetoric is allied to philosophy and to poetic, and distinguished from mere sophistry.

The first indication of the significance of rhetoric in this regard is the character of truth as Dasein's disclosedness. Since rhetoric appeals not only to reason, but also to *pathos* and to the historical specificity of an *ethos* such as finally cannot, by reason of its existential primordiality, be grounded in rationality, and since truth as disclosedness is more primordial than the statement, the 'truth of rhetoric' may well be essentially linked to the truth of disclosedness. This link in fact manifests itself in terms of the attuned understanding of Dasein, to which the orator, in appealing to *pathos* and *ethos*, also makes appeal. What then is the relation of primordial truth to the attuned understanding of Dasein? Let us recall that 'we must *ontologically* in principle leave the primary discovery of the world to "mere mood"' (*Stimmung*) (SZ 138/130). The ontological priority of attunement as disclosive of a world is the condition of the truth of rhetoric as disclosive discourse. We recall, moreover, that not only is attunement 'equiprimordial' with understanding in the existential constitution of Dasein (SZ 137/129), but 'understanding is always attuned' (SZ 143/134). Rational argumentation is a derivative form of attuned understanding. Insofar as rhetoric appeals to argument and therefore to the truth of statements, argument moves within the space opened up by the primordial attunement of Dasein.

The existential structure of Dasein, we recall, is eqiprimoridially constituted as attunement, understanding, and discourse: 'the attuned intelligibility of being-in-the-world *is expressed as discourse*' (SZ 161/151). In the act of communication, the being-in-the-world articulated by discourse is explicitly shared, grasped, and appropriated by *Mitdasein* in our being with one another (SZ 162/152). Rhetoric has to take its point of departure from the understanding, no less than from the attunement already inscribed in the articulation (or 'expression') of discourse. The already-articulated (*die Ausgesprochenheit*) of discourse pre-figures 'the possibilities of the average understanding and the attunement belonging to it' (SZ 167–8/157). An historically specific understanding of being, of the 'disclosed world' of *Mitsein*, as well as the possibilities and limits of new interpretation and its conceptual articulation, is preserved in the already-articulated. The potential of rhetoric will be circumscribed by these limits. This does not mean, however, that rhetoric, like sophistry, is a mere repetition of the already-said (*Gerede*), without reference to the things themselves (SZ 168/158). The already-said arises out of the already-articulated as its mere verbal repetition – it tends to uproot understanding from insight into the things themselves and facilitates the deracination of Dasein (169/158). Given that rhetoric is a (derivative) mode of *aletheuein*, rhetoric in its ideal form does not consist in the mere repetition of the already-said. Rhetoric would rather have as its task the work of *winning back the ground of Mitsein* in the things themselves of the public realm, or *res publica*. By implication, rhetoric would remain true to the authentic *Seinstendenz* of discourse as communication, for it 'aims at bringing the hearer to participate in disclosed being toward what is talked about in discourse' (SZ 168/157).

In undertaking to win back the things themselves of the public realm, rhetoric would have to confront both common understanding and common attunement, for 'the domination of the public way in which things have been interpreted has already decided upon even the possibilities of being attuned' (SZ 169/159). For the domination of the already-said is all pervasive: 'all genuine understanding, interpreting and communication, rediscovery and new appropriation come about in it and out of it and against it' (SZ 169/159). Yet, evidently, new interpretation and rediscovery, such as would win back the ground of *Mitsein* in the public realm, is possible, and it is precisely in this respect that rhetoric is given its task and its rights within the economy of discourse as communication. The legitimate task of rhetoric implicates a deconstruction of the concepts embedded in everyday *doxa*. Rhetoric has as its task, within the limits proper to it, of the stripping away of the 'mask' with which Dasein conceals itself from itself and from others. This mask is constituted by the average and public way of self-understanding as built into public discourse (GA63, 31–3).

Rhetoric engages language to renovate its founding possibilities of saying. The use of figurative language allies rhetoric to poetic; yet rhetoric, unlike poetry, does not engage language for its own sake, but for the sake of possibilities of action. Therefore Heidegger grants a place to poetic speech, which serves to distinguish it from and to elevate it over rhetoric: the 'communication of the existential possibilities of attunement, that is the disclosing of existence, can become the true aim of "poetic" speech' (SZ 162/152). Poetry has the potential of founding anew the attunement of Dasein to being. Since rhetoric, however, is in the first instance constrained by the attunedness (*Gestimmtheit*) of the they-self and the public sphere belonging to it, rhetoric must be derivative of the more primordial realm of poetry. The attunedness of the they-self and everyday *Mitsein* must be turned against itself. The ultimate aim of rhetoric must be to turn everyday *Mitsein* toward the existential possibilities of Dasein's primordial attunement as opened up by poetry and philosophy. The existential isolation of primordial attunement which Dasein experiences in anxiety, for example, may therefore be anticipated by a rhetoric of the public sphere which points Dasein back to itself; but rhetoric on its own account, insofar as it brings about an authentic attunement of the public, cannot disclose Dasein with equal primordiality (cf. SZ 190–1, 322/178, 297). Heidegger in effect claims that rhetoric engages neither discourse nor Dasein's attunement as essentially as poetry or philosophy.

The attunement of Dasein discloses it as thrown – as delivered over to the necessity of taking responsibility for its concrete, historically specified possibilities (SZ 134–5/127). Since rhetoric speaks to and out of the *pathe*, and since these, in turn, become historical and communal as *ethe*, what demand does the primacy of the *pathe* lay on rhetoric as political discourse? Rhetoric, in effect, speaks to the attunement of a particular, historical, and hence communal thrownness and the demand it lays on being-with. The orator speaks to the attunement of a generation, thus to arouse and guide it. This attunement itself, however, must be wrested from unconcealment, for attunement '*discloses Da-sein in its thrownness, initially and for the most part in the mode of an evasive turning away*' (SZ 136/ 128). Given this turn away, could it be that an authentic, truth-seeking rhetoric, no less than philosophy, aims to 'awaken' by turning the public toward the attunement which – albeit fundamentally unknown to the public – nonetheless guides it? Why? To open a space for fundamental decisions by winning a stand in the fundamental attunement of a generation, as opposed to fleeing it. Suppose boredom in the face of the being of beings is such a fundamental attunement. Boredom reveals our experience of the weightlessness of the things themselves in their uniformity. The meaningful differentiation of things dissolves in the face of their temporal in-difference, since they are all equally 'available' and equally insignificant as markers of existential rank and order. Inauthentic 'turning away' from the experience of boredom would take, among other forms, the shape of the consumption of beings in consumerism. The authentic awakening to and experience of this attunement calls for a return to and preservation of the things themselves in the specificity of their being. '*Mood has always already disclosed being-in-the-world as a whole and first makes possible directing oneself toward something*' (SZ 137/129). Granted the primacy of attunement in the disclosure of a world, then the first order of political action – of *phronesis* and of rhetoric as subordinate to it – would be, in conjunction with philosophy and art, – to awaken, transform, and found again the fundamental attunement of a generation, as the 'condition' of the positive constitution, law, and economics of a polity (cf. SZ 138–9/130–1). The transformation of attunement (*Stimmung*) would be the condition (*Be-stimmung*) of what is posited as the governing discourses of the polity.

In awakening and transforming, rhetoric seizes on the attuned understanding of a generation. For understanding, as part of the existential constitution of Dasein, informs its being as a thrown possibility for being (SZ 144/135). In its historical finitude as thrown, Dasein is its possibilities, that is to say, it is projective of ways of being (SZ 145/136). The task of rhetoric would be to disclose the existential possibilities open to *Mitsein*, as given by the tradition (the *ethos*) into which it is thrown. This implicates the projection of possibilities out of a specifically determined, historically founded attunement to the being of beings, for this attunement will circumscribe in advance the political possibilities open to an orator and the orator's generation. If consumerism, for example, is founded in a certain flight from essential boredom, understood as the experience of the nihilation of the being of beings, then the political economy of consumerism cannot be 'turned' in an essential way, and in new directions, without a new experience of boredom, particularly in a turn toward boredom, as opposed to a continued flight from it.

The complete concept of rhetoric, as a potential of *Mitdasein*, can only be won by way of its rootedness in Dasein's historicity. For no less than the historical disciplines is rhetoric determined by historicity to incorporate a specific potential of *Mitsein* as social being. The problem of Dasein's historicity arises out of the need to determine the unity of Dasein as founded in the temporalizing movement of its being (SZ 374–5/343–4). The historicity of Dasein, we recall, constitutes the way of its unified extension (or *bios*) between birth and death. Whereas Heidegger's analysis of the temporality of *Sorge* had shown how the anticipatory resoluteness of Dasein in being-toward-death throws it back on the concrete possibilities of its situation, the source of these possibilities was not given adequate attention (SZ 373/342). This source is the other 'end' of Dasein's temporalizing being – the throwness of its being-born (SZ 374, 376/343–5). Heidegger will unfold the concept of Dasein's birth to reveal the way in which the specific possibilities for being Dasein takes up are drawn from its heritage and developed, in authentic or inauthentic form, in community with its particular 'generation.' The task of rhetoric, therefore, consists in the liberation of the vital possibilities of a heritage for the sake of the authentic being-with of a community.

We recall that what is 'historical,' in the primary sense of constituting the possibility of history, is the historicity of Dasein itself (SZ 381/349). Dasein's historicity is determined as 'more concrete' working out of its temporality, as revealed in the structure of Care (SZ 382/350). Since this structure determines Dasein as the thrown projection of possibilities for being, the essential sense of historicity is to be sought in the way in which possibilities for being become actual for Dasein in its concrete being with others:

> The resoluteness in which Da-sein comes back to itself discloses the actual factical possibilities of authentic existing *in terms of the heritage* which resoluteness *takes over* as thrown. (SZ 383/351)

Given, therefore, that Dasein is always *Mitsein*, it follows that the destiny (*Geschick*) of Dasein, as thrown back on its ownmost, individualized possibilities, will always be wrested from the common fate (*Schicksal*) of the historical community (*Gemeinschaft*) and the generation to which it belongs. The 'happening' or temporalization of the Volk-community is determined as fate.

> In communication and in battle [Kampf] the power of destiny first becomes

free. The fateful destiny of Da-sein in and with its 'generation' constitutes the complete, authentic occurrence of Da-sein. (SZ 384–5/352)

The place of rhetoric in the happening and actualization of the fate of the community becomes clear: it is one significant way in which the community constitutes itself in ongoing dialogue (*Mitteilung*), in struggle and self-clarification concerning itself. What Heidegger specifies as communication and struggle (*Mitteilung und Kampf*) is the form through which the essential, liberating possibilities of a heritage are set free. A 'good' heritage can only be won from tradition. Its positive aspect consists in the 'making possible of authentic existence' (SZ 383/351). This is a communal task, although rooted in the radical metaphysical isolation of Dasein's being-toward-death. The retrieval (*Wiederholung*) of the vital possibilities of a heritage, moreover, is the express way in which a tradition authentically actualizes itself (SZ 385/352). What Heidegger calls 'choosing one's heroes' (SZ 385/352) in reference to the appropriation of a tradition again indicates the central place of rhetoric in the constitution of the public sphere. For the canon of heroes of a community is the result of an ongoing process of education, evaluation, reappraisal, rejection, and reaffirmation. Retrieval, in contrast to the mere repetition of the past of a tradition, implicates a critical response and disavowal (*Erwiderung*) which confronts the merely actual to wrest the possibilities still alive in a heritage from it (SZ 386/353). The public site of this making-manifest, insofar as it is explicitly concerned with the public good of the polity and hence governed by *phronesis*, is the site constantly clarified and renovated by rhetoric.

Dasein integrates its birth into the destiny it lives by taking up its heritage as a set of possibilities and retrieving these for its own existence and for the tasks which its concrete sitedness as *Mitdasein* reveals (SZ 391/357). This implicates a rejection of the mere factuality of the present such as the already-said of discourse has inscribed in the body politic (SZ 391/357). Within the limits prescribed by its determination by the public realm, rhetoric has the task of the critical evaluation and renewal of the governing concepts and fundamental attunement of a polity.

The 'object' of history as a discipline, given its derivation from Dasein's historicity, is the possible: historical science constitutes and interprets the 'facts' of the past as they are revealed by the fundamental possibilities of a heritage (SZ 394/360). These possibilities are themselves traced into the facts of the past, and must be won from them (SZ 395/361). The question arises whether rhetoric can be conceived on the model of historical science, at least in this respect: Does rhetoric take its departure from the possibilities of the communal existence of a polity to question and reconceive its actuality, whether the actuality of a constitution, of positive law, or of the canon of heroes? The ideal of rhetoric, given that it keeps its eye on the good of the polity, must conform to this demand. But insofar as rhetoric confirms the laws and constitution of a state, this, too, derives from a grasp of the possibilities for being which gave rise to them. In both cases the ideal of rhetoric implicates retrieval, as opposed to a mere repetition, of the thrown possibilities for being granted by a heritage.

2.3 The Limits of Rhetoric: Philosophy, *Weltanschauung*, Rhetoric

Central to Heidegger's reflections in the Address is the relationship of science and attunement to being. In the *Nachwort* to *What Is Metaphysics?* (1943), Heidegger claims that modern representational science is rooted in a fundamental attunement to being as presence.[33] The question at issue is how the alienation of knowledge from concrete historical existence, which arises with the objectification of beings, can be overcome to root science once more in the *ethos* of the people. Insofar as philosophy, *Weltanschauung*, and rhetoric, each in its own way, attempt to awaken, guide, and transform the attunement of a people, they engage the historically founded *ethos* out of which a science has arisen and to which it still responds, if only in alienation from its origins. But how is the engagement of rhetoric with Dasein's attunement distinct from that of philosophy, on the one hand, and *Weltanschauung*, on the other? The answer to this question will allow us to specify further the reach and limits of rhetoric, in Heidegger's account.

In *Die Grundbegriffe der Metaphysik* (*Welt–Endlichkeit–Einsamkeit*), Heidegger claims that the act of philosophy, if it be authentic, will be founded in and motivated by a fundamental mood, a mood which is itself an expression of Dasein's openness to being. Moods (*Stimmungen*) are expressive of Dasein's attunement to itself, to others, and to its world: moods 'set the tune' of our being to determine how things will manifest themselves to us (GA29/30, 100–1). Not to be confused with the flightiness of mere 'emotions' and whims, moods signify ways of being-attuned through which beings – including our own being – become accessible to Dasein. The *Stimmung* constitutes the 'primordial How' of our being-open to give Dasein 'its stand and possibility' (GA29/30, 101). As the 'How' of the manifestation of beings, being-attuned constitutes the temporal order, or 'melody,' of manifestation. To be in a mood, as Heidegger specifies in great detail by reference to the mood of boredom, is to experience a specific form of the temporalization of Da-sein (GA29/30, 101, 191). A form of being-attuned is a form of standing-in-relation, of being-related-to other beings and 'oneself.'

To engage in philosophy, on Heidegger's account, is to take up a fundamental way of one's own, historically concrete being-attuned and to allow oneself to be seized by it. The mood of our philosophizing, therefore, is not to be objectified, not to be rendered up to consciousness for analysis, for this would be to uproot ourselves from the fundamental being-attuned which 'sites' us. Heidegger insists that a mood must be 'awakened' to allow it fully to be and, in being, to seize hold of us (GA29/30, 92–3). Thought takes its stand in the clearing opened up by fundamental ways of being-attuned, such as boredom, and anxiety. In its encounter with the fundamental being-attuned of its own facticity, Dasein is led back to *itself*, to con-ceive or 'grasp' the concept of its own *finitude*, as the 'beginning' which holds Dasein in its grasp (cf. GA29/30, 9–10). For only insofar as Dasein takes a stand in being-attuned, does the conceptual work of metaphysics find its ownmost ground. Allowing its own, most intimate being-attuned to being to awaken, Dasein is thrown back on itself to question itself. This questioning, in turn, forces Dasein to go to the root of the mood which motivates questioning and which calls for the concept. The mood of boredom, once fully awakened as a source of questioning, leads Dasein back to the experience of the in-difference of the temporalization of time, and thus to an experience of *world* (GA29/30, 222).

The phenomenological description of the mood of boredom offers Heidegger entrance to the problem of Dasein's being-in-the-world as a temporal structure. The entrance thus won – and the concept of Dasein's finitude and worldhood thus constructed – is prefaced by a deconstruction of the contemporary 'mood' or situation (*Lage*), as evidenced by the work of Spengler, Klages, Scheler, and Ziegler (GA29/30, 103–16). Works of these authors, in each case an exercise in the 'philosophy of culture,' offer an account or representation of the contemporary mood, without, however, bringing Da-sein to the point of taking a stand, of taking responsibility for itself (GA29/30, 113). If, then, philosophy serves this purpose, as opposed to offering merely a 'diagnosis' and 'prognosis' of the times, what can be said of rhetoric? Insofar as it also works to awaken Da-sein's being-attuned, rhetoric shows itself allied to philosophy. Rhetoric cannot be content with an account of the public mood, for it aims to lead to decision; and therefore rhetoric must transpose itself into a mood, thus to allow the mood to awaken and unfold itself. For the object of rhetoric is not the objectification and analysis of the fundamental moods of the public – it rather works to clarify and stabilize a fundamental way of being-attuned, so as to make action and preparation for it possible. This work of clarification, moreover, will call for a transformation of the governing public mood, and its *doxa*, to uncover their fundamental ground in *Mitdasein*'s being-attuned. In this respect, rhetoric no less than philosophy has both a deconstructive and a constructive task. Rhetoric departs from philosophy, however, in that it does not engage Dasein's being-attuned for the sake of questioning itself, and the intensification of it, but for the sake of dialogue and action in the public sphere. Conversely, however, the temporality of the rhetorical situation, which is intent on decision, rather than contemplation, implicates, as Kisiel notes, a resolute openness to the 'particular human situation.' The kairological temporality of rhetoric, in its service to the political life, offers the possibility of generating 'concepts' imbued with the primordial, passionate intensity of life.[34]

Does rhetoric as ideally conceived serve philosophy? On Heidegger's account this is only the case if philosophy, in remaining true to itself, does not for its part rest in mere contemplation of the conceptualized and stable – it must seize the kairological moment defining rhetoric and grasp life still more radically. As Heidegger admonishes a student in the Heraclitus seminar (with Eugen Fink) of 1966–7, 'we have to rethink the concepts anew every day.'[35] If we allow that rhetoric serves philosophy in this endeavour, what is the fate, conversely, of a rhetoric that falls short of its highest possibility?

The ideal of rhetoric we have proposed indirectly acts as a handmaiden to philosophy. It challenges the governing opinion and the public, collective moods of a polity to prepare the collective decisions of the public sphere. But in doing so, rhetoric ideally opens a space within the public realm for more fundamental modes of being-attuned, and in this way it anticipates philosophical questioning. But insofar as rhetoric fails to challenge governing *doxa*, it is liable to contribute to the inculpation of the norms and ways of being-attuned which organize and guide a society. As early as 1919, Heidegger had defined such a system of cultural values and the attunement to transcendental being proper to it, as a *Weltanschauung* (GA56/57, 9). A *Weltanschauung* is itself a philosophy of culture, or *Kulturphilosophie*, such as propagated by Spengler. Heidegger still held this view in the *Beiträge* of 1936–8: a *Weltanschauung* serves to supplement science and critical philosophy by crowning their merely technical and scholastic endeavour with an aura of 'ideals' (GA65, 37). Whereas philosophy is defined by Heidegger as a way of questioning which ever begins, as perpetual homesickness, a *Weltanschauung* is set in unquestionable certainties, even and especially if these certainties are the relative certainties of a perspective (GA 29/30, 1–8; GA65, 37).

The perspectival nature of the *Weltanschauung*, which defines the origins and nature of the concept, reveals its origin in a mode of being-attuned; and this creates the appearance of kinship to philosophy. For this reason alone, Heidegger must insist so tenaciously on the essential difference of the two as founded in the *Ent-schlossenheit*, the openness of Da-sein, as a questioning, founding being, to being. To misconceive *Ent-schlossenheit* is to ascribe to Heidegger a 'decisionism' which is proper to a *Weltanschauung* as the setting-into-position of a system. The strength of such a system of values is its ability to instrumentalize all resources, including those of rhetoric, to mobilize the public domain. Consequently, the dissolution of rhetoric as a way of truth-finding comes about with its integration into the socio-technical management of society as organized by modern 'world-views,' be they liberal or totalitarian (GA65, 38–41). Rhetoric surrenders the power of the word and the task of the renovation of common attunement to the theatrical display and intensification of emotion (cf. GA65, 131–34). This signifies the final collapse of the political realm and the triumph of socio-technical management.

We have seen that rhetoric is not an independent mode of *aletheuein*. Yet it serves the unconcealment of those fundamental moods which in a given situation can found Dasein in its historical specificity. The address of 1933 is an intervention in a concrete revolutionary situation. Heidegger aimed to arouse an attunement to fundamental metaphysical and political questions to guide the revolutionary energies of the 'Movement' – thus to turn it away from the mere repetition and institutionalization, in crude and simplified form, of metaphysical positions (SU 23). This intervention in the revolutionary situation of 1933 attempted to redirect the National Socialist breakthrough toward a fundamental re-ordering of the national community, and to do this Heidegger was fatally constrained to appeal to the common opinions of the Movement – such as the primacy of the Will, the Volk, and the struggle against intellectualism – as his point of departure. Heidegger's intervention implicated a certain homology of terms, but not necessarily of concepts. It is a commonplace of the critical literature that Heidegger seemingly 'takes over' Nazi phraseology in the Rector's Address, as well as in his programmatic speeches of this period – *Kampf, Wille, Zucht,* and *Volksgemeinschaft,* for example. But we cannot assume that Heidegger's uses of these terms – 'struggle,' 'will,' 'discipline' or 'cultivation,' the 'community of the Volk' – were filled with National Socialist content. They were not. The fact that, as Fritsche argues, Heidegger shared vocabulary with the Right and the National Socialists in itself proves nothing.[36] Heidegger's understanding of language is not positivistic – language for Heidegger articulates the moodful understanding of our being-in-the-world. Hence he did not repeat terminology in recognition of the concepts they signify. He appealed rather to a common fundamental mood, and to common *doxa,* in an effort to transform the understanding of his audience.

At issue in the Address is the nature and task of the university as a community of knowledge, and its leadership in the state. The speech is a 'political' exhortation, in the essential sense that it proposes to arouse a fundamental attunement commensurate to the true nature of science and the appropriate task of the university, thus to prepare the site of the polity as a community of knowledge. In Halliwell's terms as applied to Aristotle, the Address can be characterized as a species of deliberative oratory which has the 'longer-term perspective of a city's continued existence and flourishing' as its proper theme.[37] Thus Heidegger needed to undertake the deconstruction of the *doxa* of his audience, regarding the character of the university, the position of its faculties, and the mission of knowledge in service to the state and the people. The nature of the leadership role of science in the polity, furthermore, calls for reformulation. Since these *doxa* are implicitly guided by a certain attunement to being, the rhetorician's task of turning the *pathe* of the audience must be founded in philosophical insight into the question of being itself. This makes for an essential ambiguity, inherent in political engagement, which was only complicated by the heterogeneous composition of Heidegger's audience of traditional academics, their ideologically engaged counterparts, Party functionaries, and student radicals committed to National Socialism. The essential ambiguity the Rector's Address inscribes – caught as it is between the essential questioning of philosophy and the rhetorical necessity of engaging the *doxa* of an audience to turn it toward fundamental questioning – would entangle Heidegger in the politics of National Socialism in ways he did not anticipate.

3 Heidegger and the Conservative Revolution

3.1 Heidegger's Retrieval of Aristotle and the Relation of Volk and Science in the Rector's Address of 1933

Heidegger's 'Rector's Address' has drawn perhaps inordinate attention in recent years, particularly as evidence of Heidegger's 'involvement' in National Socialism – which it undoubtedly offers. The interpretations of Ott, Rockmore, Philipse, Köchler, and Fritsche, among others, are typical in the sense that they implicate Heidegger in the totalitarian designs of National Socialism, even if they allow that Heidegger's version of Nazism was not necessarily racist, and that it was, in fact, unorthodox in its entire tendency.[1] Yet the philosophical grounds of Heidegger's invocation of the fundamental interrelation of Volk, work service, and science in the Address remain insufficiently clarified by these interpretations. In what follows, I propose to show that Heidegger's deconstruction and retrieval of Aristotle, in particular, prepare the way for his understanding of Volk in its relation to the historicity of science, and that, consequently, the Address reflects some of the central theses of Heidegger's thought, and is not merely an opportunistic response to the political situation of 1933.

3.1.1 The Grounds of Science and 'The Self-Assertion of the German University'

The title of Heidegger's Rector's Address insists that the University must win back its essential ground in the unity of knowledge, which can only arise out of our response to the being of beings. In this sense the University 'asserts' itself; its assertion of its political independence, in Humboldt's sense, is not only derivative of a more fundamental self-assertion, but overtaken by the necessity of leading the Volk, in submission to the demand of the historicity of Volk (GA16, no. 155, 301–7). This does not mean that the University, and philosophy, should serve a political agenda, but that both take their measure from the historicity of being. The University does not assert itself by following the ideal of 'value-free' science: its self-assertion consists in the overcoming of the separation of science, or *theoria*, and *praxis*, for in doing so it affirms the power of being in its presencing.

Heidegger's Address responds to the perceived deracination of knowledge from its essential ground and the consequent transformation of the University. Perhaps the inaugural address of 1929 articulates this problem, which had concerned Heidegger since 1919, most pointedly:

> The scientific fields are quite diverse. The ways they treat their objects of inquiry differ fundamentally. Today only the technical organization of universities and faculties consolidates this burgeoning multiplicity of disciplines; the practical establishment of goals by each discipline provides the only meaningful source of unity. Nonetheless, the rootedness of the sciences in their essential ground has atrophied. (WM 104/94)

What is at stake is the unity of the sciences in their 'essential' ground. Evidently Heidegger holds that the idea of the University propagated by Humboldt had been so undermined by the increasing primacy of the applied sciences that it could no longer prevent the disintegration of the University into a technical research apparatus. Although Humboldt's central theses – 'the freedom of research and teaching, the unity of teaching and research, the unity of the sciences, and the priority of *Bildung* over vocational training'[2] – still tended to determine the terms of the debate regarding the idea of the University and the possibility of university reform, Humboldt's fundamental premise, that philosophy could found the fundamental unity of all disciplines, no longer seemed tenable (GA16, no. 155, 294–7). It therefore comes as no surprise that in 1933, Heidegger, along with many others, contemplated the reform of the University to found its essential unity anew, thus to facilitate the return of the sciences to their source (GA16, no. 155, 292–7). As Hans Sluga has shown, Heidegger would briefly ally himself to reformers such as Krieck and Baeumler in his effort to fundamentally restructure the University. These efforts finally failed, in Heidegger's account, due to the opposition of conservative academics and because of Heidegger's speedy estrangement from his National Socialist allies, Krieck and Baeumler.[3]

The reform Heidegger aspired to, moreover, presupposes the unity of the Volk and the political will to establish knowledge on new foundations. University reform, Volk, and state are linked and unified, in Heidegger's mind, in the upsurge of a 'revolutionary' political will to unity and in the return to fundamental sources. In 'The German University,' an address held 15 and 16 August 1934, Heidegger makes this point:

> *Education of the Volk, through the state, to become a Volk* – that is the meaning of the National Socialist movement, that is the essence of the formation of a new state. *Such* education for highest knowledge is the task of the new University. (GA16, no. 155, 307)

Whereas it is clear that Heidegger shared with the 'movement' the will to re-educate the German body politic, it must be made equally clear that his premises are of a different order, and we must unfold these premises out of his own essential thought.

Ernst Krieck, in an article of 1933, published in *Volk im Werden*, typically insists that the source and ground of the unity of the sciences, and therefore of the organization of the University and its faculties, is the 'life-process' of the Volk in its 'historical becoming.'[4] This process of becoming articulates itself as a *Weltanschauung* which is the source of a people's science, as well as the goal which it attempts to realize. The applied sciences or technical disciplines are conceived as particular applications of philosophy or fundamental research.[5] A science justifies itself in its practical application to the well-being of the Volk community. In Krieck's own terms, therefore, the unity of the sciences, technology, and the organization of the University is to be founded in anthropology – that is, in the 'racially' conceived Volk and its *Weltanschauung*. This solution to the problem of the deracination of science is totally rejected by Heidegger. As we shall see, he insists on the necessity of a new *Grundstimmung*, founded in the presencing of being, and actualized in the *historicity* of Volk.

What did he understand the essential place of science (*die Wissenschaft*) and the University to be in the new state?

> The will to the essence of the German university is the will to science as the will to the historical mission of the German people as a people that knows itself in its own state. *Together,* science and German fate must come to power in this will to essence. (SU 10/471)

First of all, I propose to focus simply on the notion of 'essence' enunciated here. The responsibility of leadership and the right to lead and educate the people, which the University as the site of knowledge claims for itself, must be founded, if they are to be legitimate, in the will to essence of the University and of science. A being's 'essence' (*Wesen*) designates the temporal and local unfolding of a being as founded in its own originating limit, and as granted by the destiny of unconcealment in which it comes to stand. The essence of science, thought in remembrance of the first beginning, is called 'the *questioning, unguarded holding of one's ground in the midst of the uncertainty of the totality of what-is*' (SU 14/474). This will to essence alone 'will create for our people its world, a world of the innermost and most extreme danger, i.e., its truly *spiritual* world' (SU 14/474). The will to the essence of science brings the being of beings to a stand. This happens only in the decisive, history-founding act of a questioning of the being of beings which first opens up a site for beings to appear in their determined outline.

Heidegger's explanatory notes of 1945 refer to 'Platons Lehre von der Wahrheit' (Plato's Doctrine of Truth) as one of the philosophical keys to the Address (SU 22/482). Recalling this essay, we know that beings are brought to a stand in the aspect, the *eidos*, through which being presences to site itself in the image and the gestalt (WW 219). In this way, a 'world' first comes to be, thus to allow beings to stand forth in their being as tree, temple, as work of art and act of state. The 'world' thus opened up and brought to a stand is called 'spiritual' in the sense that a world is founded in the attuned understanding, the resolute openness of Dasein to the presencing of being: 'spirit is primordially attuned, knowing resoluteness toward the essence of being' (SU 14/474).

Heidegger rejects the Hegelian concept of spirit which Derrida ascribes to him.[6] But as his commentary on Hegel's philosophy of state reveals, Heidegger retrieves *Geist* in the sense of historically rooted existence, from the idealist interpretation.[7] In an address of August 1934, introducing the idea of the German university, Heidegger defines *Geist* as the 'inner essence' (*inneres Wesen*), or 'the *comportment* [*Haltung*], out of which the University actualizes and defends its task' (GA16, no. 155, 289). The sign of the retrieval of historicity is the determination of spirit as 'attuned': through the enactment of its questioning resoluteness, spirit is rooted in being-toward-death and in the earth. It is delimited by the temporal and local singularity of the site which questioning brings to a stand. '*Geist must be given gestalt* [*Gestalt*]' (GA36/37, 7). Consequently Heidegger does not follow, and in fact implicitly rejects, Ludwig Klages' understanding of *Geist* as intellect in conflict with the soul.[8] The Address foreshadows the 'Origin of the Work of Art,' inasmuch as the site of the historical specificity of the presencing of spirit is referred to the earth. Therefore, Heidegger appeals to the 'spiritual world' of a people as the 'power that most deeply preserves the people's strengths, which are tied to earth and blood.' In the 'spiritual,' that is, in the historical singularity of the presencing of being, an earth, to which the powers of 'blood' belong, comes to stand (SU 14/474–5); no less, however, again in antici- pation of the 'Origin,' does a world call for rootedness in an earth, if it is not to degenerate into the empty, merely analytic play of rationality.

Heidegger's reference to 'blood' has given offence, arousing the suspi- cion that he was prepared to compromise and contaminate his thought by recourse to racism and biologism. His response, in lectures of 1933–4, to Kolbenheyer's biological interpretation of the Volk, is to unequivo- cally reject it (GA36/37, 209–13). What Heidegger calls the sustaining powers of earth and blood rather circumscribe the singularity and histor- ical specificity of the presencing of being. The first beginning happens as a 'Greek' founding, arising out of the powers of the Greek people (*Volks- tum*) 'by virtue of [its] language' (SU 11/471). The appeal to 'blood' refers a people back to its earth, hence back to the historicity of a world as founded in the resolute openness of a questioning which unlocks 'in all things what is essential' (SU 13/474). The powers of 'earth and blood,' therefore, are not racial and biological categories, but refer to the necessity of self-limitation founded in a people's act of decision to belong to its 'native soil.' This implicates an ethic of responsibility for the finitude of the earth which has economic as well as political and cultural consequences. Heidegger's motivation is profoundly anti-cosmopolitan, but by no means racist or nationalist, inasmuch as modern nationalism descends from the abstraction of a general, or collective, will which Heidegger's critique of metaphysics rejects.

What is essential in all things, including the being of a people, is the unfolding of its own potential for being as determined by the *arche* and *telos* which govern it. Since the essence of science is in question, this means that science must be founded – or re-founded – in response to the historical necessity imposed on a people in the entire unshelteredness of its response to the being of beings. This in turn demands of a people, no less than of science and the University, a self-imposed delimitation (*Selbst- begrenzung*), as the surety of its proper unfolding into its ownmost possibil- ities (SU 10/471).

Questioning, as the 'highest form [Gestalt] of knowing' is the enactment of self-delimitation. In 'The German Student as Worker' (25 November 1933), Heidegger insists that the demand for knowledge must be guided by what is worthy of knowledge, which, in turn, 'sets off the limits [Grenzen] within which genuine questioning can found and preserve itself' (GA16, no. 108, 201). The sciences, guided by the specificity of their historical task, as the way of knowledge of a people in its response to being, are carried 'back from their endless and aimless dispersal into isolated fields and corners' (SU 13/474). Questioning 'shatters the division of the sciences' to expose them to the necessity of responding to 'the world-shaping powers of human being [Dasein] such as: nature, history, language; people, custom, state; poetry, thought, faith; disease, madness, death; law, economy, technology' (SU 13–4/ 474). It is precisely this response, and the singular character of it, which roots a people in its homeland and *sets the limits of science.*

Heidegger's appeal to the retrieval of the first beginning issues a challenge to the Germans to re-found knowledge in response to the 'destiny of being.' This phrase is not the empty sound it first seems, for it intimates an event which makes itself evident almost everywhere, in practically all domains of life, in our own history. It intimates the history of the abandonment of the being of beings (*die Seinsverlassenheit*) in the event of the increasing dis-integration, and functional integration, of entities. The destitution of beings is attended by the expropriation of what is most proper to them in their historical, local, and temporal specificity, in favour of their generalized availability. Heidegger's allusion to Nietzsche and the devaluation of all values (SU 13, 39/474, 498) establishes nihilism conceived as the abandonment of the being of beings, as the hermeneutic context of the Address. For this reason, he broaches the problem of the de-construction and recovery of science, thus to place it in the service of the world-building powers of Dasein. Science must be made to serve 'life' (to echo Nietzsche's untimely reflection on history) if it is not to become definitively the lord of the living.

The retrieval of science Heidegger undertakes begins with an acknowledgment of the superior power of necessity over knowing, and of the failure of knowledge in the face of 'overpowering fate' (SU 11/472). Nihilism has become a destiny. The deracination of peoples also belongs, and in fact belongs essentially, to this destiny, and calls for a response in the form of the founding of the unity of 'science and German fate' (SU 10/471). Heidegger evidently holds that the prerequisite to a newly founded unity of science and a people in its historical specificity would be the transformation of the fundamental attunement of 'theory' in its supposed objectivity. What is at stake is the reality (the being) of the real, which is concealed by the re-presentational forms of scientific reflection on nature and history. Claims to universal validity made by the human sciences, no less than by the natural sciences, in the wake of the Enlightenment are founded in the separation of theory and concretely embodied existence. The retrieval of *theoria* implicates the engagement of knowledge, for the sake of beings, and in recognition of the finitude and historical specificity of knowing. This makes not only for the passion (*Leidenschaft*) of *theoria*, but also for the overcoming of the distinction of theory and praxis (SU 11–12/472). We know, in fact, that since his earliest lectures Heidegger had called for the engagement and realization (*Vollzug*) of thought in confrontation with the entire facticity of its hermeneutic situation. The lifeworld is to be given creative form (*schöpferische Gestaltung*): this becomes possible inasmuch as the situation of Dasein is permeated by the 'spontaneity of the living Self,' to grant existence its primordial significance. Heidegger calls for the engagement and realization of the Self in its factical situation, thus to transform and found anew the meaning inherent in a context of relations (*Bezugsinn*); thus, for example, the idea of the scientific or the religious life as objectively given is existentially founded in the life of the individual (GA58, 260–1; cf. SU 23/483).

Key theses of the Address are evidently founded in Heidegger's Aristotle interpretation of the 1920s and early 1930s. In the Address, Heidegger claims that the Greeks 'struggled precisely to conceive and enact' the engagement of scientific observation or contemplation (*Betrachtung*) as 'the highest mode of *energeia*, of man's being-at-work' (*am-Werke-sein*) (SU 12/472). According to Heidegger's Aristotle lectures of 1924, *energeia* names the How, or way of being, the actuality of being setting itself to work in the limit (*peras*) set by Dasein's engagement with beings. Dasein is being-limited (*Begrenztsein*): its engagement with others and with beings is bound by the horizon of a limit and end (*telos*) which arises out of Dasein's way-of-being-actual (*energeia*) itself, not out of anything external (GA18, 65–68, 97–101). In this interpretation of the Greek *energeia*, Heidegger proposes to found the need of his time in a retrieval of the authentic Greek sense of *theoria* as *energeia*: 'theory was to be understood as itself the highest realization of genuine practice (*Praxis*)' (SU 12/473). This does not mean, as Taminiaux claims, that Heidegger follows Plato to grant 'theory' supremacy over the properly political realms of *phronesis* and *praxis*.[9] Exactly the opposite is true. The realization of *praxis* consists in the actualization, or being-at-work, of *theoria* in the life-world of *praxis*.

In the 1924 lectures, Heidegger had insisted that being-in-the-world, as *energeia*, actualizes the potential of Dasein to engage beings in the *praxis* of setting concern to work in the work (GA18, 76–9, 100).

This interpretation is supported by Heidegger's comments on the relation of *theoria* and *praxis* in the *Metaphysische Anfangsgründe der Logik* of 1928: the tendency of antiquity in the wake of Plato to interpret 'the phenomenon of world' in terms of the being-present of Ideas, in their accessibility to pure contemplation, has one of its essential grounds in the fact that 'from early on transcendence was grasped as *theorein*.' And this means, Heidegger immediately adds, that the nature of 'transcendence was not sought out in its primordial rootedness in the essential being of Dasein' (GA26, 236/183). According to the argument of *Being and Time*, transcendence belongs to the structure of Dasein as being-in-the-world. In the existential analytic, it reveals itself, in the first instance, in our everyday involvements. The theoretical attitude of 'just looking,' of pure perception, has its 'existential genesis' in the 'circumspection that guides "practical" taking care of things' (SZ 358/328). The objectification of a realm of entities, which characterizes science, arises out of our pre-scientific, everyday ways of experiencing and interpreting a domain of being (SZ 9/7). Furthermore, if

> the thematization of what is objectively present – the scientific project of nature – is to become possible, *Da-sein must transcend* the beings thematized ... But if the thematization of innerworldly beings objectively present is a change-over from taking care which circumspectively discovers, then a transcendence of Dasein must already underlie 'practical' being together with things at hand. (SZ 363–4/332)

The retrieval of the primordial rootedness of transcendence in the being-in-the-world of Dasein's practice implicates the leadership of practice over theory, for the condition of theory (in transcendence) is more primordially realized in practice. In the Rector's Address, consequently, Heidegger calls for the re-founding of theory in the primordial ground out of which it arises. The Greeks 'were not concerned to assimilate practice to theory; quite the reverse: theory was to be understood as itself the highest realization of genuine practice' (SU 12/472–3). Theory is not to be pursued 'for its own sake' but for the sake of *praxis*. In this sense, as actualized *praxis*, science was for the Greeks 'the innermost determining centre of all that binds human being to people and state' ('des ganzen völklich-staatlichen Daseins') (SU 12/473). Heidegger's commentary on the relation of *theoria* and *praxis* in the Address arises directly out of one of the essential concerns of his thought. As Bernasconi, for example, has shown, Heidegger's attempt to deconstruct the metaphysical primacy of *theoria* and *techne*, and to root both in the primordial transcendence of *praxis*, weaves its way through his entire philosophy.[10] It is also evident from the Address that Heidegger recognizes in the National Socialist attack on 'intellectualism' a crude copy of his own interpretation of the history of metaphysics, for intellectualism denotes the alienation of theory from practice.

Praxis, as noted, realizes theory as *energeia* – that is, in the founded and finite forms of being-at-work. For *energeia* means, in Heidegger's interpretation of Aristotle, the actualization of the finitude of beings as bounded by the unfolding (*kinesis*) of their potential for being into the form and limit (*morphe* and *telos*) proper to them. The specific *energeia* of *praxis* consists in the actualization of the *kinesis*, and therefore the temporality, of Dasein. To call for a transformation of science into the enactment of thought as *energeia* is to found science in the finitude and historical specificity of a community. For this reason, following the Greek model which he hopes to retrieve for the Germany of 1933, 'science is not a "cultural good," but the innermost determining centre' of communal being: science lays out ways of approach to beings, responds to the differentiation of beings to set limit, rank, and measure, and thus constitutes the 'centre' (the supporting pole) in terms of which a people can constitute a state. Heidegger does not argue for an ideologically committed science, such as propagated by the new regime, and in fact decisively rejects the '"new concept of science"' (SU 10/471). Heidegger rejects this initiative no less firmly than the liberal ideal of 'value-free' science. This science, as Heidegger argues in the Plato lectures of 1931–2, has lost its rootedness (*Bodenständigkeit*) in Dasein, and therefore is in no position to determine what an 'object' is, for a conceptualization of beings without the founding experience of being remains formal and external (GA34, 210). Thus the difficulty of the challenge Heidegger envisions first becomes evident: How can the sciences of nature and history engage the historical specificity of a people's native soil to generate a form of life which does not surrender the singularity of place and historicity to a set of universal, cosmopolitan categories of political, economic, and technological determination? Heidegger's early conception of the potential of National Socialism made this question appropriate, in his mind, to the new situation of 1933 (SU 23, 39/483, 498).

Heidegger's response to this question again takes up the necessity of a determining limit which binds science to its essence. This determining limit, itself, sets the measure of the authentic freedom of scientific study and work. In the first instance, Heidegger appeals to three services, or bonds, which together constitute the concrete realization of the freedom of the university student: these are the bonds of labour service to the community, of armed service to the nation, and of service in knowledge to the 'spiritual mission of the German people' (SU 16/476). Freedom is understood as the actualization of the governing, self-given law through which Dasein enters into its proper, historically concrete essence and limit (SU 15/475). Heidegger's appeal to labour service has typically been interpreted as a concession to Nazi ideology. Thus the significance of work, and of the work-world in its relation to the existential motivation of science, in the Address has rarely been recognized – James Ward's commentary on the text offering a significant exception.[11] Work has to be referred back to a world, founded in knowledge, understood in its finitude, and historicity, as the world of a particular people. Work, science, and Volk share a common root in the historicity of being – that is, in the event of presencing as realized in the making-present of beings. Only insofar as the three services are united in '*one* formative force,' Heidegger argues, can the freedom of self-delimitation be concretely founded, and the University enter into its essential gestalt (SU 18/478).

Heidegger calls the unity of the three bonds – '*by* the people, *to* the destiny of the state, *in* a spiritual mission' – 'the primordial and full essence of science.' The 'realization' of this unity 'is our task – supposing that we submit to the distant command of the beginning of our spiritual-historical being [Dasein]' (SU 16/477). Wherein does the realization, or setting-to-work, of the unitary unfolding of science consist? In the differentiation of the being of beings, insofar as beings are brought to stand and are fulfilled in the enactment of all the realms of making, thought, and action. Heidegger calls the deployment of differentiation 'struggle' (*Kampf*), which he expressly glosses as *polemos*, in the commentary of 1945 (SU 28–9/488). The retrieval of Heraclitus's fragment 53, thus of being-as-*polemos*, is the 'distant command of the beginning' to which Heidegger appeals. Heidegger's reference of *Kampf* to *polemos*, and thus to Heraclitus, is not the belated effort of 1945 to 'clean up' his record of 1933, for as early as 1933, while writing to Carl Schmitt, Heidegger interpreted fragment 53 in this sense.[12]

In a public address to former classmates in May of 1934, moreover, he insists that World War I – in its spiritual significance – must be internalized as *Kampf*, and *Kampf*, understood as *polemos*, must be grasped as the inner law of our being. This inner law calls for founding and saving the site (Da-sein) of the differentiation of the being of beings, for *polemos* articulates not only the generation of all things but also the law of their preservation (GA16, no. 154, 283). Therefore Heidegger interprets *polemos* as the differentiation (*Aus-einander-setzung*) of being in beings (SU 28/488). 'The essence of *polemos*,' Heidegger writes in 1945, 'lies in the *deikunai*, to show, and in *poiein*, to produce, as the Greeks say, to make-it-stand-out in open view' (SU 29/489). This happens pre-eminently as the *logos* which engages (*i*) self-emergent *phusis* to bring the differentiation of beings to light; (*ii*) the *eidos* (including the *eidos* which guides *techne*) which brings beings to stand-forth in the light of their emergence; (*iii*) the enactment (*Vollzug*) of *energeia* in the stand Dasein takes; and (*iv*) the incorporation of truth in the work. The *presencing* of the differentiation of being governs the *unity* of the 'world-shaping powers of human-historical being' in which beings disperse and manifest themselves (SU 13/474). Hence *polemos, the differentiation of the being of beings*, calls for a site of differentiation – for Da-sein – as the site of the unfolding of a people, their state, and the spiritual mission of knowledge.

Mitdasein takes its stand in being to enact the differentiation of the being of beings. This 'stand' is the resolute, attentive openness (*Ent-schlossenheit*) of Dasein to the presencing of being. Da-sein's rootedness in the event of being, as the differentiation of being, determines both its fundamental attunement, and consequently the 'hold' Dasein has on itself, and the gestalt in which beings manifest themselves to it (GA34, 237–8). The 'gestalt' of Dasein, itself, implicates a certain rhythm (*mousike*), or mode of attunement – a way of being-open to the manifestness of beings.[13] '*Mousike*, the rhythmical, which holds itself to an inner order and thereby forms [Bilden]' gives order and gestalt to the philosophical life (GA61, 50).[14] The form is the temporal structure of a way of being-open that holds to itself and thus holds-open a way of making-manifest. As a way of being–under-way, we can speak of a gestalt of Dasein without falling back into the metaphysics of the paradigmatic idea. Perception (*aisthesis*) itself, although of nature, is not part of Dasein as nature, but only as integrated into the erotic (transcendent) nature of Dasein, insofar as this nature has brought itself to stand in *paideia*; and this happens as the history of Dasein, that is, in its founded ways of being-open and holding-open (GA34, 235).

Since *polemos* happens as the differentiation of being, the attunement proper to it, as Heidegger intimates in 1945, is the attunement of the letting-be of beings. The Address brings into question the 'essence of truth as the letting be of what is, as it is' (SU 27/487). In the *Logik* of 1934, as well as in the public lectures of this period, Heidegger gives the name of 'work' (*Arbeit*) to the event of the differentiation of being in beings (GA16, no. 108, 205). Work is defined by the making-present of the present out of the unity of the temporalization of Volk: this unity is defined by a vocation (*Sendung*) and task (*Auftrag*) – the 'past' and future of Volk's historicity, which, in their mutual determination, open up a present, understood as a particular way of the disclosure of beings (GA38, 126–30). Differentiation implicates the recognition of the proper limits belonging to all entities and to every action and enactment, including acts of leadership, of obedience, and of the legitimate rights and inherent limits of the state (cf. SU 19/479). The will to the essence of science, and of the University, must also be turned toward the presencing of being, and away from the illusion of the ahistorical objectivity of science. In this sense the appeal to a fundamental attunement responsive to *polemos* is an attempt to re-found science in the historicity of Da-sein's being on the earth. Of the three services, as Heidegger emphasized in 1945, knowledge is the ground of the other two, for knowing consists in the stand Dasein takes to attend to the presencing of differentiation. The unity within particularity of the faculties within the University derives from this stand.

But insofar as this stand is not won, Heidegger warns, the mere semblance of culture triumphs over the sitedness of being (SU 19/480; cf. GA16, no. 155, 300). Transcendental categories of being are themselves the condition of the semblance of reality, in the sense that the *chorismos* Plato and the metaphysical tradition set between being and beings degrades beings to a mere image of the real (GA40, 113/106). The metaphysics of collective subjectivity as posited by the proponents of liberal democracy, nationalism, or international Marxism generates, in Heidegger's terms, a semblance of political being, far removed from the authentic 'ground' of the polity within the historicity of Da-sein. All derive from the planetary unfolding of the will to power (SU 24–5/485).

The philosophical grounds of Heidegger's Address, especially as it articulates a conception of the Volk, its relation to a 'state,' and the role of the University as the leading site of knowledge in the state are beginning to come into view. These grounds are to be found in his understanding of the historicity and actualization of Dasein, as developed in *Being and Time* and the interpretation of Aristotle. The lectures of 1931 (GA 33, *Aristoteles, Metaphysik Theta 1–3: Vom Wesen und Wirklichkeit der Kraft*) are especially significant. These lectures – as those of 1924 – lay out the deconstruction of *ousia*, *arche*, *peras*, and *energeia* as metaphysically conceived to undertake a deconstruction of the metaphysical Aristotle in the wake of Heidegger's re-reading of Greek ontology as it developed under the influences of Luther, Augustine, and St Paul. As van Buren's *The Young Heidegger* has shown, this deconstructive work is essential to Heidegger's thought leading up to *Being and Time*.[15] The Aristotle interpretation offers us a gateway to Heidegger's concept of Volk, and thus an entrance into the fundamental grounds of the Rector's Address. Heidegger's retrieval of Aristotle allows us to establish the ontological grounds of his understanding of Volk.

3.1.2 Volk, or Volksein, as the Movement of a Way-of-Being

The question of what the Volk 'is' can only be won by reference to the question of being, in the sense that the being of the Volk is a way-of-being. The existential analytic defines Dasein as a way to be, rather than as anything 'substantial' in the metaphysical sense. Dasein's way of being manifests itself as existence, and thus as held in comportment toward its own being in constant interpretation and re-interpretation (SZ 12/10–1). John van Buren has noted that Heidegger's 'fulfilment-sense or temporalizing-sense of being was a retrieval of the Aristotelian theme of human *praxis* as a kind of coming-forth (*physis* [alternative spelling of *phusis*]) in the sense of movement (*kinesis*) towards ends that are fulfilled in situations (*kairos*).'[16] This indicates that the nature of Volk excludes both the subjectivistic and the substantial interpretations of the being of Volk. Heidegger – following his retrieval of Aristotle – understands the being of a being as the movement (*kinesis*) of a being into its own proper limit and form, as determined by its inherent principle of unfolding (*arche*). *Arche* points to the self-reserve of *phusis*. It governs the unfolding of motion without exhausting itself; it is the 'origin' and 'principle' which continues to presence without reduction to the merely-present (cf. GA22, 34–5). The limit of Dasein is not that of the completed product, but the gestalt of a certain attunement, a specific staying-on-the-way or engagement with be-ing. The 'how' of this fulfilment sense of temporality is granted a certain regularity and stability by Dasein's comportment (*Haltung*). A comportment gives the praxis of Dasein its *arche* and *telos*; the end of *praxis*, moreover, is internal to itself, as opposed to the *telos* of production (*poiesis*). Moreover, since *praxis* 'includes its own goal, and, as such, is *teleia*, or complete ... *praxis* unifies what it previously was and what it will be, its past and future, whereas the *kinesis* of which *poiesis* is a species, leaves its past and future unrelated to one another.'[17] Heidegger's interpretation of *phronesis* and *praxis* in his *Sophistes* confirms this (GA19, 48–51). *Arche* and *telos*, therefore, are not restricted to the being of entities brought forth by production. Dasein itself, and therefore Volk, may be said to be structured by an 'origin' and an 'end.' The end cannot be that of a finished product; nor the origin, that of an initial cause. The question of how this structure, in its unity and differentiation, is to be understood will be answered by Heidegger in terms of the historicity of Volk as a potential (as *arche* and *dunamis*) for being. This interpretation goes back to *Being and Time* (SZ, sec. 74), and is elaborated in the *Logik* of 1934. Thus the *Logik* determines the historicity of Volk within the unified temporalization of vocation, task, and work (see GA38, 128–9, 161–4). The vocation, or *Sendung*, of Volk denotes the unfolding of its potential, the way of its being-sent on a path of disclosure. This way unfolds itself as the task it takes up, and in its engagement with beings in work, thus to bring them and itself into their limit. This gives us our first clue as to where to seek out Heidegger's understanding of Volk.

The second clue is offered by the Rector's Address itself and follows from the understanding of being I have just noted: Volk is defined by way of the powers of earth and blood. Far removed from the dogmas of a 'biological' interpretation, 'blood' can signify no more nor less than 'earth' understood as the powers of birth, kinship, custom, and the chain of the generations. 'Blood' conveys the prior determination of a generation in its way of belonging to its 'earth,' or homeland, hence the historicity of its way of being. Yet, being 'itself,' for Heidegger, is finite, and unfolds itself in and through the historicity of Da-sein – that is, through the Volk and in a way of knowing which order themselves, in turn, 'politically,' as a 'state' (GA38, 165–66). The *polis*, Heidegger had claimed, in Aristotle lectures of 1924, is a possibility of human being arising out of *phusis* (GA18, 49). In the Address, Heidegger intimates that being, or *phusis*, comes to stand in the light of the open, through the Volk, a way of knowing, and their articulation by the structure of a state. Volk is understood as the manifestation and articulation of *the historicity of being*, as one essential way in which being as *phusis* comes to unfold itself. Volk is therefore a power, or potential, of *phusis, understood as the historicity of the earth disclosed in the intelligibility of a world*. As such, Volk is a way of the movement of being, held in tension between earth ('blood') and world (knowing, science): the appeal to 'blood' indicates *the movement of withdrawal from all forms of objectification and calculation* (all socio-technical discourses of the modern state).

Why does this movement of self-withdrawal implicate and necessitate the 'category' of Volk? Why not ascribe this saving movement to the autonomous individual in the liberal tradition? Or to the transcendental ego? Because the movement of saving withdrawal from conceptual, discursive reason is the 'gift' of historicity. Whereas 'history' may be conceived as the experience of a 'collective,' the historicity of the Volk expresses a potential of self-reserve (*An-sich-halten*) inaccessible to rational transparency. Volk names a movement of realization, of self-articulation (*Vollzug*), and in-corporation (*Am-Werke-sein*); at the same time, its being is reserved in what is sent to it as a vocation. The movement into actualization is always already a movement of withdrawal from conceptual fixation and ideological formation. This does not make, as typically claimed of Heidegger's concept of Volk, for a politics of will and identity, unified in the realization of a model or idea of the Volk,[18] but for a 'politics' of the differentiated actualization of a pre-reflective potential of being in its particularized historicity. As pre-reflective understanding, Volk denotes the historicity of Dasein's pre-ontological understanding of being, such as is already embodied, as Dreyfus argues, in the 'social practices' reflective of the ethos of a people (cf. SZ 12/10–11).[19]

To support this thesis, let me turn to the Aristotle lectures of 1931, which investigate the question of the nature of *dunamis* and *energeia* in book 9, chapters 1–3 of the *Metaphysics*. Heidegger translates *dunamis* (*potentia*) as *Kraft* or *Möglichkeit* – as power or potentiality – and it is the threefold character of *dunamis*, in a text which has nothing explicit to say regarding *polis* or Volk, which offers us a guiding thread of how to understand Volk as a way of being.

At stake is the unity of *dunamis kata kinesin*, where the question of how this unity is constituted and articulated is guided by the question of the being of beings (GA33, 49). Being is understood as presencing in the differentiated specificity of beings (*ousia*), for being (*to einai*) represents the participle 'be-ing' (*to on*) (GA33, 15, 31). Now, when we consider movement and things-moved, Heidegger argues, we speak of a potential which moves things, and of an activity which is at work in the work (GA33, 50). All forms of *dunamis*, as modes of activity, have the sense in common of being the 'origin for a change or transformation [Umschlag (*metabole*)]' of one thing into another, or of one thing in respect to itself (GA33, 68).[20] A *dunamis* denotes the *arche*, the originating power of the mode of unfolding of a thing. As such, as we shall see momentarily, it holds a being on the path of unfolding proper to it.

The potential of movement is bound to, and appears as, a being-at-work (*Am-Werke-sein*): 'the most evident and general character of *kinesis* is *energeia*' (GA33, 51). *Energeia* conveys, as Frede notes, the actuality of an activity,[21] but no less is the being of a substantial thing (*ousia*) the being of activity.[22] The '*energeiai* are the modes of activity, of working [*ergon* in the first sense as activity] ... which are engaged in a work [*ergon* in the second sense]' (GA33, 50).

Where movement unfolds itself as the activity of making, producing a work, it is guided by the *eidos* understood as the *telos* or consummation of the thing, and this 'is in essence the limit, *peras*' of the thing made (GA33, 138). Making, moreover, is guided by a knowing (*episteme*), which itself belongs to the disclosive power, or *logos*, of the soul. The *logos* is a potential of dis-closure which makes manifest the *eidos*, and consequently the being of beings in their determined gestalt, or *peras* (GA33, 136–44).

In what sense, however, does the possession of the *logos* define the *dunamis* of the human soul as a potential of change in respect to itself, in respect to its own end? In his consideration of *dunamis*, and the *arche* of motion, Aristotle explicitly distinguishes between soulless beings and beings which have souls and are characterized by the possession of *logos* (*Metaphysics*, 1046a36–b2; GA33, 117f). All living beings (*zoe*), furthermore, have an inherent *telos*, and of these, humans alone have life (*bios*) 'in the sense of a life-history,' hence 'the possibility of a freely chosen and formed Dasein [gestaltbaren Daseins], which holds itself in what we call a comportment [Haltung]' (GA33, 123). This implicates choosing and seeking out a way, of taking one stand and not another, in every act of dis-closure (*Kundschaft*). In this way, the *movement of dis-closure* which belongs to Dasein (*bios*), and which articulates the *logos* of Dasein, finds its own 'inner limit.' Inasmuch as it grants Dasein a stand, thus to delimit the stability of a comportment, this limit alone grants 'the greatness of the engagement of human existence [der Grösse des Einsatzes menschlicher Existenz]' (GA33, 145). The lectures of 1924 interpret the Aristotelian *arete* as the capacity to actualize a specific potential for being, thereby to bring Dasein into the 'perfection' of its own inner limit (GA18, 97–100; cf. GA22, 188). 'Comportment,' or *Haltung*, designates *arete* in this sense.

Being and Time, moreover, established that Dasein's relation to its own having-to-be constitutes its most fundamental comportment (*Verhalten*) (SZ 14–5/12). In *The Basic Problems of Phenomenology*, Heidegger holds that 'comportments have the structure of directing-oneself-toward, of being-directed-toward.' In the *terminus Verhalten*, Heidegger characterizes the intentionality and transcendence of Dasein, which founds the possibility of the subject-object sphere of metaphysics (GA24, 81/58). Dasein's comportment encompasses the relation-to (*Bezugssinn*); the How, or way of enactment (*Vollzugssinn*); and the temporalization of the enactment in 'factical life and existence' (*Zeitigungssinn*) (GA61, 53). Comportment holds to something in a certain way while holding to itself as a way of being-open (of temporalization). In holding to itself (to its situated finitude), and therefore to its own limit, Dasein is first able to enact its openness-to, its relation-to, the other.

The transformation of Dasein's existential intentionality into a specific, historically founded way of being (*Haltung*), such as is proper to the being of a Volk, implicates the formation and actualization of this existential structure through the decisions of a community, whereby a community takes responsibility for its own being. Thus Heidegger's proposals for university reform (more precisely, for the special training of *Dozenten*), specifically call for the development of a new comportment (*Haltung*), one which would exemplify the will to transform the sciences, from their foundations (GA16, no. 156, 308–9).

The 'decisions' (*Entscheidungen*) of Dasein are the forms of self-limitation founded in Dasein's belonging to a generation. Every decision arises in dialogue, out of a heritage, and within a situation, and puts Dasein on a track of self-disclosure, which eliminates another divergent road. The decisive point of book 9 of the *Metaphysics*, Heidegger concludes, is the 'inner finitude of every potential' (GA33, 158, 128). This also applies to the 'potential' of a community: its inner limit arises for it, not because a *dunamis* runs up against an external limit, but because the decisions which actualize the potential of a community-in-dialogue decide for one direction or another. *Logos* as dis-closure implicates the decision of embarking on one way rather than another, hence signifies inherent self-limitation. Given that *Volk-sein* happens as dialogue, its *telos* is not an ideal of limitless communication (Habermas), nor empty 'decisionism,' but the specificity of actualized, engaged being (*energeia* as *Vollzug*), unfolded out of its own inner limit and articulated as comportment (*Verhalten*). Heidegger holds that Dasein signifies self-delimitation in the sense of the achievement of its 'end' – that is, entrance into the way of being which actualizes its potential. *Volk-sein* as limit is the historically founded appropriation – that is, the authentically realized historicity – of the 'mineness' of Dasein. *Volk-sein* means the entrance of a people into its own limit.

We have now distinguished two primary senses of *dunamis*. *Dunamis* as the actualization of a potential in being-at-work: in working a potential sets itself into the work as the inner limit of the work (GA33, 218–9).[23] *Vollzug* is the act of the realization of the potential, e.g., in the production of the work. It designates being-at-work in the work, or *energeia* (GA33, 171). Production presupposes, however, the ability to produce (GA33, 185). Actualization in its full sense includes both senses of *dunamis*, and signifies the consummation of activity in the work as a delimited entity (*entelechia*) (GA33, 224), as well as signifying the actualization of a potential, as the realization of a comportment. The unity of the movement (*bios*) of Dasein consists in acts of decision to which it holds, and which compel it to hold to the comportment (*Haltung*) proper to it.

In lectures on Plato's *Republic* and *Theaetetus* (1931–2), Heidegger explicates comportment, or *Haltung*, by way of a retrieval of *paideia*:

> *paideia* does not mean 'education' [Bildung], but *he hemetera phusis*, that which rules as our ownmost being ... *paideia* signifies the reserved stability [Gehaltenheit] of humanity, as arising out of a 'comportment' [Haltung] which takes a stand and asserts itself; taking a stand in the midst of beings through its own free choice, mankind takes the measure [den Halt] of its own essence – that for the sake of which and through which it empowers and authorizes itself to be. (GA34, 115)

In accordance with the argument of *Republic*, book 7, which recounts the 'analogy' of the Cave, this measure is the idea of the good: the idea is the determining, delimiting *telos* which actualizes the liberation of the cave-dwellers, insofar as they hold to and bind themselves to being (GA34, 96). *Paideia* is the movement of the enactment (*Vollzug*) of Da-sein, as a potential for being. This movement will always be defined by a certain historical specificity of the in-corporation of Da-sein, emerging from the stand Dasein takes. As the mutual 'hold' which Da-sein and being have on each other, this stand, or comportment, constitutes the inner limit and possibility of the actualization of the community of knowledge. The third sense of *dunamis* that Heidegger specifies is that of 'having' a potential (*dunamin echein*): to have a potential is the ability-to-be-active even when the activity proper to the potential is not being performed. One 'holds oneself in this potential,' and one holds to oneself in maintaining oneself in the potential (GA22, 33, 183). Not only is the potential held in reserve, but this particular reserve 'holds' – in the sense of granting a certain stability of being – the being having the potential. What grants and holds in this way remains the unreflected origin (*arche*) of activity and actualization. It constitutes *the reserve of being* from which the delimited being of a particular entity springs, and as such it also grants to Dasein the hold and measure of a *Haltung*, or fundamental comportment which governs activity.

It is our thesis that Volk is not the image of a transcendental Ideal (Herder), nor, like the modern concept of 'the people,' the 'organic' unity of an artificial body (Hobbes), not the unity of a collective will (Rousseau), nor the contractual unity of individual wills (Locke), but a movement of self-reserve and actualized self-differentiation (*dunamis* in the three senses noted). As opposed, moreover, to the tendency of contemporary discussions of nationality, Volk cannot be equated with the pre-political ethnic condition of the 'nation,' as articulated in the Romantic tradition, in its opposition to the tradition of civic nationality.[24]

Our point of departure is Heidegger's interpretation of *dunamis kata kinesis*: this interpretation has as its goal to specify the singularity of motion or movement as a way of being-actual (GA33, 172). The being of movement in its full or consummated sense as *energeia*, moreover, offers us our most complete insight into the character of being as singular 'substance,' or *ousia*. Commenting on Heidegger's Aristotle of 1924, Kisiel writes that Heidegger takes *ousia* to signify the being of 'each thing in its particularity.'[25] Moreover, given that the being of 'substance in general,' as Aryeh Kosman writes, 'is revealed as an entity whose very *ousia* is *energeia*, that is, whose essential nature is activity,' then 'substance' has to be understood as a kind of motion.[26] As noted above, *Volksein* is an activity of self-actualization (*energeia*). In this sense, *Volksein* is a kind of *kinesis*, and as *praxis*, its '*energeia* is contained within the activity, more precisely within the agent himself, who, as agent, always has the potential of acting or not acting.' The *energeia* of *praxis* is distinct from that of *poiesis*, where it is 'within the *ergon* (the product) that *energeia* (i.e., effectiveness) is implemented.'[27] *Volksein* can never be the realization of a 'product,' not even in the 'national-aesthetic' sense of the production of an ideal, as Lacoue-Labarthe claims.[28] The unitary being of Volk, therefore, is misconceived by analogy with 'an autonomous individual with a unique identity and mission, which it chooses to realize or fulfil in resolving to be itself.'[29] Because the being of Volk, in Heidegger's estimation, is a kind of motion it can never be identified with the metaphysical substance of a collective will or with a 'biological' and hence 'racial' substance. We have seen, rather, that *energeia* (actuality) is not the presence (*Vorhandenheit*) of a being but the tension of being-between *arche* and *peras* (self-reserve and differentiated gestalt) which *dunamis* unfolds and holds together. It is precisely this movement of presencing-in-gestalt which determines the way of being of a Volk, as the actualization of the differentiated presencing of being in beings. The *way of actualization* attunes Volk to being and grants its unity.

But why take movement or motion as our starting point in the consideration of the being of a Volk? We recall that *Sein und Zeit* defines Dasein as *Mitsein* in its historicity as a structure of motion, or the movement of the self-appropriation of a community, through the retrieval of its heritage, thus to authentically grasp its ownmost possibilities as revealed by its situation. This movement of self-appropriation brings *Mitdasein* into its proper limits. The question of the mode of the self-identity of a Volk, which therefore arises, asks us to consider how a Volk can be one, and yet differentiated. In choosing to be itself (*sich entscheiden*), the *Mitda-sein* of a community takes its hold and measure from the presencing of the being of beings (in their own singularity) as presencing reveals itself in its historical specificity. Therefore *the oneness of its stand in presencing* differentiates itself (*ent-scheidet sich*) in attentiveness to the specificity of beings. What is held in common is the truth of beings, and this truth 'shows itself to all, to whom unconcealment is given in common': a *way of the unconcealment* of beings is 'shared' in being-with-one-another (GA27, 106, 109–10). It is not the collective subject of Volk which grants self-identity, but rather a way of disclosure, a certain stand in, and exposure to, the presencing of being in beings. The openness of this site of disclosure is the condition of the fixation of subject and object, including the collective subject of a metaphysically conceived Volk identity.

Given that unconcealment, however, is always a project – the encounter through which Da-sein, in grasping the being of a being, binds itself to its measure – and that this event of truth founds a 'history,' then the ways of unconcealment must be themselves finite and founded (cf. GA34, 71–2, 91). 'In other words, truth is not a unchanging possession ... but unconcealment rather happens only as the history of ever-renewed (self-)liberation' (GA34, 91). Furthermore, insofar as a 'history' is always understood as a 'destiny,' as a project and task given to be performed, it is performed by a people insofar as it takes up a way of being as a way of unconcealment. If we understand Volk as a way of being founded in the happening of truth, then we are led to seek out, in Heidegger's own thought, the structure of this way, or movement, as the actualization of Dasein's historicity.

Brief reflection shows, moreover, that perhaps the central, motivating question of modern political philosophy is that of the nature of the 'motion' proper to humanity, and the relation of this motion to the state, or community of action, to which individuals bind themselves. Thus Hobbes takes his point of departure from the limitless passion of humanity, which articulates itself as the fear of death and the desire for glory, and binds this motion to the Leviathan, or 'Artificiall Man,' which the limitedlessness of individual passion demands, and into which it integrates itself. In taking passion, or desire, as his starting point, Hobbes follows Aristotle's definition of the soul as being in motion, in either aversion from or attraction to some end.[30] The Hobbesian state of war is governed by one attunement, common to all, which articulates itself as the oscillation between fear and desire. The concept of the Leviathan responds to the following question: How can the unlimited motion (passion) of humanity, which is not bound or consummated by a highest good, be integrated into a commonwealth, or state, so as to tame, channel, and 'organize' this motion for the common good by means of the socio-political mechanisms of the polity? Although the motion of individual will and passion is controlled and managed in the polity, the fundamental attunement on which the state rests remains the same. And this is also true of Locke's 'Man,' because the 'unease of desire' motivates the search for self-identity characteristic of Locke's individual in the polity no less than in the state of nature. The motion of the unease of desire is the fundamental attunement of the polity, which demands and legitimates particular forms of comportment such as are grounded in the autonomy, rationality, and calculability of action. What grounds the unity of the Volk as a way of being? Heidegger holds that this unity is granted by the fundamental *Haltung*, or comportment, of a people. Essential to the movement of *Volksein*, given that it is understood as a *dunamis*, is the moment of holding-to-itself, that is, to its own *arche*, as a way of being (cf. GA33, 7, on *Ansichhalten*). Comportment is grounded in the self-reserve of holding to itself: this grants the differentiation of a *dunamis* – as work of art, as modes of production, as rites of leadership – its unity in a way of being. Already in the *Grundprobleme der Phänomenologie* of 1919–20, Heidegger claims that 'life' consummates itself, out of its own inherent drive toward form, in the 'historically motivated gestalt' proper to it (GA58, 42). It belongs to the structure of life itself to be an 'in itself' (*an sich*), in the sense that it contains the possibility of the consummation of its own motion in the gestalt proper to it. In this sense, Heidegger claims, we speak of the 'religious' or the 'aesthetic' life. Therefore,

In understanding a context of relations, Dasein has been referred to an in-order-to in terms of an explicitly or inexplicitly grasped potentiality-of-its-being for the sake of which it is, which can be authentic or inauthentic. (SZ 86/80)

The ability to be is the potential which Dasein explicitly or inexplicitly attempts to actualize. Actualization expresses the engagement with beings and with itself which brings Dasein into its *telos* and the circumscribed limit (*peras*) prescribed by the possibilities for being it takes up. And this pertains, in a superlative sense, to Volk, since Dasein's temporality fully unfolds itself only in terms of the historicity of Volk.

The 'unrest' – or unease – inherent in life can find rest only in a living relation to the ways and the forms of fulfilment of the factical possibilities of life (GA58, 59). Life, in effect, tends to give itself stability in gestalt. The gestalt of the Volk, as a way of being, would rest in what Heidegger calls the 'how' or the mode of a way of being: at stake is not the content (*Wasgehalt*), still less an essential, ideal pre-figuration of being, but the 'factical mode of attunement (*Weise*), in which experiences are factically registered, a functional rhythm which life in its facticity itself forms and expresses' (GA58, 85). The 'facticity' of life denotes its historical rootedness, which gives it a coherent attunement or rhythm (cf. GA58, 112). *Weise* in fact means both mode and melody, and therefore the unified order of a way of making manifest. Hence, although experience is subject to 'manifold modifications,' a certain 'fundamental style of being (*Grundstil*) conserves itself' to determine *how* things are experienced (GA58, 100).

The *arche* of the *kinesis* of the soul is the desired (*das Erstrebte*). Aristotle holds that the soul has the *arche* of its movement and change (*metabole*) in itself. The object of desire, in turn, is what holds the soul in a given direction and governs its comportment (GA33, 151). Given that the Volk itself, as the potential for being of *Mitdasein*, has an *arche* which governs it, would this *arche* not be inscribed in the ethos of a Volk as the singular rhythm of its comportment to beings?

This question can be clarified by reference to the relation of rhetoric to the public realm. Rhetoric is a *dunamis*; its *ergon* is the persuasion of the listener, hence the transformation of the listener's mood and beliefs (*Rhetoric*, 1355 b26). Given rhetoric is a *dunamis*, how is it related, as *dunamis*, to the community? In speaking to the concerns of the public realm, the orator speaks to the ethos of the community, which the orator seeks to move and to turn in a certain direction. This ethos is the *dunamis* of the community, for the ethos articulates the potential ways of being and the pathways of actualization proper to a community. The kinds of things which are sought and avoided by the soul, and to which the orator appeals in appealing to *pathe*, are pre-figured by the ethos of the community, and will be unique to each community.[31] A *dunamis* is actualized by the orator insofar as the fundamental mood of the community is turned, thus to win new insight and possibly to prepare the community for decision. Ethos implicates a fundamental comportment to being, which unfolds itself in a style of 'national' being to permeate all spheres of life, including the rituals of politics. According to Aristotle, as Schütrumpf argues, ethos is fundamentally the firmly held mode of comportment, or *Haltung*, of a community.[32] Consequently we can say that the ethos of a community, its way of being, is the *dunamis* and hence the *arche*, of the motion of a Volk. The *telos* of the unfolding of a Volk would be the actualization of the potential for being of its particular ethos. The state, and in fact the form of state proper to that particular people, would be one way in which the ethos is actualized. In Heidegger's estimation, the task of the state in 1933 would be to prepare the fundamental attunement requisite for a new stand-in-being, i.e., to prepare the founding of Da-sein. This is *paideia*. It is not, conversely, the task of the state to construct and organize an image of the Volk, for this would signify the socio-technical manipulation of the saving reserve of being, the movement of withdrawal from representation, which the Volk actualizes.

Evidently the polity as the embodiment of a truth of being must be conceived as an historically specific founding of the event of truth. It does not derive from suprahistorical values supposedly grounded in the essence of humanity as rational, autonomous being. No less is scientific knowledge determined by the limitation of its sitedness. The central political question which thus emerges for Heidegger may be formulated as follows: *How can the event-character of all being be politically founded and articulated?* Heidegger's turn to the work of art, to the enactment of forms of life and of leadership, is the attempt to safeguard the event of being as the unified movement of manifestation in the phenomena, and as simultaneous self-reserving withdrawal. Only the movement of self-withdrawal, or holding-to-itself, of each being bars the tendency of the modern state to consummate itself in forms of transparency, in the techniques of discipline and self-regulation, with which Foucault, for example, has made us familiar. Postmodern technologies of life, such as the human-genome project and reproductive technologies, only accelerate this tendency.

We have seen that the 'self-assertion' of the University implies the overcoming of the separation of theory and practice as the condition of the founding of the presencing of being in beings. The realization of *praxis*, in effect, consists in the actualization, or being-at-work, of *theoria* in the life-world of *praxis*. The historical necessity of this actualization – which arises out of the fragmentation of the sciences and the dis-integration of beings – motivates Heidegger's linkage of the questions of the being of a Volk, of the University as the site of leadership within the state, and of the historicity of science. The founding of a site for science calls for the mutual delimitation of knowing and Volk to allow for the unfolding of their potentialities as the unconcealment, and the founding, of being in its destined specificity. Volk and knowing must mutually define each other to together articulate the historicity of being. Both are to be sited in the finitude of the historical earth as homeland. The limits of science are to be set, Heidegger implies, by its fidelity to the historicity of the earth as it articulates itself in a Volk. This would allow science to be actualized in the enactment of the differentiation of the being of beings. *Volk-sein*, in turn, as a movement of being, means the actualization of self-limitation understood as the movement of a Volk's historicity: the actualization of a potential, as inscribed in the vocation and task of a Volk. Its entrance into a delimited gestalt, conceived as the governing rhythm of a specific comportment realized in all the modes of the making-present of beings, is realized through work as the making-manifest of beings in their differentiated specificity.

3.2 Heidegger's Confrontation with the Discourses of National Socialism and the Conservative Revolution

Who constituted the 'public' to which Heidegger turned in the Rector's Address and in the programmatic speeches of 1933–4? To what ideological positions and discourses was he responding in his lectures and treatises of the 1930s and early 1940s? What follows, as an attempt to answer these questions, is an analysis of key works of conservative and National Socialist discourse. Although the survey I have undertaken is not comprehensive – ideally it would be supplemented by reference to additional authors and public pronouncements, including those of Adolf Hitler – this review of the relevant literature will serve to map out the contemporary territory within which Heidegger's political engagement moves.

Given the great diversity of political tendencies, even within the anti-Weimar camp, it will always remain difficult to circumscribe the 'public' to which Heidegger appeals. The attempt to isolate correspondences between Heidegger's essential thought and the opinion of his generation is likely to be still more unsatisfactory. Both the public to which Heidegger appeals and the possibility of such correspondences are functions of the 'hermeneutic situation' of the Rector's Address and of subsequent texts. How can this situation be circumscribed? In historical terms, as I propose, the hermeneutic situation could be defined as co-extensive with the birth and demise of the Weimar Republic and, more precisely, as the period between 30 January 1933 and 30 June 1934, which marks the inauguration, and the definitive installation, of the National Socialist dictatorship. The hermeneutic situation of later works, down to the *Parmenides* of 1941, is evidently extensive with the unfolding of the Nazi dictatorship and the advent of World War II. In the first instance, however, from the point of view of the conservative right, the dislocations of the Weimar period of 1919–33 are consummated in the crisis of 1933–4. The Rector's Address appeals to a public in a state of crisis, in a revolutionary situation, the final outcome of which was, at the time of the Address, still uncertain.

The installation of Hitler as chancellor on 30 January 1933 did not yet create a Hitler cabinet (only three of eleven members were National Socialists), much less a National Socialist regime. To contemporary observers, the reactionary conservatism of Alfred Hugenberg, which called for a presidential dictatorship, seemed more radical and dangerous than Hitler's policies, which still paid tribute to the legal forms of the Republic.[33] As the leader of the Deutschnationale Volkspartei (DNVP), Hugenberg emerged as the centre of rightist opposition to Hitler after October 1931 (which marks the failure of the attempt to create a common front with the NSDAP [the National Socialist German Workers' Party]).[34] The period between 30 January 1933 and the resignation of Hugenberg from the cabinet, on 27 June 1933, witnessed the failure of the conservative opposition to suborn and 'control' Hitler, and the consequent emergence of a brownshirt revolution from below.[35] Heidegger's Rector's Address falls within this highly volatile period. It takes place after the *Enabling Law* of 24 March 1933, which gave Hitler sweeping power to govern by decree. But only with the events of 30 June 1934, which saw the liquidation of the SA leadership, along with the conservative and national Bolshevik opposition, did the dogmatic contours of the regime fully emerge.[36]

My account of the public opinion of this period is largely descriptive. My aim is to illuminate potential points of commonality between Heidegger, the conservative revolution, and National Socialism, not to offer a critique of the crimes of Nazism as revealed by subsequent events.

Following the critical literature, judgement of Heidegger's Rector's Address often assumes a certain context, above all the persecution of the Jews. Insofar as it has been documented, Heidegger's insensitivity to the plight of his Jewish colleagues, and to German Jewish citizens, brooks no excuse.[37] Yet the relative ambiguity of the situation in 1933 is reflected in the fact that the German-Jewish veterans association, on the one hand, and the Zionists, for reasons of their own, both supported the new regime. The Nazis collaborated with the Zionist program by allowing vocational retraining centres to be set up across Germany for German Jews willing to emigrate to Palestine.[38] Of those who stayed, approximately 150,000 men of partially Jewish descent served in the *Wehrmacht*, often with the express permission of Nazi authorities and Hitler himself. Some rose to senior ranks; Erhard Milch, for example, held the rank of Field Marshal in the Luftwaffe.[39] Given the initial fluidity of the new regime's Jewish policy which this indicates, evaluation of Heidegger's willingness to support the regime in 1933 appears in a different light. This is not to underestimate the egregious nature of discriminatory legislation (passed 7 April 1933) against 'Non-Aryans' in the public service and professions. Yet insofar as the anti-Semitic measures of the regime were, as Noakes and Pridham document, 'far from being planned and coordinated from the top, in fact developed in a largely incoherent and *ad hoc* fashion,'[40] Heidegger perhaps conceived reason to believe that they did not express the true and final will of the national government. According to Claudia Koonz's *The Nazi Conscience*, 'antisemitism played little role in attracting voters to Nazism' between 1928 and 1932. In contrast, moreover, to the current popular perception, the new regime did not constantly harp on the 'Jewish problem.' Koonz writes that between 1933 and 1939 'only two comedies and one historical drama among approximately 2000 films approved by Goebbels and his staff ... featured overt anti-Semitism.'[41] In addressing the 'general public,' Hitler discussed racial issues on 'only three occasions between April 1933 and the invasion of Poland in September 1939.'[42] Hitler and Goebbels' propaganda ministry rather concentrated on the injustices of the Versailles *Diktat*, the menace of communism, and, on the positive side, the virtues of ethnic pride and social solidarity.[43] It is quite likely that Heidegger, along with the vast majority of Germans, approved of this emphasis, but this does not make him what today is popularly conceived of as a 'Nazi.'

A balanced judgement must also take other aspects of the contemporary context into account to avoid anachronism. Among other, now largely forgotten or ignored contexts of the appeal to national unity in

1933, a number are significant, not least because they figured prominently in Nazi propaganda. First, there was the oppressive situation of millions of Germans who in 1918 were placed under foreign rule; Heidegger makes reference to this (cf. GA16, no. 124, 233). Throughout the Weimar period, certainly, the common perception in Germany was that the treatment of ethnic Germans in Poland and Czechoslovakia was very discriminatory. As a consequence of the redrawing of borders under the Versailles Treaty, moreover, many ethnic Germans were forced to flee their homes in the newly created states of Central Europe. Second, there was the forced starvation of some 6 million Ukrainians by Stalin; the Nazis gave very extensive publicity to this crime, even as they presented themselves as the last hope for the salvation of Germany and Europe from the 'Red menace.' Soviet communism targeted the national independence of the Ukrainians by killing the landowning yeomanry (Kulaks), and attempted to 'liquidate' them as a class.[44] Given Heidegger's attachment to the land, it is hardly surprising that he is liable to have thought the Nazis a lesser evil, and perhaps the only party capable of meeting this threat. Third, if one does want to make an issue of Heidegger's appeal to the necessity of military service in the Address, it is also necessary to note that until 1935 Germany was effectively disarmed and at the mercy of hostile neighbours. Heidegger had, of course, written a eulogy for Schlageter – not merely a 'Nazi hero,' as some call him, but honoured by the entire spectrum of the national resistance to the French occupation of the Ruhr.[45] This is worth noting because one of the oft-repeated accusations levelled at Heidegger is that he praised Schlageter as a resistance fighter and a model of conduct (GA16, no. 285, 759–60). Fourth, there were the class division, unemployment, and the social and political chaos of the unloved Weimar regime, a regime widely perceived as internally corrupt, as well as impotent on the international stage. The Weimar 'system' was despised by both the Left and the Right as the child of Versailles. As the final component of the concrete historical situation we have to take note of, the internal communist threat had led to a communist uprising in 1918 and remained a potent danger in the form of the Soviet-directed German Communist Party.

We have little ground to suppose, moreover, that Heidegger expected, much less wanted, a Nazi dictatorship as the means to Germany's renewal. 'Never did [Nazi ideologue Gottfried] Feder, or any major Nazi writer before 1933, prophesy a dictatorship,' write Lane and Rupp in their evaluation of Nazi ideology.[46] The Party which took power in 1933 did not have an original and distinctive program. It rather drew support from the entire spectrum of the opposition to Weimar, from the national Bolsheviks of Ernst Niekisch on the left, to 'racialist' (*völkisch*) groups on the right. In the period before 1933, the influence of the racialists on the Nazi movement decreased, in favour of the conservative revolutionaries and revolutionary nationalists (who are generally associated with Ernst Jünger).[47] 'The strength of the national socialist movement,' wrote Niekisch, in 1931, 'has hitherto been its formless lack of a distinct [ideological] profile.'[48] 'Hitler remained a sphinx even after 1933.'[49] Hitler was able to draw on a wide range of support, and the movement could mean many things to very diverse critics of Weimar liberalism, of capitalism, and the Versailles system. This has to be taken into account in evaluating Heidegger's response of 1933. As Mohler notes, moreover, the situation between January 1933 and 30 June 1934 – when Ernst Röhm and the SA leadership were liquidated – remained extremely fluid and open to many possibilities.[50] We have no reason to suppose, therefore, as Rockmore claims, that Heidegger supported the new regime because his 'conception of Being' demands 'some type of antidemocratic, totalitarian politics.'[51] Not only was this type of government by no means inevitable in 1933, but Heidegger's understanding of the differentiation and strife inherent in being, as we shall see, is at odds with totalitarian politics.

Polt summarizes seven types of interpretation of 'Heidegger and National Socialism':[52] 1) Heidegger's political commitments show he was of bad character; therefore, his philosophy must be disreputable. 2) There is no relation between his thought and his actions. 3) Heidegger was politically naive in thinking he could influence National Socialism. This thesis in itself, however, says nothing about the potential of his thought. 4) Heidegger's actions are understandable, or at least comprehensible, in view of the options open to Germany in 1933; this thesis is subject to the same objection as thesis 3. 5) Heidegger failed to act on his own concept of authenticity, as developed in *Sein und Zeit*; in 1933, he fell into the inauthenticity of *das Man*. 6) *Being and Time* is 'a crypto-fascist book. Its ontology of Dasein is really a "political ontology" that prepares the way for Nazism.'[53] 7) 'Heidegger succumbed to Nazism because he was still under the sway of the metaphysics of presence'; only the deconstruction of metaphysics would allow us to 'undermine authoritarian and repressive regimes.' This constitutes the postmodern critique and rehabilitation of Heidegger.[54]

I think we can ignore the first, *ad hominum* line of interpretation, and all the evidence speaks against the second thesis. Not only does the third fail to take Heidegger's philosophy into account, but it assumes a grasp of the historical situation – thus to show what is naive and what is not – which commentators on Heidegger have not demonstrated. This applies to Ott and Fritsche, as well as to Sluga and Bourdieu, for example, and they are among the few who have engaged the historical context of Heidegger's thought. In agreement with thesis 4, I will argue that Heidegger's actions and commitments of 1933–4 are comprehensible, given the concrete political situation. Since the complexity of this situation has hitherto been underestimated, the options Heidegger perceived to be open in 1933 were far greater than evident in 1945, or even 1935. These commitments, moreover, are at least in part acceptable consequences of his thinking.

Furthermore, in opposition to thesis 6, I have argued, in discussing Heidegger and the question of rhetoric, that in *Being and Time* he develops a concept of *Mitsein* at odds with totalitarianism. Given his concept of authenticity and of *Mitsein*, Heidegger did not – as thesis 5 claims – 'fall into' inauthenticity in 1933, but rather attempted to actualize his philosophy through his political commitment. His mistake was in assuming that the actualization of creative *Mitsein* and historicity would be possible under National Socialism. This error shows that his action was not so much inauthentic – that is, lacking in resolute, and hence liberating, being-with-one-another – as it was not genuine, inasmuch as he failed to appreciate the factical situation of his action (cf. SZ 146/137). I am prepared, finally, to give some credence to the postmodern argument, to the extent that Heidegger's discourse of 1933–4 is not entirely free of the metaphysics of the will.

Philipse, in line with thesis 5, and to some extent thesis 6, attempts to resurrect the decisionist argument that Heidegger develops a concept of resoluteness which leaves him no recourse, in *Being and Time*, and consequently in 1933, but to opt for National Socialism. The first stage of this argument is that Dasein is 'justified by resoluteness alone,' for the rejection of all moral and cultural norms radically individualizes and isolates Dasein. This radical individualization, in itself empty of content and without hold in any moral principle, is, however, Philipse continues, impossible to endure. Therefore, in section 74 of *Being and Time*, Heidegger turns to a collective notion of destiny and Volk, primarily for psychological reasons, for his fundamentally individualistic Dasein cannot implicate a notion of authentic *Mitsein* or historicity.[55] As we have seen, however, resoluteness is not 'individualistic,' as Philipse would have it (SZ 298/274). He ignores the fact that Dasein, as Dasein, is always already *Mitsein*, and that resoluteness is always factically situated. Decisions are not made in a decisionistic vacuum, but are released by possibilities granted by a heritage. Since these possibilities, moreover, must be won from a heritage through communication and struggle (SZ 384/352), and since being-with-others, in struggle and communication, is authentically for the sake of others in authentic letting-be, a totalitarian commitment does not follow from the text of *Being and Time*, and is in fact precluded by it. It follows that if Heidegger was true to his own philosophy in 1933 he could commit himself to National Socialism without self-contradiction only on the assumption that its 'inner truth and greatness' was not totalitarian. Clearly, Heidegger held, and was mistaken in holding, this assumption. I argue, however, that Heidegger did not contradict himself, and that he had legitimate reasons to read the historical situation as he did.

With reference to the authors I consider below, we know that Heidegger was familiar with at least some of the works of Spengler, Schmitt, Baeumler, Krieck, and Ziegler. Heidegger expressed sympathy for Schmitt's *The Concept of the Political*.[56] He clearly distanced himself from Krieck, but no less from the *Lebensphilosophie* of Klages, which helped to found the political irrationalism of the period.[57] According to Ott, Heidegger may have initially hoped to work with Baeumler and Krieck on the common project of university reform, but these plans quickly collapsed.[58]

I have not, however, restricted myself to a survey of works and authors that Heidegger manifestly knew. I hope it will become evident that certain ideas of Walther Darré and the geopolitical school of Haushofer, for example, reveal a limited commonality of presuppositions and aims with the political thought implicit in Heidegger, quite independently of his possible acquaintance with these works. However, I propose to consider Heidegger's confrontation with Carl Schmitt, and with Ernst Jünger, separately.

This is not to say, conversely, that Heidegger's thought can be identified with that of any of these writers, but that he shares with them the public space of opinion common to the conservative Right. This space is that of the 'conservative revolution' and of 'revolutionary nationalism' as originally defined by Armin Mohler and elaborated by many others, including Sontheimer, Klemperer, Bourdieu, Palmier, Herf, and Woods. Mohler's account still remains in many respects the most refined. The conservative revolution encompassed, as we know, the entire spectrum of conservative critique of modernity. Hence it included a critique of individualism and the class struggle, in favour of social and national unity; of analytic disintegration and 'intellectualism,' in favour of organic totality; of technology, in favour of holism and ecology. This critique, founded on a common attunement to the spiritual situation of the time, aimed to recover the sources of action in the unity of life.[59] Paul de Lagarde, Moeller van den Bruck, George, Spengler, Klages, Ernst and Friedrich G. Jünger, and Niekisch are some of the names we associate with the critique of 'civilization,' the call for a national revolution and a new mythic consciousness commensurate with the challenge of mass democracy, industrialization, and the disintegration of the formative power of art, tradition, and religion. As Ott has shown, Heidegger was at home in this climate of opinion.[60] Zimmerman has noted Heidegger's debt to Spengler's and Scheler's critiques of technology.[61] The attempt of Ott, however, to reduce Heidegger's engagement in 1933 to its social and institutional context remains blind to the philosophical content of Heidegger's *action* no less than to his thought.

Nor is it justified, for example, simply to align Heidegger with the particularist nationalism of the tradition of Fichte, Arndt, and Jahn, any more than with the cosmopolitan nationalism of Herder, to recall common historiographical distinctions within German nationalism.[62] The revolutionary nationalism which emerged after 1918, as distinct from the old-style nationalism of the Second Reich, was much more radical than the previous nationalist tradition in its philosophical presuppositions and aims.[63] But here, too, distinctions have to be made in respect to Heidegger's affinities: for if Heidegger was willing to learn from Jünger, he had nothing to learn from Krieck. It is significant that many revolutionary nationalists, including the Jüngers, became opponents of the new regime after 1933. Given Moeller van den Bruck's early death, we cannot know what his reaction to 1933 would have been. But the conservative revolution he preached 'has no difficulty in reconciling the ideals of a conservative and a democratic state.'[64] The 'Third Reich' of Moeller had only the name in common with that of Hitler; for it was the Reich, in Moeller's terms, of a new synthesis of the oppositions defining Germany history – of the confessions, of centralized state and the *Stämme* (the Franks, Saxons, Bavarians, for example), of universalism and nationalism, of capitalism and socialism. The Reich would bring about a synthesis within diversity.[65] The conservative revolutionaries, rather than recognizing the Nazi state as their own offspring, initially saw Hitler's assumption of power as a means to the end of a true German revolution.[66] This position is very close to Heidegger's own: Heidegger's provisional acceptance of the new state in the Rector's Address anticipates a revolution yet to come. This is supported by his lectures of the summer semester of 1933 (GA36/37, 7–8).

Still less is the sociology of Bourdieu up to the task of grasping the intimate relation between Heidegger's 'ontology' and the dialogue of his generation with itself and its tradition. It is Bourdieu's claim that 'a philosophical stance is no more than the homologue, in a different system, of a "naïve" politico-moral stance.'[67] The 'social unconscious' of a given cultural period, Bourdieu claims, speaks through homologous systems of discourse – e.g., scientific, political, philosophical – which compose linguistic 'fields' of meaning, ultimately defined by their market value.[68] Philosophy is only a system among systems. The priority it claims for itself as 'first philosophy' is spurious. Bourdieu aims to reduce the philosophical content of Heidegger's work to a homologue of political and academic discourse, to which he grants the priority proper to his own (unexamined) materialist presuppositions.

In what follows, I grant correspondences between Heidegger's political thought, as implicit in his understanding of being, and the conservative discourse of his 'generation.' The concept of 'generation' implicates a dialogical model: Heidegger, in dialogue with his generation, consequently shares with it an historical situation, speaks out of it and to it. But his dialogue with the Western tradition as a whole cannot be identified with or reduced to the rhetorical space of his speaking. He shares, at least in certain fundamental respects, a common *attunement* with his generation, but the way he enters into and transforms this attunement is his alone. At issue is the relation between concept (*Begriff*) and attunement (*Stimmung*). Authentic concept formation, according to Heidegger, is a matter of being-seized (*Er-griffen*) by the issue in question. All 'being-seized derives from and rests in attunement' (GA29/30, 9). The fundamental forms of attunement in which Dasein rests must be sifted and wrung, moreover, from the dominant moods of the public sphere of the They. To say that the concepts proper to different 'discursive fields' are homologues of each other fails to take the formation of concepts in the existential (factical) situation into account. The character of the concept formed will depend on the rootedness of Dasein in a fundamental attunement (GA61, 56–61). The so-called homology of concepts remains merely formal and external.

Hans Sluga's *Heidegger's Crisis* evidently has certain methodological elements in common with Bourdieu, but Sluga approaches the problem of the political implication of philosophy with greater sophistication. He is dismissive of Bourdieu's attempt to account for 'Heidegger's politics' as a rebellion against neo-Kantianism, and in fact, Sluga offers a more subtle picture of the political conflict of 'philosophical conservatives and philosophical radicals.'[69] Like Bourdieu, however, Sluga rejects 'the inclination to treat the whole issue [of Heidegger's political engagement] in psychological terms,' and rather proposes 'to look not for hidden meanings but for manifest relations and structures.'[70] The structure Sluga examines is the institution of philosophy in Weimar Germany. He offers a sociology of philosophy and philosophers, and of the University, as articulated through the discourse of philosophy into the early 1930s: 'the views of even the greatest thinkers cannot be fully understood in isolation. In order to know the performative function of their statements ... how they were understood at the time, what role they played in the contemporary debate ... we need to know the discursive setting in which the statements were made.'[71] Sluga isolates several key concepts which served to organize the cultural criticism of philosophy in response to the challenges and dislocations of the 'political field' of Weimar Germany, within which the institution of philosophy operated. 'I argue,' he writes, that there were 'four major concepts' which 'served to bridge the usual gap between philosophical thinking and political engagement' – 'crisis, nation or race, leadership, and order.'[72] He places the philosophical and political articulation of these concepts in a tradition going back to Fichte, whose *Addresses to the German Nation* Sluga grants an almost paradigmatic function in defining the terms of the debate. In simplified terms, the crisis of the identity of the nation subsequently comes to be defined in racial terms, and leadership and order are defined as articulations of the unique identity and mission of the German nation.

Like Bourdieu, Sluga offers a kind of sociology of knowledge, based on the primacy of discourses, and hence fails to appreciate the existential and historical specificity of concept formation. He claims that the sense of crisis experienced in 1933 lacks empirical foundation in the historical course of events – it rather exemplifies a crisis constituted, articulated, and repeated by institutional and discursive formations. He cautions that political engagement should think in terms of 'patient explorations and continuous, partial shifts' rather than allow itself to be captivated by a sense of national identity and mission, for these are concepts posited a priori.[73] In effect, Sluga betrays a certain failure of historical imagination: he treats the 'concepts' he considers as symptoms of an immature political culture. Nations are properly speaking mere 'constructs.'[74] Given that national identity is a construct, it calls for construction – and what the terms of this construction are is precisely the question at issue. Concept formation derives from the power of a tradition, which also gives the construct of the nation its ground of possibility.

To complain that the conservative Right was incapable of constructing 'Germany' along the lines stipulated by parliamentary debate ignores the character of the German tradition and the situation inherited by Weimar. Sluga implicity posits the terms of 'parliamentary democracy' as an ahistorical ideal of political culture, while ignoring the character of real, existing democracy and international power politics in the 1920s and 1930s.

In attempting to circumscribe Heidegger's rhetorical situation of 1933, I take a number of related currents of opinion into account. In the most inclusive sense, the conservative Right included a wide spectrum of writers and artists, from Mann and Hofmannsthal to expressionists such as Benn and Wigman, who supported the concept of a German third way, both revolutionary and conservative, distinct from East and West. Thus the anti-Western conservatism of the Thomas Mann of 1918 foreshadowed that of Benn in 1933, who hoped to see the creation of a truly national community. That Expressionist artists could also enthusiastically welcome Hitler is perhaps indicative of the diverse expectations engendered by National Socialism. For example, the most innovative German dancer of her time, the expressionist Mary Wigman, also greeted the new regime in 1933 in the spirit of national renewal.

Hugo von Hofmannsthal's famous address of 1927 – 'Das Schriftum als geistiger Raum der Nation' – in fact calls for a 'conservative revolution,' and in this respect the author may also be associated with the defence of Germany's unique path and mission. Von Hofmannsthal understands the nation as a spiritual and linguistic community affirming a common tradition and a destiny.[75] In coining the term 'conservative revolution,' Hofmannsthal defines it as the search for a new 'form' of existence, 'a new German reality' conceived as the spiritual space of the nation.[76] These authors of the avant-garde 'right' in varying ways and degrees expressed the will to national regeneration on an explicitly German model, in the years leading up to 1933. Heidegger evidently shared these aspirations.

To define politically conservative and revolutionary opinion more precisely, (i) reference pre-eminently to the following authors and tendencies will prove useful: Leopold Ziegler, Spengler, Ernst Jünger, the Germanist Josef Nadler, Hans Freyer, and Edgar J. Jung clearly accept the central theses of the conservative revolution without committing themselves to the ideology which emerged after 1933; the same may be said, in a much more qualified way, of Carl Schmitt. Also (ii) reference to racialist authors Ludwig Ferdinand Clauss, Hans F.K. Günther, and

Schultze-Naumberg serves to establish a relatively 'orthodox' position in racial studies in 1933. Mohler describes Günther, professor for social anthropology at Jena, Berlin (1935), and Freiburg im Breisgau (1940–5), as the 'most well known German racial anthropologist [Rassenkundler] of this period.' After 1933, he devoted much of his work to essays on the family, marriage, and the peasantry.[77] Nonetheless, according to Billig, Günther remained in professional contact with leading Nazi ideologues, such as Eugen Fischer, Darré, and Rosenberg, and published on racial questions in semi-official journals.[78] Clauss, student of Husserl, sometime professor in Berlin, attempted to develop a phenomenological approach to the study of 'racial' identity. Mohler calls him the 'most significant' German racial theorist of his time. According to Mohler, Clauss caused himself difficulties after 1933 by deviating from the party line, but continued to publish.[79] As well (*iii*) the works of both Moeller van den Bruck and Karl Haushofer will be worth examining. Mohler categorizes these two as 'Young Conservatives'; Moeller himself emphasizes the distinction between the revolutionary conservatism he represents, and for which he was later lauded by the National Socialists, from the merely reactionary conservatism of the monarchists. Moeller's *Das Dritte Reich* represents one of the key political statements of the Weimar period. We shall seek to evolve, writes Moeller, 'a conservative-revolutionary thought as the only one which in a time of upheaval guarantees the continuity of history and preserves it alike from reaction and from chaos.' For the conservative, unlike the reactionary, 'creates by giving to phenomena a form [Gestalt] in which they can endure.'[80] Haushofer was the pre-eminent German representative of geopolitical thinking in Weimar Germany as well as after 1933, although attempts to demonize him as 'Hitler's strategist' are groundless. As editor of *Zeitschrift für Geopolitik* he propagated ideas on the interrelation of a people, its space, and its political development. As Ebeling notes, Haushofer was close to Young Conservatives such as Edgar J. Jung, as well as to Rudolf Hess.[81] And (*iv*) given the relative academic prominence of Ernst Krieck and Alfred Baeumler after 1933, as well as their evident commitment to the new regime, their work may serve to constitute a kind of ideological norm against which other writers, including Heidegger, may be judged, to determine their distance from the ideas of the regime. Baeumler (1887–1968) was director of the Institute for Political Education at the University of Berlin from 1933 to 1945. He made his name in the Weimar period as a Nietzsche scholar and seized on the Nazi breakthrough of 1933, whether out of conviction or opportunism, to enhance his posi-

tion. This undoubtedly compromised Baeumler's philosophical serious-
ness, as his publications in praise of Rosenberg indicate. Ernst Krieck
(1882–1947) is still more closely associated with the aims of the National
Socialist state, both as educator – his publications focus largely on problems of social pedagogy – and as editor of *Volk im Werden*, one of the leading ideological mouthpieces of the post-1933 period. This explains the
prominence I have given these two philosophers in what follows.
Another focus will be (*v*) the works of Alfred Rosenberg, Walther Darré,
and Walther Schoenichen, who all held government positions after
1933, in the fields, respectively, of cultural politics, agricultural reform,
and ecological reform. Darré and Schoenichen are of interest to us insofar as they articulate ideas consistent with the delimitation and historical
finitude of being.

My survey of the *periodical literature* of the period before and after 1933
is of necessity selective, given the plethora of publications at issue. The
selection is guided by reference to subject matter relevant to Heidegger
(questions of Volk, state, historicity, and the embodiment and enactment of being), and by an attempt to establish the rhetorical situation of
1933, as delimited by related but distinct political and cultural commitments. The journals surveyed fall in the following broad categories:[82]

i) Jungkonservative (Young Conservative) journals which represented
the essential core ideas of the conservative revolution – These were *Die
Tat, Deutsches Volkstum,* and *Zeitschrift für Geopolitik.*[83] The Young Conservatives, as noted above, are distinct from the monarchists and the
Deutschnationale Volkspartei of Hugenberg, whom they viewed as
reactionaries. Stapel, Moeller van den Bruck, Jünger, etc., wanted an
organically unified community based on new fundamental principles,
not a restoration of the social hierarchies of Wilhelmine Germany.[84]

Under Hans Zehrer, who took over the general editorship in 1930, *Die
Tat* became one of the leading conservative periodicals of the late
Republic. It was opposed to the Weimar state, but no less to the Nazi
movement. Sonntheimer calls it the most widely recognized mouthpiece
of anti-capitalist nationalism.[85] Carl Schmitt praises it as 'one of the few
current periodicals which is neither a relict of the pre-war period nor the
vehicle of progress for its own sake, but in fact contemporary, all action,
not opinion.'[86] Zehrer called for a 'revolution from above,' based on the
presidency and the Reichswehr. This made Zehrer's own position with
the paper untenable after August 1933.[87]

Wilhelm Stapel, co-editor with Günther of *Deutsches Volkstum,* studied art history, philosophy, and economics in Göttingen, Munich, and Berlin. He was awarded a doctorate in art history in 1911. Stapel called himself a student of Friedrich Naumann's idea of *Mitteleuropa*, which implicated, on largely liberal grounds, the economic and cultural unity of Central Europe under German leadership.[88] The monthly periodical *Deutsches Volkstum*, which he infused with the spirit of radical conservatism in the tradition of Moeller van den Bruck, is often credited with preparing the ideological breakthrough of National Socialism. Yet despite reliance on biological analogies of the body politic, and an increased tendency to anti-Semitism after 1933, the journal attempted to maintain some critical distance from the regime. The journal ceased publication in 1938, and Stapel withdrew into private life.[89] In the late 1920s and early thirties, he had assumed, along with many other conservatives, that the National Socialists would prepare the way for an authentic conservative revolution. His support for the 'movement' was of a tactical nature.[90] *Deutsches Volkstum* was conceived in the spirit of a radical conservativism, and therefore was both anti-modern and anti-democratic. It proposed a defence of the peasantry, of an ideal of art, of traditional customs and norms of behaviour, of an authoritarian concept of the state, of the stylistic purity of language, and of a genuinely German religious sensibility. Hence Stapel could support the new regime, but by 1938 the influence he represented had become superfluous.

ii) *Völkische* (racialist or nationalist) journals – The journals in this class, it should be noted, elaborate the question of 'race' and *Volk* from a variety of anthropological, political, social, and phenomenological perspectives, and therefore cannot be collectively reduced to a 'racist' standpoint along biological or Darwinist lines. *Völkische Kultur*, edited by Wolfgang Nufer, falls into this class. According to Mohler, this journal attempted to build a bridge between the conservatives and the new regime.[91] Nufer also edited *Das Volk: Kampfblatt für völkische Kultur und Politik*, which is still more closely associated with National Socialist ideology. *Rhythmus*, edited by Rudolf Bode, but clearly under the influence of Ludwig Klages, defines its *Weltanschauung* as follows: 'German culture is the elastic unity of spiritual and formative powers with the transmitted body and soul of German, historically determined, being [des deutschen Wesens]. In particular, German culture of the future will develop, more strongly than hitherto, the values of bodily movement in relation to language, music, and dramatic dance, expressed in speech, song, and movement, thus to bring the German community to visible expression.'

iii) Journals founded or refounded in the early years of the Third Reich in response to the advent of the new regime – The following examples of this type deserve special mention: (*a*) *Volk und Heimat* – The subtitle translates as *Monthly Publication of the Association for National Education.* This publication was 'recognized and recommended by the state Ministry for Education and Religion.' Ernst Krieck found room in its pages. It concerns itself with 'education' primarily in the sense of the ideological justification of traditional customs (*Brauchtum*). (*b*) *Das Innere Reich: Zeitschrift für Dichtung, Kunst und deutsches Leben* – This journal (edited by Alverdes and von Meechow) was re-founded in 1934, at least in part in response to the literary exiles. It claimed to be the voice of the true, 'inner' Germany. Its stated task was to support the 'unfolding of German art,' trusting that 'the re-established power of the state will preserve it, and that the united will of the entire nation will powerfully inspire it.' Between 1934 and 1944, the journal published authors as diverse as Heidegger and E.G. Kolbenheyer, Ernst Jünger, and Ernst von Salomon. Heidegger's 'Hölderlin und das Wesen der Dichtung' (December 1936) uneasily shares space in the journal with the despised Kolbenheyer, whose 'Goethes Denkprinzipien und der biologische Naturalismus' sponsors a biological and racial interpretation of genius (October 1937). This says a great deal about the ideological fluidity of the journal, as well as the lack of clear direction from the regime. And finally (*c*) Ernst Krieck's *Volk im Werden: Zeitschrift für Erneuerung der Wissenschaften* – Founded 1933, this journal represents the relative orthodoxy of the new regime.

The survey which follows is guided by the object of discovering common conceptual ground between Heidegger and the rhetoric of 1933. This ground had, firstly, to be substantial enough to allow Heidegger to believe that ideological positions – concerning Volk and race, for example – could be deconstructed and opened up to the question of being. What were the perceived 'qualities of the movement,' in Wolin's words, which led Heidegger to believe that it was 'endowed with such tremendous metaphysical potential as a countermovement to the dilemmas of European nihilism?'[92] Secondly, we may expect to find, within limits, a common attunement to Weimar and the crisis of the West. What grounds did Heidegger have to believe, as he evidently did, that his intervention could initiate the disclosure of a more fundamental, more authentic response to the commonly perceived crisis? Finally, the discussions in the sections which follow are guided by five questions, which I found to *emerge from the discourse of this period* to direct my reflections: (*i*) What is the 'origin' of the political being of mankind? This question underlies the discussions of 'Volk and Race' and 'State, Volk, Earth.' (*ii*) What are the bases of the authority and legitimacy of leadership in the state, and of the claim of science to leadership? This question guides my discussion of 'State, Science, and Leadership.' (*iii*) What are the normative ends of leadership? This question motivates 'Gestalt and Type.' Finally (*iv*) How can Volk, state, and the ends of authority be actualized? This question generates 'Volk Embodied, Enacted.'

3.2.1 Volk and Race

Common to the conservative, and the National Socialist, critique of the liberal theory of the state is the contention that the Volk is not a self-conscious discursive unity, as postulated by the contractual model of the generation of the modern state.[93] This critique holds that the contractual model implicates the scientific or discursive alienation of the Volk from the fundamental sources of its own life. Thus Leopold Ziegler, for example, whose work of 1929 Heidegger refers to in his lectures (GA29/30), claims that the modern liberal state, deriving as it does from the autonomous consciousness of contracting individuals, is not comparable to a *Volkstaat*, inasmuch as a Volk is unselfconsciously rooted in a multitude of historically founded practices which can never become fully transparent and objective.[94] This claim, which is central to the Young Conservative rejection of liberalism, insists on the historicity and specificity of 'national' being – Edmund Burke and Herder are the godfathers of this tradition. The basis of this defence of the Volk is the rejection, by Young Conservatives such as Moeller and National Socialist ideologues such as Krieck and Baeumler, of the claim of Enlightenment thought to have discovered one, ahistorical measure of reason common to all humanity. In this vein, Ernst Krieck's *Wissenschaft Weltanschauung Hochschulreform* (Science *Weltanschauung* University Reform) of 1934 proposes a critique of 'pure reason' and calls for its re-integration into 'the life-totality of the Volk' (WWH 4, 7). Science is to serve the life-totality in its historical, organic specificity, thus breaking with the metaphysical dualism of subject and object (WWH 7, 25).

In view of the subsequent history of Nazi Germany, Krieck propounds a thoroughly suspect example of his meaning, although it almost reads, at first glance, as an exercise in postmodernism. Modern medicine, Krieck argues, is based on a technical and mechanical model which separates the patient from the life-totality of the patient's historical culture, objectifies and subjects the patient to the 'pure will and technical capacity' of institutionalized medicine (WWH 30). Founded as it is in the ahistorical claims of pure reason, Western medicine is an 'abstraction,' fundamentally alien not only to other cultures, but also to the whole personality of Western humanity (WWH 32). The application of Western medicine to another culture, insofar as it is blind to its 'established custom and way of life' is simply an expression of 'Western imperialism' (WWH 32). As the art and science of true healing, medicine aims to mobilize the patient's will to live by treating the entire person as belonging to a specific culture and tradition (WWH 34). For this reason, the 'shaman' of Siberia is the true healer of his people, because he is able to arouse the healing forces of the life-totality to which the 'patient' belongs (WWH 31–2). Krieck, therefore, in the first instance, insists on the cultural relativity and specificity of knowledge: knowledge is founded in the ways of being of particular peoples. Sickness and healing, in turn, are understood in their historicity. This brings Krieck's position close to Heidegger's. For Heidegger would be prepared to concur with Krieck's claim that sickness and healing are not merely or even pre-eminently biological functions: 'What is sickness? Sickness is not the malfunction of a biological process, but belongs to the historical happening of our being, something which is in part founded in our being-attuned' (GA38, 153). Health and sickness, therefore, are historically specific modes of a Volk's attunement to being. In August of 1933, in celebration of the fiftieth anniversary of the Institute of Pathology of the University of Freiburg, Heidegger had made the same claim, somewhat more provocatively, by linking the 'health' of Germany to Hitler's leadership (GA16, no. 75, 150–1). Yet this claim does not implicate a biological or racial understanding of health. The contention that the character and definition of health and sickness are culturally conditioned is by no means in itself absurd, and in fact finds support in contemporary research (e.g., Foucault, Szasz). In his dialogue with the Swiss physician and psychologist Medard Boss, in the early 1960s, Heidegger insists that the metaphysical foundations of modern medicine are to be found in the objectification of the human body.[95] Boss's own work continues this interrogation of the foundations of modern medicine in *The Existential Foundations of Medicine and Psychology* ([1971] 1979).

What separates Heidegger from Krieck, however, and what makes Krieck's position thoroughly suspect, is the attempt, in common with Nazi ideology, to link talk of culture and Volk to a discourse of race, or even to found ways of knowing in 'racial' specificity. Krieck holds that the *basis* of Volk is race (*Rasse*), understood in the first instance in the continuity of the blood and generation (WWH 37). However, to prevent a narrowly biological definition of race, he continues by defining race in historical and cultural terms. Race 'consummates itself in custom, in the forms of the comportment of life [Lebenshaltung und Lebensführung], in an order of value, in the law' to which a form of life, an historical community, subjects itself (WWH 43). 'Volk' intimates the collectivity of historically embodied 'racial' perspectives.

Darré similarly defines *Rasse* (race) as *Art* (kind): what pertains to a 'race,' therefore, is trueness to kind, understood as a particular historical form of life and custom (*Arteigen*).[96] This definition is essentially coherent with Spengler's insistence that 'race' is an historically determined form of the expression of being, not a matter of 'scientific' classification.[97] The same opinion finds expression on the radical conservative right in the pages of *Deutsches Volkstum*: commenting on Gregor Feder's 'Program of the NSDAP and Its Ideological Foundations,' Klaus Klaasen maintains that the Nordic 'race' (*Rasse*) is not physically determined, but defined by certain values and qualities of being.[98]

Not only does Krieck not identify Volk and race, but, as he insists, race itself cannot be reduced to biological determinants. Leading Nazi ideologues in the academic sphere come to similar conclusions, thereby complicating the entire question of race. Hans Günther, for example, insists on linking 'physical traits and spiritual characteristics' in defining a race as a distinguishable group.[99] Yet despite Günther's admiration for the French racial theorist Vacher de Lapouge, and thus for quantitative analysis of racial groups (skull measurement and classification),[100] Günther finally propagates an 'idealist' concept of race: the ideal racial type of the Volk – conceived as the perfected unity of spiritual traits and embodied comportment – is to be selected for by political and eugenic education.[101] The Volk is composed of many races. No people, not excepting German or Jewish, are the simple expression of one race.[102] Nonetheless, of the seven 'races' which he identifies as composing the genetic inheritance of the German people, Günther proposes to privilege one, the 'Nordic,' which he admits constitutes a minority of 5 to 8 per cent of the population (or 45 to 50 per cent of the genetic inheritance).[103] The Nordic serves the classical function of an ideal type, which it *embodies* in spiritual as in physical terms. He identifies the Nordic with the ancient Germans, on the one hand; and sets it as the long-term goal of a racial transformation, on the other.[104] The embodiment of the spiritual in the bodily is typically understood – as in the works of Ludwig Ferdinand

Clauss – as the visible gestalt, which articulates itself in a certain delimited *style* of being.[105]

Nor does Rosenberg define the concept of 'race' by reference to the supposed 'biological constancy' of a people. Race rather expresses itself in a transhistorical 'myth,' or Idea embodied in a type (*Typus*), which is the object of conscious formation.[106] According to Baeumler's interpretation, 'blood' in Rosenberg's *Mythus* signifies the necessity inherent in life to give itself form and limit.[107] Blood is a metaphysical, not a biological determination deriving from positive science. Lacoue-Labarthe and Nancy claim that if 'the Nazi myth was initially determined as the myth of the "race," it is because it is the myth of Myth, or the myth of the creative power of myth in general.'[108] The truth of myth, however, is the truth of the gestalt, that is, of the necessity of giving form and limit to being. Limit is the concept which allows us to make sense of Rosenberg's appeal to race.

The transformation of the type, moreover, is by no means excluded, but is in fact implicated, in the idea of the self-formation of the national subject.[109] Thus the ideal types of National Socialist racial ideology cannot be identified with the racial typology of nineteenth-century racial theory. As Michael Banton has shown, typologists held that the racial type, defined by physical and psychological characteristics, remains permanent and underlies the diversity of populations. Typology derives from Cuvier, and found expression in the works of J.C. Nott in America, Gobineau in France, and Charles Hamilton Smith in the United Kingdom.[110] In fact, the emphasis in the discourse of Weimar and National Socialism on 'race' as a form of life inscribed in mores and customs undermines the exclusively biological interpretation of Nazi racial theory.

Of course, this would not make the 'scientific' ethnology of the ideologues any less racist, since they insist on ascribing negative qualities of spirit to 'the Jews' and correlating these, in turn, with the development of particular socio-economic systems. Consequently Herbert Backe links liberalism, as the economic form of deracination, to the nomadic character of Jewish existence (*das Judentum*) as that of a people without a national territory.[111] Insofar as the ideologues insist, moreover, that mores over time become imperative and definitive for a 'racial' consciousness, they subvert historicist arguments against the biological thesis.[112] The appeal to the formation of ideal types, conversely, in a certain measure re-instates the power of historicity, inasmuch as body and soul can be formed and transformed. Günther claims that the discourse of the 'ideal type' refers to an aesthetic ideal of education and discipline – it consists in the formation of the body and its corresponding qualities of

soul.[113] The art historian Schultze-Naumberg also holds that every people has its racial ideal and that it is the function of art to give expression
to this ideal.[114] Every 'race' is defined by a certain psychological comportment, and the object of art is to give expression to an ideal of harmony of body and soul.[115] In Günther's case, as in Schultze-Naumberg's,
the accusation of 'national aestheticism,' which is often levelled at
Heidegger, is warranted.

Clauss, Günther, Schultze-Naumburg, and Darré are all associated with
the 'Nordic' school of racial theory. Together with Rosenberg, Günther
was supposedly one of the 'official' race theorists of the period,[116]
although Lutzhöft, in his book on Günther, argues that the theory of Nordic racialism and Nazi practice were increasingly at odds after 1940.[117] Of
course, the Nordic group was not alone in propagating an 'official' or
semi-official racial doctrine in National Socialist Germany. The more
strictly biological-materialist interpretation of race which, drawing on
social Darwinism and the work of Mendel, Haeckel, and Galton, called
for 'racial hygiene [as] a matter of public policy' competed with the supposedly merely descriptive ethnology of racial types, and with the views of
the 'racial mystics,' such as Chamberlain and Lagarde, who postulated a
cosmic war of Aryans and Jews.[118] In short, the discourse of race before
and after 1933 cannot be reduced to any one official doctrine – not even
to the biological concept of race.

But if 'the' Nazis did not (as Banton claims) rigorously and unambigu-
ously 'subscribe to the typological thesis that race determined history,'[119]
this could help to explain Heidegger's adhesion to the regime in 1933,
and his attitude toward it as late as 1935. For according to Löwith's
account, Heidegger insists that the revolutionary import of National
Socialism lies in its confrontation with history, in effect, in the Movement's engagement with the historicity of the Volk.[120] This account is
thoroughly at odds with the essentialism of typology. Either Heidegger
was entirely deceived regarding the 'racial thought' of National Socialism, or this movement was sufficiently diverse and undogmatic – even
regarding racial questions – to allow Heidegger's interpretation of the
subordination of 'race' to historicity. This is in fact my argument. If,
nonetheless, as the subsequent history of National Socialism shows, the
emphasis on the embodiment of gestalt and of 'soul' would degenerate
into the crudest biologism, this by no means necessarily follows from
National Socialist *theories* of 'race,' of Volk, or of their relation. These theories were themselves in competition, and their relation to actual practice remains unclear. In Geoffrey G. Field's words, Lutzhöft's 'excellent

monograph,' *Der Nordische Gedanke*, serves to remind 'us that for all the intensive study and analysis of the cultural roots of National Socialism, important lacunae still exist in our knowledge of German racial attitudes both before and during the Third Reich.'[121]

The cultural determinants of Volk which Krieck considers, are to be formed and transformed under the guidance of political leadership (WWH 41). Thus, although Krieck does not determine Volk biologically, he does determine it 'technically,' as something which can be produced by a political program. This line of thought is also evident in Baeumler's *Politik und Erziehung* (Politics and Education) of 1937: the author proposes that the 'biological laws' (of 1935) are an expression of a 'political concept of Volk.' This means that 'one understands the Volk as an entity [Grösse] which can be changed by means of legal measures' (PE 48). Thus the insistence on the non-discursive 'opacity' of Volk, inasmuch as it rests in itself and its own nature, which served as the conservative and National Socialist point of departure, is vitiated by appeals to a 'political culture' and its *Weltanschauung*. A poet of Benn's stature could also hold the view (at least in 1933) that a eugenic program of selection and formation (*Züchtung*) was necessary to preserve and enhance the natural potential for leadership and creativity of a people.[122] Heidegger undoubtedly rejects eugenic proposals of this type, no less than the ideological re-education of the Volk. In these respects, as in respect to the biological interpretation of Volk, the gulf between Heidegger and the party ideologues he addresses in 1933 is evident and needs no further commentary.

Conversely, Heidegger is clearly allied to the mainstream of Young Conservatism, which rejected materialistic interpretations of race. The Young Conservatives were not initially opposed to the Republic, insofar as they hoped that the defeat of 1918 might initiate the social revolution they wanted.[123] This changed with the failure of the revolution and the perception created by Versailles and its aftermath that Weimar served primarily the interests of the West. The original cultural nationalism of the conservatives did not implicate the union of all ethnic Germans in one state; but now they insisted on the application of the ethnic principles of Versailles to German interests. For the logic of Versailles appealed to the principle of ethnicity – national self-determination – in the creation of new nation states torn from German or Austro-Hungarian territory. By the same logic, the conservatives argued (as Hitler also would) that the newly created German ethnic minorities in Poland and in Czechoslovakia, as well as the Austrian Germans, themselves, had the right to be part of the greater German Reich. As I have noted, Heidegger was sympathetic to this view (GA16, no. 124, 233). But this application of the principle of national (or ethnic) self-determination obviously does not presuppose a biological interpretation of the Volk. Edgar J. Jung, for example, refers to the biological interpretation as 'a materialism of the blood, a betrayal of the spirit, which makes it impossible to conceive of history as the realm of free action ... "Germanity" [das Deutschtum] is a question of sensibility, not of blood [liegt im Gemüte, nicht im Geblüte].'[124] In his *Herrschaft der Minderwertigen*, Jung defines Volk as a collective 'personality,' but rejects the biological interpretation. The Jews, he holds, have become 'individualistic' through the course of history, not as a result of an inherent racial essence. Zionism, understood as a social and national movement, is 'the Volkish movement of the Jewish people.'[125] Moeller van den Bruck also insists that the 'spiritual' concept of 'race' has nothing to do with biological conceptions: those defining what is German should be wary of excluding, on biological grounds, people who 'spiritually' belong to the German race.[126] This notion of a 'spiritual racial commonality' (*geistige Rassenzugehörigkeit*), defined in terms of the commonality of language, tradition, and communal destiny also determines the sense of 'blood and soil' in the geopolitical tradition of Haushofer.[127]

The discourse of the revolutionary right, in fact, was capable of a concept of 'Volk' which made no appeal to race in any sense. Thus Hans Freyer's *Revolution von Rechts* (1931), one of the classics of the period, defines Volk as the collective subject which comes to consciousness with the industrial revolution: the question at issue, according to Freyer, is whether technology shall find, or not find, a requisite social form, thus to serve the community as a whole, as opposed to remaining the instrument of class interests.[128] As this subject, the Volk embodies the historical rationale of the industrial transformation of the earth, the 'mobilization of a new humanity' for the spiritual transformation of the forces of nature.[129] Herf's account of Freyer's sociology emphasizes his attempt to develop a new kind of technological culture, commensurate with the conservative view of the German tradition: Freyer's project – anti-liberal, anti-capitalist, and anti-Marxist – aims to overcome the alienation of historical subject and objectified nature.[130] Inasmuch as Freyer claims that the Volk emerges out of the metaphysical history of the West, as a response to the challenge of technology, we may recognize a certain anticipation of Heidegger's thought. For Heidegger's reflections on the being of *dunamis* and *ousia* are responses to the discursivity and limitedlessness of the technological project. And as we shall see below, he understands the question of Volk, at least in part, as a necessary response to this project.

The complexity of the hermeneutic situation of the early 1930s is complicated, as noted, by the fact that 'the' National Socialists did not propound an unequivocal theory of race. For we have seen that the Nazis did not, contrary to popular opinion, regard the Jews as a 'race.'[131] Nor did they claim that the Germans were one 'organic' or unadulterated race. They were well aware that 'racially' the Germans are a fusion of Latin, Celtic, Baltic, Slavic, and Germanic elements, however much the Germanic may predominate. This is not the key point, however. Rather, what counts as essential for National Socialism is the perceived rootlessness of 'the Jews,' and their supposed devotion to a communistic program of uprooting peoples still rooted in their homelands.[132] This is how the Nazis read the history of Russia after 1917 – as the victory of a perceived Jewish program of the destruction of the traditional roots, and even the material substance, of a people (e.g., Stalin's genocide of the Ukrainian Kulaks of the early thirties). The key opposition, in the Nazis' view, therefore, is between a people concretely embodied in its historical landscape, customs, and institutions and an agglomeration of individuals programmed to realize some political idea of a new, Soviet humanity.[133] Although there is no evidence that Heidegger ever committed himself to this perverse interpretation of 'the Jews,' there can be no question – given his understanding of the historicity of being – of his opposition to the politics of deracination. It follows that he is liable to have conceived of the extreme Right as the lesser evil and to have been willing to make compromises with it to prevent the triumph of communism in Germany.

3.2.2 State, Volk, Earth

The distinction and consistent opposition between *Volk* and *Staat* is a common theme in the evolution of modern Germany and marks, in different ways, the Wars of Liberation, the liberal nationalism of 1848, and the foundation of the *Reich* in 1871, no less than the Weimar Republic. Yet after the failure of the revolution of 1918, Weimar was perhaps the least loved and most despised of German states. National Socialism could draw on these sources of discontent and revolutionary passion and claim for itself the task of completing the integration of Volk and state to create a living community (*Volksgemeinschaft*).[134]

It was the common critique of the conservative revolution that the failure of the revolution left Germany shackled to Weimar and Versailles. Ante-bellum Germany cannot be restored, nor is it desirable, Moeller van den Bruck writes, to restore it. The revolution must be radicalized: we 'must as a people complete our transformation into a politically minded nation' or 'as a nation we will cease to exist.'[135] The state should be 'a means towards securing' 'the community of life' and an expression of it.[136] As the awakened, historical consciousness of industrial society, writes Hans Freyer, the Volk wills its own form of state. The 'Volk, as revolutionary, is not an organism, but a field of force. The revolutionary state ... is the political and historical integration of this force field' into one active will. The state is instrumental: it serves the Volk as the means by which it may master of the challenge of industrial society.[137]

A.E. Günther, co-editor of *Deutsches Volkstum*, writes that the state finds its legitimation not in a constitution, understood as a 'static' body of principles, but rather as the dynamic unity of the will to form.[138] The birth of this will, and the experience of this unity, he holds, was first forged in the *Fronterlebnis* of World War I.[139] This claim, of course, finds its pre-eminent exponent in Ernst Jünger, whose early works – *In Stahlgewittern, Der Kampf als inneres Erlebnis,* etc. – give it definitive expression. Common to the discourse of the revolutionary right, therefore, is the insistence that the state is the historically specific *embodiment of the will* of the Volk. This proposition recapitulates a classical moment in the history of modern political philosophy. It is, in Heidegger's own terms, thoroughly metaphysical. Heidegger's appeal to the 'will' in the Rector's Address nonetheless implicates him in this discourse and marks his dependence on the politics of the conservative right.

It is generally the opinion of the authors we are considering that the state derives from the Volk. The Volk is not the creation of a state, as contemporary commentators typically assert.[140] This does not exclude, however, as Krieck asserts, the application of political 'technologies' to the formation (*Gestaltung*) of the life of a people so as to create a unitary whole (WWH 25). The idea of a governing technology of politics means, in effect, a political ideology, or *Weltanschauung*. Thus the state, Baeumler asserts, is governed by a world view and has as its aim and proper focus the creation of a new *Typus* of humanity, not imperial expansion (PE 20, 24). Even if the basis of a world view, in turn, is the 'living spiritual power of the peoples' (PE 23), the form given to this power will be determined by ideological constraints. Consequently the state would be steered by a world view, and a *Weltanschauung*, in turn, would provide the program for the 'formation' of the Volk from which both state and *Weltanschauung* putatively derive.

The subordination of Volk to *Weltanschauung* generates a program that is liable to lead to the kind of uniformity, centralization, and bureaucracy, at odds with the original aim of many supporters of National Socialism to preserve the ethnic diversity (*Volkstum*) of the German people, as historically incarnated in its *Stämme*, or 'branches' – the Saxons, Bavarians, Franks, Swabians, and so on. The concept of the Reich, as opposed to that of the State, is the historical locus of the unity of the distinct ethnic branches of the German Volk, each distinguished by custom and dialect (*Mundart*). Edgar J. Jung calls for a Volkish federalism to counteract the tendency of the modern state toward centralization: the unity of the German people can only be conceived in the 'ethnic' diversity of its historical branches and their distinctions.[141] These distinctions, which go back to the earliest times, were preserved by the Reich of Charlemagne and his Ottonian successors.[142] National Socialism, at least in theory, affirmed this ideal of diversity. As the members, or branches, of an organic Reich, the *Stämme* themselves, in their historically founded reality, compose 'racial' elements which resist the uniformity of a centralized state.[143] Evidently the conservatives conceived it possible to reconcile the unified will of the state with its 'ethnic' diversity: this in itself indicates that they did not favour the development of a homogenous, centralized state. In Jung's case, in fact, the very opposite is true: he proposes the devolution of state powers with the development of a federal political and a corporate social structure: in internal affairs the state would function primarily as the guarantor of the law.[144]

The idea of the 'Reich,' as Sonntheimer has shown, is quite distinct from the modern idea of the state. The *Reich* of the neo-conservatives intimates an idea of metaphysical and religious unity and order, a federative structure, rather than centralization on the French Revolutionary model of the state. Above all, it is conceived as the embodiment of German destiny and universalism.[145] The federal re-structuring of Germany and the reordering of *Mitteleuropa* into a co-operative economic and cultural space were perhaps the most concrete proposals for the rebirth of the Reich.[146] Heidegger's 'provincial' resistance to Berlin, and his insistence that the dialect, mores, and landscape of his Allemanic homeland be the sources which 'ground' his authentic thought, which circumscribe his 'work,' are, of course, well known. This so-called provincialism, however, reflects a commitment to the differentiated unity of the Reich, as opposed to the centralism of the state. The 'metaphysical' character of the Reich referred to above, moreover, implies that it is grounded in the natural and divine order of things, as opposed to the contractual character of the modern state.

In both his Schlageter eulogy of 1933 (GA16, no. 285, 759) and Heidegger's rejection of the call to Berlin,[147] he appeals to 'nature' as a 'political' category. As Mosse documents, the mutual determination of Volk and landscape is one of the founding premises of Volkish ideology.[148] Yet Heidegger's appropriation of this thesis does not necessarily imply his acceptance of the Volkish world view, as Young claims.[149] Not only does Heidegger reject the racialism of the Volkish ideologues, he founds the mutual implication of 'landscape' and fundamental attunement (*Grundstimmungen*) in the historicity of *Grundstimmungen*, which are integral to the ontological structure of Dasein's historicity. *Stimmung*, or attunement, opens the site or native ground in terms of which both our 'corporal' being and the 'physical' earth crystallize as Da-sein, enter into synthesis, and come to be. We could not 'stand' on the earth, Heidegger writes in 1934, 'if this stand were not permeated by our attunement, thanks to which ground, earth, in short nature first comes to carry, preserve, and threaten us' (GA38, 152). Given the situatedness of Da-sein, the Reich would be the constituted embodiment of Dasein's differentiated, historically founded being. In an address of November 1933, Heidegger grants the 'state' this formative power: it is the 'jointure' (*Gefüge*), or con-stitution, which modulates and unifies the fundamental powers of the Da-sein of the Volk. 'Nature' becomes manifest as 'landscape and homeland' (GA16, no. 108, 200).

Nature is understood as the historicity of the earth. The earth is the site of an attunement which manifests itself in the rhythms of thought and work, no less than in the rhythm of the seasons and the qualities of the landscape. Landscape gives birth to qualities of character and spirit. Heidegger's evocation of the Black Forest echoes the 'geopsychology' of the geopoliticians, who hold that the ethnic specificity of the German *Stämme* arises out of the unified unfolding of a dialect, the formative powers of landscape, and history.[150] C.G. Jung also holds, in an article of 1927, that the 'soul is conditioned by the earth' of its native landscape: this landscape, imprinted on the unconscious, grants the soul its creativity. Rootlessness is the fate of émigré and imperialist alike, until transformed and assimilated by the new land.[151] Otto Gmelin, writing in *Die Tat* (April 1925), holds that a land becomes landscape, not through aesthetic appreciation – for this is a secondary experience – but through a process of mutual assimilation of land and soul, inasmuch as the rhythm of the land

and of the soul become one. When the rhythm of the land is internalized to inform the rhythm of the soul, and when the soul stamps the land with its own, determinate rhythm and form, a land-scape takes gestalt to inform, in part, the Volk soul. The Volk soul manifests itself, for example, in the poetry and architecture of a people.[152] This thought has a certain affinity with Heidegger's emphasis on *Befindlichkeit* as the attunement of the 'soul' (Da-sein) to the historicity of being in its local gestalt. The political tendency of this discourse is undoubtedly conservative and anti-modern – insofar as it is anti-urban – but no less is it anti-imperialist. Both Heidegger and the geopoliticians (or geopsychologists) conceive the *historicity of the earth*: this constitutes their common ground. The geopolitical conception, with few exceptions, raises a national ideology to the status of myth, whereas Heidegger attempts to recover the earth as the homeland of its peoples. And this is only possible, according to Heidegger, insofar as earth and world ('nature' and 'historicity') mutually determine each other and come to word in the specificity of the dialogue of a people with itself and its tradition. The strictest confirmation and development of this thesis is to be found in Heidegger's lectures on Hölderlin, from the winter of 1934, which are already situated at a distance from Heidegger's early enthusiasm for the regime, without abandoning, however, a certain ideal of National Socialism.

The historicity of the earth demands ways of working; and thought itself is a kind of 'working' with the things themselves, in the sense that thought attends to the ways in which things manifest themselves in their being (GA16, no. 108, 200–1). Politically, this implicates the primacy of the ethos, and of the local. Heidegger's supposed 'Black Forest romanticism' is actually a return to the reserve and limits of the local, and takes shelter in the historical ecology of the local, in opposition to the claims of state centralism and the cosmopolitan. In face of the tendency to increasing centralism under the new regime, Heidegger writes, it is all the more important that the primordial ethnicity of the historical regions be decisively 'awakened and preserved'; for only in this way can the state-creating power of the Volk, as grounded in ethnicity (*Volkstum*), fully be unfolded (GA16, no. 121, 227; no. 126, 240). Under conditions of modern technology, the possibility of the option of the local is certainly open to question: it should not be confused, however, with nostalgia for a vanishing rural lifestyle and its political conservatism.

The primacy of the local rather demands, in Heidegger's view, a refounding of the state in the *historical and geopolitical conditions of its possibility*. The state must acknowledge what it owes to the earth and accept the limits the earth imposes – in this sense Heidegger appeals to the powers of earth and blood, as we have seen. 'The voice of the blood,' he writes in the *Logik* of 1934, 'arises out of our fundamental attunement' (GA38, 153); our attunement is 'embodied,' in turn, in our belonging to our native soil. The insistence of the geopolitical school around Haushofer on the geopolitical determination and limitation of the state therefore reveals an affinity of thought with Heidegger's own appeal, in 1933, to the legitimate rights and limits of the state.

The geopolitical school claims for itself a critique of liberalism and capitalism as global imperialism. National Socialism constitutes a supposed return to the limited 'living space' proper to a people, insofar as it transforms its own space through work.[153] The earth, historically occupied and developed by a people, constitutes its legitimate space and the limits thereof.[154] This concept, as such, by no means necessarily implicates the conquest of territory to increase occupied space, although this is typically imputed to geopolitics and to Haushofer particularly.[155] Ebeling's incisive critique of this misconception also comes to the conclusion that the concept of limit, or self-limitation, is central to the geopolitical thinking of Haushofer's school, and determines the concepts of Volk, state, 'living-space' (*Lebensraum*), and the relation of peoples.[156] Geopolitics presupposes *the emergence of the state from a symbiosis of Volk and space: it implicates the limitation of the state by the historicity of the 'earth' which gave rise to it and to which it belongs.* Haushofer's empirical work on the history and concept of geopolitical limits is itself informed by his sense of the metaphysical imperative, imposed on the supposedly 'Faustian' Germans, of the necessity of determining themselves by the discovery of their own proper limits of being.[157] The geopolitical critique of liberalism is typically articulated as a critique of imperialism: because liberalism, given its universal, ahistorical premises, refuses to recognize its own limits, it is inherently imperialistic and tends to formlessness.

Regarding the internal reorganization of the state, the geopolitical idea found corresponding expression in the significance the Nazi state granted to ecology. Walther Schoenichen's late work of 1942 would offer in retrospect a systematic justification of Nazi ecology. *Reich* Director of Conservation, Schoenichen links cultural and ecological conservation to a critique of imperialism in his *Naturschutz als völkische und internationale Kulturaufgabe* (Conservation as National and International Cultural Objective).[158] In *Naturschutz im Dritten Reich* (Nature Conservation in the Third Reich) (1934), Schoenichen attacks the measurelessness of capitalist rationalism and technology as equally destructive of species variation and the living, creative relation of the Volk soul and the earth.[159] The ecological commitment of the Nazi state, however unwelcome to contemporary ecologists, has been seriously documented. It found expression in innovative legislation to preserve nature and protect animals (the *Reichsnaturschutzgesetz* of 1935);[160] it was propagated by Darré's program (supported by Hess and Himmler, among others) of organic farming, and of land reform to encourage a free-holding peasantry, from whom the future political elite of the Reich would be drawn.[161]

Walther Darré, Minister for Agriculture from 1933 to 1942, proposed the development of a new elite of yeoman farmers as a means of countering the deracination of the state from the people, and of the people (the urbanized proletariat) from the land.[162] The limitations and the imperial tendencies of Darré's program are evident in the resettlement program which developed during the war. Yet more important for the purpose of taking into account the political fluidity of the new regime, circa 1933, is that Darré, no less than Schoenichen and Haushofer, lays claim to a critique of Western imperialism, conceived as a critique of the formlessness of international capitalism, urbanization, and the deracination of the national elite.

Some of these ideas, or course, were not unique to Nazism and clearly emerged out of the conservative revolution of the Weimar period and its critique of denaturation and urbanization, of the destruction of all seemingly 'natural' forms and limits. Edgar J. Jung proposes the idea of a corporate state, for example, designed to curtail the power of 'rootless' finance capitalism.[163] As Stobbe's review of Wilhelm Stapel's *Deutsches Volkstum* documents, the idea of land reform designed to generate the creation of a new elite drawn from the yeomanry found broad support on the revolutionary right.[164] It is nonetheless true that the Nazi state alone gave concrete form to the cultural critique of the Weimar period. Thus Darré's program, for example, advertised itself as an earth-saving response to the measureless imperialism of technology and modern consumer society. Evidently this echoes, in its own way, Heidegger's critique of technology. What separates Heidegger from Darré, however, is the latter's commitment to the technical organization of a new peasant class and future elite defined by one coherent 'style' of being.[165]

Insofar as Heidegger's work *can* be understood as a response to the crisis of his generation, it offers this generation's most profound reflection on the finitude of being, and on the being of limit. This allows us to recognize a certain affinity between Heidegger and the ecological and geopolitical program, insofar as both give expression to concepts of limit and self-delimitation, as founded in the historicity and finitude of a people. The implications of Heidegger's thought for ecology have been established by Foltz, for example, without, however, drawing out their implications for 1933: one essential reason why Heidegger tended toward Nazism may be found in the 'Movement's' *evocation of the earth as the measure of a people and its state.*

3.2.3 State, Science, and Leadership

In 1933, Heidegger apparently attempted to grasp the opportunity to bring about a fundamental change in the leadership role of the University within the State. How did he conceive of leadership within the existing political context? What kind of transformation must our concept of science undergo, if science is to lead in knowledge within the state, and for the 'people'? Kisiel argues that the question of the 'essence of the university,' as founded in 'the essence of science,' is the 'single most important thread' running through Heidegger's lectures between 1919 and 1933.[166] The essence of science, in turn, on Heidegger's own premises, has to be sought in the finitude of Dasein, in the concrete historical specificity of Dasein's being-in-the-world. For this reason, the question of science is a 'political' question, and stands in intimate relation to the question of Volk and state. My object in what follows is to show how Heidegger's commitment to the finitude of science could entangle him in the 'politics' of science and motivate his engagement for National Socialism.

Heidegger was evidently convinced that the 'crisis of science' calls for a return to the existential motivation of science as founded in the finitude of Dasein and the historicity of *Mitsein* as Volk (GA27, 26–45). 'Authentic' science, as existentially motivated, would serve the Volk-community in its finite historical specificity. Therefore Heidegger could conceive, at least in 1933, an alliance with the new regime, given that he believed, as he evidently did, that National Socialism represented a movement of the recovery of historicity, and thus a step back from the deracination represented by the primacy of the liberal market-place, international 'research' for its own sake, and an instrumental conception of technology.

The conservative Right of Weimar was convinced that to avoid the functionalization of command typical of the modern, democratic, sociotechnical state, the leadership of the new State would have to stay attuned to the diversified ethnicity of the historical Reich. The logic of the recovery of the 'leadership principle' (SBV 23f), as formulated by

Carl Schmitt, is based on an *Artgleichheit,* or 'similarity of kind,' between leaders and the led. This model of unity, in turn, derives from a 'unitary concept of form' which forms (*gestaltet*) all aspects of public life (SBV 33). Leadership is in this sense possible only in a unity of the common 'existential conditions of [a people's] own kind or type [*Art*]' (SVB 45). In appealing to the unity of 'form,' Schmitt explicitly rejects the arbitrariness of command and the rule of bureaucratic functionalism (SBV 42). Leadership is rather founded in the 'unmediated presence and realized actuality' of the leader, and this demands, on Schmitt's account, a common existential ground of mutual understanding, such as allows leadership, but which also limits it to prevent it from degenerating into mere tyranny (SBV 45). Hitler's charismatic leadership must be limited through the dynamic of the public space of a common attunement.

This thesis finds its correspondence in Heidegger's claim in *Being and Time* that *Befindlichkeit* is equiprimordial with understanding and discourse. A common attunement would be the condition of the dialogical situation and the mutual understanding of leaders and led. The unity which thus arises cannot be rationally founded in contract relations, which are themselves only a construct, based on the unexamined a priori of *a common attunement of a generation, as defined by its locality and historicity.*

Schmitt's attack on bureaucratic functionalism recalls Max Weber's critique of the leadership style of the liberal state, as defined by rationalization and the rule of bureaucratic experts. The truth of the rational norms of a state must be founded in the ethical and dialogical actuality of decision-making and action, which limits the claims of the autonomous self, no less than the claim to the universal validity of the norm.[167] Charismatic authority, conversely, as the antithesis of functional rule, entails 'the possibility for authentic political action – action that bears the stamp of "personal responsibility" and the "moving spirit"' of the politician's own personality.[168] Heidegger shares this view, writing in August of 1934 that 'the *Gestalt,* the direction of the will, and the ability' of the University leadership is more important than any institutional reform. Leaders should be 'effective through what and who they *are,* not though what and whereof they *speak*' (GA16, no. 156, 309).

To make personal authenticity the legitimating ground of politics is highly questionable, indeed dangerous, as Wolin notes.[169] With the functionalization of command, conversely, rule without responsibility passes over to the faceless dictates of socio-technical discourses. Socio-technical discourses were conceived as modes of deracination, by the conservative Right of Weimar, and therefore were deemed illegitimate. *The measure of*

legitimate leadership is constituted by what serves to root a people in its native soil.
In this respect, the 'leadership principle,' as conceived by Schmitt, is an
attempt to recover the autonomy of the political from the socio-technical
realm. The primacy of the political and the responsibility of leadership
are cornerstones of Hitler's personal credo, insofar as it can be established.[170] Schmitt claims that only within the terms of a clearly demar-
cated political realm can the abstractions of socio-technical 'processes'
be put into question (SBV 36). These processes, as contemporary commentators acknowledge, have increasingly come to characterize the
development of modern democracy.[171] Therefore it cannot suffice simply
to castigate Heidegger's political stance by reference to an ideal of
democracy. For this reason, conceivably, Heidegger could greet Hitler as
the embodiment of charismatic leadership, and could applaud the initia-
tion rites of a properly political realm. Subsequently Heidegger would
come to reject the Nazi state as the triumph of socio-technical discourses.

To say, as Heidegger infamously did, in a speech to Freiburg students
(October 1933), that not ideas or doctrines, but the '*Führer* alone *is* our
German reality of today and the future and its law' (GA16, no. 101, 184),
implies that the being of leadership is in the act, for the enactment (*Vollzug*) of the rite of command opens up the sphere of the political. In this
respect, perhaps, Heidegger finds himself in the company of Baeumler,
who holds that the 'action' of leadership means *to be one's historicity* – it is
action in this sense, as the rite of enactment, which founds the Reich
anew every moment (PE 9–10).

Ernst Krieck, in turn, insists that the concepts of 'leadership' and
'leader' (*Führung* and *Führer*) derive from the National Socialist 'Movement,' as opposed to the authority invested in an office of the State apparatus (or 'system,' in the critical terminology of the Nazis). These
concepts must remain in tension, even when combined in one person –
Hitler, for example, was Chancellor (an office whose authority derives
from the constitution) and *Führer* (which names Hitler's relation to the
Movement). Leadership is an organic relation between leaders and led:
it remains in force only as long as the personal qualities of a leader are
convincingly demonstrated. The authority of an office is the function of
an institutional code, not of the person holding the office.[172] Up to this
point – that is, in acknowledgment of the fundamental distinction of
Office and 'personal' authority – it may seem that Heidegger could, with
some qualifications, grant Krieck's case. This could help to explain, at
least in part, Heidegger's aversion to the Weimar 'system.'

Yet on examination, Heidegger's concept of leadership is radically at odds with Krieck's. According to Heidegger, philosophical leadership is founded in the awakening of a fundamental attunement which impels the 'led' to confront their own finite freedom and take responsibility for themselves (GA25, 39). Inasmuch as Krieck insists that 'leadership' consists in 'the creation of a true community of scientific work as founded on a *Weltanschauung*,' it is evident that he cannot grant this measure of freedom and self-responsibility.[173] The primacy of the 'racially' founded *Weltanschauung* determines in advance the 'selfhood' of leaders and the led, the direction of their 'questioning,' and of their responsibility – which is to the anthropologically understood Volk.[174]

In practice the charismatic leadership of Hitler encouraged a chaos of competing policy initiatives and competencies deriving from his decrees (*Erlasse*), as opposed to the collective decisions of the Cabinet or *Reichstag*. These decrees circumvented the traditional instances of the state and the check on arbitrary power they might impose. Insofar as the power of the Party (or 'Movement') supported by the totalitarian tendency of the state became unlimited, the original objective of the conservative critique of parliamentarianism as a system of party interests and functional bureaucracy found itself betrayed. According to Ernst Niekisch, no less, speaking for the radical left of the 'Movement,' Hitler had surrendered the German idea of the state to a Roman, or imperial, concept.[175]

The conservative critique sought to found decision-making in the unity of a common attunement and the mutual limitation of leaders and led in the dialogical situation. This project had to fail, insofar as the public space of being-attuned became the object of explicit, propagandistic manipulation. In Heidegger's terms, which offer a realistic critique of this development in the *Beiträge*, the authenticity of the *Grundstimmungen* of *Mitdasein* was to be distorted and perverted into manipulated *Erlebnisse* – the sensationalistic exploitation of the public sphere (GA65, secs. 66–69). In this way the public sphere – which authentic rhetoric is burdened with clarifying, in order to allow a *Grundstimmung* to come to word (SZ 138–9/130) – would be 'darkened' by the sensationalism of emotion generated by modern propaganda techniques. It is nonetheless the case that in 1933, Heidegger saw opportunities for the renovation of the University, opened up by a political leadership which would, as he thought, allow the transformation of the fundamental attunement of the nation and of the scientific attitude.

Within the state, the University holds a special leadership function, for not only does the University educate the leaders of the state, and regulate the transmission of knowledge from the fundamental to the applied sciences, but the University offers 'spiritual' leadership by 'making sense' of the entire enterprise of knowledge by articulating its grounds and its unity. The opening sentence of the Rector's Address reads as follows: 'The assumption of the rectorate is the commitment to the *spiritual* leadership [geistigen Führung] of this institution of higher learning' (SU 9/470). Within the context of the Address, the term 'spiritual' has to be deconstructed, to root the properly spiritual in the powers of earth and historicity. Wherein does the leadership of the University by the office of the rectorate, and the leading role of the University itself in the state, consist?

More precisely, Heidegger does not speak of the *office* of the rector, but of teachers and students. What kind of authority does the rector, as teacher and 'philosophical' leader, have in leading the University? In *Die Grundbegriffe der Metaphysik* of 1929–30, Heidegger denies that the teacher has any 'authority' whatsoever: in philosophizing, the teacher leads, but only inasmuch as he or she has the 'remarkable destiny' of having to serve as the instigator of philosophy in the listeners, by 'awakening' philosophical questioning in them (GA29/30, 19). The philosophical leadership of the University implicates the communication of 'higher and richer possibilities of human existence, which are not imposed on the other, but actualized for the other in the practice of life, thus alone to be made discretely effective' (GA27, 8).

And this means that we as listeners put ourselves, no less than the teacher, into question. To be authentic, questioning must be founded in a fundamental attunement (*Grundstimmung*), for only insofar as we allow an attunement to hold us in its grip can our questioning bring the phenomena into its 'grasp' – that is, into conceptual definition (GA29/30, 9). For phenomena presence in the space opened up by the attuned understanding of a specific way of being-in-the-world. Granted that we allow that the concept (*Begriff*) and being-grasped and moved (*er-griffen*) by a fundamental mood are related in this way, what does it say about the leadership of the University? It seems that Heidegger understands the leadership of philosophy in the University to consist in the preparation and awakening of a fundamental mood, *thus to allow new concepts to form out of an altered understanding of our life-world.* The life-world to which the Address in the first instance speaks is the University itself.

Heidegger understands this life-world, as the site of science and as defined by a passion for it, to be in a state of crisis. According to the *Einleitung in die Philosophie* (1928–9), the leadership of the University in the community ideally consists 'in the communication of a scientific education [einer wissenschaftlichen Bildung] which grants Dasein the possibility of a new stance in the whole of the world, in which Dasein's relatedness to all things undergoes a transformation' (GA27, 7). Philosophy does not name a matter to be treated, 'but the How, the fundamental mode of a comportment' to beings (GA27, 25). The crisis of science which arises out of our mode of comportment has two aspects: (*i*) the aspect of 'its position in the whole of our historical and social Dasein,' for it is by no means clear, Heidegger continues, 'in what way not only scientific results, but scientific education itself' shall be integrated into 'the unfolding of genuine education in human societies'; and (*ii*) the aspect of 'the relation of the individual to science itself' (GA27, 27). For it remains unclear what essential place science has in our existence. This is the problem of 'the existential essence of science' (GA27, 29).

Heidegger's formulation of the crisis of science recalls Nietzsche's *On the Advantage and Disadvantage of History for Life*; and in some ways, Heidegger's response, in the Rector's Address, also recalls Nietzsche's approach to the problem. Nietzsche had castigated the ahistorical formlessness of the production of knowledge in the wake of the objectification of the past. The result is that the living selfhood of the 'subject,' seduced by the equal and indifferent availability of objects of study, is hollowed out and replaced by the mechanism of a methodology. Nietzsche's insistence on the necessity to life of a limited, perspectival seeing is reflected in Heidegger's appeal to the historicity of the Volk, for the Volk imposes the limit of a perspective on the production of knowledge, thus to give our encounter with beings measure and rank.

Students and teachers, Heidegger continues in the first paragraph of the Address, must be rooted in the 'essence of the German University.' And this means that they allow themselves to be defined by the historicity of the German community of fate (SU 9/470). Evidentially, the crisis of science is to be engaged by an individual and by an existential response which roots science in the needs of the community and determines its goals accordingly. Clearly this demand reflects the priority of *phronesis* over *techne;* the deracination of science implies the triumph of *techne* over *phronesis.* Consequently, according to the *Einleitung,* the crisis of science in respect to its place in the whole of our 'historical reality' may be formulated as the question concerning 'the essentially practical character of science.' The primordial 'finitude' of science is at issue – and this means that science is 'an essential possibility of human existence' (GA27, 40–1). The finitude of existence, and therefore of science, calls for the actualization of the limit, form, gestalt (*Gepräge*) of a certain form of existence and comportment to beings. As such, the spiritual mission of the Volk imposes itself on science, and on the leadership of the University.

In the Rector's Address Heidegger refers to the new concept of science propagated by the regime, to categorically reject it. Yet, though Krieck's view of the character and role of science (*Wissenschaft*) in the new state well exemplifies the target of Heidegger's opposition, certain common concerns, if not common aims and presuppositions, also emerge. Thus Sluga's account of the conflict of the 'philosophical radicals' – Heidegger, Krieck, and Baeumler – who entered into a short alliance against the philosophical 'conservatives' – Hartmann, Hans Heyse, and others – reveals that Heidegger, in common with the 'radicals,' worked for university reform and the integration of science into the Volk community.[176] This was a central theme of a conference, for example, in July of 1933 in Berlin, where Heidegger appeared with Baeumler and other rectors.[177] This common goal, however, masks the deep dissension between Heidegger and his 'allies' of 1933.

Krieck's understanding of the relation of *Weltanschauung* and science affirms the primacy of the world view, or *Mythos*, of the state in the determination and formation of the Volk (WWH 65).[178] Krieck offers the example of Paracelsus's attempt to found a German, holistic art of medicine, to illustrate the thesis that science must be rooted in the history and character of a people (WWH 29, 78). The critique of 'liberal science' Krieck correspondingly proposes castigates its analytic character, which ignores the unity of our historical-communal being as the basis of all science. Liberal science 'is without relation to the living reality of the Volk-totality' (WWH 80). Since every Volk seeks its particular form of inner completion, or the gestalt proper to it, the aim of science as the expression of the life of a people should be to make a contribution to this end through the formation of the technical form and style of life (WWH 81–2). And since concrete and living history, Krieck's continues, consists in 'the formation of a gestalt, ever-anew, out of the subterranean life of the Volk' (WWH 7), the contribution of German science to the founding of a new history must also consist in the generation of 'a new sense of meaning, as granted by a consummate gestalt [einer vollendeten Gestalt]' (WWH 8).

In this undertaking, science must become militant, hence the necessity of a governing world view. The division of the faculties must be overcome for us to recognize the unity of life and to respond to it (WWH

79–80). Krieck rejects the (Kantian) model of the university as founded in humanism and the primacy of the philosophy faculty (WWH 86). The ideal of objective, scientific truth must be redefined in favour of a recognition of the perspectival character of science as limited by the 'totality of life and historical decision-making in living relation' (WWH 11). As Krieck writes in *Volk und Heimat*, the character of reason and ways of knowing are related to 'the reality of national characters [Volkscharaktere].'[179]

Although Heidegger rejects politically motivated science, he insists that 'genuine questioning and research' are founded in and preserved by limits set by a given 'demand for knowledge,' and this, in turn, by a 'will to knowledge' (GA16, no. 104, 191–2). Every demand and every will to knowledge is grounded in a particular comportment to beings, hence stands in the light of a specific understanding of being (GA24, 390/275). As we know from 'On the Essence of Truth,' the truth of a *comportment* is founded in Dasein's fundamental *attunement* to being and is, in turn, the ground of *truth-statements* about beings (WW 180–3/120–22). A comportment lays out the pathways of Dasein's way of being, and these grant it its 'self-identity,' or ownness; ownness implies being-limited, implies holding oneself in and toward a limit, for it is in this circumscription that Dasein and a Volk begin to be. A given will to knowledge, therefore, if it is to be genuine, must know how to limit itself; and this limit is granted by a confrontation with the things themselves in their being (*Auseinandersetzung mit den Seienden*). Heidegger insists on tying the will to the self-limitation of knowledge to the category of the Volk as one of self-limitation, and thus calls for a 'people's science' (*völkischen Wissenschaft*) (GA16, no. 104, 192). This demand is not as such at odds with the claim that the fundamental principles of science, as principles of nature, are universal: it does not commit itself to the nonsense of a 'Jewish physics,' and the like. Heidegger's claim, however, might be formulated as follows: scientific research is genuine, *in its existential motivation*, insofar as it attends to and is guided by the historical and 'ecological' sitedness of the community *for the sake of which* science wills to know. Science must be founded in, and limited by, the finitude of the earth in its historicity, that is, in and by the 'native soil' of a people. It is in this sense that Heidegger's reference, in the Rector's Address, to the power of 'earth and blood' as the source of a people's strength is to be understood (SU 14/475). The 'existential concept' of science, Heidegger writes in *Being and Time*, 'understands science as a mode of existence and thus as a mode of being-in-the-world which discovers or discloses beings or being' (SZ

357/327). The priority of being-in-the-world in the existential analytic over the detachment of the scientific attitude, demands, in Heidegger's terms, that science has a responsibility to the being-in-the-world out of which it arose, for this constitutes the existential end of research (GA16, no. 155, 306). Conversely, insofar as the will to know becomes absolute and without respect for the limits inscribed in beings themselves, it 'idolizes a rootless and powerless way of thought' (GA16, no. 104, 192). This can mean that insofar as science, in its global claim to mastery over the earth, and therefore in its rootlessness, takes power over the earth, it becomes powerless in the face of the natural forces it unleashes by overstepping all limits. Whether or not this is the case remains to be seen. It is in any case Heidegger's claim that science loses its genuine motivation, and its existential rootedness, when it is no longer guided by the measure of an historically and ecologically sited community.

We have seen that the 'existential essence of science' is at issue (GA27, 27). The recovery of this essence – understood as the historical rootedness of Dasein in its responsibility for being – demands a turn in the fundamental comportment (*Grundart des Verhaltens*) of science and philosophy (GA27, 25). Scientific consciousness itself, Heidegger had written in 1919, forms the comportment (*habitus*) of the individual (GA56/57, 4). This *habitus* is genuine insofar as the end of science is the existential-historical *life-world* of the individual and the individual's community. As an 'essential possibility of human existence,' hence as 'finite,' science must become *praxis*; *praxis* determines the comportment of scientific consciousness in concrete questions of what is worth knowing and how it is to be known. The 'how' stipulates that knowledge be bound to the genuine needs of a human community, understood as a finite life-world. Science becomes 'essential' in the *actualization* (*Vollzug*) of these needs (GA58, 261). What is needed above all is openness to the 'e-ventuation,' or unconcealment, of being in beings, for this openness alone preserves beings in their being (GA34, 160). The rootlessness of science derives from the *telos* of idealization and functionalization inherent in the objectification of beings. Inasmuch as science disintegrates beings to integrate them into functional relations, it loses its hold on beings and uproots itself from the earth. In section 18 of *Being and Time* ('Relevance and Significance: The Worldliness of the World'), Heidegger asks,

> If we thus define the being of what is at hand (relevance) and even worldliness itself as a referential context, are we not volatizing the 'substantial being' of innerworldly beings into a system of relations, and, since relations

are always 'something thought,' are we not dissolving the being of inner-worldly beings into pure thought? (SZ 87–8/82)

The 'referential context' of a system of relations, taken as an end in itself, constitutes the deracination of significance from its 'ground' in Dasein's being-in-the-world. In 'The Age of the World Picture' (AWP 80–2/122–24) and the *Beiträge* (GA65, sec. 76), Heidegger argues that the 'pure thought' of modern scientific methodology triumphs over science as a way of knowing, and over the phenomena themselves, which are constrained to show themselves according to the 'groundplan' projected a priori by science as 'research program.'[180] The dissolution of science into technology, which this paradigm portends, is contested by Heidegger in the name of the existential foundedness of science in the life-world of a community. This critical attitude toward science, it is worth adding, is developed in the discourse of the period, although in an entirely inadequate way, as the attack on 'intellectualism.' *An Introduction to Metaphysics* constitutes Heidegger's most direct philosophical and political response to the question of intellectualism understood as the deracination of Dasein, the triumph of ahistoricity, and the oblivion of being in the finite specificity of its presencing in beings.

Heidegger's *Was ist Metaphysik?*, his inaugural lecture before the combined faculties of the University of Freiburg on 24 July 1929, can give us additional clues regarding the existential genesis of the sciences in the being who poses the question of being. The University is understood as a community of knowledge defined by the passion for science; this passion is the comportment (*Haltung*) out of which questioning emerges (WM 103, 105/94, 95). The passion for science defines it in its submission to the manifestation of the being of beings, consequently in a service to beings which 'allows in its way, beings to come into their own' (WM 105/95, modified). The crisis of science, and therefore of the University – as both have lost their rootedness in their 'essential ground' and are increasingly defined by the 'technical organization of the University and its faculties' (WM 104/94, modified) – consists in their deracination from the being of the things themselves. This uprootedness stands in harsh contrast to the 'idea of science' as a way of 'entering into nearness to what is essential in all things' (WM 104/94).

This characterization of the hermeneutic situation opens the site for a remarkable turn in Heidegger's address – given his audience – which initiates its essential movement: the turn toward the Nothing as the 'condition' of our (scientific) engagement with beings. For the Nothing 'makes possible the openedness of beings as such' for Dasein (WM 114/104). Consequently Heidegger is intent on stepping back from beings in their being-present as potential objects for scientific research, to the event of the presencing out of which and in which things become present. This event 'in itself' is Nothing, or No-thing; in the Afterword to the text of 1943, Heidegger writes, 'But this Nothing presences as being' (*Wegmarken*, 304). In our experience of the Nothing, as the event of our detachment from all beings, Dasein's transcendence announces itself, and with it, the condition of our scientific being, inasmuch as it goes beyond mere entanglement in beings to pose the question of what entities are (WM 119/108–9). We come back to beings, in wonder and astonishment, from a 'position' which we ourselves are, of being beyond them, as open to the No-thing of the event of coming-to-presence (WM 119–20/109). 'Da-sein means: being-held in the Nothing' (WM 114/103, modified). To this point Heidegger has established the Nothing as the 'condition' of the being-present of beings and hence of scientific questioning and objectification.

The question arises, however, as to how an experience of the Nothing is possible, thus to give our speaking 'foundation' in the phenomena. For recourse to the presencing of being – and thus of the negativity of the Nothing – cannot be logically derived from beings, quite aside from the absurdity of saying Nothing 'is.' Nor can the Nothing be derived from negation, from the saying of the 'is not,' for negation 'can make denials only when something deniable is already granted to it' (WM 115/105). Consequently Heidegger, following the existential analytic of *Being and Time*, appeals to the evidence which moods (*Stimmung*) offer of our fundamental attunement (*Befindlichkeit*) to what is as a whole. What is revealed in this way is the 'fundamental happening of our Da-sein' (WM 110/100, modified). If, in what follows, the mood of anxiety is given exemplary status, the question arises as to why this is so. It is not just that the mood of anxiety 'reveals the Nothing' in the withdrawal of beings, and of our own being, to leave us no hold in beings (WM 111/101). According to *Being and Time*, anxiety reveals our being-in-the-world itself and therefore points to the 'structural whole' of Dasein (SZ, secs. 39–40). Nothing presences together with beings *in their withdrawal* (WM 113/102). In this movement of withdrawal, beings come into presence in a peculiar way: the Nothing 'refers' to beings as they slip away by turning away from them, thus to reveal them in their long-concealed strangeness as the completely other to the Nothing (WM 113/103). It is not simply that innerworldly significance withdraws and collapses. Beings themselves are revealed in the movement of withdrawal, or saving reserve, out of which they arise. The becoming-present of beings in their withdrawal from presence is the movement of their saving preservation from mere being-present. The event of nihilation which eventuates in presencing belongs to the being of beings.

In the movement of withdrawal, and in the nihilation of beings, we recognize the *lethe* which is the innermost heart of *aletheia*. *Lethe* belongs to the event of truth. In the presencing of Nothing (being) as the completely other to beings, being differentiates itself in beings in the event of an unconcealment which holds beings in the saving reserve of withdrawal. In this sense anxiety is the experience of the concealment at the heart of truth. The question at issue, therefore, is whether or not the sciences are capable of engaging this event and of encountering the *lethe* proper to beings. If in 1929 and in 1933, Heidegger's answer to this question was equivocal, both the *Beiträge* and the Afterword of 1943 answer it in the negative.

Granted that anxiety as a fundamental attunement has an exemplary relation to the truth of being as Nothing, what relation, if any, does it have to the fundamental attunement of science? Heidegger confirms that this relation is an intimate one (WM 120/109–10). Only insofar as beings – held in the oscillation of presencing and withdrawal, in the happening of Nothing – strike us in their strangeness, can wonder, and consequently the Why? of science, arise to move us to seek out the nature and grounds of entities. Since Aristotle wonder has been recognized as the fundamental attunement of philosophy and scientific inquiry. We come back to beings in wonder, Heidegger argues, from the nihilation of our subjectivity: we are left without familiar hold or ground, hanging in Nothing (WM 111/101). Anxiety individualizes to bring Dasein before 'itself as being-in-the-world' (SZ 188/176). This allows world in its worldliness to be 'all that obtrudes itself' (SZ 187/175). The obtrusion of worldliness as the other to the mere being-present of beings reveals them in their strangeness.

Dasein emerges from Nothing as the site of the presencing of beings. We recall that the ideal of science Heidegger enunciates here 'allows ... beings to come into their own.' In what relation does this demand to attend to beings stand to the attunement of anxiety? I have already indicated an intimate relation between anxiety and the presencing of beings in their nihilation: beings come to presence in their saving withdrawal from mere being-present. The Nothing at the heart of beings saves them, in the words of the Afterword, from 'the unconditional production' of their 'objectivity' (*Wegmarken*, 301). The collapse of the subject in the attunement of anxiety, conversely, is reflected in the disintegration of the object-being of entities. The disintegration of objectivity, in turn, is the condition of the letting-be of beings. Yet this alone would not suffice to allow beings to come 'into their own.' Beings must come to manifest themselves in the differentiation proper to each. Early in the Address, Heidegger mentions another fundamental mood, that of boredom (*die Langeweile*), in which all things merge in a 'remarkable in-difference' (WM 110/99). Heidegger devoted a detailed phenomenological description to boredom in lectures of the winter of 1929–30 (GA29/30, 117–249); nor is boredom without relation to the question of the 'metaphysical foundations of science.' Boredom brings to light the in-different, hence equally present and equally inconsequential temporalization of entities. In the *Beiträge*, Heidegger will claim that boredom in the face of the indifferent being-present of beings is the concealed end toward which modern science is racing (GA65, sec. 76). This end is founded in the re-presentational availability of all beings indifferently to subjectivity. Evidently boredom is the antipode of wonder. But boredom also stands in an essential, if oblique, relation to anxiety. Boredom conceals the specific How of the being of beings by revealing them in the uniformity of their temporalization. Given the character of modern science, this is an indication of the ontological weight of boredom as a fundamental attunement of modern mankind: it is the attunement proper to the abstraction of mathematical-physical nature in the historical indifferentiation of its mere availability.

In what sense is it possible, conversely, for anxiety to reveal beings in the sited specificity of their becoming-present in saving withdrawal from objectivity? This question is complicated by the observation that anxiety itself is accompanied by a certain indifference to all things and ourselves (WM 111/101). Yet this indifference, which shatters the self, opens the site of Da-sein as the site of a questioning which rebounds on the questioner to place his or her own being in question. The Nothing is not a general concept: it only happens in questioning and through a community of questioning which I must always make my own: questioning founds a site inasmuch as it holds itself in the openness of Nothing and I take my measure from beings, in their emergence, which happens with the withdrawal of Nothing from entities (WM 105/95). Questioning must allow itself to be grasped by anxiety, thus to be brought before the authentic possibilities of existence (cf. SZ 191/178). But how does anxiety point us back to the differentiated presencing (temporalization) of beings? By revealing beings in the finitude of their sited presencing in the differentiation (*Ent-scheidung*) which questioning itself is. Anxiety has an exceptional disclosive power because it individualizes (SZ 191/178). The spellbound calm (WM 113/102) which belongs to anxiety allows beings to be – that is, come into their differentiated temporalization as presencing-in-withdrawal – in the openness opened up by the situated historicity of questioning Da-sein. In this sense the attunement of anxiety discloses *the possibility of a scientific comportment which attends to the differentiated temporalization of entities,* thus to bring each into its own.

Questioning is the event and founding site of the finitude of the presencing (being) of beings. The passion of science in its service to beings, the comportment of the scientist, the emergence of beings in their essential ownness, constituting one rooted, unitary event, gives the 'scientific existence' of Dasein its 'passionate simplicity and sharpness' (WM 105/95, modified). Heidegger insists that being 'itself' is finite. This implies that science must be founded in the finitude of being – in effect, in the thrownness of Dasein which anxiety discloses (SZ 188/176, 343/315–6). Evidently Heidegger rejects Husserl's recourse, as Dreyfus notes, to the transcendental ego as the source of all intelligibility.[181] Only in the Nothing of Dasein do beings as a whole enter into their 'most proper possibility,' that is, reveal themselves in their finitude (WM 119/108). The radical finitude of authentic science, however, must be founded in a community of questioning. This brings to light not only the existential genesis of science, but also, if only in an incomplete way, the intimate bond between authentic science and Volk, on which Heidegger insists in the Rector's Address.

It is true that the defamiliarization of the everyday context of significance in the attunement of anxiety exposes Dasein in its not-being-at-home, in its *Unheimlichkeit* (SZ 188/176). From an existential-ontological point of view, Heidegger writes, "'*Not-being-at-home*' must be conceived ... as *the more primordial phenomenon*' than the everyday familiarity of our being-in-the-world (SZ 189/177). This reminds us that in bringing the eruption of beings to a stand, thus to give gestalt to a world and the community of knowledge, the Volk must, first, be founded. The founders themselves – in the terms of the *Antigone* commentary of the *Introduction to Metaphysics* – are *apolis*: not-at-home, without a site (GA40 162/152–3). Apparently Heidegger conceived the reconstruction of the University – in 1933, as in 1929 – as the project of founding a site of knowledge as the leadership site of the Volk. In this regard, his point may be elaborated as follows. *The ontological Not of the not-at-home must be given an ontic constitu-*

tion by being sited in the finitude of an historical community. For only in this way can questioning emerge in all its pointedness, to rebound on the questioner. Otherwise, the Not of our finitude would 'function' as the abstraction which in fact spurs and motivates modern science to make the infinite its end. The infinite – the conquest of the earth, of space and time, above all, of death – is, as it were, the unacknowledged 'existential passion' of modern science.

To reiterate a point made earlier, Heidegger cannot mean to reject the international character of scientific 'research' – there cannot be one physics for China and another for America. The question is, however, whether physics shall serve the needs of the community for the sake of which we seek to know, or serve only the end of research for its own sake. Insofar as it serves no end other than itself, it commits itself to the impossible goal of making the infinite its end. Instead of serving a community in its historical and ecological, earth-sited specificity, science attempts to dissimulate its goallessness by claiming to serve a relative abstraction, the abstraction of the 'international scientific community.' In 'The German University,' an address held in August of 1934, Heidegger makes precisely this point: 'Progress of the sciences – discovery on discovery, until an overall view became impossible; growing internationalization of the sciences. This became a cultural value as such. Research for the sake of research, no matter what was being researched, became the fundamental principle' (GA16, no. 155, 296). Heidegger would presumably object to the notion of such an 'international community' on the grounds that it is no community whatsoever, but rather the collective subject of research, and hence defined by a corresponding passion for the infinite. The same objection would apply to the notion that science serves the 'community of mankind' to find its end in the advancement of 'humanity.' For notwithstanding the 'values' to which the Enlightenment appeals, 'humanity,' and the 'research program of science' tend to mutually define each other, and increasingly so, to finally fuse, in Heidegger's terms, in the anti-gestalt of techno-animality. This process becomes all the more self-evident to the degree in which fundamental research is suborned and integrated into technology.

We have seen that the existential 'essence' of science, according to Heidegger, is grounded in our attunement to the being of beings, and in the finitude and historicity of Dasein. It is defined by attention to the modes of temporalization of entities in their sited historicity. Anxiety, as openness to being (No-thing), discloses beings in their withdrawal and differentiated presencing, and thus points to the possibility of an attunement to beings which is attentive to the immanent limit of beings, as that which shelters them from representational transparency and calculability. Therefore the task of leadership to which Heidegger dedicated himself in 1933 consisted pre-eminently in the formation of a new comportment of scientific and philosophical consciousness corresponding to the historicity of being.[182] The Rector's Address is also an attempt to open this site. The comportment that Heidegger aspires to constitutes a rejection of the ideal of 'value-free' science and the rejection of the political system which supports it. It is by no means the case, however, that Heidegger ascribes to the politicization of science. The leadership of philosophy, rather, consists in awakening and guiding a fundamental mood as the space of the intelligibility of the being of beings, for it is out of this space that a renovated comportment to entities and to the communal being of the polity can arise. Science is to be founded in the finitude of being and the historicity of Dasein, and rooted back in the earth as it articulates itself through the being of the diverse peoples of the earth.

3.2.4 Gestalt and Type

It is the evident demand of the writers we have considered that the gestalt of a people be acknowledged as the basis of its political life. The 'holistic' or 'organicist' interpretation of social life to which the thesis of gestalt typically led was susceptible to political appropriation from the democratic left, from the conservative right, and from the racist right. Gestalt theorists and holists of all political persuasions were in fact inclined to draw social and political conclusions from their scientific research, as a contribution to the solution of the ongoing crisis of Weimar Germany and the intellectualist, materialist fragmentation of modern life. As Harrington has shown, gestalt theorists such as Goldstein and Wertheimer were social democrats in politics; Driesch meant vitalism to serve democratic humanism and pacifism; von Uexküll was a conservative elitist, but not a National Socialist; and the Nazis themselves were by no means undeviating holists, for this conflicted with the social Darwinist tendency within the movement.[183] Consequently, the 'politics of gestalt' cannot be reduced to an antidemocratic *Weltanschauung*.

Gestalt expresses the finitude of the inherent, proper measure of a being. 'Measure,' writes Rudolf Kassner, 'is bound to gestalt, and being [Dasein] to the figure [Gesicht].'[184] Kassner opposes the rhythmic unity of thing and world, which grants measure and singularity to a being, to a

system of relations which determines entities as mere points of mediation between positions. The system does not allow beings face (*Gesicht*)
or gestalt;[185] it institutes a 'completely arhythmic, formless world [unge-
stalteten Welt].'[186] One of its purest articulations is Money, understood
as the power of unending circulation effecting the dis-integration and
transformation of beings into Number.[187] The opposition, in Ziegler's
terms, between *Geist* and science corresponds to that between gestalt,
which arises naturally as a form of life, and a scientific or discursive consciousness, which analytically decomposes life into functional combina-
tions.[188] For the conservative authors of this period, liberal democracy
embodies the politics of decomposition. The ground of this judgement,
in turn, is not to be sought primarily in an 'organic' idea of Volk nationalism, nor in the longing for simple solutions and autocratic leadership,[189] but in a positive concept of the perspectival nature of life, and
consequently in an idea of the inherent limitation and self-limitation of
being. In this respect, as in many others, the conservatives and their
ideological successors in the new regime are indebted to Nietzsche. The
level of philosophical sophistication with which the governing idea of
gestalt is thought out varies greatly, but it motivates Krieck and Baeumler
no less than Schmitt and Heidegger. While the claims of Nazi ideologues
are clearly at odds with the Party's racism and imperial program, it is
important to recognize the terms of National Socialism's own self-legiti-
mation, and hence the sources of its initial appeal and wide spectrum of
support. And in this respect, the concepts of self-determination and self-
limitation, as centred in the uniqueness of a form of life, played an essential role.

Thus Baeumler typically rejects the political idea of the French Revolution: he opposes its fundamental sentiment of the 'love' of 'mankind,'
without limit, to the defining sentiment of the Nazi revolution, which
gives Nazi Germany its own internal limit. This sentiment, Baeumler
claims, is the sentiment of honour (*Ehre*): 'the concept of honour, however, as an existential concept, implicates limit, and gestalt, a unity which
can be encompassed, and within which alone honour can flourish' (PE
27–8). Honour is the central ethical category of Rosenberg's *Mythos*. Precisely because the concept of Volk is determined as gestalt and limit, it is
opposed, on this account, to the limitlessness of liberal democracy and
revolution, insofar as both posit one universal subject as the carrier of all
value.

Baeumler's critique of the universal, objectifying subject of modern
thought aims to overcome the dualism of subject and object by founding

the subject in the historicity of the local. Baeumler calls the unity of spirit
and body ('*Geist/Körper*') 'potential' (*Kraft*). To begin political considerations with the concept of *Kraft* means to start with an 'inborn nature
[*Physis*],' rather than with spirit (PE 127–8). *Kraft* is an anti-imperial concept, because it defines the limits and constraints proper to a polity.
'Imperialism means, seen from inside, the breaking free of power
[Machttendenz] from all barriers set by nature, consequently the dissolution of every people's gestalt as brought forth by its inborn nature and
potential [Kraft]' (PE 132). To practice politics in the name of the Volk,
Baeumler concludes, means practicing politics for the sake of measure
and against measurelessness (PE 133).

Baeumler's arguments for a politics of gestalt are allied to the entire
spectrum of conservative thought, from the cultural conservatism of Zeigler and Naumann, to the political theory of Schmitt and the geopolitics
of Karl Haushofer. Heidegger's thought of the early 1930s also implicates
allied claims, as his call for Germany's withdrawal from the League of
Nations, for example, indicates. Heidegger justifies this measure by
appealing to the 'primordial demand laid on every being, that it preserve and save its own nature.' The national will to take responsibility for
itself articulates itself as the will of each people to find and unfold its own
proper determination. And this alone – and not the illusion of a limitless
'brotherhood of mankind' – claims Heidegger, offers the greatest possible surety of peace and mutual respect between peoples. International
community, according to Heidegger, is possible only insofar as each
member unfolds itself within its own inherent limits (GA16, no. 103, 188;
no. 104, 190–1).

In the political opinion of the period, 'limit' may be understood in
economic, as well as in historical and cultural, terms. At the root of these
determinations, however, we find the thesis, most incisively in Heidegger's own works, that 'being' differentiates and articulates itself as the
potential to actualize itself in its self-limitation. This thesis is undoubtedly contradicted by the power politics of the Nazi state. It is nonetheless
significant that the ideological self-justification of National Socialism
took this form, for only on these grounds could Heidegger have reason
to believe that his work shared a fundamental impulse with the ideology
of the movement.

But even aside from the power politics of the regime, Heidegger's
enterprise of transforming the 'Movement' and its discourse from within
is confronted by the philosophical task of *deconstructing the governing metaphysical interpretation of gestalt*, which informs the discourse of the period.

This interpretation is brought to a formula in the following statement of Baldur von Schirach (Youth Leader in the Third Reich): 'Die Organization ist die Gestalt der Weltanschauung' – 'The organization is the gestalt of the world view.'[190] All of the terms of this statement, in this form, are burdened with the heritage of metaphysics and express its consummation in the essence of technology. The challenge of overcoming this metaphysical self-understanding of the 'Movement' proved insurmountable. The distinction between metaphysical 'gestalt' and its deconstructed 'essence' (in Heidegger's sense) marks the closest approach, and the deepest abyss, between Heidegger and neo-conservative, no less than National Socialist, discourse.

In the first instance, type (*Typus*) signifies the tendency of life to manifest itself in the regularity of specific forms. The individual of a species is a variation on the form. Whereas the individual is conceived as an instantiation of the type, the conservatives do not deny the historicity of mankind, nor the freedom of self-formation: the 'type is the law of the self-regulated, ordered constitution of a form through which the power of creation wins a gestalt in the world of appearances.'[191] The *Typus* as such does not appear, does not take gestalt.[192] In the language of Cuvier's comparative anatomy, the type is the function ('form') governing a certain set of manifestations: for example, *respiration in general* is a function of living beings which governs such diverse manifestations as gills and lungs. The function takes gestalt in these manifestations. The biological concept of type, transposed into political discourse by conservative writers, proposes to provide a kind of comparative anatomy of diverse political systems and their cultural manifestations.

This mode of cultural anthropology could undoubtedly take untenable forms once appropriated by the ideologues of the new regime. For example, the psycho-anthropology of E.R. Jaensch identifies a 'French' and 'Jewish' *Typus*, founded in Cartesianism and analytic thinking, and calls for the development of a German counterweight to it, a type rooted in the organic unity of thought and action.[193] Jaensch, who became editor of the *Zeitschrift für Psychologie* in 1933 and chair of the German Society for Psychology in 1936, emerged as one of the most aggressive antagonists of gestalt theory after 1933, and attempted to supplant it with his own brand of anti-Semitic holism.[194] While still his colleague at Marburg Heidegger remarks of him in a letter to Jaspers (19 May 1925) that Jaensch's philosophy is 'even too primitive for primary school teachers.'[195]

The anthropology of Jaensch offers an extreme example of related but more plausible positions. Every political form of life (including democracy), Ziegler claims, has its particular style, based on a certain historical-existential *Typus*, or type. The concept of type echoes Plato's theory of Forms, as Jünger's recourse to the discourse of type also shows. Nonetheless the concept of type, as used in conservative discourse, owes more to Nietzsche than to Plato: the type, as the lodestar of national self-expression and development, is the posited ideal of a world view, and open to re-conceptualization. 'Type' designates a focus of value posited by a perspective. The 'style' of modern democracy – implicating a capitalist economy, the subordination of the social to technical relations, and the predominance of discursive or analytic forms of thought – is based on the triumph of functional relations. This style, in turn, is held to be the expression of a new 'type' which is 'the historical basis of the system' of discursivity and nomad money.[196] In certain respects, Ziegler's thesis holds much in common with Weber's analysis of the protestant ethic and its relation to the capitalist 'type.'

In Ziegler's case, moreover, the characterization of liberalism is free of anti-Semitism, for he argues that the latter deceives itself by misconceiving cause and effect. The Jewish diaspora is not the cause of nomad money; nomad money rather has its roots in the nominalism of the Middle Ages, which signals the triumph of logical relations over the real.[197] 'Whereas the unmediated consciousness of life allows the phenomena of the world to take shape in the living gestalt, the discursive consciousness [das verwissenschaftlichte Bewusstsein] of the European, by contrast, fundamentally dissolves all form into relations of equal parts – it disintegrates the gestalt,' breaks its wholeness down and generates an equation of analytical relations.[198]

Under these conditions of the thorough-going rationalization of life and the reduction of the social to 'economic functions' and statistic regularities, how can an authentic sense of Volk still be revived?[199] Through originary rites and cultic dance and theatre, Ziegler answers.[200] This response seems disconcertingly simple and naive. Evidently Ziegler claims that Volk comes to be in its concrete historicity in works and forms of enactment, not in the analytic relations of economic transactions, nor in forms of political re-presentation. Volk happens in the immediacy of the presentation of a non-present totality in the 'typical' instance. For this reason, theatre in all its forms is given an archetypal significance which carries over from conservative discourse into the practice of the Third Reich. In the cultic dance of Mary Wigman, for example, the personality of the dancer, concealed by the mask, fuses with the *typical*, which is expressed by the mask: mask, dancer, and the space opened by the dance compose one gestalt, for each comes to be only in the performance of the dance.[201] The sense of the necessity of embodied form as living expression of the Volk was widely shared in writings on theatre and dance. According to Raschke (1936), the new drama of the Third Reich aspires to an 'archaic world view' wherein 'the body will once again be a witness of the soul, wherein all dualism is overcome and humanity meets fellow mankind among the same gods.'[202]

The type is conceived as the expression of the unity of the whole in its individual instantiation.[203] Benn conceives a new type of being embodied in 'mythic and racial continuity' as the proper response to the dead end of 'intellectualism,' and the disintegration of life and substance into mere function, which intellectualism represents. Mythic and racial consciousness expresses itself in forms of embodiment, not in concepts, definitions. Although Heidegger avoids the language of *Typus* as thoroughly entangled in metaphysics, it is evident that the question to which the call for a new type responds also motivates his thought. In its simplest form this question may be formulated as follows, as conceived in terms proper to the conservative revolution, no less than to Heidegger: How can the analytic disintegration of being be overcome?

Heidegger's response to this question aims to open a site to allow entities and our own being a stability which is nothing merely formal, nothing merely imposed by regularities of social and technical discourse, but inherent in beings themselves, and proper to each kind of being. Where the conservative revolution calls for a new *Typus*, Heidegger appeals, as we have seen, to the stability of a comportment articulated in response to the eventuation of being in beings, and in this sense, a response to the finitude and sited historicity of being. The *Typus* is an ideal of value posited by a perspective. Heidegger anticipates a comportment which holds to the differentiated disclosure of being, and thus takes responsibility for beings. I will reserve further consideration of the question of *Gestalt* and *Typus* for my discussion of Heidegger and Jünger.

3.2.5 Volk Embodied, Enacted

Along with other authors of this period, Ziegler holds that a Volk comes to be in pre-discursive enactment and in the incorporation of works, rites, and cultic theatre. Baeumler makes the same argument in his *Bachofen und Nietzsche* (1929), specifying that only what has been pre-reflectively founded and articulated in religious rites, and in the customs of a people, discloses the depths of reality.[204] The Volk 'is' as ritual enactment, it does not have its being as Idea or substance 'behind' the phenomena. Theatre should incorporate ritual community, not a naturalistic representation of action.[205] The economic arrangements of labour are also forms of the ritual enactment of the unity of the Volk. This concept of work is appropriated by National Socialism. The idea of the Nazi state as a 'workers' state,' which has sublated distinctions of class and status in favour of the unity of the people, articulates the first order of 'embodiment' and enactment. It is an idea to which Heidegger, as the Rector's Address and other documents testify, gives his assent.

More precisely, Heidegger holds that 'the *essence* of work [will] now determine, from the ground up, the Dasein of humanity' (GA16, no. 108, 205; my emphasis). The 'essence' (*Wesen*) of work is 'spirit' (*Geist*), in the sense that every 'working,' transforming encounter with the things themselves should be guided by knowledge of the being of the thing. The things themselves limit and shape the character of work, and work, in turn, 'embodies' itself in production (GA16, no. 125, 238–9). In *Being and Time*, Heidegger argues that Dasein's transcendence is always already 'embodied,' in the sense of taking its being from the practices which constitute our being-in-the-world. Since these practices, moreover, are not mediated by 'self-referential mental content,'[206] they themselves actualize the space of Dasein's coming back to itself as 'body.' Our way of involvement with different kinds of equipment, for example, would allow different modes of corporality to emerge – to use an example of Heidegger's, the corporality of the typewriter is quite distinct from that of the pen (GA54, 125–6). Given this understanding of corporality, it is possible to extrapolate consequences for the 'social ontology' of the workplace and for the significance Heidegger attaches to labour service: the repetitive motion of 'individuals' working on the assembly line, for example, must articulate a different kind of corporality, and of *Mitdasein*, than the team assembly of a product. If this is true, and if it follows from Heidegger's understanding of corporality and *Mitsein*, then the philosopher's support of the social re-construction of labour, in the addresses of 1933–4, is founded in a fundamental decision deriving from his essential thought.

The theoretical attitude is an abstraction from our everyday involvement with and comportment to entities and others. The spiritual work of the 'intellectual' only deserves emphasis insofar as it engages more deeply the 'necessities of the historical being of a people' (GA16, no. 125, 239). Work receives its highest determination as the history-founding encounter of a people with the sources of its own being. Work is rooted in its spiritual source insofar as it attends to the differentiation of being and engages it. This engagement is the enactment of thought, through which a Volk has the possibility of being itself, of 'embodying' itself. Heidegger's *Logik* of 1934 offers a discussion of work which I will consider in detail below.

Embodiment and enactment as ways of being forge the link between race and Volk. This is illustrated by Baeumler's definition of race: the word *race* denotes the limitation and the 'circuit of possibilities' offered by heredity and life (BG 62–3). 'Life' has to be thought in its historicity. Baeumler insists that race is not a biological concept (*Naturbegriff*). Race rather incorporates 'ways of comportment' (*Verhaltungsweisen*): a 'dynamic unity of breath and rhythm, a centre of action and reaction governed by a specific comportment,' which *maintains itself over generations* (BG 66). The function of education is to awaken and transmit a way of comportment, especially as founded in the body, in breath, in rhythmic dance, speech, and choral song, for herein 'humanity manifests and expresses itself, in an unmediated way, as a self-creative racial being' (BG 70). Baeumler explicitly rejects the Enlightenment approach to race as an object of supposedly scientific study, for this abstracts from 'the unmediated actuality' of race as the principle of the transformation of the life of a people (BG 71). As opposed to this tendency to abstraction, immediacy articulates itself, for example, in the communal rites of the festival as the experience of the fundamental rhythm of life of a people (BG 71–2). Rainer Schlösser, *Reichsdramaturg* and head of the Propaganda Ministry's theatre department after 1935,[207] held associated views on the function of theatre: it is to incorporate – in dance, music, and word – the ritual, communal space of the people, thus to found a common mythic consciousness. Communal unity derives from the participatory embodiment of a common life-rhythm.[208]

The *embodiment* of an ideal of value is particularly emphasized by Clauss, whose works hold the ideological centre under the new regime: value articulates itself in a particular style of being, including the expression and comportment of the body.[209] The differences between races, Clauss holds, 'are differences of style, not of qualities [of being].'[210] It is significant that the subtitle Clauss gives his book reads *Eine Einführung in den Sinn der Leiblichen Gestalt* (An Introduction to the Meaning of Corporal Form).

But writers and artists by no means committed to the dogmas of National Socialism, such as Mary Wigman and Ludwig Klages, among many others, insist that national life incorporates itself in forms of bodily expression; and of these, pre-eminently in dance, theatre, and music. In her *Deutsche Tanzkunst* (The German Art of Dance) (1935), Wigman appeals to the unity of art and life, 'the inner fusion of vision and gestalt, the organic interaction of idea and act,' to create a dance form, and a new theatre, which will generate not just an audience but a quasi-religious community of the Volk.[211]

The concept of a *common rhythm of social cohesion* is by no means exclusive to German conservatism and National Socialism, however. As Margot L. Lyon notes, the relation between the body, embodiment, and social practices which serves to generate a collective or communal rhythm has won recognition by social anthropologists such as Mauss, Durkheim, and Plessner. These studies have been taken up by contemporary anthropology and purport to show that 'social life has rhythmic properties. Rhythm in this sense is a form of temporal patterning grounded in both biological and social functions. It is a property of structures, not an entity in itself.'[212] If this is true, it would help us to understand the conservative and National Socialist emphasis on the rhythmic embodiment of the 'body politic' as an attempt to found the Volk and the state in pre-discursive orders of meaning.

Although it is undoubtedly true, as Klaus Vondung argues, that the idea of theatre and ritual community the National Socialists propagated was intended to support the ideological aims of the regime,[213] the sources of the new sense of ritual embodiment emerging between 1918 and 1933 were too diverse to be accredited solely or even primarily to the cultural politics of the Nazis. Writing in *Rhythmus* in 1936, Werner Deubel claims that the meaning of the German revolution of 1933 realizes itself in the overthrow of the idols of intellectualism and the rebirth of the earthborn soul.[214] The opposition of *Seele* (soul) to the intellectualizing tendency of *Geist* (spirit), which Deubel posits, draws on Klages among others, and clearly pre-dates 1933. The expressionist dance of Wigman, for example, sought official confirmation after 1933 but did not originate with the ideological imperatives of the new order,[215] nor did Heidegger's appeal to destiny and the ritual enactment of community.

The *official* model of National Socialist theatre may well be derived from the civil religion of revolutionary France and therefore from the attempt to create a new collective subject of experience, as Vondung claims.[216] Heidegger's critique of the regime after 1933 clearly rejects the attempt to 'organize' a new intensity of communal experience (*Erlebnis*) from above (GA65, 131–8). Heidegger's understanding of being, as articulated, differentiated, and embodied, resists organization, for the 'organized' functions as the representation of subjectivity. What Heidegger sought – in vain, insofar as the ideological objectives of the regime are concerned – were forms of embodiment in breath, word, in song, theatre, and dance, which might in-corporate the temporality and historicity of our Da-sein. Egon Vietta, for example, a student of Heidegger's Freiburg lectures of the late twenties,[217] developed an historical critique of dance which is remarkably close to Heidegger's thought. In *Der Tanz: Eine Kleine Metaphysik* (Dance: A Short Metaphysics) of 1938, Vietta offers an account of classical ballet as the realization of Cartesian metaphysics and the *homme machine*, and the dance of the Greek chorus, conversely, as the embodied service of the divine. The epochs of dance are epochs of the articulation of being in the very pulse and breath of life.[218] What is at stake, for Heidegger, in all these forms of enactment and embodiment, is the actualization of being (*ousia*) as *energeia*, therefore as situated temporality, or *Vollzug*, of Da-sein. Heidegger did not, by this, commit himself to the triumph of aesthetics or of the theatrical over the political in the Third Reich. In fact, in recognition of the metaphysical significance of the theatrical in the new Reich, the *Beiträge* offers a critique of the 'staging' of the real (GA65 347/243). The theatrical belongs to the 'age of the world picture' and heralds the representation of beings to and for collective subjectivity. Heidegger's understanding of Dasein as defined by *Befindlichkeit*, conversely, is an attempt to retrieve our 'embodied' being. In Heidegger's *Logik* of 1934, as we shall see below, the Volk is understood as a structure of temporality unified and articulated by its fundamental attunement (*Grundstimmung*) or determination (*Bestimmung*). Inasmuch as this determination modulates the Volk's encounter with beings it constitutes the 'embodiment' of Volk.

3.2.6 Conclusion

Based on this brief consideration of the hermeneutic situation of the Rector's Address, and of public opinion relevant to Heidegger's situation in 1933, it is possible to isolate a number of claims and presuppositions, either of the conservatives or of the nominal National Socialists, to which Heidegger is liable to have been sympathetic. It is evident that Heidegger's political allegiance favoured the conservatives. In common with them, especially in the still fluid political atmosphere which defined the period between 30 January 1933 and 30 June 1934, Heidegger evidently expected a revolutionary transformation of German life. The chancellorship of Hitler, the triumph of National Socialism over the

Republic, was conceived by those supportive of a conservative revolution as the inauguration of that revolution, not as its final destination.[219] The thesis of von Klemperer, that the conservatives' rejection of the Republic left them with no choice other than the support of a dictatorship, rests on the assumption that conservative thought had no positive content or alternative to offer. The conservative revolution, as the expression of 'cultural despair,' finally exhausted itself in the affirmation of dictatorship for its own sake.[220] According to Zimmerman, Heidegger was drawn to Hitler by the same longing for authoritarian leadership and radical, but 'reactionary,' solutions to the crisis of modernism.[221]

I have argued, however, that Heidegger's understanding of the differentiation of being is incompatible with totalitarian politics. This also excludes the thesis of Julian Young, who argues that Heidegger's antimodern politics implicitly support *völkisch* totalitarianism – in the style of Pol Pot, no less.[222] Young's basic thesis is that in 1933 Heidegger attached himself to the 'ideas of 1914,' which, according to Young, still dominated the conservative Right in 1933. The ideas of 1914 were originally represented by writers such as Mann, Scheler, and Sombart, who attempted to justify the exclusivity of the German tradition in its opposition to the West. Yet Mohler and Sonntheimer, for example, demonstrate that the conservative revolutionaries, from Moeller to Jünger and Niekisch, rejected the restorative politics of the old conservatives and sought a revolutionary solution. Insofar as Heidegger's political allegiance can be specified, he identified himself with the national and social idea of Volk and state represented by the revolutionary conservatives, not with an ideal of German 'spirituality' (*Innerlichkeit*) as represented by the ideas of 1914. Young's conflation of the ideas of 1914 with radical racialism is even more questionable: he argues that conservative defenders of Germany in 1914 and in 1933 favoured an anti-modern, totalitarian *völkisch* state. According to Young, Max Scheler and the Himmler-Darré faction end up favouring the same agrarian ideology. Having proposed that Heidegger belongs to this ideological stream, Young ascribes to him a program of de-urbanization, resettlement, and conquest.[223] Certainly Heidegger and the conservative revolutionaries were critical of industrialization, and of Marxism no less than of democracy: this led them to seek a 'third way.' But this does not allow their identification with the racialists, with the Nazis, nor with a policy of de-urbanization. In the tradition of conservatism, the independent peasant, or yeoman farmer, represents an ideal of value, a model of self-sufficiency, political stability, virtue, and rootedness. This ideal of value is supported by a political philosophy which runs from Aristotle to Thomas Jefferson and beyond. But even Darré's program of encouraging a new peasant elite never proposed to offer a practical alternative to industrial society. Heidegger's attachment to this ideal cannot support Young's claim. Nor does Heidegger, despite his questioning of the metaphysical provenance of technology, ever call for a 'rejection of modern, industrial technology' in favour of a Volk dictatorship.[224] In fact, in 1933, Heidegger presupposed the possibility of a 'genuine technology,' which, rooted in the will to know of the Volk, as constituted by the state, would liberate nature (GA16, no. 75, 200–1).

In common with conservative revolutionaries such as Jünger and Freyer, Heidegger sought a national and social revolution capable of integrating technology into the community to serve its goals. Consequently, in his political addresses of 1933–4, Heidegger recognizes the priority of the Volk. Young argues that this implicates the subjection of the individual to the collective, as personified in the will of the *Führer*.[225] Young confuses, however, the concept of *individualism* with the value of the individual, with selfhood. Sontheimer's conclusion, that the radical-conservative concept of 'freedom' exhausts itself in proclaiming the dissolution of individual liberties in favour of the unity of the whole, rests on the same misconception.[226] The modern notion of individualism in political philosophy descends from Hobbes and Locke: the state derives from the contract of radically autonomous 'individuals' in the 'state of nature.' This genealogy of the state is evidently rejected by conservative thinkers. They also reject the values associated with the rational, self-constructing 'individual' that liberal theory posits. It by no means follows, however, that they despise the ontological value of individuality. The values on which conservative discourse proposes to found the state – spirituality, community, honour, self-sacrifice – are only possible as the values of highly motivated individuals.[227] Totalitarian subjection of the individual to an alien will would render appeal to these values meaningless. The terms of Heidegger's analytic of Dasein – conscience, authenticity, the dialogue of a generation with its tradition – are equally at odds with the abandonment of responsibility for one's selfhood. It is true that Heidegger acknowledges Hitler's right to lead; yet, in Heidegger's view, as well as in that of the Young Conservatives, the right to lead is contingent on leading well, hence also on an acknowledgment of the autonomous selfhood of the followers.

The abyss between the conservative revolution that Heidegger supported and the reality of National Socialism led Edgar J. Jung, like many other conservatives, into the opposition at a time, however, when it was too late to be effective. Author of von Papen's famous address to the students of Marburg, delivered on 17 June 1934, Jung hoped to crystallize resistance to Hitler: 'They call freedom a liberal concept, whereas in reality it is an old Germanic concept. They attack equality before the judge, denouncing it as a liberal degeneration, whereas in reality it is the basis for every just verdict. These people suppress that very fundament of state which at all times, not only in liberal ones, has been called justice. Their attacks are directed against the security and freedom of the private sphere of life.'[228] The state must be the highest guarantor of the rule of law. Statecraft consists in giving the state stable form, not in revolutionary dynamism without end. Jung repeated his faith in the spiritual mission of Germany in Europe. The murder of Jung by the SS on 30 June 1934 marked the effective end of the revolutionary conservative option, and any possibility it ever had of changing the course of the new regime. This was also evident to Heidegger: writing in 1945, he justifies the rectorship of 1933 on the grounds that he hoped to save and strengthen the 'positive possibilities' evident to him in the Movement at that time (SU 26/486). This was the common conviction of those conservatives who did not reject the chancellorship of Hitler out of hand in January 1933. But, following the events of 30 June 1934, 'anyone who after that still assumed an administrative office in the university was in a position to know beyond the shadow of a doubt, with whom he was bargaining' (SU 40/499).

In the course of these reflections, I have attempted to isolate a number of positive theses, common to the conservative movement, and implicated by Heidegger's philosophy, which go far beyond a mere rejection of democracy, and which cannot be assimilated to a facile affirmation of dictatorship. These are as follows:

(1) As the Schlageter eulogy of May 1933 shows, Heidegger, in common with many Germans who were by no means committed to the dogmas of Nazism, had come to regard National Socialism as an *anti-imperialist national liberation movement*, opposed to the shackles of the Versailles system of territorial annexation and financial extortion.[229] To hold this view does not necessarily implicate the anti-Semitic thesis of an international Jewish conspiracy encompassing capitalism and Bolshevism. It does imply rejection of the second-class, semi-colonial status of Germany, as inscribed by Versailles and the capitalist world order (GA16, no. 66).[230]

(2) Not only was Weimar Germany the client state of the post-war system – and hence suspect – but the liberal, capitalistic state as such is deemed to be alienated from the sources of life, and therefore incapable of *restoring the dignity of work and social justice.*

(3) Nor is liberalism capable of *preserving what is essential and proper to the nation.* The dream of liberalism, according to Moeller van den Bruck, is 'the great International, in which the differences of peoples and languages, races and cultures will be obliterated.'[231] In a harshly worded letter of 25 June 1933, Heidegger concurs, denouncing the neo-Kantian Hönigswald on the grounds that neo-Kantianism is a form of liberalism. The 'free-floating consciousness' of liberalism aims to uproot historically founded existence, in favour of a homogenous world culture (GA16, no. 65, 132). Thus Heidegger proposes to justify Germany's exit from the League of Nations by appealing to the responsibility every people has of preserving its own nature (*Wesen*). This claim cannot be understood, of course, unless one recalls the prevalent conviction of most Germans, both right and left, that the League merely served the interests of Versailles imperialism (GA16, nos. 103–4). More significantly, along with the conservatives, Heidegger committed himself to the idea of a uniquely German 'third way': he defined this in his own terms, certainly, to give the Germans an epochal mission in the overcoming of Western metaphysics.

The very concept of Volk, moreover, implicates the historical singularity of every people. Heidegger accepts this view, and in turn rejects the Enlightenment metanarrative of universal reason to which the idea of Volk is opposed. Commenting on Herder in lectures of 1919, Heidegger claims that Herder saw 'the independent self-worth of every nation, every age ... Historical reality was no longer seen exclusively in a schematic–rule-bound, rationalistic–linear direction of progress ... The goal of progress is also no longer an abstract, rational happiness and goodness ... There awakens the view for individual, qualitatively original centres of reality and contexts of reality; the categories of "ownness" [Eigenheit] become meaningful and related to all shapes of life' (GA56/57, 133–4). [232]

(4) The necessity of a new *sitedness and earth-rootedness of political thought* founded in the idea of the Volk follows from this. According to the Young Conservative critique of the liberal West, true 'self-determination' consists in each people's discovery of its own proper potential and path

of development. The rationalistic, utilitarian presuppositions of liberalism are alien to the German tradition, the young conservatives argue. The Volk, however, 'is' as a movement of being defined by historicity, not by an unchanging essence. The unity of the *Reich*, as the articulation of Germany's historical *Stämme*, is to derive from the common attunement of a Volk, and this expresses itself in a style or comportment of being, but by no means in the kind of centralization and *Gleichschaltung* which would actually develop after 1933.

(5) Consequently the necessity also arises of *siting science in the genuine needs of the community*. According to Hans Heyse, for example, the task of philosophy in the University is to restore the unity of 'spirit and life, idea, and existence' in order to overcome the problems of excessive specialization and alienation from the Volk community.[233] Heidegger is prepared to grant the conservatives that science must be rooted in our 'life-world,' but evidently departs from them radically in his interpretation of how our life and being are constituted. This is only possible, in Heidegger's terms, by recovering the *site of truth*. The crisis of science consists in its alienation from the event of the differentiation of being in beings. This crisis is the occasion of necessary decisions, such as offer the potential of releasing new possibilities for human existence.

(6) Both Volk and State are defined in terms of their *inherent limits, as articulated by the potential proper to them*. In 'The German Student as Worker' (26 November 1933), Heidegger proposes,

> What happens when the Volk comes to be as State [Staatwerdung des Volkes]? These powers, nature, history, art, technology, the state itself, are *accomplished* and in this accomplishment *set into* their limits. And thus *that* becomes disclosed, which makes a Volk secure, brightly shining, and strong. But disclosure of these powers is the essence of *truth* [Wesen der *Wahrheit*]. (GA16, no. 108, 201)

The fundamental powers of existence are 'accomplished' by being set in their limits (*Grenzen*). The state itself is set in its limits, actualized as the con-stitution (*Gefüge*) of the will to primordial knowledge. Accomplishment can only signify entering into the proper limit, or *peras*. In 'On the Essence of Truth' (1930), Heidegger had written that the 'essence of truth is freedom' (WW 183/123). Freedom 'is engagement in the disclosure of beings as such,' thus to 'let beings be as the beings which they

are' (WW 186, 185/126, 125). Letting be is the recognition and accomplishment of the being of the limit proper to each being. If the state is
the constitution which 'awakens and binds' these powers (GA16, 200),
these powers, in turn, understood as the differentiation of being, must
bind the state. Otherwise the will to know would be bound to the will of
the state, and Volk and science would become its politicized instruments.
If an authentic will to know 'sets the measure' to determine what is worth
knowing, and not worth knowing, and if this knowledge, in turn, 'sets the
limits' of genuine questioning, then the state must also be subject to a
questioning which binds its being to the accomplishment of being as the
limit in self-limiting beings. It is a measure of Heidegger's self-deception
that precisely the opposite came to be, with the progressive unfolding of
the nature of the regime.

Heidegger's understanding of being, particularly as evidenced in his
interpretation of Aristotle, conditions his reading of Volk and state and
constitutes the most evident link to the revolutionary rhetoric of the new
regime. *The concept of the self-limitation of being is Heidegger's most fundamental 'political' thesis, and the basis of his understanding of Volk, state, and technology.*

(7)   The *potential of Volk and state takes gestalt* to embody itself in works and
rituals, in social and technical organization, and in the enactment of the
responsibility of leadership. We recall that in Max Müller's account, for
Heidegger 'everything always revolved around the figure [Gestalt] ... He
did not think abstract values or norms but definite figures one could follow and comprehend were committing. The figure, or shape, that a
nation [Volk] must assume is the work. And this shape must be, on the
one hand, characteristic of the nation, but, on the other, the contradiction subjectivity-objectivity dissolves in it. It is our shape yet still objective
shape.'[234] In the meantime the truth and import of this statement have
emerged more clearly.

Finally, Heidegger's opposition to the core of Nazi ideology can be easily summarized. He rejects the concept of the state as a technical enterprise guided by a *Weltanschauung,* and with it, the primacy of the world
view as such. The imperial tendency of the new regime also falls under
Heidegger's critique, as at odds with the fundamental principle of the
self-limiting nature of every potential for being, including Volk and state
conceived as potentials. The primacy of the world view grants discursive

thought 'leadership' in the 'organization' of political life, and the life of the Volk, which cannot be reconciled with Heidegger's commitment to the thesis that being articulates itself in the singularity of beings. For this thesis follows from the deconstruction of 'being' understood as a set of transcendental categories. These categories, conversely, found the concepts from which discursive thought derives.

Biologically based interpretations of Volk presuppose the collectivity of a 'subject,' in this case one supposedly founded in material nature, which contradicts Heidegger's critique of subjectivity and his commitment to the historicity of Dasein. As opposed to Baeumler, who holds that the proper approach to the political is anthropological (BG 64), Heidegger proposes to begin with the articulation of being in Da-sein. The unfolding of the question of being, moreover, stipulates that knowledge be determined by this question, and not by the perspective of a Volk or of a race, as Krieck claims.

Since Heidegger, by all evidence, is philosophically opposed to anti-Semitism, his willingness to work with the new regime can only be explained by the mistaken expectation that the serious and 'authentic' core of National Socialism might be liberated from the dominance of the anti-Semitic ideologues. This expectation reflects an attunement to the crisis of nihilism, which however distinctive to Heidegger, was nonetheless allied to that of his 'generation.' As late as 1935, as we know from *An Introduction to Metaphysics*, he still believed in 'the inner truth and greatness of National Socialism.' This 'truth' evidently consisted, for Heidegger, in a confrontation with being – and as such, with the essence of technology – as it differentiates itself in the myriad forms of modern life. In Heidegger's conception of 1933, the dis-integration of the being of beings calls for a political revolution as the actualization of thought.

Heidegger's appropriation of the heritage of Luther, no less than that of Aristotle, insists on the enactment of being, and on being-as-actualization, in Da-sein's subjection to and transformation of its situation.[235] Heidegger's explicitly 'political' turn of 1933 presupposes his conviction that the new regime opens a space for the actualization of being in beings – and this means the opening of a site for the transformation of the essence of technology. Only such a site could save beings in their 'essence.'

The Rector's Address, as well as Heidegger's other public interventions of this period, therefore constitutes an intervention in the public sphere: its object is to turn public opinion in the direction of authenticity by arousing a more fundamental and authentic attunement to the crisis of the disintegration of 'form.' In this way, Heidegger evidently hoped to build a bridge between his understanding of nihilism (the abandonment of beings by being, *Seinsverlassenheit*) and the 'public' interpretation of this crisis on the conservative and National Socialist Right.

4 Volk, Work, and Historicity in Heidegger's *Logik* of 1934

The critical discussion of Heidegger's understanding of Volk has tended to re-inscribe Volk into the metaphysics of collective subjectivity.[1] I propose to challenge this interpretation by reference to *Being and Time* and, in particular, to Heidegger's *Logik als Frage nach dem Wesen der Sprache*, lectures delivered in the summer of 1934, shortly after his resignation of the rectorship. The editor of this volume, Günter Seubold, indicates, in his postscript to the text, that the *Logik* replaced the course Heidegger had originally announced for the summer, entitled 'Der Staat und die Wissenschaft' (The State and Science). We may expect that the state is also at issue in the *Logik*. My commentary will specify how the *Logik* serves to unfold a structure of temporality as the essential 'constitution' of the concept of Volk. To anticipate this task, a brief consideration of the aim and structure of these lectures is necessary.

The object of these lectures is to show that historicity is the specific kind of motion which is proper to, and constituent of, the being of a Volk. The lectures intend to deconstruct traditional logic by bringing to light its derivation from the metaphysics of presence. Heidegger's account begins with the question of logic and closes with the question of language. The way to language is won by turning to the being who speaks, who 'has' language. This turn allows the question of Volk to be raised, for the self that speaks, as Heidegger had already argued in *Being and Time*, is constituted as *Mitsein*, not as an isolated, self-present, and self-reflective subject. The nature of what Volk is, in turn, can only be brought to clarity through a deconstruction of its metaphysical determinations by uncovering the structure of primordial, ecstatic temporality and historicity which determines the sitedness of Dasein. This structure implicates, as we shall see, a view of *Volk-sein* as (*i*) a movement of withdrawal from objectification; and as such (*ii*) the enactment of the differentiation and finitude of being in the encounter with beings through work; (*iii*) an enactment through work founded in the stability and unity of a comportment; and (*iv*) a comportment articulating *Mitdasein* as the site of the differentiated disclosure of being in its historicity. This site is permeated by the Not of the withdrawal from representation.

4.1 Volk as Movement of Withdrawal from Objectification

The Volk is a way of the movement of being: it signifies the movement of withdrawal from all forms of objectification and calculation. Of the forms of motion proper to the various realms of being (lifeless nature, life, and Dasein), historicity, or the happening of history, is the kind of motion proper to Volk. In *Sein und Zeit*, section 74, Heidegger argues that the 'happening' of *Mitsein*, arising out of the appropriation of the possibilities of a heritage, occurs as the *Geschick* 'of the community, of a people' (SZ 384/352). Vetter raises the question as to why Heidegger moves from the temporality of Dasein to that of the community (*Gemeinschaft*) and the Volk, thereby neglecting the common temporality of society (*Gesellschaft*) as constitutive of Dasein. In Vetter's terms, not only does Heidegger conceive of society as a 'merely deficient modus' of being 'subordinated' to a romantic conception of community, but Heidegger's appeal to Volk derives less from 'phenomenological necessity,' hence from an eye to the things themselves, than from 'ideological prejudice.'[2] Fritsche has recently restated this position in the most extreme terms, claiming that Heidegger wants to expel not only the inauthentic They-self of our social being from the ideal community, but to eliminate social and racial 'others.'[3]

In the first instance, Heidegger's understanding of the Volk community, *as a structure of enacted temporality,* in no way implies a policy of racial exclusion, for Volk as the enactment of Dasein's historicity cannot be defined racially. The They-self (SZ 130/122), belongs, moreover, to the structure of Dasein – it will always be an integral, existential part of *Mitsein*. Consequently it is not possible, in the existential analytic, to designate 'society' (*Gesellschaft*) as inauthentic and oppose it to 'community' (*Gemeinschaft*) as authentic and to argue that the two social forms correspond to, and derive from, the existential structure of Dasein as constituted by authenticity and inauthenticity. Our Dasein in the most consummate *Gemeinschaft* will be constituted by inauthenticity no less than by authenticity. It is a further misconception to hold that *Gerede*, as

inauthentic, belongs to the inauthenticity of society and could be elimi-
nated, as it were, from authentic communal intercourse.[4] Fritsche is
wrong to argue that section 74 implies a 'Rightist' political philosophy of
submission, and that it implicates a call to return to an 'authentic' state
of being in the Volk community.[5] Understood as the already-said and the
articulated weight of our heritage in us, *Gerede* is integral to the *logos* of
Dasein.

Volk and community are categories of self-responsibility and authenticity (ownness). In *Being and Time* the question of the Volk emerges
from a discussion of being-toward-death and the thrown, finite transcendence of Dasein as a being delivered over in responsibility to its possibilities for being (SZ 384/351–2). Because Dasein takes up the possibilities –
not the actualities, however modified – of the tradition, this excludes
Dasein's submission to 'fate,' as well as the mere revitalization of the past.
The act of taking-up and actualizing a possibility for being implies a
founding moment, such as opens a site for the presencing of being in
beings. Mark Blitz raises the question as to how a particular authentic
possibility of Dasein gains factical priority over others. We may reply that
founding Dasein in the limit of its historicity, and thus setting beings
themselves into their inherent limits, determines which of Dasein's
authentic possibilities are 'more choiceworthy than another.'[6] The central issue of Heidegger's political philosophy, as implicated by *Sein und
Zeit* and other texts, is not the authenticity or inauthenticity of a political
or social form – the issue is finitude and the power of the inherent limit,
as opposed to formlessness and limitlessness.

This comes to word in *Sein und Zeit*, as the question of wholeness. Consequently, introducing the question of history in section 72, Heidegger
writes as follows: 'Temporality was set forth with regard to the authentic
potentiality-of-being-a-whole of Dasein' (SZ 372/341). And in section 74
(to which Fritsche devotes great attention), Heidegger adds that 'the
interpretation of the historicity of Da-sein turns out to be basically just a
more concrete development of temporality' (SZ 382/350). The question
of historicity, therefore, will in its own turn be a more concrete elaboration of Dasein's potentiality for wholeness: it is in these terms that the
questions of Volk and community arise in section 74. Heidegger raises
the question of Volk, in effect, to demonstrate that Dasein actualizes its
wholeness by way of its communal *Mitsein* and its historicity in belonging
to a Volk. In the wholeness of Dasein, the inherent limit of Dasein, such
as gives it its stability and ability to be, is at issue. The questions of Volk
and *Gemeinschaft* arise as reflections on the wholeness of Dasein, on the

possibility of an 'internal' limit inherent in the social constitution of *Mit-dasein*. If the internal limit of Dasein is being-toward-death, then the internal limit of the authentic historicity of our communal being is the historicity and finitude of our earth-sited being. Admittedly this equation is not entirely developed in *Sein und Zeit*, inasmuch as the 'earth' is not an issue.

Limit – as opposed to formlessness – is the implicit criterion of Heidegger's evaluation of social and political regimes. Community and Volk implicate the finitude and delimitation of a sited, earth-situated humanity, in ways the universality of society does not. This universality derives from the subject's theoretically unlimited power to enter into association and contract with any other subject. In the Hölderlin lectures of 1934–5 (GA39), Heidegger claims that community, as opposed to society, is founded in 'the already existing, binding relation of every individual to that which elevates each beyond himself and thus binds and determines' (GA39, 72). In common with the rhetoric of the conservative right, Heidegger alludes to the community of the front, which arose as a community in the face of a common death and common sacrifice (GA16, no. 154, 279). Death and sacrifice individualize and bind each in advance to something which transcends the contractual will of self-reliant subjects. The front community, however, is hardly intended as a factical ideal: it rather points to the possibility of community as arising out of the finite transcendence and common task and mission of a people. The experience of the front must be internalized and 'spiritualized' in the community of work (GA16, no. 155, 299–304). Volk as a temporal structure articulates the mutual implication of the specificity of a call to be – to take up the finite possibilities of a particular heritage – and the responsibility to be authentically, by entering into the limit set by historicity.

Following *Being and Time*, in the *Logik* of 1934 Heidegger conceives the motion proper to Dasein as its thrown finite transcendence. In the *Logik*, as this motion is unfolded as historicity, it becomes the ecstatic span of a duration of being-open and responsive to the being of beings ('ein in sich ausgesetzt-entrückt-erstreckendes') (GA38, 159). In being '*ausgesetzt*' (at the mercy of, exposed to), as Heidegger intimates, it becomes the thrownness proper to the determination of a Volk in the face of its tradition and mission. The motion of Volk consists in its retrieval of its thrownness in the projection of a future, thus to open a space for the emergence of the presence of beings in the present. The ecstatic unity of the three dimensions of time is the condition of the stability of a subject and the fixation of objects. Heidegger argues that the concept of Volk implicates no less than the deconstruction of the contractual subject of modern politics, of representation and discursivity (GA38, 156), and with it, the deconstruction of Cartesian subjectivity as the metaphysical basis of the collective subject of modern nationality and the modern state. Since the self-reflective moment of re-presentation is always thrown and ecstatically open, the 'stability' or 'sub-stantiality' of the subject is granted by the *unity* of the temporalization of the three dimensions of time. The being-present of the contractual, rational subject is fractured by its thrownness, which arrives as a vocation to set itself to work in the transformation of *Mitsein* and of beings (GA38, 156–7).

The moment of withdrawal from representational or conceptual fixation proper to the motion of Volk, comes to word in the temporalizing structure of *Mitsein*, in the relation between *Stimmung* and *Sendung*: for neither the *attunement* nor the *vocation* of a Volk can be discursively fixed or calculated (GA38, 129–30). Both the modern concept of 'nation' and the metaphysical concept of Volk are constructs, although in different ways (GA54, 204). Volk, on the one hand, in principle intimates an essential moment of resistance to ideological 'formation' and modern disciplines of 'socialization.' Volk is founded in the withdrawal from conceptualization implicit in the deconstruction of metaphysically conceived language (GA38, 165–8). In view of the deconstruction of logic, the power of language is understood as the primordial site of the manifestation of the being of beings. As such it is the site of our exposure to presencing and the site of the response it calls for: the historicity of a Volk consists in its openness to the presencing of beings as founded by the arrival of a tradition, and the vocation it intimates, out of the future. The grant of the self-manifestation of beings by the world-disclosive power of language cannot be captured by a discursive reflection on language. Modern nationalism, on the other hand, is an ideological construction which defines the 'nation' as the identity of a common will.

Heidegger proposes a deconstruction of the metaphysical determinations of Volk. Volk withdraws from conceptual construction insofar as the retrieval which Heidegger undertakes de-termines it as a way, or potential, of being – the being of Dasein's historicity. The preliminary analysis of the metaphysical determinations of Volk deconstructs three forms of the construction and social formation of the 'body politic.' (*i*) Volk as 'body' (*Körper* and *Leib*) – The deconstruction of the metaphysics of blood or race (*Rasse*) aims to win *das Rassige*: for '"race" does not only mean the racial in the sense of what pertains to the blood and heredity.' Rather, '*das Rassige* realizes a particular rank, lays down specific laws, and does not pertain, in the first instance, to the corporality of the family and the genders' (GA38, 65). *Das Rassige* actualizes measure and rank, enunciates certain laws in the sense of the delimitation, consummation of a way of being – it signifies a question of form or flair, of style, of the intensity of life. Heidegger uses the example of a *rassiges Auto* (car); one might equally refer to a high-spirited horse or a fine wine as *rassig*; a fiery woman can also be called *'rassig.'* In all cases, *rassig* expresses a concept of approbation, value, of 'spirit.' The step back from *die Rasse* to *das Rassige* intimates the deconstruction of the Volk as 'body' to retrieve corporality as a mode of attunement, hence as rhythm and style of being. *Rassig* intimates the consummation of a mode of being in its proper limit and end, in which it holds itself. (*ii*) Volk as soul (*Seele*) – The soul is what metaphysically still belongs to the animal-being of mankind – instincts, urges, drives, and the instability of emotions and moods. Heidegger reconceives the discourse of the soul as humanity's attuned openness to being, both as one's own bodily being and as the being of the earth and world. Heidegger attacks the metaphysical determination of 'the soul of a people,' or *Volksseele*, which is pervasive in the ideological literature of the period. This discourse links race and its expression as soul – in the forms of bodily comportment, in the style of art and custom, and in the stamp impressed on a landscape. In *Being and Time*, *Stimmung* is defined as the ontic manifestation of *Befindlichkeit*, understood as an existential co-constitutive of Dasein's finite transcendence. *Stimmung* is not, therefore, to be conceived as a quality of the collective subject. It is neither subjective nor objective, but the site of the attunement of Dasein to being. The retrieval of *Seele* therefore implies the de-termination (*Bestimmung*) of a Volk through the historicity of its attunement (*Stimmung*) to being, as embodied and enacted in the rhythms of its language, art, custom, political, and social culture. A musical culture, for example, embodies the temporality of a people. Soul conceived as attunement conveys the accord of Volk and its earth. *Stimmung* constitutes the invisible body and hence the 'supporting ground' of Dasein. Heidegger shatters the substantiality of the biological body, along with the attempt to objectify it, to open the site of the accord of 'inner' and 'outer.' As the ecstatic ex-posure (*Ausgesetztheit*) of Dasein, *Stimmung* is the site of our being-with beings, in terms of which a 'landscape,' for example, can first come to be for a 'subject' (GA38 151–2). (*iii*) The deconstruction of spirit (*Geist*) – Spirit is retrieved as the enactment of the historicity of Volk, founded in knowledge and expressed in the will to articulate its internal differentiation and order (GA38, 67). Whereas will belongs to the act of decision, the founding moment of will nonetheless is subordinate to *Ent-schlossenheit* as an open response to the differentiation of being. Labour itself, in its confrontation with 'nature,' initiates diverse responses, which will, in turn, lead to a rank order of knowledge and leadership. Heidegger's brief reflection on spirit anticipates the necessity he later enunciates that a Volk give stable form to the order most proper to it, in a state proper to its inner structure and dynamics. The deconstruction of the metaphysically conceived *Geist* consists in the retrieval of the historicity of acts of founding made in response to the differentiation of being. Spirit does not signify, as Derrida claims, a relapse into metaphysics.[7] *Geist* is integrated into the praxis of work as the enactment of differentiation. With this step back from the metaphysics of body, soul, and spirit, Volk is projected as a movement of withdrawal from collective subjectivity.

The withdrawal of Volk from objectification, finally, comes to enactment in questioning (GA38, 69). The attempt to define the Volk by answering the question 'What is the Volk?,' thus to win the general concept of what we mean by Volk, is transformed into the question 'Who is this Volk that we are?' Why is this transformation of the mode of questioning necessary? Because, on Heidegger's account, Volk cannot be defined *in abstractum* – it is only as enacted in the historically sited question, which, rebounding on the questioner, calls for decision. It is in the questioning, as opening up a space of decision, that Volk as a way-of-being comes to be.

The character of resolve or decision (*Ent-scheidung*) (GA38, 72) comprehends a decision for, a response to, and resoluteness in the openness of Dasein's exposure to the being of beings. The essence of decision is *Entschlossenheit* (resolve), understood as responsiveness to beings (*Entschlossenheit*, or un-closedness). Therefore the temporal moment of decision Heidegger emphasizes is neither the past (having-decided) nor the present (the unmediated occasion of decision as conceived by the 'decisionist' thesis of Löwith),[8] but the future: being-open for and responsive to what comes to be in the decision (GA38, 75). Being-open is the seemingly paradoxical ground of the stability and unity of Volk, and therefore founds the constancy of its differentiated self-identity. Resolve 'has its own constancy in itself': it 'gives our being its specific stamp and steadiness' (*Prägung und Beständigkeit*) (GA38, 77). Wherein does this constancy consist? Not in the act of decision, but in the movement of Dasein into the openness of its future. Dasein is moved into the future and held on the course founded by the heritage it takes over. The being-open of decision therefore implicates the surrender of calculative rationality, that is, of the attempt to 'organize' and form in advance what a Volk is to be (GA65, 319/224). It is at odds with the Platonism of 'national aesthet- icism,' which Lacoue-Labarthe falsely ascribes to Heidegger.[9]

Volk enacts a *movement of withdrawal from calculation*, which delivers it over to endure the stand in being into which it is thrown, by taking up its tradition.

4.2 Volk and Limit

Be-ing a Volk, or Volksein, *signifies entering into one's own limit. A Volk finds its specific limit in the mode of its encounter with beings, that is, in work.* We recall that 'labour service' figures in the Rector's Address of 1933 (GA16, no. 51, 113). But it remains to determine what Heidegger understands by 'labour,' or work. The question of work arises out of the determination of Volk and is founded in the historicity of Dasein. 'Work' itself has mul- tiple senses, which Heidegger does not specify in the *Logik*. Nor is work as such a theme in *Being and Time*; nonetheless the question of work is implicit in sections 15–18, which I will examine to advance our immedi- ate project. Not only does *Being and Time* implicate an understanding of work, but the *Logik* offers a more concrete development of the question of work by founding it in historicity.

In *Being and Time*, section 15, Heidegger undertakes an elucidation of the environing world of Dasein, and of worldhood as such, by reference to our everyday being-in-the-world, and in particular, by reference to our concernful dealing with things. The use of equipment is a kind of praxis governed by its own insight (*Umsicht*), proper to the ready-to-hand (SZ 67/63), as opposed to the theoretical gaze which fixes on the present-to- hand for its own sake. Equipment is integrated into an equipmental con- text, or totality. Engagement in an equipmental context is always guided by an 'in-order-to' which is founded in the disclosure of Dasein's world: 'world is always predisclosed for circumspect heedfulness [Besorgen] together with the accessibility of innerworldly beings at hand' (SZ 76/ 71). Things ready-to-hand refer (*verweisen*) within a predisclosed world – they indicate an in-order-to (SZ 69/65). Reference makes up the struc- ture of their being (SZ 74/69). Determined by the structure of reference – by being-referred – the ready-to-hand has the being of relevance (*Bewandtnis*) (SZ 83–4/78).

Within these terms, work may be defined as circumspective praxis within an equipmental totality, and as such it takes its meaning from world, for the being-in-the-world of Dasein is the final destination of the structure of relevance, or involvement (SZ 84/78). Since Dasein is always constituted as *Mitsein*, work is fundamentally being-with, or working-with, others. There is nothing in *Being and Time* to suggest, moreover, that 'work' should be terminologically restricted to the equipmental totality of the ready-to-hand (hence to the process of production). The 'theoretical' attitude is also a mode of heedful concern – it too, 'works,' and not merely in the sense of following a method or procedure (SZ 69/64–5).

Work, finally, not only takes its meaning from a world which gives an equipmental totality its sense, but work is itself a way of dis-closing a world. This follows from the experience of equipmental breakdown or disturbance. This experience makes the 'what-for' of the reference of failed equipment 'visible and with it the context of the work': the 'totality never seen before ... makes itself known' as world (SZ 75/70). In making itself known, a world can come into question. Equipmental failure implies more than the replacement of a broken tool or the repair of equipment. It can bring an entire way of working into question. Catastrophic failure can disclose a world in its commitment to a wrong way of working. What Heidegger calls the spell (*benommen sein*) of the familiar which innerworldly beings cast over Dasein is broken. With the disruption of familiarity, 'the objective presence [Vorhandenheit] of beings is thrust to the fore' (SZ 76/71). The breakdown and reconstitution of praxis as a way of working passes through the experience of the mere presence and alienness of beings. In the terms of 'What Is Metaphysics?,' praxis would have to come back to itself out of anxiety in the face of the Nothing. Breakdown awakens praxis from the false security of the familiar and brings it into the saving light of anxiety and the possibility of a different work ethic.

Relevance is said to set beings, as ready-to-hand, free, to release them into being-relevant for Dasein. Relevance is the 'a priori' condition of the being-relevant of beings (SZ 84–5/79). As such it pertains to their being and to letting 'them be *as* they are and *in order that* they be such' (SZ 84/79). Letting-be-relevant, as releasing beings ready-to-hand into a totality of involvements, 'frees' them (up) for Dasein's understanding of world (SZ 85/80). Yet, as Heidegger immediately adds, the being-discovered is not allowed to be as it is, but as ready-to-hand: we 'work over it, improve it, destroy it' (SZ 85/79). There is a fundamental disjunction between making-relevant and letting-be-relevant, between the violence of the one and the letting-be of the other. In this way the problem of 'nature' in *Being and Time* is indirectly raised, inasmuch as making-relevant as ready-to-hand appears to implicate violence against beings as not ready-to-hand. Dreyfus goes so far as to claim that the definition of equipment in terms of the totality of its context 'denies localness, thus removing the last barrier to global totalization.'[10] Nature is reduced to its being-for-equipment, integrated into technology. As I indicated above, however, the experience of breakdown has the potential of refiguring the equipmental totality, and therefore of placing the use and the kind of technology used into question. The questions nonetheless remain, whether the category of the ready-to-hand does not necessarily involve our 'alienation' from nature, and whether or not the letting-be of beings is compatible with the totality of the ready-to-hand. Both questions remain open in *Being and Time*. This conclusion is substantiated by what Heidegger has to say regarding the work (the product) which issues from the work-process.

Section 15 implicates a further sense of work: *the* work as the thing-produced (*das hergestellte Werk*): 'What everyday association initially stays with is not the tools themselves, but the work ... The work bears the totality of references within which the equipment is encountered' (SZ 71/65, modified). Heidegger enumerates five references which the work carries, or bears. The work refers (*i*) to its useability (the 'what-for'); (*ii*) to its 'from-which,' or source, in the things of nature; (*iii*) to the user or consumer; (*iv*) to the public world; and (*v*) to environing nature (SZ 70–1/ 65–7).

The act of production and the thing-produced are understood in terms of these references, hence in terms of a reference totality and Dasein's being-in-the-world. At the same time, innerworldly entities, along with 'nature' (as natural resource *and* as environment), are brought into the open through the work. In Macquarrie and Robinson's translation (which is superior here),

> Our concernful absorption in whatever work-world lies closest to us, has a function of discovering; and it is essential to this function that, *depending upon the way we are absorbed,* those entities within-the-world which are brought along [beigebrachte] in the work and with it (that is to say, in the assignments or references [Verweisungen] which are constitutive for it) remain discoverable in varying degrees of explicitness and with varying circumspective penetration. (SZ 71/SZ-MR 101)

Depending on the kind (the way or quality) of absorption, the work-world discloses, but not all work-worlds disclose in equal degree. 'Familiarity' is a kind of concernful absorption (*Aufgehen*) which can lead to a benumbing loss of self (*benommen sein*) in the equipmental totality – but it need not necessarily do so. The way or quality of absorption would signify diverse regimes of work, diverse possibilities of being-with others and things (e.g., assembly-line production, as opposed to team-production). The work itself is a node of disclosure; in the language of the later Heidegger, it gathers and bears references. Innerworldly entities are and stay disclosed through the work, in various degrees of explicitness, depending on the quality of absorption. The work itself, moreover, will be determined by the way of our absorption (by the regime of work) in the sense that different degrees of disclosure of the innerworldly are possible through the work, and through different kinds of works. The category of the ready-to-hand is not univocal, for the degree of disclosure constitutes a criterion of evaluation and of the internal differentiation of the ready-to-hand.

Does handicraft, for example, disclose more of the innerworldy – including nature – through the work produced itself than machine production? Not necessarily. The ascription of a prejudice in favour of archaic modes of production to Heidegger is ill-founded. The five references defining the work do not, moreover, restrict the 'work' to products of unmediated use or consumption. In these terms, a technical installation would also qualify as a work. A work in this sense, such as a nuclear power plant, could have an immense power of disclosure, depending on the way or quality of our absorption and on the degree of our 'circumspective penetration' of the relations gathered together in this installation.

The degree of disclosure of the innerworldly – including nature as 'resource' and as 'environment' – through work depends, not only on the quality of absorption, but also on the work as a node of disclosure. This renders a criterion for the evaluation of diverse kinds of works, as well as of diverse regimes of work, given that the disclosure of innerworldly entities is a 'value' in and of itself. If benumbment can be determined as a fallen, or inauthentic, way of absorption in the work-world, then it must be possible to evaluate the various kinds of work-worlds. The benumbment of this way of absorption implies that things are not optimally disclosed and that a greater degree of disclosure is possible and desirable. The work, moreover, as a node of disclosure, can also be concealed as such: the 'referential context that constitutes worldliness as significance can be formally understood in the sense of a system of relations. But we must realize that such formalization levels down the phenomena to the extent that the true phenomenal content gets lost' (SZ 88/82). Thus the work itself, as a bearer of references, and hence as a node of disclosure, must be actively preserved against the tendency toward concealment by formal relations.

The 'work' of the preservation of the work implicates a way of absorption in the ready-to-hand of its own. This work, in effect, calls for a certain *attunement* to beings, and a certain way of the *making-present* of the ready-to-hand. What is at stake is the transformation of praxis, as much as its limitation. Joseph P. Fell argues that the 'limits of praxis' in *Being and Time* – hence the limit of the primacy of the equipmental world and its totality – are to be found in 'Dasein's being disposed or mooded' as the key to a non-technological experience of nature.[11] The *Logik* of 1934 brings work into the limit of a founded, and founding, attunement to being. To found work in the historicity of the Volk means to let work arise out of the full, authentic temporalization of Dasein. The category of the ready-to-hand is implicitly integrated into the unity of the having-been, the present, and the future.

In the *Logik*, Heidegger argues that the threefold *Bestimmung* (de-termination) of Volk, consisting of the jointure of *Stimmung* (attunement), *Arbeit* (work), and *Sendung und Auftrag* (mission and task), constitutes the structure of Volk. This structure articulates the temporalization of a world, in the ontological-existential sense of *Being and Time* (GA38, 65/61), and consequently specifies the condition of intelligibility of Dasein's complete, authentic historicity, as well as of the intelligibility of the derived history of inner-worldly beings. The unity of this structure of historicity is granted by the *Gestimmtheit* of a *Grundstimmung*, that is to say, by a common comportment (*Haltung*) (GA38, 130). Heidegger proposes to win the structure of the historicity of *Volksein* from a transformed understanding of temporality. The gateway to this transformation is the concept of *Bestimmung*, or de-termination, in the sense of a limit-granting *telos*. The actualization of temporality is grasped as the determining, gestalt-giving attunement which grants a Volk the 'form' of its comportment and sitedness, which is to say, its historicity. Temporality is concretely actualized inasmuch as we are engaged by something and dedicate ourselves to it:

> Our de-termination is not to be understood as a definite provision of our nature, understood corporally or in some other way, or as a process of self-discipline directed toward whatever ends. Rather, we understand our de-ter-

mination as that *to which we dedicate ourselves*, that with which we engage ourselves as our *task* [*Auftrag*]. (GA38, 127)

A task, in turn, is understood in terms of the mission or call to be which
has been granted or 'sent' to us (as *Sendung*). We are called to actualize a
mission or vocation which has long since come to presence as our being,
even if in a 'distorted and misunderstood' way (GA38, 127). 'De-termination in this sense means being-carried-forward into our mission and
vocation, which approaches us as task' (GA38, 127). Given the intimate
relation between Volk, work, and the limit into which Volk sets itself, mission should not be conceived metaphysically: it is (*i*) not derived from a
transcendental command – the revealed word of God, or the World
Spirit; (*ii*) not a nationalism based on this revelation; and (*iii*) not the
secularization of this theologically based nationalism – e.g., mission of
progress, the 'rights of man,' civilization, or culture. A Volk can have a
'mission' only insofar as it founds the presencing of being in the gestalt
of beings, *thus to overcome the metaphysical separation of being and beings*
(GA65, sec. 120).

The following sets of questions have implicitly guided my consideration of the problem of 'work' in Heidegger: (*i*) Is Heidegger's discourse
on work implicated by his own philosophy? Is it merely the result of an
attempt to accommodate himself to the new regime in the early years of
National Socialism? We have seen that Heidegger's understanding of
work is rooted in his conception of Dasein and the presencing of being
in beings. It is not a tactical accommodation to Nazism, as Lacoue-
Labarthe claims.[12] (*ii*) Does Heidegger's concept of work have a contribution to make to the phenomenology of labour? Or does it remain a
vague, quasi-mystical discourse without relation to the concrete reality of
our being-in-the-world? It will become evident that work according to
Heidegger implicates certain criteria which allow us to evaluate the
praxis of diverse economic and political regimes. Finally (*iii*) given the
ideological program of the National Socialist movement up to 1933, did
Heidegger have reason to believe that the new regime would commit
itself to social revolution and the re-constitution of work? It is my thesis
that this belief was one of the essential conditions of Heidegger's engagement in 1933–4. This is evident not only from the Rector's Address, but
from practically all the public speeches Heidegger delivered in this
period, as well as from the *Logik* of 1934. Undoubtedly National Socialism portrayed itself, however deceptively, as the salvation of the working
class, as the enemy of the 'slavery of interest' (Gottfried Feder),[13] of eco-

nomic exploitation and imperialism. It would be useful to go into this question in greater historical detail than we already have, to determine Heidegger's implicit relation to the left wing of National Socialism.

Work embodies the actualization of the way a Volk comes to be by bringing itself into its own limit through its engagement with beings. Work is defined as the actualization of the spirituality (*Geistigkeit*) of Dasein: it implicates the presencing of the spirit, insofar as work sets our being into self-transforming contact with beings to liberate them in their being (GA38, 153). What Heidegger calls the liberation of beings in work means the letting-be of beings in their historically sited presencing as they unfold themselves out of their own structures (SZ 84–5/78–9). In *Being and Time* Heidegger had shown that the in-order-to of the use of equipment is ultimately guided by the for-the-sake-of-which of our being-in-the-world (SZ, sec. 18); our working with things, and on things, is non-theoretically guided by the presencing of a world, and it is in a world where both equipment and things-made gain their gestalt and come to be. Work as actualization sets itself into the gestalt of works, actualizes itself as action, to found and enact the disclosure of being in beings (GA38, 128).

· As a response to the limits inherent in beings themselves, work in Heidegger's sense would be inconsistent with a technology of functional-ization. Work, furthermore, is the actualization of our own being as set in the work, as actualized in the gestalt and order (*Prägung* and *Gefüge*) our vocation gives to beings (GA38, 128). Work is the becoming-present of the present in the specific historical determination (*Bestimmtheit*) granted by the unity of the three temporal dimensions of our historicity. This unity articulates itself as follows. Understood as the having-been of historicity, vocation (*Sendung*) presences in the actualization of work by opening up a present through the arrival (future) of the task (*Auftrag*) our vocation has sent us. This entire structure is governed by a guiding attunement (*Bestimmung*), understood as 'the fundamental e-ventuation of the power of time' in Dasein, as the originating power of dis-closure in Dasein, in terms of which beings are disclosed or concealed to us (GA38, 130). This structure defines the historicity of work and determines the How of our encounter with beings. In Heidegger's terms it is the condi-tion of the intelligibility of any socio-economic determination of work.

As the actualization of beings, founded in the finitude of our historic-ity, work denotes the realization of the motion proper to humanity: work is the setting into work of Dasein's potential as Volk. The unity of this temporal structure, which concretely realizes itself in a world's forms of 'production,' constitutes the limit set to the historical specificity of Dasein. Work gives the ecstatic unity of historicity the gestalt and limit of the concrete historical being of Volk: 'In work and through work beings first become disclosed to us in their particular regions, and as worker one is moved into the open of the unconcealment of beings and their structure ... Being moved into the openness of the unconcealment of the things themselves belongs to our constitution' (GA38, 154). Work is the response of a Volk to the finitude of being as granted by a vocation and a task. Thus Heidegger speaks of the jointure (*Gefüge*) *of beings*, not simply of an order imposed on beings.

Work is not, in Heidegger's sense, the self-production of humanity, conceived in its subjectivity, through its encounter with nature (Marx). Nor is it the case, as Zimmerman claims, that Heidegger followed Marx to anticipate the reduction of the world of work (the proletarian class) to 'sheer abstract humanity emptied of specific contents' as the condition of a turn in the nature of humanity's relation to work.[14] At least in 1934, Heidegger held that work can enter into its own essence only in its founded specificity, as the work of a people rooted in its native soil. Nor is work the transformation of nature into real and metaphysical property (Locke). In the context of his political philosophy, Locke conceives nature in terms of its abstract indifferentiation as territory. The ground of all ownership is self-ownership, or property in one's own self. Locke's subject, no less than the collective subject incarnated in the proletarian class, produces its own being by transforming nature into the products of its own labour. As Zimmerman has shown, Heidegger's critique of the modern determinations of work derive them from 'productionist metaphysics,' and thus from the claim that beings as such may be conceived in terms of the model of the production of form from matter.[15] Since both the self-production of humanity through work and the concept of nature as the object of our production rest in the subjectivity of metaphysical mankind, Heidegger's essential task must be (*i*) to establish a relation between Volk and work which overcomes subjectivity; and (*ii*) to redetermine 'nature' to allow it to presence, through work, as other than object.

Heidegger's definition of work as our *ecstatic exposure* to the disclosure of beings constitutes a critical response to the productionist model. Work is the happening of the *presencing of beings* in a certain gestalt and regulated order. The onslaught of beings is brought to stand, beings are set in their own limits through work as reception and response to beings. In the Hölderlin lectures of 1934–5 (GA39), Heidegger writes, 'Since we are as dialogue, we are ex-posed [ausgesetzt] in the midst of self-disclo-sive beings, and only since then can we encounter the being of beings as such to be determined by it' (GA39, 72). What Heidegger calls *Ausgesetzt-heit*, or exposure, reflects the demand which beings make on us. This demand binds individuals into a community. The possibility of a commu-nity (*Gemeinschaft*) rests in a common attunement (*Stimmung*) to the being of beings which determines (*bestimmt*) and limits a way of being. Given that this way is actualized as work, then work takes its binding determination from the demand which beings issue in our exposure to them. The contractual bonds of the social sphere are secondary, and thus derivative of the primordial bond with the being of beings which forges a community and allows the possibility of a society. Community is not the collective response of a people, as opposed to the contractual society of radical individuals. Dasein in its individuated selfhood and the community of work are both bound by a Third term – the disclosure of the being of beings in the configuration of a specific historical attune-ment (GA39, 72–3). Heidegger's argument is that the primordial bond of obligation is our obligation to the being of beings themselves: in our exposure to beings, we encounter the resistance of beings to arbitrary assault – we are obliged to take their being into account in all our ways of working with them, for them, or against them. The realization of this obligation, however, always depends on the specific attunement to being of an historical humanity – consequently the necessity of the question of the Volk, of the state, and of the relative primacy of the socio-economic or political realms.

'The Da-sein of mankind – that is, its being-exposed, open, to the self-disclosure of beings as such – means, being in truth and untruth' (GA16, no. 158, 328). Work is the response of a Volk to the demand which the presencing of being in beings issues. Demand and response always have a finite, situated determination. The presencing of beings as 'object,' 'product,' 'value,' or 'signifier' is only possible within the site opened up by a specific historical founding of the ecstatic temporality of Dasein, for this site alone allows 'subject' and 'object' to be. Work gives this site gestalt:

> In work as the present, understood as enpresenting [Gegenwärtigung], the making-present of beings happens. Work signifies the present in the pri-mordial sense that we are moved toward an encounter with beings in the historicity of their arrival for us, submitting to their power and transforming them in primordial moods of struggle, astonishment, and reverence, thus to enhance the greatness of beings. (GA38, 154)

What does Heidegger mean by 'enpresenting' (I follow Hofstadter's translation of GA24)? Since section 21(a) (431–45) of *The Basic Problems of Phenomenology* of 1927 (GA24) is devoted to the 'Temporal Interpretation of Being as Being-Ready-to-Hand,' we may expect it to offer us some clues. Beings, and the ready-to-hand in particular, are made-present to Dasein out of the temporal unity of the three ecstases of time. What is present is not merely present – it is not present merely as object or function of an atemporal system of relations. The ready-to-hand signifies an historically founded and modified event of presencing. 'Original familiarity with beings lies in dealing with them appropriately. This constitutes itself with respect to its temporality in a retentive-expectant enpresenting of the equipmental contexture as such' (GA24 432/304). In other words, 'appropriate' dealing (*angemessenen Umgang*) with beings has a specific kind of temporal constitution. The being-present of something present (e.g., equipment at-hand) is made-present in its being in the arrival ('enpresenting') of the context of relations ('contexture'), as retained and anticipated 'in' the being, thus to constitute it. Making-beings-present in this way, work projects beings on the temporal horizon of '*praesens*' (*Praesenz*) (GA24, 435/306). As 'removal to ...', the present [*Gegenwart*] is a being-open for entities confronting us, which are thus understood antecedently on *praesens*' (GA24, 436/306–7).

Praesens is a more primordial phenomenon than the Now, understood as the succession of time in its before and after (GA24, 434/305). Things ready-to-hand are indeed subject to the succession of Nows – they are 'in' time. Heidegger proposes, nonetheless, to determine the being of the ready-to-hand in the ecstatic unity of Dasein's temporality: 'work' designates the making-present (*Anwesendmachen*) (GA38, 154) of *beings* to 'generate,' as it were, the ready-to-hand, for the sake of the present which work itself is. In being made-*present* (*anwesend*), beings are given the stamp of being, that is, brought into their appropriate limit. The contextual limit of the equipmental totality which 'positions' the ready-to-hand as a function of a totality is merely formal. The ready-to-hand is set into its 'proper' limit by the temporality of Dasein itself, as work, in the encounter with beings. Work actualizes the overcoming of the 'inauthentic' ready-to-hand and of the inauthentic temporality proper to it. How? By integrating the making-present of beings in work into authentic historicity.

Returning to our previous, extended quotation from the *Logik*, we find it evident that 'work' is understood by Heidegger as service to the being of beings. The greatness of beings is enhanced by making-them-present (as opposed to surrendering them to the empty succession of Nows or fixing them in the sterile stability of merely formal relations). It is in this sense – work as service to the being of beings – that Heidegger defines the commitment of the state to 'socialism.' Rejecting the idea that essential socialism merely means the transformation of the economy, the redistribution of wealth, and the primacy of the common good (GA16, no. 154, 281), Heidegger proposes that socialism expresses

> concern for the measure and essential structure of our historical being, and therefore it affirms an order of rank according to vocation and work, it affirms the unquestioned worth of every kind of work, it affirms unconditional service as the fundamental form of relation to the inescapable [presencing] of being [in beings]. (GA38, 165)

Socialism affirms work as ek-static response of our being-in-the-world to the rank order and measure immanent in the historically sited, that is, finite presencing of beings. Presumably the transformation of economic relations of production is a necessary but not sufficient condition of the socialism Heidegger envisions. Socialism must be concretely founded as a response to the limits of the earth, and to the finitude of an historically rooted community. Socialism, in Heidegger's sense, is evidently Volk-socialism. In order for this claim to win content, Heidegger would have to claim that other kinds of social order – capitalism, for example – do not allow work to express an order of rank responsive to the rank order of beings. This is implicit in Heidegger's claim: the social order of (international finance) capitalism, along with the metaphysics of liberalism from which it derives, is destructive of all orders of rank. It consummates the metaphysics of in-differentiation.

Heidegger's thesis regarding the interrelation of work and Volk can now be brought to a point as follows: A Volk *finds its specific limit in the mode of its encounter with and transformation of beings, that is, in work.* As 'the fundamental comportment of humanity,' it is through work that a community comes into being (GA38, 156). Hegel had already argued this point in his *Realphilosophie.*[16] The mode of being-with will always be historically specific to a community. Being a Volk, conversely, is the condition of work, as the measure of delimitation in the encounter of a people with beings. For Volk – as deconstructed body, soul, and spirit – grounds work in the limits, and thus in the historicity, of the earth. Where this condition does not obtain, in other words, where humanity constitutes itself otherwise than as a Volk, the historicity of Dasein, and thus the historicity of the earth-as-limit, cannot actualize itself. This implicates the de-limitation, or limitlessness, of a people: now work is no longer a mea-sure-setting limit, but tends toward limitless production. This is the telos of modern production, Hegel argues, because human needs, unlike those of the animal, are not limited and predetermined. The more they are satisfied, the more they differentiate and multiply themselves.[17] Among the unsolved problems of Hegel's discussion of civil society and the question of work is the one of finding a limit determining produc-tion and the proliferation of needs. Can it suffice to leave this role to the State, as Hegel does, or is it possible to find a limit inherent in a rede-fined understanding of work? Heidegger's appeal to Volk is precisely such an attempt.

The standpoint of subjectivity, and therefore of the objectification of nature, inevitably leads to the self-alienation of mankind through the processes of production themselves, because these assume the aspect of an alien power.[18] Production is the anti-thesis of work. Whereas work unfolds the moment (*Augenblick*) wherein *beings and Dasein mutually delimit each other, thus to found the Volk in its historicity,* production repre-sents the dissolution of all limits proper to beings and their consequent integration into the in-difference of the planetary reserve of 'resources.' What Heidegger calls *Ausgesetztheit*, or exposure, intimates the demand which beings make on us. Work is the response of a Volk to the demand which the presencing of being in beings issues. Demand and response always have an historical, situated determination.

Heidegger argues the thesis that a people can be outside 'history,' can enter into and pass out of history (GA38, 84). The Volk is a potential for the founding of the historicity of being. The ways of fulfilling the criteria constituting a people's entrance into history are all instantiations of the delimited presencing of being: (*i*) the creation of 'native soil' by a peo-ple's fusion with a landscape (GA38, 84–5); consequently (*ii*) its power to will a future (GA38, 86); (*iii*) its power as granted by a vocation; and thus (*iv*) creation of a state to give vocation and task their stability and secu-rity (GA38, 165). A people has a future insofar as it recognizes its depen-dence on the native soil in which it is rooted and insofar as it gives gestalt and stability to this dependence in work and in a state. The dependence spoken of here refers to a people's response to the presencing of being, which calls on it to become sited in its soil. And this call issues a demand which, following Heidegger, is at odds with the politics and economics of internationalism.

The objection could be raised that Heidegger's understanding of work fails to take the concrete reality of socio-historical structures into account, and thereby mystifies the historical and economic character of work. It is true that Heidegger has little to say – here or elsewhere – regarding the economic re-structuring of society. But this is not his object and task. Heidegger's thesis is that socio-economic definitions of work cannot grasp the *essence* of work. This essence (mode of coming into presence) has to be grasped as the reciprocal determination of work, Volk, and the being of beings: as the founded historicity of being in bringing itself into the limit of beings.

The problem of limit can be clarified by reference to Heidegger's *Sophistes* of 1924–5, which offers a commentary on *techne* in Aristotle's *Nicomachean Ethics*, book 6, chapter 4 (GA19, 40–7). The metaphysically conceived *techne* of 'production' tends toward limit-lessness because neither the *eidos* nor the *telos* of *techne* is fully inherent in *techne* itself. For the *eidos* of *techne* is in the soul of the maker (for example, the blueprint of the architect's conception); and the *telos*, in the end of the thing made (the for-the-sake-of-which of the house). In this sense, *techne* becomes the means to ends outside itself – and therefore, because its *arche* lies outside of itself, it can become 'free-floating,' instrumental. But if *techne* is not itself bound to a limit then what grants work a limit? For, although work, as we have seen, is not *techne*, but rather the *present* actualization of Dasein's ecstatic temporality, it has a relation to *techne*, precisely as this making-present of beings. This relation can be specified in the form of a normative demand with which work confronts *techne*: the 'production' of *techne* (what is brought forth as present in the *ergon*) has to be founded in the making-present of work as the actualization of the ecstatic temporal unity of a Volk. This unity sets the limit of *techne* because it sets the limit of pro-duction in the making-present of the limits and hence differentiation of beings in and through work. The problem of *techne*, moreover, is compounded by the fact that by 1934 Heidegger may no longer have held a metaphysical understanding of *techne*.[19] The deconstruction of the metaphysical determination of *techne*, after 1934 in particular, will allow Heidegger to postulate an understanding of the *ergon* as dis-closive of the presencing of being in a being. *Techne* is retrieved as a way of disclosure, and thus divorced from its 'technical' determinations as a means to an end outside of itself, as the instrument of an origin not in itself. As we know, Heidegger advances this interpretation in *An Introduction to Metaphysics* (1935) and in 'The Origin of the Work of Art' (1936), in both cases, however, with reference to only one kind of *ergon* – the work of art. Where does this leave the question of work, and work-socialism?

Reference to a passage from 'The German Student as Worker' (25

November 1933) can clarify this question. The essence of work cannot be captured by concepts of the activity of labour, or modes and conditions of production, nor by a concept of the ends of labour, or the products of production. The essence of work 'now determines the Dasein of humanity *in its fundamental ground.*' The question of work is an 'ontological' question, or, in Heidegger's terms, an existential question which of necessity refers us back to the constitution of Dasein. As worker, 'mankind confronts [stellt sich ... in die Auseinandersetzung] beings as a whole.' As worker, confronting beings as whole, Dasein responds to the differentiation of being in beings. Confronting beings, Dasein accomplishes the differentiation (*Aus-einander-setzung*) of beings, thus to 'empower, to bring to fulfilment, to order, and to harness the world-shaping powers' of nature, history, technology, art, and the state. *With the actualization of work as the differentiation of the being of beings* 'our Dasein *begins to shift* into a different way being.' It is Heidegger's thesis that work in this sense announces the beginning of a new way of being and a new age. In *Being and Time* he had given the name of Care (*Sorge*) to the structure of the temporality and historicity of Dasein. Now Heidegger claims that *work* signifies the transformation of human being into the way of being (*Seinsart*) of *Sorge* – it announces the coming to be of Dasein, as the Da, or historically founded site, of being (GA16, no. 108, 205).

In *Sein und Zeit*, *Sorge* names the radical finitude and unity of Dasein's temporal structure. If this structure defines work, then work has to be understood as the actualization of Dasein within the limits of its historicity. The ends of *techne* are determined by these limits. Determined by Care, *techne* is conceived as disclosive of the truth of beings as granted by the finitude, the historicity, of Dasein. But this means that *techne* does not simply initiate a process of production to give beings over, as products, to the unbounded play of the marketplace. In the Nietzsche lectures, Heidegger brings *techne* into explicit relation to *melete* (carefulness of concern):

We must conceive of the innermost essence of *techne* too as such care, in order to preserve it from the sheer 'technical' interpretation of later times. The unity of *melete* and *techne* thus characterizes the basic posture of the forward-reaching disclosure of Dasein, which seeks to ground beings on their own terms. (NI 192/1: 164–5)

To ground beings on their own terms means to ground them in the historicity of work, that is, in the reciprocal limit of a Volk as belonging to the earth and of work as the making-present of beings. This shows how intimately Heidegger links the question of being to the question of work, the Volk, and the state, and how intimately he links these questions to the transformation of German existence he anticipated in 1933–4.

Clearly Heidegger's reflections on work emerge in 1933–4 in response to the challenges of the liberal, or capitalist, interpretation of the market, as well as to the Marxist critique of alienated labour. In common with Max Weber in *The Protestant Ethic and the Spirit of Capitalism*, Heidegger presupposes that liberalism has a 'spiritual' origin in a specific ethos, and that an alternative to capitalism can only emerge out of a new ethos. Heidegger's discourse on work is an attempt to prepare the ground for a new ethos of community, founded in Da-sein's *attunement* to the historicity of being. Given that Heidegger proposes to prepare the way for an alternative ethos, it is legitimate to pose the question of whether Heidegger's deconstruction of the metaphysical understanding of work, which conceives 'labour' as a mode of production constituting both self and other, renders any criterion for evaluating diverse regimes of work. We have seen that work is defined in terms of the unity of the temporal structure of historicity. Work is the founding of the limits of beings, their rank order and unity. This offers a criterion for the evaluation of diverse sociopolitical theories – e.g., Marxism, liberalism – in terms of their potential response to the differentiation of being in beings, and as such their attunement to the rank order of 'modes of production' as modes of the unconcealment of truth. There is a difference in rank, for example, between philosophy and rhetoric as modes of *aletheuein*. There is a difference in rank between authentic rhetoric and the sophistry of 'public relations.' Heidegger will later imply – in the *Beiträge*, and in the reflections on art which emerge from it ('The Origin of the Work of Art') – that, as a mode of unconcealment, the work of art possesses higher rank than the production of goods. The problem of the relation of work to the limits and rank order of beings raises significant questions. Do various technologies of the production of energy, for example, possess a different rank insofar as they express different relations to the internal differentiation and order of nature? Can technologies of food production be ranked according to their response to the natural differentiation of local ecologies?

Work in the essential sense is the institution of the differentiation of being in beings. The normative claim that Heidegger makes is that *work attains to its essential rank insofar as modes of 'production' respond to the differ-*

entiation of being. This criterion allows for a critique of both capitalist and communist systems, inasmuch as both presuppose the indifference of all beings as potential resources. The commonly raised objection, therefore, that Heidegger understands work in terms of archaic modes of production (the peasantry, the workshop) misses the essential point. Nor is it credible that Heidegger was naive enough to believe, as Young claims he did, that industrial society could be abandoned or marginalized.[20] This forlorn illusion contradicts, in Heidegger's own terms, the history of being as the history of the founding of being in beings, hence also in work. Granted that modern technology emerges out of Western ontology, a turn in its character can only be hoped for from a more fundamental attunement to the *presencing* of being. Heidegger's understanding of work, therefore, implicates the possibility of a technology which attends to the differentiation of being to preserve and shelter beings in what is proper to each. The thesis of the *Beiträge* is that the analytical character of modern technology, deriving as it does from mathematical physics and the representational space of subjectivity, disintegrates and functionalizes entities. On the evidence of the *Beiträge*, Heidegger appears to grant that with the consummation of metaphysics the power of work is integrated into a technology of in-differentiation (section 76). This process is itself intimately linked to the dissolution of the Volk and its integration into socio-technical structures and the international, consumer economy. Yet, even in the *Beiträge*, Heidegger never surrendered the *question* of technology in favour of a one-sided appeal to the saving power of art (GA65, 275/194). Based on 'The Question Concerning Technology,' we know that he continued to insist that art and technology have *techne* as their common root.

Heidegger's thesis of 1934 on work anticipates a 'differentiated' technology which responds to the differentiation of beings in all their diverse 'species,' and to the historicity of the 'homeland.' The question at issue is whether or not technology can find its limit in service to economies of scale and the ecological 'community' of a people and its native ground. Heidegger's attempt to found the essence of work in the finite and founded differentiation of being, hence within the political and economic limits of a Volk and its state, is also obviously at odds with the global economy of capitalism, the power of international corporations, and the interface of technological research and the exploitation of resources. The monopolization and propagation of seed stocks, for example, by a few great corporations undermines the bio-diversity and 'national' *ecology*, no less than it undermines the independence of national economies. The neo-colonialism of international agrarian corporations, which reduces bio-diversity by imposing controlled, standardized stocks, ultimately derives from the power of the technology of in-differentiation. At issue is the transformation of labour in the socio-technical sense into work as dwelling on the earth, and this means living in response to the differentiation of being in beings. This would allow for the possibility, in Foltz's words, of a 'new environmental ethic' founded in dwelling.[21]

This offers us another clue to the implications of Heidegger's thesis on work: not only does the finitude of being call for the founding of differentiation in historicity (in the Volk and its state), but founded historicity is the necessary site of the differentiation of being in beings. The dissolution of Volk and state into international institutions dominated by the agenda of corporate capitalism and driven by the inherent 'telos' of 'research' racing to its end is an essential, historically specific socio-economic manifestation of the consummation of the metaphysical in-differentiation of beings as stock-on-call.

According to Heidegger's address of 11 November 1933, the character of modern thought, of modern science, is 'rootless and powerless' (*boden- und machtlosen Denkens*) – in fact, in terms of Heidegger's argument, it is powerless because it is rootless. It is powerless because it is alienated from the sources of a people's life in its own tradition, in its historicity (GA16, no. 104, 193). Rootless thought generates an unlimited economy of production and consumption; it pursues the ideal of value-free science and technology for its own sake. The triumph of the socio-technical constitution of society reveals the abdication of the responsibility of the Volk and brings to light the negation of the will to give itself gestalt in the form of the state. 'Rootless thought,' in effect, denotes the liberalism of Weimar, and by extension Western liberalism, as a political, economic, and philosophical doctrine. The fact that international liberalism and its socio-economic system are Heidegger's targets becomes clear from what, conversely, he affirms in saying that the 'authentic questioning and research' of science rests in, and is limited by, the authentic, existential needs of a people (GA16, no. 104, 191–2). Only insofar as science and technology are guided by the existential needs of a people can the will of the Volk, and therefore its political will as articulated by the state, enter into its 'truth.' Only insofar as science is limited by the responsibility a Volk takes for its own historicity, that is, insofar as a Volk takes up the task of finding the governing limit proper to its being, can the primacy of the apolitical be broken.

   The actualization of science as a mode of the self-limitation of a Volk happens in work as the unity of theory and praxis. Work is posited as the enactment of a Volk's 'self-responsibility' in and through the founding of a state responsive to the powers of being and the earth. For 'work allows the Volk to recover its rootedness; work moves the state as the actuality of the Volk into the field of influence of all essential powers of human being' (GA16, no. 104, 190). The primacy of work follows from what Heidegger has to say regarding the necessity of founding research in the existence of the Volk. For, whereas work is guided by knowledge (*Wissen*), knowledge remains rooted only as long as it attends to the differentiation of being in beings. And work is the name Heidegger gives to our attentive confrontation with and transformation of beings. From the immediate context of the passage quoted above, it is evident, moreover, that Heidegger assigns to National Socialism the essential role in the transformation of work as guided by responsibility for the historical essence of the Volk. Heidegger did not merely accommodate himself to the National Socialist rhetoric of work, rootedness, and the will to self-responsibility. He was apparently convinced, at least until 1934, that he could fill the language of the 'Movement' with a new and deeper meaning, and thereby succeed in transforming it from within.
   Heidegger's argument may be reconstructed as follows. (*i*) Work implicates the recovery of the 'rootedness' of a people in the essential powers of being, and hence in its own native soil. (*ii*) This implicates an *economics of limit* guided by a Volk's response to the 'reality of all essential powers of human being.' The self-delimitation of a people is founded in the will to choose itself, to take responsibility for itself. Although this implicates the moment of 'authenticity' as realized in the community of *Mitsein*, authenticity remains a formal, empty 'category' of existence until actualized in the giving of limits to the Volk, to entities, and to being-with other peoples. As I have argued, delimitation, not authenticity, is the guiding principle of Heidegger's political thought. (*iii*) The regime of work thus envisioned must have already broken with the principles of liberalism, understood as the primacy of socio-economic thinking over the political. For the primacy of the socio-economic is one of the prime indices of deracination. Finally (*iv*) the condition of international understanding is that, taking responsibility for itself, a Volk will found the differentiation of being in work and give itself the gestalt of a state. It is apparently Heidegger's contention that insofar as a Volk enters into its own limits through work – through the specificity of its encounter with the earth – and through its state, it can enter into relatively stable,

delimited relations with other peoples (GA16, no. 104, 191–3). This is *the geopolitical moment* of Heidegger's thought.

4.3 The Attunement of Volk to Being

Volk-sein signifies the stability and unity of a comportment responsive to the differentiated disclosure of being. The comportment of Dasein is a significant theme in Heidegger's thought from 1919. In 'Vom Wesen der Wahrheit,' Heidegger unfolds the site of truth as follows: Dasein's attunement to the event of being (to unconcealment) determines how Dasein comports itself to beings, and this, in turn, is the ground of truth-statements about what is revealed of beings in our attunement to being (WW 180–3/120–2). Comportment (*Verhalten*) grounds itself, in the first instance, in the intentionality and transcendence of Dasein (GA24, 311–12/218–19). Held in the openness of being and exposed to beings, Dasein's comportment encompasses its relation-to beings (*Bezugssinn*), the How of this relation (*Vollzugssinn*), and a certain way of enactment, or temporalization (*Zeitigungssinn*), of its disclosure of beings (GA61, 52–3). This way of enactment takes form, or gestalt, in the comportment of Dasein (GA58, 42, 100). Evidently science itself actualizes a certain comportment to the being of beings (GA27, 25–35; GA16, no. 156, 308). But what is true of Dasein is pre-eminently true of the historicity of Dasein – of Volk – as the articulation of the sitedness of being. Actualized through the decisions of a community, the intentionality of Dasein is given a specific form of disclosure in the comportment (*Haltung*) of a Volk.

The character of decision (*Ent-scheidung*), as the resolute openness (*Ent-schossenheit*) of Dasein, consists in being-responsive to the differentiated disclosure of beings as it arises out of the tradition granted to a Volk. The openness of *Volk-sein* is founded in *Stimmung* (as *Ausgesetztsein*, or exposure), *Arbeit* (*Ent-rückung*), and *Sendung*, therefore in the transcendental structure of the Volk in its historicity. In fact, this structure, as the finitude and delimitation of 'collective' being, constitutes Volk as Volk, and historicity as historicity. This disclosure is differentiated in the attunement to being of a given Volk and *the actualization of this attunement* in a certain comportment to beings, including the comportment of work (GA38, 158). The historicity of Volk therefore constitutes the site of the disclosure of beings.

The disclosure of being differentiates itself in the manifoldness of beings (GA38, 157). The form and structure of this differentiation, and consequently how 'beings in their totality are opened up in their different realms,' are essentially, not merely incidentally, defined by the determination of a Volk. The unity of this determination of Volk includes the character of its potential and vocation, the nature of its ecstatic exposure to beings, the modes of work which give beings gestalt in ways of pro-duction, and *the attunement which modulates the unity of the three dimensions of time* to grant the presencing of each its specific character. Given Heidegger's key premise – that being is finite – *being can disclose itself only in the delimited finitude of an historically de-termined founding.* As the temporalizing unity of presencing and the ousiological structure of the things themselves, being 'calls for' a site. The finite stability and self-sameness of the being of beings finds its founding delimitation in the comportment of a Volk. Comportment is (*i*) founded in the self-reserve of the movement of withdrawal of a Volk from the merely present back into the sending of its vocation; and (*ii*) actualized in work as the differentiation (*Auseinandersetzung*) of being in beings. Heidegger apparently held that work, as the expression of the Volk in its state, can give technology a national gestalt and limit. The international character of modern science is not yet an argument against this thesis, because Heidegger allows the possibility that what is opened up as a realm of being by science can be taken over and transformed by work as founded in historicity.

The cosmopolitan character of modern technology, in Heidegger's terms, only substantiates the thesis that science can become deracinated from its primordial sources in the historicity of being and become measureless. Measurelessness announces itself in the dis-integration of beings. Yet Heidegger does not exclude the possibility that new forms of technology can respond in a 'measured' way to the inherent measures of the earth (GA65, 70, 275/48, 193). This thesis is also implicit in the *Logik*, unless we are to hold the unlikely assumption that Heidegger expected the National Socialist revolution to bring about a return to workshop economics. The transformation of technology in this sense, in fact, was one of the central themes of the Conservative Revolution and was carried over into the Nazi period by technologist associations opposed to measureless capitalism.

Heinrich Hardensett's *Der kapitalistische und der technische Mensch* (1932) (Capitalist and Technological Humanity), one of the best examples of this genre, opposes capitalist and technologist as two ideal types determined by fundamentally different motivations and values. The capitalist represents the dynamism of infinite striving. 'He wants infinite profits, infinite progress, and infinite expansion; he devalues the present and overvalues the future. He is faustian, measureless, restless, of extraordinary energy and dynamism.'[22] The technologist, conversely, seeks stability of form. Technical 'creation is the formation [Gestaltung] of sensuous, malleable materials and actualized energies into concrete works and forms ... [The technologist] does not want unending profit and consequently unending movement and eternally unsatisfied striving; he wants the utopian redemption of eternal, consummate duration, the eternal present instead of the infinite future.'[23] Based on a reading of Weber, Sombart, and some classical economists of capitalism, Hardensett offers a psychological and sociological typology of the capitalist and the technologist. Each is defined by a certain style of being, by a certain mode of comportment, which determines how world and nature are encountered, how time is lived. Hardensett's thesis is that the subjection of the technologist to the capitalist, and thus to the demands of a consumer economy, is fundamentally at odds with the style of being of the technologist. Far from being a part of the self-evident nature of things, this subjection is the result of the specific historical development of the liberal marketplace. Given this historical contingency, Hardensett can conclude that the 'technologist is by no means necessarily the servant of the economy.'[24]

Evidently the premises of Hardensett's critique are incompatible with Heidegger's thought. The conclusions Hardensett offers regarding the production of enduring forms, through which the present endures, are not as such commensurate with Heidegger's understanding of the 'present,' of 'form,' or of 'production.' Despite this, what unites Heidegger and the conservative technological Right is the critique of the liberal marketplace economy and its political order. This order is deemed incapable of grasping what technology is and what is at stake in the future of technology. Moreover, Heidegger does hold at least one specific premise in common with Hardensett: the 'problem' of technology arises out of the necessity of limit, of measure. According to Heidegger, as according to the revolutionary conservatives, liberal capitalism cannot solve this 'problem,' can hardly even recognize it. Capitalist comportment to beings, its fundamental comportment, is inherently at odds with self-limitation, and therefore aims at the infinite in the form of a constant acceleration of efficiencies of production and consumption.

Heidegger understands *Haltung* or comportment as the stand in the midst of beings to which Dasein holds and which holds Dasein in its ecstatic, attuned being-exposed to the being of beings. *Haltung* is Heidegger's interpretation of the Greek *paideia* (GA34, 115). Comportment is actualized in work as the differentiation (*Auseinandersetzung*) of being in beings. Moreover, as we shall see in the next section, it is founded in the self-reserve of the movement of withdrawal of a Volk into its vocation. Since the comportment of a people determines its relation to technology, Heidegger in effect postulates (at least in 1934) that work can give technology a 'national' or 'cultural' articulation which derives from the ecstatic specificity of a Volk's encounter with being, thus to found being in the historicity of beings in its own way. And it is by no means absurd to hold that given the political will, a people could make fundamental decisions regarding the kinds of technology it proposed to develop, and that these decisions in turn would have fundamental consequences for its being as a people.

In the *Logik* of 1934, Dasein's stand in the midst of beings, its *Haltung*, is given the name '*Inständigkeit*' (GA38, 163). *Inständigkeit* refers to the stand and hold we have in the midst of beings – it refers to the stability of our being in its entire, ecstatic temporality. Therefore it raises the question of selfhood. The temporal structure of Dasein shatters the self-reflective subject as the ground for the stability of acts of re-presentation. This does not mean, however, Heidegger claims, that selfhood disintegrates with subjectivity. Selfhood rather is, or eventuates, in the openness of our engagement with others and with beings in the entire concreteness of their historicity. We have already seen that the question of the Volk is posed by Heidegger as Who is this Volk?, consequently not in terms of the What? of a general concept. The selfhood of Volk realizes itself in the asking and answering of the Who?, that is, through its engagement with beings, as granted by a tradition. The mode of this engagement – conceived as the stability of a comportment or standing-exposed to the disclosure of being – grants *Volksein* its limit and brings it to expression in the stamp (*Prägung*) given to the ordered whole of a world.

4.4 The Differentiated Identity of Volk

The self-reserve of holding-to-itself constitutes the site of the differentiated disclosure of being in its historicity. Self-reserve is permeated by a Not, thus to define the differentiated identity of Volk. Bestimmung names this movement: the arrival of a vocation (future), as founded in an attunement (the presencing of the past, of tradition), to open a present in works and acts of the actualization of the being of beings (*Arbeit*). The movement into actualization is always, simultaneously, a movement back, a withdrawal of the way of being of a Volk from mere presence, into the inception of its vocation, which is sent to it and which 'sends' it on its way. This movement of presencing-in-gestalt de-termines the way of being of a Volk, as the differentiated actualization of presencing. Where, conversely, this self-reserve becomes subject to conscious, ideological formation or socio-technical discourses and their disciplines, the being of a Volk cannot enter into its own. The potential for the founding of historicity which Volk implicates begins to disintegrate. And all of the determinations of Volk we have considered are given their structural unity in the historicity of Volk: the structure of historicity constitutes the movement, the self-limitation, the stability and unity, and the self-reserve and ethos of Volk. The end of the unfolding of a Volk is the actualization of the potential for being of its particular ethos. In the *Logik*, 'ethos' is unfolded in the language of *Stimmung* and *Bestimmung*, because the *Grundstimmung* of a Volk modulates, unifies, and 'attunes' its stand in the openness of the three dimensions of time. Consequently the forms of work and of the enactment of being, the comportment which attunes a Volk to being, in effect the jointure of the de-termination of a Volk which grants it its gestalt, constitutes its ethos.

The ideological manipulation of a people constrains and distorts *Volksein*: attunement is perverted into the publicness of *Erlebnis* (heightened sensation), governed by the machination (*Machenschaft*) of socio-technical discourses. The object of the intensification of sensation puts its stamp on production; the ends of production inscribe themselves into the 'body-politic.' This implicates, in Heidegger's account, the functionalization of beings and the integration of humanity and beings into the interface of machination. This interface is not a world at all, but an 'unworld' of the mutual in-differentiation of all entities. The possibility of the differentiated manifestation of what is proper to each being arises out of the intimacy of Volk, historicity, and being in their founded delimitation. The question of Volk, therefore, arises directly out of the question of being itself. The claim of *Volksein* – which annunciates itself as the necessity of the decision to found presencing in beings – is a normative claim. According to Heidegger, response or indifference to this claim determines the rank of a people in the history of being.

The unity of actualization and withdrawal raises the question of the Not, of the 'negativity' which belongs to the being of a Volk, work and the beings themselves. In 'What Is Metaphysics?' Heidegger addresses the question of the Nothing out of which all beings presence, and which permeates all beings (WM 119–20/109). This inherent Not is also essential to the movement of Volk as self-reserving. The temporal structure of

Care is permeated by nothingness (*Nichtigkeit*): 'In the structure of thrownness, as well as in that of the project, essentially lies a nullity ... *Care itself is in its essence thoroughly permeated with nullity*' (SZ 285/263). As the thrown project of a finite possibility for being, Da-sein 'constantly lags behind its possibilities,' and this means '*never* to gain power over one's ownmost being from the ground up. This *not* belongs to the existential meaning of thrownness' (SZ 284/262). Dasein *as thrown* makes-beings-present in the openness of its encounter with beings. The exposure of work is always a thrown project. I have indicated that work, as *Ausgesetztheit*, is the ex-posure of Dasein to beings in the midst of beings. Exposure holds Dasein in the Not in the following ways. (*i*) Work is the exposure of Dasein to the Not of beings in their resistance to Dasein. This resistance, in turn, begets the violence of which *An Introduction to Metaphysics* speaks (GA40, 159/149). (*ii*) Dasein is subject to the assault of beings; negated by beings, work is the overcoming of this negation. (*iii*) Dasein is confronted by the necessity of overcoming, through work, the Not of fundamental need or distress which arises out of the ek-static temporality of Dasein itself. For not to work leaves Dasein empty. Unemployment (*Arbeitslosigkeit*) is an existential deprivation. Dasein in its nature as ecstatic, as being-moved-toward an encounter with things, is left empty by not-working:

> Because work actualizes [our] relation to beings, therefore unemployment is an emptying of the relation to being. The relation still remains, but it is unfulfilled. This unfulfilled relation is the ground of the forsakenness of someone without work. In this forsakenness, the relation of mankind to the whole of beings is as alive as ever, but as *pain*. For this reason the lack of work is helpless being-exposed [*Ausgesetztsein*].
>
> (GA38, 154)

Work does not set exposure aside but rather actualizes, or consummates, it in setting beings into the light of the open, that is, in fixing them in the gestalt (*eidos*) out of which they can begin to presence. Anticipating the *Beiträge*, we could say that in our not-working, our relation to being is emptied because it is not brought into the gestalt of beings, not founded in beings (GA65, 314–15/221). The forsakenness, or abandonment (*Verlassenheit*), of mankind – this being-left-empty – is the negation (pain) which work 'negates' in taking up and realizing Dasein's relation to beings. But this is not true of all kinds of work, for work can be 'alienated' from itself. According to Marx, it is 'in his work upon the objective world ... that man first really proves himself to be a *species being*. This production is his active species life. Through and because of this production, nature appears as *his* work and his reality.' Estranged or alienated labour, however, turns mankind's '*species being*, both nature and his spiritual species property, into a being *alien* to him, into a *means* to his *individual existence.*'[25] It is clear that Heidegger rejects the thesis of the self-production of human being through work. Yet when Marx defines alienated labour as the reduction of humanity's species being to its existence, inasmuch as labour as self-productive becomes a mere means to this end, he perhaps anticipates an essential moment of work, as Heidegger understands it: alienated labour reveals the primacy of a fallen *present* over the authentic temporalizing of the three dimensions of time in the making-present of the present.

In *Being and Time*, Heidegger refers to the spell, or numbness (*benommen sein*), which overcomes Dasein in losing itself to the processes of the work-world. In the *Grundbegriffe* of 1929–30, *Benommenheit* fixes terminologically the state of the animal in its 'world' (GA29/30, sec. 58). This is not to say that Dasein can be interpreted as animal – it cannot – but that the tendency of Dasein (as fallen) to disperse itself in the merely present can be 'institutionalized' by specific work-regimes, and thereby lead to the impoverishment of Dasein's being-in-the-world. If, furthermore, the *Contributions to Philosophy* (1936–8) anticipate the dissolution of the rational animal of metaphysics into the techno-animality of the regime of technology (GA65, 98/68), this will suffice to show that 'work' can signify the Not of the total self-alienation of Dasein, that is, the negation of its 'essence.' This alienation reflects a fourfold reduction to the present: the reduction of work to concern for the mere succession of the being-present of entities (hence its dissolution in the work-process); the reduction of the totality of beings to the present of their being-available as resources-on-call; the reduction of the worker to the present in the struggle for mere survival; and the reduction of the ek-static differentiation and unity of mission, task, and work (the historicity of a Volk) to the collective subject of production and consumption. The making-present of a product, as an available function of supply and demand for the market, implicates a privative sense of work.

Reduction to the primacy of the present signifies the concealment of the Not. Yet the Not of the exposure to beings is the fundamental 'condition of production' of works. Work as making-present allows the present to presence out of the Not-present of the other two ecstacies of time which constitute the being of work. What does this imply for the work itself? Do works ('products') as produced by work in Heidegger's sense, stand in essential relation to 'negativity,' as a condition of their being? We know that Heidegger will make this claim for *works of art*, given that the artwork incorporates the strife of unconcealment and the Not of withdrawal from unconcealment. But works of production? It is true, as we recall, that the enpresenting (*Gegenwärtigung*) of the ready-to-hand is projected on the horizon of *praesens* (*Praesenz*). Yet, Heidegger continues, the phenomenon of being able to miss something in the equipmental context shows that the Not lies as a negative moment in the being-present of the ready-to-hand (GA24, 442–3/311). A 'negative moment constitutes itself in the structure of the being of the ready-to-hand' (GA24, 442/311, modified). Heidegger does not pursue this question further, except to add that 'closer consideration shows that the not and also the essential nature of the not, nullity ... can be interpreted only by way of the nature of time.' To 'what extent is a negative, a not, involved in Temporality in general?' (GA24, 443/311). The question of the negative in the constitution of the ready-to-hand is left open.

This question could be specified more precisely at least, by way of the dynamic of earth and world as unfolded in the artwork essay. Heidegger's essay on Aristotle's *Physics*, B, 1 (1939), moreover, holds that *steresis* (privation) belongs to the unfolding of a *dunamis* into the 'actualized' work, the *ergon* (BCP 364–9/264–8). The Not belongs to the becoming-present of a being – it is not overcome or set aside.[26] This also has implications for the work of production, and not only for the artwork.

The references of the work as ready-to-hand refer to environing nature, as well as to the public world. Can we envision a 'mode of production' incorporated in a technical installation which allows the earth to come forth into unhiddenness, *as withdrawing* from being-present? The work would no longer be simply present as a product and function of the market but reveal the event of presencing and the Not of withdrawal in what becomes present. In fact, Heidegger did not abandon this question: the *Beiträge* returns to it in the form of asking what technology shall be (GA65, 275/194). Does the essence of technology conceal the possibility of giving *shelter* to the being of beings? Shelter (*Bergung*) is granted by the Not as the withdrawal from being-present in the event of the presencing of a being. The Not shelters the being from the transparency of representation, and from mere availability. Can technology, along with art, found the truth of being in beings? These questions evidently still refer us back to the essence of work, and evidently, for Heidegger, to the Volk as the 'subject' of work.

4.5 Volk and Self-Responsibility

In what relation, finally, does Heidegger's phenomenology of work and the place of science in the state, as I have attempted to unfold it, stand to his overtly political and programmatic statements of 1933? For it has become a commonplace of criticism that Heidegger allowed himself, however briefly, to be suborned by Nazi ideology and to serve the interests of the regime.

The address of 11 November 1933 in Leipzig, to which I referred above, is instructive in this regard. The immediate occasion of the address is Germany's withdrawal from the League of Nations. Heidegger justifies this step on the grounds that a people's 'will to take responsibility for itself' is 'the fundamental law of the Dasein of the Volk' (GA16, 190). Heidegger rejects the implication that Germany's No to the League is a step back into international lawlessness. Just as clearly, he identifies the politics of the League with the faith of 'international brotherhood,' and holds that this ideology is without foundation and incapable of generating a binding obligation. Evidently he considers the League, as Carl Schmitt, for example, also did, as a forum of national power politics, masked in the guise of universal brotherhood, and as being all the more dangerous for this. Given the history of the League and its origins in the wake of Versailles, this judgement is not extraordinary. It is not clear, however, how Heidegger's appeal to national self-responsibility and obedience to the self-imposed 'limit' of a people's own nature can prevent a relapse into anarchy. For it can be argued that whatever the failings of the League, an international institution of collective security and conflict resolution like the League was and is a necessity.

Two questions, it seems to me, emerge as keys to the address: (*i*) the one of obligation; and (*ii*) the one of limit. What obliges a people to recognize the rights of other peoples? Is there in any sense a law of our being, of the being of peoples, from which all positive international law may be said to derive? Although Heidegger does not pose this question explicitly, it is implied in the address by his insistence that Germany's withdrawal from the League does not open the door to lawlessness (GA16, 191). His implicit answer holds that 'the will to self-responsibility' shall be the 'law of the being-with-one-another of peoples [Völker]' (GA16, 193). How can the will to self-responsibility found an international order where, in Heidegger's words, 'every Volk can and must be for every other a teacher of the richness and power of all great deeds and works of human being' (GA16, 193)?

We have seen that in the same address Heidegger holds that modern thought is eviscerated by its own rootlessness. And therefore it is also powerless to oblige one people to enter into essential, mutually limiting relations with another. The idea of the 'brotherhood of mankind' cannot grant a stable world order, cannot found a relation of mutual obligation. Thus, he argues that

> The will to a true community of nations [Volksgemeinschaft] keeps itself as distant from the idea of the brotherhood of mankind, which is without foundation and obligation, as from the blind rule of force. (GA16, 191)

Heidegger insists that the mutual obligation of peoples has a hold in reality only insofar as each discovers and remains true to its own historical essence (*Wesen*), and thus, taking responsibility for itself, comes to be out of its own limits to affirm its own independence (*Eigenständigkeit*) (GA16, 191). These limits are suborned by the deracinated character of modern thought, which finds its expression in an unlimited economy of production and the requisite socio-technical constitution of the planetary order.

Heidegger's fundamental reason for rejecting the League now becomes clear. Evidently he holds that the primacy of economics and technology over the idea of the political under the regime of liberalism vitiates the claim of the League to speak for the nations. Only insofar as science is limited by the responsibility a Volk takes for its own historicity, that is, insofar as a Volk takes up the task of finding the governing limit proper to its being, can the primacy of the apolitical be broken. Only at this point, as it were, can a people be trusted to enter into alliances.

It is still not clear, however, how Heidegger conceives the self-governing limit of a people to actualize itself in its own political being and in its being with other peoples. The condition of actualization is a people's confrontation with beings, thus to found them in all the modes of their differentiation.

> The innermost motivation of questioning of a science rooted in the Volk [einer völkischen Wissenschaft] is the originary courage either to grow or to break in the confrontation [Auseinandersetzung] with beings. (GA16, 192)

The actualization of science as a mode of the self-limitation of a Volk happens as work.

> Yet the will to take responsibility for itself is not only the fundamental law of
> our being as a Volk, but at the same time the fundamental event of the real-
> ization of our National Socialist state. Out of this will to self-responsibility
> every work of every class in things small and great are moved into the posi-
> tion and rank of their equal necessity. The work of the classes carries and
> secures the living structure of the state; work allows the Volk to recover its
> rootedness; work moves the state as the actuality of the Volk into the field of
> influence of all essential powers of human being. (GA16, 190)

In this passage, work is posited as the condition of the actualization of
self-responsibility in and through the founding of a state responsive to
the powers of being and the earth. The primacy of work follows from
what Heidegger has to say regarding the necessity of founding research
in the existence of the Volk. For, whereas work is guided by knowledge
(*Wissen*), knowledge remains rooted only as long as it attends to the differentiation of being in beings. And work is the name Heidegger gives to
our attentive confrontation with and transformation of beings. The
place Heidegger gives to National Socialism in the transformation of
labour into the enactment of the rootedness of work is evident.

What remains largely implicit in Heidegger's address is the argument
that in willing itself, a Volk wills the self-willing and self-responsibility of
every other Volk. Choosing self-responsibility, consequently, would constitute the condition of mutual obligation in the intercourse of nations.
This is brought to word as follows: 'if the will to self-responsibility
becomes the law of the being-with-one-another of peoples,' then they
shall be teachers of greatness to one another (GA16, 193). What are we
to make of this 'law'? In the first instance, it cannot be founded in the
mutual recognition of stable, collective subjects, that is, in the metaphysical identity of peoples. For we have seen that the Volk is a *project* of selfhood, and does not have the identity of a collective subject. Heidegger's
deconstruction of the metaphysics of presence, moreover, undercuts the
possibility of self-identity as the condition of mutual obligation.[27] The
being of the Volk, no less than the being of Dasein, is only as transcendent, which is to say, it constitutes itself out of the movement of its return
to itself from its being-with things and others (GA24, 229/161). Dasein's
authenticity is not the solipsism of an isolated self, but is already marked
by its relation to the other. We recall that in *Being and Time*, Heidegger
holds that as 'being-with, Da-sein "is" essentially for the sake of others'
(SZ 123/116). Authenticity also arises out of the relation to the other, in
fact out of the recognition of the other as Dasein. The authenticity of

Dasein already implicates *Mitdasein* as a constitutive moment of authenticity. And as such to choose one's self, in self-responsibility, implies the recognition of the potential of the other as a self-responsible, autonomous being. Birmingham makes this point as follows: Dasein's purposiveness, whereby it chooses to be authentic, 'marks its heteronomy, its responsibility to the other as end. In other words, Dasein's capacity to choose, its "I am able," marks the moment of obligation.'[28] It is my argument that this structure of transcendence, which yokes together, in one moment, the choice to take responsibility for oneself and the recognition of the other as one to whom we have an obligation, is the 'law' to which Heidegger appeals in the address. Heidegger evidently holds that this is the only possible ground of mutual obligation, to the extent that the collapse of metaphysics into nihilism removes the transcendental sanction for norms of behaviour in international relations. The mutual obligation of peoples or nations to each other, however, is founded in their *common obligation* to a way of working which is rooted in the native soil, or historical earth, of each people. Heidegger apparently expected National Socialism to initiate a transformation of the economics of production which would break with the measurelessness of capitalism. The rootedness of the 'Volk,' in the postmetaphysical sense, in its native earth would be the 'condition' of this political and economic transformation, and consequently also the condition of the law of nations.

5 *An Introduction to Metaphysics* and Heidegger's Critique of 'Intellectualism'

It is the fundamental premise of Heidegger's *Einführung in die Metaphysik* that the 'political' question can only be asked in a sufficiently radical way, so as to allow a new founding project of state and Volk to institute itself, if it is asked as the question of being. This demands that the *differentiation of being be brought into knowledge in and through the practice of founding thought* in art, thinking, and leadership. National Socialism understands itself, Heidegger avers, as a necessary counter-movement to 'intellectualism' and the deracinated ideologies and political cultures of Marxism and liberalism (GA40, 130–1/122). Although the critique of intellectualism is necessary, Heidegger holds, it fails to achieve its goal, and itself falls back into political reaction insofar as it is incapable of grasping the roots of the abyss between thought and historically founded existence in the metaphysical destiny of the West. According to Heidegger, the critique of intellectualism therefore implicates the de-construction and retrieval of the metaphysical tradition. This implies the de-construction of the metaphysical concept of being (beingness) as the ground of intellectualism in the separation of being and thought, and involves the overcoming of the metaphysical interpretation of *ousia*. In Charles Guignon's words, what this 'retrieval is supposed to provide is a way of replacing the substance ontology that dominates Western thought with an alternative understanding of Being' as 'an unfolding *happening* or *event*.' This '"event ontology"' would found our experience of all that is.[1] The four determinations or 'limitations' of being – appearance, becoming, thought, and the Ought – are to be founded in the *polis*. The *polis* is projected as the site of articulation of being, that is, the site of the event of being as enacted in rites, and brought to fulfilment in labour and works of art.

5.1 Overcoming Intellectualism

We have established that Heidegger opposes himself to the actual development of National Socialism after 1933. After the purge of the conservatives and the SA in 1934, Heidegger concluded that the regime had fallen prey to its reactionary wing. This is reflected in Heidegger's attack on the concept of value, to which the ideologues of the Party, as well as the advocates of 'spiritual conservatism,' and traditional intellectuals appealed. Nonetheless, Heidegger continued to believe, at least until 1935, in the 'inner truth and greatness of National Socialism' – to recall the most notorious phrase of *An Introduction to Metaphysics*. The central political question of the *Introduction* is how this reactionary recourse to values and the 'traditional intellect' in philosophy and politics may be overcome. Heidegger still accepts the critique of 'intellectualism' as a necessary countermovement to deracination. But intellectualism can only be overcome, he will argue, by uncovering the provenance of the ahistorical intellect in the separation of *logos* and *phusis*. Intellectualism implies the triumph of logical, ideological, and logistical calculation over the *logos* as the gathered differentiation of *phusis* in the historical specificity of its unconcealment (GA40, 130–1/122). As Dahlstrom has shown, the *Introduction* questions the 'logical prejudice' of metaphysics, understood as the primacy of logic in the determination of the meaning of being.[2] Not only does the question of intellectualism arise, for Heidegger, out of the problem of logic, but both issues are rooted in the question of being and the possibility of its historical articulation in the *polis*. The deconstruction of intellectualism, moreover, to uncover the unity of *logos* and *phusis*, is simultaneously intended as a critique of value, for values in their atemporal validity are founded in the separation of the Ideal from the historically sited presencing of being in beings (NII 221–2/4: 165).[3]

'Intellectualism,' as conceived by radical conservatives and National Socialists, consists in the separation of thought, or more precisely, of the intellect, from the life world of concretely embodied historical existence. According to Houston Stewart Chamberlain 'only those representations which have been transformed into gestalt constitute the enduring possessions of human consciousness.'[4] The intellect disintegrates the gestalt. It becomes the destructive enemy of life, of the soul, of the 'spirit.' Ludwig Klages holds, in his 'Rhythmus und Arbeit' (Rhythm and Labour) of 1936, that modern industry substitutes the pulse of the machine for the organic rhythm of work, announcing the triumph of the alienated intellect over body and soul.[5] Already in *Mensch und Erde*

Klages had argued that this alienation of thought from life is the outcome not only of capitalism and the sciences, but even more fundamentally of Christianity, which prepared the subjection of appearances, in the sense of the image and embodied life-forms, to the spirit (*Geist*). The 'spirit' would take power over the earth, and in its capitalist avatar deriving from Christianity itself, reduce the plenitude of life-forms to quantitative relations 'incorporated in the possession of money.'[6] The triumph of the intellect is therefore the end result of a long historical process. Driven to its logical conclusion in the disintegration of lived totality, it opens the possibility of a countermovement. In Leopold Ziegler's words, 'With the conclusion of this movement [of the scientific and analytic transformation of the spirit] the substance of our human individuality will have evaporated into calculable economic functions – [our individuality] dispersed, indeed annihilated, an imaginary point of intersection of statistically generated laws of behavior; and at that moment resistance against this historical process will become infinitely great and invincible.'[7] The countermovement Ziegler anticipates finds expression across the entire cultural spectrum of the German Right, from politics to the arts, from ecology to metaphysics. For example, Schoenichen's *Naturschutz im Dritten Reich* (1934) attacks modern technology in the same vein, claiming that it subjects all of nature to a 'calculable and rationalist point of view' which threatens species diversity, alienates humanity from the laws of life, and uproots German humanity from the sources of its power in its attunement to the landscape.[8] Ecology and species preservation – Schoenichen goes so far as to complain without irony of the 'serious persecution' (*heftiger Verfolgung*) some species of insects have been forced to suffer – are intimately linked, in Schoenichen's thinking, to the preservation of a people in its own natural habitat.[9] Schoenichen echoes Klages on species diversity and preservation,[10] and both link the preservation of cultural and biological *form* to anti-capitalism and anti-imperialism. We have seen that an allied critique of 'intellectualism' runs through writings on university reform, and the critique of 'capitalist' humanity, as opposed to the form-giving impulse of the technologist. Ruttke insists, in an essay of 1936 devoted to university reform, that National Socialism does not pursue science 'for the sake of science, but puts science in the service of the people and thereby the coming to be of the people as an historical event' (*Volkwerdung als geschichtlichen Vorgang*).[11] All of these discourses identify the alienation of thought from a holistic conception of 'life' as the root of deracination and decline.

In Heidegger's own terms, thought is degraded to mere 'intelligence,' signifying the application of analytic faculties to the dis-integration, control, and management of life in pursuit of the greatest possible efficiencies of production and consumption. Heidegger would essentially agree with Ziegler's diagnosis that the movement of intellectualism implicates the loss of our individuality, that is, of our being, and in fact represents the hollowing out of the being of all things. Although he shares this evaluation with conservatives such as Zeigler and with National Socialists such as Krieck and Baeumler, Heidegger's analysis of the roots of intellectualism goes far deeper to uncover its origin in the *chorismos* of being and beings. The *chorismos*, or separation, of the presencing of being from beings initiates the destiny of the West. In the *Introduction*, Heidegger defines *chorismos* as follows: it was

> in the Sophists and in Plato that appearance was declared to be mere appearance and thus degraded. At the same time being, as *idea*, was exalted to a supersensory realm. A chasm, *chorismos*, was created between the merely apparent essent here below and real being somewhere on high. (GA40, 113/106)

The consequences of this chasm for the metaphysical history of the West can be summed up in two words: *Seinsverlassenheit* – the abandonment of beings, by being, which delivers entities over to their 'non-essential' functionality; and *Seinsvergessenheit* – the oblivion of being, and consequently the withdrawal of presencing from beings, thus to release them into the orbit of their mere availability and calculability as determined by metaphysical categories of presence (*Seiendheit*).

An Introduction to Metaphysics has drawn considerable commentary. Particular passages, or claims, of the text, as well as Heidegger's relation to the tradition, have received pointed attention: Heidegger's interpretation of the *Antigone*, or of *phusis*, his 'cultural pessimism,' his equation of America and Soviet Russia, the discourse of *Geist*, his notorious reference to the 'inner truth and greatness' of National Socialism, have all evoked passionate response. The potential of the lectures as a commentary on the idea of 'the political' has certainly been grasped, yet Heidegger's overtly 'political' statements have tended to overshadow the reflection on the conditions of the possibility of the political, implied in the unfolding of the lectures. In what follows, I will attempt to show how the movement of the lectures as a whole attempts to integrate the guiding question of being and a reflection on the political within the specific context of the problem of intellectualism.

Let us briefly take up the issue of National Socialism, and Heidegger's relative adherence to its 'inner truth.' Ferry and Renaut lay out a commonly accepted interpretation: according to Heidegger, the 'inner truth and greatness' of Nazism, in its confrontation with modern technology, consists in (*i*) a counter-movement to modernity and the socio-technical world, or (*ii*) in the consummation of modernity and this world, thus to reveal its horrific essence.[12] Which of these views did Heidegger hold in 1935? Based on considerations I have already laid out in detail, it seems that in 1935 Heidegger held to the first position. By 1936, however, on the evidence of the *Beiträge*, this position had become increasingly untenable for Heidegger. The fact that, despite this, Heidegger did not then, or subsequently, seek refuge in liberal democracy or democratic socialism, but rather included all three existing political directions in his critique, has aroused perhaps the most outrage – outrage overshadowed only by his incomprehensible silence on the Holocaust. Heidegger remained true to his own 'vision' in seeking a third way, even after the collapse of his hopes for National Socialism. The question remains whether the fundamental terms of this third way can be derived from Heidegger's philosophy and specified. As I have already argued, it will not suffice to assimilate Heidegger's position, as Zimmerman does, to the 'cultural pessimism' of a rejection of the Enlightenment project, in common with Spengler and many others of this period.[13] The claims and presuppositions of Heidegger's 'third way,' which he shares with the Conservative Revolution, have to be specified, and I have tried to show that in significant degree they can be specified.

Wherein does the movement of Heidegger's *Einführung in die Metaphysik* consist? It fundamentally consists in *the retrieval of the four metaphysical determinations of being in order to site the unity of the differentiation of being in the polis*, and pre-eminently in the event of the work, in the practice of thought, and in the act of leadership. The movement of the *Introduction* leads us to a retrieval of being from its determinations, or 'limitations' (*Beschränkungen*): metaphysically, being has been determined in its distinction from becoming, appearance, thought, and the 'Ought.' 'Being' is delimited against these determinations, even though it is entangled in them. The retrieval of being, for Heidegger, will consist in the transformation of each of these metaphysically conceived differentiations of being. The *chorismos* of being from appearances, its separation from becoming, thought, and the Ought, is to be overcome in the re-integration of being and its four determinations. The historical siting of the unity of these determinations as the differentiation *of being*, as 'internal' to being, will be the condition of the overcoming of intellectualism. The '*polis*' is to be understood as the possibility of a polity which would allow the presencing of being in beings to be actualized, and Da-sein is to be the site of this event (GA40, 214/205). The *possibility* of a polity which would allow the presencing of being in beings to be actualized is as such distinct from particular political institutions. In this sense it is an objective of the *Introduction* to show the 'condition of possibility' of the political, without, as such, committing itself to any specific political system.

To a large extent this movement into the 'condition of possibility' of the political is implicit in *An Introduction to Metaphysics*. The question of leadership, for example, is intimated primarily by the *agon* of Antigone and Creon, regarding the proper limit of human commanding and doing. Tragedy emerges as a founding rite of the *polis*. Through the work of art, mortality reveals itself as the source of rootedness of the *polis* in *phusis*. Receptiveness to the event of being as the event of the tragic rite intimates the limit of human knowing and of scientific *techne*. The four determinations of being – becoming, appearance, thought, and the Ought – are retrieved in their founded and founding specificity as differentiations of the sitedness of presencing (GA40, 102/95). The deconstruction of these determinations, thus to exhibit their fundamental ground in a post-metaphysical understanding of being, conditions the retrieval of the *polis*.

As a reflection on 'being and the political,' the project which is initiated here stands between the Rector's Address of 1933 and the *Contributions to Philosophy (From Enowning)* of 1936–8. Certainly the *Contributions* take up this question under changed circumstances – Heidegger's sense of distance from the priorities of the regime has only increased – and are informed by a still more radical interrogation of the tradition. In the *Introduction*, being is said to be delimited in four ways, as follows.

5.1.1 Being and Becoming

This distinction already defines Greek philosophy: Parmenides (Fragment 8, 1–6) holds that being is without becoming and without passing away, in all that is the abiding. Heraclitus holds that all is movement – *panta rhei* – and therefore that being is becoming (GA40, 103–5/95–8). The question at issue is in what sense movement and abiding are to be understood in each case. Heidegger does not engage this question directly; nonetheless, it is implied. Heidegger claims that the two thinkers do not stand, as traditionally assumed, in the most extreme opposition: they rather say 'the same.' The same, however, is not the identical, but the belonging-together of the differentiated. In 'On the Being and Conception of *Physis* in Aristotle's *Physics* B, 1' (1939), Heidegger will take up the question of the sameness of being and becoming as the differentiated unity of *kinesis* and *ousia*. This unity finds expression as *morphe*. Heidegger explicitly interprets *morphe* as *Gestalt* in 'The Origin of the Work of Art.' The distinction of being and becoming is retrieved as the differentiated unity of being-as-gestalt. This is thematized in the *Introduction to Metaphysics* in terms of the retrieval of *ousia* as the delimited presencing of beings. This puts the metaphysical interpretation of *ousia* as abiding presence into question. Since presence signifies the truth of the atemporal Idea and the precondition of the Ought as *agathon* and the normative, Heidegger's thesis of the finitude of presencing also undermines the subsequent metaphysical conceptualization of the Idea as principle and axiom, as well as the determination of the ethical as the normative. The distinction of being and becoming, moreover, traditionally finds its corollary in that of being and seeming (or appearance). But if *ousia* is reinterpreted as the differentiated unity of being and becoming, then being and appearance also enter into a new relation. Seeming is no longer understood as the non-being of the mere image, but belongs to being itself in the sited finitude of its presencing. In this sense, the way is opened for the re-integration of both becoming and appearance into our understanding of presencing as shining-forth in the gestalt. Since the site of the finitude of being is the *polis*, Heidegger's retrieval of the differentiations of being will also have a decisive import, if in the first instance only an implicit one, for our understanding of the political.

5.1.2 Being and Appearance

The mimetic theory of truth, which Plato's analogy of the cave unfolds, opens up the *chorismus* between the Idea of the *agathon* and mere appearances (GA40, 113/106). The polity is grounded in the atemporal, which appears in appearances only in the darkened form of the image. The Ideas enter modern politics as a conceptual system of fundamental theorems, which are the a priori condition of the Leviathan. With the disintegration of the specifically political in favour of the socio-technical management of society – a process which leads, in the Anglo-American tradition, from Hobbes via Locke and the *Federalist Papers* to the postmodern technopolis – the *chorismos* of being and appearing is closed in a novel way which is anticipated by the analogy of the cave itself. Being and appearing, in effect, collapse into simulation processes which produce the 'real' as simulacra of every kind of technical and socio-technical programming.[14] The postmodern 'politics' of the image 'institutes' a technopolis of the cave. Heidegger's engagement with tragedy and the work of art, in contrast, is an attempt to *close the abyss between being and image* by founding being in the gestalt; and the gestalt, in the polity.

5.1.3 Being and Thought

Schürmann has argued that the discursive grounds of politics derive from the logical principles, or *archai*, of substance and accidents, of identity and non-contradiction.[15] The deconstruction of these principles leads us back to the possibility of an attunement to being as a call to the letting-be of beings. The question of what kind of polity would be commensurate with the thought of releasement (letting-be) remains unclear in the *Introduction*. In the *Beiträge*, Heidegger will attempt to show that the essential determinations of the polity are laid out in acts of the founding of the differentiation of being in beings. But already in the *Introduction*, 'thinking' is understood, in opposition to intelligence, in its sited historicity – as a mode of apprehension which takes its measure from the things themselves. This calls for a deconstruction of 'intellectualism.'

> If we wish to combat intellectualism seriously, we must know our adversary, i.e., we must know that intellectualism is only an impoverished modern offshoot of a development long in the making, namely, the position of priority gained by thought with the help of Western metaphysics. (GA40, 130/122)

A new, more primordial measure must be found in the thought-of-being. But insofar as this taking of a measure involves the violence of *setting a measure* where none exists, an essential ambiguity runs through the text and through Heidegger's understanding of the founding acts of thought and leadership. Heidegger devotes the greater part of his discussion to this distinction. He draws on three witnesses in particular: Sophocles, Heraclitus, and Parmenides. In the *Contributions*, Heidegger will call this reflection on 'being and thought' a step in the overcoming of the Greek, and the founding of the other, beginning (GA65, 196/137). The fixation of thought in the abiding presence of beingness (*Seiendheit*) is to be deconstructed to reveal temporality as the measure of the presencing of being (*Seyn*) in beings.

5.1.4 Being and the Ought

Heidegger's thesis in the *Introduction* that Plato's thought of the *agathon* intimates the *chorismos* of being and beings, and consequently that his thought of the *agathon* reveals the origin of intellectualism, is evidently a significant departure from the position of the *Metaphysical Foundations of Logic* (GA26).[16] Now the deconstruction of the Ought necessitates the deconstruction of the metaphysical *telai* of political action – the good, progress, happiness – such as would provide normative grounds for the legitimation of a polity. To say that the Ought no longer determines action, means, for Heidegger, that thinking takes its directive from the sited presencing of being: this directive expresses itself in the ethos of being as the unconcealment of *phusis*. The normative demands of an ethics would have to give way to the history-founding specificity and singularity of the presencing of *phusis* in work and ritual. Greek tragedy is such a ritual. The deconstruction of the normative to open the possibility of an ethos as the sitedness of Da-sein again raises the problem of finding a measure for thought and action which would grant Da-sein its 'stability.' It is in this context that the question of being-toward-death arises.

In his introductory comments to his remarks on these delimitations of being, Heidegger notes that they are 'by no means accidental. What is held apart in them belonged originally together and tends to merge. The distinctions therefore have an inner necessity' (GA40, 101/94). Our objective, if we are to 'ask the question of being radically,' Heidegger adds, must be to 'understand the task of unfolding the truth of the essence of being; one must come to a decision regarding the powers hidden in these distinctions in order to restore them to their own truth' (GA40, 102/95).

5.2 The Hermeneutic Situation: Siting the Question of Being

The hermeneutic situation out of which the question of being arises is the destitution of the being of beings. This destitution calls for a new experience of the presencing of being, to found being in Dasein and thus in the primordial ways of the unconcealment of being. Heidegger's *An Introduction to Metaphysics* opens with the question, 'Why are there essents rather than nothing?' This question moves the being of beings in their entirety into the openness of the why of their possible ground (GA40, 6/4). The transformation of the question no longer seeks, in the manner of onto-theology, a first and highest cause of the being of beings.

It rather seeks to site the question in our attunement to the presencing of being. In this way the metaphysical question concerning the why, the being *of beings*, is also transformed – it becomes the question concerning being 'itself.' The question is now understood as the questioning-being-open to the presencing of being (GA40, 20–1/18). The hermeneutic transformation of the question concerning the Nothing, moreover, will bring us back to the question of logic and the *logos*. This question, in turn, will be unfolded as the question concerning the differentiation and historical sitedness of being.

What is the non-metaphysical ground to which the question concerning the Nothing leads us? In fundamental moods, such as anxiety and boredom, beings become strange, questionable to us (GA40, 3–4/1–2). 'Nothing,' writes Heidegger in *Being and Time*, 'which is at hand and objectively present within the world, functions as what *Angst* is anxious about' (SZ 186/174). Fundamental boredom, when things lose their 'weight' and we become indifferent to them also leaves us hovering in the midst of beings, detached from beings (GA29/30, 117–251). In both cases, we transcend the things to their 'site' – the open clearing out of which things emerge for us. This site is *no thing:* in *Being and Time*, anxiety is said to be called forth by '*being-in-the-world as such*' (SZ 186/174). Called forth by our being in the world, anxiety calls us back to ourselves – as beings who are themselves in question. The question recoils on the questioner. In this way the metaphysical question, which seeks a first cause of what is, becomes a question of meta-physics, of self-engagement in the transcendental ground of our being. This 'ground,' however, is not any given highest principle, physical, metaphysical, or theological, for as a first cause, and hence as a kind of entity, this ground is also shattered by the question. The only 'ground' which remains is that which is opened up by the questioning of the questioner. This 'ground' is not pre-determined in advance: it is rather the openness of a grant to the questioner. For this reason alone the strictures which Derrida raises against the 'question of the question' lose their force.[17]

The question opens up a site: Dasein in its existential-historical concreteness. For the 'self'-engagement which attunement to the questionableness of beings calls for is historical. Thus the attunement of boredom, for example, in the face of the weightlessness of entities is an historically specific response to the destitution of entities. Heidegger's subsequent reflections on the destiny of Germany and the West (GA40, 40–42, 48–53/37–9, 45–50) are also attempts to site the question in the destitution out of which it emerges. Our engagement with the question of Nothing is already conditioned by our situatedness. In this sense the posing of the question is already 'thrown.' The question can only be posed, conversely, as a leap which opens up its own ground of possibility. For every already existent ground is precisely what has been placed in question (GA40, 8/6). The thrown project of the question, therefore, opens up the site *of questioning*: the site only is in the holding-oneself-in-the-question. This holding-in is itself not an ahistorical disposition, but arises out an attunement to the historical specificity of beings (in their destitution), as a response which founds or attempts to found a site. In founding, the being-open of the question is given the gestalt of work and ritual, not as a means of closing the question, but so as to allow the question of the emergence, the presencing of beings, to pose itself ever anew.

The metaphysical asking of the Why? poses the question in terms of the cause of beings. But with the abandonment of the search for a cause of beings, the question is transformed into a response to the Nothing out of which beings emerge and in which they are constantly held, as that which differentiates them from each other (GA40, 30–3/27–30). This response to the Nothing constitutes the step back from the metaphysical formulation of the question to recover its founding moment in the historicity of Da-sein as the site of the emergence and taking-gestalt of beings.

However, to ask about Nothing, to pose the question of why beings are at all, and not rather Nothing, runs against the laws of logic, inasmuch as Nothing is posited as something (GA40, 27–8/25). But is thinking to take logic as its measure? Or is logic derivative of philosophical and poetic thinking and founding? It is in this context that the question of being becomes a question concerning the *logos* as movement of the unconcealment of the differentiation of beings. Beings emerge into their being out of the possibility of their non-being. Can this emergence and what emerges be founded, sited as gestalt? Only insofar as thinking responds to what being, understood as the *logos* of unconcealment and differentiation, offers, or sends as destiny, to an historically founded tradition. To respond to being is to respond to the sending of being as preserved by a tradition. It is in this sense that Heidegger takes up the metaphysical question concerning the Nothing, in order to recover its hidden ground in the *historicity of questioning*, and in questioning, the historicity of the presencing of being. The 'history' (*Geschick*) of being makes sense only as the response of Da-sein to what the tradition sends or apportions (the *Zusage* of language). The thesis that the 'sending' of being merely mystifies empirical history[18] reduces history to the positivity of what can be calculated in terms of cause-and-effect relations. The

'*Geschick* of being' is not a mystical cloud, however dark, hovering over history, but gives expression to the experience that possibility belongs to the actuality of the historical as that which gives it sense and direction. The question of the political, in turn, is not an addendum to the question of being, but an essential articulation of the specificity and singularity of the presencing of being. The task of siting the manifoldness of being in beings is the primordial political challenge Heidegger's philosophy poses. Because the question concerning Nothing calls for the founding of being in beings, it leads us into the question of the political. The questions of Volk, of work, and of state arise in response to the possibility of giving the presencing of being a site and articulation in beings.

5.2.1 Being as the 'Measure' of the Political

Heidegger argues that the beginning of Western thought experienced the whole of beings as *phusis*: the 'realm of being as such and a whole is *physis* – i.e., its essence and character are defined as that which emerges and endures' (GA40, 19/16). *Phusis* is the measure of all that arises, unfolds, and rules according to the measure of time accorded to it. *Phusis* is experienced as the being of beings itself: it names the *Ent-stehen*, meaning both the becoming of entities (their unfolding out of uncon-cealment) and their coming to stand in and through the limits of form (GA40, 17/15). The question concerning the whole of beings, which seeks out their ground in the experience of being which initiated Greek thought is inherently an historical question. The question posed is a response to the abandonment of beings: what Heidegger hears in *phusis* – the delimitation of beings which accords to each its own proper measure – arises out of the limitlessness of planetary ratiocination. It is within this context that Heidegger's geopolitical remarks on the measurelessness of America and the Soviet Union have to be located. The measure of the proper is what the tradition of Western thought has reserved for the technological epoch as a possible turn.

What is the task of philosophy at the present juncture, according to Heidegger? Its essence, he writes, is

a thinking that breaks the paths and opens the perspectives of the knowledge that sets the norms and hierarchies, of the knowledge in which and by which a people grasps the Dasein of its historical and cultural world and fulfils it [aus dem ein Volk sein Dasein in der geschichtlich-geistigen Welt begreift und zum Vollzug bringt]. (GA40, 12/10, modified)

Heidegger avers that the destitution of beings is itself an historically determined distress which the era of the consummation of metaphysics, our own, brings to fruition. This distress calls for knowledge rooted in the history of this destiny. It calls for knowledge founded in being, thus to unfold out of being the measure and the rank appropriate to the ways of being of a particular people and their historically grounded, spiritual world. Evidently Heidegger does not reject every concept of 'norm' and 'measure' – he rejects concepts of a transcendental norm, founded in metaphysics, and the values which can be derived from it.[19] The concept of 'value,' as Taminiaux hints, cannot be simply abandoned; it has to be replaced by a new, founding concept of responsibility.[20] Does Heidegger respond to this need? In my discussion of Heidegger on 'work,' I have tried to show that Heidegger implicitly ascribes a rank order to different ways of working. The measure that sets out an order of rank is given by the historicity of Da-sein in its response to being's differentiation in beings. This response implicates responsibility to beings as they arise and come to be in their historical specificity. Dasein measures itself against the challenge of the differentiation of being. The reduction of entities to in-different stock-on-call, in Heidegger's account, fails to takes its measure from the differentiation of being in beings, and thus mankind falls below the rank called for by the possibilities of presencing in beings.

The reference to 'historical and cultural fulfilment' in the passage just cited makes an appeal, in the original German, to the 'historical and *spiritual* world' of Dasein (this is covered up by Manheim's translation). The appeal to *Geist* should not mislead us into discovering a reversion, on Heidegger's part, into humanism and idealism, as Derrida proposes in *Of Spirit*. According to Derrida, Heidegger's relapse into the discourse of spirit opposes itself to the naturalism of National Socialism. Yet the appeal to spirit is, no less than the National Socialists' appeals to the collectivity of the Volk, contaminated by 'humanism' as a form of subjectivity.[21] However, the world which emerges out of the measure-setting knowledge of philosophy is the delimited historical world of a people, and not, as Derrida argues, the abstraction of humanist subjectivity. Already in *Sein und Zeit*, Heidegger had insisted that *Geist* be understood as the temporalization of Dasein: '"Spirit" does not first fall into time, but it *exists* as the primordial *temporalizing* of temporality ... "Spirit" does not fall *into* time; but factical existence "falls," in falling prey, *out of* primordial, authentic temporality' (SZ 436/396). As Derrida has pointed out, in *Being and Time* Heidegger distances himself from the metaphysical concept of spirit. This is the beginning of a certain retrieval, a certain

otherness, of spirit.[22] Wherein does this otherness consist? The temporalization of spirit implies the historicity of Dasein – hence not only its
finitude, but also the sited attunement of the There of being. Indeed, it
is not that *Geist*, in the idealist sense, imposes a measure, but that the finitude of the spirit unfolds itself in the measures of historically founded
ways of being – in the measure of the particular, 'typical' artforms of a
people, for example. It would be mistaken, furthermore, to suppose that
an appeal to the necessity of form, in the type, or gestalt, implicates a Platonic metaphysics, which drags with it, in turn, the spectre of spirit in the
guise of the 'national aestheticism' which is so central to Lacoue-Labarthe's argument. The emphasis on philosophy as a way of knowledge
which opens avenues of measure and rank reminds us that a historical-
spiritual world can only be what it is, as that specific world, in the self-cir-
cumscription and delimitation of its being. It must maintain and unfold
its own finite measure by giving shape and rank to the manifold tempo-
ralizations of being in beings.

In this sense the historical-spiritual world which philosophy opens, and
which is unfolded through all the ways (art, leadership, sacrifice, technology) through which measure is given and rank set, is still founded in *phusis*. For to say that *phusis* is the unfolding power of measured presencing
(*das aufgehend-verweilende Walten*) means that being differentiates itself in
and through beings, according to the measure of temporalization proper
to each. The destiny which *die Seinsverlassenheit*, in turn, brings with it,
precisely by virtue of giving beings over to functionalization, implicates
the deracination of the peoples of the earth from the measure appropriate to each. When this happens, being, as the measure of measures, no
longer comes to a stand in an historical site: it falls into forgetfulness and
withdraws in favour of the planetary, the 'cosmopolitan.' The planetary,
in Heidegger's terms, portends the in-difference of the temporalization
of entities, and hence the uniform availability of beings.

5.2.2 Ousia

Section 20 of the *Einführung* (in the *Gesamtausgabe*) unfolds the Greek
understanding of being as *ousia* and *phusis*. This section is part of chapter
2, entitled 'Zur Grammatik und Etymologie des Wortes Sein.' The Greek
understanding of language, Heidegger argues, is founded on their
understanding of being, for language is one kind of entity. Being, in
turn, is experienced in two related ways, as (*i*) 'standing-in-itself [In-sich-
stehen] in the sense of arising [*Ent-stehen*, standing-out-of] (*phusis*)'; (*ii*)

'but as such permanent [ständig], i.e., enduring (*ousia*)' (GA40, 68/63–4). The sense of unfolding, or coming-into-being (*Ent-stehen*), hence the temporality of 'presencing' which *phusis* brings out, is in tension with the second moment of being, which is the sense of coming-to-a-stand, of a stability, captured in the word *ousia*. A certain sense of stability, or 'gestalt' is integral to *ousia* itself, as Heidegger notes. The experience of being thereby revealed by *ousia* is quite distinct from that of a boundless 'substance' (*Substanz*) which 'underlies' the particular determinations of the being of beings (GA40, 65/61). What is already at stake here is the retrieval of the meaning of *ousia* from the metaphysical tradition, and hence from the discourse of *Seiendheit* (beingness), according to which being designates the boundless, unparticularized general category of beings, their most abstract condition of possibility. Indeed this is how *ousia* came to be interpreted (GA40, 202–3/194). But *ousia* has another sense in Greek usage; and it is by reference to this primary, non-technical meaning that Heidegger proposes to recover, here and elsewhere, the non-metaphysical sense of being. The 'recovery' is evidently not an historical-archaeological enterprise, but a rethinking and founding anew of the tradition.

And in this context, a note on language – to be precise, on the 'grammar of being' – is in order, for Heidegger offers an interpretation of the provenance of the oblivion of being which calls grammar to account. Gregory Fried has shown that Heidegger's determination to tie the question of the grammatical forms of 'to be' in Indo-European languages to the question of being can be justified on linguistic grounds.[23] According to Heidegger, grammar is itself a metaphysical determination of language. He takes his point of departure from the presupposition that the pre-ontological understanding of being which is expressed in saying 'is' is itself the condition, not only of saying this one word, but of saying anything. Why? Because saying (of anything) says in reference to its being; hence, it is an articulation (differentiation) of the understanding of being. But what does 'to say' mean here? To comport oneself to the being of something – in effect, saying is the articulation of the structure of Dasein as *Sorge* (care), hence of the ex-sistence of Dasein, its being-open to what is. Consequently, the multiplicity of the ways of saying 'it is' unfolds being, intimates the differentiation of being. The grammar of the 'copula,' in turn, as the link between subject and predicate, is already a particular, metaphysical limitation and determination of what being is – the emptiness of the most general category which underlies all predication concerning beings. Heidegger's reflections on the language of being in this chapter focus on the falling off of the experience of being from the differentiated saying of what is said in the finite forms of the verb to the saying of the in-finite, and thus a falling off into the atemporality and relative abstraction of the infinitive form. The infinitive is not only a later development, but it conceals the particularization of being: person, number, *tempus*, genus, modality. The infinitive fails to delimit the manifestation of what is. It abstracts from the particularity of being to name the most general, the emptiest case. In the infinitive form of to be, moreover, the saying of being already conceals and withdraws itself (GA40, 72–4/68–70). Not only this. The finite forms of 'to be' themselves shroud the root meanings of the Indo-European forms of the verb: to live, to emerge, to dwell (*leben, aufgehen, verweilen* or *wohnen*). The language of being therefore eventuates in a second dissimulation of the powers of being, for in the existing finite forms these root meanings withdraw in favour of the abstraction of the copula (GA40, 75–8/70–4). But the properly understood power or *Wesen* of being is its own differentiation, which delimits what is.

The fate of *ousia* is reflected, therefore, in the occultation of the differentiations of being in the infinitive of the verb to be. Now, in addition to its terminological usage as 'presence,' the word *ousia* also suggests a second, and actually more primordial, sense of *Anwesen*: it 'designates an estate or homestead, standing in itself or self-enclosed' (GA40, 65/61). As I noted above, the German word *Anwesen* (commonly translated as presence or presencing) shares with the Greek *ousia* the sense of 'presence' arising out of the well-defined limits, or gestalt, of an entity – that of a villa, for example. In ordinary language usage '*ein Anwesen*' refers to a well-formed edifice: a building set 'in' itself, rooted in its ground, and so able to create an aura of its own. A chateau has 'presence' and hence 'presences' out of the circumscription of its limit. Being: *ousia: Anwesen*. Not the unparticularized ground or substance, which 'founds' what is, but the differentiation of coming to presence within limits. This sense of *ousia* still implicates the stability of what abides. But it is not the unbounded or atemporal abiding of the undifferentiated. Presencing stands within and comes to presence out of the limit (*peras*) which gives a being its 'stand':

Yet what thus comes up and becomes intrinsically stable [ständig] encounters, freely and spontaneously, the necessity of its limit, *peras* . . . That which places itself in its limit, completing it, and so stands, has form [Gestalt], *morphe*. (GA40, 64–5/60)

It is significant that Heidegger retrieves a non-metaphysical sense of *Gestalt*, and interprets *Gestalt* as *entelecheia* – 'the holding (preserving)-itself-in-the-ending (limit)' (GA40, 64, 65/60). The being of beings begins with the limit: for in coming to stand in the circumscription of its proper limit, a being comes back to itself to take a stand in its own 'potential' and to bring it to a consummation. 'Coming to a stand accordingly means: to achieve a limit [Grenze] for itself, to limit itself [er-grenzen]' (GA40, 64/60).

The unbounded, by contrast, is strictly speaking *Unseiend* (nonessent). Yet as *Unseiend* it still 'is.' Insofar as it has the available and disposable being of a 'natural resource,' for example, its being consists in its availability. But the river as a natural resource of power generation, the woodland as the natural resource of the forestry industry, cannot in principle allow the river, the tree and forest, to manifest themselves out of their particularized limits: to rest in themselves and to stand forth each in their own gestalt. The forest has already been posited in advance as lumber and wood pulp, the river as kilowatt/hours.

Heidegger's use of the word *Gestalt* in section 20 determines gestalt in reference to the limit (*Grenze*) out of which something comes to stand, not by reference to the being of the idea which constitutes it in its beingness (*Seiendheit*). Being presences (*west an*) in the shining-forth of a gestalt. Where the gestalt disintegrates, being also withdraws. To say that being withdraws under the regime of beingness means that being cannot site itself by differentiating itself in beings. It remains undifferentiated in the universality of the concept (in *Seiendheit*, or beingness). In the *Beiträge* Heidegger brings this distinction, as we shall see, to a point as follows. *Das Seyn west:* 'being presences' in the historically founded forms (gestalten) in which it differentiates itself. In contrast, *das Sein ist:* 'being-ness is,' or persists, in the power of conceptualization, in the model and the program. Heidegger remarks that the highest name Aristotle gives to being – *entelecheia* – implies 'the holding (preserving)-itself-in-the-ending (limit) [das-Sich-in-der-Endung (Grenze)-halten (wahren)]' (GA40, 64/60). It is out of the end as internal limit (*peras*) that the gestalt begins to be. Inasmuch as the gestalt of beings is dis-integrated, and simultaneously re-integrated into a limitless play of signification, into the 'relay' of deterritorialized thought, the sited differentiation of being (*Seyn*) in beings is occluded under the regime of the planetary. Planetary thinking, and the integration of entities into the universality of signification and the production of value, are therefore allied processes in the deracination of thinking and creation from the earth. It is the implication of

Heidegger's argument that this movement into the unlimited play of conceptual thinking also conceals the possibility of the 'political' and institutes the regime of the socio-technical management of society.

5.2.3 Spirit and Historicity

Let us consider more closely Heidegger's appeal to *Geist*, and with it Derrida's claim in *Of Spirit* that in the *Introduction*, as in the Rector's Address of 1933, Heidegger falls back into metaphysical discourse: 'But it is still in the name of spirit, the spirit which guides in resolution toward the question, the will to know and the will to essence, that the other spirit, its bad double, the phantom of subjectivity, turns out to be warded off by means of *Destruktion*.'[24] If this claim holds, then the argument advanced here, that Heidegger's reflection on the possibility of the political is founded on the distinction between planetary and earth-sited thinking, cannot be held. Derrida argues that the question of being, although explicitly conceived as the deconstruction of metaphysics, is itself inherently metaphysical inasmuch as it contains a 'will to essence.'[25] Both the willing and the question of essence remain entangled in the metaphysics of presence. For the attempt to fix beings in the determination of an essence, of a stable presence to thought, repeats classical ontology. The metaphysical character of Heidegger's questioning, moreover, is evident in the determination of Dasein as the 'spiritual' being: Derrida argues that Heidegger's attempt to quarantine Dasein from the metaphysical discourse of biologism by the appeal to 'spirit' causes him to fall back into metaphysics. This argument assumes, however, that (*i*) in posing the question of being Dasein posits itself as the 'subject' or *hypokeimenon* which remains stable and unchanged in the act of questioning (this is precisely not the case, as we have seen); and (*ii*) that *Wesen*, 'essence,' is to be understood as the unchanging, underlying nature of a being, or of being itself. Heidegger, however, insists that *Wesen* be grasped as the way of unfolding of a being, and of being itself. *Wesen* is thought in its temporal and historical specificity and singularity. To say that Dasein is 'spiritual,' therefore, need not imply a fall back into the metaphysical opposition of body and spirit, given that spirit is re-interpreted as the historicity of Dasein, and Dasein as the site of every differentiation of being, including the metaphysical distinction between body and spirit.

Conceived as a metaphysical discourse in the Idealist tradition of the World Spirit and the humanistic concept of the humanity proper to it, the discourse of spirit founds the cosmopolitan world of planetary thinking, which is already announced in Kant's philosophy of history. In effect, 'spirit' would determine a discourse of beingness, not a thinking response to being. Derrida indeed grants that Heidegger rejects the transcendental concept of spirit. Yet, in Derrida's view, the discourse of spirit returns as the 'ghost' of the will to know and of the affirmation of essence. If this is so, then the 'spiritual world' to which Heidegger appeals is not historically founded in the differentiation of being, but rather re-inscribes an essentialist metaphysics. In political terms, this would implicate the 'typology' which Lacoue-Labarthe ascribes to Heidegger: the type is the essence posited by the self-willing of a people as a 'spiritual' people.[26] As opposed to this argument, I argue (*i*) that in the *Introduction, Geist* is understood in terms of the history of being; and hence (*ii*) that it is understood in reference to the abandonment of beings (*die Seinsverlassenheit*). Inasmuch as being simultaneously withholds and sends itself, *Seinsverlassenheit* is also an epochal way of being's arrival into presence, and so I argue (*iii*) that the historicity of *Geist* signifies the attunement of Dasein to *phusis*, as manifested, for example, in the historical earth, or homeland; and (*iv*) that the decision 'for' Spirit is a decision for open attentiveness and receptivity to the differentiated presencing of being in beings. Finally, we must constantly keep in mind that Heidegger's usage of *'Geist'*, as of *'Gestalt,'* is not predetermined by the metaphysical tradition but arises as a reflection on it.

In section 13 of the *Introduction* Heidegger asks the following: 'Is being a mere word and its meaning a vapor, or does what is designated by the word "being" hold within it the historical destiny of the West?' (GA40, 45–6/42) The question of the destiny of being, and hence of the 'spiritual destiny' of the West, arises out of and in response to the 'world history of the earth' (GA40, 48/45, modified). *It is indeed the earth, not simply world history 'on the earth' which is at stake* (GA39, 93–6). The common 'ground' of Dasein's attuned questioning and knowing is the possibility of the recovery of the earth as homeland, as intimated by being-toward-death.

In Heidegger's usage, 'destiny' expresses the re-collection and re-trieval of the creative possibilities of the tradition. The pre-eminent possibility for being reserved to us is the possibility of possibility itself – that is, the distinction between being (presencing) and beings (being present) which metaphysics knows as the ontological difference.[27] Insofar as things-present enter the light, the field of presencing itself withdraws and reserves itself (hence the *epoché of being*). The way of arrival of being, and hence the mode of withdrawal of being, opens and founds the site of an historical 'epoch.' The global destiny to which the earth as earth is driven in our time is evidently, although the word is not used here, the destiny of the abandonment of beings to the undestined, to the destitution which *Seinsverlassenheit* names. This destiny arises out of the metaphysical history of the West, where 'the West' is conceived as the site of one form of the founding of being in beings. As the site of the emergence of technology it implicates the danger of the destitution of beings, which can only be encountered essentially by going back to the roots of technology in the Greek understanding of being. To say that 'being' is a destiny means, then, that this destitution can only be overcome by posing the question of being in order to open a site for the historically singular differentiation and gathering of being. The question of being, therefore, is an historical question in the sense that founds a new history (GA40, 46/43). As such, it is already in its very unfolding an unfolding of the being of the political.

In section 15 (GA40, 48/45), this epochal measure of destitution is called the darkening of the world. Its essential events are the flight of the gods, the triumph of quantification, and the primacy of the mediocre. This 'darkening' of the world intimates the uprooting of the nations from their native soil, and the subjection of the earth to a planetary concept. As we have seen, the question of being involves an attempt to awaken a 'spiritual' sense of the earth as the homeland of its peoples that is directly opposed, on philosophical and political grounds, to the processes of 'globalization.' What Heidegger calls the disempowerment of the world of the spirit means the falsification of thinking as spirit. Its fundamental ground, Heidegger argues, is the mutation of the specificity of the presencing of being which *Anwesen* designates into the concept of the abiding presence, the substantiality of being. The falsifications of spirit referred to in section 15 – the triumph of intelligence, the concept of the instrumentality and calculability of the creative force of spirit, and its reduction to a cultural value (GA40, 50–3/46–9) – are empirical, historical manifestations of the uprooting of being itself. The deracination of being means that being (*Seyn*) no longer presences (*west nicht an*) and hence that entities are abandoned to the 'is' of conceptualization (*die Seiendheit*). With this, metaphysics is consummated, and the world of the spirit collapses. Thus the collapse of spirit, its subversion by instrumental intelligence, signals the epochal emergence of beingness (*Seiendheit*) and the concealment of the presencing of being. Now the destitution of beings, arising out of the disintegration of what is proper to each, is systematically pursued as the condition of the process of their integration into the planetary, functional economy. The question of being implicates a geopolitical thesis and, at least in Heidegger's perspective of 1935, the necessity of a geopolitical response. This does not mean that a new geopolitical concept is the condition of the question of being, but that the leap into this question is the necessary prelude to the historicity of dwelling on the earth.

Quoting from his own text of the *Rektoratsrede* of 1933, Heidegger concludes section 15 by insisting that spirit is not 'the boundless work of dismemberment carried on by the practical intelligence; much less is it world-reason; no, spirit is primordially attuned [gestimmte] knowing resolve toward the essence of being' (GA40, 53/49, modified). Spirit is to be understood as the openness of a stand in the midst of beings. In this sense, 'spirit' expresses the openness of *Ent-schlossenheit* (resoluteness), which takes its determination from attentiveness to the presencing of being. The resoluteness of spirit is not founded in the priority of subjectivity over what is, but in the attunement of an openness to the differentiation (*Wesen*) of the being of beings. *Wesen* – presencing – is already, as such, differentiation, hence not 'essence' metaphysically conceived, but the gathering (*logos*) of the differentiated in the site. *Logos* and *polemos*, understood as the event of differentiation, are one and belong together in the oneness of a differentiated site (GA40, 66, 153/62, 144). Historically founded and attuned attentiveness constitutes 'knowledge' (*Wissen*, as distinct from *Wissenschaft*). Only out of the openness of attunement is spirit, spirit; only as founded in the question of being can spirit be awakened from the falsifications of subjectivism. Lest the talk of 'spirit' be misinterpreted metaphysically, Heidegger immediately adds that the question of being is an essential condition for 'an awakening of spirit and hence for an original world of historical Dasein' (GA40, 53/50, modified). Spirit can found a world *only as historically grounded,* delimited, and attuned to the sited differentiation of being. In what follows in the *Introduction,* it becomes clear that dramatic poetry, as well as thinking itself, are differentiations of being in and through which an attunement to the whole of what is, is given gestalt. Only because *Geist* is attuned to being, and takes its determination (*Be-stimmung*) from the differentiation of being in beings, can Heidegger say 'where spirit prevails, the essent as such becomes always and at all times more essent' (GA40, 53/49–50). Beings are more or less in being, depending on whether or not being (*das Seyn*) presences through the gestalt and reserves itself in the gestalt or withholds itself in favour of beingness (*die Seiendheit*) as the transparency and availability of beings. The knowing (*das Wissen*) proper to *Geist* is the experience of the determinations of being, non-being, and appearance. It unfolds as the recognition of the 'delimitation' of what has come to stand as being ('die Ergrenzung des zum Stand Gebrachten und Gekommenen, d.h., das Sein') (GA40, 121/113). Beings must be *set into their limits, and preserved in them*, to allow them to be. For the limit of each is to each its ownmost shelter from the shelterlessness of being stock-on-call. *Wissen*, therefore, (*i*) is attuned to the destiny of being; hence (*ii*) is open to the differentiation of the presencing of being; therefore (*iii*) saves the phenomena; and (*iv*) saves the phenomena by founding the site of their differentiation according to the measure and rank appropriate to each. The founding of the differentiation of being clearly implicates the political, given that the character of a polity will be co-determined by the rank order of recognized forms of knowledge as ways of the disclosure of beings. It is the attunement of Dasein to the differentiation *of being* which opens the possibility of a transformation of the polity.

Founding and differentiation call for the word to give them gestalt; in fact, they are as word. The 'information age,' for its part, and the interpretation of tradition and of language it rests on, implicates a decision for the non-differentiated functional whole of a system of production and consumption. Hence the 'political' question and the question of being are also, fundamentally, questions of language. Heidegger's appeal to *Wissen* as historically founded knowledge offers a critique of the metanarrative of *Geist* and of the progress of science, a critique which anticipates the postmodern critique of modernity.

5.2.4 *The Founding of Being in the* Polis: Techne

Heidegger's reflections on the *Antigone*, to which I will turn shortly, contribute to the retrieval of a non-metaphysical determination of the relation of being and thinking. The guiding questions of this retrieval are as follows: How did it come about that the *logos* is interpreted by way of logic and the statement? Given the increasing power of the logical as the conceptualization of beings, does a way lead back to a more primordial determination of truth and hence of the being of beings? Heidegger's object, therefore, in appealing to Sophocles, is to prepare a deconstruction of logic by uncovering the truth of unconcealment (*aletheia*) as the 'condition' of conceptualization. What are the primordial articulations of unconcealment, given that the saying of the assertion is non-originary?

Unconcealment occurs only when it is achieved in the work: the work of the word in poetry, the work of stone in temple and statue, the work of word in thought, the work of the *polis* as the historical place in which all of this is grounded and preserved. (GA40, 200/191)

Heidegger takes up two paths. The first is that of the artwork. The work of art is conceived as a response to the letting-become-manifest of the *logos*, where the *logos* is thought as the gathered differentiation of being (*phusis*). The work of art in-corporates unconcealment. Heidegger's reflection on Parmenides, which frames the discussion of the choral ode, leads into the second way, the way of thinking. Both ways are forms of non-representational attentiveness to the unconcealment of being. The *polis*, as the site of differentiation, is the crossroads of these ways, and as such the 'condition of possibility' of the 'political.' The *polis* is, as it were, the *agora* of being, the site of the articulation of the four delimitations of being.

In his discussion of the first choral ode of Sophocles's *Antigone*, Heidegger avers that *Wissen* translates *techne*. Heidegger's attempt to retrieve *techne* as *Wissen* (knowledge) proposes to site knowledge in the historicity of a people's 'confrontation' with presencing, thus to found the differentiation of presencing. The question of what knowledge essentially is, therefore, already opens the 'political' question inasmuch as *the kind of knowledge to which a people grants the highest rank, as well as the entire rank order of kinds of knowing*, will determine the nature of the polity. These decisions determine, for example, Bacon's political and natural philosophy in such a way as to constitute essentially the modern idea of state. *Techne*, then, is knowledge: yet it is not to be conceived 'technologically' as the process of the production of a product. In this case, *techne* is understood as making and in reference to things made. What is essential to *Wissen*, rather, is the manifestation of the presencing of being through the delimited gestalt of an entity: 'Knowledge is the ability of setting-being-to-work in a being in its particular thusness' ('Wissen ist das Ins-Werk-setzen-Können des Seins als eines je so und so Seienden') (GA40, 168/159, modified). *Wissen* is the knowledge which is able to open a site for the actualization of being in beings ('eröffnendes Er-wirken des Seins *im* Seienden') (GA40, 168/ 159). Bringing being to a stand in a being, thus to allow being to presence out of the delimitation of the gestalt takes its most unmediated and exemplary form, Heidegger claims, in the work of art (GA40, 168/ 159).

Wissen unfolds in the 'violence' (*Gewalt-tätigkeit*) of the un-concealment and giving of limits (*Be-grenzung*). Only through the decisive act of the delimitation of being does a people become historical by founding a history. Knowing (*techne*) is the response of Dasein, as *deinotaton* – the most terrible, uncanny, unhomelike being – to the overpowering power (*deinon*) of beings as a whole (GA40, 159/149). Humanity gathers this power and sets it in the open, allows it to manifest itself in its being, that is, 'in limit and gestalt' (GA40, 153/144). The 'violence' – or taking-power – of *techne* in the face of the over-powering gives shape and limit to beings. Recalling the *Logik* of 1934, we can understand *techne* as *work* – as the transformation of Dasein's ex-posure (*Ausgesetztheit*) to being in and through the transformation of beings.

Hence the selfhood of historical mankind betokens the act to 'transform the being that discloses itself to him into history and [to] bring himself to a stand in it' (GA40, 152/143, modified). Being-a-people means to bring the being of beings into the limit of their in-each-case-respective gestalt. Attunement to being, which brings beings into the gestalt is always in 'essence' historical, singular, for it founds history. The same passage rejects the definition of people as a collective subject. Still less is 'people' to be conceived 'racially' (as one form of collective subjectivity), given that 'race' is understood 'biologically' and derives from a regional ontology of metaphysically conceived mankind. Race is not *phusis* in mankind, but at best a scientific (or pseudo-scientific) determination of the animality of the metaphysically conceived rational animal.

To bring the overwhelming might of being (*deinon*) to a stand by setting being into the forms of its differentiations founds a history. This history, then, will be the history of a particular 'people,' understood as a specific articulation of the differentiation of being as embodied in language and in the historical works, rites, and institutions that incorporate the rank and order of entities. Yet every founding-ordering of the uncanniness of beings as a whole is a wager set against the order (*dike/Fug*) of being. Every wager risks going-astray and even catastrophic decline into ahistoricity (GA40, 170/161).

Heidegger's attempt to retrieve the fundamental sense of *techne* from the metaphysical determination of *techne* as 'skill' and as para-deigmatic production evidently has the goal of bringing the primordial unity of science and art, in their attentiveness to the differentiation of being, to light. Given that the modern state is pre-eminently a socio-technological enterprise of the management of human and natural resources, it pertains, in Heidegger's view, to open the question of the provenance of this state, thus to bring about the kind of 'confrontation with modern technology' which Heidegger mistakenly ascribed to National Socialism. The *Introduction* of 1935 therefore still holds, at least in this respect, to Heidegger's estimation of the positive possibilities of the new regime which he enunciated in the *Rektoratsrede*. The *Beiträge* of 1936–8, however, will decisively reject this position: not only is the reality of National Socialism rejected, but science (*die Wissenschaft*) is denied founding power.

5.3   Attunement and the Dis-attunement of Intellectualism

We have seen that knowledge is always attuned (*gestimmt*). We recall that the phenomenological hermeneutics of *Sein und Zeit* grant to attunement (*die Stimmung*) equiprimordiality with understanding and discourse. The attunement of Dasein, moreover, pre-eminently conveys its sitedness – in a situation, in the temporality of its experience of the world, in a history and the historically unfolding earth to which it belongs. As a way of being-open to what is, and of concealing what is, attunement is above all the integrative force which attunes thinking to the specificity of the local, its history, customs, and landscape. The attunement of thought roots it in being as *phusis*, and this means in the differentiation of being. The attunement of Dasein is *phusis* in us. Heidegger's phenomenology of attunement is the way in which he develops the question of the earth-sited embodiment of being which Nietzsche raised for him in the misleading form of the biological and physiological. *Phusis* is not to be confused with created and fallen nature, nor with the nature posited by science and exploited by technology. *Phusis* arrives in unconcealment in the specificity of the gestalt and takes its stand in it. Given the overtly political context of this citation from the *Rektoratsrede* in the *Introduction*, the attunement of knowledge to the presencing of being Heidegger appeals to calls for attention to the modalities of *phusis* as it takes gestalt in and through the historicity of a people. The historicity of Dasein's being-attuned implicates, for example, the 'ecological' situatedness of Dasein, thus attention to the limits imposed by the historical character of a people's native soil, as limits inscribed by the differentiation of being.

Heidegger's position has implications for ecological politics which are not only at odds with the power of international finance, but which are also opposed to the politics of the de-historicization of a people in favour of the 'construction' of an amorphous 'population.' For there is a fundamental distinction between a population of individuals constituting a society defined by individual rights and contractual relations, and a people which takes its measure from the historical-ecological limits imposed by its and only its native soil. To confuse the two would be to suppose that laws propagated after the fact can legislate in favour of a sense of limit to a metaphysically conceived humanity, which in principle recognizes no measure but its own collective subjectivity. And by contrast, the appeal to measure presupposes that 'native soil' be understood as the sited differentiation of being, in which a given humanity participates, and not as the 'property' and possession of a nationality conceived metaphysically as a collective subject.

The critique of cosmopolitanism refers us back to the question of intellectualism, which is the most evident political or 'ideological' concept of the text. Though obviously marked by contemporary discourse, Heidegger's appropriation of the conservative critique of intellectualism aims to uncover its genealogy in the dissention of *logos* and *phusis*. This is the implicit political thrust of Heidegger's apparently purely philosophical disquisition on fundamental Greek 'concepts.'

Heidegger takes his point of departure in his consideration of the *logos* from *legein* as gathering: *logos* does not primordially signify speech and word, but the gathering of the unconcealment of beings itself (GA40, 136–8/126–30). *Phusis* names this gathering, which is not that of an undifferentiated unity, but rather the belonging-together of beings in the setting-apart and standing-apart which Heidegger identifies with *polemos* (GA40, 140/131). *Logos* is said to be the gatheredness of beings, which is to say, being. *Phusis* and *logos* are the same (belong in the same). The gathering which is the *logos* joins the differentiated into the whole of an order and rank in which each comes forth and stands – as *phusis* – in the gestalt of its own delimited being. Beings are *said* in the gatheredness of their proper presencing as the unfolding (*kinesis*) of the gestalt (*morphe*) which owns them. In the saying, the gathered differentiation of *phusis* is brought to word, that is, made manifest in its 'openness, delimitation, and permanence' (Offenheit, Umgrenzung und Ständigkeit) (GA40, 180–1/172).

The inner, primordial unity of *logos* and *phusis* casts the subsequent metaphysical disjunction between *logic and nature* in the role of the determining 'historical' event of Western history. We want to trace the origin of this division only insofar as it can illuminate how Heidegger's experience of the 'political' in 1935 is rooted in the history of being. We recall that 'intellectualism' is at issue. Intellectualism signifies the pre-eminence of the intellect, of the 'idea.' The idea, however, as the conceiving of the subject, finds its original ground in the Ideas as the being to which conceiving attempts to 'correspond.' In Plato's philosophy, *eidos, Idea,* are the names given to being itself, and hence also to *phusis. Phusis* passes under the yoke of the Idea in the sense that the Idea determines what truly and 'correctly' is. In the first instance, the *eidos* is the aspect in which *phusis* shows and brings itself to a stand in its differentiated presencing (GA40, 189/180). In this respect Plato's thought still echoes that of Heraclitus. The decisive import, however, of Plato's understanding of being is that the presencing of *phusis* in the *eidos* is concealed in favour of the stability of the Idea as constant presence (GA40, 191/182). *Phusis* in its presencing is reduced to mere appearance, to a mere image of the Ideas. In modern terms, what truly *is* stands 'behind' the appearances as the governing axioms from which the appearances take rise. The axioms are articulations of what remains stable in all change: they articulate the underlying (*hypokeimenon*), the abiding presence and stability of 'substance' (*ousia*) (GA40, 202–3/193–4). Thought is no longer attentive to presencing in the phenomena (*phusis*), but seeks to discover the fundamental 'categories' which order phenomena, and to correspond to them in its saying. Because the constant stability of *phusis* as Idea serves thought as *paradeigma*, saying takes its directive from the Ideas in its saying truly. The primordial significance of the *logos* as gathered, differentiated unconcealment, as *phusis*, narrows to the truth or falsity of what is gathered in the statement about *phusis.* Truth, *aletheia,* is no longer understood as the unconcealment of presencing, but rather as the correctness of a statement to the Idea. *Logos* is now understood as logic in the sense of a teaching regarding the categories of assertion and their possible interrelationships. Logic itself, as true to its own 'categories,' determines what may appear as 'real' (GA40, 195/187).

'Intellectualism,' in effect, announces *the triumph of socio-technological categories over the singularity of a people's historically founded existence.* Heidegger's deconstruction of metaphysics allows him to confirm a concept of intellectualism congruent with conservative discourse. We may assume that the charge of 'intellectualism,' in Heidegger's view, would apply equally to the social order of 'liberalism' (particularly in the avatar of international finance capitalism) and to the dialectical claims of Marxism: both systems uncritically presuppose the scientific and technological determination of nature and a conception of the 'rational animal' defined by 'humanism.' Neither offers a way of knowledge (*techne/Wissen*) which is attuned to the finitude of a people's dwelling within the limits of its homeland. Both are at war, according to Heidegger, with 'nature' no less than with the historicity of peoples.

5.3.1 Founding the Polis *in the Homelessness of Being-toward-Death*

The retrieval of the sense of a people's historicity, as founded in the history of being, is the essential counterweight, for Heidegger, to the incipient world order of information as the triumph of ahistorical 'intellectualism.' What grants a people its 'essential ground'? Heidegger answers that it is projective saying, founding, which is rooted in the openness of being-toward-death. The relation between our 'political' being (that is, the *polis*) and being-toward-death is by no means self-evident. Nor does Heidegger develop a detailed argument for this relation in the *Introduction*. Nonetheless such a relation is intimated in this text. In this section, I also will draw on *Being and Time* and the *Contributions to Philosophy* to present the outlines of an argument which may be unfolded as follows.

Recalling *Sein und Zeit*, we know that death is the 'internal' limit of Dasein, in the sense that being-toward-death consummates Dasein (SZ, sec. 62). Following the argument of *Sein und Zeit*, being-toward-death throws Dasein back on its own singularity and thus calls on it to take up the burden of its freedom and of its possibilities as they are inscribed into its tradition. In this sense, death is the limit from which and out of which Dasein begins to be, to 'own' itself. Being-toward-death is the limit which appropriates Dasein to itself. This is the first step in an argument which would allow Heidegger to 'found' the *polis* in being-toward-death.

In the *Introduction to Metaphysics*, Heidegger's commentary calls death the self-set limit of the poetic project (*Entwurf*) of opening a site for being to found itself. To say that Dasein is limited by death clearly must not be misinterpreted biologically – that humans, as all things living, die. Being-toward-death is the project of founding humanity in the *rites of mortality*. Only by virtue of being *founded* in mortality does *Da-sein* come to be. Da-sein is the site of the openness of the *letting-be of beings*. The tragic poetry of the Greeks is such a founding: it does not represent a world, but first founds the differentiation of being which allows the historical world of the Greeks to take gestalt. Being-toward-death is the form of attunement to being to which the rites and rituals of concretely embodied existence give voice and articulation to site a people in the historical specificity of its 'native soil.'

In the *Contributions to Philosophy* (GA65), Heidegger insists that being-toward-death, 'unfolded as essential determination of the truth of Dasein, conceals in itself two fundamental determinations of the differentiation [Zerklüftung]' of being: (*i*) the Nothing which belongs to the presencing of being, and which grants the *possibility* of possibility, of decision; and (*ii*) the *necessity* which belongs to being 'itself' and which being-toward-death reveals in bringing Da-sein to take responsibility for itself (GA65, secs. 160–1). Given that these two 'modalities' of being are actualized in Da-sein's being-toward-death, then how does this mutual implication of the *Da* and of *Sein* pertain to the possibility of the *polis*? Is the *polis* the articulation, the site, of this mutual implication, and consequently of the differentiation of being which belongs to it? But death, as the project of a mortality which is appropriate to the possibility of an encounter with the gods, must be sited. As a 'determination' (*Bestimmung*) of Da-sein, being-toward-death holds Da-sein in its a-byssmal grasp, 'makes it that "between" that offers moment and site to "enowning" [Ereignis] and can thus belong to being' (GA65, 285/201). In terms of *Being and Time*, 'death is connected to "time," which is established as the domain of projecting-open the truth of be-ing itself' (GA65, 284/199). Being-toward-death is the opening to the 'truth,' and that means to the un-concealment of being as that which must be founded and delimited. The question of the political emerges from this relation.

Not only is being-toward-death the limit which founds Dasein, but Dasein is called on to give gestalt to death in the rites of sacrifice. These rites are the rites of the celebration of the delimitation of being, hence a celebration of the differentiation of being, for being presences only in being brought to a stand. For this reason, Heidegger continues in his commentary on the *Antigone*, for 'us this happening of uncanniness (of death) must be primordially founded as Da-sein' ('Die geschehende Unheimlichkeit [des Todes] muß für uns anfänglich als Da-sein gegründet werden') (GA40, 167/158, modified). The *Antigone* is one way in which mortality is founded in language and ritual; the mythic games of the Roman imperium, for example, already intimate a fundamental shift in the relation of the founding powers of polity and mythos. The mythos goes on stage for the imperial eye of command. The modern 'show-trial' occludes death altogether, the juridical murder is carried out in secret, whereas the 'confession' is staged to satisfy the optic of a victorious ideology. The tragedy of *Antigone*, by contrast, allows the *agon* of Antigone and Creon to establish the limits of possibility of human command and the merely human *logos*: the posited law, or *nomos*, every normative concept of right, is subordinated to the necessity of the *nomos* which the earth-rooted powers (Hades) themselves set. The tragic work is therefore an enactment of the 'modalities' of possibility and necessity – it founds the *polis* in the openness of a way of being, or Da-sein.

But as the project which founds the site (the Da-) of the openness of being, mortality is the anchor of stability of Dasein, which roots it in the earth as earth. Death is the root of earth-sited humanity. The unease of desire which is cosmopolitan humanity must subject the earth to the calculi of consumption because it is nowhere at home on it. The occultation of mortality and the triumph of representational thought and with it, of planetary thinking, strictly condition one another. Heidegger calls death-delimited Dasein 'die geschehende Un-heimlichkeit selbst' (the happening of uncanny unhomelikeness itself) (GA40, 167/158, modified). Da-sein articulates the not-being-at-home of its death-centredness in the rites of a people, their gods, and their earth. In this sense, being-toward-death itself founds the site of the homeland, which is quite distinct from any nationalistic conception of collectivity. The *Un-heimlichkeit* (strangeness, uncanniness, unhomelikeness) of Dasein spoken of here is everything other, however, than the metaphysically conceived rootlessness of cosmopolitan humanity. This misconception reinscribes Heidegger's project back into the circuit of a supposedly deconstructed metaphysics.

The starting point, therefore, of a Heideggerian politics would have to be the in-stitution of the differentiations of being in the rites of an historical people. Not 'patriotism,' but the historical, earth-sited being of a people grants a homeland. This being is 'founded in poetry, and ordered in thinking, to be set into knowing, and enacted by state-founders rooted in the earth and historical space' (GA39, 120). It is difficult to escape this conclusion, in my opinion, however uncomfortable it makes those late representatives of the Enlightenment project for whom Heidegger's unbroken attachment to the 'homeland' makes his philosophy especially suspect (e.g., Habermas, Krell, Thiele; also Derrida, in a different way). For although homeland is not thought nationalistically, it is thought in its relation to the ethos of a people, and therefore the ontological homeland *of the Germans* must be thought in reference to the ontic realities of German history.[28] This does not exclude, but rather affirms, that *every people* has the task of unfolding its 'ontological' homeland out of the specificity of its tradition and in the struggle to retrieve its possibilities. Heidegger holds in *Being and Time* that only if the existential analytic is 'grasped in an existentiell way – as a possibility of being of each existing Da-sein – does it become possible at all to disclose the existentiality of existence and therewith to get hold of a sufficiently grounded set of ontological problems' (SZ 13/11). The priority of the ontic which Heidegger indicates here shows that the separation of the ontological homeland from the specificity of historical existence is not tenable. The 'ontological' concept of 'homeland,' in effect, no less than the ontology of Dasein itself, must submit to the 'ontic priority of the question of being.'

Conversely, Heidegger implicitly assumes that the cosmopolitan project, which begins by positing a universal, rational subject, to derive the rights of individuals and nations from it, is founded on the in-difference of peoples and traditions, and that this in-difference is founded in the in-differentiation of being as a set of transcendental categories and values. In Heidegger's terms, the heirs of the Enlightenment read internationalism as the protagonist of a metanarrative of progress. Internationalism is humanistic in the sense that it posits an Idea of humanity as its own, self-conceived ground, and actually existing historical peoples are called on to measure up to this Idea. The program of internationalism is as aesthetic (humanity is to conform to an ideal image of itself) as it is thoroughly metaphysical. For the Idea of Humanity, to which peoples are universally to conform, annunciates the triumph of a conceptual program over the possibilities of the singular tradition of a people. The interpretation of being as a conceptual system, hence the oblivion of the differentiated presencing of being in beings, is in turn the root cause of the ideo-logical fixation of being in competing perspectives of value, and therefore the cause of the global conflicts which marked the twentieth century. The results of 'progress' are seen in the 'darkening of the world,' and in the 'flight of the gods.' These poetic formulations, however, are not empty of serious content, as one might be inclined to think: they signify the process of the abandonment of beings by the presencing of being, that is, the oblivion of being as presencing in favour of being-ness as a conceptual, or ideo-logical, system, separated from and yet imposed on our historical life-world.

'From an existential-ontological point of view,' Heidegger writes, in *Being and Time*, 'the "not-at-home" must be conceived as the more primordial phenomenon' (SZ 189/SZ-MR 234). The sense of uncanniness, or *Unheimlichkeit* (the unhomelike), which characterizes anxiety as a fundamental attunement of Dasein reveals this phenomenon by undermining our everyday sense of being-at-home in the familiar. It is essential, however, to distinguish between the ontological homelessness of ex-sistence and the ontic homelessness of the cosmopolitan. Only by being ontically-historically rooted can we experience our ontological homelessness: for the 'ontological,' now understood in terms of the history of being as the presencing of being, only manifests itself in the 'ontic' works and rites in which being founds itself. The metaphysical distinction between the ontic and the ontological, moreover, is derivative of the more fundamental differentiated gathering of being and beings, which Heidegger later calls the thought of the topology of being. This means that being presences in being-sited. One might say that sitedness itself calls for 'ontic' being-at-home in the works and rites through which the presencing of being comes to presence. Yet this formulation is misleading: for precisely in dwelling in the presencing of the work of art as work, the subjectivity of the subject, in its ontic determination, is overthrown in favour of the ex-sistent being open of Da-sein. Da-sein, however, calls for a There, understood as the finitude of the arrival of being in the gestalt. What Heidegger, in the Hölderlin lectures, calls the 'unheimische Heimischsein des Menschen' – the unhomelike being at home of humanity – supposes that the properly understood ontological homelessness of humanity as an ex-sistent being founds itself in the finitude of being (GA53, 150–1). The Da of ex-sistent being, which is to say homelessness in the 'ontological' sense, is only possible as the sitedness of historicity, as Da-*sein*. The historicity of Dasein precludes the possession of the homeland and implicates alterity and openness to the guest and stranger.[29]

Thiele advances the argument that the 'ontological' homelessness of mankind, as Heidegger understands it, obviates the possibility of founding a home rooted in the specificity of a people's history and that Heidegger's 'nostalgia' for *Heimat* is 'opposed to the thrust of his philosophy as a whole.'[30] Thiele in fact misinterprets Heidegger's understanding of *Heimat* as a 'nostalgic longing for the establishment of an organic national family rooted in tradition by blood, language, and soil.'[31] The terms of this definition of *Heimat* – 'organic,' 'national,' 'blood' – are in each case metaphysical determinations presupposing the concept of a collective subjectivity which Heidegger's *Beiträge*, as we shall see below, explicitly rejects. *Heimat* is indeed the site of an 'ontological' homelessness, but 'ontological' homelessness must be sited in the finitude of being in order for the presencing of being's finitude to be experienced.

This argument is supported by the lectures on *Hölderlins Hymne 'Der Ister'* (GA53). 'Inasmuch as mankind, in the midst of beings, is in such a way as to comport itself to beings as such, it must seek to learn to be at home in a place, in conformity with its being [Wesen]' (GA53, 111). This does not mean that a Volk turns obsessively about its own axis, for it is only in 'dialogue' with other languages and peoples that a Volk, in its homelessness, finds a way home (GA53, 80, 92). The uncanniness of existence is grounded in the ontologically understood homelessness of Dasein, as ek-static. But it does implicate a decisive rejection of the cosmopolitan idea of 'mankind,' as enunciated, for example, in Kant's philosophy of history. The cosmopolitan is implicated in Heidegger's understanding of ontological homelessness as the triumph of appearances (the simulated image) over the presencing of the sited being of beings (GA53, 112). *Das Unseiende (me on/*non-being) understood as the mere appearance, is without inherent gestalt (*eidos*) and stability. The political, understood in modern terms as the conceptualization of the technical management of the real (GA53, 118), institutes the reign of appearances in the technopolis. The technopolis is atopic.

The attempt to amalgamate Heidegger's understanding of homelessness with that of postmodern cosmopolitanism, nomad thought, or a philosophy of exile, Thiele's argument notwithstanding, is fundamentally misconceived.[32] The idea of *Heimat* and the sited specificity of the presencing of being is thoroughly suspect to this thought, as Derrida indicates: Heidegger's 'solicitation of the Site and the Land is in no way, it must be emphasized, a passionate attachment to territory or locality, is in no way a provincialism or particularism ... The thinking of Being thus is not a pagan cult of the *Site*, because the Site is never a given proximity but a promised one.'[33] It is true that Heidegger's understanding of the topology of being, and thus of the sitedness of being, is not to be identified with an 'attachment to territory or locality.' Yet a people's attunement to being, such as first founds a *Heimat*, always arises out of the specificity of a tradition, hence out of the historicity of the differentiation of being in work, language, thought, and ritual. The concept of mere 'territory,' moreover, is always an abstraction from the earth-sited specificity of an historical people. Nor does the presencing of being, as Derrida correctly proposes, implicate a 'proximity,' which is to say, the actuality of being as sited; such proximity confuses being and beings. Yet Derrida still construes the site in a metaphysical way. This is evident from the implied antitheses to the terms which he uses to characterize the site: the cosmopolitan City is the antithesis of the province, the universal of the particular, the ethical (as the transcendental) of the 'pagan.' Derrida's positive concept of site as non-proximity, or exile, is also still entangled in metaphysical categories.

5.3.2 Polemos: *Founding the Differentiation of Being*

Heidegger's commentary on the third choral ode of the *Antigone* holds that the essential poetry of a people is one way in which the site of

Dasein, as the clearing of the encounter with being, is founded. The commentary is guided by the thought of the overpowering presencing of being, which presences only in being differentiated and brought to a stand in the gestalt. In differentiation, a world, or site of intelligibility, comes to be (GA40, 66/62). This guiding thought is already evident from the first paragraph of the commentary, in Heidegger's appeal to Heraclitus, Fragment 53:

> polemos panton men pater esti, panton de basileus, kai tous men theous edeixe tous de anthropous, tous men doulous epoinese tous de eleutherous.

Polemos is translated as *Aus-einander-setzung*: as 'setting-apart' or differentiation. In Manheim's translation of Heidegger's free rendering the entire fragment reads as follows: 'Conflict is for all (that is present) the creator that causes to emerge, but (also) for all the dominant preserver. For it makes some to appear as gods, others as men; it creates (shows) some as slaves, others as freemen' (GA40, 66/61–2). *Polemos* is the differentiation of being itself, through which beings are set apart, articulated and differentiated from each other in nature and rank and given over to the limit of each one's own being. The *agon* of Antigone and Creon is the enactment of a differentiation which sets the limits of the claims of each and in doing so determines the source of the 'legitimacy' of the City. Antigone proposes to satisfy the god of death to whom all mortals are finally accountable. We recall that the *polis* is the articulation of the finitude of the open site of unconcealment. This site has its root of stability in the sheltering concealment of *lethe*, which finds essential acknowledgment in the rites of death. To deprive the god of Hades of the rites which are his due, therefore, is to shake the very foundations of the City. In this sense Antigone's *agon* with Creon is the articulation (*polemos*) of limit and gestalt, and of the rank order of the human and the divine *logos*, and as such the determination of the 'origin' of rulership (cf. GA40, 153/144).

Polemos and *logos* are the 'same.' What humanity is, Heidegger proposes, is first determined by the attunement to being and hence in the *polemos* of being, so that in contention with beings, 'striving to bring them into their being, i.e., into limit and form' Da-sein founds a site for being (GA40, 153/144, modified). The differentiation of being eventuates through the Da – or the openness of Dasein's encounter with being, with itself and other beings. This happens in the project, and essentially as project, not as the repetition of the already-given. The poetic thought of Heraclitus, with which Heidegger opens this discussion, therefore anticipates the commentary on the *Antigone*, for tragedy is conceived as the enactment of the *polemos* in which the *polis*, or the site of encounter, is articulated. The drama carries the overpowering presencing of *phusis* into the openness of being-brought-to-a-stand. By contrast, insofar as being is no longer differentiated and delimited in the works of the poets, thinkers, leaders, in the rites of sacrifice, world withdraws. Beings still are, to be sure, but as the mere residue of a history, as mere stock-on-call (GA40, 67/62–3). The triumph of subjectivity which posits what is as the available stock of potential calculations signals the withdrawal of world, and with it, the destitution of beings. For this reason, inasmuch as *logos* is understood as gathering, *polemos* and *logos* are said to be the same (GA40, 66/62). The differentiation and the gathering of being are the same. This is not to say that they are identical, but that the differentiated presences as one unified, historically sited world, and the gathering of the *logos* differentiates itself through beings.

5.3.3 Parmenides: Overcoming the Chorismos of Intellectualism

Heidegger's deconstruction of the classical distinction of being and thought appeals above all to the choral ode of the *Antigone* and to Parmenides's saying of the 'sameness' of thought and being. The reflection on the *Antigone* roots thinking back in the finitude of ex-sistent Dasein. Mortality, understood as the temporal and historical structure, and hence as the internal limit, of the unfolding of Dasein, is the condition of 'normative' thought, such as posited by the word of command. Heidegger holds, moreover, that the normative conceived as the work of conceptualization, is only possible as derived from the primordial openness of apprehension, or *noein*, to the finitude of presencing. The deconstruction of conceptualization, or representational thinking, therefore, is the connecting bridge between Heidegger's consideration of Sophocles and Parmenides.

The saying of Parmenides, Fragment 5, reads as follows: 'to gar auto noein estin te kai einai.' What is at stake here, in the interpretation of this saying, Heidegger insists, is the retrieval of the primordial long-concealed truth of a saying which has been, in its metaphysical interpretation, the 'guiding principle of Western philosophy' (GA40, 154/145). Heidegger translates the passage as follows: 'Zusammengehörig sind Vernehmung wechselweise und Sein' (GA40, 154). This is rendered into English by Manheim as 'There is a reciprocal bond between apprehension and being' (GA40, 154/145). *Noein* is translated as *vernehmen* by Heidegger, as 'apprehension' by Manheim (GA40, 149/137–8). Since, in Heidegger's interpretation, apprehension is receptive bringing-to-a-stand, we may say that this receptiveness and being belong together. They belong in the Same of mutual attunement. Clearly this 'translation' already implicates an interpretation. To say that apprehension is not an attribute of humanity, conceived as the subject of what manifests itself, is the first step back out of the 'metaphysics of presence.' 'Apprehension,' rather, 'is the happening that has man' (GA40, 150/141). *Phusis* itself, as coming to stand in appearance, is the gathering (*logos*) which takes hold of humanity and calls for founding in a site and in the gestalt (GA40, 184/175). *Vernehmen* also has the secondary meaning of 'interrogation': *phusis* and Dasein mutually 'interrogate' each other in the sense of bringing each other to stand in the limits prescribed by the modes and ways of the arrival of being in beings.

Apprehension would be the in-each-case-singular, history-founding event of an encounter with being, out of which the humanity of a particular people emerges (GA40, 150/141). In Schoenbohm's words, 'being human happens with that more originary apprehension that occurs in differentiation from and together with the appearing of beings in being or *phusis*.'[34] The mode of this 'differentiation' will always be historical and specific to a people and a tradition. As such, apprehension is everything other than thinking as the abstraction of a concept, and the consequent unity of concept and conceived would also be an abstraction from the event of apprehension. In the terms of Heidegger's 'On the Essence of Truth,' apprehension is rather the primordial attunement which is the condition of representational thinking. For the attuned openness, receptivity, of the *Da* to *Sein* first founds every bearing, including rational (self)-certainty. In the encounter of relatedness, the 'relata,' understood as 'mankind' and the 'being of beings,' come to be, which is to say, Da-sein takes its stand in presencing. If we hold fast to apprehension, or thinking, as the possession of the subject humanity, as rational animal, and propose that what is enters into being by reference to the measure of rationality, then we have already leapt over the open site of the encounter in favour of the being of *beings*, which show themselves in the encounter, and only in terms of the ground it opens up.

Apprehension brings-to-a-stand in the sense of setting beings into the limit proper to them. The stand of the limit, however, is not that of a conceptual stability of essence, but arises out of 'taking a receptive attitude toward that which shows itself' (GA40, 146/138). The phenomena are allowed to come into their own, to emerge and to unfold themselves in the gestalt. Thinking is thus the attending-receptive openness to the limit, or *peras*, of the being of a being. In this respect the nature of *noein*, as responsive openness to being as gestalt-giving, recalls our earlier reflections, which are echoed, in fact, by Heidegger's unfolding of being as *morphe*. In 'The Origin of the Work of Art,' gestalt is interpreted by way of *morphe*. Likewise, in the *Introduction, morphe* is said to be 'that which places itself in its limit, completing it, and so stands, has form ...

> Limit [*peras*] and end are that wherewith the essent begins to *be*. It is on this basis that we must understand the supreme term that Aristotle used for being, *entelecheia* – the holding (preserving)-itself-in-the-ending (limit). (GA40, 64/60)

Without developing in greater detail the relation of *entelecheia* and gestalt, or *morphe*, at this point, we nevertheless find it evident that the attuned receptivity which apprehension is responds to the delimited gestalt of the phenomena. Thus *noein* in Heidegger's interpretation implicates the fundamental attitude of phenomenology, as a laying bare of the phenomena. The receptivity of apprehension is not the passive reception of the 'real,' but anticipates in its transcendental openness to being that which is unfolded by the phenomenological method as the threefold of construction, deconstruction, and reduction. For it is in precisely this sense that apprehension brings what is into the openness of its being. This bringing into the open, or the movement of unconcealment, however, is itself thrown and therefore is not to be conceived as the freedom of the self-certain subject. Were the movement of unconcealment re-presentational in this sense, as founded on the subject, so that unconcealment itself falls into oblivion, then the 'unity' of thinking and being which the saying of Parmenides expresses would take on, in fact, the sense given to it by modernity as the unity of thought with its object in the 'I think' of the self-present subject (GA65, 198–200/138–9).

This sense is transformed in the course of modern philosophy to culminate in the unity of simulation (conceptual programming, generation of a virtual reality), and simulacra, as defined by postmodern discourse. But as such, in the hyperworld of postmodernism, the phenomena precisely no longer show themselves from themselves: the simulation of the 'real' generates 'mere appearances' only. The mere appearance, to recall the distinction *Being and Time* develops between phenomena and mere appearances, does not manifest what is, but rather shines forth as the effect of an analytic de-composition and programmatic re-integra-tion of the phenomena. Consider, for example, the experience of live performance of music, as opposed to the process of its recording, digital inscription, and the translation of the digital code into music by a techni-cal apparatus. What the latter pro-duces is the effect of the technical transformation and re-iteration of the phenomenon, not the phenome-non itself. This is reflected in the term 'reality-effect' as it is used in the discourse of postmodernism (Baudrillard, Derrida). The digital code is the inscription of the unity of thought, to be precise, of representational thinking, and the being of an entity (the music).

In Heidegger's terms, the digital program encodes not so much a world, but the withdrawal of world – it renders present a non-world, or 'unworld.' The encoded unity, and the 'world'-on-call which it 'founds,' is at the most extreme remove from the world of the saying of Parmenides, from which this unworld nevertheless derives. The unworld signals the withdrawal of the presencing of the temporally sited differentiation of being to give what is over to mere appearance and the being-of-stock-on-call.

With the collapse of world as 'original emergence' and epiphany (GA40, 67/63), the things withdraw in their being to offer themselves in the aspect of their availability, as images on stock and at command. 'Epiphany becomes a visibility' of the 'already-there'; vision degenerates into 'mere optics'; and beings become objects of 'pure cognition' (GA40, 67/63). We enter the postmodern scene, as evoked by Baudril-lard's reflections on the disappearing body and the dissolution of sub-stance into the electronic flicker of the technotopia. The triumph of optics is a triumph over the phenomena in favour of mere appearances, of simulacra, as generated by simulation processes. The political order proper to the power of simulation is the technopolis, understood as the non-essencing of the *polis*, the non-essence of phenomena, and hence of the reduction of the world-founding power of language to the transmis-sion of bytes of information. But a sterile order is a great chaos. To say that the *polis* does not essence, and that the phenomena are defined by their non-essence, means that the site of the unconcealment of being appears to be the unchanging stage-set of the already-given of a concep-tual-functional order. This stage-set not only bedazzles us with the sem-blances of the real, but the distinctions of self and other, of image and world, of conceptual program and copy, disintegrate and are re-inte-grated into the hyperworld unity of simulation and simulacra. It is in this sense that the postmodern world has begun to experience the realization of the word of Parmenides (Fragment 5) which frames Heidegger's commentary on the founding power of tragedy and its articulation of the differentiations of being.

In what sense, therefore, is apprehension the Same – *to auto* – as being, where the Same is understood as the differentiating belonging-together of the differentiated? Being is understood as differentiated, as the belonging together of receptive bringing-to-a-stand, and that which comes to a stand, in the gestalt. For being means 'to appear, to enter into unconcealment' (GA40, 147/139). The Same happens in the happening of unconcealment: 'where being prevails, apprehension prevails and happens with it; thus the two belong together' (GA40, 147/139). The two belong together in the Same, *to auto*. The Same is the open site of the Da as the history-founding encounter of humanity and being. In the questioning, which is to say, in the differentiating bringing-to-a-stand of the being of beings, mankind itself comes to be, to give itself a stand in the midst of beings. Being comes to a stand in being brought to a stand: being presences as emergence into *morphe*, which is to say, into the delimitation of a measure of being. But measure is always the singular, history-founding measure of the differentiation of beings. Apprehension, as founded, brings beings to a stand, and only in and out of the delimitation of their proper limits are they in being. Only in maintaining itself in the receptivity of this knowledge, as bringing to a stand in the limit, is apprehension fully apprehension. In Heidegger's sense, therefore, conceptualization, understood as the fixation of entities as objects of knowledge for a subject, is already a falling-off from apprehension. The metaphysical distinction of 'thinking' and 'being' conceals the open site of the belonging together of emergence and reception. Receptive thinking is the openness of bringing-to-a-stand of what shows itself as standing-in-itself (GA40, 147/139). In the *Antigone* commentary, the nature of humanity, as *deinon*, or the uncanny being (*der Unheimliche*), is exposed to the uncanniness of being in mankind's power to bring being to a stand.

In the second part of the Parmenides commentary the violence of bringing beings to stand is called *techné*, knowledge (*Wissen*) (GA40, 174/165). *Techne* in this sense, clearly, is not to be confused with the positing power of representational thinking. *Wissen* is not 'science' (*Wissenschaft*), but still implicates a receptivity to the presencing of the things themselves in their phenomenal being. As such, *techne* responds to *dike*, to the gathered differentiation of being (GA40, 160/169). *Dike* is usually interpreted as justice or norm. This interpretation is derived from the sense of *dike* as custom, judgement, and the relation of propriety or rightness. Heidegger understands *dike* as the gathered-differentiated 'order' of being itself. He therefore translates the word as *Fug*: jointure, governing order. *Dike* is the governing order of the differentiated belonging-together of the presencing of beings. In this sense, it is *polemos*, understood as the open site of differentiation and hence mutual delimitation of beings in their coming to be and ceasing to be. The bringing to a stand of beings by *techne*, therefore, is founded in the receptivity of apprehension to the possibilities of the gathered-differentiated, in such a way as to found the differentiated in the work, rites, rule, art, and thought of a particular people (GA40, 62/66–7).

But if a tradition falls off and away from the knowledge of the necessity of decision, such as articulates being, and entrenches itself in the management of the already-known, then the violence of founding gives way to another violence and another danger: now man 'turns round and round in his own circle,' entangled in appearances and its own pre-conceptions (GA40, 166/158). This circle is the circle of representation, of the re-iterative presentation of beings as already-sent and conceptually circumscribed to and for the subject. Now mankind turns away from the *logos* and hears only itself: intent on its own conceptual schemata and simulation-processes, it no longer has an ear for the *withdrawal* of being from beings, which leaves them hanging in the cyberscape of their functionality (GA40, 138–9/128, 129).

It is essential to distinguish the limitation and gestalt of beings which arise out of the presencing of being (*das Seyn*) from the stability of entities under the regime of representational thinking. The stability of the latter is the prelude of the functionalization of beings. The signifiers of a text, for example, have a functional stability which derives from the linguistic codes and the discourses which order the metaphysically conceived field of language. The limitation of the gestalt, conversely, rests in the temporal differentiation of being itself, which grants to each the time of its while. What is comes into its gestalt as obedient to its own *arche* and *kinesis*, hence as obedient to the time-space of its unfolding into the limit (*peras*) of its own *telos*, for in this way it brings itself into self-manifestation and reserves itself in the sheltering concealment proper to its being. The metaphysics of the will-to-power, in turn, signifies the de-limitation of the power of representational thinking: beings are granted being only insofar as they become present to subjectivity in terms of the perspective which posits them in advance (hence the 're-' of representation). The unbounded power of representation strictly circumscribes how beings may manifest themselves – e.g., as objects, products, concepts, functions. The distinction between the delimitation of the gestalt and the limitlessness of representational thinking offers the necessary point of departure for thinking Heidegger's political thought in its essential rootedness in the history of being.

Heidegger's discussion of the *Antigone* ode evokes the *polis* as 'the historical place, the there *in* which, *out of* which, and *for* which history happens' (GA40, 161/152). The *polis* is the *there* of the site of founding, out of which a history emerges. The founders themselves, precisely as founders – the poets, thinkers, rulers – are *apolis*, without the City, for they must found it (GA40, 162/152–3). Yet the *polis*, as the site of the encounter of the gods, mortals, and 'nature,' most fully is in the project of founding, which brings being to a stand and shelters it in sacrifice, the work and the constitution of a polity. This moment of giving place to the uncanniness of being in the gestalt is one of utmost danger of going astray. However, Heidegger insists that the danger of being *apolis*, hence of having to found a measure, passes over into another danger: coming to be at 'home' in the already-known, to thoughtlessly accept the appearance of being for what is, and to become entangled in words without insight into the experience of things, their presencing and withdrawal from conceptualization. These two dangers define the hermeneutic situation of the early 1930s in its 'political' as well as its metaphysical dimension. In terms of the second danger (the greater danger?), humanity is abandoned by being, and left to spin on its own axis (GA40, 167/158). The *polis* enters into its own non-essence of the repetition of the same. According to the thesis of *Sein und Zeit*, *Gerede* is the already-said of the conceptual inscriptions of a tradition, which prefigure the ways of interpretation of a generation and thus conceal the fundamental sources of Dasein. The crisis of modern science, in Heidegger's estimation, consists in its rotation around the axis of its own *conceptual system*, in its inability to shatter in face of the mystery of being and found anew. In this sense, caught in the circularity of the already-written, humanity is *pantotopos aporos*: finding a way to master beings in all things, it is *aporos*, without a way through or a way out, because caught in the circle of its own representations, and hence blind to the presencing of being.

The falling-off of the *polis* into the circularity of the repetition of 'operative' definitions and concepts is founded on a categorical and functional definition of the being of beings which comes fully to light only with the destitution of beings in the era of the consummation of metaphysics. Heidegger, in common with the Conservative Revolution, believed that the liberal-technological conception of the 'people' as a contractual association of independent, deracinated individuals is founded on an ahistorical conceptual schema. To say that a political philosophy is founded on conceptual deracination means that its fundamental premise is an ahistorical concept of humanity as such and in itself. In Heidegger's view, still very much in evidence in the *Introduction*, the triumph of conceptualization over history posits a set of conceptual stabilities which aim at the transcendence of historical specificity and its limits in the discourse of nations.

What might this mean in reference the frequent target of Heidegger's critique – liberalism in political philosophy and social organization? Locke's *Second Treatise of Civil Government*, for example, predicates political life on the premise of the conceptually posited deracination of historically founded peoples, substituting in their place the idea of a 'state of nature' wherein identity is produced by the transformation of territory into property. In the liberal tradition deriving from Bacon, Hobbes, and Locke, the imperial conception of the state as founded on the conquest of nature, the appropriation of territory as 'property,' and the determination of humanity as a calculable and calculating animal mutually supplement each other. The premises of this tradition determine mankind and nature a priori by reference to the respective laws of natural and moral 'motion.' *The Federalist Papers*, for example, posit a social organization of self-aggrandizing individuals whose fundamental egotism must be managed by governing mechanisms, but who cannot be formed to higher ideals of civic or philosophical virtue in the classical sense. This political 'program' is founded in the de-limitation of the 'subject.' What emerges is not so much a political 'state' as the social organization of the 'unease of desire' – to recur to Locke's pregnant definition of the fundamental metaphysical disposition of liberal humanity. The unbounded unease of desire and the un-leashed subjectivity of the subject mutually complement each other to institute the dynamics of modern society. The critique of intellectualism, in Heidegger terms, would address the preeminently bureaucratic-technological concept of the polity which, in his view, determines this political tradition, as well as the Bolshevik regime of Soviet Russia. On these grounds we can make sense of Heidegger's remark in the *Introduction* that America and Russia are *metaphysically the same* – which is *not* to say that they are *identical* – a common and important distinction in Heidegger's terminological usage we should not overlook. What the *Introduction* offers in response to this purported metaphysics of the production of the human animal is a philosophical project for a 'politics' of finitude rooted in the structure of Dasein itself, and in particular in being-toward-death.

Heidegger's retrieval of being as becoming, appearance, thought, and the Ought proposes to set these differentiations of being back into the primordial unconcealment of being. The retrieval is itself a project which responds to the differentiation of being in the wager of a decision. As historically rooted and determined questioning, moreover, this engagement of thought is already 'political' in the sense that it engages the gathered differentiation of being. The site of this gathering, which thinking seeks to prepare, is the *polis*. Finally, I will consider two of the 'limitations,' or differentiations, of being – that of thinking and that of appearance – in their implicit import for the question of the political.

Being presences as shining-forth. In the shining-forth, being brings itself to a stand in beings. Shining-forth is nothing subsequent or supplementary to being, but the manifestation of being itself. The shining-forth of being, in this sense, is understood as the unconcealment of *phusis* (GA40, 108/101). The work of art, action, rite, and ritual also bring the unconcealment of *phusis* to a stand within the determinate limits proper to each. In the limit proper to each being, the shining-forth of being gives itself in an aspect (*Ansehen/doxa*). 'Being is thus dispersed among the manifold essents' (GA40, 110/102). For this reason, because the presencing of unconcealment is not separate from beings, the question of being is inherently already a reflection on the founding of beings in being. This reflection thinks the differentiation and the together of being and appearing without reducing the shining-forth of being to a mere appearance separate from being. With the inception of Western 'political philosophy' in Plato's *Politeia*, a fundamental decision regarding the relation of being and appearance occurs. Now appearance comes pre-eminently to signify what merely appears, hence as what darkens and conceals being (GA40, 113/106). With this reduction of the shining-forth of being to the mere image as reflection and copy, the possibility of the *polis* as the site of the differentiation of being in beings is also undercut.

The founding of the differentiation and unity of being and appearance calls for a primordial knowledge (*Wissen*) more fundamental than science (*Wissenschaft*). Only in this way can the 'limitation' of being which opposes it to thinking to give rise to intellectualism be overcome for the sake of a receptive apprehension and response to being. This more fundamental knowledge does not presume to replace science as a way of rendering 'service to the nation' (*Dienst am Volke*) (GA40, 114/107). But the engagement of primordial knowledge, including the preparatory thinking of philosophy, is the precondition of such a transformation of science as will allow the 'transformation of beings into the openness of [the truth] of Dasein' (GA40, 115/107). The rank order which Heidegger implies here is evident. The new National Socialist state calls for a science which will serve the people: the goal of science and technology is to be the transformation of beings in the sense of Dasein as historically founded and delimited existence. While, finally, he acknowledges the justice of this demand, Heidegger holds that only primordial knowledge, as founding thinking, can prepare the way for a new science. At this point in his argument Heidegger turns to Greek tragedy as a way of knowing in which the primordial relation of being and appearing is founded in the work so as to preserve the inner differentiated unity of their strife (GA40, 115/107). The preservation of this unity and this strife is essential to the constitution of the *polis*. *An Introduction to Metaphysics*, therefore, is an attempt to waken primordial, founding knowledge. With this knowledge alone comes the readiness to wager (*tolma*) a decision regarding the differentiation of being which will be responsive to the presencing of being itself and to in-corporate this decision in the work, thought, rite, and action (GA40, 121/113). It is in the saying of the differentiated unity of the presencing of being in the gestalt of beings that thought serves the polity by laying out pathways of knowing and orders of rank. The knowing stance (*techne*) in the midst of beings of the being who is most uncanny (*deinotaton*) is the 'condition' of the political, for knowing wagers an order of beings against the might of the over-whelming power of being (*dike*). The making-manifest of being in the limit that is set-into-beings opens the space of the political. Therefore Fóti is wrong to claim that Heidegger's interpretation of Sophocles is 'dichotomous,' 'never countenancing the possibility of conjoining ontological insight with sociopolitical concern and efficacy,' thereby neglecting the realm of the political.[35] The 'sociopolitical' is in fact already prefigured in an 'ontology' of the mutual delimitation of beings as founded in the differentiation of being. The sociopolitical is implicated in the choice of ways of knowing and the rank assigned to different ways of knowing. Art, belief, science, technology are all ways of knowing. The primacy of technology, in the essential sense, which has come to dominate all other ways of knowing to determine what beings are, is by no means self-evident.

The possibility of another founding, such as Heidegger anticipated in 1933, is premised on the healing of the breach between nature and thought, *phusis* and *logos*. What kind of political order could begin to do this – according to Heidegger's conception of 1935? In conclusion, I venture to summarize the political implications of *An Introduction to Meta-*

physics, if only in a schematic and thoroughly provisional way, in terms of the following theses. They integrate certain conclusions we have already encountered in previous chapters. Certainly they are questionable, and they are intended to raise questions.

The political order Heidegger envisions would have to be self-limiting and particularistic, rather than cosmopolitan, in founding its claims to legitimacy. Following from this, it would be committed to the primacy of the earth in its historical specificity, and hence to an ecological order of economics. Concepts of 'responsibility' and 'justice' would have to be founded in the limits the earth calls for, and in the limit set by Da-sein's own mortality. Furthermore, recalling Heidegger's reading of *Antigone*, this political order would be the expression of a ritual order of leadership based pre-eminently on personal authenticity and authority, rather than on the primacy of institutional arrangements. Authenticity and authority take their measure from being-attuned to the historicity of earth-sited Da-sein, and do not, therefore, give free rein to the 'decision-istic' subject. The historical and ecological order of the earth sets the limit to human authority. Furthermore, the 'highest good' (or for-the-sake-of-which) of the polity would incorporate itself in the will to bring the differentiated being of beings into the gestalt in all essential realms – in technology and work, no less than in art, thought, sacrifice, and rule. The will to the differentiation of being in beings has implications for mankind's shepherdship of nature, in the sense of species preservation, for example. As such, the polity would be the intersection (*polis*) of these realms of unconcealment, and would lay out the con-stitution of their rank and order. Essential decisions could not, in principle, be left to the 'market.' This polity, finally, would have to take its 'condition of possibility' from a fundamental attunement to the presencing, or unconceal-ment, of beings, very different from the will to certainty and mastery which has founded modern socio-technocratic society since Bacon and Hobbes. All of the implications of Heidegger's political position, as I read them, are fraught with danger, perhaps none more so than the rejection of the universal order of a global politics, and the notion of a ritual mode of leadership.

In the *Introduction to Metaphysics* the outlines of a new attunement, which Heidegger's philosophy proposes to prepare, are evident, although given much fuller development in the *Beiträge*. *The unity of ques-tioning, which rebounds on itself, of attunement and knowledge, of being-toward-death and historicity, open the site of the possibility of the political.* Being is understood as the presencing of gestalt. This fundamental attunement consists in Dasein's openness to the differentiated presencing of the being of beings and consequently in attention to the inherent, proper limits of beings. Heidegger's interpretation of the choral ode of *Antigone* intimates that humanity's ontological homelessness, which the ex-sistent finitude of Dasein incorporates, founds the letting-be of beings. The homelessness of Dasein's existent being announces the abandonment of the *nomos* as law or principle. Letting-be denotes that the conceptual, categorial determinations of beings are deconstructed in favour of the specificity of their local-historical presencing. The letting-be of *noein*, receptive apprehension, however, implicates at the same time the *violence of founding and shaping knowledge*, which brings presencing into its differentiated forms. The deconstruction of the classical differentiation of being which the *Introduction* undertakes leads back to Dasein as the site of the inner strife of being. The strife between the letting-be of presencing and the giving-gestalt to presencing also conditions the nature of the polity: Heidegger's praise of the potential of National Socialism as a creative confrontation with technology implicates that the violence of giving-gestalt is responsive to the differentiation of being: *dike* itself is the 'jointure' of 'responsibility,' which joins response and giving-gestalt in one order of rank which it is the mission of the new state to found. Yet as politically reactive, the new regime is conceived as imposing the metaphysical form, or schema, of a 'value' system on the reception of nature and history. These two conflicting judgements mark the essential ambiguity of Heidegger's response to National Socialism in 1935 and the reflections of the *Beiträge* that follow.

6 Heidegger and Carl Schmitt: The Historicity of the Political

Heidegger explicitly rejected the 'concept of the political' which Carl Schmitt developed in the attempt to salvage a notion of political being from the all-inclusive claims of socio-technical society. In the *Parmenides* of 1942–3, Heidegger maintains, without mentioning him by name, that Schmitt's understanding of the political does not suffice to grasp the nature of the *polis* (GA54, 135). Heidegger's late disavowal notwithstanding, it remains necessary to determine to what extent his understanding of modernity accepts the thesis of Schmitt's *Der Begriff des Politischen*, particularly since Schmitt and Heidegger have so often been linked, categorized, and 'accused,' as political 'decisionists.'[1] My discussion will identify, by reference to key works of Schmitt's *oeuvre*, the common ground the two thinkers share to establish the essential points where Schmitt and Heidegger agree, or part company. This common ground may be staked out in two movements: the critique of liberalism as founded in subjectivity; and the question of the historicity of the political.

6.1 Schmitt's Critique of Liberalism

The central issue in Schmitt's text is the independence of 'the political' from the claims of economics and the technological determination of society (BP 57/75). This is a constant theme of Schmitt's political philosophy, equally evident in *Staat, Bewegung, Volk* (1933), *Politische Theologie* (1934), *Leviathan* (1936), and the prison text of 1945–7, *Ex Captivitate Salus*, as well as in *The Concept of the Political*. As the 'first product of the age of technology,' the Leviathan of Hobbes held within itself the seeds of its own destruction: social institutions arising out of the individual liberties Hobbes allowed made it possible for liberal ideas to 'cut up the

Leviathan and divide his flesh among themselves. Thus did the mortal god die for a second time' (LTH 118/73–4). The modern liberal state has become a 'great business': there 'must no longer be political problems, only organizational-technical and economic-sociological tasks' (PT 82/65). The primacy of socio-technical organization follows from the theological premises of the modern state in the mechanistic world view of Deism, no less than from the principles of modern science (PT 49/62). Guided by the 'fundamental principles' of security and calculability, every aspect of communal life is governed by normative abstractions laid down in advance (SBV 36). The 'new paradise' which this society propagates is that of a 'technologically determined earth and a thoroughly organized humanity'; am I on earth, Schmitt asks rhetorically, to be transformed by technology into pure radiant energy? (ExCS 83, 86).

The political in Schmitt's sense is won by way of a delimitation of the special essence of political being. In common with Heidegger (GA65, secs. 19, 76), Schmitt offers a critique of liberalism understood as the socio-technical management of production and consumption. Liberalism is incapable of recognizing its own limits, and is therefore inherently expansionist and imperialist. As such Schmitt offers a critique of modern society with which Heidegger concurs. It is my argument that in 1933 both thinkers were motivated by *the question whether the political being of mankind, as opposed to its socio-technical organization, is still a possibility.*

Heidegger's letter to Schmitt of 22 August 1933 praises *The Concept of the Political* as a work of great import.[2] With special reference to Heraclitus's Fragment 53, Heidegger intimates that the *basileus* is the ordering principle of the differentiation, or *polemos*, of the being of beings. In the figure of the *basileus* the differentiation of being into the limits of the gestalt proper to each being is founded in acts of leadership and rule. I argue, therefore, that Heidegger read Schmitt's work as a contribution to a concept of the political as the founding of the differentiated unity of a polity in its limited, historical specificity. This implicates the mutual recognition and delimitation of polities. In an address to German scholars held in Leipzig on 11 November 1933, Heidegger insists that it is purely out of 'the mutual allegiance to this unconditional demand of self-responsibility that there arises the possibility of taking each other seriously in order to affirm a community [of peoples]' (GA16, no. 104, 191). Self-responsibility is founded in the historicity of Dasein and of a Volk. Heidegger will oppose it to the imperialism of unlimited technical organization as founded in subjectivity (AWP 108–9/152). The question arises whether Heidegger's understanding of the historicity and sited specificity of being also informs Schmitt's 'concept of the political.' Is the political, in Schmitt's sense, a category of self-limitation? If so, then Schmitt and Heidegger undertake projects which have something essential in common, even if Schmitt develops his project very differently. If this is Schmitt's project, moreover, then the rhetorical situation of 1933 takes on contours which further clarify Heidegger's intervention in political life. If Heidegger, in other words, could justifiably read *Der Begriff des Politischen* as a reflection on the essential self-responsibility and self-limitation of the authentic polity, then his estimation of the situation of 1933 and his hopes of finding allies and actively intervening in the course of the new regime also become more comprehensible.

Like Heidegger, Schmitt evidently committed himself to the new regime in 1933 in the name of the conservative revolution. On the eve of Hitler's chancellorship, Schmitt favoured a presidial solution to prevent a totalitarian triumph and later collaborated with the Nazis, still hoping 'to save as much as possible of the traditional state from the all-pervasive interference and transformation inherent in universal Nazification.'[3] In attempting to accommodate the regime Schmitt compromised himself, perhaps for merely opportunistic reasons, far more than Heidegger, particularly by his anti-Semitic publications. Yet the theses of *The Concept of the Political* belong to the conservative revolution, not to National Socialism, in *the specific sense of a meditation on limits, and on the limitlessness of liberal, socio-economic discourse*. By 1936, moreover, Schmitt also found himself at odds with a regime he could not influence, and which regarded his professions of loyalty as hypocritical. He had become an 'outcast.'[4]

Before I develop my argument further, it will be useful to sketch the reception of Schmitt which has long been standard, and which is still often assumed in discussions of Heidegger and Schmitt. Since Schmitt's death, in 1985, the scholarship on him has unfolded a much more nuanced analysis of his thought and discovered the contemporary relevance of the central questions he poses. The crisis of liberalism has led to the recognition that liberalism is itself an historical product, that it has a '*particularistic*' nature, and consequently that its claim to ahistorical universalism is questionable;[5] in the wake of the Cold War, problems of world order have given added impetus to the re-emergence of geopolitics, and with it Schmitt's concept of *Grossraumordnung* (mutually limiting regional power blocs) has come under renewed scrutiny; the realization has occurred that the rise of ethnic nationalism and the claims of competing 'civilizations' pose a challenge to liberal ideology as the engine of historical change calls for a re-thinking of the liberal project;[6] and the post-modernism of Derrida, Lyotard, Baudrillard, finally, has demanded a re-examination of the Enlightenment project and the claims of universal reason and the prerogatives of socio-technical categories of thought. The questions of the historicity of peoples, of the self-assertion and responsibility of polities, of their legitimacy and mutual limitation, and of their relation to the earth's finite resources and their own 'native soil' have reasserted themselves.

This effort of scholarship has set itself against an older orthodoxy, which I propose to map out by reference to Mathias Schmitz's *Die Freund-Feind-Theorie Carl Schmitts*. Schmitz argues that the concept of the political in Carl Schmitt's thought follows from the devaluation of a transcendental ground for politics. The devaluation of universal rational grounds, and therefore the collapse of the attempt to found politics in objective reason and natural law, generates, in Schmitz's account, a series of consequences leading to the thoroughly nihilistic conclusions of Schmitt's political philosophy:[7] 1) 'If our belief in *ideés generales* loses its power, then the Norm becomes a mere fiction.'[8] The idea of the Norm, as realized in the proclamation of laws, only serves to conceal actual conflicts of power. Liberalism, and the condition of endless parliamentary discussion in which liberalism expresses itself (PT 75/59), finds its possibility in the fiction of a rational, universal ground of politics and the norms which reason grants. But with the collapse of natural law, the metaphysical foundations of parliamentarianism and liberalism also collapse.[9] 2) 'The situation as a whole becomes a state of exception.'[10] The ground of political action and order shifts to the power of decision of political actors; the exception reveals the sovereign.[11]

Politics is founded in decisions; decisions express the will of a political actor in commands which make laws. The state of exception becomes the norm. 'Now decisions are sought for their own sake, decisiveness and resolve take on a model, exemplary character.'[12] With reference to Schmitt's *Politische Theologie*, Schmitz claims that in a situation without inherent meaning the only meaning possible open to Schmitt is generated by the resolve to decide.[13] Löwith makes essentially the same argument.[14] The echo of Nietzsche's dictum that the will to power would rather will nothing than not to will at all is clearly audible. 3) The only criterion of rank distinguishing decisions is the intensity of a decision. The highest intensity of decision takes the form of life or death decisions. 'For this reason existential resolve fully discloses itself only in life-or-death struggle, in which a political entity *wagers* its existence.' Schmitz argues that war, in consequence, must be the defining instance of political being for Schmitt.[15] In *Politics of Friendship*, Derrida makes the same claim.[16] 4) The distinction which constitutes the political, that of friend and enemy, is derived from the act of decision: in a free-floating act of decision, unsupported by any universally recognized norm, we posit the enemy as enemy. Schmitz claims that just as decision is for its own sake and justifies itself in terms of its intensity, without reference to content, or to *what* is decided, so the concept of the enemy is not defined by reference to the material or ideological 'content' which the enemy represents. What the enemy concretely represents is a matter of indifference. 'What is rather decisive, is the existential attitude [Haltung] with which an issue, in itself a matter of indifference, is defended.' The 'foundation' of Schmitt's political theory is the 'willingness to die.'[17] The enemy is the objective correlative of the intensity of commitment to our decision; the decision implicates a negation; it generates, in the act of negation, an enemy, but one without particular content. The enemy is simply what is to be negated.

This account of Schmitt's political thought is seriously open to question. In the first instance, let us briefly consider the question of Schmitt's 'decisionism.' The necessity of a founding decision arises with the breakdown of normality. Civil war, for example, constitutes a state of exception to the acceptance of norms and the functioning of laws. The sovereign decision which founds a state establishes the possibility of a norm and is the condition of laws (BP 47/64). It is true that Schmitt does not grant the reality of an objective rational order, or of natural law, to determine norms from which laws may be derived. The decisionism of Hobbes, Schmitt writes, may be expressed in the dictum that '*autoritas, non veritas facit legem*' (PT 66/33). 'Sovereignty is outside the law, since the actions of the sovereign in the state of exception cannot be bound by laws.'[18] As founded, or supposedly founded, in a rational order, norms are expressions of what ought to be – of the Ought which stands over against concrete historical existence. *Veritas* reveals itself as what ought to be. Schmitt's theory of state and of law is thoroughly modern and positivistic in the sense that he insists that laws are posited by sovereign decisions of the will. According to the premises of Schmitt's political thought, the *Being* of will is opposed to the *Ought*, and it has a higher reality than the ahistorical ratio it represents. Kervégan summarizes his discussion of Schmitt's 'decisionism' by insisting that 'contrary to currently accepted opinion ... it is less decisionism as such than hostility to every form of normative thought which characterizes Schmitt's approach to law.'[19] This does not mean, however, that decisions are made *ex nihilo*. The decisionism from which law derives is not decision for its own sake, as Herf claims, for in Schmitt's terms this would be mere 'occasionalism.'[20] Occasionalism, as I indicate below, seizes on concrete historical situations as the mere occasion for a decision for decision's sake. Decision is rather rooted in the historical specificity of a people's traditions (SBV 42). The absence of binding norms cannot mean that decisions are made in an existential vacuum. Therefore the founded, delimited historicity of decision, and the specific embodiment of the will it represents, becomes an issue. The condition of decision in a metaphysics of the will and the possibility of uncovering the ground of decision in the historicity of being offer essential points of contact and contention between Schmitt and Heidegger.

Schmitt opens his account of the concept of the 'political,' conceived as an independent realm of being, by claiming that it is based on the distinction between friend and enemy (BP 7/26). This distinction founds political thinking just as the distinctions between good and evil and between the beautiful and the ugly, respectively, found ethics and aesthetics. The 'enemy' is defined as an opponent with whom existential conflicts are possible, and at times necessary. Yet this does not mean, as Schmitz claims, that Schmitt propagates war for its own sake, for *the enemy is by definition* granted recognition as a commensurate and legitimate other: 'political unity presupposes the real possibility of an enemy and therefore presupposes another co-existing political entity' (BP 35/53). The distinction of friend and enemy receives its full existential weight only in terms of the distinction between enemy and 'criminal' (ExCS 57–8). The authentic sense of the political allows the possibility of an enemy without criminalizing him. In *Ex Captivitate Salus*, the 'other' is in fact defined as my 'brother.' For whom can I acknowledge as my 'enemy'? Only someone who is capable of placing my way of being into question. And who can do this? Only I myself, or my brother: 'the other turns out to be my brother, and my brother my enemy' (ExCS 89). In the figure of my enemy, the fundamental existential question I pose myself takes gestalt (*Gestalt*) (ExCS 90). War in the purely political sense signifies the intention of maintaining the limits (*Grenzen*) which properly define the being of each party (ExCS 19, 32). Mutual recognition implicates reciprocal delimitation; this is Schmitt's fundamental thesis, not, as Derrida claims in *The Politics of Friendship*, the destruction of the enemy.[21]

If the mutual differentiation of friend and enemy is the fundamental distinction of Schmitt's political thinking, then the political must be defined as the possibility of differentiating conflict – not conflict, war, for its own sake, still less destructive indifferentiation, which reduces both parties to one form of being, ending in the triumph of the lowest common denominator. Political conflict, as the enactment of difference, sets each party to conflict into the limits which define it in its own proper being. The *unity* of a political form arises out of the self-recognition and self-limitation attendant on differentiating conflict. The concept of the state, as a particular organization of political unity, presupposes the political dimension, and therefore the dimension of conflict.[22] This mode of statehood and of conflict, Schmitt argues, was concretely realized in the European state system and the international law which regulated it between the seventeenth and twentieth centuries. Therefore, Schmitt links the state and the political intimately, on historical grounds, practically identifying the modern state with the political, and opposing both to liberal society.

Yet Schmitt introduces the thesis that the political, understood simply as conflict, is inherent in the nature of mankind. 'The political or polemic dimension is inscribed in human nature,' as Kervégan writes, of the anthropological premises of Schmitt's thought.[23] I have already alluded to this dimension by way of Heidegger's reference to *polemos* in his letter to Schmitt of 1933. For Schmitt, the political is indeed defined by the presence of conflict. As such, the political is not bound to any one political form; it is definitive even of forms such as liberal society, which historically constitute a depoliticization of political structures (BP 49/ 69). Precisely this depoliticization leads to a totalization of society and a new unity of ideological and socio-economic discourses, which in another sense implicates the total 'politicization' of society. Everything of public interest is in some way 'political.'[24] But conflict between totalized (but not necessarily totalitarian) states is no longer defined by mutual differentiation and delimitation. Liberalism, as a form of the total integration of all social forms into one system, presupposes a metaphysics of indifferentiation which serves to legitimate universal, ahistorical institutions and unconditional warfare as the means of bringing about this end. The opponent is denied the status of enemy and criminalized as outlaw (BP 19/36; ExCS 57–8, 71).

Therefore 'the political' receives two opposed senses, which Schmitt attempts to integrate into one coherent history of modernity. (*i*) The political in the authentic sense, incorporated in the classic state, is understood as a category of mutual recognition and limit. Liberal society signifies the dissolution of the state and of the political in this sense. (*ii*) The political returns in the form of an indifferent totalization, in socio-technical form, to constitute an unconditional assault on rank order, authenticity, and ownness, thus to consummate the functional indifference of all entities (LTH 63/98–9). This account has evident similarities with Heidegger's understanding, in the *Introduction to Metaphysics* of 1935, of the abandonment of the being of beings, of the 'darkening of the world' in the era of technology, as the epoch of the consummation of metaphysics (GA40, 41/38). For the abandonment of the being of beings intimates their dis-integration into functions. The liberal state is one form this development takes; other forms of the movement toward totalization are communism, fascism, and National Socialism.

However, at least in 1933–4, Schmitt evidently hoped National Socialism would initiate a countermovement to functionalization and totalization. This countermovement, insofar as it is still conceived as a possibility in 1933, originates in the Volk and the historically founded orders which emerge out of its ethos. Neither Heidegger nor Schmitt are under the illusion that the past order can be re-established. The collapse of classical politics, and with it the friend-enemy distinction, in the era of depoliticization and total war does not allow for a return to classical politics – *but it does raise the question whether the logic of mutual recognition and delimitation can be established on other grounds.* Schmitt, like Heidegger, will evoke the historicity of the earth, hence the native rootedness of peoples, and on this ground both part company with the politics of globalization. And Heidegger evidently thought, at least in 1933–5, that National Socialism in its 'authentic' form could initiate a mutually delimiting differentiation of polities, founded in historicity and the 'native' earth.

The 'political,' in Schmitt's terms, is a category of limit, and the friend-enemy distinction is a principle of mutual recognition and limitation. Authentically existential conflicts are possible only insofar as the opponent is recognized in his or her being as 'other.' The term 'existential,' therefore, refers not only to conflicts generated by the confrontation of different modes of being; the mode of being of the other demands recognition as a mode of being, and thus imposes a limit on one's own mode of being. Modes of being are given concrete, historical specificity as the modes of being of diverse peoples, of *Völker.* In this way the friend-enemy distinction is given content; and conflict, the rationale of the defence of the historical specificity and mode of existence, or ethos, of a Volk (BP 8–9, 19, 32/27, 36, 49). Although Schmitz acknowledges that Schmitt makes this claim, Schmitz nonetheless insists that the conflict of 'modes of existence' is an abstract determination of conflict tending toward the mere negation and annihilation of the enemy. Yet Schmitt's argument implicates the historicity and situatedness of political being, and hence of the friend-enemy distinction. This saves it from the charge of 'abstraction,' for conflict arises out of specific historically founded interests, not out of mere decisionism and negation for its own sake. Insofar, moreover, as conflict is understood as the conflict of political entities in the classical sense, it must remain limited, for the negation of the mode of existence of the other would create a state of in-difference which would obviate the very end of political being – the maintenance of a mode of existence in its difference from others. Since the absence of mutual recognition generates unlimited conflict, conflict is revolutionalized: it becomes a category of indifferentiation as opposed to differentiation. The sublation of all 'political' differences into one universal state is precisely the termination of classical politics, and cannot, therefore, be the goal of conflict in Schmitt's sense. Schmitt claims that liberalism, conversely, subsumes the historical specificity of political existence under the ahistorical universality of reason as incorporated into socioeconomic institutions.

The friend-enemy distinction, therefore, is founded on a concept of the inherent and proper limits of all states. The recognition of the enemy as enemy is the event which enacts one's own self-recognition and affirmation. 'Friend' and 'enemy' – one's own and the other – mutually determine and condition each other. The reciprocal determination of 'the political' and 'self-limitation' is what essentially distinguishes it from the inauthentic political form of 'political romanticism,' which aims at the sublation of all limits (*Grenzen*) (PR 91). Political romanticism represents the triumph of a transcendental idea of politics, which imposes an ethical idea of the universal brotherhood, of abstractly conceived 'humanity,' on historically rooted existence (PR 91, 110). It is determined by the need for totality, hence it uproots the historically specific to 'found' the polity in the abstraction of the concept. The 'occasionalism' of this doctrine reveals the theological origins of modern society. As a political doctrine occasionalism is a form of transcendental discourse which founds political association in the wake of the collapse of the belief in a transcendent God (PR 86). The 'occasionalism' of political romanticism, more specifically, implicates that the historically given concreteness of events, peoples, and polities are merely 'occasions' for action which determine themselves by ahistorical concepts of political being posited a priori. Occasionalism signals the triumph of the ahistorical transcendental subject over history (PR 122–5, 135). It is not surprising that Schmitt approvingly refers to Edmund Burke as an anti-romantic political thinker who insisted on a politics founded in living tradition (PR 135).

Since liberalism, by contrast, defines itself in economic and moral terms and claims the superiority of its values, it cannot recognize other kinds of polities as legitimate forms of life. Because the other is not recognized as legitimate, it is denied the status of enemy and reduced to being an outlaw and criminal (BP 61/79). For this reason the wars of liberal society against non-liberal states take an especially inhumane character, for liberalism denies the moral worth and right to exist of these states (BP 19/36). The 'state' as a political entity and therefore as a higher order of unity than the socio-technical management function of liberal society is already, metaphysically speaking, a threat to the claims of liberalism. These claims derive from the primacy of the individual as a self-constituting entity in the Lockean sense. Referring to Paine, Schmitt defines liberalism as the attempt to subject the political to the ethical and economic nature of humanity. This definition of mankind's 'nature' derives from Locke and Hobbes. Conceived as the 'result of the rational management of needs' (BP 42/61), liberal society is an attempt to codify a metaphysical understanding of human nature as self-production. Heidegger is in essential agreement with this critique of liberalism (GA65, secs. 19, 76). Liberalism, therefore, may be conceived as a metaphysics of 'property' in both the economic and moral sense. Since the state, in Schmitt's terms, lays claim to a higher order of being than the social mechanisms of self-constitution, and since it, the state, claims the status of a form of life distinct from these mechanisms, it must enter into conflict with liberal society. This conflict, however, is not determined by political categories, for liberalism implicitly aims at one world order. The political, conversely, announces the differentiation of humanity into mutually limiting and distinct life-forms or states. Liberalism claims to speak for 'humanity.' The 'concept of "humanity," however, is a particularly useful instrument of imperial expansion' (BP 37/54).

Schmitz raises the critique that Schmitt neglects the categories of friend and friendship in his determination of the political. Aristotle founds his investigation of politics in the friendship (*philia*) which members of a community bear one another.[25] Why does Schmitt, on his part, insist on the priority of the 'enemy' in determining the political realm? The answer is not far to seek: the modern revolutionary tradition proclaims the 'brotherhood of mankind' and claims to found politics in the 'love of mankind.' This implicates a politics without limit. To wage war in the 'name of humanity' implies an ideology of the dehumanization of the enemy, and consequently an inhumane war (BP 37/54). For the enemy is no longer acknowledged in its concrete historical specificity. It becomes an absolute enemy because it is defined as the pure negation of highest values, posited a priori; therefore war also becomes absolute, total war.[26] In 'Überwinding der Metaphysik' ('Overcoming Metaphysics'), Heidegger, on his own grounds, will also recognize the total character of modern war as founded in the dis-integration of the being of beings and their integration into an in-different, unlimited, resource base of stock-on-call (sec. 26). The question of the 'political,' for Heidegger no less than for Schmitt, is a response to this 'process.'

Since the category of the enemy is one of recognition and self-limitation, the claims of political entities are subject to mutual limitation. Whereas Schmitt's critique of liberalism is evidentially inspired by the First World War and its aftermath at Versailles, the import of this critique cannot be reduced to reactionary nationalism, as Herf claims.[27] For *Der Begriff des Politischen* was first published in 1927, under conditions of the colonization of Germany by the Entente powers. As a political tract, it is anti-imperialist in its intention and tendency.[28] Schmitt astutely identifies, moreover, the complex of economic imperialism and 'human values' which has frequently served to legitimate the foreign policies of the liberal West since 1914. Winfield, for example, supplements his critique of Schmitt with a theory of territorial rights – the right to possess and acquire territory – which justifies the imperialism of 'just,' i.e., liberal-democratic, states.[29] Schmitt in fact emphasizes, furthermore, that the preferred policy of these states is not open warfare but economic imperialism, expressed in the blockage of credit, the destruction of foreign currencies, and the denial of raw materials, or of markets for raw and finished materials (BP 60/78). Schmitt's most fundamental point, however, is that the 'politics' of liberalism is founded on the metaphysical claim to represent the essence of humanity. The concept of the political denies this claim, just as liberalism must negate a political sphere based on the mutual limitation of competing, but in principle equally legitimate, states.

The features of Schmitt's political philosophy which have hitherto emerged stand in essential agreement with Heidegger's understanding of the metaphysical nature of socio-technological society. The governing principles of this society insist on the indifference of humanity and nature as resources on call. The insistence on the indifference of all beings, and with it, the inability to acknowledge the historical specificity of peoples and traditions, also results in the denial of the authentically political. Inasmuch as Schmitt's concept of the political is based on the mutual limitation of historically founded polities, his political philosophy finds resonance in Heidegger. This agreement regarding the politics of liberalism, however, should not obscure the fundamental disagreement between Heidegger and Schmitt in respect to the metaphysical provenance of liberalism; nor should it lead us to think that the essence of the political is the same for both thinkers.

In *Staat, Bewegung, Volk*, Schmitt had defined the political state, in its internal constitution, as determined by its own, proper concept of form or gestalt (SBV 33). This demand for a cohesive concept of form could be misused for totalitarian purposes if it were taken as a call to impose form on the 'body politic.' Yet this interpretation is not demanded by the concept of *Gestaltung* or form-giving itself. The concept of form is not conceived as paradigm, but as the historically rooted condition of proper self-unfolding inherent in the tradition of a people (SBV 45). The concept of the political presupposes self-delimitation as the self-formation of a people; hence, as derived from the primary value of the historically determined specificity of a people, the concept gives Schmitt's understanding of the political a normative function which has often gone unrecognized.[30] The metaphysical claim of the normative value of the self-determination of a people as rooted in its historical specificity grounds Schmitt's concept of the political as the opposition of friend and enemy. Were it not ultimately derived from an ontology of limit and self-limitation, the opposition of friend and enemy would be merely formal and without content. Given the metaphysical foundations of Schmitt's idea of the political in the concept of limit, he does implicitly provide what has been denied him – 'norms for evaluating diverse regimes.'[31]

The notion of the historicity of a people which Schmitt propagates, moreover, should not be confused with some ideal of an 'organic' state modelled on the work of art.[32] Schmitt explicitly rejects this model as integral to political romanticism. Evidently Schmitt recognizes that so-called 'national aestheticism' is grounded in a metaphysics of self-production which takes the givenness of tradition as the mere 'occasion' for the imposition of a state-forming idea (PR 157, 172–3). The aesthetic model posits an idea, or paradigm, of state as the precondition of the production of a polity. Wherein, therefore, might the unity of the political state rest, according to Schmitt? Schmitt intimates that the place-granting power (*Raumkraft*) of the word tells of the unity of word and place (*Ort*) and therefore of self-delimited and historically founded being (ExCS 91). The unity of the state would have to be founded in the power of place as it brings itself to word. The Leviathan of Hobbes was one such political '*Mythos*' which liberal society slaughtered, Schmitt claims, to replace it with its own mythos of a technically managed society (LTH 118). Every polity rests in the power of the word, but the decisive question is whether a governing mythos allows a multiplicity of places (*Orte*) to unfold themselves within the unity of the whole, or integrates all places into one pre-determined dimension. Given the foundations of Schmitt's political theory in the concept of limit, the 'state,' to remain true to its nature, could only be a differentiated unity.

Heidegger would also concur with Schmitt that 'humanity as such cannot go to war, for it has no enemy, at least not on this planet' (BP 36/54). This is evident. Yet, insofar as 'humanity' is an idea laid claim to by the elect of humanity, this elect will find occasion to wage war against peoples and states that do not 'measure up' to the rational criteria of this idea. Schmitt's point may be extrapolated, moreover, in the following way: once given that mankind has overcome political divisions to establish a technocratic world order, another 'enemy' emerges. For having loosed itself from the delimitations imposed by historical existence, and having defined itself as techno-animality, then the genetic, biological 'basis' of humanity, insofar as it is imperfect, becomes mankind's enemy, as will death itself. His intimation of the sublation of the friend-enemy distinction already allows Schmitt to anticipate, without fully grasping in his own terms, Heidegger's reflections on the technological destiny of metaphysics.

In his *Theorie des Partisanen* of 1963, which is conceived as a supplement to the 'concept of the political,' Schmitt recognizes that the struggle for world power which follows from the dissolution of all limits reduces the earth to a single, planetary dimension determined by technology.[33] This dimension is ultimately defined in its technological uniformity by the transcendental subjectivity which Schmitt, as we have seen, nominates political romanticism. The 'transcendence' of the historical givenness of traditions and limits and the reduction of the earth as a multiplicity of places to the uniformity of the planetary are corollaries of the same historical process. Dissolving every founded gestalt and tradition, this process posits the planetary as a system of human and natural resources. The stability of this system, however, is doubtful, in Schmitt's view. In his *Nomos* (1950), he proposes that only by taking its measure from the elemental order of our being on the earth can humanity find lasting security and stability.[34] With the triumph of techno-planetary thought over the concept of the political, mankind as it is (mortal, imperfect) becomes its own enemy. And this distinction between technicity or techno-animality, on the one hand, and mortality, on the other, will become all-determining. Yet this distinction cannot finally be grasped by the rational animal, as Schmitt still presupposes, and it cannot be brought to a decision, because humanity so conceived cannot put itself into question.

6.2 The Historicity of the Political

Schmitt's account of modernity is premised on the movement of political being from delimited, historical specificity toward an unlimited, technocratic society which has subjected the earth to the idea of a universal planetary dimension. This movement toward totalization is simultaneously a movement toward the ahistoricity of mankind. His thought, therefore, is confronted by the necessity of giving adequate expression to the historicity of the political. This task imposes itself in the following moments: (*i*) the necessity of winning an adequate understanding of Volk as a movement of withdrawal from the objectification of socio-technical discourse; (*ii*) the questions of subjectivity and representation in their relation to the political; (*iii*) the definition of the nature of the state in its relation to Volk; and (*iv*) an explication of conflict, or *polemos*, commensurate to the founded historicity and differentiation of beings. The *questions* of subjectivity and representation, Volk, the state, and *polemos* reveal the common ground which Heidegger and Schmitt share in 1933.

6.2.1 Volk

Heidegger's understanding of Volk may be derived from section 74 of *Being and Time*, and as such, from the concept of the historicity of Dasein. The *Logik* of 1934 offers a more explicit working out of Heidegger's premises, and it is to this text I will turn, however briefly, for the question of Volk in Heidegger's philosophy demands an extended treatment of its own. In common with Schmitt, Heidegger understands Volk as a countermovement to rational transparency and functional disintegration; understood in its historicity as the unity of temporalization, Volk moves into the future of its task (*Auftrag*) only inasmuch as it is moved back into and is sent on its way by its mission or vocation (*Sendung*). This movement back signifies the retrieval of being-thrown. The thrownness of

Volk, which sets it on its path of historicity, can never be brought into the rational transparency of ideological formation. Thrownness intimates *the movement of withdrawal from representation* inherent in the being of Volk. The taking-up and enactment of a task opens the future allotted by a Volk's mission: in this enactment, Volk actualizes its potential by bringing itself into *the achievement of its inherent limit*, as set by the movement and unity of its historicity. Having-been (mission) and task (future) are concretely actualized in the making-present of beings in work – in *the differentiated disclosure of the being of beings* (GA38, 126–31).

An examination of the concept of Volk in Schmitt will allow us to anticipate the terms of Heidegger's implicit critique – to the effect that Schmitt's political thought is founded on an inadequate concept of historicity. The first question at issue is whether or not the concept of Volk fills an essential need in Schmitt's thought in 1933–4, or whether he recurs to it for merely opportunistic reasons. I concur with Piccone that although 'decisionism is prominent in Schmitt's writings during the 1920s, he gradually came to emphasize *Ordnungsdenken*, the primacy of traditional institutional orders, as a more stable source of legitimacy and as such, a possible alternative to liberal depoliticization and disintegration.'[35] In 1933–4, Schmitt abandoned the dualism of decision and norm, and with it the metaphysical opposition of Being (the will, as incorporated in decision) and the Ought (the objective rational order, which founds norms), in recognition of the power of historically founded orders or institutions.[36] This revision is implicit in *The Concept of the Political* and carried through in *Staat, Bewegung, Volk* (1933) and *Über die drei Arten des rechtswissenschaftlichen Denkens*. In response to the dynamism of National Socialism, Schmitt evidently wanted to exclude the decisionistic misinterpretation of his political thought to which *The Concept of the Political* had given rise: thus decisionism is further limited in favour of the founding power – not of ahistorical reason and the Norm – but of historically founded orders and institutions, such as are embodied in the ethos of the Volk. In this sense, Schmitt's reflection on orders is an attempt to give a more concrete articulation to the concept of Volk as a constitutive political moment. Therefore, Schmitt's reflections on the Volk, in the publications of 1933–4, should not be construed as opportunistic attempts to ingratiate himself with the *völkisch* and racialist thinking of National Socialism.[37] Volk is the moment of stability and rootedness in face of the dynamism of the Movement – a moment which expresses itself in leadership, in revolutionary acts of decision – and in face of the normative structures of the State, which tend at least in theory to rational transparency (cf. the Preface to the *Politische Theologie* of 1934). Therefore, I cannot agree with Kervégan that the Volk is merely the 'static and as such non-political pole' of Schmitt's tripartite structure.[38] In the first instance, Schmitt recurs to 'concrete' – that is, historically founded – orders and the community of action which antedates the normative structures of society (UAR 17). The unity of these orders is granted by the Volk, for it alone expresses the sited historicity of the political and as such generates the possibility of concrete, historically specific norms of law and decision making. To a significant extent the Volk as founding moment remains implicit in this text and becomes manifest only through Schmitt's citation of Fichte's appeal to Volk (UAR 48–9, note to 48). Volk is therefore an essential political moment of the tripartite conflictual nature of the political. This moment, however, is inadequately developed according to the terms demanded by Schmitt's own theses of 1933–4.

If, as Kervégan argues, Volk is conceived by Schmitt as a relatively passive object of the dynamism of the Movement, which in itself constitutes a historically concrete political order by mediating between Volk and State, then Schmitt has indeed opened the door to the combination of state functionalism and arbitrary decisionism which would in fact characterize the National Socialist state. Admittedly Schmitt leaves the concept of the historicity of the Volk, and therefore the political moment of the withdrawal from both rational transparency and decisionism, undeveloped. His attempt to limit the possible arbitrariness of leadership, of the Movement, by reference to a homology of kind, by reference to the common attunement of leaders and led (*Artgleichheit*), is too vague, for he never specifies how, concretely, the sovereignty of leadership is limited by the competency of Volk. Given that Volk is understood as a category of limit and rootedness, it would be incumbent on Schmitt to develop this moment of the idea of Volk as a counterweight to the claims of functional structures and arbitrary command. The racination of the Volk in its ethos would be opposed to forms of deracination. This motif, however, as Schmitt's *Leviathan* shows, leads Schmitt away from an authentic confrontation with modernity into the murky waters of anti-Semitism, inasmuch as he identifies the Jewish intelligentsia with the forces of deracination (LTH 92–3). Schmitt's anti-Semitic turn substitutes – in a negative way – for his failure to more systematically unfold a theory of the historicity of Volk. As such, the possibility of a countermovement to totalization, to which I referred above, also becomes questionable. This leaves the field open for the ideologues of the regime, for the National Socialist state itself actualized a form of the triumph of socio-technical functionalization by instrumentalizing a primitive idea of Volk. The terms of Schmitt's confrontation with the new regime were, therefore, undermined by an inadequate concept of Volk as *the articulation of Dasein's historicity* and vitiated by the realities of 1933.

6.2.2 Subjectivity and Representation

In his *Staat, Bewegung, Volk* of 1934, Schmitt reverses the emphasis of his earlier argument, as developed in the *Verfassungslehre* (Theory of the Constitution) (1928), that the Volk is in itself non-political, and only becomes present to itself by the mediation, or re-presentation, of the state. There is no state without representation: for a state cannot be without form, and form derives from the apprehension of political unity which representation, as the space of mutual recognition, first constitutes (VL 207). Representation – whether in the form of the symbolic and material identity of the sovereign with one person, or in the form of the delegation of the will of the people to an assembly – constitutes 'the political sphere, because it manifests, or stages, political unity.'[39] Representation constitutes the identity of a people through an act of self-objectification – a people goes on stage to enact itself, as it were. Short of being-represented, the unity and identity of a people is only a fictive idea, for as the realm of natural desires and private wills, the 'people' is a non-political category (VL 215).[40] Schmitt stands fully in the modern tradition of Hobbes, Rousseau, and Hegel. What one commonly understands as Volk, Hegel writes in the *Grundlinien der Philosophie des Rechts*, are 'the many as individuals' who constitute a collective, but as a 'formless mass' whose 'movement and action remain elemental, irrational, wild and terrible' (sec. 303). As opposed to this realm of natural and particular desires, the state represents the 'highest, concrete generality' of a will which consciously affirms itself (secs. 303 and 270).

The modern tradition identifies representation with the sovereign power of a state. It subordinates the merely 'natural' and non-political realm of desire – as expressed in the inchoate mass of what is not yet a 'people,' not yet historical – to the constituting act of representation. Political representation is defined as the re-presentation, or 'staging,' of a founding or sovereign subject *of itself* (as a 'people') *to itself* (as the Leviathan of state). In Schmitt's terms *political* representation, moreover, is a form of *presentation* distinct from, and superior to, every form of delegation of powers or agency in the socio-economic realm (RK 26): representation makes present and publicly visible what was invisible. The coming-forth into public manifestation (*in das öffentliche Sein*) and taking-form (*Heraushebung*) of the invisible is what Schmitt calls *Existenz* (VL 210). *Existenz* intimates the taking of form, of standing-forth into the open. Representation defines the realm of the political as the site of the emergence of a people's communal being into the definitive outlines of a determinate form. Given the primacy of the socio-economic over the political under the 'regime' of liberalism, it is evident why Schmitt insists that liberalism signals the triumph of formlessness. Heidegger evidentially shares Schmitt's critique of formlessness and seeks to give the 'political' a gestalt in and through the presencing of being in the state as the articulate will of the Volk (GA38, 165). The 'presencing of being' (i.e., the event of truth) in Heidegger's sense, finds, within limits, a corresponding measure in what Schmitt understands by 'representation' and '*Existenz.*' Being presences – takes gestalt to manifest itself – in beings: in the work of art, acts of leadership, and in the founding of a state (UK 48/186; GA 65, 71/48). Schmitt attaches himself to the tradition of representation only to seemingly abandon it in 1933–4, in favour of a theory of state founded on the 'natural' and even racial 'substance' of the Volk. The 'substantial similarity and equality of kind' (*Artgleichheit*) of the Volk are interpreted in a racialist way (SBV 42–5). This recourse to Volk, to be sure, is implicit in the *Verfassungslehre*, although in ways which betray no commitment to a natural or racial substratum of national identity, such as founds the unity of the state. Identity, understood as the presence of a people to itself, is required by every state, to a greater or lesser degree. 'With the word "identity," we signify the existential reality of political unity, as opposed to any sort of normative, formal, or fictive equality. Democracy [not to be confused with liberalism] presupposes in every part and in its whole political existence a people equal in kind [gleichartiges] who have the will to political existence' (VL 208, 235). It is by no means self-evident, however, that the distinction Schmitt makes in the *Verfassungslehre* between polities founded in *the mediated unity of representation* and those founded in *the unmediated unity of identity of a Volk* calls for a 'substantial' or racialist theory of the unmediated unity of identity (VL 204–6). The two ideas of unity are not even opposed to each other, for although one form of unity is liable to predominate, they typically supplement each other in the historical constitution of any given state. The unity of identity, therefore, as presented in the *Verfassungslehre*, does not implicate a racialist interpretation. Schmitt, moreover, leaves open the possibility, on the Greek model, of an *identity of attunement* to the earth as homeland, as the ground of the unity of a Volk.[41] Yet in 1933, Schmitt capitulates, as it were, to the new orthodoxy of racial identity, and fails to develop the notion of *Artgleichheit* in the direction of the Greek model. The representational unity of the state gives way to a spurious racial unity of identity.

Schmitt's incomplete development of the concept of the unity of identity has unfortunate consequences. In *Staat, Bewegung, Volk,* he insists that the idea of *Führung* 'does not derive from baroque allegory and representation, nor from Cartesian general concepts,' but represents 'unmediated presence and realized actuality [unmittelbarer Gegenwart und realer Praesenz]' (SBV 41). The condition of leadership is the *Artgleichheit* of leader and led: 'commonality of kind' establishes a common attunement, a common way of knowing, feeling, existing, which alone allows the possibility of being understood by others, of coming into conversation with the other (SBV 45). Those alien to this community of understanding will feel and think differently. Political unity is produced (*hergestellt*) by representation; it is manifested or enacted (*dargestellt*) by a state founded in identity.[42] The *Führer* is conceived as the incarnation, the manifested presence, of an identity of kind grounded in a common attunement. This position has evident weaknesses. The abrogation of the re-presentational space of the state as the public site of the conversation of leaders and led eliminates constraints on the misuse of power. The erasure of the distinction between the private person of the *Führer* and his public function as the enactor and author of a common attunement tends to uncouple the private will of the *Führer* from the general will. In his *Römischer Katholizismus,* Schmitt had argued that the Roman Catholic Church, as an institution, manifests the transcendent reality of the incarnate God through the function of the priesthood – for example, in the administration of the Mass (RK 26).[43] Function is subordinate to a superior, transcendent reality. If the leader, in turn, is conceived as a kind of priest, enacting the rites of state, as Kervégan suggests,[44] he too, must act in the name of the unitary will of the people. This demands a measure of accountability to which Schmitt fails to give concrete, institutional expression.

Heidegger's existential hermeneutic of *Befindlichkeit,* as the power of *phusis* in us, shows that a deconstruction of the 'natural,' thus to retrieve *Volksein* from the metaphysics of biologism and found it in historicity, is a possible path for the politics of Volk. Heidegger could commit himself to the political unity of identity, founded in the Volk, as opposed to the unity of representation, without committing himself, as Schmitt did in

1934, to a racialist interpretation of identity. Since *Befindlichkeit*, moreover, is not identical with the realm of unreasoning feeling but is constituted by understanding and discourse, the politics of identity demands, no less than the politics of representation, an open, public site of dialogue (SZ, sec. 29). This would be one way the political takes definitive gestalt. Rhetoric is the articulation of this site: as a kind of *aletheuein* it brings the attunement of the Volk into the clarity of the concept, and grounds the concept in the fundamental, authentic attunement of a generation. The identity of a common attunement is the condition of dialogue and the possibility of mutual understanding in the public sphere (GA38, 12–30; GA39, 72). No less is the public sphere of dialogue the condition of the ongoing work of wresting truth from the distortions inherent in the common interpretation of the attunement of a generation. The dialogical space imposes reciprocal restraints on each participant in dialogue, inasmuch as each is bound by responsibility to the threefold temporalization of Volk. The politics of identity, therefore, does not necessarily implicate an arbitrary exercise of power. In Heidegger's terms, moreover, the identity of the Volk has to be understood as differentiated, or 'fractured': this follows from the fact that identity is conceived as a movement of temporalization, as opposed to the self-presence of subjectivity. Therefore Heidegger's understanding of Volk offers an explicit critique of subjectivity as the re-presentation of the subject to itself (GA65, sec. 196).

What Schmitt, following the modern tradition, calls the self-objectification, re-presentation, or 'staging,' of the Volk to and for itself shows the derivation of Volk, or people, and the modern state from the founding metaphysics of Descartes. Heidegger's most explicit statement linking re-presentation to the metaphysics of the subject going on stage for itself is found in 'The Age of the World Picture' (1936): under the regime of representation,

> man sets himself up as the setting in which whatever is must henceforth set itself forth, must present itself [sich ... praesentieren], i.e., be picture. Man henceforth becomes the representative [der Repraesentant] of that which is, in the sense of that which has the character of object. (AWP 89/132)

Heidegger's rejection of the metaphysics of representation raises the question whether his position still allows for a public sphere, for the public is constituted by the self-representation of a people to itself. The rhetorical moment is one way a generation articulates its response to the claims of a heritage. Following *Being and Time*, we know that Heidegger attempts to break with representational subjectivity, as the ground also of political discourse, by establishing Da-sein as the site (the Da-) of the unconcealment of the claim of being. This claim, which articulates itself as the 'voice' of the tradition in its threefold temporalization, embodies itself as 'language.' It is the condition of the self-presence of subjectivity. Hence the public sphere must be reconceived as the enactment and actualization of the power of language, as opposed to the self-realization of individual subjects or the collective subject of the nation. Language, as primordial *logos*, articulates the event of the differentiation of the being of beings. Heidegger attempts to reconceive the public sphere as the site of ongoing response to this event, wherein the response actualizes itself in questioning, works, and acts. For example, the community of research, as founded in questioning, wins its 'actuality,' or being, from the deconstructive rebound of the question on the self-presence of the questioner (GA27, 40–1; SU 9/470). The 'public space' of research gains its stability from the constancy of being-held-open by the question, and not by reference to the self-presence of subjectivity (WM 119/109).

Only the deconstruction of the subject and the founding of Da-sein would allow the still metaphysical position of Schmitt's concept of the historical specificity of rational humanity to be overcome. What is fundamentally lacking in Schmitt, therefore, out of Heidegger's perspective, is a concept of historicity founded in the history of being. This history calls for the founding of Da-sein in the situated, concrete form of the temporalization of a Volk. In this sense, the question of Volk is the gateway to the question of being. Only as founded can the historicity of Dasein be brought to bear on the essential decision between techno-animality and mortality which arises with the technocratic totalization of the state. This decision is the response of a resolve which opens itself to the differentiation of being in beings, thus to preserve each in its own being, and Dasein in its being-toward-death (GA65, secs. 44–6, 61). Decision and preservation are not derived from the re-presentation of the subject to itself: they are rather conceived as the condition and the enactment of the making-present of beings. The making-present of beings, thus to set each into the limits proper to it, is what Heidegger understands by 'work.' Volk actualizes itself in the making-present of work. Consequently the Volk is constituted neither by the re-presentation of subjectivity for itself (thus to derive it from the state) nor by the unmediated self-identity of presence to itself. As the concretely enacted temporalization of the situated finitude of being, Volk 'is' in being in ek-static being-with beings, thus to actualize itself as work (GA38, 153–5).

6.2.3 State and Volk

The thematic of enactment and actualization, as attempts to break with the logic of representation, are supported by Heidegger's effort to found the state itself in the temporality of Dasein. In the *Logik*, Heidegger insists on the necessity of the State as the form of the 'historical being of the Volk' (GA38, 165). The passage reads as follows:

> Because the being of the historical Dasein of mankind is founded in temporality, that is, in Care, therefore the state is essentially necessary. Not as an abstraction and a right derived from the imagined and timeless nature of humanity as existing in itself, but the state as the essential law of historical being. The force and order of this law first allows the Volk to secure for itself its historical duration [Dauer] – that is, the preservation of its mission and the struggle for its task. The state is the historical being of the Volk. (GA38, 165)

A number of questions immediately arise. Why, in the first instance, is it necessary to make the move from Volk to state? How is the idea of the state related to the governing principles *of* Volksein *as limit, withdrawal, and the differentiated disclosure and unity of comportment?* Why does Heidegger insist on opposing the state to society, and how is this distinction significant? In what respects is Heidegger's understanding of the state based on the existential analytic of *Being and Time?*

I will begin with a consideration of the last question. Heidegger holds that the state arises as an essential necessity because 'the being of the historical Dasein of humanity is founded in temporality, that is, in Care' (GA38, 165). We recall that the analytic of Dasein reveals the Care-structure as the condition of the unity (*Ganzsein*) and ability-to-be of Dasein (SZ 317/292–3). This structure articulates the selfhood of Dasein, hence deconstructs the metaphysically conceived subject and grounds it in the temporality of Dasein as a thrown project. Heidegger defines the Kantian subject as follows: 'the I think is not something represented, but the formal structure of representing as such, and this formal structure alone makes it possible for anything to be represented' (SZ 319/294–5). Kant conceives the I as subject, Heidegger holds, and thus Kant conceives it in an 'ontologically inappropriate' sense, for 'the concept of the subject does *not* characterize *the selfhood of the I qua self, but the sameness and constancy of something always already objectively present*' (SZ 320/295). The deconstruction of the subject breaks with the substantiality of an abiding, underlying presence (SZ 322–323/296–7). This leads to the implication that if the state is founded in the non-substantiality of the structure of Care, then *the state cannot be conceived by analogy to the metaphysical subject.* This merely negative determination calls for considerable clarification.

Heidegger designates the state as a *Fügung* – an articulated, unifying structure. As *the articulation of unity* the state preserves a certain constancy. It is important to distinguish the constancy Heidegger imagines from that propagated by ideologues of the regime, such as Krieck. For Krieck, the unity of the state derives from the cultivation of a particular racialist form or character (VGE 81). This is not the case for Heidegger. Since the state is founded in the Care-structure, we must turn to Heidegger's formulation of the non-metaphysical constancy of Dasein to gain insight into the unity and constancy of the state. Wherein is the authentic, existentially founded constancy of Dasein to be sought? Heidegger answers as follows: 'in terms of Care the *constancy* [*Ständigkeit*] *of the self,* as the supposed persistence of the subject, gets its clarification' (SZ 322/296). The constancy of the selfhood of Dasein implicates 'having-won-a-stand' (SZ 322). Dasein stands in the resoluteness of its anticipation of death, which opens up an authentic present for the thrown project it is. Dasein wins a stand by grasping its finitude, and thus the possibility of being-a-whole.

This allows a first, preliminary interpretation of Heidegger's idea of the state. Given the state grants a Volk its 'historical duration,' or constancy (*Dauer*) (GA38, 165), then the state actualizes the principle of constancy: the state con-stitutes the temporalization of Volk to win a stand and hold a stand in the midst of the presencing of beings. The state is the gestalt (*Fügung*) of this stand (GA38, 165). The thesis of the non-substantiality of the state – meaning that it is not derived from the metaphysics of subjectivity, hence of presence and representation – is confirmed by Heidegger's insistence that the state is not founded in some atemporal law of humanity's nature (GA38, 165). The historicity of the state is confirmed in the rejection of the idea of the state as *Abstractum*: the state as the representation of an ideal of being, as conceived in the tradition of the metaphysical interpretation of Plato's *Republic*. If the state is conceived as the essential law of our historical being, then the state must arise as the authentic form which *Mitsein*, understood as Volk, gives to itself. The state must be founded in the existential determinations of *Volksein*, therefore determined as temporalization, as the delimitation of a unified comportment to being rooted in an earth-sited disclosure of the differentiation of being.

Heidegger poses the question of the unity of selfhood, understood as the unity of the Care-structure, in a more radical way, by unfolding the sense or direction (*Sinn*) of this structure (SZ 324/298). The structure of Care is an articulated, non-substantial, temporalizing whole. It is the 'condition of possibility' of the differentiated presencing of the being of beings. If the state is to be understood as the actualization of this structure, then the state must be constituted in such a way as to allow the differentiation of beings to manifest itself and to be founded. *This renders a norm for the evaluation of diverse kinds of states.* If, furthermore, the structure of Care is that of a thrown project, then the state must be understood as a founding project, as the retrieval of the authentic possibilities of the heritage to which a Volk is delivered over (SZ 325/299). The primacy of the project – hence of the dimension of the future (SZ 327/300–1) – implies, furthermore, that under certain conditions of historical necessity the state must become the founding project of the re-constitution of our communal being. Heidegger evidently believed that these conditions obtained in 1933. His openness to a new, revolutionary founding is based on the assumption that an 'authentic' German state had yet to be founded, not on the abstraction of his supposed decisionism.

The present which arises out of the structure of Care is a letting-be-present: 'only as the *present*, in the sense of making-present, can resoluteness be what it is, namely, the undistorted letting what it grasps in action be encountered' (SZ 326/300). The 'undistorted' letting-presence of beings *actualizes itself as work* in the sense of setting the presencing of being into the delimited gestalt of works and acts in our encounter with beings. This would call for the differentiation and delimitation of beings, and therefore for a rank order of modes of production.

Given that the state is founded in *Sorge*, the state becomes necessary as the articulation of a modus of temporalization. Evidently the temporal unity of our being-in-the-world can be structured in many different ways. We know that Heidegger distinguishes, in the first and most primordial instance, between authentic and inauthentic modi (SZ 328/302). This distinction can offer a criterion for the evaluation of states as forms of the constitution of Dasein's being-in-the-world. The modus of a state's articulation of the finitude of Dasein, its articulation of being-toward-death in relative authenticity or inauthenticity, offers an essential indication of the 'authenticity' of a state, and therefore a norm of evaluation of diverse kinds of political regimes. *Authenticity grounds in a recognition of finitude.*

Heidegger's concept of sacrifice as a 'value' in and for itself, for example, follows from the need to give the authenticity of being-toward-death a public face. It is not simply or primarily a question of the assimilation of Nazi ideology. Consider another example: granted that there is an essential distinction between 'health' and the technical prolongation of life, then the social articulation of this distinction gives expression to the way in which a community is attuned to death. If Dasein is authentic in being-toward-death, and inauthentic in everyday dispersal and flight from its ownmost possibility for being, then this provides an evaluative criterion for states, given that states 'constitute' our relationship to death by a multitude of discourses and practices (cf. GA16, no. 154).

The political projects of both Hobbes and Locke, for example, found the state in mankind's fear of death, and in its corresponding desire for acknowledgment and security. The fundamental attunement of Locke's Man – the 'unease of desire' – is a response to the infinity of desire (which knows no highest good), and the finitude of our being (which has no transcendent destination). Our dispersal in the present, in the pursuit of objects of momentary desire, understood as the fundamental attunement of humanity, calls for a corresponding con-stitution, or an articulating, unifying structure.

The state is founded in the temporalization of Care, Care in historicity, as a more concrete elaboration of temporality (SZ 382/350). Let us briefly recall how Heidegger joins the issue of temporality to that of the historicity of the Volk. Historicity, Heidegger avers, poses the 'riddle of being and ... of *movement*' (SZ 392/358). At stake is the unity of motion: this unity is disclosed by 'Dasein's primordial historizing, which lies in authentic resoluteness ... in which Dasein hands itself down to itself, free for death, in a possibility which it has inherited and yet has chosen' (SZ 384/SZ-MR 435). Given that

> fateful Dasein, as Being-in-the-world, exists existentially in Being-with-Others, its historizing is a co-historizing and is determinative for it as *destiny* [*Geschick*]. This is how we designate the historizing of the community, of a people. (SZ 384/SZ-MR 436)

Destiny is understood as the authentic and at the same time *finite temporality* of Dasein, which it actualizes in its *Mitsein* in taking over, or retrieving, the possibilities of its heritage (SZ 385–6/SZ-MR 437). The unity which arises out of the temporality of *Mitsein*

> is in itself a *steadiness which has been stretched along* – the steadiness with which Dasein as fate 'incorporates' into its existence birth and death and their 'between,' and holds them as thus 'incorporated,' so that in such constancy

Dasein is indeed in a moment of vision for what is world-historical in its current Situation. (SZ 390–1/SZ-MR 442)

In the *Logik*, the state is explicitly defined as the means by which a Volk secures its 'historical duration' (*Dauer*). In the terms of *Being and Time*, Volk is 'as such' defined by primordial historicity; it does not require the 'addition' of the state to become historical. To suppose otherwise would be to hold, in common with metaphysics, that the Volk is a construct of the state. In fact, the state 'only *is* insofar as it *becomes, comes to be* the historical being of beings called *Volk*' (GA16, no. 158, 333). The state arises out of the Volk as a structure of historicity. Nor can Heidegger consistently hold that the state grants the happening of the community, or destiny, its 'steadiness,' or continuity (*Stätigkeit*). The state 'secures' the 'duration' of the historizing of the Volk. The duration Heidegger speaks of here cannot refer primarily to the formal continuity of forms of government, for example. Rather,

The state only *is* insofar and so long as the will to rule – which arises out of a mission and a task, and which, conversely, is actualized in labour and in works – is carried out and accomplished. (GA38, 165)

The will to rule is not its own ground – it arises out of the historicity of a mission which is granted to a Volk. Heidegger holds that the state is the actualization of this will in works and action – it *is* in actualization. While the state secures the historical being of a Volk, it is not the origin of the Volk, in the sense of producing the Volk as a concept or ideal form, for this would indeed signify a fall back into the metaphysics of 'national aestheticism.' Heidegger's appeal to the 'will,' nonetheless, appears to be a dangerous concession to the times, and to hark back to the metaphysics of the 'common will.' He explicitly refers to the will *to rule* – that is, to decide. Decision would have to engage and respect both the unconcealment of being in beings and the resistance of Volk to rational transparency (i.e., ideological formation through the institutions of the state). The state signifies the will to be-in-historicity. Yet the question remains whether this clarification alone can suffice to extricate Heidegger from a metaphysics of the will. In the absence, or collapse, of this will, moreover, does a Volk decline into the status of an unactualized potential? Does the dissolution of this will into forms of socio-technical discourses characterizing a 'self-managing society' signify the dis-integration of a Volk into a contractual society of individuals?

6.2.4 State and Society

It is characteristic of the movement of the *Logik* of 1934 that Heidegger attempts to answer the question of who we are by asking about Volk and that the question of Volk emerges out of the concretely questioning We of the University, as a community of inquiry into its present actuality, tradition, and future. This shows that the Volk is not an abstract mystical body 'behind' the phenomena of social institutions in which we are involved, but is rather a way of being, a sense of the *actualization* of these institutions.

Consequently, it is not a matter of discovering the linguistic, ethnic, or ethical reality of a Volk, in contradistinction to the practices and discourses which constitute our social being. It is rather a question of *bringing to light the structure of temporalization which gives these practices and discourses their horizon of intelligibility* and full, authentic sense. Fritsche's contention, that Heidegger simply insists on 'cancelling' society (*Gesellschaft*) in the will to retrieve a mythical community or *Gemeinschaft*, is misconceived.[45] It is true that Heidegger identifies the advent of the 'individual' and of the contractual theory of society as a key characteristic of modernity; the concept of the Volk which arose with German Romanticism already attempted to initiate a countermovement to modern 'society' (GA16, no. 155, 290–1). But the Romantic notion of Volk also has to be deconstructed by uncovering the non-subjectivistic temporality of a Da-sein which founds both the contracting individual and the collective subject of the Romantic idea (GA54, 204).

Heidegger holds that the state is the constituting, unifying will of a Volk to its own historicity. As opposed to the modern tradition from Hobbes to Hegel, this cannot mean that the Volk, 'in itself,' denotes a non-political, unreflective way of being. Because the political is a category of the differentiation of modes of being, Heidegger's understanding of Volk leads to the conclusion that he grants Volk 'political' being in the most primordial sense, as the articulation of the differentiated and differentiating structure of time.

Heidegger insists that the state is not merely the 'contemporary and at the same time calcified form of organization of a society' (GA38, 165). The question therefore arises as to why society cannot realize the being of Volk in its historicity. The distinction of state and society, and with it the valuation of the state as a qualitatively higher will than the system of relations composing a society, is central to conservative discourse and the critique of Weimar. Heidegger also holds that the state is in being 'only inasmuch and only so long as the will to rule – arising out of a mission and a task and actualized in labour and in works – accomplishes itself' (GA38, 165). 'Society' is evidently determined, in the first instance, as the interplay of socio-technical discourses. It is the form of organization of the impersonal 'they' and constituted by *Gerede* as the already-said of stratified concepts, practices, and forms of attunement. This is not to say that Heidegger denies the necessity and inevitability of social institutions and discourses in modern society – nor is the inauthenticity of these institutions an argument against them. Inauthenticity belongs to the structure of *Mitdasein*, and for the most part our social intercourse takes this form, whether in dealing with the nurse in the medical clinic, arguing with the taxman, or riding the bus with faceless 'others.' Social institutions call for critique and authentic actualization, *just as* Gerede *calls for deconstruction and retrieval* through the enactment of authentic discourse. Were this not the case, then Heidegger's commitment to university reform would make no sense whatsoever. But then how can Heidegger justify, on his own premises, a normative critique of society in favour of the state?

Heidegger implicitly appeals to the criterion of self-limiting wholeness as founded in historicity. Socio-technical discourses have no inherent limit, and tend to dis-integrate all realms of life into one integrated, functional system. The state is conceived as a counter-movement to the socio-technical tendency to transparency and a totally self-managing society. Because the state is understood as the will to rule, grounded in the self-reserve of the Volk, it articulates the movement of withdrawal from the social system of rational transparency. As such, as the articulation of withdrawal, it preserves the site of truth as the strife of *a-letheia*, of unconcealment and saving reserve.

Volk and state are of necessity allies as constituting a *counter-movement to the tendency toward rational transparency inherent in the social and technical discourses of a totally managed society.* The state enacts this counter-movement in the will to fulfil its own historicity. The question remains, nonetheless, whether the appeal to the will does not signify a fall back into the metaphysics of subjectivity and representation. The will inherent in the state is itself in conflict with the Volk as a movement of withdrawal from all forms of objectification, from what the will posits. Liberal theory ascribes to the atomistic individuals of the 'state of nature' certain inalienable rights – finally and fundamentally, the right to self-preservation. Hence it acknowledges the will to be of the individual. The state cannot abrogate this will, and therefore inscribes a moment of self-reservation, of withdrawal from the claims of the state, into the constitution of the state. Although the liberal tradition ascribes this moment to the individual, Heidegger understands it as belonging to the Volk in its authentic and unified structure of temporalization.

6.2.5 Polemos

Schmitt added a note on Heraclitus in the third edition of his text, published after Hitler's assumption of power. In the copy he sent to Heidegger, Schmitt presumably mentions Fragment 53 of Heraclitus, and this serves Heidegger as the occasion of his letter.[46] Based on the interpretation of *The Concept of the Political* I have offered, I conclude that Schmitt understands *polemos* as the power of being, that is, as the power of bringing into being by the differentiation which generates entities and holds each in its being. As opposed to Derrida's *Politics of Friendship*,[47] we have to insist that the political distinction of friend and enemy *as subjects* presupposes this ontological thesis. The opposition of friend and enemy, in this sense, is not the enmity of already existing, substantial entities, but the relation which gives to each its limit, nature, and rank, hence its being as a way of unfolding. The relation is 'prior' to the *relata*. If this is so, then friend and enemy cannot be conceived in terms of a metaphysical dualism. Schmitt writes, we recall, that in my enemy the question of my own being takes gestalt to place my being in question. The distinction of friend and enemy, therefore, is not simply an 'external' mark of difference, but a movement of differentiation which issues in a call to self-discovery and self-limitation. Schmitt's response to National Socialism, however, will lead me to qualify this account in certain respects.

Heidegger's letter to Schmitt of August 1933 refers explicitly to Fragment 53 and therefore offers us a somewhat cryptic indication of how Heidegger might have read *The Concept of the Political*. Therefore it gives us some sense of what Heidegger might have understood by the distinction of friend and enemy as the founding distinction of the political. As a basis of interpretation to help us understand Heidegger's thoughts on Heraclitus at this time, the letter offers equally cryptic pointers. For this reason I will draw Heidegger's Hölderlin lectures of the winter of 1934 and a number of other texts to our aid.

Fragment 53 of Heraclitus reads as follows: 'War [*polemos*] is the father of all and king [*basileus*] of all, and some he shows as gods, others as men; some he makes slaves and others free.'[48] In his letter to Schmitt, Heidegger writes,

Your quote from Heraclitus appealed to me particularly, because you did not forget *basileus* (king), which gives definitive meaning to the whole maxim if one interprets it completely. I have had such an interpretation set down for years, with respect to the concept of truth – the *edeize* (proves) and *epoiese* (makes) which appear in Fragment 53.

But I myself am in the middle of *polemos* (war) and all literary projects must take second place.[49]

Based on Heidegger's 'commentary' of 1945 on the Rector's Address, we have a sense of his interpretation of *polemos: polemos* is the *Aus-einander-set-zung*, or differentiation, of beings into their being (SU 28). If we are correct in assuming that Schmitt, no less than Heidegger, understands *polemos* in this sense, then the differentiation of being is the common ground which allows Heidegger to read the friend-enemy distinction of Schmitt as an ontological thesis.

Differentiation separates, gives to each its rank, its own. The harmony of the cosmos arises out of the mutual delimitation of beings. Heidegger's *Die Grundbegriffe der Antiken Philosophie* (1928) tends to support this interpretation, although admittedly his commentary on Heraclitus consists largely of incomplete lecture notes (GA22, 59). More substantial support can be found in lectures dating from the winter semester of 1933–4 – *Vom Wesen der Wahrheit* (GA 36/37) – in *An Introduction to Metaphysics*, Heidegger's *Heraklit* of 1943–4 (GA55), and the Heidegger-Fink seminar of 1966. The lectures of 1933–4 explicitly interpret the *polemos* of Fragment 53 as that which gives rise to and preserves beings in their being (GA36/37, 91–2). *Polemos* shows and sets beings forth as beings by setting each into its determinate limit, for in and out of its limit it wins a stand, stands forth (GA36/37, 93). Heidegger confirms this interpretation in the *Introduction*, referring directly to *polemos* as 'the conflict which sets (being) apart,' and adds,

> It is only such conflict that *edeixe*, that *shows*, that brings forth gods and men in their being. We do not learn who man is by learned definitions; we learn it only when man contends with the essent, striving to bring it into its being, i.e., into limit and form, that is to say when he projects something new (not yet present), when he creates original poetry, when he builds poetically. (GA40, 153/144)

This passage brings the differentiation of being and the founding of differentiation in beings – in the site of the *polis* – into clear relation. Being is unequivocally understood as 'limit and form.'

Turning to the *Heraklit* of 1943–4, the *basileus* of Fragment 53 is thought as lightning and fire in Fragments 64 and 66. Lightning 'steers' the cosmos: in the light of this 'fire' the whole (*ta panta*) is illuminated and differentiated in the sense that everything first appears in the ordered limits of its proper, spatio-temporal gestalt ('erscheint erst jedes Erscheinende in den gefügten Grenzen seines Gebildes'; GA55, 163). In Eugen Fink's words, as recorded in the seminar of 1966, just as 'lightning tears open the field of *panta* and works there as the driving and reigning, so war as ruler directs and reigns over *panta*.'[50] Heidegger responds by saying that for Heraclitus 'the origin [*arche*] of movement is also the origin of ruling and directing.'[51] Lightning-*polemos* grants to each its 'time' and 'space' within the differentiated order of the whole: it 'originates' in granting the measure of unfolding proper to a being.

Furthermore, Heidegger especially emphasizes the *basileus*: understood as king or ruler, *polemos* holds each being on the path of its unfolding. Strife is *integral to beings themselves* as the motion which grants them their being. In an address of May 1934 to commemorate the twenty-fifth anniversary of his *Abitur*, or graduation, Heidegger advances precisely this interpretation: 'the power of strife [des Kampfes] in the being of all things and in mankind reigns in a double way: as the power of generation [Erzeugung] and as the power of preservation' (GA16, no. 154, 283). On this point Heidegger would concur with Zeller;[52] Guthrie also holds that war 'is common because the *Logos* that is the law of all becoming (fr. 1 [Heraclitus Fragment 1]) is a law of strife, of simultaneous opposite tensions.'[53] The question at issue is how 'tension,' or motion, as opposite and simultaneous, belongs to the proper being of an entity. Heidegger's interpretation of *basileus* leads to the conclusion that he understands *polemos* as the *arche* of *kinesis* of entities. The interpretation of *polemos* put forward by Kirk, that *polemos* consists of the strife and unity of opposites deriving from the mere succession of states, fails to grasp *polemos* as the principle of the differentiated unity, or motion, of each individual being.[54] Rather, according to Heidegger, *basileus* is the name given to *polemos* as *the principle of individuation* of beings. The letter, finally, introduces the question of truth, which for Heidegger means the question of *aletheia*: *polemos* and *basileus* draw their full import from truth as unconcealment. What this implies for the character of 'the political' is a question to which I will return shortly.

In *Hölderlins* 'Germanien' *und* 'Der Rhein,' Heidegger glosses Fragment 53 as follows:

Strife [Kampf/*polemos*] is the power of the genesis of beings, but not in the sense that strife withdraws from beings once they have arisen out of it; but rather, strife precisely preserves and oversees beings in their essential being [Wesensbestand]. Strife is indeed the genesis, but also the ruler. (GA39, 125)

The translation of *Kampf* is a problem, since neither 'war,' nor 'struggle,' nor 'strife' entirely catches Heidegger's meaning. No more does *Kampf* serve Heidegger well as a translation of *polemos*. Yet evidently Heidegger understands *polemos*, and *Kampf*, as the power of differentiation into being, *and* as the power of preservation within the limits of being. As the power of preservation proper to each being, *polemos* is implicitly read as the 'origin of movement' of beings. *As that which preserves and oversees, polemos is the* arche *of* kinesis *which holds beings on the path of their being.* In this sense 'father and ruler' name the unity of temporalization (*kinesis*) of beings: *polemos* is the *arche* out of which things arise, not to abandon them to the in-difference of having-been-generated (along with all other beings), but to hold each being in the gestalt which grants to each the limit (*peras*) which preserves each in its way of unfolding. *Wesensbestand* refers to the rootedness, or stability of a being in its own 'nature,' where nature (*Wesen*) is understood as a way of coming to be. *Polemos* differentiates in two ways: as genesis, by granting each its being, in and through distinction from other beings; and as ruler, as the principle of differentiated unity and identity.

Polemos is the power which differentiates-into-being by setting each being in its own limit; only as differentiated, de-limited, does each entity first come to be: 'there are no gods and humans, as such and in themselves,' for each comes to be through being-as-differentiation. With reference to Fragments 48, 51, and 54, Heidegger holds that 'strife opens up' the possibility of the harmony or cor-respondence of beings: the strife of contraries (*Widerstreit*) 'sets the counterpoised powers each into its limits [Grenzen]. This de-limitation [Be-grenzung] is no constraint, but releases from constraint [Ent-schränkung], de-termination, and consummation of the being of a being' (GA39, 124–5). An entity begins to be out of the internal, self-reserving limit which holds it on its proper path. In this sense, de-limitation (the rootedness of a being in its internal limit) is understood as the movement of release of a being into the full measure of its possible unfolding. The dissolution of internal limit – of *arche* and *peras* – means confusion, dis-integration, and death; the maintenance of an external, imposed limit signifies the sterility of a merely formal, functional order.

Therefore, *polemos* is understood as the *basileus*, or 'ruler,' of differenti-ated self-identity. It is not just that *polemos* is the power of differentiation between entities, but 'internally' to each being *polemos* names a differen-tiated unity. That Heidegger interprets Fragment 53 in this sense is evi-dent from the fact that he brings Fragments 48, 51, and 54 to bear on Fragment 53. Fragment 48 intimates that life and death, being and not being, belong together as one: 'For the bow the name is life, but the work is death.' The 'most extreme contraries of being' are brought together in a harmony, which is unapparent, but stronger than the apparent (GA39, 124; see Fragment 54). Fragment 51, in turn, reads, 'They do not apprehend how being at variance it agrees with itself: there is a connection working in both directions, as in the bow and the lyre.'[55] It is the tension of the strung bow, and of the strings of the lyre, Heideg-ger writes, which is the life of bow and lyre (GA39, 124). Bow and lyre signify a movement of striving apart internal to the being of each; and it is precisely this strife which holds each in its *Wesensbestand*, or way of unfolding. *Polemos*, therefore, has to be understood as the movement of the internal differentiation and unity of a being.

In his *Parmenides* of 1942–3, Heidegger will claim that the space of Da-sein institutes the site of the difference of mortals and divinities, of the strife of concealment and unconcealment which Heidegger calls *aletheia*. This space is the *polis* itself as the site of the presencing and differentia-tion (*polemos*) of being (GA54, 130–75/88–118). The letter to Schmitt already suggests this interpretation. As the site of the differentiation of being in beings, which allows beings to enter into the limit of their own, the *polis* entails a concept of political pluralism, and cannot in principle tend, as Harries claims, toward 'totalitarianism.'[56]

The *polis* is said to be the site and axis of the manifestation of the being of beings (GA54, 133/90). Thus beings appear in the historical depth of the possibilities of their being, not merely in the actuality of their avail-ability, as cut off from the unity of their temporal unfolding. The tree, to recall Emerson's *Nature*, is not merely or even primarily the lumber of the timber merchant, but the tree of the poet and the sagas of a people. As lumber, the tree is defined in terms of the commodity exchange of the international market. Its rhythmic specificity dissolves, dis-integrates, into the cycles of exchange – its being is integrated into the hyperworld of international finance. Conceived as an electronic function of this 'world,' an entity loses the specificity of its delimiting gestalt. Where-as the *polis* allows the emergence of entities into their determinate gestalt, the integration of entities into the hyperworld subjects them to the limitless (*des Grenzenlosen*). Gestalt implies the coming-to-stand of a being out of the rhythm proper to it. In this sense it presences (*west an*) (GA54, 121/82). Gestalt implicates the strife of unconcealment in emergence and withdrawal – it incorporates the *lethe* of self-reserving concealment to which the *polis* gives a site (GA54, 133/90).

Heidegger avers that the *polis* cannot be identified with the Greek city-state, and still less is it identical with the modern state. For 'the *polis* is as little something "political" as space itself is something spatial' (GA54, 142/96). Yet the *polis* is called the place of the presencing of the polity (GA54, 133/90). In some sense the *polis* is the pre-condition of what we call city and state. Heidegger does not elaborate this point. We may suppose, however, that in order for a polity to correspond in its nature to the *polis* as the site of unconcealment it would have to allow beings to presence and take a stand in the gestalt proper to them. But insofar as the artwork, for example, under modern conditions becomes a function of discourse and commerce, the state reveals its deracination from the *polis*. The technical availability of the word as 'information' generates a hyperworld of functions on call which conceals emergence into being.

The *polis* is the site of the differentiation of being which founds the realm of the friend-enemy distinction as an historical and existential distinction. The socio-technical regime of liberalism disallows even this secondary distinction between friend and enemy. As such, it denies the possibility of political leadership and decision in the strict sense, in favour of the discursive management of the polity. Whereas Schmitt still insists on the power of leadership to decide, this appeal to power and rank, according to Heidegger, does not reach the central issue of what 'decision' means: the differentiation of being as founded through the rank order of the possibilities of saving unconcealment through work, in leadership, sacrifice, thought, and works of art (GA65, sec. 173). The 'political' in Schmitt's sense is just one derivative way in which being differentiates itself and founds itself in the rituals of rule and rank. The 'concept of the political' implicates the historical, existential difference and mutual limitation of polities as the ground of political being. This difference, however, is derivative of the differentiation of being itself in its founded specificity in the *polis*. The condition of the modern state as an inherently imperial construct is the collective subjectivity of modern humanity. Because, according to Heidegger, metaphysics also defines the concept of a people (*das Volkhafte*), which, deriving from Herder, arose in opposition to the institution of the state, the *polis* does not derive from the notion of the 'people.' Without Descartes, Herder's concept of Volk is not thinkable (GA54, 204/137). Neither the state nor the Volk, as founded in subjectivity, can found the *polis*. In the crucial period leading up to 1933, moreover, Schmitt fails to develop sufficiently the twofold sense of *polemos* as the origin of differentiated unity, that is, differentiation in respect to the identity of the individual being and in respect to the identity of the whole. I suggest, this is the philosophical reason why Schmitt could allow himself to be seduced by the idea of a unity of identity founded in the 'substantiality' of race, and thus fall back into the metaphysics of subjectivity. The issue, therefore, remains one of giving an adequate articulation of the historicity of Volk and State.

7 The *Beiträge zur Philosophie* and the Differentiation of Being

The *Beiträge zur Philosophie (Vom Ereignis)* – translated by Emad and Maly as *Contributions to Philosophie (From Enowning)* – has been called Heidegger's second *magnum opus*. The *Contributions* 'first traces out and brings into the open the transition to the other beginning of Western history, it attempts to prepare for the other beginning by providing a site for the truth of be-ing [Seyn] in Da-sein.'[1] In the fundamental word *Ereignis* – enowning, or, the event of appropriation – Heidegger intimates the event of an encounter of Da-sein and being, granted or sent by the historicity of being, which apportions to all entities its own measure of being. Since this event names the grant of ownness, the existential structures of Dasein in *Being and Time* are not abandoned. They are rather founded in the historicity of Da-sein's response to the grant – the historicity – of unconcealment. This interpretation is not universally accepted, and the *Beiträge* has been read (or mis-read) as a surrender of the ownness of Da-sein to the 'essentialism' of 'being' conceived 'cosmolologically' or 'mythically.'[2] We shall see that this is indeed a fundamental misreading of the *Contributions*. Being does not presence without Da-sein. 'The relation of Da-sein to being belongs in the essential unfolding (*Wesung*) of being itself' (GA65, 254/179). The problem is to grasp this founding relation without reducing it to a subject-object, or any kind of metaphysical, relation. The relation is terminologically emphasized by Heidegger's re-writing of *Dasein* as *Da-sein* – that is, the Da is experienced as the There, or openness, the site, of being (*Seyn*).

On a basic level of interpretation the *Contributions* allow us to 'place' Heidegger's previous and subsequent work in three respects: (*i*) the fundamental ontology and analytic of Dasein of *Being and Time* may be placed within the 'history of being'; (*ii*) Heidegger's engagement with the classical works of the history of philosophy takes its place within his deconstruction and retrieval of the tradition; and (*iii*) 'regional' investigations of particular kinds of beings, such as the artwork, are revealed as contributions to the project of founding being (*Seyn*) in beings.

The history of being has to be distinguished from the metaphysical history of beingness (*Seiendheit*), which marks the distinction of being and beings. The metaphysically understood ontological difference, as a determination of the difference of beingness and beings, is 'reappropriated' by being in the sense that *Seyn*, in its finitude and historicity, differentiates 'itself' and founds 'itself' in Da-sein, and therefore in beings as illuminated and brought to shelter in the site of Da-sein. Da-sein 'belongs' to being as the thrown project of the grant of being which Da-sein receives and founds in beings. The 'turn' frequently attributed to Heidegger is into the clearing of being as the Da of *Seyn*, but as such it is not a turn away from the historicity of Da-sein. It is, rather, a turn toward the 'ground' of Da-sein's historicity in the history of the epochs of being. The 'turn' in truth, already prefigured by 'On the Essence of Truth' (1930), turns toward the withdrawal (*lethe*) at the heart of unconcealment. The 'being-historical thinking' of the *Contributions* is an internal transformation of fundamental-ontological thinking,[3] and as such the turn into the event of the finitude and singularity of being.[4] This event must be founded. The 'turn' toward the work of art founds sheltering withdrawal in a being, in the strife of earth and world. The work of art is exemplary as one way of founding the site of Da-sein and therefore the historicity of being. The question of Volk arises out of the historicity and oblivion of being, and out of the challenge of the abandonment of beings, as the necessity of a founding decision.[5]

The difficulty of the *Contributions to Philosophy* derives not only or even primarily from its often aphoristic style, but more fundamentally from its attempt to enact a founding leap in the history of being. This leap is a leap into Da-sein, and as such, raises the question of the relation of Da-sein and *Seyn*, of the historicity of the site of the Da and *Ereignis*. As Schürmann notes, it is Heidegger's 'thesis' that the 'event of appropriation' transmutes metaphysics and therefore breaks with every totalizing ground and *telos* – the supersensory world, the Ideas, God, Progress, and so on.[6] The transmutation (*Verwindung*) of metaphysical categories (e.g., *arche, morphe, peras*) intimates the retrieval and transformation of fundamental possibilities. This also pertains to Volk as a possibility for being no longer defined in terms of collective subjectivity.

We have seen that Volk has to be understood as a movement of withdrawal from representational thinking, and hence as a post-metaphysical enactment of being. If this point is not grasped, then, as Reiner Schürmann claims, the *Beiträge* indeed suffers from an internal contradiction fatal to its entire project. According to Schürmann, the *Contributions* (*i*) questions any metaphysical ground, *arche*, or totalization in the thought of *Ereignis*; and yet (*ii*) proposes to found being in Da-sein, in Volk, as collective subjectivity.[7] Schürmann understands the event of truth, which comes to word in *Ereignis*, as the strife of appropriation and expropriation. Appropriation reconstitutes an *arche* in the metaphysical sense, and Volk as collective subjectivity institutes a (self) appropriation. *Expropriation*, or the *lethe* of *aletheia*, is 'anarchic.' Therefore the appeal to Volk dissimulates the strife, the fissure at the heart of truth and being and reinscribes a totality. As 'arche' in the form of collective subjectivity, Volk is the 'monstrous site' to which the *Contributions* is riveted. This interpretation, however, misconceives what is at stake in the event of *aletheia*: *lethe* intimates not simply concealment, but saving shelter (*Bergung*). Still less does it signify expropriation, rather the opposite: the shelter which holds each in its own, and as such in its singular *arche* and movement of unfolding. Given that Volk, as founded in Da-sein, enacts the historicity of the event of truth, it enacts a movement of withdrawal from the mere being-present of representational truth and its totalization. The temporal-historical structure of Volk constitutes its *arche*, but not a metaphysical totality, and therefore the contradiction Schürmann postulates does not obtain.

What follows is not a comprehensive interpretation of the *Contributions*. I will, rather, following the lead of F.-W. von Herrmann, focus on a set of related issues as unfolded by the text: pre-eminently Volk, technology, and the work of art. For 'insight into the historicity of being itself now opens up the possibility of moving technology, politics, and art, in its being-historical essence, into the perspective of the historicity of the question of being.'[8] Every interpretative effort is founded in the perspective of the interpreter. My explication of Heidegger's text will also be guided by an interpretation of our hermeneutic situation, understood, in what follows, as the event of the dis-integration and simultaneous functional integration of entities into the postmodern order of things.

In the *Contributions* the 'historicity of the crossing' into Da-sein as the site of *Seyn* is structured as a 'jointure' of six movements:

Der Anklang (Echo)
Das Zuspiel (Playing-Forth)

Der Sprung (Leap)
Die Gründung (Founding)
Die Zukünftigen (The Ones to Come)
Der letzte Gott (The Last God) (GA65, 5/6)

Heidegger writes,

> What is said is inquired after and thought in the 'playing-forth' unto each other of the first and other beginning, according to the 'echo' of be-ing in the distress of the abandonment of beings, for the 'leap' into be-ing, in order to 'found' its truth, as a preparation for 'the ones to come' and for 'the last god.' (GA65, 7/6, modified)

This passage indicates the path I will attempt to follow: in response to the hermeneutic situation of the abandonment of beings, the question of Volk, of art, and of technology will be posed in anticipation of the possibility of a founding Leap into Da-sein.

7.1 Volk, Differentiation, Founding

7.1.1 Volk and the Differentiation of Being

Despite his growing estrangement from the actuality of National Socialism, Heidegger did not abandon the question of Volk in the *Beiträge zur Philosophie* (1936–8). The question of the differentiation of being and the question of the coming to be of the Volk are intimately related, for both are founded in the question of the historicity of being. The differentiation of being opens up a site. A people that takes up and endures *the founding of the differentiation of being* as a task may call itself a Volk (GA65, 97/67). My continued use of the term 'Volk' is not intended to bind Heidegger's reflections on Volk to the place and destiny of the German people within the history of being. Obviously, Heidegger hoped and believed that 'the Germans' 'have' a special mission within the destining of being. This remains concealed. However, I am using the word Volk to emphasize a fundamental philosophical distinction between Volk (in Heidegger's sense) and metaphysical concepts of 'people' or 'nation,' or any concept of collective subjectivity.

The community which Heidegger envisions could not be a contractual experiment of autonomous subjects, for the selfhood of Da-sein, in which the Volk rests, comes to be only in the enactment (*Vollzug*) (GA65,

96/67) of the differentiation of being. Heidegger intimates that a people is gathered into a Volk by those especially called, or marked (*die Gezeichneten*), to bring about this gathering. They are also called 'the future ones' and fall into three groups: The *solitary ones* (*die Einzelnen*) prepare the sites and moments of decision by establishing the essential ways in which Da-sein founds itself in poetry, thought, deed, and sacrifice. As such they 'create the essential possibility for the different forms of sheltering concealment in which Da-sein becomes historical' (GA65, 96/67, modified). The *fraternity* (*die Bundischen*) takes its measure from these founding sites to unfold the laws of the transformation of beings (in the social constitution of labour, in technology, in art, etc.) to preserve the earth and project a world, preserving their strife. The *compatriots* (*die Zueinanderverwiesenen*), have a common historical heritage; heritage is understood as being rooted in the local, the Heimat, hence it is called '*erdhaft-welthaft.*' They work to transform beings in such a way as to give stable form (*Bestand*) and constitution to the founding of the unconcealment of truth (GA65, 96/67). The primordial gathering which makes the Volk possible is governed by the event of the differentiation of being in the gestalt of ritual, works, and leadership.

Heidegger adds that the gathering of these founders of a Volk at least in part still emerges out of the established order of the state (GA65, 97/67). He presumably has the University, among other institutions, in mind. This casts a light on Heidegger's hopes for the internal reform of the University in 1933 – new life might yet emerge out of old structures. He insists, however, that the gathering of the new cannot be programmed, or co-ordinated from above, for it rather has the character of a concealed, grass-roots movement, and only thus has it the possibility of effecting a sudden, unexpected transformation of the fundamental attunement of a people. Heidegger rejects, as we already know, cultural politics or planning, whether in the totalitarian or in the more subtle liberal mode (GA65, 149/102). It may be that Heidegger's insistence on the spontaneous gathering of creative forces reflects the tension within National Socialism itself between State and Movement, between people and Volk, and between Volk and State.

To found the differentiation (*Ent-scheidung*) of being in decision (*Entscheidung*) demands preparation in all the realms of our attunement to the presencing of being in beings. The gathering of a people in a state is one such realm, and in this regard Heidegger was still inclined, in the period of 1936 to 1938, to give some qualified assent to the possibilities, if not the actual politics, of National Socialism. For 'the reflection,'

Heidegger holds, on the 'nature of the Volk [das Volkhafte]' is essential (GA65, 42/30). This assent, however, is restricted to two related aspects of the movement and excludes all other ideological elements which characterize Nazism. Heidegger's fundamental move is to reject every form of Platonism in regard to the Volk, such as defines the body of the Volk in terms of the already-posited (as idea or model, meaning, value). As noted above, Volk can only be founded in the leap which opens up the site of Da-sein (GA65, 43/30).

First, in the *Beiträge*, without mentioning National Socialism by name, Heidegger implies that what is at stake in the new movement is a reaction to the historical deracination of the people, and the attempt to reverse it (GA65, 97–101/67–9). Deracination in this context would signify the alienation of a people from the ownmost possibilities of its singular history as a people belonging to the Occident, as defined by the Greek inception of philosophy. It is likely that in Heidegger's eyes the most urgent danger of deracination in the interwar period takes the form of international communism, although western liberalism would present an allied but more subtle form of deracination.[9] In both cases, deracination has to be understood as a symptom of nihilism; and nihilism (as the triumph of collective subjectivity, technicity, and of the will to power), as the will to 'valuate' being (GA65, secs. 19, 25, 74). In the *Parmenides* Heidegger describes Leninism as the conjunction of the Party (the collective subjectivity of a class) and electricity (technicity) (GA54, 127). In common with the conservative right, Heidegger also rejected the techno-bureaucratic order of the Weimar Republic and the liberal order on which it was based. Both systems are held to be incapable of founding the differentiation of being. They rather conceal and accelerate the destitution of beings and the transformation of the human subject into the 'technicized animal' (GA65, 98/68).

Second, the task of an 'authentic' National Socialism would be to prepare the transformation of the fundamental attunement of the people in order to open a space of decision for the task of founding being anew in the differentiation of being (cf. GA65, 86/59). Only in these terms, as differentiated, are beings brought into the limit of their proper gestalt. Heidegger's critique of Nazism is in part a response to its failure in this respect: he recognizes the danger of failing to make fundamental decisions in favour of the bureaucratic transformation of the 'Volk' into an instrument of politics (GA65, 43, 97–8, 149/30, 67–8, 103). The cultural politics of National Socialism, as the will to produce a higher ideal of the Volk in accordance with a particular world-view, mistakes the Volk for an end in itself. To make the people – its political and economic power and increase – its social improvement and education, an end in itself, is to assume that human being is nothing other than collective subjectivity. Yet this is precisely what is in question (GA65, 318/323–4). Thinking engages the question of being to respond to the distress of beings and to bring them into shelter (GA65, 100/69). Precisely this fundamental attunement is what Heidegger found lacking in National Socialism. The 'gathering of the people' (*des Volkes*) effected by this movement is drawn back into a subjectivistic interpretation of Volk in terms of a politics of race. The formlessness threatened by technology is not overcome, nor is technology integrated into the earth-sited historicity of the Volk. Thus the singularity of being in its differentiated presencing, including the singularity of peoples, is occluded in favour of an essentially technological conception of 'humanity' as a human resource on call. Heidegger's private National Socialism, if such it was, conceived the attempt to think and to found the singularity of being, and of an historical people, in Da-sein, *not to found Da-sein in the Volk* (GA65, 98/68).

Heidegger's point of departure in the history of being holds that the destruction of the earth as the homeland of its peoples, as a result of the processes of acceleration and quantification under the purview of representational thinking, arises out of the withdrawal of the non-representational being of beings. The non-representational reserves itself. Representational thought ensures, conversely, that 'self-sheltering as such, as determining power, is no longer allowed entry' ('das Sichverbergen als solches in keiner Weise als bestimmende macht noch Einlass findet') (GA65, 123/86). Being abandons beings to their mere representational availability. This historical event, which as we know, Heidegger calls *die Seinsverlassenheit*, implicates the technology of transparency, the technology of the interface of humanity and machine under the regime of mutual reliability and availability.

Every merely socio-political interpretation of Heidegger's critique of modernity will fall short of its full import, insofar as it fails to recognize that the mutual implication of the *mode of presencing* – which releases things into their way of being, *and* the things-present themselves – prefigures the how and where-for of the socio-political realm. A socio-political critique of Heidegger's experience of the disintegrative power of modernity, therefore, offers no counter-argument by claiming, for example, that technology advances the freedom of the individual in a democratic society, and so forth. This may even be so, granted that we know what 'freedom' is, what the 'individual' is. What is at stake, however, for

Heidegger, is presencing and withdrawal of being in beings, not the facti-cal being-present of something. Advances in medical science, for exam-ple, allow life-saving heart transplants. What does this practice implicate for our way of being – for the presencing of being – as opposed to our facticity? In socio-political terms it can be affirmed as a contribution to the progress of mankind, and Heidegger's unease in the face of technol-ogy can be brushed aside. But this affirmation implicitly commits itself to a mode of presencing (to a thesis concerning being), even if it only wishes to reap the benefits, as it were, in the kingdom of facticity. A socio-political reading of Heidegger's interpretation of modernity can never be neutral in regards to being, for it will always have to presuppose not only our comportment to beings as present, but also implicitly commit itself to a specific way of their becoming-present. This pre-supposition is the issue in question.

Seinsverlassenheit implicates a mode of the presencing of beings in their destitution, disintegration, and 'abandonment.' We recall, more specifi-cally, that

> the abandonment of the being of beings [is] brought nearer by being mind-ful of the darkening of the world and the destruction of the earth in the sense of acceleration, calculation, and the claim of the quantitative. (GA65, 119/83, modified)

What is at stake in all three determinations of *Seinsverlassenheit* is the tem-porality of the unfolding of being in beings: the acceleration of experi-ence; indifference to the seldom; the inability to endure anticipation and the singularity of the moment; the presumption that everything is in prin-ciple knowable, calculable, and therefore present for representation; and the triumph of Number as the all-pervasive measure of beings, which therefore become equally available (present) for everyone. Two ques-tions arise at this point: (*i*) Is this account of beings phenomenologically founded, or does it merely reflect Heidegger's anti-modern instincts? How can we decide this question? and (*ii*) How is this account related to the question of Volk?

The abandonment of the being of beings is the Echo of being in its refusal and withdrawal from beings. Entities are abandoned to them-selves in their mere calculability and availability (GA65, 108–9/76–7). The Echo of being attunes Da-sein to and for the necessity of the Leap into Da-sein as the Founding of being in beings in the other beginning. The de-termining ground, therefore, of the experience of the destitu-tion of beings is an attunement to being:

The *guiding-attunement of echo* is the *shock, the horror,* of the disclosure of be-ing's abandonment of beings and at the same time the *deep awe* before the resonating enowning [Ereignis]. (GA65, 396/277, modified)

What is the 'status' of the attunement (*Stimmung*) of horror in the struc-ture of Heidegger's account? Does it merely reflect the cultural pessi-mism of his generation? Or does it intimate an epochal turn, a turn from beings to being under the shock of the destitution of beings? What kind of insight necessitates the Leap into the founding of Da-sein, to make it, in the words of Klaus Held, a 'binding task'? 'Bindingness means that which binds our thinking. In binding lies a compulsion, a necessity [Not-wendigkeit]. The ontohistorical forethinking with respect to the *kairos* of the other beginning possesses a necessity because it obeys the compul-sion of a need or distress [Not]'[10]

We recall that according to *Sein und Zeit*, mood, or *Stimmung* – under-stood as the ontic expression of the existential of *Befindlichkeit* (sec. 29) – '*has always already disclosed being-in-the-world as a whole and first makes possi-ble directing oneself toward something*' (SZ 137/129). We recall, moreover, the exemplary status of the *Stimmung* of anxiety in disclosing Da-sein's own, individual being-in-the world as the for-which of anxiety (SZ 188/176). Anxiety reveals Da-sein to itself in the necessity of taking respon-sibility for its being. The *Stimmung* of anxiety, therefore, discloses; in disclosing, attunes (*stimmt*) Da-sein to its own being; and in attuning, de-termines (*bestimmt*) and binds it as subject to a claim (*Bestimmung*). The *Stimmung* addresses a demand to Da-sein to which it must respond, if only in the mode of turning away. In this sense anxiety is a binding call-to-be. The *Stimmung* of anxiety grants the 'phenomenological founda-tion' for the claim[11] – articulated by the existential analytic of Dasein – that Dasein is bound by the call-to-be authentically.

The 'historical referentiality of moods,' as Held notes,[12] emerges only after *Being and Time*, particularly in *The Fundmental Concepts of Metaphysics* (GA29/30). We know that this lecture course of 1929–30 devotes great attention to boredom as a fundamental mood, or attunement (*Grund-stimmung*), with a view to bringing the temporality of Dasein's finite, soli-tary being-in-the-world to light (see GA29/30, sec. 39). For our present purpose, a few brief points will have to suffice. Heidegger is apparently concerned with the fundamental attunement of Dasein in its historicity, that is, with the attunement of a generation. This becomes evident through his reference to the works of contemporaries (Scheler, Klages, Ziegler, Spengler), as attempts to diagnose, as it were, the mood of the time. While these efforts are of limited value, they reveal the problem of determining *where 'we' stand, of how 'it stands' with us.* The title of chapter 5 of part I of the text, moreover, addresses profound boredom as 'The Fundamental Attunement of Our Contemporary Dasein' (GA29/30, 238/160). In fact, since Dasein is always *Mitdasein,* and historicity belongs to its being, we can speak of the attunement to being of a generation without departing from the premises of *Being and Time.*

The question arises, however, whether the mood that Heidegger identifies as fundamental – in this case, boredom – is indeed fundamental, and granted that it is, whether it binds or obligates us in a way which is analogous to the place of anxiety in the existential analytic. What does boredom reveal about our being-in-the-world, and the being of beings, which demands a response? Heidegger indeed proposes to show, in the course of a refined phenomenological description of three, progressively more profound 'levels' of boredom, that essential boredom reveals the emptiness in which we ourselves, together with beings, hang: boredom reveals a way of the temporal unfolding of beings, reveals them in their in-difference and inconsequence (GA29/30, 243/162). Beings refuse themselves in their being, that is, in accordance with their proper temporalization. The mood is 'fundamental' in the sense that it reveals the 'ground' on which we 'stand' as the indifferent temporalization of time (GA29/30, 235–7/158–9). It is ultimately time itself which *refuses itself* as the right or the wrong time, thus to hold itself in in-difference. This in-different expanse of empty time, in which beings hang, however, has the potential to reveal the power of time in Da-sein, thus to bring time 'to a point,' as it were, in the instant of the blink of an eye. In Michel Haar's words, we 'rediscover all *possible* time':[13]

> It is not beings that properly refuse, but time, which makes possible the manifestness of these beings as a whole. What properly refuses is simultaneously that which announces itself, in turn, as that which gives Dasein the possibility of making itself concretely possible as this Dasein in each case within and in the midst of beings as a whole. (GA29/30, 226/150–1)

Dasein's recognition and actualization of its own possibility of being in all its concreteness bring time to a point in the 'moment of vision' *(Augenblick)* (GA29/30, 224/149). The moment of vision is the eruption of temporality in the in-difference in which Dasein hangs suspended, the breach of Da-sein which opens the possibility of authenticity in the sense of a response to a fundamental need. The moment of vision articulates the urgency of a decision thus to take into care the whole as whole as determined by the finitude of our historicity (GA29/30, 223–4/149).

Heidegger's reflection on boredom of 1929–30 anticipates section 76 of the *Beiträge*, in which he assigns to technology the goal, concealed from its own self-understanding, of racing toward the consummation of boredom in the functional management of beings. Yet boredom is allowed the possibility of a turn arising out of the temporality of in-differentiation itself: this is the 'shock' of the disclosure of 'the gaping abandonment of beings by being' (GA65, 157/109). Following the *Grundbegriffe* of 1929–30, we can say that in shock and horror the wide, empty expanse of the in-different temporalization of beings is brought to a point, and potentially reversed: the shock consists in the simultaneous recognition of the *power of temporality* in Da-sein and in the *refusal of time* as differentiating. Beings, and Da-sein itself, are experienced in the void of their indifferent being-present. This same refusal, however, as we have just seen, reveals time as that which grants Da-sein its possibility of being. As a fundamental revelation of Da-sein's epochal temporality, profound boredom issues a demand. Da-sein must take up its being-possible in the midst of beings. In this sense boredom calls on Dasein *to respond in awe* to the singularity of the temporalization of beings. The horror, or shock, of which section 76 speaks, arises out of the disclosure of the in-differentiation of the presencing of beings. In what way is this demand analogous to the obligation which anxiety places on Da-sein? Does Da-sein, in order to be Da-sein, have an obligation to beings, to the unconcealment of beings in accordance with the 'form' of their ownmost temporal unfolding? If this is so, on Heidegger's own premises, then, horror in the face of the in-differentiation of being would be the phenomenological foundation of a call which binds us to the being of beings, the call of a turning toward being. The response to this call is the Leap into Da-sein, and thus into the Founding of the Da. 'The creation of works that have the power of initiating historical change becomes the binding task for Dasein.'[14]

I will now turn to the second of the two questions I posed above: How is Heidegger's account of *Seinsverlassenheit* related to the question of Volk? This question leads back to another one, more fundamental: Why should Volk be? What necessity calls for the being of a Volk? For either Volk is a necessity in the founding of the other beginning or it is nothing at all.

The destitution of the being of beings implicates their deracination under the impact of acceleration, calculation, and the power of the quantitative (GA65, 119/83). The coming to be of Volk is understood as a counter-movement to deracination (GA65, 97/67). To avoid a superficially 'political' reading, it suffices to bear in mind that as counter-movement the meaning of Volk can hardly be defined as the totalitarian mobilization of the masses. Volk is defined in its opposition to *Seinsverlassenheit*, and this means it is defined as response to the distress (*Not*) of the being of beings. Since *Seinsverlassenheit* – as the abandonment of beings to the being-present of their availability – signifies the uprooting of historicity, the Volk becomes necessary as the way of the in-stituting of Dasein's being-historical. This necessity (*Notwendigkeit*) is only recognized in the experience of the need, or distress (*Not*), of deracination. Need calls for a turn (*Not-wendigkeit*) (see GA65, 97–8/67–8). This is only possible as a decision *for being*, that is, as the decision to found the differentiation (*Ent-scheidung*) of being in beings. *The decision to found the historicity of being as Volk, therefore, is only enacted by turning away from the Volk as a modality of the political organization of a collectivity.*

But if essential decisions are to be prepared – under the conditions and style of the time – by establishing a 'gathering of the people,' *or at least* by establishing the conditions of existence (*Bestand*) of the Volk, then this entails 'the utmost danger of completely missing the domain of decision' (GA65, 98/68). Given that this is a reference to the policies of National Socialism (as it almost certainly is), then Heidegger's equivocation between Volk and a mere *Bestand* is telling. The gathering of the Volk can easily be diverted into the establishment of an organized reserve on call (*Bestand*).

If the decision for the Volk is to be a decision for the historicity of being, then the Volk, as a way of being which founds being in beings, must serve the in-stitution of the ownmost temporalization of beings.

> In its origin and destiny this people is singular, corresponding to the singularity of be-ing itself, whose truth this people must ground but once, in a unique site, in a unique moment. (GA65, 97/67)

The founding of the truth of being in a site is the response which the disintegration of beings itself calls for. It is instructive that already in the *Grundbegriffe* of 1929–30 the fundamental mood of essential boredom reveals the necessity of decision and communal action, in the same instant that it reveals the power of temporality in Dasein:

> The absence of an essential need in Dasein is the *emptiness of the whole* (of our being), so that no one stands with anyone else and no community [Gemeinschaft] stands with any other in the rooted unity of essential action. (GA29/30, 244/163, modified)

Only in response to the distress which arises out of the emptiness of in-different temporalization revealed by boredom (GA29/30, 243/162) is Dasein bound to beings as a whole, that is, obligated to actualize the being (the temporalization) of beings. The absence of an essential dis-tress of our Da-sein as a whole refers us to the wholeness of Da-sein and to its historicity as a Volk. The *absence* of essential need must itself first become oppressive for Da-sein. We must first become aware of the in-dif-ference of temporalization in which beings hang, for this very indifferen-tiation affords us with limitless diversions. Time is not brought to a point of decision, because the need is not felt, and therefore essential commu-nal action also becomes impossible. Volk, conversely, is in being as a response to being, that is, as the enactment of the necessary differentia-tion of being in beings. As such, it is a condition of the founding of the uniqueness and delimited determination of beings in the gestalt which shelters them from the disintegration of acceleration, calculation, and the quantitative. Only in this way does the question of Volk gain a neces-sity in terms of the epochal shift in the history of being which Heidegger intimates.

7.1.2 *The Experience of the Destitution and Sheltering Unconcealment of Beings*

We have seen that the hermeneutic situation which motivates the ques-tion of Volk – as a response to the question of being – is the distress of the experience of the destitution of beings (*die Seinsverlassenheit*). This desti-tution implicates a loss (in being) of the being of beings, yet this loss is experienced as an intensification of being, with the consequence that the distress of the withdrawal of being is not felt. We recall that the abandon-ment of being veils itself in an increased intensity of lived experience, in the acceleration, quantification, and calculability of the 'aesthetic' envelope of the body-mind, which has only begun to be exploited by chemical and electronic technologies of sensation. The integration of the deconstructed 'individual' of modern philosophy into the interface of technology is predicated on the historical-metaphysical process of the deracination of being, understood as the surrender of the sitedness of being in favour of transcendental and ahistorical categories.

The need proper to the distress of the destitution of beings arises with the abandonment of beings by their being: the things themselves are given over to objectivity and functionality because being (*das Seyn*) no longer presences through beings to found itself in them (GA65, 115/

80–1). The pain of the reduction of the full unfolding of entities to their mere functionality is the need which must be felt if a turn in the history of being is to become possible. What Heidegger calls the 'Ver-wesung des Seyns' implicates the restriction of *Wesung* – the incalculability and historicity of the presencing of beings – to mere presence as the representation of the calculable. Representational thought is itself caught up in the *Verwesung des Seyns* as the decay (*die Verwesung*) of the meditative receptiveness of Da-sein to the spontaneous arrival (*Wesung*) of being which founded Greek thought. This decay is nothing merely negative, however, but the sign of a dissolution of all hitherto accepted certainties and historical forms as the necessary prelude to the founding of a new gestalt. The gateway of the turn, however, is projected by Heidegger as the possibly long-entrenched global order of the calculable, wherein beings are schematized in reference to the constancy of transcendental categories (GA65, 25, 115/18–9, 81). In this sense, beings themselves, as mere copies or instances of being in its universality are sacrificed to the transparency of representation. Yet being, conceived as the most universal and emptiest of categories, itself falls into oblivion – its presencing in and through beings in the founding moment of a history withdraws (GA65, 116/81). Therefore Heidegger insists that the founding of Da-sein implicates the 'sheltering concealment of the unconcealment of being in beings as the recovery of beings' ('Bergung der Wahrheit des Seyns in Seienden als eines Wiederbringung des Seienden') (GA65, 27/20, modified). Only insofar as being in its unaccountable arrival takes gestalt in beings, to found them in their historical specificity, are beings sheltered from representational transparency, and being 'itself,' no longer the transcendental emptiness of a category, becomes the historical site of the encounter of Da-sein and the last god in the *Ereignis* (GA65, 26, 116/20, 81).

In part VI of the *Beiträge*, entitled 'The Future Ones,' Heidegger holds that non-metaphysical selfhood is rooted in searching, in questioning. The future ones are governed by the measured reserve of the open questioning and searching out of 'where and how the truth of being may be founded and brought into sheltering unconcealment' ('wo und wie die Wahrheit des Seins sich gründen und bergen lasse'). Only in the searching is the searcher brought to himself, that is, 'into the selfhood of Da-sein, in which the clearing and concealment of beings happens' (GA65, 398/279). The selfhood of Da-sein is not the already given of a subject which seeks and confirms itself. No more is the selfhood of a Volk the confirmation of the already-given. The leap into Da-sein and only Dasein is the 'ground of possibility' of a Volk (GA65, 98/68). The Volk is not its own ground, nor an end in itself. The Volk comes to be as the gathering of Da-sein understood as the differentiated site of being as founded in beings. With this leap, the possibility of the concrete transformation of beings in their historical specificity is first opened up. The leap, therefore, is everything other than 'empty of content,' without concrete relation to the life of a people in all its realms, as Schwan claims.[15] A Volk comes to be in the movement of self-transcendence, not, however, in the metaphysical sense, but as the movement of its own enactment (in deed, sacrifice, thought) and in the in-corporation of beings.

This movement is guided by its discovery of what Heidegger calls the singular 'god' of a Volk. The god is what roots a Volk in its history and sends it on its way into its singular encounter with the presencing of being: 'A Volk *only* is a Volk, when it has been apportioned its own history in finding its god; this is the god which forces it to overcome itself and thus sets it back [into the work of founding being] in beings' ('in das Seiende zurückstellt') (GA65, 398/279, modified). Heidegger continues: 'Only then does a people avoid the danger of circling round itself and of idolizing as its *unconditioned* what are only conditions for its existence' (GA65, 398/279). The essence of a Volk is said to lie in the self-belonging of a Volk to itself as granted by its belonging to its god. The event of appropriation ('en-owning,' in the sense of coming into one's own) is the event of the founding of this mutual belonging of Volk and god. In this event, the earth becomes historical and history is grounded back in the earth (GA65, 399/279). Earth, in this context, is understood as '"life," body, generation and the generations, tribe,' but this means that the earth articulates the historicity of Da-sein's embodiment (GA65, 399/279). 'Earth,' therefore, is necessarily understood in terms of its historicity, and not in separation from it, as has been suggested.[16]

Is Heidegger's recourse to the 'god' of a people the 'highest stage of mythification' of his philosophy? Is it the definitive turn away from a phenomenological encounter with the things themselves, including the meaning of Volk, state, and history? If, in the *Logik* of 1934, Heidegger could propose to articulate the historicity of Dasein as *work*, how is it possible that in the Hölderlin lectures of 1934–5, and subsequently in the *Beiträge*, the talk of a 'god' comes to overshadow, as it were, the concretely embodied historicity of Dasein? Can we bring the question of work and the question of a god into any kind of relation? How, finally, does the question of 'god' and historicity touch on a hermeneutic situation defined by the abandonment and destitution of the being of beings?

I will attempt, however briefly and incompletely, to engage these questions in order to relate the question of 'god' to the historicity of Dasein. But of course the question of god in the *Beiträge* and in the Hölderlin lectures of 1934–5 goes far beyond what we can attempt here.

If Volk articulates a moment of withdrawal, or sheltering unconcealment, in respect to the state and social discourses in their tendency to transparency (as we have seen), then the god is the moment of withdrawal determining the Volk which holds it on the path of its historicity. Volk is forced to 'overcome itself' in its tendency toward self-representation, for therein it mistakes itself for a collective subject: it *circles round itself* and takes its conditions for the unconditioned. Since this is indeed the danger which emerged in all its virulence after 1933, Heidegger's turn to Hölderlin is motivated at least in part by his own experience of this danger and the need to confront it.

Yet this does not mean, as Philipse claims, that Heidegger's appeal to a god is an act of faith intended to proclaim a new 'Nazi religion,' an act of faith which arose out of his disappointment with real existing National Socialism, inciting him to give Nazism its proper, anti-Christian, spiritual foundation.[17] Within the architectonic of the *Beiträge*, as I argue, 'the last god' is a contribution to Da-sein's historicity, and to our being-in-the-world, and not the subject of a 'faith' replacing Christianity. Nor can the last god signify the object of a new state cult, or 'religion,' for as such it would be entangled in the toils of our collective subjectivity and lose any power to transform our being. And the transformation of our being – not by our doing, but not without the leap into our Da-sein – is the *project* of the *Beiträge*. The Volk *comes to be* only in finding a god. Volk, as a *founding project* of historicity, is opened to a specific kind of encounter with the being of beings by 'its' god. And since 'historicity' articulates the delimited, founded finitude of Volk as a structure of temporality, the 'god' is the name given to the mode and measure of presencing which takes gestalt to articulate the historicity of a Volk. In the metaphysical history of being, the God of Calvinism, for example, determines the attunement of a people, and with it the comportment toward beings that Max Weber calls the spirit of capitalism.

Therefore, since work intimates the differentiation and founding of being in beings, the god announces the *grant of a measure* which articulates *the order and rank* of beings in their differentiation. The god does not alienate Da-sein from beings, but rather 'sets Volk back' into the task of founding being in beings. And while this happens as work, work requires a measure of differentiation. The 'concept' of work implicates a differentiated response to the differentiation of being in beings, for the concept of work, as that of Volk *Socialism*, is intended by Heidegger as a critical response to the undifferentiated production of products and the consequent impoverishment of beings under the regime of capitalism. Work demands a measure. If Heidegger now appeals to the need for a god, is this because the things themselves, in their increasing in-differentiation, hardly evoke in us a sense of obligation, hardly issue a demand for differentiation? And did this become evident to Heidegger only after the debacle of National *Socialism* after 1934? Is a 'god' the measure set against the destitution of beings arising out of their measureless objectification, and disintegration, as functions of a system of production?

The turn toward the possible arrival of a god, however, only arises with the experience of distress in the face of this destitution, and with it the transformation of our fundamental attunement to being. The poet, Heidegger avers, endures the flight of the gods *and* goes in advance to arouse a *Grundstimmung* of receptiveness for a god, and for a measure which guides our openness to beings (GA39, 144, 184).

> But insofar as the gods entirely pervade [durchherrschen] historical Dasein and beings as a whole, the attunement simultaneously moves us out of our transport (toward the gods) back into a mature and measured relation to the earth, the landscape, and the homeland [Heimat]. (GA39, 140)

The fundamental attunement of openness to the god 'first of all discloses beings as such' (GA39, 140). In the attunement, a particular historically specific disclosive exposure (*Ausgesetztheit*) to beings sets Dasein into the midst of beings, and this happens as the historicity of the being-with one another of the Volk (GA39, 143). If, as Heidegger still holds in the Hölderlin lectures, this fundamental attunement to being is given its de-termination (the gestalt of its unfolding) by the founding of a state (GA39, 144), then our attunement will be actualized in work as the founding transformation of beings, for in Heidegger's terms we cannot think the 'state' without reference to 'work' as Da-sein's encounter with beings.

Work, then, finds its possibility in a new founding discourse, which transforms our being-open to beings, and renders us receptive to a new measure of rank and order. The 'poet founds [stiftet] being [Seyn],' that is, brings the historicity of Dasein to word (GA39, 184). Work would have to take its measure from the word of the poet. By letting the holy come to word, poetry opens up possible pathways of encounter with the things

themselves which are no longer defined by the metaphysics of production. What is at stake is the transformation of production, founded in
subjectivity, into work in the specific sense Heidegger gives it. The holy,
the advent of a god, however, itself awaits the transformation of the earth
as mere territory into the homeland of a people (*Heimat*): 'inasmuch as
the earth becomes *Heimat* it opens itself to the power of the gods' (GA39,
105). *Heimat* presages the historicity of the earth. Our historical being
has to be founded, Heidegger writes, by the word of the poet, but no less
'ordered [gefügt] and brought to bear as knowledge [Wissen] by
thought, rooted in the earth and historical space by the deeds of the
founders of the state' (GA39, 120). In the *Logik* of 1934, the questions of
the state and of work and socialism are so intimately intertwined that neither can be thought without the other. If, therefore, Heidegger 'down-
plays' the question of work, and eschews the discourse of work, in the
Hölderlin lectures, this perhaps reflects his revulsion from the misuse of
this discourse, but it cannot undermine the essential place of the question of work in his thinking. This place is reflected no less in the question
of 'god' than in the question of technology. In fact, *Heimat becomes the
measure of work* as founded in our response to the being of beings, as
opposed to the measureless demands of socio-technical production for
its own sake.

7.1.3 The Presencing of Being (Wesung)

The possibility of the site as the unfolding of the historicity of being presupposes a retrieval of essence (*Wesen*) as *Wesung* (presencing or 'essential swaying,' in Emad and Maly's translation). Only with this step can the
chorismos of being and beings be overcome. In section 165 of the *Beiträge*,
Heidegger insists that the *Wesen* of *ousia* is no longer to be understood as
koinon, hence is no longer defined in terms of the Platonic Idea. *Wesung*
is the 'happening of the truth of being and, in fact, in its entire historicity, which always implicates the sheltering concealment of truth (unconcealment) in beings' (GA65, 287/202, modified).

We recall that truth is so far from being a characteristic of the proposition, in Heidegger's understanding of the history of being, that it founds
the open site of sheltering and saving unconcealment (*die Lichtende Verbergung*) which allows beings to presence according to the measure appropriate to each (GA65, 70/48). To say that truth presences as sheltering
unconcealment means that the manifest is saved and sheltered in its own
being. But unconcealment itself calls for the shelter of the gestalt, sets

itself into the transformed gestalt of beings (*in den veränderten Gestalten des Seienden*) (GA65, 70/49). The forms of being which Heidegger pre-eminently emphasizes as giving gestalt to unconcealment are things, equipment, technological ordering, the work, action or leadership, and sacrifice (*Ding, Zeug, Machenschaft, Werk, Tat, Opfer*) (GA65, 70/48). In each case, truth is in some sense concretely, historically embodied and sited. It is not an attribute of the proposition.

As historically embodied, truth unfolds as the dynamic movement of temporalization: '*Truth* is sheltering that lights up, sheltering which occurs as removal-unto and charming-moving-unto' ('Wahrheit ist die lichtende Verbergung, die geschieht als Entrückung und Berückung') (GA65, 70/48). The temporalization of truth, the open site of *ecstasis*, comes to pass in Da-sein and as Da-sein (GA65, 71/49). Da-sein is in being, and thus brings what is into the manifestation of its gestalt, in acts of attentive concern (*Be-sorgung*): in the manufacture of equipment, in the design and application of technical installations, in artistic creation, in founding a state, in sacrifice. These are modes of bringing forth into the manifest (*Weisen der Hervorbringung*, GA65, 71/50). Equally signifi-cant is Da-sein's taking of responsibility, within the world thus opened, for the encounter of living and unliving (*Stein, Pflanze, Tier, Mensch*) in such a way as to allow what is made manifest, through productive-creative activity, to hold itself in the limits of its own, to maintain its own measure of being by rooting itself in self-concealment. The sending of Da-sein, as the 'shepherd of being,' is not to master the earth, but to allow it to unfold its manifold forms – herein consists the ecological ethic of Heidegger. Insofar as what is holds to this measure it is sheltered 'in the earth' (GA65, 71–2/50). The 'earth' is not, to be sure, conceived as the physical mass of the planet, but the grant of the in-each-case historically founded images and forms in which things give themselves to found a homeland (GA65, 72/50).

Consequently, 'the people' of Heidegger's political thought is not moulded on an idea in respect to which it is to be educated, unfolded, or imitated. Wherein, therefore, does the presencing of being take its stability (*Beständigkeit*), if not in reference to the Idea? Only as founded in the work, in thought and ritual: these give a stand to beings, far removed from the abstraction of the genus, in the concretization of knowing. Being wins a stand. Philosophy is conceived as a path of think-ing; and the stability which grants gestalt unfolds as the loyalty of hold-ing to the path of questioning. *Wesung*, or presencing, as the happening of being in thought, the work, and ritual is never 're-presentational, but rather is only grasped in the knowing [Wissen] of the time-space of truth and its always singular, sheltering unconcealment' (GA65, 287/202, modified). The time-space is the site of the simultaneousness of being and beings (GA65, 289/203). Knowledge which stands in the open draft of presencing calls for and 'is itself the leap into Da-sein. For this reason this knowledge can never be won from the merely general contemplation of the given and its already determined explication' (GA65, 287/202, modified).

The 'stability' of taking a stand in the 'root unfolding' (presencing) of being is a leap. The leap is thought as the experience (*Er-fahrung*) of entering into (*ein-fahren*) the There, to take a stand in presencing and to bring it to a stand in beings (GA65, 289/203). With this leap, the realm of beings is illuminated as the domain of the true. Presencing 'does not lie "above" beings separated from them, but beings stand in being and have only in it, as standing in this openness and rising out of it, their truth as the *true*' (GA65, 287/202, modified). The historicity of being emerges as the inseparability of being and its historical site – the rhythm of unfolding in thought, poetry, and the rites of a community.

This raises the question of what happens to the ontological difference of being and beings in Heidegger's transformation of 'essence.' The unity of being and beings is founded in the differentiated unity of the *event* of differentiation (*Seyn*) *and* the *differentiated* (beings). In the rhythm of presencing and withdrawal in what-presences-and-withdraws being articulates itself.

7.1.4 Founding

What Heidegger understands as 'founding' (*die Gründung*) is intimately related to the time-space of the site and the event of appropriation. The founding founds being in the recovery of the being of beings. It requires a Leap, which is itself prepared by a shift in fundamental attunement. Despite the apparent abstraction of the project which Heidegger intimates under the name of *Ereignis*, it delimits certain 'political' implications, as I propose to show in what follows, precisely because it is a founding project.

In harmony with our guiding thread of the question of the fate of beings in the technological epoch, let us continue by asking what the founding of the site of Da-sein implies for the transformation of beings. Beings are. 'Das Seiende ist' (GA65, 269/189). Beings 'belong' to the founding-presencing of being ('das Seiende gehört in die Wesung des

Seyns') (GA65, 269/189–90). As an object of representation the entity is not yet *seiend.* The object (*Gegenstand*) first takes being from the face-to-face event of an encounter (*Begegnung*) in which it comes to stand (*Gegen-stand*), and hence to stand-in-itself. If the object in its represent-edness for subjectivity no longer truly stands in itself to presence as the over-against, still less could a function of a nexus of calculations make itself known to us out of the saving limit of its own being. As a function its being has already imploded. Heidegger's deconstruction of the meta-physically understood object attempts to prepare the recovery of beings from the weightlessness of a mere representation. Only the open space of the region of the encounter, understood in its temporal movement and historicity, grants beings their measure of being. Therefore Heideg-ger insists that a being is *seiend* insofar it 'always belongs to being accord-ing to a particular mode of *sheltering unconcealment*' ('je aus einer *Bergung* in ihrer Weise zugehörig ist dem Seyn') (GA65, 269/190, modified). The temporal-historical movement of the site, of *Er-eignis*, which implicates the coming to stand of beings in the encounter, and thus also their with-drawal from the transparency of representation, opens the possibility of a measure of shelter (*Bergung*).

Bergung always has an historically determined, specific character: its measure (*die Weise*) and its constitution (*Verfassung*) together determine the 'what,' the 'how,' and the 'that' of beings, according to the rhythm and the attunement proper to each and the time-space of its site. The turn to 'measure' and 'constitution' as determinations of beings is an attempt on Heidegger's part to overcome the metaphysical distinctions of the *hoti estin,* or *existentia,* and the *ti estin,* or *essentia* (GA65, 270/191–2). *Die Weise* means way or measure, but also melody: down to its inner-most being Da-sein is attuned to being. Da-sein is the song of being. What is at stake is the transformation of metaphysical categories that determine the difference of beings and beingness (*die Seiendheit*), into the founding project of post-metaphysical thought. Measure (*Weise*) and constitution (*die Verfassung*) mutually determine each other as the historically specific rhythm of coming into presence to take a stand in appearance (to take gestalt). The de-termined presence of a being's constitution, which always arises out of the attuned delimitation of Da-sein's openness to being, is not to be understood as an atemporal essence. Beings are de-ter-mined (*be-stimmt*) in accordance with Da-sein's attunement (*Stimmung*). They mutually accord to each other, and it is the governing rhythm of this accordance which gives beings their 'essence.' The metaphysical inter-pretation of *ousia* as constant presence (*beständige Anwesenheit*) demands a retrieval which brings beings back into the stand, or constitution, appropriate to the aspect of their delimited presencing (their *Anwesen*, thought temporally and by reference to the delimitation of the *eidos* and the *peras*). The site of the appropriated and hence delimited presencing is the time-space from which the metaphysically understood *ousia* is an abstraction. Da-sein institutes the possibility of a site and the moment of a turn in which beings are released from their metaphysical determinations and raised into the light of the presencing of being:

> The t/here [Da] is the occurring, *en-owned and inabiding* site for the moment of the turning [Wendungsaugenblickstätte] for the clearing of beings in enownment. [Das Da ist die geschehende, *er-eignete und inständliche* Wendungsaugenblickstätte für die Lichtung des Seienden in der Ereignung.] (GA65, 273/192)

The enownment (*Ereignung*) of Da-sein arises out of the event of appropriation (*Ereignis*) in and through which Da-sein and the gods are differentiated (*die Ent-scheidung*) and brought into an encounter (*Ent-gegnung*) with one another (GA65, 470/331). What Heidegger calls the site of a turn, or transformation, in the blink of an eye, intimates the site of the time-space of an encounter between humans and the non-human. This is the site of mutual recognition of gods and mortals, of human and non-human. The word *Wendungsaugenblickstätte* implies that the site is opened in the exchange of a glance of the eye, in a moment of seeing and being-seen. This gaze, however, in opposition to a certain discourse of modernity, is the completely other to the objectifying gaze of representation and subjectification. It is not the gaze of 'theory,' it lays down no first principles; nor is it the gaze of 'theatre,' opening the space of political representation. The Da of Da-sein is itself this site, where a new kind of humanity, thought in its historical specificity, in each case comes to be. The Da is the site of a blink of an eye, the moment of an exchange in which beings come to stand, each in its own being. The experience of this temporally conceived site of coming to stand in being is understood by Heidegger as the project of the retrieval of *ousia*, thus to overcome its metaphysical determination as abiding presence and to root *ousia* in its primordial ground.

This encounter (*Ent-gegnung*) is the origin of the strife between earth and world which 'holds sway by setting a being free [entsetzt] from its lostness in mere beingness' (GA65, 470/331). *Ent-setzung*, or setting-free, releases beings of the determinations to which they are subject under the regime of metaphysics ('mere beingness'). The *Ent-setzung* literally is a de-positioning of these metaphysically posited (*Setzung, Satz*) determinations. The de-construction of the posited allows beings to come into the limit of their own, proper being. *Entsetzen* means to view with horror, to be appalled. Da-sein, attuned to the disintegration and destitution of beings under the regime of technicity, recoils in horror, thus to initiate the release (*ent-*) of beings from their entanglement in what has been posited (*setzen, gesetzt*) by metaphysics. Setting-free is Da-sein's response to the abandonment of beings: with the consummation of metaphysics, entities lose their conceptual stability, the objectivity of the posited, to the degree that they are integrated into the functionality of technological ordering. In this sense, the attunement of horror, which reflects the subject's loss of a stable ground, responds to *Ent-setzen* as the *withdrawal* of being-posited. Furthermore, since *Entsetzung* has a military sense as the relief of a 'position,' *Ent-setzung* reverberates with the sense of de-militarization, the *de-commissioning of beings from the standing reserve of total mobilization in the planetary epoch of technology*.

The Da is the historical grant of a site of encounter. What 'turns' on this encounter and with this encounter? A turn away from planetary thinking, which is founded on the interpretation of *ousia* as abiding presence, into the measure of appropriation, which the time-space of a locality founds. The Da of Da-sein is the event of the coming to stand of beings in their proper *morphe*, thus to open a space wherein Da-sein can take a stand. 'Das Seyn west als das Ereignis': 'Being holds sway as enowning' (GA65, 256/181). Being is not, it holds sway or presences (*west*) in and through beings as released into the open by the constituting event of the mutual appropriation of the Da (the site) and *Seyn*:

> Finally, however, enowning [Ereignis] cannot be *re*-presented as an 'event' and a 'novelty.' Its truth, i.e., *the* truth itself, holds sway only as sheltered in art, thinking, poetizing, deed – and therefore requires the inabiding of Da-sein, which rejects all illusion of immediacy of mere re-presenting. (GA65, 256/180)

The truth of *Ereignis* calls for 'shelter' in works, thought, and deed. This is a clear statement that Heidegger has not abandoned beings to an obscure fate or mysterious 'entity' behind the phenomena, but that the question of *Ereignis* is a more fundamental working-out of our concrete being-in-the-world, as enunciated in *Sein und Zeit*, and of the question of work and 'socialism' in the *Logik* of 1934.

Representational thinking (*das vor-stellende Denken*) aims at the transparency of beings to rationality – transparency has calculability as its end. Heidegger calls the presentation of beings to and for subjectivity *the mere appearance of immediacy*. Yet this appearance is what fascinates and seduces in the aspect of moments of intensity of experience which the technology of representational thinking produces and regulates.

The interface of humanity and machine in virtual-reality programs already offers a promise of the hyperimmediacy of simulacra which the technological consummation of metaphysics is beginning to realize. This 'reality' is 'founded' in the efficacy of the present, and entities are only insofar as they can impact in the dimension of the present. In the 'other beginning,' however, Heidegger writes, 'a being is never actual in the sense of this "being-present"' (GA65, 257/181). According to the dominant metaphysical conception of time in Aristotle, only the present is, insofar as time itself is, for the past and future are no longer and not yet; and therefore the present must be the most real; and things being-present are real. Yet Heidegger insists that the present is least in being because the present as present is founded in the time-space of the interplay of recollection and the anticipation of preparation (*Erinnerung und Bereitung*). What is present (*das Anwesende*) shines forth into the present (*die Gegenwart*), into the encounter (*das Gegenwärtigen des Anwesenden*), only out of the echo of the concentrated innerness of the memory of past and anticipated future. For in memory (*die Erinnerung*) we hear innerness (*die Innigkeit*). The sheltering reserve (*Innigkeit*) of the temporal site of Da-sein is the crossroads of the encounter which brings truth into the measure of its own, into the gestalt, as artwork, poetry, thought, and deed. What takes measure in the gestalt to 'present' itself out of the interplay of the past and future is in being (*Seiend*). It is in being precisely because it is not given over to the transparency of calculative thought and to the appearance of the intensity and immediacy of the unreserved. The manufactured appearance of immediacy, for its part, is no less the echo of memory and anticipation: it is the final interiorization (*Er-innerung*) of metaphysics in the anticipation of the dissolution of subjectivity into technicity. The boundless dimension of this process of dissolution is itself founded in a certain attunement to being. Planetary thinking is governed by an enthusiasm which manifests itself in various forms of technomania – for planetary exploration, virtual reality, designer drugs, genetic programming, and so on. Technological thinking is attuned to the dissolution of subject and object and their re-integration into a kind of immediacy of the 'real' which is not real at all, but rather a simulation of reality which is experienced as being more intense, more real than the 'things' themselves, more real than the object in the classical sense of that which still stands over against a subject. 'Reality' indeed becomes a 'show,' and is for show. The simulation of reality 'founds' the techno-interface as the dimension of the distance-less and undifferentiated.

Why then the appeal to the god, to the divine, in speaking of being and *Ereignis*? Could it be that the advent of a god is the starkest measure of distance and rank-order? The last god is the measure of a reserve, a refusal, which in its advent as *Wink* (hint, or indication), draws beings, as belonging to the Da of *Seyn*, into the sheltering unconcealment of being, which shelters them from the non-being of functionality under the regime of metaphysical categories (*Seiendheit*):

> and this again and again only historically in the stages and domains and degrees of the sheltering of truth in beings, by which alone – within the boundless but dissembled extinguishing into not-being – a being again becomes more-being. (GA65, 410/288, modified)

The preparation of such advent, however, calls for the receptivity of an attunement which is itself a way of knowing founded in the historicity and hence the differentiation of being. 'How few know that god awaits the grounding of the truth of be-ing and thus awaits man's leaping into Da-sein' (GA65, 417/293). Da-sein is the site of truth which

> imparts to beings the prerogative of standing in the remotest remoteness to the passing of a god, a prerogative whose imparting occurs only as history: in the transformation of beings unto the ownmost of their destiny and in freeing them from the misuse of machinations, which, turning everything upside down, exhaust beings in exploitation. (GA65, 417/293, modified)

The god, therefore, would seem to intimate the advent of a measure of differentiation within the in-difference of the undifferentiated exploitation of beings. In its remoteness and alien otherness, the god re-establishes the possibility of remoteness and nearness. Is this a mystification of Da-sein as being-in-the-world, or is it a response to the flattening of our being-in-the-world, a response as wager and as founding project? We recall that Da-sein is thought only as project, in effect, as the project of historicity. To speak of god, therefore, in Heidegger's sense, is to speak of the actualization of Da-sein's historicity in the passage from metaphysics, through technicity, into the *possibility* of a different beginning.

It is evident that Heidegger thinks of historicity as the ground of beings, and that this ground, which is thought as the presencing of being (*die Wesung des Seyns*) must be founded in the different orders of being. Founding is itself the project of an *Augen-blick*. With this inception of differentiation a history begins (GA65, 255/180). Thus the entity is in being insofar as it is integrated into the time-space of an historical site, for the site appropriates to each limit and measure. Conversely, the deracination of the presencing of being, in Greek thought, and with it the eventual triumph of the planetary dimension of representational thinking, is the corollary of the economy of the 'real.' The world order of the real demands and pursues the factual deracination of the peoples of the earth as its necessary consequence, for rootedness implicates measure and self-limitation. This world order aims at a measureless dimension of inter-changeability, a hyperreality of simulations 'founded' in the software of the techno-interface. The mere appearance of immediacy which thus arises implicates the non-presencing of the site (e.g., the 'community' of the Internet, as a simulacrum of community). The program grants a certain stability derived from the functional encoding of presence, and this betrays its heritage in the metaphysical interpretation of *ousia*. The functional inscription of the object, as of the subject, signifies the overthrow of the final remnants of such standing-in-itself which still defines the object as *Gegen-stand*. The economy of functionalization, moreover, makes evident the antiquation of political systems which – however modern, progressive, or totalitarian in other respects – still appeal to the collective subject (of nation, class, race) or to classical (Lockean) individual autonomy. The functional refiguration of socio-political relations to favour a post-modern economy is founded on and in turn unfolds its own fundamental attunement to the hyperreal. This attunement must lay bare for stimulation and consumption any reserve or withdrawal from 'reality' in order to integrate it into the circuit of the intensification of sensation, which is the last and highest 'value' of the hyperworld. The postmodern economy produces 'signifiers' of intensity, and what is emerges as a relative intensity generated by the economy of signification. Yet the disintegration of entities into mere cyphers of signification also has the possibility of creating the need to found being in beings. One exemplary kind of being, Heidegger insists, in and through which the truth of being can be articulated, is the work of art.

7.2 The Artwork and the Site of the Political in the *Beiträge*

Heidegger's *Contributions to Philosophy* constitutes the historical and systematic site of 'The Origin of the Work of Art' (1936). I will show that the

Contributions also maps out the groundplan of the relation of the 'political' and the 'aesthetic' realms as modes of the 'con-stitution' and institution of being in and through the artwork. The proper point of departure into the question of the artwork, as von Herrmann correctly insists, is the question of being, not any cultural-anthropological or aesthetic standpoint).[18] In section 247 of the *Beiträge* – the last section of part V, 'The Founding' – Heidegger explicitly refers to the artwork essay as an investigation into the 'founding of Da-sein and the ways of sheltering truth.' This formulation implicates a number of theses which will guide this discussion: The artwork is one way in which the truth, that is, the unconcealment of being (*Seyn*), is founded in beings, thus *to overcome the separation, or 'ontological difference,' of being and beings* (GA65, sec. 266). 'Being' is nothing 'behind' the phenomena, in the way of the metaphysical tradition, as a significant number of commentators still claim.[19] Being rather disperses or differentiates itself in beings. Evidently Heidegger understands Da-sein as the site of this dispersal, and asks us *to comprehend being in its finitude and historicity.* The hermeneutic situation out of which the *Beiträge*, and therefore also the 'Origin of the Work of Art,' speaks is the desolation and dis-integration of beings (*Seinsverlassenheit*) (GA65, secs. 56–8). The founding of Da-sein calls for ways of giving shelter (*Bergung*) to beings, as founded in the historicity of Da-sein and the finitude of being, thus to allow beings *to refuse rational transparency and technical manipulation.* The 'political' and the 'aesthetic,' as renovated in the community opened by the work, find their common ground in this refusal or withdrawal (the *lethe* of *aletheia*). My fundamental claim is that *being 'takes gestalt' in beings,* and in the comportment of Da-sein, and that this event overcomes the separation of being and beings to found the historicity of Da-sein and the being of entities. Consequently, I will argue that 'gestalt' should be understood in a non-metaphysical sense as *the time-space of the event of truth,* as set into the work, as enacted in leadership, thought, sacrifice. The entity as 'object,' and as resource, has no gestalt in Heidegger's terms: the object is defined by its relation to a subject (to re-presentation), and the 'resource' is merely present as the function of the system of relations into which the dis-integrated object has been integrated. Defined in terms of its availability as stock-on-call (GA65, secs. 55, 67–70), the entity cannot come to presence out of the singularity of its own time-space (GA65, secs. 242–3). In approaching the artwork essay in this way, my account will be guided by the question of how Heidegger's reflections on his hermeneutic situation anticipate our own, as defined by the dis-integrative power of post-modern technicity and functionality.

7.2.1 Artwork and Community

By 1936 the essay had already entered its third version (following the first draft of 1931 or 1932, and the Freiburg address of 1935),[20] indicating that the question of *the relation of world to earth*, which lay dormant in *Being and Time*, had come to increasingly occupy Heidegger. The artwork essay is in fact an attempt to overcome aesthetics, and this means, as Bernasconi has noted, that the work must become an *origin* in the sense of founding truth. The political dimension, therefore, although muted, pervades the essay: Shall art remain the object of 'aesthetic experience,' or shall it once again, in Hegel's terms, become an 'absolute need'?[21] In the first draft of the essay, which apparently dates from 1931 or 1932 according to von Herrmann,[22] Heidegger insists that the work must establish its own 'openness' as the condition of entering into the 'public space' (*Öffentlichkeit*) of its reception. The 'public' or audience of the aesthetic object is 'destroyed' by the work (UK-HS 8). This would be the condition for opening a space for a people in its historicity. Bernasconi argues that the *Holzwege* essay of 1936 already marks a first step in Heidegger's estrangement from politics in favour of the saving power of art. But the reception, or preservation, of the work of art belongs to its being as work. And the work is only as an absolute need of Da-sein in its historicity, that is, for a Volk (UK 61/199). One essential way in which the Volk is founded, and this is the claim of the *Beiträge*, is through the space opened by the work. It is not the case, as Bernasconi (and Pöggeler before him) claims, that Heidegger turns toward art in progressively turning away from the political question of Volk, thus to entangle himself once again in an aesthetic of art alienated from the community.[23]

Given that the modern state is determined, as Heidegger's critique of science claims, by discourses of representation (GA65, sec. 76) founded in subjectivity, the work of art becomes perhaps the pre-eminent way in which being is given shelter in a being, thus to open a non-representational space for community. In the words of Françoise Dastur's commentary on the second (or Freiburg) version of 1935, art is not an 'ontological representation, but an ontological effectuation,' and in this sense a response to the tyranny of representational thinking. The work is not a representation (*Darstellung*) but an original thesis, or setting-into-work of truth.[24] If the advent of the work breaks with representational thinking, it would be a condition of the coming into being of a postmetaphysical community, whereas the modern state, in Heidegger's estimation, is the creature of the self-representation of subjectivity (GA38, 156–7, 165).

The deconstruction of the received metaphysical interpretation of the work of art therefore becomes an essential gateway to the political problematic of Heidegger's thought. Heidegger's reflection on the work of art opens the space of a possible non-metaphysical order of politics. This by no means implies an 'aestheticization' of politics.

After 1934, this turn toward the founding power of art follows in Heidegger's thought from his turn away from the earlier attempt to reconceive and reorganize the sciences by way of a national program of university reform. In the *Beiträge*, Heidegger draws the conclusion that this failure was not merely due to unpropitious political circumstances, but inherent in the historical essence of science itself: the sciences are not a mode of foundational knowledge (*Wissen*), but rather function as the technical organization and development of the being of beings as long since founded by metaphysics (GA65, sec. 76). The thrown project of philosophy, however, constitutes such knowledge as can prepare a turn, and thus also prepare the site of art as the arena of a post-metaphysical community. The artwork is granted the power, given that it unfolds the 'self'-knowledge of an historical community, to found a history. It does this by sheltering the truth (the coming to presence) of being in a being. Pre-eminently the artwork shelters coming to presence in the image (*Bild*) and the *Gestalt*.

> The poetic projection of truth that sets itself into work as gestalt [Gestalt] is also never carried out in the direction of an indeterminate void. Rather, in the work, truth is thrown toward the coming preservers, that is, toward a historical group of human beings. What is thus cast forth is, however, never an arbitrary demand. Truly poetic projection is the opening up of that into which human being as historical is already cast. This is the earth and, for a historical people, its earth, the self-secluding ground on which it rests together with everything that it already is, though still hidden from itself. (UK 62–3/200, modified)

In taking-gestalt, truth sets the limit and measure of the political being of an historical people and inscribes this limit in what becomes native soil (UK 61/200).

We recall that the artwork incorporates the strife of earth and world. 'Earth' designates the movement of withdrawal at the heart of unconcealment (UK 32/172). The artwork, as the opening of a communal site, has the possibility of attuning politics to the movement of withdrawal from representation intimated by the historicity of the earth as manifested through the work. This withdrawal from the claim of representational schemata intimates the necessity of the recovery of *phusis*, understood as the in-corporation of the unconcealment of being in the sheltering *forms* of being. These modes of incorporation, in the image and in poetry, music, dance, architecture, as well as in thinking, sacrifice, political leadership, and technology, give aspect and gestalt to the historical presencing of being (GA65, secs. 225, 244). The earth-rootedness of Da-sein, as opened up by the communal site of the artwork, would implicate a political order founded in, and belonging to, the limits of the historical earth. It is Heidegger's claim that until 'economic humanity,' understood as the collective subjectivity of scientific-technological thinking, shatters and in shattering attunes itself to the locality and singularity of the presencing of being, the earth remains forgotten in favour of planetary management, and its versions of political ecology. Heidegger in effect claims that the attunement of humanity to the presencing of being – as opposed to the limitlessness of representational thinking – is the condition of any possible political ecology or 'world order' which might presume to constitute a global future.

Conversely, the technological order, which grounds in what Heidegger calls 'machination' (*Machenschaft*), establishes a political order of transparency and availability to representational thinking. Machination reveals the beingness (*Seiendheit*) of beings as that which can be made, produced (GA65, secs. 61, 67). In the techno-scientific realm, for example, the human-genome project represents a mapping of the 'raw material' of 'humanity' in the service of its efficient use and therapeutic manipulation. The genome project is perhaps the most striking evidence of the ultimate dissolution of politics into technicity and of the collective subject of humanity into the unlimited planetary 'energies' of machination. According to Heidegger, the measurelessness of technological, or representational, thinking, including socio-political technologies, constitutes the urgent danger which impels us to contemplate the question of being, as the question of the abandonment of beings to machination, conceived as the governing form of the epochal disclosure of beings (GA65, secs. 58–9). This danger consists in the senselessness of the schematization of all entities – including mankind – according to one design, the design of transparency and calculability (GA65, sec. 70). The design of transparency is founded on the metaphysics of transcendence, even where the transcendental has been re-interpreted as a system of functional relations. The things themselves are functionalized, hence no longer presence out of the reserve (*lethe*) of their proper being. It is within this context that the question of the 'origin' of the artwork arises in the *Contributions to Philosophy* as a reflection on the necessity of founding being in beings, thus to allow things each their own way of unfolding.

7.2.2 Truth as the Sheltering Unconcealment of Being in Beings

Da-sein is the site of the presencing of being, hence the temporal site of the in-corporation of being in works of art. The following passage from part V ('Grounding'), section 243, of the *Beiträge* clearly lays out the systematic place of the artwork essay within the plan of this work:

> Leaving out of consideration that truth is never extant, sheltering is not a subsequent housing of the truth as extant in itself within a being.
>
> Sheltering belongs to the presencing, or essential swaying (*Wesung*), of truth. This truth *is* not essential swaying if it never holds sway in sheltering.
>
> Therefore, when by way of indicating 'what is ownmost' to truth is called clearing (*Lichtung*) for self-sheltering, then this happens only in order first to unfold the essential swaying of truth.... Clearing needs that which keeps it in openness, and that is in each case a different being (thing-tool-work) ...
>
> Thus it must be possible – with, of course, the corresponding leap ahead into be-ing – to find the way from 'a being' to the essential swaying of truth and in this way to make manifest the *sheltering* as belonging to truth. (GA65, 389/271–2, modified)

As Heidegger immediately adds, the Frankfurt lectures of 1936 – that is, the essay on art – constitute precisely such an attempt to 'find the way' from a being to the *sheltered in-corporation of truth* in a being. In finding this way, we undertake the leap into the site of being as Da-sein. For

> Da-sein does not lead away from beings and does not vaporize beings into spirituality. On the contrary: In accordance with the uniqueness of be-ing, Da-sein first opens up the unsettledness of beings, whose 'truth' is endured and sustained only in the renewed inceptual struggle of bringing them into shelter in what has been created by historical man. *Only that which we, inabiding in Da-sein, found and create and in creating let face us in its onrush, only that can be what is true and manifest and accordingly be recognized and known.* (GA65, 314–5/221, modified)

The 'inabiding' of Da-sein – Da-sein *as* inabiding (*Inständlich*) – means nothing other than the ex-posure of Da-sein to beings in the midst of beings, *and therefore* 'the power of sheltering truth' in the granting of gestalt to beings ('die Kraft der Bergung der Wahrheit in das gestaltete Seiende') (GA65, 315/221). The 'fourfold' of Heidegger's late works – gods, mortals, earth, and sky – belongs to the uniqueness of being as it in each case gives itself in and through the creations of a particular human-ity. Da-sein takes its stand in beings: its authenticity is not a moral quality, but the knowledge which brings the being of beings each into its own. Thus the Da is creatively 'brought to stand in one or the other manner of sheltering the truth (in thinking, poetizing, building, leading, sacrific-ing, suffering, celebrating)' (GA65, 302/213, modified). The *Instän-digkeit des Da-seins* intimates that a 'humanity' takes its stand in the creative modes of bringing the singularity of the being of beings to stand in beings, and that humanity, being nothing other than this, *the movement of bringing being into the sheltering gestalt*, holds the openness of the Da open, and releases itself into the openness. What Heidegger calls the *Wesen des Da-seins* (GA65, 308/216) unfolds as the attentive openness of Da-sein to the being of beings, the openness of concern for being.

Da-sein and 'humanity' are evidently not the same, for Da-sein is said to be the openness of the 'Between' of an historically founded and founding humanity and the gods (GA65, 311/219). The openness of the Between is the ground of a particular historical humanity, which comes to be in and through the founding of the Between in beings. The 'found-ing of the Between' allows the self-withdrawal of Openness to presence and thus brings entities into shelter: 'Da-sein is the very own self-ground-ing ground of *aletheia* of *phusis*, is the essential swaying of that openness which first opens up the self–sheltering-concealing (the essential sway of be-ing) and which is thus the truth of be-ing itself' (GA65, 296/209, modified). The relation between the presencing of the openness of truth spoken of here, in the *Beiträge*, and the founding of being in the work of art is unfolded in the following passage from 'The Origin':

> The openness of the open region, that is, truth, can be what it is, namely, this openness, only if and as long as it establishes itself within its open region. Hence there must always be some being in this open region in which the openness takes its stand and attains its constancy. (UK 47/186)

The openness of truth must establish itself in beings, and in this respect the work of art is exemplary. Openness is brought to a stand in the work, and in such a way as to reveal the being of the thing and of equipment.

The openness of truth, however, is the truth of *phusis*, which is to say, arrival of the self-withdrawal of the earth from representation to take shelter in its own forms and images. The interplay of arrival and withdrawal constitutes the strife which is brought to a stand in the work: 'Because truth is the opposition of clearing and concealing, there belongs to it what is here to be called establishing [Einrichtung]' (UK 47/186). Openness needs the shelter of beings to manifest itself in the strifeful singularity of this particular (historical) openness, in this gestalt – the Greek temple, the gothic cathedral.

It belongs to the presencing of truth to institute itself in the order and arrangement of beings in all their modes – no less in the tool and the nuclear power station, in the biochemical laboratory, than in architecture, poetry, or sculpture. Yet it appears that Heidegger does not grant the scientific disciplines and the technologies the same degree of founding power as art, thought, or the leadership which brings a polity into being (UK 48/186–7). Why is this? Presumably because the openness of Da-sein primordially founds itself as the open site, or clearing of self-concealment, as the manifestation of sheltering self-withdrawal, and the tendency of the technologies toward representation occludes self-concealment. The movement into the shelter of their own propriety gives beings, and hence Da-sein as the Between of the being of beings, their founding power. By contrast, the 'production of equipment never *directly* effects the happening of truth ... For equipment to be ready means that it is released beyond itself, to be used up in usefulness' (UK 50–1/189; my emphasis). Equipment, moreover, conceals unconcealment in usefulness, while the work is more evidently an event of the differentiation of unconcealment as it disperses itself in beings. This is what setting-into-the-gestalt in Heidegger's non-metaphysical usage means.

Beings win a stand only insofar as they are allowed to stand in their own light, thus to bring the openness of Da-sein to a stand (cf. UK 48/187). For this reason, because Da-sein gains its stand as the Between of beings, the sustaining endurance of Da-sein in the midst of beings is exemplified in 'The Origin' as the stand of Da-sein in the openness of beings as in-corporated by a work (UK 53/192). The work itself must be 'preserved,' in fact, it only is a work insofar as it is 'received' by a community. The community, conversely, comes to be through its reception of the work. To 'preserve' means to endure the event opened up by the work, to endure and stand one's stand in the demand for self-transformation the work poses.

The work of art is one way the possibility of a limited community is opened, but this does not imply 'ontological aestheticism,' as Zimmerman claims, for the art-work is not an object of contemplation, but the event which allows reconstitution of 'subject' (community) and 'object' (things in the historicity of their belonging to the earth).[25] Hence the political, in Heidegger's sense, cannot be founded in a mimetic relation of political education and the Volk (GA65, 390/272), or of the leader to the led, as the 'national aesthetic' thesis of Lacoue-Labarthe claims.[26] For the mimetic relation implicates both the formation of an idea of Volk, and the refusal of the self-reserve of Volk. National aestheticism implies that the Volk must be on-call as available energy. It must be integrated into the limitlessness of signification. Heidegger rejects these premises.

Heidegger argues that the open space of the challenge the work poses is 'prior' to the subject-object relation, not only in respect to the experience of art, but also in the demand which political leadership poses for the 'follower': to lead is to open the space of communal self-transformation, and in this space the follower does not follow, but must find himself. Heidegger names the 'state-founding deed,' along with the work, sacrifice, etc., as one way in which truth presences (UK 48/187). Leadership therefore con-stitutes the differentiation of being in the singularity of a site: it formulates the law of the appearance and withdrawal of beings from manifestation, the law of their taking gestalt in the propriety of the rites which order a community.

Heidegger's understanding of the truth of being does not allow for a political order founded on technological and sociological discourse any more than it would allow for a political order based on a mimetic order of being. In this regard it matters little, according to Heidegger, if political order is conceived as a 'dictatorship' or a 'liberal democracy,' for the dictatorship of rationality determines both (GA65, sec. 76, no. 10). Perhaps Heidegger underestimates, in this regard, the potential of democracy to open a dialogical space for the critique of instrumental reason. Extrapolating from Heidegger's reflections on the artwork, we can say the essential point of his 'political' project is to lead to the founding of a political order based on *the institution of the rites and laws which allow a community to preserve itself in the self-withdrawing propriety of its own, historically granted limits.* The determination of a people to preserve its historical character and to unfold it according to that people's own rootedness in its native soil is liable to bring it into conflict, as a political entity, with the global economic order of unlimited production and consumption.

In Heidegger's view, liberalism, as the socio-technical management of society, tends toward limitlessness. Heidegger's rejection of 'liberalism' in the *Beiträge*[27] follows from this, since he understands liberalism in philosophical terms as the institution of the boundless, ahistorical primacy of the subject, which determines all cultural, economic, and political realms. Yet this anti-liberal position by no means results in a return to a traditional idea of Volk. Rather,

> *It is only from Da-sein that what is ownmost to a people can be grasped* and that means at the same time knowing that the people can never be goal and purpose and that such an opinion is only a 'folkish' [*völkische*] extension of the 'liberal' thought of the 'I' and of the economic idea of the preservation of 'life.' (GA65, 319/224, modified)

The ideological concept of Volk, even if it rejects the 'state of nature,' and the institution of a polity by contract, nonetheless presupposes (along with Hobbes and Locke) that the purpose of the state is the security and well-being of the 'people.' It extends the concept of the primacy of the individual to the collective of the Volk. The deconstruction of this ideological concept implicates the turn away from 'Volk' to a community of work and action which is founded only by a turn toward the founding of the self-reserved presencing of being. In this sense a Volk comes to be in terms of the Da, the site of the encounter with being. Da-sein '*moves away from the relation to man and reveals itself as the "between" that is unfolded by be-ing itself* as the domain where beings tower up, where above all a being returns to itself' (GA65, 299/211; my emphasis). The Volk is founded in the Da which comes to light and takes a stand in the work. In the words of 'The Origin of the Work of Art,'

> Preserving the work does not reduce people to their private experiences, but brings them into affiliation with the truth happening in the work. Thus it grounds being for and with one another as the historical endurance of Da-sein out of its relation to unconcealment. (UK 54/193, modified)

The *endurance* spoken of here (*Ausstehen*) is to be understood as the endurance of the ex-posure (*Ausgesetztheit*) of Da-sein in the midst of being, which founds a history. Ex-posure in this sense also defines work, that is, labour, in the *Logik* of 1934: in the ex-posure of Da-sein to beings in labour, entities are brought to a stand in the particularity of their becoming-present (GA38, 128).

The truth which comes to pass in the work of art, however, is given exemplary status in the founding of the space of a community. This community grounds in the knowledge (*Wissen*) which the work itself brings into play. What kind of knowledge is this? Knowledge is said to be the *Ent-schlossenheit* of Da-sein for the unconcealment of being. The decision to take a stand in being and to bring being to a stand in beings is not the 'action of a subject' such as sets and posits its own goals (UK 53–5/191–3). Rather it is the liberation of Da-sein from the bedazzling 'reality' of entities for the sake of the openness of the space of the coming to be of the differentiation of being. This space must be endured and founded, that is, inscribed in the singular design of a singular site. The site is the self-inscription of Da-sein, in which the subjectivity of the rational animal suffers the dismemberment of the *polemos* of being thus to be torn open to, and for, the presencing of being (UK 53–5/192). The *polemos* of being, in allusion to Heidegger's commentary (1945) on the *Rektorsrede* of 1933, is said to intimate the *Aus-einander-setzung*, or differentiation of being: Dasein takes its stand in the site of differentiation (SU 28/488). The belated self-interpretation of *Kampf* (strife or war) as *polemos* is substantiated by Heidegger in the *Introduction to Metaphysics* of 1935 (GA40, 153/144).

This site, Heidegger avers, is inherently that of an historical tradition: its 'nature' as site implicates the arrival and differentiation of being in the delimited aspect (gestalt) of beings. This site has to be won again and again in the struggle against the decadence of merely taking for granted what has been founded: 'At each time the openness of beings had to be established in beings themselves by setting truth into the gestalt [Gestalt]' (UK 63/201, modified). With the falling-off from the event which opens up a realm in and through the gestalt, a falling off into the mere maintenance of what has been, the world of the work decays (UK 26/166). The merely represented work may belong to the culture industry of a society, but it cannot found the *Volksein* of a people. For the being of a people is only engaged and constituted by a work of art insofar as the event of worldhood still reverberates through the work. Only as long as a community is still attuned to the singular differentiation of being which a work manifests is a people in being as a people (UK 30/170).

The world, or structure of significance, which a work manifests, constitutes the pathways of the essential decisions of a people (UK 30/170). Heidegger claims that the ground of these decisions is never fully mastered and transparent to reason, and where this seems to be the case the rites of essential decision making have been replaced by the attempt to institutionalize them, thus to cling to the illusion of certainty this offers. Still less does the earth, which manifests itself historically in and through the singularity of a world, give itself to the life of representational thought, except to conceal and withdraw itself. The work brings this double movement of un-concealment in which earth and world, in turn, are locked together, into the 'figure,' or gestalt: 'this strife is fixed in place in the gestalt [Gestalt] of the work and becomes manifest by it' (UK 56/ 194–5, modified). The gestalt fixed in the work is a creative projection and yet a response to what 'lies hidden in nature': a 'rift-design, a measure and a boundary [Grenze] and tied to it, a capacity for bringing-forth – that is, art' (UK 57/195). The gestalt fixed in the work, therefore, is the actualization of a potential of nature (*phusis*) itself. As Kockelmans intimates, the gestalt of the work articulates the retrieval of the ontological difference as set into the event of the work: the 'rift-design' unites earth and world, their differentiation, and the difference of unconcealment and sheltering withdrawal.[28] The metaphysical difference of being and beings is overcome in the event of truth as being comes to be (presence) in a being.

What we call 'nature' emerges in its multidimensional forms out of the mythos of a particular site, which the historicity of the work mediates, and to which it gives exemplary shape. *The reduction of the work to an object of consumption, of nature to the uniformity of raw material, and of the community to the techno-social institution of productive capacities are correlative events in the institution of the measurelessness of representation.*

The presencing of the truth measures itself out, apportions itself to beings and takes gestalt in beings (GA65, 389/271–2). The in-corporation of the openness in its self-concealing shelter manifests the presencing of being. In founding the truth of being, Da-sein 'does not go from a being over to its being. Rather, the founding of enowning [Ereignis] happens as sheltering of truth in and as a being' (GA65, 322/226, modified). Methodologically speaking, the artwork essay attempts to make the mutual belonging together of sheltering unconcealment (*Bergung*), and truth, evident by way of an exemplary kind of entity. The appeal to the work of art arises out of the necessity of bringing beings into the shelter (the propriety) of the self-withdrawal of being. Hence the primacy that the artwork is granted over the thing and things-made. The event of the self-manifesting withdrawal into shelter which founds being in beings, can also be, as we have noted, an act – an act of leadership or sacrifice, for example. Yet all the ways and modes of giving shelter to the coming to pass of truth in beings in order to found the self-reserved openness of Da-sein in its historicity are equally 'political' in the sense that the polity is constituted through the differentiation of being in all its modes.

What is essential *in every mode* is the movement of bringing into shelter.

Only when self-sheltering thoroughly dominates all interswaying regions of what is produced (*des Erzeugten*) and created and acted upon and sacrificed, when it determines the clearing and thus at the same time sways counter to what is closed off within this clearing, only then does world arise and along with it (out of the 'simultaneity' of be-ing and a being) earth emerge. Now for a moment there is history. (GA65, 349/244)

The 'interswaying' (*ineinanderwesend*) spoken of here designates a certain degree of mutual reciprocity of the coming-to-presence of the various regions of being. Is it therefore misleading to ask which mode of the institution of being, technology or art, has the greater potential to respond to this demand of giving shelter? No, not as such. It is likely, however, that Heidegger held that the fusion of the two will play a leading role in overcoming the desolation of the being of beings. What kind of political order follows from this for the unfolding and preservation of the earth? Must technology, art, and a political order fuse in a new way, take on the power of an absolute cult, to let the earth, her creatures, be, come to presence as strange, other, and incalculable – as strange and incalculable as Da-sein 'itself,' as the open site of the strife of earth and world?

7.2.3 Truth and Untruth of the Image

The work of art is said to belong solely to that realm which it itself opens (UK 26/167). The realm thus opened founds, and is founded in, the stand which Da-sein takes to institute the arrival of presencing in the gestalt of beings. The realm of the artwork is integral to the space of the differentiation of being (GA65, 311/218). The movement of differentiation-as-appropriation this passage appeals to is developed in the artwork essay by way of the example of the Greek temple, which manifests the god, opens the space of essential decisions, and brings the being of each into the limit of its own presencing (UK 27–8/167–8). Who sees, who stands in this space to apprehend tree and stone, the animal and the god? (cf. GA65, 311/218). Not the representational subject, but a being who first comes to be in the encounter with being opened up by the work (UK 28/168–9). The statue of the god is not as copy or representation, but rather as the delimited presencing of the 'locality' of being. In this sense being presences as 'image.' Being 'is' in the presencing of 'spatio-temporal' specificity and singularity, and this singularity is gathered in the image of the god (UK 29/168). The temple incorporates the court (*Geviert*) of a singularity which gives things their 'face' (*Gesicht*). The four-square of the courtyard is the open centre of the edifice (*das Anwesen*) of being, and it is only by way of the directions laid out by the fourfold that a humanity brings itself into view, not in its givenness as subject, but as 'captured' in the aspects of the things themselves.

The uprooting of the image from its site and its integration into the planetary image-bank of the global economy and the cyberworld is a key event in the process of the generation of the electronic animal of post-modernity. This animal is precisely not-at-home, not sited, but the Away of being (*Weg-sein*). For Da-sein presences as the site of the blink of an eye in which the openness of the Between enters into the gestalt. This instant situates the eye-to-eye encounter of the Da and the presencing of the truth of being in beings. 'Man "is" the Da only as historical, i.e., as history-grounding and inabiding in the Da in the manner of sheltering the truth in beings' (GA65, 324/227). What, then, might humanity in its ahistorical unsitedness, in the dis-integrated gestalt of 'internationalism' and 'cosmopolitanism,' be called? Not Da-sein, but *Weg-sein*. In its ahistoricity, mankind

is 'away' *from* the steadfastness of the Da and completely with *beings as being-present* (forgottenness of being). Man is the *away*.

Being-away is the *more originary* title for Da-sein's *inauthenticity*.

Being-away [is] the manner of *pursuing* the extant as seen from the stance of the Da and belonging to it. (GA65, 323–4/227)

Weg-sein is in fact integral to the structure of Da-sein. For we recall that according to the analytic of Dasein in *Being and Time* the inauthenticity of Dasein belongs to its structure. This manifests itself in the fallen-ness of Dasein and its dispersion and lostness in beings. In the first instance, then, the Away is the surrender of the open space of the There in favour of entanglement with the actuality (*Vorhandenheit*) of beings. The presencing of the actual is already a derivative, in-authentic manifestation of the historicity of being because the openness of the withdrawal of presencing (the *lethe* of *aletheia*) itself is occluded. Yet being-away has its own historical necessity and its own 'epoch,' which only modern technology and the discourses of deracination make possible. For when the being-away of concern with the actual, which is integral to the structure of Dasein, is transformed into a program of being-away for its own sake, as the 'business' of deracination for the sake of the consumption of images, then the hyper-space of cosmopolitan representation begins to enter its own and to 'found' its own 'epoch.' This follows from Heidegger's reflection on the dynamics of the image. Deracination is an event in the history of being, but no less a function of socio-political structures, ideologies, and their attendant technologies of information. The Away, therefore, which belongs to the structure of Da-sein itself, finds its confirmation in empirical history, as an event in the history of being.

A further sense of the Away, as the most extreme and most intimate possibility of being-away (GA65, 324/228), is revealed in being-toward-death. This Away is not the termination of the There, but the Away in Nothing presences in Da-sein as the innermost mystery of its being: 'the reciprocal relation of the Da to the away that is turned toward the Da – is the mirroring of the turning in the essential sway [Wesen] of being itself' (GA65, 325/228). Therefore we see that the epochal Away of humanity in its entanglement in 'actuality' consummates a flight away-from finitude, hence from being-toward-death. The essence of technology inscribes this flight in postmodern humanity. This flight, however, is nothing negative, for in its consummation it disintegrates beings, strips them of their purported 'reality,' in revealing their functional interdependence and mutual indifference. Their in-difference is revealed, and with it, the holding-sway of the Nothingness in which they hang. The epochal being-away of a bedazzlement entangled in mere actuality turns us toward the Nothing from which we flee. In this turn, we are turned toward the 'essential sway of being itself' as revealed in the Nothing.

Metaphysically conceived the movement of Da-sein is the movement of representation (*Vorstellen*) as the movement of the transcendence inherent in subjectivity. The deconstruction of re-presentation, in turn, shows that representation is, thought in terms of Da-sein, the ek-stasis of Da-sein, its *movement into the open* (GA65, 316/222). Insofar as representation merely re-presents itself, the movement of ek-stasis is only repeated and is only determined in terms of representation. The open as open remains concealed. The *Inständigkeit* of Da-sein, however, signifies holding oneself in the open thus to bring the presencing of the open into shelter in beings without passing over into the metaphysically determined being of beings. The '*self* is never "I." The *with-itself of the self* holds sway as inabiding [Inständigkeit] in the taking-over of en-ownment' (GA65, 322/226). The 'selfhood' of Da-sein is not a function of representation. En-ownment (*Er-eignung*) intimates the endurance, the bearing-out of the strife of earth and world in the event of appropriation. This movement of bringing the open into shelter sets the open in the *eidos*, the image, the gestalt.

As thrown projecting-open grounding, Da-sein is the highest actuality in the domain of the imagination, granted that by this term we understand not only a faculty of the soul and not only something transcendental (cf. Kantbook) but rather *enowning [Ereignis]* itself, wherein all *transfiguration* reverberates. (GA65, 312/219)

In the image (*Bild*) as gestalt, the event of the clearing (*Lichtung*) of being crystallizes, takes 'form.' Da-sein founds the realm of the 'imagination' (*Einbildung*) in the things themselves. This founding is a thrown project, hence it intimates a 'world' in its historicity and specificity. The image brings *aspects of a world* to light in the gestalt. The image no less reserves, shelters what is – as opposed to delivering beings over to representation – and therefore *roots what is in the earth*. The *selfhood* of Da-sein is nothing other than the open site of the unfolding of the strife of earth and world: the movement of the self-reserved crystallization of earth and world into the image constitutes the realm of Da-sein as the actualization of 'imagination.' The attunement of measured reserve accepts the 'measure' of an historically founded earth and world, and, attuned to the finitude which this implies, takes on itself the responsibility of decision, that is, of founding the differentiation of being in the There (GA65, 69/48).

The triumph of simulacra, of virtual reality, over the things themselves, and hence the transformation of the vis-à-vis of the site into the interface of animality and the machine, is already anticipated, as we have seen, by Heidegger's thoughts on machination as the integration of the machine and the body. If we follow Heidegger's interpretation of technology as the consummation of metaphysics, the political order of the hyperworld itself belongs to the presencing of the Openness of self-concealment, and more precisely must be thought as its deracination (*Unwesen*). The dis-placement of the Open, and hence the distortion of the incorporation of the image in beings, is thought in its historicity by Heidegger as the triumph of theatricality (GA65, 347/243). The metaphysical root of theatricality, as 'The Age of the World Picture' argues, is the self-certain stage of representational thinking, whereon the phenomena, and the ego itself, must appear in order to be granted being. Thought in terms of the history of metaphysics, what Heidegger calls the 'shaping of the actual as task for the stage-designer' and what is referred to as the triumph of the theatrical (GA65, 347/243) are essential anticipations of the simulated 'worlds' of postmodern electronic 'reality.' The hyperworld is the electronic stage of the image-manipulators and programmers, wherein the singularity (*Einzigkeit*) of the localization of being is dis-integrated and re-incorporated into the generality of relatively few and basic schemata, and the past enters into the distanceless present of competing but in fact in-different discourses. The 'theatrical comes to power' as the deracination (*Unwesen*) of the 'ownmost' (*Wesen*) (GA65, 347/243). Founded in the formalized 'languages' of computation, the hyperworld belongs to the sending of being itself, for herein the *logos* announces itself in the guise of logistics and programmatics. The integrated hyperworld of discourse and the imagebank, precisely because it is devoid of the distance which shelters phenomena, each in its own being, signifies the distortion of the Openness of self-concealment in favour of the shelterless arena of thorough-going availability. If we now recall that the work of art makes manifest the movement of self-concealment, the withdrawal of a being into the delimiting shelter of its own opacity, then it again becomes evident why the artwork is treated as an exemplary instance of the presencing of the Open (UK 49–50/188–9). Insofar as we are drawn into the space the work opens for itself, the possibility of a shift of fundamental attunement to the whole of what is also arises (UK 53/191–2). Attunement to the sheltering self-withdrawal of beings would have to guide all our essential doing and thinking in order for the site of the There to be founded. Beings are thus appropriated to their own (GA65, 348–9/244). The place of technology, and the politics of technology in the 'organization' of the social order would have to be re-thought in terms of the preservation and unfolding of the being of the earth and in acknowledgement of the limits of representational, technicist thinking. This calls for acceptance of the 'place' of humanity in the service of the being of beings. The present 'world order,' insofar as it is governed by technological and 'liberal' claims legitimating the biotechnical exploitation of the earth's genetic resources in the name of increased production and consumption, is only possible in the light of a transparency of beings inscribed by the conceptualization of being (*die Seiendheit*). This order is dependent on the oblivion of the 'simultaneity' of being and beings. In the instant of presencing, being withdraws into the gestalt of beings, thus to grant the shelter of withdrawal from being-present. The primacy of availability as definitive of the being of entities expresses the attunement of mankind and nature in the interface of their mutual challenge and response, their integrated 'actuality.' Each is available, 'on call' for the other: 'subject' and 'object' become integrated functions of one interface. Thus the hyperworld constitutes its own 'space,' or mode of openness, and the attunement proper to the in-different availability of the Same. For despite the variety of what is on offer, what *is* indiscriminately presences as information and sensation. The planetary dimension must in principle undermine the rootedness and temporal singularity of being in beings.

This dimension is structured by the 'reality' of the actual and the conceptual formalization which generates the actual. These discourses submit themselves to the fascination of the immediacy of the actual, thus to attune themselves to an ever-changing present, which nonetheless remains constant in the mode of its presencing. Heidegger raises the question whether, and how, the illusion of the constancy of beingness (*Seiendheit*) as the conceptualization of a reality which 'is' in the immediacy of being-present can be shattered. The self which experiences being in its certainty and immediacy must be broken and come to be anew out of the singularity of the incalculable presencing of being. What presences in this way is the event of appropriation, or enowning (*Ereignis*).

> Finally, however, enowning cannot be re-presented as an 'event' and a 'novelty.' Its truth, i.e., *the* truth, holds sway only as *sheltered* in art, thinking, poetizing, deed – and therefore requires the inabiding of Da-sein, which rejects all illusion of immediacy of mere re-presenting. (GA65, 256/180–1)

This event attunes Da-sein to give it its stand in the midst of beings. In the space thus opened up beings are never actual (*das Wirkliche*) in the sense of being-present:

> *Actual*, i.e., what is [seiend], is only the remembered and what still awaits [Bereite]. Remembering and preparation [Bereitung] open the free-play of the time-space of be-ing, with regard to which thinking must disavow 'presentness' as the heretofore only and sole determination. (GA65, 257/181, modified)

The space of attunement to the temporal sitedness of being, opened up by memory and anticipation of the awaited, first allows the present to presence in its uniqueness (*Einzigkeit*). It is this uniqueness which gives the present its 'stand' in the other beginning. It is still in this context that Heidegger elsewhere raises the question whether Greek tragedy is not to be understood as an originary, history-founding site (GA65, 374/261). The temporality of the site which Greek tragedy opens up generates the shock of an encounter with the presencing of the Open, as incorporated in the work. Can the work, given the aesthetics of production and consumption, still generate its own space within the planetary dimension?

And if not, what kind of state, and what kind of socio-political 'pre-conditions,' would have to exist to allow the work to be a work?

Given that the 'state,' as Heidegger still thought in 1933–4 (GA38, 165), has a role to play, can the renovation of the intimacy of Volk and artwork avoid falling back into the metaphysical nationalism of 'people's art,' organized and ordered from above? Can a different kind of polity be conceived and founded in the finitude of the earth, thus to allow the artwork to emerge out of the strife of earth and world? Does the 'recovery' of the historicity of the earth, understood as the labour of recovery of *the 'native soil' of a people in its geopolitical limits,* open a way to the founding power of the 'art-work'? All of these questions revolve around the finitude and historicity of being as founded in Da-sein and *set to work in the gestalt of beings.* Being discloses itself in the gestalt, that is, in beings, in the plentitude and delimitation of their temporality and locality. Despite their apparent abstraction, these questions fundamentally confront the international world order of technicity and the globalization of measureless production and consumption.

7.3 Limit and Gestalt: Heidegger's Retrieval of Aristotle, the Work of Art, and the Possibility of the Political

Can Heidegger's understanding of the work of art as an in-stantiation of truth serve to reveal fundamental aspects of the nature of the political? Alexander Schwan, among others, has forcefully made the claim that to understand Heidegger's political thinking we must understand his conception of the artwork.[29] In 'The Origin of the Work of Art' Heidegger grants the artwork, together with other founding ways of being, the power to open a 'world' of action and decision, hence to establish a space for political being in the narrow sense (UK 30/170). The work is set to work through its reception, preservation. The truth opened up by a work founds a community in its specific historicity. The 'political,' Schürmann has argued, is 'situated in the confluence of words, things, and deeds': 'From the topological viewpoint [of the historicity of being], relative to the loci of presencing, the political is the transcendental opening in which words, things, and deeds find their site, it is the "locality" [Ortschaft] of linguistic, pragmatic, and practical loci.'[30] This opening reveals *the origin* of the confluence of words, things, and deeds, *as an event,* as opposed to a 'principle that dominates society by organizing it.'[31] I will argue that one way the event of the political is opened up is through the art-work as event. In the presencing of the work, thing and word and deed arising out of one common attunement to being mutually condition each other and come to be articulated. Dauenhauer writes that the political is the space opened up and held open by 'the domain of projective speech' rather than by 'fabrication.'[32] To this degree the work already implicates the political. Evidently this thesis necessitates not only the neutralization of the claim that the political is thereby reduced to aesthetics, but also deconstruction of the metaphysics of origin, thus to recover the origin of the work as event.

I argue that Heidegger's retrieval of *eidos* in the *Republic,* and of the *energeia* of Aristotle, allow for an understanding of being (*ousia*) which informs the artwork as event. The site of this event is one essential way in which the site of the political is opened up and structured. The event of the work, which includes its 'reception' by a community, grants communal experience a 'form,' understood as the structure of its historicity. Heidegger's retrieval of *eidos* and *energeia,* therefore, seeks to uncover the historicity of being. Insofar as the work gives site to historicity, it enacts the site of the political.

What are the questions regarding the art-work especially pertinent to a reflection on the possibility of the political? Let us consider those of (*i*) the relation of art and truth: the answer to this question will determine whether the nature and experience of art have any place or priority in the constitution of the community as the locality of unconcealment; (*ii*) the self-identity of the work: for given that the artwork has a founding character, the quality of its self-identity, together with other founding modes of thought, will constitute the self-identity of the community; (*iii*) the relation of the 'origin' (*Ursprung*) of the work to the 'origin' of the political.

Lacoue-Labarthe holds that the mimesis of Form and copy, as exemplified by the artwork, serves Heidegger as a model of the identity of a people with itself.[33] The truth of the polity, therefore, is inscribed into a fundamentally Platonic discourse of re-presentation. It matters little that Plato's philosophy is inverted insofar as a people posits for itself a Form which they *will themselves* to be, for the model of the polity which emerges is still that of self-production. The polity wills to produce itself according to a form which serves the process of production as paradigm. The coming-to-be of the polity, therefore, is modelled on both aesthetic and technical discourse. Aesthetic, insofar as the form is posited as the ideal to be re-presented; and technical, because the representation is to be produced by reference to the already-given of the form.

The thesis of Heidegger's covert implication in 'national aestheticism,' which Lacoue-Labarthe has made popular and perhaps best represents,[34] calls for deconstruction along the following lines. The mimetic model of Form and copy must be deconstructed to reveal its derivation from the more fundamental truth of unconcealment. Reference to Heidegger's 'Plato's Doctrine of Truth' and to 'On the Essence of Truth' will allow us to see how Heidegger proposes to retrieve the presentation of truth in the *eidos* from the metaphysics of representation. This prepares the ground for the deconstruction of the mimetic theory of art. And granted that Heidegger does not define art mimetically, his philosophy of art cannot serve as a model for a mimetic theory of the political. Hence we may reject the claim that Heidegger determines the polity according to the truth of representation and a paradigmatic discourse of production. Given that the identity and stability of the work of art, moreover, is not defined by its representation of the form which it reproduces, the claim that Heidegger understands the self-identity of a people to be defined by the undifferentiated unity of a monoethnic culture may also be put into question. For according to the thesis of national aestheticism, mono-ethnicity is the ideal form of the *Volk*, which the founders of the polity propose to produce.[35] Schwan's conclusion, later re-iterated by Harries, that the concept of the work implicates a totalitarian politics because the polity is modelled on the unitary idea of the work, becomes equally questionable.[36]

The thesis of national aestheticism, together with the concept of art on which it is founded, implicates the imposition of a form on a material. Heidegger's retrieval of the fundamental 'categories' of Aristotle's 'physics,' as undertaken in 'On the Being and Conception of *Phusis* in Aristotle's *Physics* B, 1,' also places this concept of the artwork into question. At stake is the character of the self-originating movement (*kinesis*) of *phusis* into form (*morphe*) so as to unfold its inherent *telos* within the limits (*peras*) of its proper being. Key to Heidegger's analysis is his deconstruction of the substance ontology of *ousia* in order to recover the meaning of being (*ousia*) as the instantiation of being in beings. The recovery of being-as-founded in beings implies the post-metaphysical retrieval of *energeia* and *entelecheia*. These founding words of Western metaphysics are now reinterpreted as being's (*phusis*) setting itself into the limit of a being. This interpretation reflects Heidegger's attempt to recover from Aristotle a non-metaphysical concept of form: form as *morphe* implicates form-in-being to signify the sited, historical presencing of being in and through beings.

Heidegger claims that the work of art, as work (*ergon*), sets unconcealment into the limit of the 'Gestalt' (UK 52/191). I argue that the fundamental 'categories' of the artwork essay are ultimately founded in Heidegger's retrieval of an Aristotlean ontology of the delimitation and instantiation of being (*ousia*) in beings. I will show that this implies that the work, in Heidegger's terms, means 'gestalt,' and that gestalt, freed of its metaphysical determinations, signifies the simultaneous movement of unconcealment *and* of sheltering withdrawal from conceptualization, as fixed in the limit of a being in its locality and temporality. Although implicit in Heidegger's early Aristotle lectures (GA33), this comes fully to light only *after* the composition of the artwork essay, in the Aristotle essay of 1939.

The work of art is one, exemplary way, in which the movement and differentiated unity of an entity brings itself into the limits of its own 'form.' The character of the differentiated unity of the gestalt, however, does not derive from the stamping of a form on a 'material.' The gestalt has the mode of being of the movement of unconcealment and withdrawal. As the in-corporation of the movement of unconcealment the work does not offer a paradigmatic model for a polity, but it allows the articulation of the *Volk* and the polity through the rites of unconcealment. As such the *Volk* no more has an undifferentiated self-identity with itself than does the work of art, conceived as an event of the unfolding of *phusis* according to the law of its inherent limits. Given that the *polis* is co-constituted by the work in the event of the work's in-stantiation of unconcealment, the polity is determined and limited by concepts of locality and temporality fundamentally at odds with subjectivity and the universalism of the modern state. Heidegger's retrieval of *phusis* in the Aristotle essay, therefore, founds not only the fundamental terms of 'The Origin of the Work of Art,' but also opens a way to the post-metaphysical understanding of the political as implicit in Heidegger's reflections on art.

7.3.1 The Retrieval of Eidos and the Question of Truth

The hierarchy of the true and less true which the allegory of the cave in book 10 of the *Politeia* develops is the basis of the idea of mimesis which has dominated the tradition. Let us see how Heidegger treats this question in 'Plato's Doctrine of Truth.' Truth is understood comparatively as a movement away from the image-world of the cave toward the truth of the Ideas (PL 218/258).[37] The movement out of the cave offers an allegory of the movement toward a more correct way of seeing. The main thrust of Heidegger's essay is to undertake a deconstruction of the truth of correctness or correspondence in order to reveal the possibility of correspondence in the site of unconcealment, or *aletheia*, itself.

Given the understanding of mimesis implicated in the correspondence notion of truth, art makes-manifest, not the Forms themselves, but an image. The work of art is a mere reflection of true being.[38] The first movement of the allegory is away from re-presentations of the Ideas back to the Ideas. This implies that art, as an image, points beyond itself to the Idea, or in modern terms, to the concepts or discourses which determine the truth of art. Hence, in Derrida's terms, the *parergon* is the condition of possibility of the *ergon*.[39]

Yet Plato's relation to the truth of art remains ambivalent, for the *Phaedrus* tells us that beauty itself awakens in us a remembrance of true being.[40] This ambivalence regarding the nature of the manifestation of being through beings is the starting point of Heidegger's reflection on Plato's 'doctrine' of truth. In his consideration of the cave analogy, Heidegger begins not with the shadows in the cave, but with the things themselves, as they show themselves in the light of being. The things show a 'face': they present themselves. The self-presentation of the thing to sight reveals its *eidos* or Idea, which allows us to grasp its manifold manifestations (PL 212/254). According to Heidegger's account, self-presentation already implicates an ambivalence inscribed in mimesis itself: mimesis is both a *movement* of self-presentation and the *imposition* of a form, the form of the Idea, on the entity. In the latter case, mimesis indicates the relation of Form or original and a copy, or mere image; in other terms, the relation of being and seeming. However, given that we conceive the Idea as presenting-itself, as a movement, as a process of making-itself-manifest, then the emphasis falls on the disjunction between (*i*) the unconcealment of the Idea, which allows us to see it at all; and (*ii*) the darkening of the Idea as it presents itself in this particular thing. This disjunction is quite distinct from that of copy and original. For now the thing (or the artwork) is not a copy, but an in-stantiation of the Idea, which darkens (conceals) the Idea in its unadulterated non-particularity. In book 10, the mirror is said 'to make' (*poiein*) the image.[41] In Heidegger's terms, 'making' can only mean 'bringing-forth' into manifestation. What is brought-forth, Plato avers, darkens the Form. On the evidence of the *Phaedrus*, however, it is equally possible to hold that the Idea shines most brightly through the beauty of a particular form.

The allegory of the cave consists not only in the movement out of the cave toward the light of being, but also in the movement of the liberated cave-dweller back into the cave to free the fellow prisoners. This movement mirrors the process of education (*paideia*). As *Bildung* (education), this process gives form to the self-manifestation of the Ideas to the mind. In an essential turn of Heidegger's argument, *Bildung* as education is interpreted as the unfolding of the image (*Bild*) into self-manifestation (PL 213–16/254–7). The movement of *paideia*, which is the movement back to being, passes by way of the image. We can conceive of the image as a reflection of the Idea. We aim at the Idea itself, and in respect to it the image is merely a copy: the image is re-presentative of the already-given and atemporal. However, Heidegger's retrieval of *paideia* as *Bildung* opens another way: now the emphasis falls on the image as the unfolding of the presencing *and withdrawal* of being. This other possibility is overlooked by the argument for national aestheticism.[42] Education through the image instigates the transformation of our whole being into the openness of being (PL 216/257). The open manifests itself through the image to constitute a communal realm. In Schürmann's terms, being 'symbolizes itself in the entity,' to open up a space of unconcealment.[43] This openness, however, is not to be conceived as the transparency of reason. For the image shelters the presencing and withdrawal from presencing of being. Not only is the image conceived as the event of the unconcealment of being, rather than a copy, but the 'darkening' of being in the image is re-interpreted as a withdrawal from presencing. In the movement of withdrawal or concealment at the heart of *aletheia*, the being of a being *is sheltered from the grasp of conceptual representation*. According to 'Vom Wesen der Wahrheit,'

> Precisely in the levelling and planing of this omniscience [of representation], this mere knowing, the openedness of beings gets flattened out into the apparent nothingness of what is no longer even a matter of indifference, but rather is simply forgotten. (WW 190/129)

As the sheltering in-stantiation of the presencing of being in a being, the image represents not at all. In fact, the full nature of *aletheia* as the sheltering unconcealment of beings realizes itself by founding itself in the historicity of the image, in the gestalt. Insofar as unconcealment is set into beings, and beings incorporate the movement of withdrawal from representation, beings are defined by an immanent limit, which shelters them from the grasp of representation to reserve their being.

The polity and *paideia*, opened up by way of the image, which belongs to what Schürmann calls the symbolic realm,[44] are essentially related. The space of the political is held open by the incorporation of being in the gestalt of beings, where gestalt enacts the unconcealment of sheltering reserve. This implies, following Heidegger's reading of Plato, that the 'political' announces a movement of withdrawal from re-presentation and objectification, hence from socio-technical discourses, including the discourse of collective subjectivity. Gestalt incorporates being-as-limit. Given that the site of the political is held open by being setting itself into gestalt, the political must be defined as the enactment of limit and delimitation.

Heidegger's retrieval of *aletheia* in this text already implicates the founding of *aletheia*. The retrieval of *aletheia* and of the *eidos* mutually support each other. This becomes possible because *eidos* and idea are re-interpreted in terms of the image through which the delimited gestalt of being shines forth. Better said, being 'is' as the movement of presencing in the gestalt – it is not the atemporal, ahistorical, and most general concept under which all beings fall. For the openness of being, into which the liberated cave-dweller emerges, is 'not the unlimited of a mere expanse,' but the delimitation of illumination, which shines forth in beings under the light of the sun. Seeing, in fact, only becomes free in grasping and being grasped by the 'secure boundaries' of things standing forth into appearance (PL 219–20/259). The light of being shows itself not only *through delimited things, but as the limit* which gives beings their being. For whereas the unity of presencing and withdrawal is always delimited, the unlimited strictly speaking has no being (PL 225/263).

Yet 'unconcealment goes under the yoke of the Idea' (PL 228/265). The atemporal stability of the Idea determines the measure of the true. This means that the open site of unconcealment is itself concealed in favour of the truth of correctness, or correspondence to the Idea. The correspondence of perception to the Forms manifest in entities founds the correspondence theory of truth (PL 228/265). Following Aristotle, this means that the site of truth now shifts to the statement as the expression of correspondence to what is (PL 230/266). The concept is the light or 'essence' through which the being of a thing manifests itself. As statement and concept become the site of truth, being is uprooted. Secondly, however, the occultation of unconcealment means that the delimitation of the *eidos* in its coming to presence is interpreted in reference to the stability, atemporality of the Idea. In this way the site (*aletheia*) and the structure (gestalt) of the movement of presencing and withdrawal are occluded to allow the triumph of the stable shining forth of the Idea. In political terms this means, as Schürmann has argued on his own grounds, the reign of metaphysical principles which found action.[45] The triumph of the socio-technical discourses of the modern state derives from the principial.

The movement of disclosure, which Heidegger understands in its historical specificity, is the condition of the correctness or incorrectness of a statement about an object. Subject and object must already stand in an open realm of unconcealment in order for a statement about an object to become possible. The question of the 'essence' of truth, as Heidegger develops it in 'On the Essence of Truth,' revolves around the deconstruction of the metaphysical 'site' of truth in the statement, in order to lead us back to the site of the disclosure of being and our attunement to it. The 'essence of truth' now denotes the historical unfolding (*wesen*) of the unconcealment of the being of beings (truth). 'Essence' in its primordial sense is no longer fixed in the concept, and the concept is no longer fixed in the statement, as the unchanging, ahistorical nature of an entity. Because the essence of truth is understood as the historical unfolding of unconcealment, the correctness (*stimmen*) of statements becomes derivative of our attunement (*Stimmung*) to unconcealment. For only insofar as we are *attuned* to the movement of the disclosure of being can we *comport* ourselves toward beings. The way of this comportment, in turn, is the condition of our making propositional *statements* about what is revealed of beings in our attunement to being (WW 180–3/120–2).

The concept of reason to which the statement gives expression itself presupposes a certain attunement (e.g., a belief in the stability and self-identity of what is). The relatedness of subject and object which comes to word in the statement (understood as evidence of a particular kind of comportment) is therefore founded on the preconceptual attunement of a tradition to being. Hence the representational relation is grounded in what cannot be fully represented, is grounded in the ek-static openness of Da-sein to being. The mode and structure of this ek-static openness constitute the measure of our comportment to things. Our relation to nature as object of science and technology, as a 'natural resource,' or as a manifestation of the gods, for example, is founded in our attunement to the disclosure of being. Statements about 'nature' cannot found this realm of disclosure, nor can they found our attunement to it, but are thoroughly dependent on what shows itself in its light.

The disclosedness of being must site itself, that is, it must become historical in the sense of founding a history (WW 186–7/126–7). One way this happens is through the in-corporation of truth in a work; another way is through the polity-founding decisions of leadership. Thus the 'sitedness' of truth as unconcealment means that truth is articulated. For example, through *works* of art – the classical ballet is one such articulation, modern expressionist dance another; the space of the gothic cathedral 'in-corporates' unconcealment in one way, the space of the baroque in another.

The act of founding a polity is equally grounded in a particular attunement to unconcealment. A political constitution would articulate and 'incorporate' a mode of unconcealment. For this reason Heidegger's reflection on the essence of truth, as the attunement of a specific unconcealment of being which founds the being of a particular people, rather than 'humanity' in general, is already a reflection on the 'essence' of the political. The 'people' who thus come into being, however, should not be conceived as a collective subject. For insofar as the work of art, for example, is a work – hence giving structure to unconcealment – it is not an object for a 'subject,' for it throws the subject as its own self-certain ground into question. *Who* sees? is the question. The viewer comes to be through the encounter with the work. The concept of 'people' which Heidegger's understanding of the essence of truth implicates, therefore, is not to be found in a notion of collective subjectivity and identity. The essence of the political is enacted in the perpetual re-founding of the site of attunement in the gestalt of the image, in rite and ritual, for only thus does a 'people' come to be and hold itself in being. This implies what Schürmann calls 'symbolic praxis,' that is, the political realm where word, thing and action cohere.[46] Only in this sense would I concur with Schürmann that Heidegger holds an 'an-archaic' (non-principial) concept of the political.

7.3.2 The Mode of Being of the Work of Art

The work of art is one essential way in which unconcealment takes gestalt. In the first instance, therefore, it pertains to determine the mode of presencing of the work, how its mode of presencing is distinct from other, allied modes, and what the rank of art is in the polity as a way of founding unconcealment. Following Heidegger we may distinguish a number of modes of the presence of a 'work' (for example, of a Communion cup): (*i*) The 'thing' – The cup in the communion service 'communicates' the possibilities for being of the ritual in which the believer participates. This experience would be defined by both our antiquarian and our 'monumental' historical being, in Nietzsche's terms. (*ii*) The 'object' – The cup conceived as the target of historical research, which investigates the material and socio-historical causes which brought it into being, as well as investigating its formal 'aesthetic' qualities. The object (may be) integrated into a narrative defined by the categories of historiography (cause-effect, agent, intention, evidence, etc.). Insofar as the cup is in principle objectified, it can become 'evidence' for an historical 'fact.' (*iii*) The 'function' – The cup in this mode is taken as a signifier of value in the art market. It loses the relative autonomy of a self-subsisting object. The cup's 'presence' (the being it has) is dependent on the economies of sale and resale of art objects of a certain historical period. As a function, for example, of the tourist industry, the cup takes the measure of its being from the 'interest' it arouses, the revenues it generates.

Are these modes of presence mutually exclusive? The museum, as a scientific institution, and as a tourist site, would allow the cup to appear alternatively as object and as function. Churches themselves are tourist sites, and an integral part of the tourist industry. In this case, the cup would appear almost simultaneously in the mutually exclusive perspectives of the believer and the tourist. Perhaps 'postmodernism' initiates the epoch of the incipient triumph of the merely 'functional' presence of entities. Information storage and processing technologies would be the most visible sign of the re-inscription of 'things' and 'objects' as a data-base of 'signifiers' on call, and of history of a reserve stock of images. What place would be reserved for the *work* of art in the midst of the functional reduction of entities?

In 'The Origin of the Work of Art,' Heidegger first engages this question by way of a distinction between the work, the 'mere' thing, and equipment. The purpose of this distinction is to establish the priority of rank of the artwork as founding mode of the unconcealment of being: the being of thing and equipment is revealed by and through the work as a founding site. All three kinds of entity exhibit the self-containment of resting-in-itself (*Insichruhen*) (UK 13/154). This already indicates that the goal of the essay is the recovery of *phusis*, for *phusis* manifests itself as self-reserved unconcealment. These entities, however, also evidence the self-differentiation of *phusis*: for while the thing is self-shaping out of *phusis* (*Eigenwüchsig*), equipment is not. It is rather a human form of production, based on a paradigm, and a mode of *techne* in the narrow sense. Following *Being and Time*, moreover, we know that equipment is defined by the referential context of the world which determines it: equipment serves the structure of an in-order to (SZ, sec. 16). In the artwork essay, Heidegger therefore establishes the being of equipment in its 'handiness' as resting in its serviceability. Serviceability, in turn, presupposes reliability (UK 19/161). Given that equipment is integrated into the references of its in-order-to, it lacks the self-sufficiency (*selbst genügsames Anwesen*) which characterizes both the mere thing of nature and the artwork (UK 13/154). Does the work of art also have a self-shaping quality by analogy with entities arising directly out of *phusis*? To propose that it does would be to hold that the work has its *arche* of *kinesis* in itself, and that it is not essentially a paradigmatic *techne*. The 'origin' of art would be a mode of self-reserving unconcealment itself, not the 'making' of 'man.' Without our entering into this question in any more detail for the moment, it is evident that the starting point of Heidegger's reflections on art presupposes an understanding of *phusis* as the movement of the differentiated unconcealment of beings. Based on *Being and Time* and 'The Origin,' and extrapolating from these texts, these distinctions may be schematized as in Schema I.

Schema I – Modes of presencing of 'thinghood'

	Gathering	Handiness	Objectivity	Function
Mere thing	*Phusis*[a]	–	Classical science	Quantum science[b]
Equipment	Heirloom	Ready-to-hand	Present-at-hand	Economic signifier
Artwork	Locus of community	–	Aesthetic object	Aesthetic 'value'

[a]Self-contained, self-shaping self-sufficiency
[b]Cf. Heidegger, 'Question of Technology.'

Yet the relation of the artwork and *phusis* is not immediately evident in the essay. The retrieval of *phusis* calls for a prior deconstruction of the metaphysical concept of the thing, and in particular, of the substance interpretation of being (*ousia*) which underlies them. Heidegger in fact distinguishes three related concepts of the being of the thing: (*i*) the thing as the unity of substance and its accidents (UK 7/149); (*ii*) the thing as the unity of form (*morphe*) and matter (*hyle*) (UK 11/152–3); (*iii*) the thing as *aistheton*, or the unity of a manifold given to sense (UK 10/151). The second interpretation fundamentally derives from the first, because the form-matter distinction presupposes the substance interpretation of *ousia*. A form is imposed on matter. The unity of a manifold, in turn, posits subjectivity itself as the *hypokeimenon*, or the underlying 'substance' which grants unity to sense. The task Heidegger sets himself, therefore, is the deconstruction of *ousia* as substance and hence of the form-matter schema of the thing. The first movement of this deconstruction is to show that the form-matter schema does not pre-eminently derive from an interpretation of the thing at all, but rather from the experience of equipment, from whence it is carried over to both thing and work. As I have already indicated, Heidegger shows that the form-matter determination of equipment distorts the being of this kind of entity as well. It does this by abstracting equipment from the referential context of its world, in which terms alone it has its being as a way of becoming-present. For the choice of material and form, as causes of a piece of equipment, are guided by the final cause of reliable serviceability. This final cause, in turn, relies on the quality of resting-in-itself of the thingliness of the 'matter' from which equipment is made (UK 20/160–1).

Heidegger's approach to the work of art has led us from the thingliness of the work back to the metaphysical determination of the mere thing and from the form-matter definition of the thing back to equipment from which this model derives. I have indicated that Heidegger deconstructs the form-matter schema to arrive at the serviceability and reliability of equipment as its proper mode of being. But how does Heidegger make this manifest? How, in effect, is the world, or the context of intelligibility, of equipment revealed? The way Heidegger chooses to iluminate the being of equipment is through the work of art (UK 17/158): the elucidation of van Gogh's painting of a pair of peasant shoes brings a world and an earth to light (UK 19/159–60). The painting reveals the earth of the peasant world through the thingliness of the shoes as equipment. Yet what equipment is, as one mode of the manifestation of the unity of earth and world, the work of art itself reveals. Through the work of art the being of equipment, as well as the thingliness of the mere thing, is made manifest. The work, moreover, reveals the unity of reliability and the resting-in-itself of the equipment's thingliness as the unity of earth and world. As the revelation of the being of this entity, the work of art is granted a priority of rank in terms of in-corporating the event of unconcealment (UK 24/165), which means that the movement of *phusis* is brought to light. Unconcealment (truth) is said to be set to work in the work (UK 68/207). In the 'setting,' or bringing to a stand, of the event of truth, Heidegger's formulation already points to the character of *phusis* as he develops it in the Aristotle essay: *phusis* is understood as *en-ergon*, hence as being-set in a gestalt. *Phusis* is *morphe*, *morphe* the movement of bringing being into the gestalt (UK 69/209).

Therefore the work cannot be defined by reference to its thingly substratum (UK 23/164). For the form-matter and substance conception of the thing presuppose the event of truth: being understood as substance (*ousia*) is derivative of the temporalization of being (*aletheia*) in ways Heidegger's commentary on the *Physics* B, 1, will clarify for us. For the moment, it is important to see that as the in-corporation of the event of unconcealment, the work cannot be determined in terms of the atemporality of substance ontology. To determine the work as the imposition of a form on a material substratum, moreover, is to misread it as a kind of equipment, for the form-matter schema derives from the being of equipment. The aesthetic formulation of the question of art, in fact, is determined by metaphysics, hence by the governing understanding of *ousia* as abiding presence (UK 24/164). Since the work is an exemplary way of revealing the being of beings (UK 24/164–5), the question concerning the nature of the work arises in terms of the Greek founding of metaphysics. The substance ontology of *ousia*, in effect, would have to be deconstructed to allow Heidegger's claim that the work sets truth to work in the work. For the movement of unconcealment unfolds the presencing of being (*ousia*) in beings. Since the claims of 'The Origin of the Work of Art' are implicitly founded in the deconstruction of the substance interpretation of *ousia*, it becomes necessary to read this essay in conjunction with Heidegger's interpretation of Aristotle's *Physics* B, 1, to which I shall now turn. For ease of reference, I will refer to the marginal pagination of the *Wegmarken* text, because this is the pagination used by the Thomas Sheehan translation.

7.3.3 The Artwork in the Light of Phusis

Let me prepare the place of Heidegger's 'On the Being and Conception of *Phusis* in Aristotle's *Physics* B, 1' (BCP) by reference of these reflections: (*i*) art and technology are two allied ways of bringing *phusis* to light; (*ii*) art as imitation and the realm of aesthetics are founded on the matter-form interpretation of *phusis* which is deconstructed here; (*iii*) the artwork as the strife of earth and world, set in the gestalt, thus to let the singularity of the sited truth of being appear, is founded on the understanding of *phusis* as *morphe* and *entelecheia* developed in this essay; (*iv*) the artwork is not *phusis*, but one way of bringing *phusis* to light, and in fact one way which is necessary and exemplary for the technological epoch – the artwork is an essential *techne* as a way of knowing (*Wissen*) which discloses *phusis* to set truth forth in the gestalt (UK 45–6/184–5); and (*v*) Heidegger distinguishes between *phusis* in the narrow sense as things-of-nature and *phusis* as being, with the aim of recovering being as *peras, morphe, energeia, ousia,* and *entelecheia.* Once the basic movement and argument of the Aristotle essay have been established, it can be brought to bear on the artwork essay to determine the place of the work in the differentiated unconcealment of being.

7.3.3.1 KINESIS AND METABOLE

It is evident, Aristotle claims, that all things which take their being from *phusis* are determined by being-moved.[47] This serves Heidegger also as his point of departure (BCP 313/225). Beings from *phusis* have their *arche* of *kinesis* within themselves, moreover, as opposed to having the 'originating ordering' (*arche*) of their unfolding (*kinesis*) in some other being (BCP 316–7/227).[48] It is essential to note that Heidegger interprets *arche* as the ordering principle of a movement into the proper unfolding of an entity, in effect, that which abides to bring it into its *telos* as an individualized being (BCP 316–7, 321/227–8, 231). *Arche* is not merely the 'push' which sets something into motion. *Kinesis*, in turn, includes every form of transformation, or *metabole*, and not only or even pre-eminently change of place (BCP 318/228–9). Rest, in turn, is only to be thought in terms of movement, for the unmoving – the number three, for example – cannot be said to 'rest' (BCP 317/227). Beings which take their movement from *phusis* come to stand in constancy, according to their own inherent *arche*: '*Phusis* is what is responsible for the fact that the constant has an individualized standing-on-its-own' (BCP 316/227). The constant implicates, in the first instance, 'that which stands-"forth,"' and secondly, 'the enduring, the lasting' (BCP 316/227). Crucial to Heidegger's argument as a whole is that the constancy of a being from *phusis* stands-forth as that individualized being. And as such, it takes its being from the self-differentiating movement of the 'form,' or *morphe*, proper to it. The constancy it has is determined by the law of its own temporalizing, hence by its *arche* of *kinesis*, understood as its proper rhythm. *Morphe*, therefore, is not to be understood as the purdurance of an atemporal 'form.' The sense of *morphe* as the standing-forth of a being out of its proper rhythm of unfolding also determines that of *Gestalt* as it is used in 'The Origin of the Work of Art' (UK 69/209). An artifact, conversely, is a kind of entity, not directly from *phusis*, which does not have the *arche* of its *kinesis* in itself: for the pro-duction (*techne*) of an artifact is guided and governed by the form (*eidos*) which is seen beforehand by the producer. Therefore the *arche* of the artifact lies in the seeing of the *eidos* by the producer (BCP 320–2/230–1).[49] We may conclude that an artifact is not *morphe*, not gestalt, in the full and proper sense. Nor is the work of art, in turn, an artifact. This is not to say, evidently, that a work derives from *phusis* in the manner of a plant or an animal, but that it is a distinct way of being through which *phusis* is brought to stand as gestalt. We may already suppose that the human subject is not, in Heidegger's regard, the 'origin' of the work. Heidegger rather holds that art is the origin of artist and artwork (cf. UK 1–2/143–4). But how can 'art' be an 'origin' except as a movement (*kinesis*) of the self-unfolding of *phusis* in which human being, attuned to *phusis*, responds and participates? *Phusis* itself is the origin. The origin 'originates' as the event of appropriation of being to beings, which apportions to each its proper limit. The origin in this sense is the common origin of both art and the political.

It is essential to distinguish the non- or post-metaphysical sense of *arche* from its metaphysical determination. Schürmann defines this determination in terms of the 'primacy of production': with 'the pair *arche* and *eidos*, "pro-ducing" definitively ceases to mean "bring forth into the open" and henceforth coincides with "fabricating," and the work of leading an *eidos* to complete visibility.'[50] Heidegger's objective is a retrieval of *arche* from its metaphysical definition, as inscribed in Aristotle's text. But he is by no means intent on an abandonment of the *arche* of beings. For the *arche*, in Heidegger's sense, is *what gives shelter to the singular unfolding of a being as this being* – it has to be understood in terms of the sheltering unconcealment, or *lethe*, inherent in the event of truth. The *arche* is what shelters from 'complete visibility,' be it the being of the work, of a thing, or of the *Volk*. The withdrawal into shelter of *lethe* is what Schürmann overlooks, and this, therefore, leads to his misconception of the weight and place of the question of *arche* in Heidegger's thinking.

7.3.3.2 *OUSIA* AND *PERAS*

Aristotle holds that all entities from *phusis* have the being of *ousia*.[51] This is the point of departure for a decisive step in Heidegger's argument (BCP 329/237): the deconstruction of the 'essence' and substance-concept of *ousia* as the underlying, the *hypokeimenon* (BCP 330–1/238). This deconstruction serves to bring *ousia* as the limitedness of becoming-present in a being to light. Heidegger begins with a return to the historically determined usage of *ousia* as distinct from, and yet related to, the terminological usage. According to the principles of Heidegger's hermeneutic practice, the terminological concept emerges from the life-world of its everyday usage. Here Heidegger is aided by the fact that *ousia* in its common signification as 'house and holdings,' 'real estate,' finds commensurate expression in the German *Anwesen*. *Anwesen* indeed designates *das Vorliegende* or that which lies present, and in this way corresponds to the sense of *ousia* as *hypokeimenon*. In everyday usage, however, *Anwesen* equally means, with the Greek *ousia*, 'estate' as house and holdings. Such an *Anwesen* has the 'presence' of its own self-determined and limited gestalt, in the character of a villa or chateau, for example. What do these reflections win for Heidegger's argument? This: that the lying-present of *phusis* as *ousia* is *in something lying-present: ousia* presences in be-coming-present in the presence of a particular, determined thing. In this sense, *phusis* as *ousia* is *morphe*, presencing-in-gestalt.

At this turn in his argument, Heidegger, following Aristotle, is forced to take into account the challenge offered by Antiphon's interpretation of *ousia* as the unchanging, elemental which underlies all change, thus to constitute the being of the changeable (BCP 335/242).[52] Because the non-elemental, Antiphon claims, has the character of *rhythmos* as the 'articulating, impressing, fitting and forming' of the elemental, hence as a departure from the original stability of the elements out of which all things are formed, therefore non-elemental *rhythmos* is less in being (BCP 337/243). *Rhythmos* and *diathesis* (measure, proportion, rhythm; disposition, arrangement) are conceived to be merely temporal modifications of primordial being. *Phusis* is the 'primary formless which sustains everything that is'; only the formlessness of the elemental truly is *ousia*, is being (BCP 337/243).

Is *ousia*, therefore, as elemental, limitless in duration, and unformed, or is *phusis*, as *ousia*, emergence into the limit of a *rhythmos*, wherein this limit alone gives the kind of self-grounded stability which is proper to the being of *phusis*? But what are we to understand by 'limit' (*Grenze*), *peras*?

> Limit is always that which limits, determines, gives footing and stability, that by which and in which something begins and is. Whatever is present and absent without limit has *of itself* no becoming-present, and it deteriorates into instability. (BCP 339/245)

The *peras* of *ousia* is what allows beings to become present of themselves, whereas non-*ousia* becomes 'present *only* on the basis of something that is already present' (BCP 339/245). At issue is the presencing of an entity out of its own *arche*, as opposed to its re-presentation by way of the 'elemental,' understood as the conceptual field which generates it. The conceptual-elemental may well be limitless in duration. Why, therefore is it not *ousia*, not more fully in being than the merely temporal and limited? Because the criterion of *ousia* is not *unlimited duration, as opposed to the transitory, but rather the owness or non-ownness of a being*, depending on whether it presences out of its own *arche* or not.

The digital recording, or re-presentation, of a musical performance, for example, offers an in principle unlimited duration of its availability for repeated listening. As a studio production, moreover, it offers a more 'perfect' realization of the score, freed of all the 'accidents' of live performance. Yet it lacks the fundamental character which the singularity of a live performance brings to light: the digital recording does not have the *arche* of its unfolding in itself, for what it is, is determined by the technical apparatus of the conditions of its production. Hence the studio recording is a product of *techne*, governed by the 'paradigm' of the perfect realization of the score by technical means. The live performance, conversely, precisely through the unrepeatable singularity of its presencing, has the potential of bringing of itself its own gestalt (*morphe*) to light. As such, a live performance, whatever its imperfections may be, can unfold the *arche* of a musical score in a way in which in principle a studio digitalization cannot.

The studio production would have, in Heidegger's words, '*of itself* no becoming-present.' It becomes 'present *only* on the basis of something that is already present' (BCP 339/245). The digital program and the entire technical apparatus of the studio constitutes the 'already present' which generates the musical 'product.' This product, moreover, would not be a 'work,' in Heidegger's sense, for the *arche* of its movement into presence, into the unhidden, does not lie in itself. Yet it is precisely being-moved – as *becoming-present in unhiddenness* to take a stand in its own, proper *morphe* – which the being of *ousia* is. *Ousia* is in-stantiation: the movement of taking a stand in the gestalt. As such it is at the furthest remove from the elemental formlessness of unending duration which defines Antiphon's understanding of *ousia* as substance and essence (BCP 342–3/247).

7.3.3.3 MORPHE AND HYLE

Morphe 'has the honour of determining the Being of *phusis*' (BCP 343/248).[53] It remains to see why this is so, and why *morphe* should not be interpreted as the 'form' which is imposed on a material (BCP 344–5/249). *Morphe* is said to be a '*placing* [Gestellung] *in the appearance*'; as such it is 'being-moved, *kinesis*, which "moment" is radically lacking in the concept of form' (BCP 347, 346/251, 250). The movement of an entity from *phusis* into the appearance in which it holds itself for a time (the *Jeweiligkeit* of the being; BCP 346/250) constitutes the mode of being of *ousia* as *morphe*. As *das Jeweilige* – that which holds itself in the appearance for its own proper time – *morphe* denotes the *mode of temporalization* of a being. By appearance, we understand *eidos*. Consequently '*morphe* must be understood from *eidos*' (BCP 345/249). We recall that in 'Plato's Doctrine of Truth' Heidegger proposes to retrieve a sense of *eidos* as the shining-forth of the being of a being, as opposed to a manifestation of the stability of the Idea. Now Heidegger insists that the 'appearance and the placing into appearance must not be taken Platonically as standing apart unto themselves, but rather as the Being in which an individual being stands at the moment' (BCP 351/254). The *eidos* is 'the aspect' which a being 'offers and only can offer because the being has been put forth into this appearance and, standing in it, becomes present of itself – in a word, is' (BCP 345/249). The *eidos*, therefore, is not the stability of what is common to many appearances and thus 'something,' as Plato held, 'present in itself' (BCP 345/249) – it is rather the particularity of a being's becoming-present as this being.

We have noted that *morphe* must be understood in terms of *eidos*; *eidos*, however, in relation to the *logos* (345/249).[54] Thus *logos*, as the saying which addresses a being as *this being*, is a constituent of the placing into appearance which *morphe* is. It is by way of the *logos*-quality of *morphe* that the character of *hyle* also comes to light. In this way Heidegger counters the interpretation of *hyle* as the 'matter,' or 'raw material,' on which a form is imposed (BCP 350–1/253). 'Aristotle characterizes *hule* as *to dunamei*. *Dunamis* means the capacity, or better the appropriateness for' (BCP 350/253). As such *hyle* is the appropriate or 'orderable' as that which has been brought into *morphe* in the gathering of a *logos*. In the *logos* the unity of the movement of the appropriated (*hyle*) and the placing (*morphe*) into the stability of an appearance (*eidos*) is brought to word, i.e., unconcealed. For it is only in the placing-into-appearance that *hyle* also comes to light. As the mere formlessness of an 'underlying material,' *hyle as hyle* would never show itself in its specificity as being-appropriate and in its appropriateness-for. In its being-appropriated-for, *hyle* is always individualized. As such, *hyle* is not the formlessness of 'material' on which a form is imposed, for the form-matter schema occludes the locality and temporalizing of *ousia* as the presencing of a being in its sited specificity. This interpretation of *hyle* is anticipated in 'The Origin of the Work of Art' in terms of the self-revealing and self-concealing 'earth' which manifests itself in the 'thingliness' of mere things, equipment, and artwork. The specific thingliness of a tool, for example, shows *hyle* in its appropriateness and as appropriate for the quality of the tool. *Morphe* is the 'breaking out of the appropriation' of the appropriated (*dumanis*) (BCP 357/258).

7.3.3.4 MORPHE AND ENERGEIA/ENTELECHEIA

Hyle comes to light in *morphe*. For this reason, Aristotle holds, *morphe* is '*phusis to a greater degree* than the "order-able" [*hyle*] is. For each individual is said to be [a real being] when it "is" in the mode of having-itself-in-the-

end [*entelecheia*] rather than when it is (only) in the state of appropriateness for' (cited in BCP 352/254).[55] In this way, Heidegger, following Aristotle, introduces the question of *entelecheia*. *Entelecheia* is traditionally
translated as actuality. The question is, however, in what way is the
'actual,' actual – in being? The 'being-moved of a movement consists
above all in the fact that the movement of a moving being gathers itself
into its end, *telos*, and so gathered in the end, "has" itself: *en telei echei*,
entelecheia' (BCP 354/256). This interpretation of *morphe* preserves the
being-moved and the placing-into-appearance in the gathering of *kinesis*
and *metabole* in the 'actuality' of a being's coming-to-presence (BCP 355–
6/256–7). *Entelecheia* is the 'gatheredness' of *ousia* into the delimited
gestalt of a 'work.' In this sense, *entelecheia* is *en ergon* (*energos*), at-work in
the work, *energeia*. The Afterword of the artwork essay in fact explicitly
appeals to this deconstructed sense of *morphe, energeia,* and *ergon* (UK 67/
206) to establish the being of the work. *Energeia* is traditionally interpreted as the 'actuality' which realizes a 'potentiality' (*dunamis*). Yet Aristotle claims that 'actuality is prior to potentiality' (BCP 356/257).[56] The
'priority' of *energeia* consists in bringing the being of *phusis* as *ousia* to
light in the gatheredness of coming-into-the-gestalt (*morphe*) (BCP 357/
258). Otherwise it is difficult to see why the condition of possibility of a
being – its potentiality – should derive from the actuality of the actual.
The 'actual' rather is as coming-into appearance, as the *movement of presencing* in a being. Therefore, what is merely stabilized in the stability of a
concept, in the objectivity of an 'object,' is less in being. Still less in being
is the unlimited potential of an unbounded 'energy' on which form is
imposed.

7.3.3.5 *POIESIS* AND *STERESIS*

Phusis is the movement into the stability of the appearance proper to a
being. It would seem that the *kinesis* of *morphe* as *entelecheia* is a kind of
'pro-duction,' conceived as a coming-forth into unhiddenness. It is
essential, however, to distinguish the pro-duction (*Her-stellen*) of *phusis*
from the 'making' (*Machen*) of *poiesis* (BCP 359–60/260). *Her-stellen* is
the self-placing in the appearance (*Gestellung*) of a being out of its own
arche. The *techne* that defines the art-work (UK 45/184) is a setting-forth
of truth (*phusis*) in precisely this sense. The appearance emerges out of
the movement of the being's own unfolding. But where the appearance
(the *eidos*) shows up only as *paradeigma* to guide *techne*, 'production' is
properly 'making,' *poiesis*. In this case, the *eidos* as *paradeigma* determines
the making and the thing made, as the stable, abiding form. The 'this-

ness' (*Jeweiligkeit*) of presencing in the appearance is concealed. The stability of the abiding form, moreover, conceals an essential aspect of the *kinesis* and *metabole* of *morphe*: *steresis* (BCP 364/264).[57]

Steresis is not merely 'deprivation' or absentness. It rather belongs to the movement of self-placing in the appearance, or becoming-present, as the movement of withdrawal from presencing in which presencing roots itself: 'the fruit comes to light when the blossom disappears. The placing into the appearance, the *morphe*, has a *steresis* character' (BCP 367/266). Thus '*steresis* as becoming-absent is not simply absentness, but rather is a *becoming-present* [*Anwesung*], the kind in which the *becoming-absent* (but not the absent *thing*) becomes present' (BCP 366–7/266). The unity of this movement is the being-on-the-way (*hodos*) of *morphe*. 'As such a becoming-absent *phusis* is always a going-back-into-itself, and yet this going-back is only the *hodos* of a going-forth' (BCP 369/268). As the unity of this way-of-being, *morphe* is as distinct from the mere stability of form as it possibly can be. *Morphe* is the way in which a being remains true to the hidden law of its own being. In the becoming-absent of *steresis*, *morphe* is rooted in the sheltering concealment (*lethe* as *kruptesthai*) which belongs to the unconcealment of *phusis*.

7.3.3.6 *PHUSIS* AS *OUSIA* AND BEING

The integration of *steresis* into the movement of *morphe* also initiates the final turn of Heidegger's interpretation: the retrieval of *phusis*-as-being, as opposed to the being of one realm of beings. The founding thinkers thought being as *phusis*, 'such that the *phusis* which Aristotle conceptualized can only be a late derivative of the original *phusis*' (BCP 370/268). Heidegger recurs to the saying of Heraclitus: *phusis kruptesthai philei*. In what sense does *phusis* 'love to hide itself'? In the sense of going back into itself, thus to root itself in the *arche* proper to each *morphe*, even as it comes forth to reveal itself. Being is the 'self-concealing revealing, *phusis* in the original sense. Self-revealing is the coming-forth into unhiddenness, and that means: preserving unhiddenness as such in its becoming-present' (BCP 371/269). In this sense, as self-concealing revealing, *phusis* is *aletheia*, the 'truth' of the unconcealment of beings. Therefore *phusis* as 'nature' is only one kind of *ousia*. And *ousia* (*Anwesen*) as the movement of placing into the appearance of the gestalt defines all the various kinds of being in which being differentiates and founds itself. The in-stantiation (*ousia*) of being always presences as the singular temporalization of a being's taking a stand as gestalt. The concealment of the truth of being, in turn, originates with the separation of the gestalt (*eidos*) from the movement of presencing and withdrawal; the oblivion of being implies the abandonment of beings, now reduced to mere images of the atemporal Ideas.

7.3.3.7 *PHUSIS* AND *TECHNE*

The question of *techne* calls for further elucidation. In the *Sophistes* of 1924–5 (GA19), Heidegger follows Aristotle's interpretation in the *Nicomachean Ethics*, book 4, chapter 4, to designate the *eidos* in the soul of the maker as the *arche* of the thing made, the *ergon*. The *arche* is not in the *ergon* itself, in distinction from beings of *phusis* (*phusei onta*), which have their *arche* and *telos* within themselves. Moreover, 'inasmuch as the *telos* con-stitutes the *arche*, the *arche* is in a certain degree not at the disposition of *techne*' (GA19, 41). This is because *techne* has the thing made in its grasp, as it were, only so long as it is not finished: as finished product, delivered over to use, its *telos* is determined by its use. This leads Aristotle to hold, Heidegger adds, that the '*ergon*, as soon as it is finished, is *para*, "beside," *techne*' (GA19, 42). Two significant consequences follow from this: (*i*) *techne* is a derivative mode of *aletheuein*, because the *telos* (and the *arche*) of the thing lies outside – or 'beside' – it; (*ii*) moreover, 'the *telos*, in its ontological character, is *peras*' and the *arche* is also in a certain sense *peras* (GA19, 44).[58] Because both *telos* and *arche* are not in *techne* as such, but fall outside or beside it, *techne* is not in essential relation to the *peras*. *Techne* is not only a derivative way of unconcealment, but it fails to set beings into the *peras* out of which they begin to be.

Taminiaux has noted that Heidegger's understanding of *techne* undergoes a transformation after the Rector's Address of 1933 to prepare the ground for the place of *techne* in the artwork essay: he distinguishes between the *techne* of mere production of a product, and a 'higher' *techne* of the unconcealment of beings.[59] The transformation of the concept of *techne* goes hand in hand with overcoming the prejudice that works of art are things made and present at hand, and as such have their origin (or *arche*) outside of themselves.[60] This is precisely what Heidegger denies. If the *eidos* is to be retained as origin, it cannot be an origin in the soul of the artist, but an origin in the work itself.

'The Origin of the Work of Art' indeed offers a very different understanding of *techne* from the *Sophistes* lectures. *Techne* is now understood as a 'way of knowing' (UK 45/184):

> *Techne*, as knowledge experienced in the Greek manner, is a bringing forth of beings in that it *brings forth* what is present as such *out of* concealment and

specifically *into* the unconcealment of its appearance; *techne* never signifies the action of making. (UK 45/184)

By 'appearance' (*Aussehen*) we may understand the *eidos* of the thing. And this 'all happens in the midst of the being that surges upward, growing of its own accord, *phusis*' (UK 46/184). Thus we can say that *techne* serves *phusis*, for in bringing-and-setting-forth, *phusis* is brought to light in the entity.

The work of art is *techne*, according to *An Introduction to Metaphysics*, because it brings being to a *stand*:

> The Greeks called art in the true sense and the work of art *techne*, because art is what most immediately brings beings (i.e., the appearing that stands there in itself) to stand, stabilizes it in something present (the work). (GA40, 168/159)

Techne, therefore, implicates making *phusis* – in its rising and holding-sway – manifest in the *aspect* of beings. The knowing of *techne* involves standing-within the openness of beings thus to bring about the 'dis-closive realization [Er-wirken] of being *in* beings' (GA40, 168/159, modified). To the degree *techne* is brought into explicit relation with the standing-forth and the aspect of beings as arising out of *phusis*, *techne* reveals the *eidos* of the being. Within the terms of the artwork essay, *techne* is reconceived, or retrieved, not only as an authentic mode of *aletheuein*, but, as a bringing-and-setting-forth into unconcealment, it *allows* a work to set itself into its *peras*, or gestalt.

But now *eidos* is thought as the self-showing of *phusis* in the differentiation of its aspects, not as the *eidos* in the soul of the maker. The retrieval of *techne* presupposes the deconstruction of metaphysically conceived *eidos*. Yet conversely, in the *Sophistes*, Heidegger argues that *techne* is the basis of the interpretation of being by way of the *eidos* (GA19, 44f); for being is interpreted according to the guiding question of *techne* as something-made, and the making is directed by the *eidos*. To liberate being from the ontology of production (and Aristotle, Heidegger notes, regards *phusei onta* as self-making or self-producing [GA19, 42]): (*i*) the *eidos*, or the self-showing aspect, must be set back into *phusis*; and (*ii*) *techne* must be retrieved as responsive bringing-to-stand of what thus shows itself. Since the *eidos* is first sighted and made-present through the seeing of *techne* as production (GA19, 47), the deconstruction of this way of seeing is a condition of letting *phusis* manifest itself in its differentiated aspects.

The *Beiträge* signals and responds to the need for 'the great reversal,' in which beings are no longer founded in mankind, but human being will be founded in being. Metaphysically conceived, *techne* is the 'fore-grasping' (*Vorgriff*) of mankind which determines a being as a thing-made (*poioumenon*). Things-made become the determining optic of *phusis* itself (GA65, 184/129). But clearly '*phusis* is not *techne*': *techne*, as a knowing questioning concerning the being of beings, sets itself over against *phusis* to let them stand forth – in the light of making and having-made. So *techne* determines the interpretation of beingness. Yet *techne* arises out of *phusis*. For *phusis*, 'in rising out of itself and by itself' offers itself in the *eidos*:

> *Phusis* is not *techne*, i.e., what belongs to *techne*, the well-versed look ahead into *eidos* and *re*-presentation and bringing before oneself of the outward look is precisely what happens *by itself* in *phusis*, in *on he on*. *Ousia* is *eidos*, *idea*, as rising (*phusis*), [as] coming forth (*aletheia*), and yet *offering a view*. (GA65, 191/133–4)

Being guided by *this eidos* means that *techne* is guided by how a being comes to manifest itself in terms of its immanent *telos* and *peras*. For this is what happening 'by itself' means: that the *eidos* gives itself to view *out of itself* – in terms of its own *telos* – and in terms of its own limit (*peras*), for *ousia* is in being in coming into the *peras* of its own limit.

Only insofar as this *peras* is recognized will *techne* recognize a limit. If, conversely, *telos* and *peras* fall outside or beside *techne* as metaphysically conceived, *techne* revolves around itself, abandons beings to being-used. As long as the *eidos* is in the soul of the maker, *techne* will not come on a limit. In political terms, this implies the determination of the polity by socio-technical discourses. The Leap of the *Beiträge*, which 'posits' the work of art as origin – as an exemplary entity, in von Herrmann's words – intimates the re-integration of *techne* and *peras*.[61] The marriage of *techne* and the work of art, therefore, brings *phusis* to light in the *eidos* (gestalt), and therefore in terms of the immanence of a limit.

7.3.4 Setting-into-Work the Historicity of Earth and World

In our consideration of the relation of 'The Origin of the Work of Art' to the Aristotle essay it was important to consider the fate of mimesis and that of substance in 'The Origin' and how the deconstruction of this heritage is undertaken hand in hand with a recovery of *phusis* and *energeia*.

The work of this recovery, which is carried out in the name of 'earth' and 'world' fully anticipates Heidegger's essay on Aristotle's *Physics* B, 1.

Heidegger's deconstruction of the metaphysical tradition, as we have seen, aims at a recovery of 'earth' as the carrying power which transfuses not only the thing as thing, but also, each in its own way, the being of equipment and of the work. The three metaphysical determinations of the thing conceal the earth as earth. Earth is thought as the moment of self-withdrawing self-manifestation: it manifests itself pre-eminently (although not exclusively) in the work, because the work fixes the strife of earth and the openness of an historical world in the inscription (*Riß*) of the gestalt (UK 50/188). In fact a twofold sense of gestalt emerges: (*i*) as world (the unity of the ways and relations through which humans win their destiny) (UK 27/167); and (*ii*) as earth (the gestalt into which things enter with their coming into appearance, thus to manifest themselves). Gestalt is thought simultaneously in its historicity and in terms of the recovery of *eidos* as *morphe* (UK 28, 32–3/168, 172–3). What Heidegger calls the earth as homeland (*der heimatliche Grund*) (UK 28/168) expresses *phusis* in the full sense: the retrieval of *ousia* as temporalizing, limited presencing-in-gestalt. The work is an exemplary manifestation of the historicity of *phusis*, which in its temporal unfolding sets truth into the stability of limit, or *peras* (UK 47, 57/186, 195).

Ousia is *gestalt, in the double sense of the historicity of the homeland as earth and of the presencing of beings as* morphe *in the space opened up by this ground.* The authentic sense of the political finds its ground – and originating limit – in this double sense of gestalt. Specifically, political action would consist in the realization of historicity and in the institution and guardianship of the ownness of the being of beings as set by the earth.

The being of the thing, and as Heidegger shows, in part II of 'The Origin,' the being of equipment is made manifest in and through the artwork. Art is said to be 'fixing in place of self-establishing truth in the figure [Gestalt]' (UK 57/196). The circumscription of truth in the gestalt is not the subsequent inscription of the pre-existing, but the event through which a world first gains the specificity of its site. The truth of the work which is appealed to here, therefore, is not to be confused with the mimetic truth of a work understood as the representation of the real (UK 21/162). It is not the re-presentation of the Idea, but the manifestation of a founding gestalt. This becomes evident insofar as the atemporality of metaphysically understood *eidos* is deconstructed in favour of the shining-forth of *eidos*. In the stability of the shining-forth, the movement of *eidos* into the limit which gives each thing its being comes to light.

I have noted that essential to the manifestation of truth in the gestalt of the work is the coming into appearance of the *Insichruhen* of the thing. In the *Eigenwüchsige* of the thing, the movement of the earth, as the power of *phusis* and hence the arrival of self-reserving withdrawal from representation, comes into the open. Earth is not conceived as the self-sameness of substance, but as the arrival of the 'wesende Ding' (UK 9/150–1), which is to say, the thing in its temporally sited specificity. Elsewhere, in 'Der Spruch des Anaximander,' Heidegger calls this the *Jeweiligkeit* of being: the in-stantiation of the specificity of arrival and departure of being in a being (GA5, 354/41). The appeal to the resting-in-itself of the thing and of things-made (UK 19/160–1) is won from the phenomena by way of the deconstruction of the metaphysical schematization of beings, and hence constitutes a recovery of what is, in its singularity, from the transparency of the concept. The work, in turn, gathers the resting-in-itself of thing and equipment into its own standing-in-itself (*Insichstehen*) (UK 25/165), which is the delimitation of the happening of truth in the gestalt. What Heidegger unfolds, in 'The Origin,' as the artwork's gathering of movement into the gestalt (UK 34, 43, 50/ 173, 182, 188–9) expresses the unity of *arche* and *kinesis.* The work's temporalization (*kinesis*) is the happening (*metabole*) of the unfolding of its own ordering principle (*arche*) into the historical specificity of its instantiation (*morphe*). *Morphe* signifies gestalt (UK 69/209). The strife of earth and world which the work gathers in the gestalt, allows the emergence of both in and through the movement of their self-concealing withdrawal from representation. This may be schematized as follows:

Schema II – Earth and world

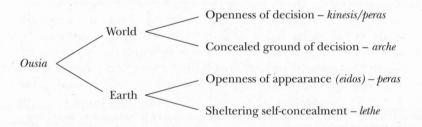

The truth which the work opens in this way as the truth of beings is in each case founded in the strife of the self-reserving self-manifestations of world and earth (UK 24/165).

Reading 'The Origin' from the perspective of the Aristotle essay of

1939, we find it apparent that earth is not Heidegger's mythological invention but the phenomenological recovery and re-interpretation of *phusis*. The setting-itself-into-work of truth in the artwork, which Heidegger understands as the giving of gestalt to the strife of earth and world, implies the delimitation of *energeia*. *Energeia* is rethought as *en-ergon-echon* (having-itself in the work) and hence as bringing being into the *peras*, or limit, of the work. The Addendum of 'The Origin' (1956) explicitly interprets the setting-into-work of truth by reference to the delimitation (*peras*) of being (UK 68–9/209). Being (*ousia*) as *energeia* presences as *en-ergon*, hence as the delimited resting-in-itself of the temporal movement of a being.

This characterization of being also gives the criterion of evaluation of the *polis* as the open site of being in its differentiation and historicity. The normative claim which this implies may be stated as follows: A polity gains its rank in being from the measure of its enactment of historicity, or the finitude of being as sited in beings. The historicity of being is enacted in the differentiation of beings: each is brought into its own limit.

In his discussion of Heidegger's implicit political philosophy, Schürmann argues that being as letting-be implies the abolition of teleology in action, and of 'arche' as the first principle of action. There is no primordial ground of political legitimization; action has no goal, but consists in releasement from goals. This in itself constitutes a political response and protest against technical domination.[62] Dauenhauer's critique of Schürmann emphasizes that an-archy 'makes no political sense' for 'political action must have both an *arche* and a *telos* of some sort' – that is, be rooted in the past and responsible for the future.[63] We have seen that Heidegger does not abolish or deconstruct *arche* and *telos*, but rather retrieves both. *Arche* is understood as the unfolding of motion out of the reserve of sheltering unconcealment. The telos of political action would be being-toward-a-limit, thus directed toward the revelation of the limit which lets each being be. Political action is legitimated by the act of setting beings into their proper limits. Political action in this sense takes responsibility for the polity and for beings in the face of the in-differentiation and thus functional activation of all beings under the regime of technology. The question remains whether the primacy of the political, as founded in *phusis*, over the socio-technical, can be established.

The *ergon*, or work, is conceived as *Ge-stell* (UK 69/209). In the word *Gestell*, we know from Heidegger's late philosophy, the destiny of *phusis* announces itself in the interface of nature and technology, and mankind goes on stage as the functionary of this conjunction. Yet the artwork is called the *Ge-stell* of a gathering which allows the manifestation of the delimitation (*Umriß* as *peras*) of truth. The work as *Gestell* gives gestalt to the event of this gathering, to the delimitation of and withdrawal from representational transparency, in the sense of setting-up the 'clearing of self-concealment' in a work (UK 69/209). The gestalt is not the impression of a 'form,' or Idea, on the passivity of a primordial substance or 'energy' (UK 69/208): the 'strife that is brought into the rift and thus set back into the earth and thus fixed in place is the *figure* [*Gestalt*]' (UK 50/189). What is essential to the *Riß* – the inscription of limit, as determined by the work's own self-manifestation – however, is the revelation of the self-reserve of the earth in the differentiated and sited singularity of beings. Because the artwork manifests the in-each-case-differentiated and self-reserved differentiation of the being of beings, it is strange to hear its being-in-the-gestalt brought into relation to the *Gestell*, for this becomes Heidegger's name for the essence of technology. *Gestell* implicates a technological order of the functional determination and availability of beings. As the essence of technology, the *Gestell* implicates the refusal of *steresis*, the withdrawal from presencing which pertains to both earth and world. This withdrawal (*lethe*) is the movement of sheltering concealment proper to truth, hence it is what saves the phenomena brought to light in the unfolding of *phusis* in the work (*en-ergon*). *The saving of the historically thought earth is the 'essence' of Heidegger's political thought.* The technological order of the *Gestell*, conversely, establishes a political order of representational transparency.

We have seen that the work is not conceived mimetically, but as the founding of the gestalt of the strife of manifestation and self-withdrawal. The insistence on the movement of self-withdrawal, which is the movement into the shelter of the unconceptual, guards Heidegger's sense of gestalt from the Platonic reading, otherwise tempting, of the gestalt as the form and imprint of the Idea. Insofar as the work becomes the focus of a site it opens the space of the mutual attunement and hence gathering of a people – given that 'people' is not misunderstood as the collective subject of a pre-conceived idea, but is de-termined by the event of an encounter of an historical tradition and the earth. A people can begin to come to be insofar as an earth – the resting in itself of *phusis* – takes manifestation in the gestalt.

The attunement of a people to the historically mediated manifestation of the self-transforming and withdrawing earth 'constitutes' the rootedness of a people. The conceptualization, conversely, of the collective subjectivity of a people by a people, or political movement, such as occurred in Germany after 1933, occludes and distorts the movement of withdrawal from representation which philosophically conceived earth-rootedness implicates. A 'political' moment – as Derrida, for example, has noted – is inscribed in the artwork essay by way of the appeal to the 'peasant' shoes of van Gogh's painting, which serves as one of Heidegger's central examples, in this text, of the coming to pass of the truth of beings in the work of art.[64] Yet what we may nominate rootedness in the philosophical sense should not be misunderstood as a 'peasant ideology' of 'blood and soil,' but should be taken in the sense of the coming to pass of the withdrawal from representational schemata in the gathering and 'formation' (*Bildung*) of a people, in the rites and works proper to the earth as homeland. It is necessary to distinguish between the 'ontic' conception and rootedness of a people, and the 'ontological' appropriation of a people by an 'ontology' of limit. Heidegger had not, evidently, fully addressed this issue in 1933. It comes to word in the essay on the origin of the work of art, given that we understand this origin 'essentially,' and hence also out of the perspective of Heidegger's deconstruction of Aristotle.

7.4 Style and the Gestalt of Global Technology

The question of the work of art arises in response to the planetary epoch as the question of whether the things themselves can still be saved in the autonomy of their non-calculability. According to 'The Origin of the Work of Art,' the work has the potential of founding the earth in the gestalt, even as the work itself is set back into the shelter of the earth. The dynamism of this movement, moreover, calls for a political leadership which can at the very least preserve the space and time of the homeland, so as to give it time to come into its own, time to find its own gestalt in the wake of the inevitable processes of the dis-integration of traditional forms. The economics and cultural politics of the international 'entertainment' industry are fundamentally at war with the temporality of un-concealment, however, given that they tend toward an acceleration of experience which in itself, even without any special ideological intention, destroys and homogenizes indigenous artistic forms. It is in terms of this world-historical situation that the 'question of style' emerges for Heidegger as a question of being.

Gestalt can be clarified by reference to the idea of style (*der Stil*). In reference to beings, style is the line and aspect in which things give themselves, present themselves *in their being*, as opposed to the activity of sub-jectivity intent on the aesthetic 'stylization' of reality. The latter, understood as the *Unwesen* of self-manifestation, is nonetheless a possi-bility related to the authentic concept of style. Baeumler, for example, propagates this notion of style under the aegis of National Socialism. Furthermore, Da-sein itself is said to be determined (*bestimmt*) by a style. Truth actualized in the gestalt of beings intimates the inscription of a style, as *founded* in the (self-)certainty of Dasein's own self-given law:

> Style: the self-certainty of Dasein in its grounding *legislation* and in its with-standing the fury.
>
> The style of *reservedness* is the remembering awaiting of enowning, because reservedness thoroughly attunes the inabiding ...
>
> As grown certainty, *style*, is the law of the enactment of truth in the sense of sheltering in beings. Because art, for example, is setting-into-*work* of truth and because in the work the sheltering comes *in itself* to stand unto itself, therefore style, although hardly understood, is especially visible in the field of art. (GA65, 69/48, modified)

'Stil ist als gewachsene Gewißheit das Vollzugsgesetz der Wahrheit im Sinne der Bergung in das Seiende' (GA65, 69). Style is the law of the manifestation of the historicity of truth as made manifest in and through beings, insofar as they are brought into the saving shelter of their own measure. Da-sein itself, as the site of *aletheia*, enacts this law. The historic-ity of Da-sein implicates, in Charles Spinosa's words, 'a style of revealing' as 'the source and ground of how things show up' in their being.[65] The style of Da-sein intimates the fundamental attunement of Da-sein to being which grants to beings the site and the modes of their presencing in the 'fury' of the encounter of earth and world. Style becomes particu-larly visible through the work of art. Why is this? Because the work sets truth to work in the work (*das Ins-Werk-setzen der Wahrheit*) by bringing the double movement of sheltering, saving, and of manifestation to a stand. As inscribed in beings, style is the movement of the tension between shel-tering concealment and unconcealment which grants to each its unique measure. In the strife of earth and world of the artwork, a space is opened which manifests beings in their delimited gestalt.

Two fundamental senses of style, therefore, emerge, in a first, prelimi-nary way: the style of Da-sein's attunement, and the style of the work of art as the incorporation of the making-manifest of the being of beings. In the gestalt of the work, as sited in the Da-sein of an historically founded people, we also discover horse and tree and stone in their being. The style of Da-sein's attunement will also determine how beings become manifest in a practical economy, or regime of work, and therefore found our engagement with technology. What Jünger calls the gestalt of the Worker is one, but only one, style of revealing. 'Productivity comes in various sorts of styles,' each determined by a specific temporal structure.[66] We recall from the *Logik* of 1934 that work implicates a temporal structure founded in *Sorge* and the historicity of the Volk. The transformation of a regime of work (an economy) presupposes a shift in the style of Da-sein which founds it in the historicity of Volk.

In the other, or new, beginning, Heidegger argues, Da-sein is determined by the style of *Verhaltenheit* (GA65, 69). Determination (*Be-stimmt-sein*) is not to be understood as conceptual positing, but as the hold, or stability, granted to Da-sein by the governing comportment of Da-sein to being. *Verhaltenheit* (the bearing of measured reserve, or 'reservedness') is the attunement of Da-sein to the whole of the open site of an historical destiny which the challenge of the essence of technology itself calls for. Measured reserve 'determines the style [of Da-sein] because it is the fundamental attunement [of Da-sein]' as the event of the sheltering concealment of being in beings. Style unfolds as the structure of temporality and historicity which attunes Da-sein to being and *measures out the ways in which beings become manifest*. Style, therefore, does not implicate the giving of form to a pre-existing material, for the temporal-historical rhythm of attunement first opens up a space of manifestation.

The earth-sited historicity of Da-sein gives it its style, and only in terms of this measure does what Heidegger calls Volk come to be (GA65, 33–4/ 24–5). A Volk comes into its own in submission to the law of its ownmost history, as it emerges in the founding leap (GA65, 43/30). The law is what limits and determines, thus to give gestalt. The 'organized masses' are without gestalt precisely because they are deracinated from the 'ground' of beings in the presencing of being (sec. 25). As the manipulation of beings becomes an end in itself the blindness to being which this implicates reduces the humanity of mass society itself to a 'human resource.' As such it is no longer rooted in its delimited historical possibilities. As resource it becomes a function of technicity and is integrated into it. A Volk, conversely, takes its stand in the sited presencing of being.

Attunement is to be understood as the ek-static temporalization of Da-sein, hence as the thrown project which first gives Da-sein a stand in its openness to being. In *Being and Time*, Heidegger explicitly refers to the attunement of *Verhaltenheit* as the 'ground' of Care (SZ, sec. 13). The attunement of *Verhaltenheit* designates the reserve of resting in itself, not in the sense of encapsulating oneself in the self-insistence of the already-known, but as the loyalty of an historical humanity to the *possibilities* (not necessarily the actualities) of its ownmost tradition. As the ground of Care, moreover, reservedness would encompass all the modes of taking-care of things, and of being-with others. Reservedness, furthermore, is an historically specific attunement: it arises out of the hermeneutic situation of our response to the tradition in the epoch of the consummation of metaphysics. It is the centre, Heidegger insists, of two other, distinct but allied, forms of attunement to being (GA65, 15/11): horror (*Erschrecken*) in the face of the destitution of beings in their abandonment by being; and awe (*die Scheu*), understood as the step back from beings into the presencing of being, thus to give beings the stillness and the space of their self-manifestation. The destitution of beings arises out of the loss of all measure, which follows, in turn, from the imposition of one universal schema of calculability on what is. This schema is without reserve in respect to beings.

As the style of Da-sein, *Verhaltenheit* determines and com-poses (*bestimmt*) the site of the presencing of being in such a way as to hold Da-sein open to being and to bring beings to a stand in the gestalt proper to them (GA65, 35/25). Da-sein takes its stand in being-open to presencing. The being-open of the reservedness of Da-sein is *gathered* in attentive *stillness* to the unconcealment of being. These senses of holding-open, taking a stand, and bringing to a stand are captured by Heidegger's use of *Inständlichkeit* (inabiding): 'reservedness thoroughly attunes the inabiding' (GA65, 69/48). The stand which Da-sein takes, however, is clearly not that of the self-identity of a subject. Da-sein signifies the 'stand' of an attunement to being, and of a comportment to beings which 'instantiates' Da-sein in the various 'modes and on the pathways of sheltering truth in beings' (GA65, 308/217, modified). Hence Heidegger speaks of 'taking one's stand' *in Da-sein* as the condition of all creation and all knowing of an historical humanity. Da-sein is the openness of the movement of the founding of being in beings:

> Only that which we, inabiding in Da-sein, ground and create and in creating let face us in its onrush, only that can be what is true and manifest and accordingly be recognized and known. Our knowing awareness reaches only so far as the inabiding in Da-sein extends, and that means as far as the power of sheltering truth in the gestalt [we have given] to beings [in das gestaltete Seiende] (GA65, 315/221, modified)

Given that Da-sein is as the movement of the founding of being in beings, what does this implicate for the character of the selfhood of Da-sein? Can we conceive of a selfhood which is not determined by the self-representation of subjectivity? The ego of subjectivity determines the self as the 'self-sameness of representing and the represented' (GA65, 319/224). The selfhood of Da-sein, however, is not to be conceived as re-presentative. How then does Da-sein return, come back to itself? The selfhood of Da-sein arises as the specificity of the historically founded movement of the incorporation of being in the gestalt of beings. The event of the endurance (*Beständnis*) of this movement constitutes the *Inständigkeit* of the Da-sein (GA65, 320/225). The stability, or return of Da-sein to 'itself,' consists in the endurance of the movement of the presencing of being in beings, consists in holding itself ever anew in the openness of its attunement to being. We recall this motif from the *Logik* of 1934.

Since Da-sein incorporates the open site of the coming to pass of truth in the gestalt of beings, *Verhaltenheit* is the reserve of a humanity which enters into relation with what is from the ecstatic position of having already left subjectivity behind, thus to allow what manifests itself to hold to its own measure. *Verhaltenheit* anticipates the *Gelassenheit* of letting beings be. The resting-in-itself of *Verhaltenheit* grants Da-sein's ecstatic project, the project of the letting-go of subjectivity in favour of the Da: the attentive concern with the ways in which truth brings itself to stand in beings. *Verhaltenheit* points to the temporalization of attentive concern that is the 'condition' of work in the sense of the *Logik* of 1934.

The delimitation of the gestalt is the condition of the resting in itself of an entity, through which alone it fully comes into being. In reference to beings, what the *Beiträge* unfolds as *Stil* and *Gestalt* is a reflection on the rootedness of entities in their own *arche*, hence on that of the temporalization proper to their unfolding. *An Introduction to Metaphysics* called for a retrieval of *ousia* as *Anwesen*, presencing out of the gestalt. Heidegger's commentary on Aristotle's *Physics* B, 1, moreover, offers an extended reflection on and recovery of *energeia* and *entelecheia*. The question at issue is the movement of an entity's arising and holding itself in being out of the limit (*peras*) which consummates its unfolding into its proper form (*morphe*). This movement defines the sense of 'style' at issue in Heidegger's reflections on the style of beings, as opposed to the style of Da-sein's own fundamental attunement. If the concept of *arche* indeed has a non-metaphysical sense for Heidegger, then the thought of style and gestalt is not an aesthetic refiguration of metaphysics, but a deconstruction and retrieval of metaphysical categories.

The intimate relation between Heidegger's retrieval of Aristotle and the reflection on style in the *Beiträge* is made evident in the *Nietzsche* lectures, where Nietzsche's understanding of form is deconstructed in terms of the Greek *morphe* (NI 139/119). Based on this understanding of *ousia* as *morphe*, the movement of becoming and the stability of being is re-interpreted in terms of *morphe* as the gathering of *kinesis* and *metabole* into the limit (*peras*) of the gestalt (cf. NI 160/135). Being as *Anwesen* (presencing, *energeia*) is the differentiated unity of the movement of a being into its proper 'form,' as determined by its own *arche*. Nietzsche holds that the 'grand style' which manifests most fully the unfolding of the will to power, points to the unity of active and reactive, being and becoming (NI 160/135). This unity is the unity of movement (*kinesis* and *metabole*) into the limit of the gestalt, into which the being of the thing is set. Heidegger's retrieval of Nietzsche's discourse on style moves to limit the limitlessness of the will to power by a determination of 'style' which understands not only the artwork, but also every being, in terms of the *arche* of unfolding proper to it.

The self-alienation of beings, their *Ent-äusserung*, conversely, gives them over to the disintegration of a functional economy. This economy indeed impresses a form on entities, thus determines them according to the paradigm of a code or discourse, but it cannot allow them their own style. The test of this assertion is the determination, in any given case, of whether a phenomenon manifests itself according to the measure of its own temporality or is constrained to show itself according to the parameters of an alien order. In this way the questions of 'style,' or of gestalt, temporality, and appropriation (or, conversely, expropriation), are brought into relation.

7.4.1 *Ernst Jünger and the Gestalt of Technology*

In section 152 of the *Beiträge* – 'Die Stufen des Seyns' (The Stages of Being) – Heidegger raises the question whether a hierarchy of the categories of beings can be established by reference to their power of siting truth. This means that the relative power of siting the conflict of concealment and unconcealment will be decisive:

> then the question remains: how to rank what is alive in nature, equipment, machination, work, deed, sacrifice and their power of truth (originariness and sheltering of truth and thereby the essential presencing of enowning) ... How is it with 'machination' (technicity) and how is all sheltering gath-

ered in it? Above all how does the intrusion of the abandonment of beings consolidate it? (GA65, 274/193, modified)

At stake is *Seinsverlassenheit*, the abandonment of beings by being (GA65, 115/80). The question of the siting of truth (or *Bergung*) takes its impetus from the historical need, arising out of the destitution of beings, to bring truth to manifestation in beings and to shelter beings in the coming to pass of truth. The Da-sein–founding power of the sheltering of being in beings is a necessity arising out of the history of being – it is the task of the epoch of the consummation of metaphysics (GA65, sec. 152). Heidegger asks to what extent technology, as distinct from the work of art, or sacrifice, for example, can incorporate the creative strife of concealment and unconcealment in the strife of earth and world, thereby to give the manifestation of being and the true a stand in beings. Technology is also a possible mode of *Bergung*. The inclusion of *Machenschaft* on Heidegger's list of possible modes of sheltering concealment (GA65, secs. 32, 152), may seem strange, given that *die Machenschaft* refers to the process of technological deracination. For the strife of earth and world is occluded insofar as technology conceals sheltering unconcealment, and hence the self-reserve of beings, each in its respective, appropriate gestalt, in favour of the ex-propriation of what is, thus to subordinate beings to the regime of total transparency and availability. The manifestation of the truth of being gives place to the crystallized order of functionality. But this is not the last word on technology.

It would seem that in our historical epoch, the task of giving gestalt to beings is granted pre-eminently to the work of art, not necessarily as a modus of being opposed to technology, but perhaps as the 'founding moment' of technology. Perhaps art is even capable of transforming technology from within. In any case, the question of technology is still undecided, still demands decision:

> What shall technicity be? Not in the sense of an *ideal*. But how does technicity stand within the necessity of overcoming the abandonment of beings, respectively of putting this abandonment to decision, from the ground up. Is technicity the historical pathway to the *end, to the last man's falling back into a technicized animal – or can technicity be above all taken up as sheltering and then enjoined into the grounding of Da-sein*? (GA65, 275/194, modified)

Insofar as the essence of technology intimates the disintegration of classical subjectivity – and it does – the question is not whether our concept of mankind will be transformed, but what this unavoidable transformation will signify. Subjectivity can reconstitute itself in the de-centred functionalized forms Derrida celebrates, forms of total programming already anticipated by mankind-machine interfaces. Alternatively, technology can enter the service of Da-sein to give shelter to the earth and to give image and gestalt to a world. For sheltering is always the empowering of the 'strife of earth and world' (GA65, 275/193): it is the actualization or the in-corporation of the play of self-reserved withdrawal within the realm of the unconcealed. It is in this context that Heidegger's engagement with Ernst Jünger's *Der Arbeiter* (1932) and the idea of total mobilization become significant for our reflections.

In what follows I will focus fairly narrowly on *The Worker,* and on texts immediately associated with it, since a comprehensive interpretation of Jünger's immense *oeuvre* is not possible or necessary here. But first, a few preliminary remarks. Jünger has long had a significant reputation in France, where his social and political critique of modernity, as well as his qualities as a writer and witness to his times, is taken seriously. For example, Jean-Michel Palmier devotes considerable space to Jünger in his *Les Écrits politiques de Heidegger* (1968), and the book still offers one of the best treatments of Jünger and Heidegger.[67] Until recently, however, Jünger has been largely disregarded in the English-speaking world, and for the most part he has received attention only as a forerunner of Nazism or has been castigated for his supposed 'reactionary modernism' (Herf). Neaman's recent study is still in this tradition, although he offers a much more nuanced treatment than Herf. There is no doubt that the Jünger of Weimar identified with the revolutionary conservative camp, such as Albrecht Erich Günther, editor of *Deutsches Volkstum,* and even with the left wing of Niekisch and the 'National-Bolshevists' – in whose journals he published – but Jünger was finally too individualistic and elitist to commit himself to any party.[68] Despite sharing anti-liberalism and a loathing of Weimar with the National Socialists, he quickly distanced himself from them after 1933, and subjected the totalitarian regime which emerged to a veiled critique in his allegorical novel of 1939, *On the Marble Cliffs.* Jünger did not share the racialist bias of National Socialism. His study of the figure of the Worker, which emerged from his experience of World War I, is a contribution to a phenomenology of industrial civilization in its totality, and not the bible of a new nationalism and its superman.

In what follows I will argue that Jünger's *The Worker,* as a critique of liberalism and a phenomenological description of technological humanity, anticipates postmodern discussions of the telos of modernity and its disintegration. Jünger's significance for Heidegger, the degree of their affinity and disaffinity, emerges out of the question of technology and its ramifications.

Michael Zimmerman suggests that Heidegger's response to Jünger can be divided into three phases: (*i*) an appropriation of Jünger's 'vocabulary about the worker in order to *counter* Jünger's vision of the worker';[69] (*ii*) a shift from work and the worker to the founding powers of art, understood as a countermovement to the technological disclosure of beings; and (*iii*) an acceptance of the triumph of technology, as forecast by Jünger, as the necessary gateway to a possible alternative to technological determination. Whereas the first two phases are linked, in Heidegger's mind, to the possibly creative potential of National Socialism, the final response acknowledges that National Socialism itself is entangled in the nihilism of technological thinking.[70] To begin with I want to consider the first of Zimmerman's theses, but in such a way as to engage the third. The question of art is unavoidably linked to the question of technology, for the founding of truth in the transformed gestalt of beings is at issue. And it is everywhere at issue in Heidegger's confrontation with Jünger.

Although Zimmerman's view is substantially correct, he underestimates the radicality of Jünger's position – as Zimmerman's acceptance of the thesis of Jünger's 'reactionary modernism' indicates – and therefore the measure of the challenge which Jünger poses for reflection on technicity. So it will prove necessary to unravel Jünger's theses in considerable detail, thus to establish his distance from and proximity to Heidegger's thought. My discussion of Jünger's position will demonstrate that the 'reactionary' category into which most commentators have traditionally slotted his thinking is fundamentally mistaken. Jünger actually stands closer to postmodern critics of metaphysics than to political reactionaries, and his distance from Heidegger must, therefore, be staked out on completely different ground.

The first question, therefore, is to what extent Heidegger's theses on work, in the 1933–4 period, can be assimilated to or distinguished from those of Jünger. We know that in the programmatic speeches of this period, as well as in the *Logik* of 1934, Heidegger uses the terminology of work, formation, and imprint, or stamp (e.g., GA16, no. 108, 204). In fact, in 'The German Student as Worker' (25 November 1933), Heidegger appeals explicitly to Jünger. According to Heidegger, based on a creative understanding of Nietzsche and the experience of the First World

War as a battle of logistics, Jünger has 'designated the mode of being of the mankind of the next epoch as [determined by] the gestalt of the worker' (GA16, 205). Heidegger immediately adds, however, that 'work trans-poses and integrates the Volk into the fields of force of the essential powers of being' (GA16, 205). Heidegger's understanding of being, and of Da-sein, cannot be assimilated to Jünger's. Heidegger can nonetheless appropriate Jünger's description of the worker as phenomenologically 'correct,' even if still burdened with the ontology of the will to power. In Heidegger's writings of 1933–4, including the *Logik* of 1934, *work* designates the ex-posure (*Ausgesetzheit*) of Da-sein to the differentiation of being, and *Worker* designates the thrown yet creative founder of being in beings. In 'On the Essence of Truth,' Heidegger holds that truth as freedom, rooted in Dasein's ecstatic being, is 'exposure [die Aus-set-zung] to the disclosedness of beings as such' (WW 187/126). I have already argued that the discourse of work is not primarily an indication of Heidegger's assimilation of National Socialist terminology, but evidence of his attempt to master the question of socialism, and Dasein's being-in-the-world, more concretely. Work as being-open, or ex-posed, positioned, in the midst of beings, and under the necessity of bringing them to an ordered stand, is the truth within which Dasein stands and into which it is thrown.

After 1934, and thus in the *Beiträge*, the discourse of work – as *a name for the possibility of overcoming metaphysics through the founding of Da-sein* – practically (but not entirely) disappears from Heidegger's texts. Does this indeed mean that Heidegger accepts the thesis that work implicates the achievement of the will to power, and thus that he abjures the possibility of a creative transformation of work and social relations? This is Zimmerman's position. It would appear to be substantiated by Heidegger's *Grundbegriffe* of 1941: 'the shape of the real is thoroughly determined by "the worker" and "the soldier,"' not as names for particular professions, but as 'metaphysical titles designating the human actualization of the being of beings which has become manifest, being which Nietzsche anticipated and grasped as the '*Will to Power*'' (GA51, 36). One nevertheless would have to distinguish between work as defined by technology and work as defining the transformed essence of technology. The latter sense signifies work as the achievement of *techne*, work as the disclosive bringing to a stand of the being of beings. In the *Grundfragen der Philosophie* (1937–8), Heidegger appeals to the recovery of *techne* in precisely this sense (GA45, 178–9). In its primordial sense, *techne* is the bringing of beings to a stand, in their emergence from *phusis*. A *techne* which brings entities into the circumscription of their proper limit is the achievement of work in the full sense of the *Logik* of 1934. This shows, as Zimmerman fails to appreciate, that Heidegger continues to insist on the distinction between work in the sense of the *Logik* of 1934, and work and worker as the realization of the will to power. Heidegger explicitly makes this distinction in the same passage: technology in the sense of Jünger's 'total mobilization' is a falling-off from the astonished openness of Da-sein to *phusis* into another kind of attunement to *phusis,* governed by the greed to know and to secure beings in their calculability (GA45, 179–80). The *techne* of authentic work, conversely, is rooted in the historicity of Volk and its way of belonging to the earth.

Moreover, if 'work' and 'worker' are understood in such a fundamentally different, non-metaphysical way in Heidegger, then 'the work' as what is produced, or what is created as artwork, will also have a different meaning. The 'gestalt' of beings must also be thought non-metaphysically. Heidegger's critique of the metaphysical concept of gestalt is pervasive in Heidegger's commentaries of the 1930s and 1940s, including those devoted to Jünger's *The Worker* (collected in GA90). Yet the metaphysical meaning cannot be presumed to exhaust the possible senses of gestalt. 'The Origin of the Work of Art,' for example, clearly speaks against this. What is at stake is the retrieval of *idea* and *morphe* in a non-metaphysical sense. This retrieval, most clearly enunciated in the Aristotle essay of 1939, allows us to posit a sense of 'gestalt' not only opposed to Jünger's metaphysical determination, but won from the overcoming of the essence of technology as *Gestell* and machination. The 'Gestalt' of the worker in Jünger's sense must be overcome to allow the gestalt of beings to emerge as the in-corporation of the sheltering concealment (*a-letheia*) of being. I will now attempt to elucidate Jünger's central theses to prepare us for a fuller discussion of the relation of his central ideas to Heidegger's thought.

7.4.2 Jünger's Der Arbeiter

The world-historical context, or hermeneutic situation, from which Jünger's reflections on *Gestalt*, the Worker, and work emerge, is the order of the 'total mobilization' of the planet which becomes visible with modern technology. Although Jünger's experience of total mobilization undoubtedly finds its origin in the trenches of World War I (cf. DA 307), the import of this totalization of resources is infinitely more far-reaching. This has not entirely escaped those critics of Jünger not completely obsessed with his role as a 'forerunner of fascism.' Karl Heinz Bohrer, for example, argues that Jünger offers a convincing aesthetic critique of the disintegrating effects of rationalism and technology. In Heidegger's terms, the experience of the war leads Jünger to offer a phenomenology of the being of beings as determined by technology. We should not be misled by the often impressionistic flow of Jünger's *Der Arbeiter*. Nor does the sociological approach of Herf, for example, which reduces Jünger's work to a species of reactionary modernism and nationalism, touch the essence of Jünger's insight.[71] As Palmier argues, the concept of total mobilization rather rethinks Nietzsche's thought of the will to power.[72] Heidegger's commentary on Jünger as recorded in *Zu Ernst Jünger* in fact everywhere confirms that Jünger takes over the fundamental metaphysical position enunciated by Nietzsche (GA90, 214–22). Total mobilization names the process of the dis-integration of entities, their functional redefinition and integration into one all-encompassing system of the production and consumption of energy. Far from reifying technology by separating it from 'any apparent connection to social relations,'[73] Jünger not only has a refined insight into these relations, but also a grasp of their metaphysical possibility.[74] In more narrowly political terms, mobilization consummates the ultimate dissolution of limits and boundaries – between political entities, classes, traditions, and races – in order to create one unified space, defined by the gestalt of the Worker (DA 75). Hence the Gestalt of the Worker, which mobilizes the world through technology, is not the expression of the nation-state. Nor can the nation-state control technology for the purposes of the nation. Technology rather makes the traditional state redundant, as the expression of an historical ordering of the manifestation of being. At the same time it creates the possibility of new states defined by the gestalt of the worker. Heidegger's dialogue with Jünger takes its point of departure from their mutual recognition of the nihilism evidenced by the dissolution of the being of entities to engage the question of the possibility and nature of the world order which technology is capable of generating. Jünger nominates this order the gestalt of the Worker.

7.4.3 Gestalt

The gestalt is the form through which the unity of the whole becomes visible to give the particulars of a world order their sense or meaning. It is more than the sum of its parts; it is nothing external to 'content,' and cannot be accounted for by an analytic procedure (DA 37). In the gestalt, the being of an entity comes to light. 'The perception of forms [Gestalten] is a revolutionary act insofar as it recognizes a form of being in the wholeness and unitary fullness of its life' (DA 46). With the gestalt, Jünger avers, the law of cause and effect is subordinated to a 'different kind of law, that of stamp and imprint' (*Stempel und Prägung*) (DA 37). Whereas the imprint may be said to re-present, or imitate, the stamp, what is perceived is an autonomous form of self-sufficient life, not the effect of a cause or set of causes. Jünger claims that thinking in terms of cause-effect relations not only dis-integrates 'life' after the fact, but is incapable of grasping the nature of the living at all. Although Jünger holds (in a letter of 1978) that the *Gestalt* more closely corresponds to Goethe's *Urpflanze*, or Leibniz's *monad*, than to the Idea in the Platonic sense, the Platonist origin of Jünger's concept of gestalt would nonetheless seem to be evident (DA 390). In fact, this is also Heidegger's interpretation (GA90, 22, 81, 94). Jünger holds that 'the imprint which space, time and humanity [now take] derives from a single gestalt, that of the Worker' (DA 37). This view would also be supported by the seeming ahistoricity of the gestalt, at least insofar as history is determined as 'progress': 'the history of progress does not render the history of the gestalt, but is at most a dynamic commentary' on it (DA 86).

The Platonist interpretation of Jünger's understanding of gestalt, however, is questionable, for it is at odds with the rejection of substance metaphysics which founds Jünger's phenomenology of modernity as the epoch of the dissolution and refiguration of beings. His refusal of the Enlightenment metanarrative of progress, moreover, does not automatically implicate an ahistorical determination of being, but rather leaves open the question of the character of the epochal shifts. In his *An der Zeitmauer* (Before the Wall of Time) (1959), Jünger anticipates the subsumption of the world-historical concept of mankind by the earth-historical, and with it, the emergence of a morphological account of mankind as a manifestation of the earth. This earth-historical poetic is opposed to a causal and narrative understanding of humanity as self-transforming subject (DA 79; cf. 100, 111). Jünger expresses a sense of the destiny of mankind which is not defined by reason or the 'world spirit,' but by incalculable transformations of the whole to which humanity belongs. This whole is the earth, hence not the ideal and transcendental, but the immanent powers of the historical specificity of peoples as earth-sited. As entities, moreover, the particulars, are not, according to Jünger, mere images of the gestalt conceived on the Platonic model. The individual thing itself, as the singularity of *this* being, possesses gestalt (DA 41). The epoch of total mobilization, as the age of disintegration and reintegration, may be the possible bridge to a new dwelling on the earth (DA 231; *Adnoten* in DA 333).

Whereas the era of liberalism and individualism is 'in essence without gestalt,' and based on 'the purely theoretical equality of the individuals who compose its building blocks' (DA 147), the 'completion of the mobilization of the world through the gestalt of the Worker' will give existence its measure and rank order and therefore gestalt (DA 187). Hence the gestalt of the Worker does not ultimately result in a reduction to uniformity of the being of beings. This is merely the preliminary stage of its history. 'Rank order' is neither inherited nor ascribed by convention, but is earned through commitment to a tradition, and a willingness to sacrifice for the future. This consciousness is what creates a new aristocracy. The gestalt is 'symbolic of the fact, that today, as in the past, life has rank,' that is, every form of life has its rank within the whole (DA 87). Measure and rank emerge out of the immanent unity of the whole, out of the gestalt as the unity of the Worker and the earth. The earth is permeated with spirit and manifests itself as 'spiritualized' energy in the machine: 'matter and *bios* are magically undivided.'[75]

7.4.4 Being and Limit

The space of the Worker is planetary because it is identical with the expansion of technology (DA 224). The unity of the planetary, however, will first emerge from the results of the competition – perhaps peaceful, perhaps warlike – between different claims to most fully represent the gestalt of the Worker (DA 224, 232). Only then can the question of how to give form to the unitary space of the planet be answered (DA 248).[76] The *emergence of this unitary space* is the direct result of total mobilization: the 'task of total mobilization is the transformation of life into energy, as it manifests itself in the economy, in technology and communications ... or on the battlefield as firepower and motion' (DA 224). Although mobilization releases the potential energy crystallized in nature and tradition, thus to speak the language of becoming, the determination of limit and gestalt (*Gestaltung*) calls on the language of form to make manifest the being of beings (DA 224).

Jünger, finally, anticipates a stable world order, defined by a certain constancy of institutions, customs, economic arrangements, and political structures. This will also allow the emergence of typical forms of industrial design, no less than of art and behaviour. The character of self-limitation proper to the 'race' which thus appears on the world stage will be analogous to forms of instinctual life as modes of giving gestalt to an entity (DA 248). This does not implicate, according to Jünger, an all-encompassing uniformity, but the greatest possible multiplicity of specialized, purposeful forms representative of the character of being as Work. The being of each entity takes its character from the stamp imposed by one of the many types which reflect the gestalt of the Worker (DA 248).

Art as the formation (*Gestaltung*) of a material serves as the model for politics as rule (DA 225). Whereas this seems to imply the subordination of politics to aesthetics, Jünger's examples call for a more nuanced judgement. The most comprehensive task which rulership can give itself is the art of 'landscaping,' most significantly as manifested in sacred gardens dedicated to the gods of holy streams, such as the Nile and the Ganges (DA 225). Both 'art' and 'politics' derive from a higher power, which is the earth itself and its gods. Both art and politics would most fully enter into their essence only in their correspondence to this power. Jünger in fact anticipates, with the event of the stabilization of the planetary dimension, 'the awakening of a new attachment to the earth' (DA 231). The earth itself, once *grasped as a unity by the Worker's will to form*, gives birth to a new feeling of responsibility for the earth. This sense includes an ecological awareness of the limitations of purely economic thinking as the founding order of the planet (DA 227–8). In the *Adnoten* (1964) Jünger writes that the Worker 'like Antaeus is the direct son of the earth' (in DA 333). What follows is perhaps Jünger's central thesis, at least from the retrospective of 1964: 'the earth transforms itself, out of the fatherlands, back to the homeland [Heimat]. Matriarchal signs gain in strength and power' (DA 333). The patriarchal power, which the form of the nation-state represents, represents the transcendental, both in the avatar of a transcendental god and in the ontological structure of metaphysics. The gestalt of the Worker, therefore, ultimately heralds the recovery of *Heimat*, but presumably only insofar as the earth again becomes a mythic and matriarchal – a religious – power.

7.4.5 *Gestalt and Archetype*

The *Typus* (archetype) is the most perfect and direct expression of the form and character of being as Work (*energeia*) (DA 249–50). 'Technology is the world revolutionary means through which the gestalt of the Worker mobilizes the world, and in the world revolutionary archetype the same gestalt creates for itself a ruling race' (DA 231). Through the archetypal, the gestalt of the Worker manifests itself in the movement of the manifold 'as a system of refined, precise, purposeful' entities (DA 249). The archetype, therefore, *represents* the gestalt and crystallizes it in stable *forms*, which are not, however, substantial entities or reflections of a transcendental idea, *but rhythmical and hence temporal regularities of a set of relations* (DA 148–9). In a way which anticipates postmodern discussions, the person of the archetype is defined as the co-ordinate of a set of discursive systems or fields – the fields, for example, of transportation, the news media, advertising, the financial marketplace, defence, and sport. Unlike the classical, rational and autonomous, individual of liberalism, the archetypal person is entirely integrated into these field relations, which in fact constitute this person, and on levels more profound than those merely of conscious choice and behaviour (DA 151, 239). Jünger insists that the archetype is not just a uniform product of the discursive fields to which it belongs (DA 246). It may be objected that given the primacy of the discursive field in the constitution of selfhood, the nature of the 'individuality' of the selfhood of the archetype is totally determined or determinable. According to Jünger's account in *An der Zeitmauer,* however, the selfhood of the archetype manifests the organic construction of earth-historical powers which ultimately remain opaque to calculating reason. This position will later be confirmed by Jüngers 'Über die Linie,' which offers the occasion of Heidegger's open letter, ultimately published as *Zur Seinsfrage,* to Jünger.[77]

Jünger begins from what he perceives as the end of the 'individual': the Idea of the bourgeois individual is supplanted by the archetype of the Worker (DA 125). The technological conditions of the production of democracy themselves prepare the emergence of the archetypal. For example, the modern media produce archetypes of behaviour and character (DA 283) which are defined by the medium itself as image-generator, rather than by a conceptual system of rights and duties, such as determines the individual (DA 240, 286). Whereas the individual is defined by the 'I' as a set of values, the type is defined by the regularity of spatial-temporal rhythms (DA 148). The world of the individual is a world of concepts; that of the archetype, the world of the gestalt, which it represents in the work character of a multitude of forms, such as the archetypes of the soldier, scientist, technologist, artist (DA 158, 239–40). The modern individual is the obverse of the modern mass population (DA 233). The two concepts mutually determine each other, but the archetype takes its functional, work-specific character from the emerging unity of Work and the formative power of the earth. The notion of *Typus* is thought by reference to the self-limiting forms of nature, each determined by its 'natural' niche – hence the inherent drive of nature 'to maintain forms within their measure and limits' (DA 235). The archetype of the Worker will constitute a new race of humanity, possessed of its particular limits, like everything living in nature (cf. DA 243).

7.4.6 *Work and the Worker*

What does Jünger understand by 'work' (*Arbeit*)? 'Work' is defined as the process of the formation of the in-every-case-distinct gestalt of the being of beings – the being of mankind, of war, of art, even of the solar system (DA 72). In the first act of its historical movement, work announces the dissolution of the rank-differentiation of beings to facilitate their total mobilization in the service of being as represented by the gestalt of the Worker (DA 74–5). The unity which thus emerges, as we have seen, is the condition of the creation of new forms and types (cf. DA 224). In terms of the history of metaphysics, Jünger's concept of *Arbeit* is comprehensible as the metaphysical interpretation of the *energeia* of Aristotle: it denotes action, operation, and actuality. In the same terms, the 'Worker' is the functionary of actuality – the gestalt which mankind takes in the epoch of unconditioned production and consumption (GA90, 6).

The identity of Work and being 'is able to grant a new security, a new stability' to the epoch of technology (DA 95–6). This identity, which the gestalt of the Worker is, allows the dynamism of the will to power (Life) to take a form proper to this epoch. In its actuality (*Wirksamkeit*), Work is the 'principle' of beings: in respect to mankind, it determines a new way of life (*Lebensart*); and in respect to the forms that beings take, it imposes a new style (DA 96). The style of the gestalt of the Worker emerges last, and for a long time remains concealed by the process of the dissolution of traditional structures and their reduction to the uniformity of the functional world (DA 97). The humanity of the work-world itself takes on a new style of archetypal simplicity which Jünger sometimes calls 'race' (*Rasse*). The new race of the Worker is the manifestation of the imposition of the form of Work on technological humanity. Race is not, Jünger insists, a biological determination:

> let it be repeated here, that within the work-world race has nothing to do with biological concepts of race. The gestalt of the Worker mobilizes the

entire reserve-stock without exception ... In the work-space nothing other than efficient performance, through which the totality of this space is expressed, is decisive. (DA 156)

The Worker's character as expressive of a new race of humanity emerges from the education, training, and discipline imposed on mankind by the work-world: it gives humanity a new style. Because the style of the Worker fixes the limitless energies released by technology in stable forms, it 'legitimates' technology:

the task of the Worker consists in the legitimation of the technical means through which the world has been mobilized, that is, has been transposed into the condition of unlimited motion. (DA 287)

Given, as we have seen, that for Jünger, Being signifies the limit of form, and form emerges from the limitlessness of Life (from becoming, in Nietzsche's terms), then the style of the Worker, as form, actualizes the movement of becoming into Being which gives the chaos of becoming its meaning, and in this sense 'legitimates' it. Following Nietzsche, we could say that the *gestalt of the Worker grants value to being* (cf. GA90, 39, 57–8, 170–1). The gestalt is not a psychological concept, nor is the Worker the general concept for the collective being of individual workers.[78] The gestalt of the Worker rather represents the way of being, that is, *the mode of disclosure* of beings in the era of total mobilization. Being is disclosed as Work, as actualization – as being-in-operation.

Actualization grants beings their value. Only then does the meaning of the apparently senseless dissolution of traditional structures become evident:

the Worker is accordingly confronted with the task of the organic construction of the limitless motion of the masses, and the energies, which the process of disintegration of civil society has left behind. (DA 288)

Only the Worker, *as the embodiment of a style of life and of the activity of giving form to entities*, sufficiently corresponds to Work as the character of being to give order to the planetary dimension:

to hold power, that is, to establish a new order by overcoming anarchy, thus to claim planetary legitimacy, is only possible today through the representation of the gestalt of the Worker. (DA 205)

The style of technological mankind is representative, and 'represents' in the sense of making-manifest in form. *Repräsentation* echoes the *eidos* of Plato. Technological humanity represents the gestalt of the Worker. Now mankind takes the stamp of being as Work (*energeia*) and in turn imposes a style of work on all beings.

The stability of form which this race embodies finds its highest realization in a new concept of the state, although it is not always clear whether Jünger is referring to a multiplicity of states, all of which represent the planetary dominion of the Worker in allied ways, or to one, all-encompassing world-state. Race is 'the final and most unequivocal imprint of the gestalt. More than any other power, the state – as the most comprehensive representation of the gestalt' is called to realize the imprint of the new race of the Worker (DA 299; cf. 310). Jünger intimates however, that entrance into a consummate world of forms is not to be expected until the great political decisions, on a global scale, have in some sense fallen and the competition of empires and cultures has given way to one superior power (DA 248).

7.4.7 Mobilization

Technology, then, 'is the way through which the gestalt of the Worker mobilizes the world' (DA 160). Humanity and machine are only 'organs' of the 'language' of technology. The *Gestalt* alone is the 'unmoving centre' of a movement of dissolution which transforms mankind and nature from their foundations (DA 160–1). Although Jünger sometimes calls technology a 'means' for the mobilization of the world (DA 195), his concept of technology is not instrumental, for technology is not an instrument of humanity or progress, but a transformation of being in which mankind participates. This becomes especially evident through Jünger's notion of 'organic construction' as

> the intimate and consistent fusion of humanity with the tools at its disposal. In respect to these tools themselves we can speak of 'organic construction' when technology has reached that highest degree of self-evident development which is immanent in the limbs of animals or the parts of plants. (DA 191)

Organic construction, therefore, signifies (*i*) the emergence of a new mankind through the fusion of technology and humanity; and (*ii*) the self-production of the technological world. Jünger anticipates the integration of humanity and machine in ways computer technology is only now beginning to imagine. We stand on the threshold, Jünger avers, in *An der Zeitmauer*, of an epoch in which 'our technology signifies not only a world of abstraction, but also the immediate actuality of the spiritualized earth [erdgeistige Wirklichkeit].'[79] The reproduction of the machines themselves, furthermore, intimates the rise of a race of androids. Both humanity and technology are conceived as the expressions of being as Work, and so Jünger abandons the standpoint of the subject which founds the instrumental and anthropological conception of technology. The collapse of the subject has already become evident, moreover, insofar as the type, which supplants the metaphysically conceived individual, organizes the 'individual' as a field of forces, rather than as a substantial ego. The deconstruction of the classical subject does not, however, signify overcoming subjectivity in the metaphysical sense of the ground of the subject-object relation. The gestalt of the Worker, Heidegger tells us, reveals the 'absolute subjectivity' that consummates itself in the essence of technology (*Machenschaft*) (GA90, 6).

Jünger does not so much overcome the subjectivity of the subject as reduce it to a function of its involvements. The *techno-animality* which Jünger envisions takes its nature from being-in-operation, from being-as-actualization. The disintegration of the subject would only affirm the transcendental character of actualization which inscribes itself in the fusion of humanity and machine. Jünger's understanding of Work would be allied to the post-modernity of Derrida, at least insofar as he also deconstructs the subject to reveal the governing power of functional operations and actualization. In Derrida's case, this concept of 'being' is called Writing and 'différance.' Both terms signify program, and the program, given that it is nothing substantial, only has being in operation.[80] Elsewhere Derrida identifies Writing and *energeia*, which is not surprising, since the inscription of a program is the operation of actualization.[81] Jünger also holds that technology takes its being from 'language': it is the process of the logical symbolization of the world; it actualizes itself as the creation of models, of purely formal relations (DA 172).

But whereas Derrida insists on the limitlessness of the play of significations, Jünger perceives the formation of new stabilities in the form of the entities themselves, as opposed to the stability of a conceptual order underlying and generating the phenomena. The process of dissolution, which technology brings about to destroy the symbols and structures of tradition, is itself founded on an occluded religious understanding (DA 172). Hence the war of technology with tradition is understood as a war of *Gestalten* – of forms of totality, or metaphysical conceptualizations of being – rather than as a history of progress or emancipation, as conceived by the metanarrative of the Enlightenment. The movement of reason does not have its end in itself. *Technology itself is the 'symbol' of a superior power* (DA 200): *this power is being as actualization-in-form.*

In this respect the question arises whether Jünger's thought finds a limited point of contact with Heidegger's interpretation of Aristotle in the essay on the *Physics* B, 1, wherein Heidegger retrieves the Aristolean *energeia* as being-*energon*, which is to say, as the in-stanciation of being in *morphe*. For Jünger, to think mobilization in terms of the gestalt means 'to grasp the image of the world [Weltbild] as a closed and well-determined totality' (DA 175): the gestalt of the Worker is what gives technology its limit, its consummate completion and *telos*. Jünger, however, thinks the totality of the 'world picture,' hence a represented totality. The question arises, moreover, whether Heidegger and Jünger conceive of limit in the same way. Is limit, as Heidegger proposes in his interpretation of Aristotle, the immanent limit of a being's resting in itself? Or is the limit of the Worker's gestalt, the limit of the ordered arrangement of the field of representation? The concept of total mobilization demands the dissolution of the immanent limit of the being of entities, thus to facilitate their movement and functional arrangement. If this is so, then Jünger's concept of gestalt is radically distinct from Heidegger's, since Heidegger deconstructs the metaphysical concept of form to retrieve a sense of *morphe* as the unity of the temporal movement that grants the singularity of a being. Yet there is a sense in which style is to be understood as bringing the movement of disintegration into the stability of form (cf. DA 177). New 'organisms' and styles of being, each limited in itself, would ultimately arise out of the fusion of mankind and technology. Does this point to an internal contradiction in *The Worker* as the thought of mobilization *and* gestalt, or does the concept of 'organic construction' resolve this contradiction by a metaphysics of the will to power? If the latter is the case, Jünger advances a metaphysical concept of limit and gestalt.

7.4.8 Totalization and Modernity

'In the same measure,' Jünger writes, 'in which individuality dis-integrates (into a greater unity), the force of resistance with which an individual may refuse his mobilization also decreases' (DA 154). Finally, the totality which Jünger has in view here is not at all that of the classical, absolute and autocratic, state nor that of modern totalitarian structures (as Herf assumes),[82] but the de-centred and yet disciplined societies of postmodernity. This 'totalized space' is not represented in a 'centre': here 'every point much rather simultaneously possesses the potential significance of a centre' (DA 284). In fact, a substantial part of Jünger's *Der Arbeiter* is devoted to a consideration of democracy, both as a force for totalization and as an incomplete form of totalization. In the first instance, democracy is a more complete form of mobilization, both in peace and in war, of the potential energy of a society than monarchy, and for this reason the First World War had to end in the triumph of democracy (DA 255). For under the regime of liberal democracy the autonomous individual is conceived as a social atom; 'there are no substantial bodies any more to which [the individual] has obligations. The remnants of these ties are reduced to mere associations, to common attitudes or contractual bonds' (DA 262). By 'substantial bodies' (*substantiellen Gliederungen*) Jünger apparently means pre-reflective or unmediated bonds of community, such as the family or (at least in some conceptions) the 'people.' According to Hegel's *Philosophy of Right*, both the family and the people are a community of this kind. In the liberal tradition, Locke's *Two Treatises of Civil Government* already constitutes a systematic deconstruction of this kind of unmediated bond, with the result that even the familial bond is determined as a construct of reason and of the pragmatics of feeling. Precisely the high degree of homogeneity of democracy allows for a more complete, sudden, thorough mobilization.

Mobilization is not commanded from above, but consists in the ongoing expansion of perspectives of power on the part of every segment of society – thus the women's movement, for example, demands that women be integrated into the workforce (DA 263). The 'consumers' command, not authoritarian leaders. In the *Adnoten*, Jünger puts still greater emphasis on the consumer, and the process of consumption, as integral to the Worker's gestalt (DA 363). Democracy aims at uniformity, and brings it about by encouraging differences of opinion: these differences are without substance because the public sphere of education and the production of opinions is not only highly homogenous, but encompasses every informal as well as formal institution (schools, church, press, sport, fashion, etc.) which might allow substantive differences to arise (DA 263). Though this evaluation of the totalizing tendencies of democracy echoes a long tradition going back to Burke and de Tocqueville, Jünger antedates McLuhan and Baudrillard in holding that not the message – the opinions produced in the media – but the technical medium itself is decisive. It re-determines the 'individual' in terms of its discursive structures: 'technicity is of far greater consequence than the individual who produces an opinion within technicity' (DA 278). What counts, are not opinions – but the feeling of the communication of the 'unmediated temporal and spatial presence' of an event (DA 280). In this respect, Jünger not only articulates an essential aspect of what Heidegger calls *Erlebnis*, or the sensationalism of intensified experience, but also sets a precedent for the primacy of the 'reality effect' in postmodern discourse.

Heidegger's understanding of the 'phenomenology' of total mobilization, if not its origins, is very close to Jünger's. This is evident from a brief comparison of Jünger's theses to Heidegger's 'Überwindung der Metaphysik' (Overcoming Metaphysics) (UM) of 1936–46. *Total mobilization is ongoing in peacetime*, as revealed in the transformation of industry and the workforce for the ends of higher productivity and increased consumption (DA 305). Heidegger concurs with this view, on the grounds that nihilism, as the abandonment of the being of beings, denotes the mobilization of the entire 'stock' of beings for the sake of ever greater order and security. Representational thinking operates as the making-secure of beings for the sake of representation. This becomes an end in itself, as the only end in the absence of ends (UM, sec. 26). Again in the *Adnoten*, Jünger refers to '*standardization*' *as indicative of the* '*total work character*' *of modern society* (DA 361). In this evaluation Jünger is in agreement with the critical tradition from Weber to Foucault that has recognized the instrumental telos of rationality, concealed behind the mask of emancipatory reason. In the same section of 'Overcoming Metaphysics' as cited above, Heidegger refers standardization, or uniformity, back to its provenance in the will to power: because the will everywhere aims at the secure order of a standing reserve of beings, beings can manifest themselves only in the aspect of their calculability (sec. 26). Total war, moreover, conceived as the erasure of the distinction between home and front, attacks on civilians, etc., follows from the total mobilization of productivity, which makes the producers of the enemy a 'legitimate' target, and from the structural totality of the war process, which is the battle between systems of production. Total war has the implicit object of determining *which system implicates the greatest efficiency*, a view to which Heidegger also subscribes in 'Overcoming Metaphysics' (sec. 25). In all these respects, Jünger argues, liberal democracy has hitherto effected the most efficient mobilization and hence totalization.

7.4.9 Postmodern Jünger

I have intimated that Jünger holds theses in common with certain aspects of postmodernism. Collectively, these theses manifest the total mobilization of beings, which is, in effect, the often still unacknowledged truth of postmodernism, and hence of our own hermeneutic situation. They may be summarized as follows, by reference to key poststructuralists: (*i*) the dissolution of individuality into a set or field of relations (Barthes, Foucault). Both the individual and the collective subject (class consciousness) are dissolved into signifying relations as determined by social discourses and the communications media (Foucault, Baudrillard); (*ii*) the disintegration of substance (objects) into energy, or functions of a system (Derrida) (dis-integration of entities serves their 'acceleration' in the sense of their integration into the system of total mobilization); (*iii*) the creation of a homogeneous political spectrum which tends toward mere simulation of political decision-making (Baudrillard). The public sphere of political consciousness is thoroughly schematized. The conceptual schematization of reality re-figures the real as a reality-effect. In Roland Barthes's terms, the real is rendered mythological by the language of clichés. Thus the telos of democratization as a world-historical process also becomes evident, as instrumental reason takes pre-eminence over emancipatory reason. With the collapse of the metanarrative of emancipatory reason, micro-narratives of efficiency, as Lyotard has shown, become ends in themselves.

In Jünger's terms, what we now call postmodernity indicates the character of total mobilization, and its primacy over rooted, historical existence. But whereas the postmodernism of Derrida, for example, identifies the powers of dissolution, it remains captured by the logic of undecidability, hence incapable of willing a new gestalt, or even of recognizing its emergence. The functional 'play' of signifiers in the absence of the signified is affirmed in and for itself as liberation from metaphysics, but the possibility of new stable forms emerging from technology is denied. The *critical modernism* of Jünger consists in the discovery of the possibility of new form, gestalt, and therefore 'being' in this process of disintegration. Form alone gives sense and meaning to the movement of becoming. In common with Nietzsche, Jünger rejects the language of number, of scientific discourse, as a betrayal of Life, and seeks a concept of form as gestalt and style which is not merely intellectual, but rather rooted in Life itself. Liberal democracy, Jünger holds, refuses to recognize that its own logic of disintegration and mechanical organization gives rise to new totalities, orders of rank and typologies. It still clings to an obsolete ideology of individualism. This ideology is out-dated, Jünger claims, because superseded by the technical organization of society as a functional system.

We have seen that Jünger engages three related questions, all of which emerge out of a phenomenological description of the end of modernity as the coming to power of technology: (*i*) the dis-integration of traditional forms; (*ii*) the re-integration of beings into the system of total mobilization; and (*iii*) the emergence of the gestalt of the Worker, and with it, of the organic construction and a sense of form immanent in beings. Does this concept of form, understood as a response to the merely functional being of total mobilization, derive from Jünger's phenomenological description, or does it already constitute a project, an implicit attempt to found the new era he anticipates?

7.4.10 Heidegger and Jünger

The *Beiträge zur Philosophie* and the commentaries on Jünger published in GA90 offer us our most direct clues as to how Heidegger read Jünger in the 1930s and early 1940s. Section 74 of the *Beiträge* is entitled '"Total Mobilization" as Consequence of the Originary Abandonment of the Being of Beings' (GA65, 143/100). This gives us a significant insight, inscribed into the *Beiträge* itself, as to how to read Heidegger's understanding of Jünger in the mid-1930s. The same section opens as follows: total mobilization signifies

> pure setting-into-motion, and the emptying of all traditional contents of what is still operative as education.
>
> The priority of procedure and of institutional arrangement in [securing] the comprehensive preparedness and serviceability of the masses ... (GA65, 143/100, modified)

Evidently total mobilization pertains to the education and transformation of the masses in the sense of their integration into a new order of preparedness and service. This implicates the dissolution of traditional social relations. Movement itself, hence the availability of the masses as a resource on call, becomes the defining feature of this new order of humanity. Total mobilization, however, encompasses not just education and the masses, but all entities in their abandonment. For total mobilization is the consequence of the withdrawal of being from beings, the consequence of the abandonment of beings (*Seinsverlassenheit*). Abandonment intimates that beings are given over to their objectness and come to presence only as what has been made, produced. 'The beingness of beings fades into a "logical form," into what is thinkable by a thinking which is itself ungrounded' (GA65, 111/77).

The determination of beings as product, object, and logical form (or function) is what Heidegger calls *Machenschaft*, or machination. The term *Machenschaft* points to making, hence to *techne* and *poiesis*. It signals the breakthrough of the beingness of beings as made and self-making. Total mobilization signifies the triumph of subjectivity (*die Sujektivität*) in the actualization of beings through the work-process (GA90, 53–4). This breakthrough, which belongs to the history of being itself, was prepared by the metaphysics of presence and the theology of beings as *ens creatum,* which alienates them from their originary ground in *phusis* and forces them into the straitjacket of cause-effect relations (GA65, 126–7, 132/88–9, 92). The reduction of beings to objectness follows from the interpretation that they are things-made or effected. Being-present holds the field and the presencing of being falls into oblivion (GA65, 128/89).

As the 'consequence' of the destitution and abandonment of beings, total mobilization is nothing other than the consequence and actualization of machination. Therefore, like machination itself, it is a way of presencing, of the coming-to-presence of beings, but precisely in the mode of not-presencing, in which beings are given over to their mere represented availability as product and function (GA65, 135/94). The functionalization of beings allows their interchangeability – it is the condition of their motion and of their subjection to arrangement. This functional arrangement has the peculiar character of instituting a nexus of relations of the unrelated:

> What does *machination* mean? That which is let loose into its own shackles. Which shackles? The schema of generally calculable explainability, by which everything draws nearer to everything else equally and becomes completely alien to itself – yes, totally other than just alien. The relation of non-relationality. (GA65, 132/92, modified)

Representational thinking institutes the systematic arrangement of entities in the schema of calculability. Why does this signify, as Heidegger claims, a 'relation' of non-relation? As drawn into the network of functionality, things become even more than alien *to themselves* – that is, they have been abandoned by being to be given over to calculability. If alien to themselves, they must also be incapable of entering into relation with other beings, except in terms of a calculus of explanation and function. Relation between beings presupposes self-relation. The calculus of functionality institutes a kind of 'relation' – that of non-relationality – founded in the self-alienation of beings.

Why are beings without relation? Because they no longer presence as beings out of their own being. This self-presencing, which allows self-relation, and therefore a relation to the other, is granted by the immanent limit of beings, that is, by the sheltering reserve (*Bergung*) at the heart of unconcealment. We recall that sheltering reserve is the moment of withdrawal from mere availability and calculability. Representational thinking is the attempted overcoming of the limit of self-reserve:

> Projecting-open of re-presentation in the sense of a *grasping* that reaches ahead, plans and arranges everything before everything is already conceived as particular and singular – this re-presentation recognizes no limit [Grenze] in the given, and *wants* to find no limit. Rather the limitless is what is deciding, not as mere flux and mere 'and-so-forth,' but as that which is bound to no limit of the *given*, bound to no *given* and to no giveable *as limit.* (GA65, 135–6/94–5)

Why no limit? Because re-presentation recognizes no limit in beings themselves, and finally not even the limit of their objectivity. For as representation it is a bringing-before, an overcoming of 'distance' for the sake of making-secure and certain (132/92).

> As *systematic*, re-presentation turns this distance and its overcoming and securing into the basic law of determination of the object. (GA65, 135/94)

Whereas this is most evident through the project of quantification, we have seen that the representation of beings in terms of their causal relations in the 'historical sciences' also integrates them into an order of objectivity. The primacy of method over the phenomena, and of the operational function of knowledge over the 'truth' of the known, both for the sake of the production of results, ensures that entities are grasped in advance and ordered in the in-different space of their 'being' as product and function.

In his commentary on Nietzsche (1936–7), Heidegger explicates the immanent limit which sets a being back into itself, so as to come forth out of itself, as follows:

> Form, *forma* corresponds to the Greek *morphe*, the circumscribing limit [Grenze] and delimitation which forces and sets a being in that which it is, so that it stands in itself: the gestalt [Gestalt]. (GA43, 138)

As such it comes into appearance in the *eidos*, 'presents itself, makes itself manifest' and shines forth (GA43, 138). Form and gestalt in this sense constitute not the merely external frame, opposed to 'content,' but the movement into being of a being as rooted in the sheltering reserve of its own 'truth' (un-concealment), as rooted in its withdrawal from the emptiness of the merely formal (GA43, 139–40). Re-presentation brings this movement to a stand in the being-present of the calculable, and thus institutes the arrangement of the in-different.

The notion of *Gestalt*, as just cited from the Nietzsche lectures, which 'The Origin of the Work of Art' also articulates, has to be clearly and radically distinguished from Jünger's concept of the *Gestalt* of the Worker. According to Heidegger, gestalt in Jünger's sense is *posited* in the reversal of Platonism as the will to master the chaos of becoming (GA90, 22, 134). The gestalt of the worker is posited as the ground of certainty, the self-certain form of subjectivity that 'actualizes' entities under the regime of technology. Therefore entities have no gestalt in themselves, but only are in being as calculable functions of the gestalt of the worker, and its will to self-affirmation (GA90, 6, 134). However, if the gestalt as such, *das Gestalthafte* (the gestalt-like), is an articulation of being (*Wesung des Seins*) in a way (as Heidegger emphasizes) Jünger does not think (GA90, 141), then this already intimates that the thought of gestalt has other, non-metaphysical possibilities.

Our consideration of total mobilization, however, is still incomplete, for *Seinsverlassenheit* implicates a second moment, which is the obverse side, as it were, of machination. And thus total mobilization must also, in Heidegger's estimation, be defined by the same second moment. This is *Erlebnis*, or lived experience. The collusion of machination and the primacy of lived or intensified experience announces the end, or rather consummation, of the rational animal of metaphysics. *Erlebnis* refers to the integration of technicity and animality as it is brought to pass today, for example, by ever more subtle chemical and electronic means, from the mapping of the human genome and its therapeutic applications, to designer, mood-altering drugs, to the 'bionic man' of modern medicine, to the 'sensationalism' of a myriad forms of consumption. In all these ways mankind is 'mobilized,' is 'called up,' and keeps itself 'on call.' The human being of metaphysics finds its consummation in techno-animality.

Total mobilization, in Heidegger's understanding, involves the dis-integration of beings and their reintegration into the in-different space of a system of functional relations, as a resource on call. *As a phenomeno-logical description of the end of modernity* this concept of total mobilization has essential points of contact with Jünger's. Heidegger clearly differs from Jünger, however, in the understanding of the provenance of total mobilization in the history of metaphysics. The triumph of representa-tional thinking and the transformation of *techne*, under the influence of Christian theology, into the technology of production, are the most evi-dent conditions for the advent of the operational thinking of machina-tion, and thus for the mobilization of entities. Further, given that organic construction is a kind of self-production arising out of the fusion of humanity and technology, it brings machination to light in the consum-mation of the rational animal, in techno-animality. Finally, Heidegger understands *Seinsverlassenheit*, and thus machination – precisely because they intimate the oblivion and *withdrawal* of the presencing of being – as the possible gateway of a turn into being as the founding of being in beings. This withdrawal is the threshold of a possible turn into the shel-tering reserve of the being of beings – as the withdrawal from representa-tion. This demands a leap into the site of being as Da-sein. The leap calls for decision, the decision, for the step back into the first beginning as the retrieval of its concealed possibilities. There can be no founding of Da-sein without the leap into the differentiation of being in beings.

Does Jünger overlook the necessity and the need for decision and the leap? And if so, is it because he assumes a certain 'logic' of technology? Is this logic that of the will to power? This logic implicates a movement of the differentiation of beings, but only as functions of the in-difference of the Same. Resistance to the necessity of a decision founded in the *dif-ferentiation of being in beings* is precisely what characterizes liberalism. This resistance apparently arises out of the failure to experience the need inherernt in the destitution of beings *in its historical dimension*. Insofar as Jünger shares this undecidability (Derrida) with liberalism, it would place him in an unaccountable proximity to his most intimate opponent.

In the attempt to determine Heidegger's later critical response to Jünger, Heidegger's 'Zur Seinsfrage' (On the Question of Being) (1955) offers us important insights. The complexity of this essay, joining as it does the history of being and the question of nihilism, is such that the following discussion can only hope to open the door to further ques-tions. The hermeneutic situation out of which this reflection on nihilism arises is the challenge of planetary thinking and a planetary order (ZS

418–9). We know that in *Der Arbeiter*, Jünger takes his point of departure from the necessity of *founding – in the sense of positing legitimating values –* the planetary regime which technology imposes. The planetary order is conceived as the two-stage consummation and overcoming of nihilism in the gestalt of the Worker. But whereas Jünger apparently assumed that the process of total mobilization in its second, form-granting moment, deriving from the stability of the gestalt of the Worker, already implies the overcoming of nihilism, this position is modified in his later works. In the essay 'Über den Schmerz' (On Pain) of 1934 and in 'Über die Linie' (1950), Jünger holds that the new forms of organization produced by technology do not yet signify the positing of corresponding and commensurate values.[83]

As a reflection on nihilism, Jünger's 'Über die Linie' offers Heidegger significant points of contact, which allow dialogue and therefore meaningful critique. The essay defines nihilism as the will to the thorough organization of the work-world, and thus the reduction of beings and relations to purely functional values (UL 249, 269). The infinite expansion of perspectives of power feeds on the inner emptiness of the 'subject' of this process in the sense that the 'organization' of the 'world' is motivated by our horrified revulsion from the emptiness of our own being (UL 270). Throughout the essay, Jünger employs the medical analogy of the diagnosis of nihilism, prognosis, and possible cure. In 'Overcoming Metaphysics' Heidegger had come to essentially the same conclusion, to the extent of defining nihilism as the process of the organized exploitation of the world, as 'the organization of lack' (UM, sec. 26). The reduction of beings to raw material for the sole purpose of production and consumption implicates the withdrawal of their being and therefore generates the void, or emptiness, in which they and we ourselves hang. 'This emptiness must be filled.' Despite itself, and without being conscious of it, technology is defined by its relation to this emptiness, in the sense that production and consumption vainly endeavour to fill the lack of being which arises out of the depths of our own existence to pervade our every encounter with beings (UM, sec. 26). The atrophy of the being of beings, however, also raises the question, for Jünger, whether the realization of the functional world of work perhaps intimates the consummation of nihilism, and therefore the possibility of 'crossing the line' of nihilism into a new era. 'The moment in which the line is crossed, being turns [toward us] anew, and then begins to shimmer what truly is' (UL 267). The intimate relation between nihilism, the emptiness at the heart of the being of beings, and the possibility of a turn within nihilism, constitutes the common point of departure of 'Über die Linie' and 'Zur Seinsfrage.' But the medical analogy Jünger employs already engenders a serious problem, because it assumes a standpoint outside of nihilism and its inherent negativity, which is our own.

What remains constant in Jünger's thinking between 1931 and 1950 to offer Heidegger significant points of contention are the assumptions that nihilism can be overcome (transcended), and that the sign of this overcoming will be the emergence of new values. The form of Heidegger's questioning is to take the step back from the thought of transcendence into the origin of transcendence in the presencing of being in beings. The same step back implicates the abandonment of planetary representation in order to open a space for the earth-sitedness of presencing as *Heimat.*

Heidegger's response to the planetary, therefore, is to take the step back into earth-sited dwelling (*Bauen*) as founded in the Saying (*die Sage*) of being (ZS 417–8). Saying opens the site of being as Da-sein. With the opening of this site, the struggle for planetary *Herrschaft*, which Nietzsche's thought announces, is transformed into the *polemos* of the differentiation of being in the gestalt of beings (ZS 418). *Polemos* allows the non-metaphysical gestalt of Da-sein as mortal (the placeholder of the presencing of the Nothing which belongs to *Seyn*) to come into its own (ZS 418; cf. 413). It is implicit in Heidegger's argument that the gestalt of mortality is at the furthest remove from that of the Worker, but no less intimately related to it. Because the gestalt of the Worker signals the disintegration of classical subjectivity, it opens the possibility of a decision between mortality and techno-animality (cf. ZS 395; and GA65, sec. 45).

Heidegger's commentary holds that Jünger's thought remains caught in metaphysics: the engagement of Jünger's thought, as devoted to 'crossing the line' from nihilism to a new era, remains especially problematical. The concept of total mobilization of *Der Arbeiter* expresses the will to transcend the nihilism of the metaphysical dissolution of beings to found a world-order in the stability of the gestalt. Heidegger brings the following moments of this thought into question: (*i*) the apparent derivation of the gestalt of the Worker from the stability of the Platonic Idea (ZS 388–90); (*ii*) the idea of the transcendence of nihilism (ZS 391); (*iii*) the will to justify (legitimate) the senselessness of beings, hence to give value (ZS 390–1); and (*iv*) the negation and reduction of the negativity belonging to presencing to mere annihilation (ZS 412–15). The retrieval of negativity as the withdrawal of presencing is the gateway to a turn within the domain of nihilism, and would signify, although in a transformed sense, 'crossing the line' of nihilism.

Heidegger repeats the claim that Jünger's understanding of gestalt in *The Worker derives from the Platonic Idea* as the being of beings (ZS 389). The gestalt has the abiding presence of true being. But whereas Plato pre-figures Jünger's sense of gestalt, the metaphysical mode of this thought is ultimately that of the *will to power* as the movement of becoming which *mobilizes* the actual, hence generates the actuality of the actual (ZS 389; GA90, 22–3). The will to power is the *movement of transcendence* as the actualization of the actual. In this sense 'transcendence' refers to the passage from the stability of the gestalt to the instability of beings, to form and transform them (ZS 391). It is characteristic of the essence of metaphysics, Heidegger holds, that it determines every kind of *chorismos* between true and less true being in terms of the idea of transcendence.[84] He argues that the actualization of the will to power in beings defines Jünger's concept of 'work' and of the gestalt of the Worker (ZS 392). But because the gestalt of the Worker is the source of the meaning and value of beings, transcendence no longer signifies the passage beyond beings to their ground in being, but recoils back on itself; presence (understood as being, as the source of the being-present of entities) inscribes itself in re-presentation. Presence (the gestalt of the Worker) unfolds itself as Work, that is, as total mobilization. Total mobilization is the re-presentation of presence (ZS 392–3). The gestalt of the Worker, however, should not be understood as some kind of Platonic form 'behind' the things themselves. The 'presence' and the 'being' it has only are as operative in the movement of re-presentation. This movement 'actualizes' beings in mobilizing them, and it mobilizes as the movement of differentiation which first grants each entity its work-character, and therefore its quantum of being. The gestalt, in Jünger's terms, 'is' the movement of differentiation and totalization.

The limitations of Jünger's position become evident for Heidegger in the implication that the will to power imprints the stamp of form and therefore of value on beings. The *will to 'legitimate' beings* follows from the metaphysical *chorimos* of being and beings. It can only be overcome by the step back into the site of being as Da-sein. Heidegger holds that Jünger's understanding of the will to power interprets Zarathrustra as the gestalt of the Worker (ZS 390, 384). Yet the 'Overman' and the Eternal Return which Zarathustra teaches remain caught in the will to justify life. In the will to justification, the will to revenge against time, which defines metaphysics, is not overcome.[85] The gestalt of the Worker, there-fore, is posited as the transcendental ground of the justification of life in the actualization of form and meaning. The Worker figures transcenden-tal subjectivity, hence the essence of a humanity which is posited as the '*subiectum*' of all that is (ZS 390): the gestalt intimates an idea of human-ity 'which as presence already constitutes the ground of all beings in their being-present, thus to first allow "representation" in beings so as to "legitimate" beings *as* beings' (ZS 391; GA90, 5–6, 31). Heidegger avers that the *Typus*, or type, through which the gestalt of the Worker actual-izes and mobilizes itself in every articulation of technicity, composes the most extreme realization of subjectivity (ZS 390; GA90, 194). One could object, however, that insofar as the gestalt of the Worker announces the disintegration of classical subjectivity in the form of its integration into functional networks, it already presages the *Ge-stell* which is itself the gateway to the event of appropriation (*Ereignis*). In this respect, the gestalt of the Worker, as that of Zarathustra, remains ambivalent.

Being as actualization, furthermore, implicates the operative thinking of science, *the fixation on beings to the exclusion of being as No-thing* (ZS 412–13). The Nothing which belongs to the presencing of being as Da-sein is also occluded (ZS 405). Therefore the founding of presencing in the Da, the site, and thus in beings is concealed. From our consideration of Heidegger's commentary on Aristotle's *Physics* B, I, we know that the movement of withdrawal, of the negation (*steresis*) inherent in the *kinesis* of *morphe* cannot be brought to light as long as the Nothing is reduced to mere negativity. But with the oblivion of the movement of sheltering with-drawal, the concept of gestalt falls back into metaphysics. The meta-physical gestalt realizes the stability and transparency of the Idea. This offers us a fundamental point of distinction between Jünger's and Heidegger's understanding of the gestalt and style of the being of beings. For in Heidegger's sense, the 'form' of the work of art, and of every being in some degree, incorporates the movement of withdrawal (the *lethe* of *aletheia*) into its coming into form out of the strife of earth and world. But insofar as the thought of the 'organic construction' fails to integrate negation as the movement of withdrawal into the gestalt of beings, this gestalt is determined as the re-presentation of the gestalt of the Worker, which is to say, of the stability of being. The stability of beings as standing reserve (*Bestand*) conceals the presencing of being in beings (ZS 390). In Heidegger's view, the gestalt of the Worker, as it consummates itself in the organic construction (the unity of being, or of 'nature' and thought) affirms the metaphysics of form, of abiding presence.

The fundamental move of Heidegger's reflection on total mobilization and the Worker is the step back from transcendence. This implicates the deconstruction of the Line which separates the consummation of nihilism and the possibility of another beginning in favour of the Site of the presencing of being in the Da of Da-sein. The sign of this deconstruction is the crossing through of being as beingness. The X of the crossing marks the differentiated presencing of being as sited, as founded in Da-sein (ZS 404–5). Transcendence, as passing over the Line to go beyond nihilism (ZS 380), forgets the Nothing which belongs to the presencing of being, and therefore this thought remains caught in the metaphysics of the gestalt of the Worker (ZS 415). The non-metaphysical way of the Site does not pass over into the stability of the gestalt as *Bestand*, but opens a place for the presencing of being (as *aletheia*, therefore as the together of manifestation and withdrawal) (ZS 417). Nihilism, we could say, following Nietzsche, is the most 'unfamiliar' (*der unheimlichste*) of guests. Nihilism wills the unfamiliar, wills world-universal homelessness (ZS 381). The step back from nihilism, and from the nihilistic conception of negativity, is also already a step on the way to the new, non-metaphysical rootedness which is named in the word *Heimat*: the differentiated unity of presencing and the negativity of withdrawal from presencing.

Heidegger avers that the step back from nihilism into the withdrawal from representation at the heart of truth is announced by the essence of technology, or the *Ge-stell*, itself (ZS 395), precisely because nihilism, as the reduction of beings to a standing reserve, implies the nihilation, the reduction and emptying-out, of beings, as Jünger also recognizes (UL 257). But the 'atrophy [Schwund] of what was as being-present does not signify the disappearance of presencing.' Presencing indeed withholds itself in favour of the standing reserve, and it appears as if being were nothing, not at issue (ZS 408–9). Yet this self-concealing concealment of presencing-as-withdrawal is the turn within nihilism, within the *Ge-stell*. It intimates the possibility of the sheltering unconcealment of beings to the degree that beings – reduced or a-nihilated in their object-being through the consummation of metaphysics in nihilism – recover their being in the grant of the *Ereignis* as founded in Da-sein (cf. ZS 409–10).

Could it be, Heidegger asks, that the essence (*Wesen*) of the *Gestalt* of the Worker originates in the *Ge-Stell* (ZS 395)? We recall that a reference to *Ge-stell* (written in this way, rather than as *Ge-Stell* or *Gestell*), appears in the Addendum to 'The Origin of the Work of Art' (UK 69/208): it points back to the text itself, joining the question of gestalt and *Ge-stell*.

> The strife that is brought into the rift and thus set back into the earth and thus fixed in place is the *figure* [*Gestalt*]. Createdness of the work means truth's being fixed in place in the figure ... What is here called figure [Gestalt] is always to be thought in terms of the particular placing [Stellen] and enframing [Ge-stell] as which the *work* occurs when it sets itself up and sets itself forth. (UK 50/189)

Evidently Heidegger holds a deconstructed understanding of gestalt as the coming-to-stand of beings within the clearing of being (Da-sein). The retrieval of *Gestalt* is carried through by rethinking gestalt in terms of the event of truth, and therefore in terms of the movement of sheltering concealment – the *Bergung*, the *lethe* – which belongs to this event. The gestalt sets back into the earth. It is also evident that in 'The Origin' – and Heidegger will recur to this thought in his response to Jünger – *Ge-stell* is not yet the name for the essence of technology, the name for the event of the expropriation of beings as standing reserve. The *Ge-stell* rather articulates 'the gathering of bringing-forth, of the letting-come-forth-here into the rift-design as bounding outline (*peras*). The Greek sense of *morphe* as *Gestalt* is made clear by *Ge-stell* so understood' (UK 69/209, modified). *Ge-stell* is the *gathering* of bringing-forth, and of what is brought forth in its determinate being. For the limit or boundary (*Grenze/peras*) through which things are manifest, 'sets [them] free into the unconcealed': the limit 'fixes or consolidates' (UK 68–9/208).

The 'setting free,' however, precisely as a fixing or consolidating, is not without essential relation to *techne*, and thus to technology, and to gestalt in its metaphysical sense. In the *Grundfragen* of 1937–8, *techne* itself is conceived as a grasping of beings in their *eidos* in order to allow beings to manifest themselves 'according to their own measure,' thus to preserve the unconcealment of *phusis* (GA45, 179–80). *Techne* is 'the way of proceeding *against phusis*,' yet in the first instance it is for the sake of *phusis* (GA45, 179). For in bringing beings in their coming-forth into appearance, and thus into the stand of the *eidos*, *techne* holds them in the limit out of which they manifest themselves. The essence of technology arises out of *techne* in this sense: the limit (the gestalt) into which beings are set is *represented* as the *position* which they are challenged to take in order to secure and consolidate the arrangement of what is posited by representational thinking (GA45, 180–1; cf. UK 69–70). Metaphysically conceived, the *Ge-Stell* intimates that humanity and being mutually challenge each other and reciprocally position each other in the exposed openness of their mutual belonging. In *Ge-stell*, we hear *vor-stellen* (setting-before, or re-presentation), *stellen* (to position, challenge, interrogate), *Stellung* (a position, e.g., in the military sense), as well as the order and arrangement, the gathering of entities, implicit in *Ge-stell*. *Gestell* could be translated as 'Exposition' to signify the essence of the discursive system of language in which humanity, as it were, hangs ex-posed, which essence mankind is constrained to be, and wills to be, in the consummation of its metaphysical essence as a resource on call. Ex-posure (*Ausgesetztheit*) to beings in the midst of beings determines, as we have seen, Heidegger's understanding of work in the *Logik* of 1934. As the 'presencing' of the technological arrangement of this exposure, the *Gestell* expresses the essence of work as total mobilization, for mobilization operates as the re-presentative challenging, positioning, and arrangement of entities as standing reserve.

Consequently Heidegger advances the following argument: (*i*) The artwork and technology have a common 'essence,' for '*Gestell*' will serve him in 'The Question Concerning Technology' as the name for the essence of technology as the challenging-bringing-forth of beings. The *Gestell* is the gateway to the non-metaphysical in two senses: (*a*) as the *echo* of bringing-forth into appearance; and (*b*) as the *anticipation* of sheltering unconcealment, since *Gestell* signifies the withdrawal of beings from re-presentation. Thus (*ii*) in the artwork essay, *Ge-stell* is still understood as a *letting*-come-forth into unconcealment. (*iii*) The retrieval of Greek *peras* and *morphe* intimates a non-metaphysical sense of limit, of standing in unconcealment. Finally (*iv*) this sense of limit is designated the *Gestalt* of a being. This suffices to show that Heidegger does not abandon gestalt to the language of metaphysics, despite the metaphysical heritage of the word, which he finds inscribed in Jünger's discourse. It makes sense, in fact, to read Heidegger's dialogue with Jünger as the deconstruction of the 'gestalt of the Worker,' intended to set free the gestalt *of beings* as founded in Da-sein as the locus of the historicity of being.

Given the essential relation, moreover, between art and technology which is reserved for us in originary *techne*, and reappropriated in *Ge-stell*, it is evident that Heidegger allows the possibility that 'technology' can shelter beings, but precisely to the extent that it brings beings into their *peras*, that is, sets them into the gestalt of their own temporalization and localization. By 'localization,' I mean the event of their coming to presence in and through and for the sake of a locale, which comes to light through beings, and which in turn allows the self-reserved withdrawal of beings into sheltering. Despite the metaphysical thrust of Jünger's fundamental concepts, there is an intimation of 'sheltering' in his works to the extent to which he appeals to the earth as a formative and mythic power. This offers an additional point of correspondence between Jünger's and Heidegger's thinking.

We recall that for Nietzsche art is exemplary of the being of beings as the will to power. The 'grand style' expresses the unity of the relations through which art manifests the will to power (NI 162/137). But since art, in Nietzsche's thought, is not limited to artworks in the narrow sense – for it includes 'organizations,' such as the Jesuit order or the Prussian officer corps – the Worker can also be conceived as a work of art possessing a distinctive style.[86] This is in fact the thesis of Jünger's *Der Arbeiter*: the gestalt of the Worker calls for the embodiment of a particular style of being, as a response to the being of beings in the planetary epoch. The question which Heidegger's critique of Jünger poses more or less explicitly is whether or not this style is sufficiently *attuned to the earth* in its withdrawal from representational thinking.

The question of the earth is a question of 'style' in at least two senses: (*i*) the style of Da-sein in its attunement to being; and (*ii*) the style of beings as the 'form' into which they are set, or in which they come to 'set' themselves, thus to be. In his discussion of Nietzsche's aesthetics of the 'grand style,' Heidegger attempts a deconstruction of the aesthetics of 'rapture' (*Rausch*) and form in order to open a site for Da-sein as the strife of earth and world, without, however, explicitly addressing this strife in the lectures. Reading the Nietzsche lectures through the optic of 'The Origin of the Work of Art' and the *Beiträge*, we may hazard that 'rapture' in Nietzsche's 'physiological' or 'biological' interpretation implicates, in Heidegger's terms, the attunement (*Stimmung*) of the 'body' to beings, more precisely, the living, embodied unity of earth and Da-sein.

Attunement wills to take 'form,' thus to determine itself. The form, in turn, gives measure, articulates attunement (NI 139/118): whereas 'the bodily state as such continues to participate as a condition of the creative process, it is at the same time what in the created thing is to be restrained, overcome, and surpassed' (NI 152/129). In the form of the created, the will to power, which rapture itself is, takes form, sets itself into form:

> Rapture in itself is drawn to major features, that is to a series of traits, to an articulation. So we must once more turn away from the apparently one-sided consideration of mere states and turn toward *what* defines this mood in our attunement. In connection with the usual conceptual language of aesthetics, which Nietzsche too speaks, we call it 'form' ... Form founds

the realm in which rapture as such becomes possible. (NI 139–40/118–9, modified)

As the intensified intimacy of rapture and order, form brings the 'force and plentitude' of being into the open in a being (NI 139/119). Therefore art is a 'gestalt of the will to power' (NI 143/122). Binding all things without force or constraint (for power is not 'compulsion or violence'), 'the will releases all things to their essence and their own bounds [Grenze]' (NI 161/136–7). Because the being of the thing is given free in the form, Heidegger can appeal to a non-metaphysical sense of form as 'limit and boundary,' as 'gestalt,' granted that the movement into form (*morphe*) implicates a *withdrawal from 'formalization,'* from representation (NI 139/119). 'The Origin of the Work of Art,' therefore, rethinks the question of 'form' as the preservation (*Bergung*) of a moment of withdrawal in world as well as earth. This transforms the question of style, for it sets Da-sein as the site of beings, and beings themselves, back into the historicity of the self-secluding earth. Herein the style of work, and of the Worker, would find their measure.

Heidegger claims that 'Über den Schmerz' (On Pain) takes the position of *The Worker* the furthest (ZS 398). In this essay, Jünger insists that work implicates the self-objectification of the Worker and of beings. In this self-objectification, the Worker (unlike the bourgeoisie) no longer flees pain, but accepts it as the price of a self-discipline which wills an increase in power.[87] Metaphysically understood as annihilation of the subject, pain is integrated, in all its negativity, into the technicity of the work process. Jünger intimates, however, that this process of self-objectification is no less *the denial of pain as an elemental power*,[88] for it annihilates not only the subject, but the entire subject-object constellation of being. The gestalt of the Worker remains hanging in metaphysics insofar as it deconstructs the classical subject without being able to move beyond it. The problem is how to conceive the negativity inherent in Work as the being of beings. The dis-integration of the objectivity of beings could open the way to the experience of the presencing and withdrawal of being in the non-metaphysical gestalt of beings. Jünger takes up this thought, in 'Über die Linie,' to the extent of allowing a new shining-forth of beings beginning with the crossing of the line (UL 267).[89] The alternative, metaphysical possibility, which Heidegger sees especially in Hegel (ZS 398), is that the negation and dis-integration of entities become the spur to the systematic actualization of the real.

Because Jünger brings work and pain into explicit relation, he recalls an essential moment in the history of metaphysics: pain, metaphysically understood, inscribes our being-delivered over to beings. Heidegger claims that the unity of pain and work, as Jünger thinks it, leads to the heart of Hegel's metaphysics (ZS 398).[90] As such, a few brief, truncated remarks will have to suffice here. Pain is the concentrated rending which gathers into oneness even as it tears open into utmost exposure in the midst of beings. As exposure, it figures the essence of work, since Heidegger understands work as *Ausgesetztheit*, being ex-posed, open to beings in the midst of beings. Work and pain stand in an intimate relation founded in the differentiated wholeness of Da-sein. Then why does Heidegger insist that Jünger's grasp of this relation is still caught in the net of Hegels's metaphysics? Because work – as the being of beings – is conceived as the actualization of the real through the negativity of the concept. Work passes through negativity (the exposure of 'pain') to bring the real into being and to legitimate it.

Nonetheless, in the thought of pain as 'the innermost gathering,' Heidegger sees a relation to Work as the exposure to beings, which is no longer metaphysical (ZS 398). The Greek word for pain, *algos*, is 'presumably' related to *alego* and *lego*, hence to saying, gathering. In 'Die Sprache,' a lecture held in October 1950, Heidegger takes up the relation of saying, of language and pain, in a reading of Trakl's 'Ein Winterabend.' Pain is the threshold, the jointure which cuts the unity of a design, which endures and carries the differentiated. Now pain is understood as the differentiated unity of world and thing. This unity presences as the differentiated gathering of language, which grants each its own, and gathers it into the jointure.[91] In attempting to follow the thread of Heidegger's dialogue with Jünger we began with the question of gestalt, of style. Work and the gestalt of the Worker in the age of technology led us to the question of language. Language gives gestalt. It gives gestalt in the saying of the poem; it gives form in the discourses of the sciences. In this sense the question of the Worker is a question concerning language, that is, a question of mankind's response to the historicity of what has been sent, granted to it in the age of the consummation of metaphysics.

7.5 Freedom and the Ethos of Da-sein

In conclusion to this discussion of the *Beiträge*, I will briefly consider how the question of freedom impinges on Da-sein as the site of the truth of *Seyn*. To this end, I will draw especially on aspects of Heidegger's lectures on Kant and Schelling, without presuming to offer a full account of the issues they unfold. In lectures of 1930, entitled *Vom Wesen der Menschlichen Freiheit: Einleitung in die Philosophie* (*The Essence of Human Freedom: An Introduction to Philosophy*) (GA31), Heidegger states that freedom is the 'condition of the possibility of Dasein,' and the ground of the questioning of metaphysics (GA31, 94/134). Though this Kantian formulation reflects Heidegger's point of departure, in these lectures, from Kant's position, Heidegger's objective is to retrieve the fundamental ground of freedom by uncovering the letting-be of the being of beings as the ground of Dasein. This ultimately calls for a critique of Kant's understanding of being, and of his determination of freedom in relation to causality.[92] The two questions – the question of being and the question of freedom – are linked by way of causality, for the causal determination *of beings, including human being,* presupposes a certain understanding of *being.* This understanding of being has to be won from the entity which has an understanding of being, that is, from human being, and as we recall, this is the task of *Being and Time.* In *Being and Time,* freedom is at issue in terms of Dasein's being-in-the-world, understood as the finite transcendence of Dasein which is the condition of the unconcealment of beings. Any mode of comportment toward beings, or of Dasein toward itself, is rendered possible only on the basis of the structure of disclosedness which Dasein itself is (SZ, sec. 44). For this reason, it becomes evident why freedom cannot be, in its most fundamental sense, a possession or quality of human being, but must be the structure of openness that allows beings to manifest themselves, hence to be as beings. The essay *Vom Wesen der Wahrheit* ('On the Essence of Truth') (1930) explicitly addresses this question, by showing that truth in the sense of the truth of statements finds its ground in freedom as 'freedom for what is opened up in an open region.' Only because Dasein is structured as finite transcendence, hence as freedom-for the open, can beings manifest themselves, and can we ourselves make correct or incorrect statements about them. Therefore, 'freedom for what is opened up in an open region lets beings be the beings they are. Freedom now reveals itself as letting beings be.' The letting-be of beings implies the possibility of *the release of the will* to master beings. More than this, Heidegger insists, letting-be 'means to engage oneself with the open region and its openness into which every being comes to stand, bringing that openness, as it were, along with itself' (WW 185–6/125). As this condition of our engagement with the being of beings, as the 'disclosure of beings as such,' thus to bring them to a stand, freedom is 'not merely' the caprice of human choice, to incline in one direction or another. Nor is it merely, or most fundamentally, the negative freedom of the absence of constraint, nor primarily the positive freedom of the will to obey a higher law which the will itself sets and acknowledges (WW 186/126).

Heidegger's lectures of 1930 devote detailed attention to Kant's treatment of the causality of nature, the causality of freedom, and the possibility of their unity, which is concretely given in humanity as rational being. Whereas the first way is an attempt to show the possibility of freedom from a cosmological perspective, in a general ontology, the second treats reason in humanity as itself a kind of causality, and thereby points to real practical freedom as specific to humanity as a rational being.[93] Reason in itself has the power to originate a causal series, and since freedom is defined by causality, this implies that the origination of a causal series reveals humanity as in a certain respect free, even though as a natural being it is subject to the causal series of nature (GA31, 257–8/173–4). The rational essence of humanity is defined by Kant as personhood (*Persönlichkeit*): this means that humanity is a 'being capable of accountability' and self-responsibility (GA31, 262/182).[94] Self-responsibility is the kind of being specific to human action, to ethical praxis. The actuality of freedom as practical reason consists in will-governed action, that is, in the '*capacity to effect according to the representation of something as principle.*' Will and reason belong together, because 'to will there belongs this determining representation of something' (GA31, 275/190). In other words, willing implies the representation of a concept – this is what distinguishes an act of will from a mere urge or impulse. The will, in determining, is always addressed to itself, that is to say, the will is co-represented with the object of action. The will wills itself, and this is the condition of all willing; as such, in self-willing, it wills to take responsibility for itself. Consequently, 'the *basic law of the pure will, of pure practical reason,* is nothing else than the *form of law-giving*'; in the case of a finite being, this law takes the form of a command, of the Ought of the categorical imperative (GA31, 279/192). Heidegger concludes this discussion of Kant by saying that the essence of freedom as practical is '*self-legislation, pure will, autonomy.* Freedom now reveals itself as *the condition of the possibility of the factuality of pure practical reason.* Practical freedom as autonomy is self-responsibility, which is the essence of the personality of the human person, the authentic essence, the humanity of man' (GA31, 296/202–3).

Heidegger's critique of Kant's position holds that the questionable nature of both the cosmological and the practical determination of freedom consists in the fact that both begin with causality, yet causality as such is never put into question in respect to the understanding of being which it supposes. If this question is posed, then causality would be revealed as 'a character of the objectivity of objects' (*Gegenständlichkeit der Gegenstände*). In agreement with the metaphysical tradition, being is understood as being-present (*Vorhandensein*), and this also determines the nature of causality (GA31, 189–200/132–8). But beings 'can only show themselves as *objects* if the appearance of beings, and that which at bottom makes this possible, i.e., the understanding of being, has the character of letting-stand-over-against.' In *letting*-stand, comportment responds to and acknowledges the 'binding character' of what becomes manifest within the realm of the open. The letting-be of beings implies a being free for the demand that their being makes on us. Freedom is revealed as 'the possibility of the manifestness of the being of beings, of the understanding of being,' and causality is shown to be *one kind* of ontological determination of beings. In effect, freedom is not a problem arising out of causality, but causality is '*grounded in freedom*' (GA31 300, 302/205, 207). The understanding of being as being-present, which Kant presupposes, is dependent on an understanding of being and time, and on the way in which the interdependence of being and time is made manifest in the finitude of human being. Heidegger's critical appropriation of Kant, as Schalow shows, is directed toward uncovering human finitude and facticity as the condition of freedom in the Kantian sense of the autonomy of the self-willing will and therefore of the moral comportment proper to a being capable of willing a law for itself.[95]

With the emergence of human being in its temporal finitude and throwness, both the character of 'ground' and the being of humanity are transposed into another arena, one which is no longer defined by the self-affirmation of the will as the fundamental trait of human freedom. Whereas for Kant, freedom consists in the grounding act of the rational will in its self-affirmation (GA31, 257/173), Heidegger insists that freedom, as the fundamental problem of philosophy, means grasping the root of Dasein as that which claims Dasein (GA31, 303/208). Although Heidegger does not say so explicitly here, this leads us in the direction of the finitude of Dasein as a *thrown* project responsible for its own existence (SZ 266/245). Thus Dasein 'may become essential [wesentlich] in the actual willing of his ownmost existence' (GA31, 303/208). In this way, as becoming essential, the actuality of the will is transposed into the resoluteness (*Entschlossenheit*) of being-toward-death, which throws Dasein back on the necessity of grasping its heritage in the moment of vision (*Augenblick*) which illuminates the concrete situation of action (SZ

385/352). Willing its own existence, Dasein wills the event of its being-open for its ownmost possibility. In his commentary on Kant, Heidegger emphasizes that the reality of freedom is 'not an objective reality' – its factuality is that of praxis, or 'practical will-governed action' (GA31, 272/188). The resoluteness of being-toward-death is the opening to authentic being and action. The *Entschlossenheit* of being-toward-death, moreover, already shifts the being of action into the openness (*Ent-schlossenheit*) of another ground, distinct from the self-affirming will as ground. This ground is the structure of thrownness: in Dasein as thrown project lies an essential nullity (*Nichtigkeit*) which Dasein itself *is* in taking over the possibilities into which it has been thrown (SZ 284–5/262). As such, the entire concept of 'ground' is transformed at the root, and with it, the ground of possibility of free, responsible ethical action. In being-toward-death, Dasein becomes free for its ownmost possibilities, which are disclosed to it in and for its being-with-others (SZ 264–5/244). Ethical action, therefore, in the sense of the letting-be of the being of others, finds its ground in being-free for one's ownmost possibility and in assuming responsibility for the nullity which it reveals as the ground of one's being.

The resolve of the will implicated in its own self-affirmation, and with it, the grounding act of the will in the positing of the Ought, is dependent, in Heidegger's reading of Kant, on the self-presence of subjectivity. The *Ent-schlossenheit* of Dasein in the freedom of being-toward-death already implies a resolve and a praxis which is no longer based in subjectivity, but stands in the openness of response to the being of beings. Dasein is the site of this openness in the project of the *Contributions to Philosophy*. The question arises as to how actual practical freedom is articulated in this work, given that freedom is neither mere absence of constraint, nor pre-eminently the positive freedom of the self-legislation of the will in giving itself its own law.

As Thiele has pointed out, both concepts of freedom are predicated on a model of mastery, or control – the control of one's private space in negative freedom, and the mastery of the self in positive freedom. The latter, moreover, insofar as it implies submission to a higher, universal law, also implicates, according to Thiele, the submission of the self to the organic state and its collective law. Thiele adds that the postmodern attempt, which he associates with Foucault, to escape this dilemma by defining freedom as the self-invention of the autonomous self in opposition to the totalizing impulses of socio-technical discourses, still conceives the self as the object of self-production, and thereby confirms the fundamental determination of freedom as mastery.[96] Thiele recognizes that in response to the subjectivism of both concepts, Heidegger understands freedom in terms of the disclosive structure of Dasein, which means that freedom is actual in the guardianship of letting beings be, rather than in the mastery of the individual or collective self and its world.[97] This still leaves the question open as to how the actual practice of freedom is to be understood within the constellation of disclosive freedom and the ethics of letting-be. On the one hand, Theile explicitly separates freedom in this sense from a politics of Volk (which he sees as leading to totalitarianism), and on the other, he attempts to relate disclosive freedom to an ecological politics of 'environmental care and technological restraint.'[98] The question I wish to raise in response is whether disclosive freedom in its actuality, including practices of ecological responsibility, is possible otherwise than as part of a community of destiny, that is, as Volk in all the senses we have established.

In response to this question, let us see what clues the *Contributions* can offer, and in particular, whether we can establish a link between the disclosive structure of Dasein in its finite transcendence and an ethics of freedom in its actuality, that is, as a praxis or comportment toward the being of beings. I have already suggested that *Entschlossenheit* in the senses of resoluteness and openness expresses the actualization of the finite transcendence of Dasein, in the sense that returning to itself out of being-toward-death, Dasein takes responsibility for itself and responds to the being of the other and to innerworldly beings, as revealed by the situation into which it is thrown. In the *Contributions*, as we have seen, this taking of responsibility for beings is understood as *Bergung* – the sheltering unconcealment of the truth of being in beings. We recall that the founding attunement (*Grundstimmung*) which articulates the style of the other beginning, and attunes the comportment of Da-sein in its openness to the being of beings, is measured reserve (*Verhaltenheit*). *Verhaltenheit* is said to be the 'ground of care' (*Sorge*) (GA65, 35/25). As the *ground* of care it signals the *gathering* of the temporal unity of the thrown project of Dasein in the *turn* of being-historical thought: gathered in this turn, Da-sein turns *into* the historicity of being (*Seyn*). As such, Da-sein turns into the withdrawal of being in the abandonment of beings (*Seinsverlassenheit*) to endure this withdrawal and oblivion (*Seinsvergessenheit*). Reservedness is the ground of care because it names the turn of Da-sein *into* the abysmal ground of Da-sein. *Verhaltenheit* is the 'creative sustaining' or endurance (*Aushalten*) of the temporalizing of the abysmal ground (*Ab-grund*) (GA65, 36/26). This creative endurance is already intimated by the nullity of Dasein (in *Being and Time*), for the authenticity of Dasein is wrested from being-toward-death and the thrownness of Dasein as possibilities which Dasein must be. In taking over its own nullity Dasein becomes free for the possibilities of its heritage in the concrete situation as revealed by the *Augenblick*. Freedom as letting-be of the being of beings becomes actual in taking-up one's being as nullity. In the *Contributions*, the creative endurance of the *Ab-grund* is understood as the endurance of, and exposure to (*Ausgesetztheit*), the swaying-unfolding of truth as sheltering unconcealment. In sheltering, there is a moment of withdrawal from being-present, which Da-sein endures in holding itself in the openness of the withdrawal of all ground. This withdrawal presences in what is founded as ground and site in the works and acts of Da-sein. In this sense, the *Ab-grund,* or Un-ground, presences as ground in beings (GA65, 379–81/264–6). The steadiness of Da-sein in the face of this withdrawal of ground, which permeates all creative founding of unconcealment in the unconcealed, is the way in which the endurance of essential anxiety, as articulated in *Being and Time*, is transformed by the turn of Dasein into the event of its appropriation by and for being, in the thinking of the *Contributions*. Freedom as the letting-be of beings becomes actual in the acts and works, labour, thought, and sacrifice of the founding of the site of Da-sein. Freedom becomes an ethos of dwelling, not the fixation on any ground, but the staying in the draft of the open, thus to bring the emergence of beings to a stand.

Precisely as an ethos, we can see why freedom must be linked to the question of Volk, and why the question of *Bergung* is inseparable in the *Contributions* from the necessity of a reflection on Volk (GA65, 42/30). We recall that in Heidegger's projective anticipation, the being of Volk is understood as a countermovement to deracination, as the site of the differentiation of being in the rank order of beings and as a movement of withdrawal from representation. Freedom as letting-be and as sheltering actualizes a comportment of openness to the non-representational being of beings in all our working and doing. But this openness cannot be an actuality, as an ethos, in the form of an isolated subject – nor in that of a collective subject – but only as the praxis of the authentic selfhood of Da-sein as *Mitsein*, as a community of work and common destiny. As opposed to any concept of universal rationality, or humanity as an ideal of reason, Volk is the enactment of the '*finitude, temporality, and historicity* of mankind' (GA36/37, 166). Whereas Volk in its engagement for the historicity of being, and the possibilities which it concretely reveals, is not bound by an atemporal norm, it is bound by what reveals itself in the openness of being (GA36/37, 166, 164); and consequently it is bound to respond to the abandonment of all beings, including mankind, to technicity, in the epoch of total mobilization. The bond *inheres in freedom itself,* for freedom as letting-*be* can be actual only as an active engagement for the being of what is. Both the freedom from constraint of an autonomous being and the positive freedom of obedience to the law the will posits for itself as a rational, self-responsible being presuppose the possibility of a being capable of responding to what shows itself and of being bound by it. The project of the historicity of Da-sein shifts this relationship, that of unconcealment and response, onto the ground of its possibility in the historicity of being. The question of Volk arises necessarily, for Heidegger, out of the question of the historicity of being, and this means that it arises out of Da-sein's responsibility for the being of beings.

The emergence of beings has to be thought within the horizon of the historicity of being. Therefore the praxis of freedom, in the sense of an ethics of responsibility, implies a response to the being of beings in their abandonment to the order of causality, for under the regime of technicity beings increasingly manifest themselves as determined and determinable. As Heidegger intimates in his lectures on Schelling's *Of Human Freedom,* this order takes the *systematic* form of the calculability and functionality of beings.[99] Founded in the predominance of the mathematical in the definition of system (GA42, 60/34), hence in the self-certainty of representation, the system of being as conceived by German idealism is nothing merely external in the form of an arrangement imposed on beings, but is integral to the jointure of the being of beings itself (GA42, 86, 112–13/50, 64–5). In the terms of the *Contributions,* this system unfolds itself in the mutual implication of machination and *Erlebnis,* and hence in the total mobilization of beings in the era of the essence of technicity. The system of total mobilization, in effect, is the hermeneutic situation to which the project of the *Contributions* responds and the question of freedom is integral to this response. As Heidegger notes, Schelling raises the question of freedom in terms of the opposition between freedom and determinism, where determinism, together with the casual order proper to it, is conceived in terms of system (GA42, 143–53/83–8). How can this opposition be overcome, if indeed it can? This is the key question for both Schelling and Heidegger. In this context, I can only offer a few clues as to how Heidegger approaches this problem, and not so much in terms of the historical distinctness and otherness of his thought from that of Schelling, but as a deconstruction and retrieval of Schelling's metaphysics from the horizon of the leap into the other beginning. This implies seeing what it is in Schelling's treatise on freedom that offers Heidegger ground for this leap. In the first instance, Schelling's attempt to elaborate a system of freedom points us to the necessary relation of being and its articulations or jointures; for insofar as 'we understand "Being" ("Seyn") at all, we mean something like jointure and joining' (*Gefüge und Fügung*) (GA42 86/50). In other words, the question of the 'system of freedom' leads us directly to the heart of the *Contributions* – the jointure of *Seyn* and Da-sein.

As I have suggested, the question of the system of being (beingness or *Seiendheit* in Heidegger), concretely articulated as the total mobilization of beings, is the hermeneutic situation from which we begin. What is at stake in the *Contributions* is nothing other than the leap into *an ordered whole* of beings, of mankind and *Seyn*, which will no longer be determined by the exclusive measure of representational thinking in its representation of beings. The project of the jointure (*Gefüge*) of being-historical thought is the anticipatory articulation of this ordered whole. In this founding leap, freedom cannot be grasped in opposition to nature in its being-present as an order of causality. The opposition of freedom and system is inevitable 'as long as we take freedom to be "unlike" nature and opposed to it, and system to be merely the end product of thought's efforts.'[100] The key to the interdependence of nature and freedom is to rethink the concept of identity to unfold the belonging-together of human freedom and nature, of freedom and system.[101] As Heidegger points out, in a 'metaphysical sense' Schelling holds that love is 'the inmost nature of identity as the belonging together of what is different' (GA42, 154/89). Heidegger attempts to think this belonging-together as Da-sein, that is, as the mutual appropriation of *Seyn* and human being. The Jointure of *Seyn* is Heidegger's attempt to rethink and to initiate the *system of freedom* that Schelling enunciates in his treatise.

Schelling understands being as Will: the jointure of God and creation, of ground and existence, presences as will (GA42, 171, 235/99, 135). In Schelling's understanding of God as a becoming God, it is the 'self-seeing of the God himself in his ground' which induces the separation which is 'intrinsically in-forming individuation' (GA42, 236, 240/136, 139). Will resides in God as the self-striving inherent in the becoming of God as an emergent God, as the striving against the ground which brings forth the 'opposite of itself' (GA42, 236/136). The system of freedom is possible for Schelling because being is understood as will, and because will is understood as freedom; freedom is integral to being itself (GA42 171/99). Schelling's attempt to understand evil within a theological conception of one, all-powerful God leads him to hold that there is something within God which allows for evil, without ascribing evil to God himself. This means that evil will be ascribed to the will in its self-insistence upon itself, in its separation from the universal will (GA42, 244, 247, 257/141, 143, 149). This understanding of evil as arising out of being itself in its universality, and as actual in the self-insistence of individual being, offers Heidegger an understanding of the nature of self-hood which informs his reading of the subject and of modern subjectivity. Evil is not a mere absence of the good, it is inherent in being itself. Freedom is now understood as the capability for good *and* evil (GA42, 167/97). Evil arises out of the possibility of individuation, out of the self and the '"life dread" present in the ground of Being (that) drives it to emerge from the center, that is, to cling to separation and further it, and thus to pursue its inclination' (GA42, 263/152). The question of evil is now understood in terms of the 'inner possibility of being human.' Self-will as evil elevates itself above the universal will to define itself as 'a way of being free in the sense of being a self in terms of its own essential law' (GA42, 246–7/142–3). The 'most positive element of nature itself, the ground's willing to come to itself' is the negative, 'is' evil, and for this reason a merely moral or ethical confrontation with evil cannot reach its essence (GA42 251/145).

Heidegger interrogates the problem of evil as a metaphysical question 'in regard to the essence and truth of being' (GA42, 252/146). As such, evil is understood not only as something spiritual, and hence an aspect of human decision, but also as historical, in the form of its manifestations. The one-sidedness of the self-insistent will, which fully unfolds itself in the system of representational thinking, is also a manifestation of the fundamental negativity of the 'evil' which, for Heidegger, inhabits being 'itself' as its counter-essence. The 'hunger of self-craving' of evil 'dissolves all bonds more and more in its greed to be everything,' until it 'dissolves into nothingness' (GA42, 271/156–7). This hunger, as the evil of the self-willing will, is spiritual and arises out of freedom in its historicity (GA42, 271/156). Therefore the dissolution of bonds, and the breaking of all bounds, has to be thought, and is thought, in the *Contributions*, in terms of the essence of technicity, and hence in respect to the functional disintegration of beings and their integration into the system of total mobilization. If this is the historical – that is, the destined – form in which the negativity of evil sends itself to modern humanity, then the question arises whether this system itself reserves the possibility of another order of being. Heidegger argues that this possibility arises out of the withdrawal of representational being-present, and through this, the opening to the unconcealment of being in beings in the jointure of the dispersal of *being* and the founding sheltering of beings.[102] The jointure, or *Gefüge*, of the *Contributions to Philosophy* is consequently an attempt to found the order of being and beings on a new ground, that is, in the clearing opened up by the site of Da-*sein*. With this site, the fanaticism of the will to representation releases itself into the openness of the resolve of staying-open to the presencing of being. Staying-open to being (*Ent-schlossenheit*) is the ground of an ethos of dwelling, that is, of practical freedom as the letting-be of beings as articulated in acts and works of founding.

The transformation of the question of ethics into one of the ethos of dwelling, which Heidegger addresses in the *Letter on Humanism* (1946), is central to the movement of part V, or 'Grounding,' of the *Contributions*. What Heidegger evokes as 'inabiding in Da-sein,' understood as dwelling in the openness of being, thus to bring beings into sheltering unconcealment (GA65, 315/221), is addressed in the *Letter* as the 'ecstatic inherence' (*ekstatische Innestehen*) of mankind in being (LH 327/233). Mankind is ek-static in the sense of standing in the open of the temporalization of time and the historicity of *Seyn*. The hermeneutic situation of mankind's homelessness (LH 336/243), arising out of the deracination of modern humanity that unfolds from the representational self-certainty of the will, itself intimates the necessity of a turn into an ethos of dwelling. With this turn, freedom would be transformed and re-founded on the ground of Da-sein's responsibility for the being of beings, making it, in Heidegger's memorable phrase, the 'shepherd of being,' rather than the master of beings (LH 338/245). The leap into Da-sein, however, calls for decision. This decidedness of humanity as a finite being exhibits the capability of good *and* evil, in their concrete historicity, actuality (GA42, 255/147). The most primordial decidedness (*Entschiedenheit*), which decides for freedom as the ground of mankind, is the decision of human being to be its own essence as freedom. This decision, Heidegger continues, does not fall in time, but is the moment (*Augenblick*) wherein human temporality reveals itself to an individual existence and is grasped, decided for, in its concrete historicity. The moment of vision reveals human being (Da-sein) as the Between of good and evil, and with it, the necessity of enduring the truth of being to bring beings to a stand in it. Only what is 'wrested' from unconcealment is brought to stand in the open. Da-sein is the historical necessity of ordering the open 'so that the bond of beings may come into play' (GA42, 268–8/154–5).

In Heidegger's understanding of a 'presubjective or ontological ground-ing of freedom,'[103] the order of beings can no longer be *grounded* in cau-sality, nor can freedom be determined by reference to the self-affirming will, insofar as both 'nature' and 'mankind' are founded in the project of Da-sein as the Between of beings and being. The Between, as the site of the encounter and mutual coming-into-presence of humanity and nature, offers the possibility of a recovery of *phusis*, wherein 'nature' would no longer be determined solely by the order of causality.[104] Heidegger's reflections on the work of art as an origin from *phusis*, not subjectivity, points to the event of the work as opening up a space for the actuality of freedom in the letting-be of nature, and in the founding of the community of an historical people.

What comes into presence and is brought to stand in beings in this way, as the 'worlding' of Da-sein's being-in-the-world, is grounded in freedom as the finite transcendence of Da-sein; freedom is now thought as the originating leap of the inaugurating ground, hence as the free-dom to ground and to give grounds (WG 162). The measures of ground-ing which Heidegger unfolds in 'Vom Wesen des Grundes' (1929) as the projective opening of a world (*Weltentwurf*), as attuned being-involved with beings (*Eingenommenheit*), and as the grounding of beings in an understanding of being (*Be-gründen*), are the ways in which freedom grounds the transcendence of Da-sein (WG 162–9). The event of tran-scendence, as grounding in this threefold sense, opens up an historically determinate space for the facticity of human action and comportment, and hence for freedom as practical reason or praxis in all its modes. Freedom is the possibility to be ground and to give grounds, as such to found the being-in-the-world of an historical humanity. Only in ground-ing the unconcealment of *Seyn*, thus to 'let this ground (enowning) *be* the ground' does the 'inabiding [Inständlichkeit] of Da-sein succeed in the modes and on the pathways of sheltering truth unto beings' (GA65, 307–8/216–7).

Conclusion: Imperial Truth and Planetary Order

In an essay originally written as a foreword to the German edition of Farias's *Heidegger et le nazisme* (1988), Habermas claims that Heidegger's history of being 'rigidly maintained the abstraction of historicity (as the condition of historical existence itself) from actual historical processes.' In place of a measured response to these processes, Heidegger's thought takes, in the 1930s, first, an ideological form, allied to the Conservative Revolution and National Socialism; and then, in further withdrawal from historical reality, the 'fatalistic form' of attending to the eventuation of being.[1] Other commentators have made essentially the same point.[2] In what follows, I will show that Heidegger's understanding of the transformation of the truth of *aletheia* into the truth of *veritas* – which is perhaps the central event in the history of being – founds the 'actual historical processes' associated with the name of 'imperialism.' I will focus on the wartime *Parmenides*, in an effort to elaborate Heidegger's understanding of the grounds of imperialism in the midst of an imperialistic war. Evidently Heidegger will not offer an economic, a sociological, or a political analysis of the origins and structure of imperialism. Nonetheless, his understanding of the triumph of *veritas* over *aletheia*, as a founding event of the history of being, implicates a concept of 'the imperial' as a 'mode of being of historical humanity' (GA54, 62/42). This concept of the imperial, in turn, implicates a set of theses which can be argued, and plausibly supported, by recourse to the methods of historical enquiry and an empirical concept of imperialism. Heidegger's understanding of the 'history of being,' therefore, need not leave us hanging in the void of his supposed 'mysticism.'

I therefore propose to map out a number of theses implicated by the notion of the imperial as an event of the truth of being, and to sketch the relation of these theses to the 'politics' of the imperial. In addition to the *Parmenides*, my primary source will be the *Beiträge zur Philosophie*. I read the *Parmenides* as an attempt to deconstruct the truth of *veritas* and thus to re-think *aletheia* as the post-imperial site of truth. Frings calls the account Heidegger renders of this translation in the *Parmenides* the 'most convincing' one he has to offer, in fact, a 'classical piece' of reading.[3] The central issue of this text is indeed its confrontation with the deracination of truth, conceived as a conceptual system, from concretely embodied and sited historicity. Heidegger's appeal to the seemingly mythological figure of the goddess Aletheia is an attempt to dis-cover the bounded finitude of presencing (being) in beings. The 'anti-imperialism' of Heidegger's thought derives from a concept of limit (*peras*/gestalt). The non-imperial polis is founded in the reciprocal limitation of beings in their historically concrete presencing. The imperial, conversely, mobilizes the de-limitation of representational thinking and the consequent dis-integration of beings, which implicates their simultaneous integration into the functional systems of the planetary.

The opening pages of Heidegger's *Parmenides* direct our gaze to the gestalt of truth. Truth takes gestalt as goddess (GA54, 7/5). To think the gestalt of truth – hence the delimitation of truth, its incorporation and inscription in the gestalt – calls for attention to *the event of the founding manifestations of being*. In the *Einführung in die Metaphysik*, Heidegger had retrieved a non-metaphysical sense of *Gestalt* as *morphe* and *entelecheia*. In this interpretation, gestalt is the limit, or *peras*, out of which an entity, as limiting itself, begins to be (GA40, 63–5). To speak of truth as gestalt means to allow that the openness of *aletheia* sets itself into the gestalt to reveal presencing in the delimited presence of a being. 'The Origin of the Work of Art' supports this interpretation, since *morphe*-as-*Gestalt*, freed of its metaphysical constriction and hence of the primacy of the Idea, unfolds as the setting-into-the-work of the happening of truth. Truth presences, or eventuates, in the temporal and local finitude of the bounded gestalt (UK 30–1, 64, 69).

We may begin to glimpse the rootlessness of scientific truth and of the truth of the concept, if we allow ourselves to be estranged by the intimation of the founding and founded gestalt of truth in its manifestation as goddess. This estrangement from the modern abstraction of a truth, which has its 'site' in the proposition, will immediately lose its force if we re-integrate the truth of the goddess into metaphysics by recourse to the opposition of philosophy and science to mythology and poetry. The experience of truth-as-goddess rather intimates that truth presences out of the limit of the historically particularized gestalt; as the presencing of the limit, it founds the measure of the true and the untrue. The presencing of the limit in and through beings gives to beings the stability (*Beständigkeit*) of their being (GA54, 241).

Heidegger argues that the delimitation of presencing which the gestalt of truth intimates is brought to word in the strife of concealment and unconcealment. We recall that the event of *aletheia* is a bringing into the open which preserves the unconcealed in the sheltering limit of its own self-concealing reserve (*lethe*). 'The unconcealed is what has entered into the rest of its pure self-manifesting "appearance"' (GA54, 197/132, modified). This implies the 'removal of concealment' (*Aufheben einer Verbergung*) (GA54, 198/133) and therefore the arrival into openness. The movement of an entity's coming into the ownness of its self-manifestation, however, is founded in its withdrawal from openness to root itself in the sheltering limit of its own mode of being and presencing. Thus *Ent-bergen* now intimates, at the same time, '*to bring into saving shelter: that is, to preserve the unconcealed in unconcealment*' (GA54, 198/133, modified), and thus to also preserve the moment of saving withdrawal at the heart of emergence into the open. *Ent-bergen*, understood as 'un-concealing,' remains a granting of shelter.

In this context, Heidegger's reflection on the imperial truth of *veritas* in his *Parmenides* arises in response to the deracination of Western thought. Yet if his critique of imperialism speaks for 'rootedness,' it does not, as Fóti has also noted, speak for 'nationalism,' given that modern nationalism is founded in subjectivity and tends toward imperialism.[4] Because *veritas* is opposed to the false as *falsum*, truth establishes itself as the secure and certain, as the commanding gaze which brings the untrue to a fall. The truth of *veritas* founds the imperial in the history of being.

Greek thought sets *aletheia* into opposition to *pseudos*, for *pseudos*, not *lethe*, is the Greek word for the 'false' (GA 54, 42–67/28–45). Heidegger's argument, however, offers a retrieval of *pseudos* which brings *pseudos* into the realm of *lethe*: in its opposition to *aletheia*, *pseudos* is a form of sheltering concealment (GA54, 56/38). To the extent the sheltering self-concealment of *lethe*, which allows to each its stand, is re-interpreted by Roman thought as *falsum* – as that which has been brought to a fall – the fundamentally imperial direction of Western thinking has already been set (GA54, 57–72/39–49). This is Heidegger's fundamental thesis regarding the imperial turn and with it the uprootedness of Western thought. The 'translation' of Greek *aletheia* into Roman *veritas* is the primordial 'political' turn of Western history, precisely because the interpretation of truth as *veritas* founds the imperialism of representational thinking. The representational thinking which comes fully into its own with modernity cannot admit the withdrawal from conceptualization inherent in the differentiated nature of truth as *aletheia*. The withdrawal of which the *lethe* of *a-letheia* speaks shelters beings in their own gestalt. Since the Roman *veritas* interprets Greek *lethe* as *falsum*, the sheltering self-concealment inherent in the event of disclosure is constrained to manifest itself as the merely false. Truth stands over against the false and fallen as the over-seeing measure of the closed off and unfallen:

> *Ver-* means to be steady, to keep steady, i.e., not to fall (no *falsum*), to remain above, to maintain oneself, to keep one's head up, to be the head, to command. Maintaining oneself, standing upright – the upright. Thus it is from the essential domain of the imperial that *verum*, as counter-word to *falsum*, received the sense of established right. (GA54, 69–70/47)

Veritas denotes the undisclosed and as such expresses an experience of being which is the exact opposite of the Greek *aletheia* as unconcealment (GA54, 71/48). As the concealed and self-asserting, *veritas* sets itself up as the measure of beings and subjects the movement of withdrawal from unconcealment to its standard. The truth of *verum* directs and controls in over-seeing the unfolding of beings: it commands and in commanding already determines what is right. Over-seeing commanding is the root of the imperial (GA54, 71, 74/48, 50). Truth as command, moreover, shifts the site of unconcealment. The site is no longer the unconcealment founded in the historical specificity of the things themselves, but rather the rightness of relation between *rectitudo* as *adaequatio* and the things (GA54, 74/50). The *Wesensraum,* or site of unfolding, which Heidegger appeals to here is the history-founding Da of the *polis,* which constitutes the order of the essential gestalten of a people. The imperial has lost this ground, not, however, without substituting for it a subject territory obedient to the truth laid down by command.

Heidegger's account of the transformation of unconcealment into the imperial truth of command raises many questions. These questions revolve around the following issues: (*i*) the relation of *veritas* and command; (*ii*) the truth of *veritas* and the first principles of nature, as of the state; and (*iii*) truth and the fundamental disposition of Da-sein in its openness to being. For the transposition of *aletheia* into *veritas* brings with it a transformation of Da-sein's openness to the presencing of being in beings. This transformation marks the turn from the *arete* of the *polis* to the 'virtue' of the socio-technical state.

What is the relation of imperial command to nature? How does this relation, in turn, found the modern state? The relation between the command and nature becomes evident if we consider that *modern science 'commands' nature to manifest itself in the experiment*. In Bacon's account, only

> let the human race recover that right over nature which belongs to it by divine bequest, and let power be given it; the exercise thereof will be governed by sound reason and true religion.[5]

The 'right' over nature appealed to by Bacon is to be established by 'inquisition': Bacon calls on the constraints of the experimental chamber to force nature to reveal her true face. When nature is 'forced out of her natural state and squeezed and moulded' the conditions are established for the step-by-step determination of certain truths.[6] The experimental method takes command over the phenomena – it constitutes the secure vantage point of truth which over-sees nature and brings her to a fall. In 'Of Truth,' Bacon metaphorically defines truth as a stable point of view – 'a hill not to be commanded' – which overlooks the instability of the sea, that is, the phenomena of nature.[7] Bacon's technological and imperial program, therefore, anticipates the essence of modern science by appealing to the truth of a self-certain and stable foundation.

Modern experimental science is ultimately founded on laying down axioms of nature. Heidegger's account of Galileo and Newton emphasizes that nature is constrained to reveal herself according to axioms laid down in advance. These axioms compose the systemic conceptual site of truth, to which the phenomena are forced to conform.[8] Modern science, moreover, confirms a further transformation of the essence of truth: *veritas* is determined as *certitudo* (GA54, 76/51–2). In Descartes's philosophy the axioms of modern science take their self-evidence from the self-certainty of the *cogito*. The self-certainty of the *cogito* constitutes the site of the truth of the experimental method and thus of the truth of command to which nature is subjected (NII 189–92/4: 136–8).

It is a commonplace of criticism that the conquest of nature and the project of founding a modern imperial state are intimately linked in Bacon's philosophical program.[9] The new Atlantis which Bacon proposes derives from the subjection of nature to the commands of science. Bacon's 'De Augmentis,' Robert Faulkner argues, 'virtually announces the imperialism of Baconian politics;[10] his 'Of the True Greatness of Kingdomes and Estates'[11] offers 'formulas for the constituting of an imperial nation-state, and they are openly imperial and ruthless to an extent unique in the *Essays*.'[12] In the imperial, the nature of *veritas* as the truth of command becomes especially evident. Bacon's project presupposes the axioms which ground the experimental method. The same project requires a socio-technical concept of the state, adequate to the imperial ambitions of experimental science. In his *On Human Conduct*, Michael Oakeshott acknowledges Bacon as the founder of the state-as-economy, as distinct from a state which has an economy.[13] This calls for, as Faulkner points out, 'a nation that can be mobilized.' Bacon's 'councils' on governing are attempts 'to produce the attitudes and incentives for mobilizing.'[14] Mobilization takes on the essential character of 'holy war': 'the true holy war will be an enlightened war against religion and against nature on behalf of liberty and the real progress of humanity.'[15] Bacon's understanding of holy war, as he develops it in 'An Advertisement Touching Holy War,' is founded on the recognition of the mutual implication of the scientific project and the socio-technical transformation of modes of human behaviour to favour rationalism and commercial progress. Communities which do not measure up to these criteria of an enlightened polity are in principle objects of holy war, for they challenge pre-conceived axioms of what a polity should be.

Within the essential unfolding of the founding of modernity, Hobbes's *Leviathan* offers a requisite model of the state. The 'natural' passions which motivate humans in the 'state of nature' – the fear of death and the desire for glory – must be integrated into a machinery of state which would allow the functional application of passion to the common good. The theory of the natural passions, the state of nature, and the contractual relations which serve to establish the Leviathan together constitute *a theory of the command and management of the moral nature of mankind* which not only supplements Bacon's program of the inquisition of nature, but which also establishes the grounds for the systematic, rational application of this program. The sovereign power takes its legitimacy from the command inscribed in a 'nature' posited by the new philosophy. Promulgated law formalizes principles of comportment founded in the principles of motion and in the command inscribed in the fundamental passions of the fear of death and the desire for glory. These principles are themselves a higher law and the source of all command and positive law. Hobbes indeed hesitates on the question whether the fundamental 'theorems' (or axioms) of his political philosophy – the 'laws of nature' – should indeed be called 'laws.' For, as Alan Ryan comments, 'laws, properly, are commands rather than theorems, and thus exist only when someone issues them as commands.'[16] Yet Hobbes concludes by insisting that 'if we consider the same Theorems, as delivered in the Word of God, that by right commandeth all things; then they are properly called Lawes.'[17] The appeal to God's command serves to legitimate the command inherent in the positing of the theorem as the ground of nature and the commands that nature issues. Hobbes's entire enterprise as a political philosopher, Ryan argues, was to 'secure universal agreement that only *one* source of law existed, and that whatever that source declared as law *was* law.'[18] The Leviathan is this one source of law because it derives its legitimacy from the theorems posited a priori as the governing commands of nature.

This imperial turn is no less evident in Locke. The 'unease of desire' is the fundamental 'natural' disposition of mankind, according to Locke.[19] This unease is not directed to any higher good, such as serves the polity. Hence reason, understood as the will to make certain of nature – in this case, the moral nature of mankind – commands us to establish a theatre wherein this 'natural' unease can be integrated into one coherent system of mutual obligation. This theatre is the Lockean state. It, too, like the Hobbesian state, derives from a theory of natural passions, a fictional state of nature, and the contract relations which integrate the natural passions into a system of self-management and control. The 'state' as construct ultimately loses in significance, but only because the modern character of truth as the conceptual command determining the manifestation of entities is inscribed in the 'conscience' of the rationalized individual by social institutions.[20]

As Neal Wood has demonstrated, in *The Politics of Locke's Philosophy*, Bacon's injunction to master nature underlies Locke's natural and political philosophy.[21] The Lockean 'individual' 'actualizes' itself as individual only by way of the transformation of 'nature' into property. Locke's theory of property unfolds the implications of Bacon's imperial science, for God gave the world 'to the use of the industrious and rational.'[22] Locke derives the necessity of transforming the earth into property from the rational nature implanted in mankind by God. The creator gave mankind reason so that he might 'make the use of those things, which were serviceable to his Subsistence.'[23] Therefore the *veritas* of the command and actualization of mankind's rational, moral nature founds the Lockean state no less than the Baconian and Hobbesian. Heidegger avers that the all-overseeing gaze of the imperial command, which aims to bring what is to a fall, actualizes itself in unceasing action, in applied operation (GA54, 60/41). The Leviathan, as a construct of the integration and manipulation of natural passions into the machinery of the modern state, is the political condition of imperial 'operation.' The autonomous and rational entity of Locke's political theory is commanded by its rational nature to actualize itself by transforming the abstraction of nature and mere territory into the 'properties' of its own identity.

Heidegger's history of being holds that theoretical discourse establishes the site, the open space, or *theatrum*, of the truth of modernity. The power of the statement, or discursive truth, over the unconcealment of beings becomes possible because the mind's theatre, the subject of modern metaphysics, posits itself as the stage whereon all that is must appear, to make itself manifest (AWP 89/132). With modernity the shift from the Greek theatre as the site of the unconcealment of gods and mortals to modern 'theory' as a set of discourses prefiguring the givenness of the 'real' becomes fully evident. Indeed, according to Christopher Pye, the origin of sovereignty in Hobbes's account is 'theatrical.' The contracting subjects of the Leviathan are conceived as actors, or persona.[24] Conceived, moreover, 'from the point of view of the spectator, the figure of the King's eye as a sun, of a regal sight that brings forth what it sees, would convey the uncanny power of a spectacle which is the source of the gaze which beholds it.'[25] In Heidegger's terms, the gaze opens the space of a stage on which the subjects come to be as subjects. The collective subjectivity of the gaze founds the space of their being. With this re-presentative scene, the 'mythos' of the goddess *Aletheia*, which opens the space of the disclosure of humanity and god and nature, is brought to a fall: what rules, and hence is true, is the imperial word of command. Hobbes's Leviathan, as the artificial body which constitutes our social nature, is the founding myth of our collective being. The 'myth' of the artificial man is the *logos* from which the discourse of the modern subject derives.

Heidegger argues that the Roman interpretation of truth, which founds imperial thinking, is taken up by the Church. Dogma incorporates the command of the Church, the determination of true and false belief, and with it, the distinction of the justified and unjustified (GA54, 67–8/45–6). Armed with the all-overseeing truth of dogma, the justified already see, in anticipation and imagination, the fallenness of the untrue. Thus, in the same treatise on theatre, in which Tertullian condemns the 'pagan' rites of the Empire, he offers a vision of God's *theatrum mundi*, of the final revelation of human history which brings all of unjustified humanity to a fall and puts it on display.[26] The play of being is played out on God's stage. Insofar as the Curia of the Pope is the one legitimate source of interpretation of God's theatre it lays claim to far greater power than the Emperor. The vision of God's theatre 'legitimates' the Vatican's claim to command, to determine belief.

The *theatrum mundi* of God's providence ultimately derives from his incomprehensible and arbitrary will. This comes fully to light with Calvin's theology. In the *Institutes* Calvin insists on the distinction between 'providence' and 'fate' in order to safeguard the sovereignty of God's will.[27] Hence, God's 'will is, and rightly ought to be, the cause of all things; whatever God wills, by the very fact he wills it, must be considered righteous.'[28] The will of God, moreover, maintains what is in being for as long as it exists. God's will, therefore, opens up the space of the being and manifestation of entities. All that *is* appears by virtue of, and in the light of, the viewing space or *theatrum* of God's providence.

The common source, therefore, of the truth of the *imperium* and Christian dogma is the command. The 'Word' of the God of the Old Testament is the word of command, such as laid down in the Decalogue. In both cases, the commanding word constitutes the site of truth – and this all the more as the Church took over the imperial mission of Rome and claimed for itself the exclusive right to interpret God's word of command and lay down this interpretation in dogma.

Heidegger's argument regarding the foundations of the modern state implies that the commanding word remains the site of truth even after it is detached from the authority of scripture, and from the authority of autocratic rule, to found itself in socio-technical discourse. The sovereign Leviathan is re-figured as the discursive regulation of a society. The unease of desire, in Locke's formulation, commands us to act: the character of the polity emerges from the determination to regulate the consequences deriving from the fundamental command of nature in us. The shift, therefore, from the imperial command of a sole ruler, and the sole authority of God's word, to the decentralized and dissimilated commands of modern socio-technical discourses (in Foucault's sense) in no way undermines Heidegger's argument regarding the imperial character of modern politics.

In what senses, therefore, does the *veritas* of the modern Leviathan in its liberal, socio-technical form *bring mankind to a fall?* For it belongs to the *veritas* of imperial truth to bring the false to a fall and to determine it 'from above,' that is, to command it. First, 'human nature' itself is brought to a fall. In fact, it is already fallen because brought to fall by the 'theoretical' eye of Christian dogma. Second, because the socio-technical discourses of the modern state, according to Hobbes and Locke, posit an ahistorical 'state of nature' as the theoretical ground of the polity, the historical specificity of peoples is brought to a fall.

This tendency is only radicalized by the Revolutionary tradition deriving from Rousseau. Thus, in opposition to the ahistorical idea of the polity which follows from Rousseau's understanding of the state of nature, Edmund Burke could point out that the geometric method of the reorganization of the national territory practised by the Revolution treats the nation like a conquered population.[29] Just as the geometric method, moreover, reduces an historical landscape to the abstraction of administrative departments, the theatre of revolution and the goddess of Reason presiding over it serve to reduce the history of the French Church to a catalogue of crimes. The theatre of Reason becomes a court of inquisition presided over by the 'merely theoretic system' of the Revolution.[30] Historical continuities and traditions are uprooted and subjected to an idea of theoretical reason. In this sense the courtroom-theatre anticipates the twentieth-century concept of 're-education.' The more thorough the proposed re-education, the more fallen a subject 'population' is posited, a priori, to be.

The space of theatre in the Greek sense, as the ritual space of the self-manifestation of the gods in the delimitation of the gestalt proper to them, begins to enter the final stage of its 'non-essence' (in Heidegger's sense) when it is transformed into the 'show-trial.' The concept of the 'collective guilt' of a class or subject population, and hence the distinction of a superior and inferior humanity, constitutes the ideological foundation of the show-trial. In these respects, it is arguable that the show-trial manifests the will inherent in 'justice' (*iustitia/Gerechtigkeit*) metaphysically conceived – that is, as the will inherent in *veritas* to make a certain position of power secure, unshakable (GA54, 78/53). This metaphysical will, moreover, only unfolds itself completely when the day arrives for all of humanity, as fallen, to be treated as an experimental and criminal case. This happens when humanity is seen as a biological and behavioural problem: genetic engineering serves to supplement ideological indoctrination. Mankind can treat itself as an experimental case when the metaphysical essence of justice empowers itself in the name of the will to power (cf. NI 642–8). The Last Judgement of Tertullian's vision would finally be realized in the name of technicity.

The 'false' belongs to the essence of imperial politics as that which has been brought to a fall. The false historically enters the discourse of politics in the Christian-Roman form of the heretic, the pagan or heathen, the witch, the unbeliever, Satan's nation, the 'guilty nation.' Hence the Crusade – against the pagan, against Islam, the Greeks, the native in European eyes. The 'crusade' is an expression of the sense that the elect of God are called to subjugate Satan's progeny. As the collective of a class, a race, or a people, the 'false' is determined as collectively guilty.

The concept of 'collective guilt' derives from the falsity of the fallen. It is in this context that Heidegger's remarks in the *Parmenides* on Bolshevism and the power of the Party have to be understood: the Party embodies the theoretical and discursive system of truth, which determines the guilt of a class and brings it to a fall. Bolshevism consummates the integration of 'electricity' – that is, technicity – and the word of command proper to it (GA54, 127/86). The anthropology of collective guilt and the false and fallen derives from the essence of the imperial – from the determination of *the movement of withdrawal at the heart of aletheia* as the false and fallen and therefore as a mere negation of true being (GA54, 64, 66/44, 46). Because the true is understood as the unfallen, the errance inherent in the open, free realm of unconcealment shows itself merely as error (WW 178–9, 194). The fallen nature of mankind is an 'error' which must be 'kept down' – and conversely the will becomes 'free' to remake, reconstruct itself.

Heidegger holds that *aletheia* is in itself the differentiated realm of a strife which establishes the order and rank of beings (GA54, 134/90). In this sense *aletheia* is *polemos*. Greek tragedy, Heidegger continues, is the ritual embodiment of polemic *aletheia*. As such, the terrible, the 'demonic,' is integrated into the open site of manifestation which gives beings the space of their freedom. The *polis* is the constitution of the 'agonal,' ritual play of the masks of being. But where *lethe* is reduced to the 'falsehood' of an error, being cannot unfold itself in the *agon* of ritual enactment; the 'false' is put on show, and subjected to the command of imperial truth. Consequently, the form of the incorporation of *lethe* into the polity, as error or as errance, as the ritual of sheltering unconcealment or mere falsehood, must co-determine the nature of the polity.

The nature of imperial truth insists that politics be re-presentative: a re-presentation of the founding theoretical ground, such as has been posited in advance. The theoretical ground of the metaphysically conceived political humanity of modernity is the concept of the rational animal specific to the modern polity. As *rational* the 'animal' engages in contractual self-limitation to found the state. As *animal* the rational being is agitated by the founding dispositions of liberalism – the fear of death and the hunger for security which accompanies it, the desire for glory, and the unease of desire. The rational animal, as the theoretical ground of the modern polity, is re-presented (*i*) by way of socio-technical discourses of desire, its production, increase, manipulation. The most recent genealogy of this discourse takes us from Marx and Freud to Derrida and Deleuze. Jean Baudrillard, among others, has pointed out the metaphysics of production, and therefore the fundamentally technological model, which determines this discourse.[31] And the modern, rational animal is re-presented (*ii*) by way of the management of rationality to produce and confirm legitimacy, consensus, transparency. The ideal of 'distortion-free communication' re-presents the ideal of the rational, autonomous subject. As we recall, Heidegger argues that the production and intensification of sensation and the paradigm of rational transparency complement each other in the integrated unity of *Erlebnis* and *Machenschaft*, which finds its ultimate telos in the post-modern integration of flesh and machine (GA65, 126–8/ 88–9).

Given that the truth of imperial politics is representative in the above senses, what does it, in principle, posit as false? *The false is the non-representational*: that which resists representation, hence the incalculable, including the 'sublime' and the divine. As such, an essentially non-technological understanding of death, nature, art, selfhood, and the being of a people is already posited in advance as false. Understanding of these realms of being is 'technological,' in Heidegger's terms, because their truth derives from the metaphysics of production and self-production which is ultimately founded on the paradigmatic function of the Idea (PL 234).

The paradigmatic function of the Idea rests on a transformation of the nature and site of truth. '*Aletheia* falls under the yoke of the *Idea*' (PL 228). *Aletheuein* is still conceived by Aristotle, Heidegger argues, as a comportment (*Verhalten*) which lets the revealed come to word in its own being (GA54, 72/49). Yet, at the same time, correspondence (*homoiosis*) comes to 'represent' or stand in for *aletheia*. In the train of this transformation of *aletheia* as the site of truth, *homoiosis*, over the byway of Roman thinking, is transformed into *adaequatio* (GA54, 73/50). The re-presentation of *aletheia* as *adaequatio*, or correctness, founds the essence of the imperial as re-presentative politics: the 'imperial arises out of the essence of truth as correctness in the sense of that which gives direction, to establish the security and certainty of rule' (GA54, 74/50, modified). Because the site of truth has shifted from the realm of unconcealment to the proposition, 'the essence of truth as *veritas* and *rectitudo* is without site and ground' (GA54, 74/50, modified). The unsited truth of the proposition uproots an historically given humanity from its sitedness in the unconcealment of being. *The imperial signifies the deracinated*. In the course of the unfolding of imperial truth in modernity, the conceptual system it posits as the 'ground' of political action is already an abstraction from the experience of the realm of unconcealment. It is an attempt, more-over, to determine this realm a priori, according to the paradigm of a sys-tem. The truth of the system of liberal politics, as Hobbes already made clear, derives from the propositional 'site,' or rather non-site, of truth, not from the historically founded unconcealment of being. Because Hobbes reduces being to the function of the copula, the Leviathan determines itself a-historically, in the creative fictions of its conceptual system, even as it uproots itself from the site of unconcealment. As Heidegger observes of Hobbes's *Logica*, the place of truth becomes the no-place of the copula, in complete alienation from the world-context, or being-in-the-world, out of which signs and signification emerge (GA24, 260–73). In Heidegger's later understanding of the 'topology' of being, the truth of the copula stands in the most extreme opposition to the time-space of earth-sited thinking in its attention to the presencing of being in beings.

As Michel Foucault, for example, has shown, the conceptual system of modern politics unfolds itself historically as a set of socio-technical dis-courses of surveillance, command, and control.[32] These discourses derive from the essence of the imperial in precisely the sense Heidegger indi-cates, i.e., as the discursive means of establishing the security and cer-tainty of rule. Power, therefore, is not solely or even pre-eminently to be conceived as the embodied dictatorship of command. More fundamen-tally, it is the re-presentative and reflexive unfolding of the discourses of power/knowledge which 'generate' the power-structures of modern society.

The discursive system derives from the fundamental attunement, in the sense of the type of openness to being, which founds modernity. Recalling the argument of 'Vom Wesen der Wahrheit,' we know that Heidegger holds the truth of the proposition to be derived from the truth of our fundamental attunement to being in its historical specificity (WW 182, 188). Now, the Leviathan of Hobbes is founded on the 'geo-metric' model of truth, and therefore on the certainty and self-certainty of representations. Hobbes wished to establish a science (*sapientia*) of politics: 'political science sets out what men rationally must do,' it is a 'blueprint' for a polity.[33] The model of certain, hence true propositions, is given by the propositions of the mathematical and natural sciences as sciences of motion. These propositions, applied to humanity, set the measure of its being and the measure of the proper organization of the state. The nature of humanity is also determined by the two funda-mental 'motions' of fear and desire, which are not limited, according to

Hobbes, by any higher end beyond themselves.[34] These motions of the soul constitute the basic disposition of Hobbesian mankind – in Heidegger's terms, the *Grund-stimmungen* of the historically specific being of Hobbes's humanity. The dispositions, in turn, find the ground of their possibility in the mode of the fundamental attunement, or openness, of the rational animal in the truth of the will to certainty. The will to certainty cannot accept the limit of death as mankind's internal, proper limit. Turning against death, it turns back on itself in the will to become certain of itself. The ceaseless striving of the desire for glory turns toward what-is as the object of the subject's will to be certain of itself – for the 'glory' of the self consists in its self-certain subjection of the world-as-object to itself.

The founding propositions of the Leviathan, therefore, as propositions concerning the origin and ends of action and the polity, presuppose historically specific, existential dispositions and the attunement to being in which they are founded. The attunement of the truth of certainty, and the dispositions in which it manifests itself, together determine, in advance, how beings become manifest, and therefore are themselves the open site which makes the truth of the propositions 'evident.' For the correspondence of proposition to thing presupposes this open site. The *propositions*, moreover, as laid down in Hobbes's theory of contract and sovereignty, are the articulation not only of the understanding inherent in these metaphysical *dispositions*, but also of the *comportment* to beings which these dispositions call for. The willingness of Hobbesian or Lockean man to engage in the social contract which ends the state of nature – and with this willingness, the determination to codify it in the propositions of a constitution and a legal order arises out of fear and the desire to make the satisfaction of desire more certain, more calculable. The authority of the Leviathan, once constituted, justifies or legitimizes itself by regulating and intensifying the satisfaction of desire. The desire for certainty motivates the individual's contractual self-limitation of his will in favour of the sovereign will. But insofar as the contractual-discursive system of the Leviathan 'locates' truth in the proposition, and 'reduces' being to the predicative function of the copula, the relation of truth as unconcealment to its historically founded dispositions, from which a mode of comportment and the propositional system emerge, is concealed. The occultation of unconcealment in favour of the non-site of the proposition is already the most fundamental form of the deracination of the polity. The proposition, which 'locates' being in the emptiness of the copula, grounds the abstraction of a 'territory':

under the regime of *veritas*, '*terra* becomes the *territorium*, the colony as a realm subject to command' (GA54, 88–9/60). According to Locke, in the 'beginning' all was 'America' – a supposedly empty territory awaiting transformation into 'property.' Hence, the concepts of the 'state of nature' and of 'America' may serve Locke as conceptual fictions from which a politics a priori is derived.[35] This thesis is not only Locke's most fundamental political proposition, but also the pivot of his understanding of our human be-ing: 'America' announces the emptiness of being as defined by the abstraction of the copula. As opposed to 'America' in Locke's political philosophy, wherein the earth in principle is conceived as an ahistorical dimension, the *polis* calls for the rootedness of political action in our attunement to and responsibility for the earth in its historical givenness, i.e., as the mythos of a people. The earth comes into its own as mythos, by taking its stand in the gestalt.

I would venture, therefore, to derive the following theses from the course of Heidegger's argument in the *Parmenides*. First, imperial truth is founded in re-presentational thinking. Re-presentational politics implicates equally the production of desire and the ideal of rational transparency. Second, imperial truth and the imperial state are founded in the truth of command. We have seen that the truth of command preeminently takes the impersonal form of socio-technical discourses. Third, because imperial politics is founded in re-presentational and hence propositional truth, it implicates the deracination of truth. The imperial in this sense realizes the will to uproot historically founded existence. The site of truth becomes the no-place of the copula, which means that the theatrum of the manifestation of the divine is occluded in favour of the truth of 'theory.' Fourth, and finally, theory posits the dimension of an administrative 'territory,' but mythos founds the homeland. The imperial truth of the copula – which is the truth of the technopolis – implicates the de-territorialization of the homeland to institute and organize the regime of the planetary.

In his reflections on the 'history of being' in works of the Second World War period, and evidently in response to the hermeneutic situation of the war and the total mobilization of entities it signifies, Heidegger explicitly raises the question of the 'planetary' as an epoch of being. The advent of the 'planetary' (*der Planetarismus*) announces the political avatar of the abandonment of beings and the oblivion of being. Metaphysical humanity makes itself at home in the abandonment of beings: it pursues the realization of functionality, holds to this, and finds its sense of security in this. The planetary, Heidegger proposes, is itself the 'essential ground' of 'equality' (*Gleichheit*) in its constitution of a new world order. The will to equality unfolds itself in the organization of the masses in the service of world power, and in the empowerment of the masses as a means to power, for the sake of establishing the necessity of planetary organization (GA70, 34). The planetary is the first essential feature of mankind's sojourn (*Aufenthalt*) in the abandonment of the being of beings. As the system of world order the planetary takes the will to equality into its service. Equality points to a second essential feature of the abandonment of entities and the oblivion of being: the in-difference of all beings within the order of the same. This is an historically specific event which arises with the consummation of metaphysics. It signifies that everyone seeks their own (*sein Eigenes*, or *idion*) in the same, and as the same (*das Gleiche*) as the own of every other. The own (*idion*) is lost to the same, to the 'equality' of the mass, and in this sense the planetary is reflected in a loss of ownness which Heidegger – somewhat playfully, perhaps – nominates *Idiotismus* (madness, idiocy or idiotism) (GA70, 34–5). Since the Greek *idiotes* denotes a private person, one cut off from the whole and the concerns of the *polis*, perhaps Heidegger also means to imply that the planetary realizes the surrender of the political as a realm of decision to the organizational forms of the technopolis, of the surrender of one's own to a sameness inscribed by sociotechnical discourses. Indeed, he concludes this section of his text with the comment that in terms of the history of being, 'the unconditioned way of unfolding [Wesen] of *das Man* is idiotism' (GA70, 35). The planetary form of the They is the dispersal of the being of Da-sein into the conceptual grids of machination and the manufactured intensities of lived-experience. These are the planetary determinations of the existential characteristics of our everyday being-in-the-world Heidegger brings to light in *Being and Time* (secs. 35–8). The planetary empowers itself as power in the 'equalization' of all peoples and all entities. As such, it implicates the normalization and uniformity of beings, their integration into planetary power and the unfolding of all that is, as a quantum of power. This is the only 'truth' allowed to what is (GA69, secs. 64–5). The truth of Da-sein, as the site of the unconcealment of beings into the gestalt proper to each, falls into oblivion.

We have seen that the planetary epoch institutes the total mobilization of beings. The question of National Socialism arises for Heidegger in response the metaphysically founded mobilization of planetary resources, and of the possibility of a response to it. Mobilization assimilates labour to technological functionalization, the artwork to the installation and the interface, the state to the technopolis, and a people to the global population as a resource-on-call. The homelands of the peoples of the earth are integrated into the limitlessness of an imperial order. The creatures of the earth, in all the distinctiveness of their diverse species, are integrated into the in-differentiated being of stock-on-call. Openness to the event of presencing is occluded by the functional stability of the posited. The gestalt of beings is simultaneously dis-integrated and integrated into the order of mobilization. These events shape our own postmodern hermeneutic situation. The consummation of metaphysics in technicity shows its face in the global competition for resources, in the neo-imperial control of seed stocks, and in the manipulation of genetic materials by international biotech industries, to mention only a few of its many manifestations. For Heidegger, the question of National Socialism consisted in posing the question of being as a question of community: What kind of social order would be commensurate to the challenge of the planetary? We are still confronted by this question. The passion of metaphysical mankind for the planetary finds voice in the ideologies of globalization and in the utopias of technicity. These ideologies can be subjected to a phenomenological de-construction, and the dis-integrative, functional integration of beings into the planetary technotopia can be brought to light in phenomenological description. This would follow from Heidegger's own practice and from the method of phenomenology. Yet, to bring planetary mobilization into question in a still more fundamental way requires, according to Heidegger, insight into the history of being, and with it, a shift in our collective attunement to the being of beings.

Notes

Unless otherwise noted all emphases in citations are in the original text.

Introduction

1 Farias, *Heidegger et le nazisme.*
2 Derrida, *De l'esprit*; Lacoue-Labarthe, *Heidegger, Art, and Politics*; Thiele, *Timely Meditations*; Rickey, *Revolutionary Saints*; Ward, *Heidegger's Political Thinking*; Schürmann, *Heidegger on Being and Acting*; Zimmerman, *Heidegger's Confrontation with Modernity.*
3 Sluga, *Heidegger's Crisis*; Herf, *Reactionary Modernism*; Ott, *Martin Heidegger.*
4 See Mohler, *Die Konservative Revolution in Deutschland*; Sontheimer, *Antidemokratisches Denken.*
5 See Barash, *Heidegger et son siècle*; Kisiel, *The Genesis*; Löwith, *Martin Heidegger and European Nihilism*; Stambaugh, *The Finitude of Being.*
6 Jünger, *Der Arbeiter*; Hardensett, *Der kapitalistische und der technische Mensch.*
7 Haushofer, *Grenzen*; for a recent critical review of Haushofer's geopolitical vision, see Ebeling, *Geopolitik.*
8 Darré, *Neuadel aus Blut und Boden*; Schoenichen, *Naturschutz als völkische und internationale Kulturaufgabe*; and his *Naturschutz im Dritten Reich.*
9 Ferry, *Le Nouvel Ordre écologique.*
10 Palmier, *Les Écrits politiques de Heidegger.*
11 Ash, *Gestalt Psychology in German Culture*, 85.
12 Harrington, *Reenchanted Science*, 53, 106–8, 178.
13 Ash, *Gestalt Psychology in German Culture*, 272–99.
14 Goethe, *Werke*, 13: 5–6.
15 Ibid., 13: 164; see also Stephenson, *Goethe's Conception of Knowledge*, 59.
16 Ibid., 8, 12.

17 Goethe, *Die Schriften zur Naturwissenschaften*, 1: 10.

18 Goethe, *Werke*, 13: 55.

19 Langan, *Merleau-Ponty's Critique of Reason*, 21.

20 Lewin, *Dynamic Theory of Personality*, 47.

21 von Ehrenfels, 'On "Gestalt Qualities"' (1890), 83.

22 von Ehrenfels, 'On "Gestalt Qualities"' (1890), 93.

23 Gurwitsch, *Studies in Phenomenology and Psychology*, 7, 10.

24 Ibid., 10, 14, 23.

25 B. Smith, *Foundations of Gestalt Theory*, 51.

26 Ibid., 18.

27 von Ehrenfels, 'On "Gestalt Qualities"' (1890), 107, 108.

28 Koffka, *Principles of Gestalt Psychology*, 22.

29 von Ehrenfels, 'On "Gestalt Qualities"' (1890), 94, 101, 106.

30 von Ehrenfels, 'On "Gestalt Qualities"' (1890), 110.

31 Ibid., 106.

32 B. Smith, *Foundations of Gestalt Theory*, 42.

33 See Heider, *Life of a Psychologist*, 46ff.

34 Köhler, *Gestalt Psychology*, 105.

35 B. Smith, *Foundations of Gestalt Theory*, 58.

36 von Ehrenfels, 'Gestalt Level and Gestalt Purity,' 93–6. This selection of Smith's anthology is taken from von Ehrenfels' *Kosmogonie* (1916).

37 von Ehrenfels, 'Gestalt Level and Gestalt Purity,' 118–20.

38 B. Smith, *Foundations of Gestalt Theory*, 68.

39 Ibid., 61.

40 Ibid., 62–5.

41 Gurwitsch, *Studies in Phenomenology and Psychology*, 27–8.

42 Harrington, *Reenchanted Science*, 157.

43 Goldstein, *Organism*, 371.

44 Lewin, *Dynamic Theory of Personality*, 29–30, 40; see also de Rivera, *Field Theory in Human Science*, 24–33.

45 Gurwitsch, *Studies in Phenomenology and Psychology*, 49.

46 Ibid., 252.

47 Husserl, *Logische Untersuchungen*, A234; see *Logical Investigations*, 442.

48 Husserl, *Philosophie der Arithmetik*, 203.

49 Husserl, *Ideen I*, 265–70. Köhler postulated the synthesis of gestalt qualities on the neurological level: see Köhler, *Selected Papers*, 115, 244. See also Holenstein, *Phänomenologie der Assoziation*, 298.

50 Tiemersma, 'Merleau-Ponty's Philosophy as Field Theory,' 42–5.

51 Holenstein, *Phänomenologie der Assoziation*, 278.

52 Gurwitsch, *Studies in Phenomenology and Psychology*, 253; see also Holenstein, *Phänomenologie der Assoziation*, 294–5.

53 Gurwitsch, *Studies in Phenomenology and Psychology*, 176, 178.

54 Ibid., 189.

55 Ibid., 193, 195.

56 Ibid., 198, 203–4.

57 Ibid., 209–10.

58 Ibid., 207.

59 Dillon, *Merleau-Ponty's Ontology*, 70, 74.

60 Merleau-Ponty, *Primacy of Perception*, 15. On the influence of Goethe's theory of colour on Merleau-Ponty's *Phenomenology of Perception*, see Gandelman, 'Goethe as the Precursor,' 128; and van Eynde, *La libre Raison du phénomène*, 87.

61 Langan, *Merleau-Ponty's Critique of Reason*, 8, with reference to Merleau-Ponty, *Primacy of Perception* 18, 39.

62 Mirvish, 'Merleau-Ponty,' 454.

63 Ibid., 456, 473.

64 Merleau-Ponty, *Primacy of Perception*, 12.

65 Dillon, *Merleau-Ponty's Ontology*, 67.

66 Merleau-Ponty, *Phenomenology of Perception*, 327; cf. Dillon, *Merleau-Ponty's Ontology*, 79.

67 Merleau-Ponty, *Primacy of Perception*, 24.

68 Dillon, *Merleau-Ponty's Ontology*, 75–80.

69 Øverenget, *Seeing the Self*, 8 (and 7–33, 174–81).

70 Heidegger and Bodmershof, *Briefwechsel*, 21.

71 Ibid., 18.

72 Ash, *Gestalt Psychology in German Culture*, 216–7, 275–6.

73 Kapferer, 'Diese Art von Philosophiedozenten ist unser Ruin.'

74 Heidegger and Blochmann, *Briefwechsel*, 50.

75 Heinz and Kisiel, 'Heideggers Beziehungen,' 108.

76 Gelb and Goldstein, 'Analysis of a Case,' 319.

77 Ash; *Gestalt Psychology in German Culture*, 279.

78 Goldstein, *Organism*, 47.

79 Krell, *Daimon Life*.

80 Hamburger, *Heritage of Experimental Embryology*, 64–7.

81 Harrington, *Reenchanted Science*, 52.

82 Goldstein, *Organism* 117.

83 See R. Smith, *Inhibition*, 1–26.

84 Goldstein, *Organism*, 375–6.

85 Goldstein, *Organism*, 370.

86 See, e.g., Lewin, *Dynamic Theory of Personality*, 47.

87 Schrag, *Experience and Being*, 61.

88 Husserl, *Ideen I*, 209.

89 Husserl, 'Erneuerung als individualethisches Problem,' 26, 20.
90 Schrag, *Experience and Being*, 57.
91 Ibid., 170–1.
92 Husserl, 'Formale Typen,' 62, 61.
93 Husserl, *Crisis of the European Sciences*, 139–41.
94 Bernhard Waldenfels, 'Despised Doxa,' 33.
95 Heidegger, 'Martin Heidegger,' 180.

1 The Challenge of the Planetary

1 See Radloff, 'Total Mobilization of Art,' 231–60.
2 Ibid., 237.
3 See Radloff, '*Das Gestell*,' 23–46.
4 Ibid., passim.

2 Rhetoric and the Public Sphere

1 Schwan, *Politische Philosophie im Denken Heideggers*, 86.
2 Carr, 'Die fehlende Sozialphilosophie Heideggers,' 242–3.
3 Löwith, *Martin Heidegger and European Nihilism*, 137–59.
4 Köchler, 'Zur Frage der systematischen Wertung,' 210.
5 Rockmore, *On Heidegger's Nazism and Philosophy*, 282–93.
6 Barash, 'Die Auslegung der "Öffentlichen Welt,"' 121; Harries, 'Heidegger as Political Thinker,' 327–8.
7 Grassi, 'Why Rhetoric Is Philosophy,' 74–5.
8 Gebert, *Negative Politik*, 117.
9 Johnstone, 'Aristotelian Trilogy,' 17; cf. Aristotle, *Rhetoric*, 1356a25–6, and *Nicomachean Ethics*, bk 1, ch. 2.
10 Arnhart, *Aristotle on Political Reasoning*, 75.
11 Reeve, 'Philosophy, Politics and Rhetoric,' 191.
12 Aristotle, *Politics*, 1252a1ff; cf. Gebert, *Negative Politik*, 39.
13 Cf. Aristotle, *Nicomachean Ethics*, 1106b24 sq.
14 Cf. Ibid., 1142b34–1143a24; Halliwell, 'The Challenge of Rhetoric,' 178–9.
15 Grimaldi, 'Rhetoric and Truth,' 173.
16 Cf. Aristotle, *Rhetoric*, 1354a1.
17 Cf. Plato, *Phaedrus*, 275a2 sq.
18 Cf. Ibid., 276a8 sq.
19 Reeve, 'Philosophy, Politics and Rhetoric,' 203.
20 Halliwell, 'Challenge of Rhetoric,' 181, 179–80, 183; cf. Aristotle, *Rhetoric*, 1360b7.

21 Halliwell, 'Challenge of Rhetoric,' 185.
22 Wörner, *Das Ethische in der* Rhetorik, 70; cf. *Rhetoric*, 1355a30–9.
23 Leighton, 'Aristotle and the Emotions,' 220; cf. Aristotle, *On the Soul*, 403a16–19.
24 Engberg-Pedersen, 'Is There an Ethical Dimension?' 133.
25 Ibid., 117, 122–3; cf. Aristotle, *Rhetoric*, 1355a37–8.
26 Leighton, 'Aristotle and the Emotions,' 209.
27 Ibid., 213; Aristotle, *De Somnis*, 460b1–16.
28 Nussbaum, 'Aristotle on Emotions,' 303–4.
29 Hellwig, *Untersuchungen*, 241–2; cf. Chaim Perelman, 'Rhetoric and Politics,' 131.
30 See Hellwig, *Untersuchungen*, 256, 241.
31 Gebert, *Negative Politik*, 31.
32 See also Ibid., 58n4.
33 In Heidegger, *Wegmarken*, 301.
34 Kisiel, *Genesis*, 299, 298.
35 Heidegger and Fink, *Heraklit*, 126.
36 See Fritsche, *Historical Destiny*, esp. ch. 1.
37 Halliwell, 'Challenge of Rhetoric,' 185.

3 Heidegger and the Conservative Revolution

1 In addition to Ott, *Martin Heidegger*, 150–8; Rockmore, *On Heidegger's Nazism and Philosophy*, 54–72; Philipse, *Heidegger's Philosophy of Being*, 268–9; Köchler, 'Zur Frage der systematischen Wertung,' 205–9; Fritsche, *Historical Destiny and National Socialism*, 217–24; and the works of others on this topic already cited, see Philipse, *Heidegger's Philosophy of Being*.
2 Gebert, *Negative Politik*, 121, 122–8.
3 Sluga, *Heidegger's Crisis*, 144–51, 167.
4 Krieck, '"Allgemeinbildung" und Technische Hochschule,' 51.
5 Ibid., 53.
6 Derrida, *De l'esprit*, 66, 72–3/40, 45–6.
7 See Barash, *Heidegger et son siècle*, 132–3.
8 Cf. Klages, *Mensch und Erde*, 31–4.
9 Taminiaux, *Heidegger and the Project*, 133–7, 143.
10 Bernasconi, *Heidegger in Question*, 2–24.
11 Ward, *Heidegger's Political Thinking*, 116–27.
12 Heidegger, Letter to Carl Schmitt, 132.
13 Cf. van Buren, *Young Heidegger*, 234.
14 Cf. Plato, *Phaedo*, 61a.

15 van Buren, *Young Heidegger,* 220–34.

16 van Buren, 'Young Heidegger,' 172.

17 Taminiaux, *Heidegger and the Project,* 125.

18 Cf. Sikka, 'Philosophical Bases of Heidegger's Politics,' 250–1; Schalow, 'Question Concerning Heidegger's Involvement,' 124.

19 See Dreyfus, *Being-in-the-World,* 16–9.

20 Aristotle, *Metaphysics,* 1046a10f.

21 Frede, 'Aristotle's Notion of Potentiality,' 181.

22 Kosman, 'Activity of Being,' 207.

23 Cf. Aristotle, *Metaphysics,* 1047a24–6.

24 See Schnapper, 'Beyond the Opposition,' 219ff.

25 Kisiel, *Genesis,* 291; cf. *Metaphysics,* 1017b23–6.

26 Kosman, 'Activity of Being,' 205; *Metaphysics,* 1071a1–4, 1071b14–20.

27 Taminiaux, *Heidegger and the Project,* 123.

28 Lacoue-Labarthe, *Heidegger, Art, and Politics,* 62–70.

29 Sikka, 'Philosophical Bases of Heidegger's Politics,' 250.

30 Aristotle, *On the Soul,* 432b28; cf. GA33, 150.

31 Cf. Hellwig, *Untersuchungen zur Theorie der Rhetorik,* 236.

32 Schütrumpf, *Die Bedeutung des Wortes* ethos, 16.

33 Leopold, *Alfred Hugenberg,* 137–8.

34 Ibid., 104–27.

35 Ibid., 151–63; see also Noakes and Pridham, *Nazism 1919–1945,* 122–6.

36 Noakes and Pridham, *Nazism 1919–1945,* 161–2, 167–87.

37 Ott, *Martin Heidegger,* 187–92.

38 See Nicosia, *Third Reich,* 41–9, 58–60; Brenner, *Zionism,* 45–91; and Black, *Transfer Agreement,* 246–50.

39 Rigg, *Hitler's Jewish Soldiers,* 1–5, 29–30, 76ff.

40 Noakes and Pridham, *Nazism 1919–1945,* 528.

41 Koonz, *Nazi Conscience,* 10, 12.

42 Ibid., 100.

43 Ibid., 3, 12–13.

44 Courtois et al., *Black Book of Communism,* 146–59.

45 See Baird, *To Die for Germany,* 13–40; and Sontheimer, *Antidemokratisches Denken,* 161.

46 Lane and Rupp, *Nazi Ideology before 1933,* xii.

47 Sontheimer, *Antidemokratisches Denken,* 38–9, 169–73.

48 Quoted in ibid., 169.

49 von Klemperer, *Germany's New Conservatism,* 198.

50 Mohler, *Die Konservative Revolution in Deutschland,* 4–7.

51 Rockmore, *On Heidegger's Nazism and Philosophy,* 284.

52 Polt, *Heidegger*, 159–64.

53 Ibid., 162.

54 Ibid., 163.

55 Philipse, *Heidegger's Philosophy of Being*, 258–64.

56 Ott, *Martin Heidegger*, 237.

57 Sontheimer, *Antidemokratisches Denken*, 44–53, 75.

58 Ott, *Martin Heidegger*, 193–4; Palmier, *Les Écrits politiques de Heidegger*, 93–100.

59 Cf. Sontheimer, *Antidemokratisches Denken*, 64, 75–8.

60 See Ott, *Martin Heidegger*, 133–260.

61 Zimmerman, *Heidegger's Confrontation with Modernity*, 26–31.

62 See Iggers, *German Conception of History*, passim.

63 See Bullivant, 'Conservative Revolution,' 49f.

64 van den Bruck, *Das Dritte Reich*, 256; trans., Lorimer, *Germany's Third Empire*, 210.

65 van den Bruck, *Das Dritte Reich*, 308/250; cf. von Klemperer, *Germany's New Conservatism*, 162.

66 Bullivant, 'Conservative Revolution,' 64–6.

67 Bourdieu, *Political Ontology of Martin Heidegger*, 42.

68 Ibid., 105, 56–7, 72.

69 Sluga, *Heidegger's Crisis*, 10–11.

70 Ibid., 6.

71 Ibid., 8.

72 Ibid., 23.

73 Ibid., 74, 121.

74 Ibid., 124.

75 von Hofmannsthal, 'Das Schriftum als geistiger Raum,' 394.

76 Ibid., 412–13.

77 Mohler, *Die Konservative Revolution in Deutschland*, 367.

78 Billig, *L'International raciste*, 54–5.

79 Mohler, *Die Konservative Revolution in Deutschland*, 368.

80 van den Bruck, *Das Dritte Reich*, 230, 238/192, 197.

81 Ebeling, *Geopolitik*, 121–2.

82 These distinctions follow Mohler, *Die Konservative Revolution in Deutschland*, 286–94.

83 *Die Tat* (1909–38) was continued as *Das XX. Jahrhundert* from 1939 to 1944. *Deutsches Volkstum* was edited by Wilhelm Stapel and Albrecht Erich Günther and published 1919–38. Haushofer edited the *Zeitschrift für Geopolitik*, which ran from 1924 to 1944.

84 Leopold, *Alfred Hugenberg*, 46.

85 Sontheimer, *Antidemokratisches Denken*, 345.

86 This statement appeared as an advertisement for the journal in Freyer, *Revolution von Rechts*. 'Action' and 'opinion' are in English in the original.

87 von Klemperer, *Germany's New Conservatism*, 130–3, 205.

88 Ibid., 101.

89 Stobbe, 'Die Bildersprache des "Deutschen Volkstums,"' 65–72, 149, 232–3.

90 Ibid., 105–6.

91 Mohler, *Die Konservative Revolution in Deutschland*, 290.

92 Wolin, *Politics of Being*, 105.

93 Cf. van den Bruck, *Das Dritte Reich*, 257–8/211–12.

94 Ziegler, *Fünfundzwanzig Sätze*, 33–4.

95 Heidegger, *Zollikoner Seminare*, 197–8.

96 Darré, *Neuadel aus Blut und Boden*, 135–6; cf. Ruttke, 'Recht und Recht,' 8–9.

97 Spengler, *Decline of the West*, 2: 124–31.

98 Klaasen, 'Die sozial-philosophischen Grundlagen des Nationalsozialismus,' 482.

99 H. Günther, *Kleine Rassenkunde*, 57.

100 Jennifer Hecht, 'Vacher de Lapouge,' 293ff.

101 H. Günther, *Platon als Hüter des Lebens*, 44, 56; *Kleine Rassenkunde*, 147.

102 H. Günther, *Kleine Rassenkunde*, 11–12.

103 Ibid., 91–2, 142–4.

104 Ibid., 142, 146.

105 Clauss, *Rasse ist Gestalt*, 11–19; *Rasse und Seele*, 73.

106 Rosenberg, *Der Mythos des 20. Jahrhunderts*, 493, 513–22; see also von See, *Barber Germane Arier*, 309.

107 Baeumler, *Alfred Rosenberg*, 70.

108 Lacoue-Labarthe and Nancy, 'Nazi Myth,' 306–7.

109 Baeumler, *Alfred Rosenberg*, 13, 53.

110 Banton, *Racial Theories*, 44–80.

111 Backe, *Das Ende des Liberalismus*, 46–8. National Socialist support for Zionism, as the movement for a Jewish national home and territory, is intimately related to the anti-liberalism of the regime. Backe was State Secretary in the Ministry of Food and Agriculture, as of 1933, and replaced Darré as Reich Agriculture Minister in 1944.

112 See, for example, Schultze-Naumberg, 'Rassengebundene Kunst,' 10.

113 H. Günther, *Platon als Hüter des Lebens*, 41–56.

114 Schultze-Naumberg, *Kunst und Rasse*, 7–28.

115 Ibid., 10–11.

116 Hecht, 'Vacher de Lapouge,' 293.

117 Lutzhöft, *Der Nordische Gedanke in Deutschland*, 20; and Field, 'Nordic Racism,' 531–5.

118 Mosse, *Toward the Final Solution*, 94–112.

119 Banton, *Racial Theories*, 90.

120 Löwith, *Martin Heidegger and European Nihilism*, 75.

121 Field, 'Nordic Racism,' 523.

122 Benn, 'Der deutsche Mensch,' 230–1; 'Geist und Seele künftiger Geschlechter,' 234–9.

123 von Klemperer, *Germany's New Conservatism*, 76–91.

124 E. Jung, *Herrschaft der Minderwertigen*, 121, cited in Ebeling, *Geopolitik*, 132.

125 Ibid., 8, 51.

126 In Ebeling, *Geopolitik*, 138–9.

127 Ebeling, *Geopolitik*, 153–55.

128 Freyer, *Revolution von Rechts*, 41–2.

129 Ibid., 40, 52.

130 Herf, *Reactionary Modernism*, 121–9.

131 Cf. von See, *Barber Germane Arier*, 222.

132 See Weinreich, *Hitler's Professors*, 75–8.

133 For a typical expression of this view, see Ehrt, 'Der imperialistische Krieg,' 149–53. Brepöhl, 'Der nordische Mensch,' emphasizes the common idea that the Nordic individual is defined by a sense of belonging to the earth (p. 24). Although this implicates anti-cosmopolitanism in both its liberal and communist varieties, it does not necessarily implicate racism.

134 See Rosenberg, *Der Mythos des 20. Jahrhunderts*, 526.

135 van den Bruck, *Das Dritte Reich*, 23/35.

136 Ibid., 292/236.

137 Freyer, *Revolution von Rechts*, 62–3, 65.

138 A. Günther, 'Nationalismus,' 501.

139 Ibid., 498.

140 Morris, *Essay on the Modern State*, 230ff.

141 E. Jung, *Herrschaft der Minderwertigen*, 152.

142 Arnold, *Medieval Germany, 500–1300*, 13–74.

143 Nadler, *Das Stammhafte Gefüge*, 194–5; cf. van den Bruck, *Das Dritte Reich*, 139–149/123–133; to translate van den Bruck's use of *Stämme* as 'races' is of course misleading.

144 E. Jung, *Herrschaft der Minderwertigen*, 124–33; cf. Mohler, *Die Konservative Revolution in Deutschland*, 139–40.

145 Sontheimer, *Antidemokratisches Denken*, 282–6, 295.

146 Ibid., 282, 292–3.

147 Heidegger, 'Warum bleiben wir,' 216–18.

148 Mosse, *Crisis of German Ideology*, 13–30.

149 Young, *Heidegger, Philosophy, Nazism*, 27.

150 See, for example, Schmidt-Rohr, 'Die Sprache als politische Grösse,' 252; Schmitt, 'Landschaft und Geschichte,' 581–4; Haase-Bessell, 'Volk und Rasse,' 662.

151 C.G. Jung, 'Die Erdbedingtheit der Psyche,' 135–6.

152 Gmelin, 'Landschaft und Seele,' 32–5.

153 Vowinkel, 'Der zweite Reichsbauerntag,' 764; 'Zum Begriff Lebensraum,' 638–9; Jelden, 'Vom Raumgefühl im deutschen Menschen,' 205.

154 Offe, 'Geopolitik und Naturrecht,' 243; Brepöhl, 'Der nordische Mensch,' 24.

155 Murphy, Heroic Earth, 72.

156 Ebeling, Geopolitik, 137–8, 143–62, 209–19.

157 Haushofer, Grenzen, 2, 11–12.

158 Schoenichen, Naturschutz als völkische, 85, 409–11.

159 Schoenichen, Naturschutz im Dritten Reich, 1–7.

160 Reichsnaturschutzgesetz, 821–5.

161 See Bramwell, Ecology in the 20th Century, 200–8; Ferry, Le nouvel ordre écologique, 147–67; Darré, Neuadel aus Blut und Boden, esp. chapters 5–6.

162 Darré, Neuadel aus Blut und Boden, 84–5.

163 E. Jung, Herrschaft der Minderwertigen, 124–33.

164 Stobbe, 'Die Bildersprache des "Deutschen Volkstums,"' 230–41.

165 Darré, Neuadel aus Blut und Boden, 178–90, 216–20.

166 Kisiel, 'Heidegger's Apology,' 44.

167 Grisebach, 'Der wahre,' 114–16.

168 Lee, Politics and Truth, 85.

169 Wolin, Politics of Being, 197.

170 Sontheimer, Antidemokratisches Denken, 174–5.

171 See, for example, Coleman, Hobbes and America; Diggins, Lost Soul of American Politics; and Pangle, Spirit of American Republicanism.

172 Krieck, 'Führertum und Hochschulreform,' 57–63.

173 Krieck, 'Führertum und Hochschulreform,' 61–2.

174 Krieck, 'Die Erneuerung der Universität,' 11–12.

175 Niekisch, Hitler, 8–13.

176 Sluga, Heidegger's Crisis, 125–33.

177 Schneeberger, Nachlese zu Heidegger, 76–80.

178 See also Krieck, 'Die Erneuerung der Universität,' 11–14.

179 Krieck, 'Wissenschaft als Gestalterin,' 230.

180 See Kockelmans, Heidegger and Science, 152–62; 220–8.

181 Dreyfus, Being-in-the-World, 177.

182 Cf. Gebert, Negative Politik, 141–150.

183 See Harrington, Reenchanted Science, 164, 113–14, 190–2, 59, 195.

184 Rudolf Kassner, *Das Physiognomische Weltbild*, 160.
185 Kassner, *Das Physiognomische Weltbild*, 165–71, 138–9.
186 Ibid., 126.
187 Ibid., 216.
188 Ibid., 89, 115.
189 Woods, *Conservative Revolution in Weimar*, 87.
190 von Schirach, *Die Hitler-Jugend*, 66.
191 Haeberlin, 'Organischer Typus und Freiheit,' 277.
192 Ibid., 278.
193 Jaensch, 'Zur Neugestaltung,' 67–9.
194 Ash, *Gestalt Psychology in German Culture*, 343.
195 Heidegger and Jaspers, *Briefwechsel*, 50.
196 Ziegler, *Fünfundzwanzig Sätze*, 35, 38.
197 Ibid., 39, 52–3.
198 Ziegler, *Der europäische Geist*, 80.
199 Ibid., 115.
200 Ziegler, *Fünfundzwanzig Sätze*, 68.
201 Wigman, 'Der Tänzer und sein Instrument,' 673–6.
202 Raschke, 'Bemerkungen zum deutschen Tanz,' 47; see also Bach, 'Das Wesen,' 213.
203 Cf. Benn, 'Züchtung I,' 215–18.
204 Baeumler, *Bachofen und Nietzsche*, 25.
205 Stumpfl, *Unser Kampf*, 35–52.
206 Dreyfus, *Being-in-the-World*, 59.
207 Steinweis, *Art, Ideology, and Economics*, 55.
208 Schlösser, *Das Volk und seine Bühne*, 7, 41–61.
209 Clauss, *Rasse und Seele*, 28–9.
210 Ibid., 165.
211 Wigman, *Deutsche Tanzkunst*, 23, 62f; see also Guilbert, *Danser avec le IIIe Reich*, 35–9.
212 Lyon, 'Emotion and Embodiment,' 200–1.
213 Vondung, *Magie und Manipulation*, 39–70, 159–93, 200.
214 Deubel, 'Die Kunst und das Volk,' 65–9.
215 Sorell, *Mary Wigman*, esp. 153–67.
216 Vondung, *Magie und Manipulation*, 9–16, 39.
217 Petzet, *Encounters and Dialogues*, 100.
218 Vietta, *Der Tanz*, esp. 12, 17, 23, 51, 96–7, 112.
219 Bullivant, 'Conservative Revolution,' 65; von Klemperer, *Germany's New Conservatism*, 199–200.
220 von Klemperer, *Germany's New Conservatism*, 223, 231.

221 Zimmerman, *Heidegger's Confrontation with Modernity*, 33.

222 Young, *Heidegger, Philosophy, Nazism*, 49.

223 Ibid., 34.

224 Ibid., 27.

225 Young, *Heidegger, Philosophy, Nazism*, 22–3.

226 Sontheimer, *Antidemokratisches Denken*, 337–41.

227 E. Jung, *Herrschaft der Minderwertigen*, 55.

228 Cited in von Klemperer, *Germany's New Conservatism*, 210–11.

229 On Schlageter's significance, see Baird, *To Die for Germany*, 13–40.

230 van den Bruck, *Das Dritte Reich*, 249/206.

231 Ibid., 98–9/90.

232 Cited in Zimmerman, *Heidegger's Confrontation with Modernity*, 20.

233 Heyse, 'Die Aufgabe der Philosophie,' 52, 38–9.

234 Heidegger, 'Martin Heidegger,' 180.

235 See van Buren, 'Martin Heidegger, Martin Luther,' 161, 168–71; and Volpi, '*Being and Time*,' 203.

4 Volk, Work, and Historicity in Heidegger's *Logik* of 1934

1 Sikka, 'Philosophical Bases of Heidegger's Politics,' 250–1.

 2 Vetter, 'Anmerkungen zum Begriff des Volkes,' 244, 246.

 3 Fritsche, *Historical Destiny*, 188–91.

 4 Ibid., 132.

 5 Ibid., 18–19, 132.

 6 Blitz, '*Heidegger's* Being and Time,' 204.

 7 Derrida, *De l'esprit*, 66, 72–3/40, 45–6.

 8 Löwith, *Martin Heidegger and European Nihilism*, 160.

 9 Lacoue-Labarthe, *Heidegger, Art, and Politics*, 32–4.

10 Dreyfus, 'Heidegger's History,' 182.

11 Fell, 'Familiar and the Strange,' 68.

12 Lacoue-Labarthe, *Heidegger, Art, and Politics*, 53–4.

13 See Feder, *Das Prgramm der N.S.D.A.P.*, 20.

14 Zimmerman, *Heidegger's Confrontation with Modernity*, 90.

15 Ibid., 166–90.

16 Hegel, *Jenaer Realphilosophie II*, 213, 428–30.

17 Hegel, *Grundlinien der Philosophie des Rechts*, secs. 190, 195.

18 Hegel, *Realphilosophie I*, 237.

19 Cf. Taminiaux, 'Origin of "The Origin,"' 396.

20 Young, *Heidegger, Philosophy, Nazism*, 34.

21 Foltz, *Inhabiting the Earth*, 154–76.

22 Hardensett, *Der kapitalistische und der technische Mensch*, 62–3.

23 Ibid., 127–8, cited in Herf, *Reactionary Modernism*, 184, translation modified.

24 Hardensett, *Der kapitalistische und der technische Mensch*, 128.

25 Marx, *Economic and Philosophic Manuscripts*, 114.

26 de Boer, *Thinking in the Light*, 208–9.

27 See Hodge, *Heidegger and Ethics*, 21, 192–3.

28 Birmingham, 'Ever Respectfully Mine,' 115.

5 *An Introduction to Metaphysics* and Heidegger's Critique of 'Intellectualism'

1 Guignon, 'Being as Appearing,' 36.

2 Dahlstrom, 'Scattered *Logos*,' 83–102.

3 Cf. Taminiaux, 'Heidegger on Values,' 227–30; Schalow, 'At the Crossroads of Freedom,' 250ff; see also the extended survey of the problem of values in Mongis, *Heidegger et la critique*, esp. 79–177.

4 Chamberlain, *Die Grundlagen*, 77.

5 Haag, 'Rhythmus und Arbeit,' 10.

6 Klages, *Mensch und Erde*, 34–7.

7 Ziegler, *Der europäische Geist*, 115.

8 Schoenichen, *Naturschutz im Dritten Reich*, 6–7, 76.

9 Ibid., 46, 59–60, 81.

10 Klages, *Mensch und Erde*, 28, 31.

11 Ruttke, 'Recht und Recht,' 7.

12 Ferry and Renaut, *Heidegger and Modernity*, 60–71.

13 Zimmerman, 'Ontological Decline of the West,' 192–204.

14 For a post-modern development of this question, see Baudrillard, *Selected Writings*, 166–84.

15 Schürmann, *Heidegger on Being and Acting*, 87, 106–19.

16 See Taminiaux's account in 'Heidegger on Values,' 237–9.

17 Derrida, *De l'esprit*, 36–7/17–18; see also McNeill, 'Spirit's Living Hand,' 107–8; and Sallis, 'Flight of Spirit,' 130.

18 Habermas, 'Work and *Weltanschauung*,' 193.

19 Cf. Schalow, 'At the Crossroads of Freedom,' 250ff.

20 Taminiaux, 'Heidegger on Values,' 239.

21 Derrida, *De l'esprit*, 66, 72–3/40, 44–5.

22 Ibid., 73/45.

23 Fried, 'What's in a Word,' 134–41.

24 Derrida, *De l'esprit*, 67/41.

25 Ibid., 63/35.

26 Lacoue-Labarthe, *Heidegger, Art, and Politics*, 32–4.

27 Cf. Okrent, 'Truth of Being,' 153; and Taminiaux, 'Heidegger on Values,' 227–8.

28 See Ward, *Heidegger's Political Thinking*, 214–15; the relation between ethos and homeland, which is central to Heidegger's lectures and works of the 1930s and 1940s, is preserved in the post-war works, in the *Letter on Humanism*, for example.

29 See McNeill, '*Heimat*,' 341–7.

30 Thiele, *Timely Meditations*, 172; see also Dallmayr, *Other Heidegger*, 146–7; and Fynsk, *Heidegger, Thought and Historicity*, 215.

31 Thiele, *Timely Meditations*, 173.

32 Ibid., 178n8.

33 Derrida, 'Violence et métaphysique,' 215/45; cf. Thiele, *Timely Meditations*, 172n3.

34 Schoenbohm, 'Heidegger's Interpretation of *Phusis*,' 153.

35 Fóti, 'Heidegger, Hölderlin, and Sophoclean Tragedy,' 180.

6 Heidegger and Carl Schmitt: The Historicity of the Political

1 Löwith, *Martin Heidegger and European Nihilism*, 141–6.

2 Heidegger, 'Heidegger and Schmitt,' 132.

3 Bendersky, 'Schmitt and Hobbes,' 127.

· 4 Ibid., 123.

5 Ulman, 'Return of the *Foe*,' 5; Piccone et al., 'Ostracizing Carl Schmitt,' 87.

6 Gottfried et al., 'Ostracizing Carl Schmitt,' 97.

7 Schmitz, *Die Freund-Feind-Theorie Carl Schmitts*, 154–65.

8 Ibid., 154.

9 Ibid., 135.

10 Ibid., 154.

11 Schwab, *Challenge of the Exception*, 50.

12 Schmitz, *Die Freund-Feind-Theorie Carl Schmitts*, 133, 154.

13 Ibid., 154–5.

14 Löwith, *Martin Heidegger and European Nihilism*, 141–6.

15 Schmitz, *Die Freund-Feind-Theorie Carl Schmitts*, 155; Löwith, *Martin Heidegger and European Nihilism*, 150.

16 Derrida, *Politics of Friendship*, 132.

17 Schmitz, *Die Freund-Feind-Theorie Carl Schmitts*, 155.

18 Hirst, 'Carl Schmitt's Decisionism,' 20.

19 Kervégan, *Hegel, Carl Schmitt*, 39, 46.

20 Herf, *Reactionary Modernism*, 118n30.

21 Derrida, *Politics of Friendship*, 161–2.

22 Kervégan, *Hegel, Carl Schmitt*, 72, 77.

23 Ibid., 73.

24 Schmitt, *Der Hüter der Verfassung*, 111, cited in Kervégan, *Hegel, Carl Schmitt*, 79.

25 Schmitz, *Die Freund-Feind-Theorie Carl Schmitts*, 92; Aristotle, *Politics*, 1262b7f.

26 Schmitt, *Theorie des Partisanen*, 96.

27 Herf, *Reactionary Modernism*, 115–21.

28 Maschke, *Der Tod des Carl Schmitt*, 58–9.

29 Winfield, *Freedom and Modernity*, 298–300.

30 Cf. Ibid., 272.

31 Ibid., 270.

32 Cf. Herf, *Reactionary Modernism*, 117.

33 Schmitt, *Theorie des Partisanen*, 83.

34 Schmitt, *Der Nomos der Erde*, 20.

35 Piccone et al., 'Ostracizing Carl Schmitt,' 91.

36 Cf. Kervégan, *Hegel, Carl Schmitt*, 39–42.

37 Bendersky, 'Carl Schmitt and the Conservative Revolution,' 32.

38 Kervégan, *Hegel, Carl Schmitt*, 41.

39 Ibid., 310.

40 Cf. Kervégan, *Hegel, Carl Schmitt*, 311.

41 See Schmitz, *Die Freund-Feind-Theorie Carl Schmitts*, 162n20.

42 Cf. Ibid., 164n26.

43 Kervégan, *Hegel, Carl Schmitt*, 312.

44 Ibid., 314.

45 Fritsche, *Historical Destiny*, 101, 121, 139–40.

46 Piccone, editor's note, 132.

47 Derrida, *Politics of Friendship*, 116, 249.

48 Kirk, *Heraclitus*, 245.

49 Heidegger, Letter to Carl Schmitt, 132.

50 Heidegger and Fink, *Heraklit*, 24/42–3.

51 Ibid., 24/43.

52 Zeller, *Die Philosophie der Greichen*, 831.

53 Guthrie, *History of Greek Philosophy*, 447.

54 Kirk, *Heraclitus*, 216–17, 223.

55 Ibid., 203.

56 Harries, 'Heidegger as Political Thinker,' 327.

7 The *Beiträge zur Philosophie* and the Differentiation of Being

1 Vallega-Neu, *Heidegger's* Contributions to Philosophy, 36.

2 van Buren, *Young Heidegger*, 378–84.

3 von Herrmann, '*Contributions to Philosophy*,' 105.

4 McNeill, 'Time of *Contributions to Philosophy*,' 137.

5 Cf. Risser, *Heidegger Toward the Turn*, 5.

6 Schürmann, 'Riveted to a Montrous Site,' 314.

7 Ibid., 321–2.

8 von Herrmann, 'Das Ereignis,' 248.

9 Cf. Schwan, *Politische Philosophie im Denken Heideggers*, 76–8.

10 Held, 'Fundamental Moods,' 287.

11 Ibid., 287.

12 Ibid., 289.

13 Haar, 'Empty Time and Indifference,' 310.

14 Held, 'Fundamental Moods,' 290.

15 Schwan, *Politische Philosophie im Denken Heideggers*, 85.

16 Haar, 'Empty Time and Indifference,' 198–204.

17 Philipse, *Heidegger's Philosophy of Being*, 270–2.

18 von Herrmann, *Heideggers Philosophie der Kunst*, xviii.

19 See, e.g., Rockmore, *On Heidegger's Nazism and Philosophy*, 205; Wolin, *Politics of Being*, 147; Philipse, *Heidegger's Philosophy of Being*, 164–5.

20 Taminiaux, 'Origin of "The Origin,"' 392.

21 Bernasconi, 'Greatness of the Work,' 99–100.

22 Ibid., 115n4.

23 Ibid., 113–4; Pöggeler, *Philosophie und Politik bei Heidegger*, 122–2.

24 Dastur, 'Heidegger's Freiburg Version,' 121, 126.

25 Zimmerman, 'Ontological Aestheticism,' 70.

26 Lacoue-Labarthe, *Heidegger, Art, and Politics*, 32–4.

27 Cf. Polt, 'Metaphysical Liberalism,' passim.

28 Kockelmans, *Heidegger on Art and Artworks*, 175, 187.

29 Schwan, *Politische Philosophie im Denken Heideggers*, 86.

30 Schürmann, *Heidegger on Being and Acting*, 81, 85.

31 Ibid., 91.

32 Dauenhauer, 'Renovating the Problem of Politics,' 636.

33 Lacoue-Labarthe, *Heidegger, Art, and Politics*, 66–70, 85–6, 94–6.

34 Ibid., 110.

35 Ibid., 68, 93–6.

36 Schwan, *Politische Philosophie im Denken Heideggers*, 86; Harries, 'Heidegger as Political Thinker,' 328.

37 Cf. Plato, *Politeia*, 515d.

38 Plato, *Politeia*, 595a–597e.

39 Derrida, *La Vérité en peinture*, 65–71/59–61.

40 Plato, *Phaedrus*, 251a–253a.

41 Plato, *Politeia*, 596d.

42 Lacoue-Labarthe, *Heidegger, Art, and Politics*, 80–1.
43 Schürmann, 'Symbolic Difference,' 26.
44 Schürmann, 'Ontological Difference and Political Philosophy,' 106.
45 Schürmann, *Heidegger on Being and Acting*, 102–5.
46 See Schürmann, 'Symbolic Praxis,' esp. 39–40.
47 Aristotle, *Physics*, 185a12ff.
48 Ibid., 192b.
49 Ibid., 192b16–20.
50 Schürmann, *Heidegger on Being and Acting*, 103, 102.
51 Aristotle, *Physics*, 192b32–193a2.
52 Ibid., 193a9–21.
53 Cf. Aristotle, *Physics*, 193a28–31.
54 Ibid., 193a30–1.
55 Ibid., 193b6–8.
56 Aristotle, *Metaphysics*, 1049b5.
57 Aristotle, *Physics*, 193b18–20.
58 Cf. Aristotle, *Metaphysics* V, 17; 1022a sqq.
59 Taminiaux, 'Origin of "The Origin,"' 396.
60 Ibid., 401.
61 von Herrmann, *Heideggers Philosophie der Kunst*, 119.
62 Schürmann, 'Political Thinking in Heidegger,' 198–209.
63 Dauenhauer, 'Does Anarchy Make Political Sense?' 374.
64 Derrida, *La Vérité en peinture*, 315/276.
65 Spinosa, 'Derrida and Heidegger,' 274.
66 Ibid., 278–9.
67 Palmier, *Les Écrits politiques de Heidegger.*
68 Neaman, *Dubious Past*, 35–7.
69 Zimmerman, 'Ontological Aestheticism,' 64.
70 Ibid., 64ff.
71 Herf, *Reactionary Modernism*, 81–2; cf. Schwarz, *Der konservative Anarchist*, 74–6; Zimmerman, 'Ontological Aestheticism,' 58–61. See also Bohrer's *Die Aesthetik des Schreckens*, for an interpretation of Jünger's aesthetics.
72 Palmier, *Les Écrits politiques de Heidegger*, 202.
73 Herf, *Reactionary Modernism*, 71.
74 See Schwarz, *Der konservative Anarchist*, 23–40.
75 Jünger, *An der Zeitmauer*, 130.
76 Cf. ibid., 181.
77 Ibid., 276; 'Über die Linie,' SW 7, 244.
78 Cf. Palmier, *Les Écrits politiques de Heidegger*, 204–7.
79 Jünger, *An der Zeitmauer*, 137.

80 Cf. Derrida, *De la grammatologie*, 19/9.
81 Derrida, *La Vérité en peinture*, 92–3/80–1.
82 Herf, *Reactionary Modernism*, 72.
83 Jünger, 'Über den Schmerz,' 190.
84 Heidegger, 'Wer ist Nietzsches Zarathustra?' 118.
85 Ibid., 118.
86 Cf. Nietzsche, *Der Wille zur Macht*, aphorism 796.
87 Jünger, 'Über den Schmerz,' 165, 173–4.
88 Ibid., 174, 183–4.
89 Cf. Figal and Schwilk, *Magie der Heiterkeit*, 190–1.
90 Cf. Palmier, *Les Écrits politiques de Heidegger*, 210–11.
91 Heidegger, 'Die Sprache,' 24–30.
92 Heidegger pays particular attention to the Third Antimony in the *Critique of Pure Reason*; the distinction between transcendental freedom and practical freedom is developed in reference to the first Critique, the *Critique of Judgement* (esp. sec. 91), and the *Critique of Practical Reason*. For a detailed examination, see Schalow, *Renewal*, note 93.
93 See GA31, esp. 242–54, 258, 260ff/165–70, 174, 181ff.
94 Heidegger's *Grundprobleme der Phanomenologie* (GA24), 199–218 offers an intepretation of personhood in Kant, with the objective of laying bare the understanding of being as substance (*Vorhandensein*) which grounds it.
95 Schalow, *Renewal*, 249–304.
96 Thiele, 'Heidegger on Freedom,' 280–1.
97 Ibid., 282–4.
98 Ibid., 285.
99 Heidegger's lecture consists primarily in a close reading of Friedrich W. Schelling, 'Philosophische Untersuchungen über das Wesen der Menschlichen Freiheit,' 223–308.
100 Emad, 'Heidegger on Schelling's Concept,' 161.
101 Ibid., 165.
102 Heidegger, *Schelling's Treatise*, 169.
103 Dallmayr, 'Ontology of Freedom,' 228.
104 Cf. Schalow, *Renewal*, 290, 303.

Conclusion: Imperial Truth and Planetary Order

1 Habermas, 'Work and *Weltanschauung*,' 190, 198.
2 For example, see Heller, 'Parmenides,' 251; Schwan, 'Zeitkritik und Politik,' 96; Wolin, *Politics of Being*, 164.
3 Frings, '*Parmenides*,' 22.

4 Fóti, '*Aletheia* and Oblivion's Field,' 78.

5 Bacon, *Novum Organum*, 539.

6 Bacon, *Great Instauration*, 447, 456.

7 Bacon, *Essays or Councils*, 8.

8 Heidegger, *Die Frage nach dem Ding*, 69–74/288–95.

9 Whitney, *Francis Bacon and Modernity*, 50.

10 Faulkner, *Francis Bacon*, 149.

11 Bacon, *Essays and Councils*, 29.

12 Faulkner, *Francis Bacon*, 185.

13 Oakshott, *Of Human Conduct*, 287–8, cited in Faulkner, *Francis Bacon*, 202.

14 Faulkner, *Francis Bacon*, 185.

15 Ibid., 220.

16 Ryan, 'Hobbes' Political Philosophy,' 223.

17 Hobbes, *Leviathan*, 111, cited in Ryan, 'Hobbes' Political Philosophy,' 223.

18 Ryan, 'Hobbes' Political Philosophy,' 210–11.

19 Locke, *Essay concerning Human Understanding*, bk 2, ch. 21, sec. 44; bk 2, ch. 33, secs. 1–6.

20 Diggins, *Lost Soul of American Politics*, 235, 239.

21 N. Wood, *Politics of Locke's Philosophy*, 77.

22 Locke, *Two Treatises of Civil Government, Second Treatise*, sec. 33.

23 Locke, *Two Treatises of Civil Government, First Treatise*, sec. 6.

24 Citing Hobbes, *Leviathan*, ch. 16.

25 Pye, 'Sovereign,' 100.

26 Tertullian, *De Spectaculis*, sec. 10, fr. 5.

27 Calvin, *Institutes of the Christian Religion*, bk 1, ch. 15, sec. 1, p. 207; cf. Dakin, *Calvinism*, 97.

28 Calvin, *Institutes of the Christian Religion*, bk 3, ch. 23, sec. 2, p. 949.

29 Burke, *Reflections*, 194–5, 285.

30 Ibid., 249, 285.

31 Baudrillard, *Selected Writings*, 104–114.

32 Foucault, *Surveillir et punir*, 32–3, 195–6, 208–11/27–8, 194, 206–9.

33 Ryan, 'Hobbes' Political Philosophy,' 213.

34 Hobbes, *Leviathan*, ch. 6.

35 Locke, *Two Treatises of Civil Government, Second Treatise*, sec. 49.

Bibliography

Arendt, Hannah. *Between Past and Future*. New York: Viking, 1969.

Aristotle. *Basic Works*. Ed. Richard McKeon. New York: Random House, 1941.

– *On the Soul, Parva Naturalia, On Breath*. Translated by W.S. Hett. Loeb Classical Library. Cambridge, MA: Harvard University Press, 1964.

– *Metaphysics*. 2 vols. Translated by Hugh Tredennick. Loeb Classical Library. Cambridge, MA: Harvard University Press, 1958, 1980.

– *Metaphysik*. 2 Vols. Revised translation by Hermann Bonitz. Edited with commentary by Horst Seidl. Hamburg: Felix Meiner, 1984, 1989.

– *Nicomachean Ethics*. Translated by H. Racham. Loeb Classical Library. Cambridge, MA: 1947.

– *Physics*. Introduction and commentary by W.D. Ross. Oxford: Clarendon, 1936.

– *Physics*. 2 vols. Translated by Philip H. Wicksteed and Frances M. Cornford. Loeb Classical Library. Cambridge, MA: Harvard University Press, 1963.

– *Politics*. 2nd ed. Translated Richard Congreve. London: Longmans, 1874.

– *Rhetoric*. Commentary by E.M. Cope. Edited by J.E. Sandys. Cambridge: Cambridge University Press, 1877.

Arnhart, Larry. *Aristotle on Political Reasoning: A Commentary on the* 'Rhetoric.' Dekalb: Northern Illinois University Press, 1981.

Arnold, Benjamin. *Medieval Germany, 500–1300: A Political Interpretation*. Toronto: University of Toronto Press, 1997.

Ash, Mitchell G. *Gestalt Psychology in German Culture, 1890–1967: Holism and the Quest for Objectivity*. Cambridge: Cambridge University Press, 1995.

Avineri, Shlomo. *Hegel's Theory of the Modern State*. Cambridge: Cambridge University Press, 1980.

Bach, Rudolf. 'Das Wesen des Sprach- und Bewegungschores.' *Völkische Kunst* 5 (1934): 213–17.

Backe, Herbert. *Das Ende des Liberalismus in der Wirtschaft*. Berlin: Reichsnähr-standverlag, 1938.

Bacon, Francis. *Essays or Councils Civil and Moral*. 1597–1625. In Dick, *Selected Writings of Francis Bacon*, 6–149.

– *The Great Instauration*. 1620. In Dick, *Selected Writings of Francis Bacon*, 423–51.

– *The New Organum*. 1620. In Dick, *Selected Writings of Francis Bacon*, 455–540.

Baeumler, Alfred. *Alfred Rosenberg und Der Mythus des 20. Jahrhunderts*. Munich: Hoheneichen, 1943.

– *Bachofen und Nietzsche*. Zürich: Verlag der neuen Schweitzer Rundschau, 1929.

– *Bildung und Gemeinschaft*. Berlin: Junker & Dünnhaupt, 1942.

– *Politik und Erziehung*. Berlin: Junker & Dünnhaupt, 1937.

– *Nietzsche: Der Philosoph und Politiker*. Leipzig: Reclam, 1931.

– *Weltdemokratie und Nationalsozialismus*. Berlin: Duncker and Humblot, 1943.

Baird, Jay W. *To Die For Germany. Heroes in the Nazi Pantheon*. Bloomington: Indiana University Press, 1990.

Banton, Michael. *Racial Theories*. 2nd ed. Cambridge: Cambridge University Press, 1998.

Barash, Jeffrey Andrew. 'Die Auslegung der "Öffentlichen Welt" als politisches Problem: Zu Hannah Arendts Heidegger Deutung.' In Papenfuss and Pöggler, *Zur Philosophischen Aktualität Heideggers*, 112–27.

– *Heidegger et son siècle: Temps de l'Être, temps de l'histoire*. Paris: Presses Universitaires de France, 1995.

Barthes, Roland. 'Analyse textuelle d'un conte d'Edgar Poe.' In *Sémiotique narrative et textuelle*, edited by Claude Chabrol, 29–54. Paris: Larousse, 1973.

– 'De l'oeuvre au texte.' *Revue d'esthétique* 3 (1971): 225–32. Translated by Stephen Heath as 'From Work to Text,' in Roland Barthes, *Image Music Text*, selected and translated by Stephen Heath, 155–64. New York: Hill and Wang, 1977.

– 'Le mythe, aujourd'hui.' In *Mythologies*, 213–68. Paris: Seuil, 1957. Translated by Annette Lavers as 'Myth Today,' in *A Barthes Reader*, ed. Susan Sontag, 93–149. New York: Hill and Wang, 1986.

– *Le plaisir du texte*. Paris: Seuil, 1973. Translated by Richard Miller as *The Pleasure of the Text*. New York: Noonday Press, 1975.

Baudrillard, Jean. *Selected Writings*. Edited by Mark Poser. Stanford: Stanford University Press, 1988.

– *Simulacra and Simulations*. Translated by Paul Foss, Paul Patton, and Philip Beitchman. New York: Semiotext(e), 1983.

– *Simulacres et simulation*. Paris: Galilée, 1981.

Bendersky, Joseph W. 'Carl Schmitt and the Conservative Revolution.' *Telos* 72 (Summer 1987): 27–42.
– 'Schmitt and Hobbes.' *Telos* 109 (Fall 1996): 122–9.
Benn, Gottfried. *Essays, Reden, Vorträge.* 2 vols. Wiesbaden: Limes Verlag, 1965.
– 'Der deutsche Mensch: Erbmasse und Führertum.' In *Essays, Reden, Vorträge,* 223–31.
– 'Geist und Seele künftiger Geschlechter.' In *Essays, Reden, Vorträge,* 232–9.
– 'Züchtung I.' In *Essays, Reden, Vorträge,* 214–22.
Bernasconi, Robert. 'The Greatness of the Work of Art.' In Risser, *Heidegger Toward the Turn,* 95–117.
– 'Heidegger's Destruction of *Phronesis.*' In *Heidegger and Praxis.* Edited by Thomas J. Nenon. *The Southern Journal of Philosophy.* Suppl. no. 28 (1989): 127–48.
– *Heidegger in Question: The Art of Existing.* Atlantic Highlands, NJ: Humanities Press, 1993.
Billig, Michael. *L'Internationale raciste: De la psychologie à la 'science' des races.* Translated by Y. Llavador and A. Schnapp-Gourbeillon. Paris: Maspero, 1981.
Birmingham, Peg. 'Ever Respectfully Mine: Heidegger on Agency and Responsibility.' In Dallery, et al., *Ethics and Danger,* 109–24.
Black, Edwin. *The Transfer Agreement: The Untold Story of the Secret Pact between the Third Reich and Jewish Palestine.* New York: Macmillan, 1984.
Blitz, Mark. *Heidegger's* Being and Time *and the Possibility of Political Philosophy.* Ithaca, NY: Cornell University Press, 1981.
Bohrer, Karl Heinz. *Die Aesthetik des Schreckens: Die pessimistische Romantik und Ernst Jüngers Frühwerk.* Frankfurt am Main: Ullstein, 1978.
Bonnafous-Boucher, Maria. *Le libéralisme dans la pensée de Michel Foucault.* Paris: L'Harmattan, 2001.
Boss, Medard. *Grundriss der Medizin.* Bern: Hans Huber, 1971. Translated by S. Conway and A. Cleaves as *Existential Foundations of Medicine and Psychology.* New York: Jason Aronson, 1979.
Bourdieu, Pierre. *The Political Ontology of Martin Heidegger.* Translated by Peter Collier. Stanford: Stanford University Press, 1991.
Bramwell, Anna. *Ecology in the 20th Century: A History.* New Haven, CT: Yale University Press, 1989.
Brenner, Lenni. *Zionism in the Age of the Dictators.* London: Croom Helm, 1983.
Brepöhl, Wilhelm. 'Der nordische Mensch, sein Lebensgefühl und seine Heimat.' *Die Tat* 1 (April 1925): 23–32.
Brogan, Walter. 'A Response to Robert Bernasconi's "Heidegger's Destruction of Phronesis."' In Nenon, *Heidegger and Praxis,* 149–55.
Bullivant, Keith. 'The Conservative Revolution.' In *The Weimar Dilemma. Intellectu-*

als in the Weimar Republic, edited by Anthony Phelan, 47–70. Manchester: Manchester University Press, 1985.

Burke, Edmund. *Reflections on the Revolution in France* [1790]. Edited by Conor Cruise O'Brien. London: Penguin, 1988.

Calvin, John. *Institutes of the Christian Religion.* 2 vols. Edited by John T. McNiell. Translated by Ford Lewis Battles. Vols. 20–1, Library of Christian Classics. Philadelphia: Westminister Press, 1960.

Caputo, John D. *Demythologizing Heidegger.* Bloomington: Indiana University Press, 1993.

Carr, David. 'Die fehlende Sozialphilosophie Heideggers.' In Papenfuss and Pöggeler, *Zur Philosophischen Aktualität Heideggers,* 234–46.

Cassirer, Ernst. 'Implications of the New Theory of the State.' In Machiavelli, *The Prince,* 166–80.

Chamberlain, Houston Stewart. *Die Grundlagen des Neunzehnten Jahrhunderts.* Munich: Bruckmann, 1899.

Chierghin, Franco. 'Physis und Ethos: Die Phänomenologie des Handelns bei Heidegger.' In Margreiter and Leidmair, *Heidegger,* 115–32.

Clauss, Ludwig Ferdinand. *Rasse ist Gestalt.* Munich: Zentralverlag der NSDAP, 1937.

– *Rasse und Seele: Eine Einführung in den Sinn der leiblichen Gestalt.* Munich: Lehmanns Verlag, 1937.

Coleman, Frank. M. *Hobbes and America: Exploring the Constitutional Foundations.* Toronto: University of Toronto Press, 1977.

Courtois, Stéphane, Nicolas Werth, Jean-Louis Panné, Andrzej Paczkowski, Karel Bartosek, and Jean-Louis Margolin. *The Black Book of Communism.* Edited by Mark Kramer. Translated by Jonathan Murphy and Mark Kramer. Cambridge, MA: Harvard University Press, 1999.

Couture, Jocelyne, Kai Nelson, and Michel Seymour. *Rethinking Nationalism.* Calgary: University of Calgary Press, 1998.

Critchley, Simon. *The Ethics of Deconstruction: Derrida and Levinas.* Edinburgh: Edinburgh University Press, 1999.

Dahl, Norman O. *Practical Reason, Aristotle, and Weakness of the Will.* Minneapolis: University of Minnesota Press, 1984.

Dahlstrom, Daniel. 'The Scattered *Logos:* Metaphysics and the Logical Prejudice.' In Polt and Fried, *A Companion,* 83–102.

Dakin, A. *Calvinism.* Port Washington: Kennikat Press, 1940.

Dallery, Arleen B., Charles E. Scott, and P. Holley Roberts, eds. *Ethics and Danger: Essays on Heidegger and Continental Thought.* New York: SUNY Press, 1992.

Dallmayr, Fred R. 'Ontology of Freedom: Heidegger and Political Philosophy.' *Political Theory* 12, no. 2 (May 1984): 204–34.

– *The Other Heidegger.* Ithaca, NY: Cornell University Press, 1993.

Darré, R. Walther. *Neuadel aus Blut und Boden* [1930]. Berlin: Lehmanns Verlag, 1943.

Dastur, Françoise. 'Heidegger's Freiburg Version of the Origin of the Work of Art.' In Risser, *Heidegger Toward the Turn*, 119–42.

Dauenhauer, Bernard P. 'Does Anarchy Make Political Sense? A Response to Schürmann.' *Human Studies* 1, no. 4 (October 1978): 369–75.

– 'Renovating the Problem of Politics.' *The Review of Metaphysics* 39, no. 4 (June 1976): 626–41.

de Boer, Karin. *Thinking in the Light of Time: Heidegger's Encounter with Hegel.* Albany: SUNY Press, 2000.

Derrida, Jacques. *De la grammatologie.* Paris: Minuit, 1967. Translated by Gayatri Chakravorty Spivak as *Of Grammatology.* Baltimore: Johns Hopkins, 1976.

– *De l'esprit: Heidegger et la question.* Paris: Galilée, 1987. Translated by Geoffrey Bennington and Rachel Bowley as *Of Spirit: Heidegger and the Question.* Chicago: University of Chicago Press, 1989.

– 'La différance.' In *Marges de la philosophie*, 1–29; 'Difference,' in *Margins of Philosophy*, 1–27.

– *L'Écriture et la différance.* Paris: Seuil, 1967. Translated by Alan Bass as *Writing and Difference.* Chicago: University of Chicago Press, 1978.

– *Marges de la philosophie.* Paris: Minuit, 1972. Translated by Alan Bass as *Margins of Philosophy.*

– *Margins of Philosophy.* Translated by Alan Bass. Chicago: University of Chicago Press, 1982.

– *The Politics of Friendship.* Translated by George Collins. London: Verso, 1997.

– 'Le retrait du métaphore.' *Analecta Husserliana* 14 (1977–8): 273–300.

– 'Sending: On Representation.' Translated by Peter and Mary Caws. *Social Research* 49, no. 2 (Summer 1982): 295–326.

– 'Signature évément contexte.' In *Marges de la philosophie*, 365–93. 'Signature Event Context,' *Margins of Philosophy*, 307–30.

– 'La structure, le signe et le jeu dans le discours des sciences humains.' In *L'Écriture et la difference* 409–28. 'Structure, Sign and Play in the Discourse of the Human Sciences,' in *Writing and Difference*, 278–93.

– *La Vérité en peinture.* Paris: Flammarion, 1978. Translated by Geoff Bennington and Ian McLeod as *The Truth in Painting.* Chicago: University of Chicago Press, 1987.

– 'Violence et métaphysique.' In *L'Ecriture et la différance*, 117–228. 'Violence and Metaphysics,' in *Writing and Difference*, 79–168.

– *La voix et la phénomène.* Paris: Presses Universitaires de France, 1964. Translated by David B. Allison and Newton Carver as *Speech and Phenomena.* Evanston: Northwestern University Press, 1973.

– *Writing and Difference*. Translated by Alan Bass. Chicago: University of Chicago Press, 1978.

Deubel, Werner. 'Die Kunst und das Volk.' *Rhythmus* 14, no. 3 (1936): 65–9.

Dick, Hugh G., ed. *Selected Writings of Francis Bacon*. New York: Modern Library, 1955. Based on James Spedding, Robert Leslie Ellis, and Douglas Denon Heath, eds, *The Works of Francis Bacon*. London: Longmans, 1857–74.

Diels, Hermann, and Walther Kranz. *Die Fragmente der Vorsokratiker*. Vol. 1. Berlin: Weimannsche Verlagsbuchhandlung, 1960.

Diggins, John Patrick. *The Lost Soul of American Politics: Virtue, Self-Interest, and the Foundations of Liberalism*. New York: Basic, 1984.

Dillon, M.C. *Merleau-Ponty's Ontology*. Bloomington: Indiana University Press, 1988.

Dreyfus, Hubert L. *Being-in-the-World: A Commentary on Heidegger's* Being and Time, *Division I*. Cambridge, MA: MIT Press, 1991.

– 'Heidegger's History of the Being of Equipment.' In Dreyfus and Hall, *Heidegger*, 173–85.

Dreyfus, Hubert L., and Harrison Hall, eds. *Heidegger: A Critical Reader*. Oxford: Blackwell, 1992.

Ebeling, Frank. *Geopolitik: Karl Haushofer und seine Raumwissenschaft 1919–1945*. Berlin: Akademie Verlag, 1994.

Ebert, Theodor. 'Phronesis – Anmerkung zu einem Begriff der Aristotelischen Ethik (VI5 und 8–13).' In *Aristoteles: Die Nikomachische Ethik*, edited by Otfried Höffe, 165–86. Berlin: Akademie Verlag, 1995.

Ehrt, Adolf. 'Der imperialistische Krieg im System des Terrors.' *Das Volk: Kampfblatt für völkische Kultur und Politik*, July 1936, 149–53.

Emad, Parvis. 'Heidegger on Schelling's Concept of Freedom.' *Man and World* 8, no. 2 (May 1975): 157–74.

Engberg-Pedersen, Lars. 'Is There an Ethical Dimension to Aristotelian Rhetoric?' In Rorty, *Essays on Aristotle's* Rhetoric, 116–41.

Erickson, Keith V. ed. *Aristotle: The Classical Heritage of Rhetoric*. Metuchen, NJ: The Scarecrow Press, 1974.

Farias, Victor. *Heidegger et le nazisme*. Paris: Éditions Verdier, 1987.

Faulkner, Robert. *Francis Bacon and the Project of Progress*. Lanham, MD: Rowman and Littlefield, 1993.

Feder, Gottfried. *Das Programm der N.S.D.A.P. und seine weltanschaulichen Grundgedanken*. Munich: Eher, 1933.

Fell, Joseph P. 'The Familiar and the Strange: On the Limits of *Praxis* in the Early Heidegger.' In Dreyfus and Hall, *Heidegger*, 65–80.

Fell, Joseph P., and Alain Renaut. *Heidegger and Modernity*. Translated by Franklin Philip. Chicago: University of Chicago Press, 1990.

Ferry, Luc. *Le Novel Ordre écologique: L'Arbre, l'animal et l'homme.* Paris: Grasset: 1992.

Field, Geoffrey G. 'Nordic Racism.' *Journal of the History of Ideas* 38, no. 3 (1977): 523–40.

Figal, Günter, and Heimo Schwilk. *Magie der Heiterkeit.* Stuttgart: Klett-Cotta, 1995.

Figueroa-Sarriera, Heidi J. 'Children of the Mind with Disposable Bodies: Metaphors of Self in a Text on Artificial Intelligence and Robotics.' In *The Cyborg Handbook,* edited by Chris Hables Gray, 127–35. New York: Routledge, 1995.

Foltz, Bruce V. *Inhabiting the Earth: Heidegger, Environmental Ethics, and the Metaphysics of Nature.* Atlantic Highlands, NJ: Humanities Press, 1995.

Fóti, Véronique. '*Aletheia* and Oblivion's Field: On Heidegger's *Parmenides* Lectures.' In Dallery, et al., *Ethics and Danger,* 71–82.

– 'Heidegger, Hölderlin, and Sophoclean Tragedy.' In Risser, *Heidegger toward the Turn,* 163–86.

Foucault, Michel. *Histoire de la sexualité.* 3 vols. Paris: Gallimard, 1976–84. Translated by Robert Hurley as *The History of Sexuality.* 3 vols. New York: Vintage, 1978–86.

– *Surveiller et punir: Naissance de la prison.* Paris: Gallimard, 1975. Translated by Alan Sheridan as *Discipline and Punish: The Birth of the Prison.* New York: Vintage, 1977.

– 'La technologie politiques des individus.' In *Dits et écrits,* Vol. 4. Paris: Gallimard, 1994.

Frede, Michael. 'Aristotle's Notion of Potentiality in *Metaphysics* Theta.' In Scaltsas, et al., *Unity, Identity, and Explanation,* 173–94.

Freyer, Hans. *Revolution von Rechts.* Jena: Eugen Diedrichs, 1931.

Fried, Gregory. 'What's in a Word? Heidegger's Grammar and Etymology of "Being."' In Polt and Fried, *A Companion,* 125–42.

Frings, Manfred S. '*Parmenides*: Heidegger's 1942–1943 Lecture held at Freiburg University.' *Journal of the British Society for Phenomenology* 19, no. 1 (January 1988): 15–33.

Fritsche, Johannes. *Historical Destiny and National Socialism in Heidegger's* Being and Time. Berkeley: University of California Press, 1999.

Fynsk, Christopher. *Heidegger, Thought and Historicity.* Ithaca, NY: Cornell University Press, 1986.

Gandelman, Claude. 'Goethe as the Precursor of the Phenomenological Approach to Color.' In *Goethe in the Twentieth Century,* edited by Alexej Ugrinsky, 123–28. New York: Greenwood, 1987.

Gebert, Sigbert. *Negative Politik: Zur Grundlage der Politischen Philosophie aus der*

Daseinsanayltik und ihrer Bewährung in den Politischen Schriften Martin Heideggers von 1933/34. Berlin: Duncker and Humblot, 1992.

Gelb, Adhémar, and Kurt Goldstein. 'Analysis of a Case of Figural Blindness.' In *A Source Book of Gestalt Psychology*, edited by Willis D. Ellis, 315–25. London: Routledge and Kegan Paul, 1969.

Gethmann-Siefert, Annemarie, and Otto Pöggler, eds. *Heideggers Praktische Philosophie*. Frankfurt am Main: Suhrkamp, 1988.

Gmelin, Otto. 'Landschaft und Seele.' *Die Tat* 4, no. 1 (1925): 32–42.

Goethe, Johann Wolfgang von. *Die Schriften zur Naturwissenschaften*. Weimar: Hermann Böhlaus, 1947.

– *Werke: Hamburger Ausgabe*. 9th ed. 14 vols. Hamburg, C. Wegner, 1981.

Goldstein, Kurt. *The Organism: A Holistic Approach to Biology*. 1939. Boston: Beacon, 1963.

Gottfried, Paul, Gary Ulmen, and Paul Piccone. 'Ostracizing Carl Schmitt: Letters to *The New York Review of Books*.' *Telos* 109 (Fall 1996): 95–7.

Grassi, Ernesto. 'The Original Quality of the Poetic and Rhetorical Word.' *Philosophy and Rhetoric* 20 (1987): 248–59.

– *Rhetoric as Philosophy: The Humanist Tradition*. University Park: Pennsylvania State University Press, 1980.

– 'Why Rhetoric Is Philosophy.' *Philosophy and Rhetoric* 20, no. 2 (1987): 68–78.

Grimaldi, William M.A. 'Rhetoric and Truth: A Note on Aristotle's *Rhetoric* 1355a 21–24.' *Philosophy and Rhetoric* 11, no. 3 (1978): 173–7.

Grisebach, Eberhard. 'Der wahre und der wirkliche Staat.' *Die Tat* 4, no. 2 (1927): 92–116.

Grondin, Jean. *Le tournant dans la pensée de Martin Heidegger*. Paris: Presses Universitaires de France, 1987.

Guignon, Charles. 'Being as Appearing: Retrieving the Greek Experience of *Phusis*.' In Polt and Fried, *A Companion*, 34–56.

Guilbert, Laure. *Danser avec le IIIe Reich: Les danseurs modernes sous le nazisme*. Paris: Éditions Complexe, 2000.

Günther, Albrecht Erich. 'Nationalismus.' *Deutsches Volkstum* 8 (July 1927): 497–501.

Günther, Hans F. K. *Kleine Rassenkunde des deutschen Volkes*. Munich: Lehmann, 1933.

– *Platon als Hüter des Lebens: Platons Zucht und Erziehungsgedanken und deren Bedeutung für die Gegenwart*. Munich: Lehmann, 1928.

Guthrie, W.K.C. *A History of Greek Philosophy*. Vol. 1, *The Earlier Pre-Socratics and the Pythagoreans*. Cambridge: Cambridge University Press, 1962.

Gurwitsch, Aron. *Studies in Phenomenology and Psychology*. Evanston, IL: Northwestern University Press, 1966.

Haag, Herbert. 'Rhythmus und Arbeit.' *Geistige Arbeit* 4 (February 1936): 9–10.

Haar, Michel. *Le chant de la terre.* Paris: L'Herne, 1985.

– 'Empty Time and Indifference to Being.' In Risser, *Heidegger Toward the Turn,* 295–317.

Haase-Bessell, G. 'Volk und Rasse in ihren Beziehungen zueinander.' *Zeitschrift für Geopolitik* 16.2, nos. 8–9 (1939): 657–74.

Habermas, Jürgen. 'Work and *Weltanschauung:* The Heidegger Controversy from a German Perspective.' In Dreyfus and Hall, *Heidegger,* 186–208.

Haeberlin, Carl. 'Organischer Typus und Freiheit.' In *Der Leuchter.* Bk 7, *Gesetz und Freiheit,* edited by Graf Hermann Keyserling, 277–87. Darmstadt: Reichl, 1926.

Halliwell, Stephen. 'The Challenge of Rhetoric to Political and Ethical Theory in Aristotle.' In Rorty, *Essays on Aristotle's* Rhetoric, 175–90.

Hamburger, Stephan. *The Heritage of Experimental Embryology: Hans Spemann and the Organizer.* New York: Oxford University Press, 1998.

Hardensett, Heinrich. *Der kapitalistische und der technische Mensch.* Berlin: Oldenbourg, 1932.

Harries, Karsten. 'Heidegger as Political Thinker.' In *Heidegger and Modern Philosophy,* edited by Michael Murray, 304–28. New Haven, CT: Yale University Press, 1978.

Harries, Karsten, and Christof Jamme, eds. *Martin Heidegger: Politics, Art, and Technology.* New York: Holmes and Meier, 1994.

Harrington, Anne. *Reenchanted Science: Holism in German Culture from Wilhelm II to Hitler.* Princeton, NJ: Princeton University Press, 1996.

Harvey, Irene E. 'Derrida, Kant, and the Performance of Parergonality.' In *Derrida and Deconstruction,* edited by Hugh J. Siverman, 59–76. Continental Philosophy II. New York: Routledge, 1989.

Haushofer, Karl. *Grenzen: In Ihrer Geographischen und Politischen Bedeutung.* Berlin: Kurt Vowinkel, 1927.

Hecht, Jennifer Michael. 'Vacher de Lapouge and the Rise of Nazi Science.' *Journal of the History of Ideas* 61, no. 2 (2000): 285–304.

Hegel, G.W.F. *Grundlinien der Philosophie des Rechts.* Vol. 7 of *Werke.* Frankfurt am Main: Suhrkamp, 1970.

– *Jenaer Realphilosophie I: Die Vorlesung von 1803/4.* Edited by J. Hoffmeister. Leipzig: Felix Meiner, 1932.

– *Jenaer Realphilosophie II: Die Vorlesungen von 1805/6.* Edited by J. Hoffmeister. Republished as *Jenaer Realphilosophie.* Hamburg: Felix Meiner, 1967.

Heidegger, Martin. 'Ansprache am 11. November 1933 in Leipzig.' In *Reden und andere Zeugnisse,* no. 104, 190–3.

– *Aristoteles, Metaphysik Theta 1–3: Vom Wesen und Wirklichkeit der Kraft.* 1931. Vol. 33 of *Gesamtausgabe,* 1981.

- 'Aufruf zur Wahl.' 10 November 1933. In *Reden und andere Zeugnisse*, no. 103, 188–9.
- *Aus der Erfahrung des Denkens: 1910–1976*. Vol. 13 of *Gesamtausgabe*, 1983.
- 'Aus der Tischrede bei der Feier des fünfzigjährigen Bestehens des Instituts für pathologische Anatomie an der Universität Freiburg.' Beginning of August 1933. In *Reden und andere Zeugnisse*, no. 75, 150–2.
- *Basic Writings*. Edited by David Farell Krell. New York: Harper, 1993.
- *Beiträge zur Philosophie (Vom Ereignis)*. 1936–8. Vol. 65 of *Gesamtausgabe*, 1989. Translated by Parvis Emad and Kenneth Maly as *Contributions to Philosophy (From Enowning)*. Bloomington: Indiana University Press, 1999.
- *Besinnung*. 1938–9. Vol. 66 of *Gesamtausgabe*, 1997.
- *Briefe an Max Müller und andere Dokumente*. Edited by Holger Zaborowski and Anton Bösl. Munich: Karl Alber, 2003.
- 'Der deutsche Student als Arbeiter.' 25 November 1933. In *Reden und andere Zeugnisse*, no. 108, 198–208.
- 'Die deutsche Universität.' 15–16 August 1934. In *Reden und andere Zeugnisse*, no. 155, 285–307.
- *Einführung in die Metaphysik*. 1935. Vol. 40 of *Gesamtausgabe*, 1983. Translated by Ralph Manheim as *An Introduction to Metaphysics*. New Haven, CT: Yale University Press, 1959.
- *Einleitung in die Philosophie*. 1928–29. Vol. 27 of *Gesamtausgabe*, 1996.
- 'Erläuterungen und Grundsätzliches.' 15 December 1945. In *Reden und andere Zeugnisse*, no. 184, 409–15.
- *Die Frage nach dem Ding*. Tübingen: Niemeyer, 1987. Partially translated by W.B. Barton Jr and Vera Deutsch as 'Modern Science, Metaphysics, and Mathematics,' in *Basic Writings*, 267–306.
- 'Die Frage nach der Technik.' In Heidegger, *Vorträge und Aufsätze*, 9–40. Translated by William Lovitt as 'The Question Concerning Technology,' in *Basic Writings*, 311–41.
- 'Gedenkworte zu Schlageter.' 26 May 1933. In *Reden und andere Zeugnisse*, no. 285, 759–60.
- 'Die gegenwärtige Lage und die künftige Aufgabe der deutschen Philosophie.' 30 November 1934. In *Reden und andere Zeugnisse*, no. 158, 316–34.
- 'Das Geleitwort der Universität." 6 January 1934. In *Reden und andere Zeugnisse*, no. 121, 227.
- *Gesamtausgabe*. General Editor, Friedrich-Wilhelm von Herrmann. Frankfurt am Main: Klostermann, 1975–.
- *Die Geschichte des Seyns*. 1939–40. Vol. 69 of *Gesamtausgabe*, 1998.
- *Grundbegriffe*. 1941. Vol. 51 of *Gesamtausgabe*, 1981. Translated by Gary E. Aylesworth as *Basic Concepts*. Bloomington: Indiana University Press, 1993.

– *Die Grundbegriffe der Antiken Philosophie.* 1926. Vol. 22 of *Gesamtausgabe,* 1993.
– *Grundbegriffe der Aristotelischen Philosophie.* 1924. Vol. 18 of *Gesamtausgabe,* 2002.
– 'Die Grundbegriffe der aristotelischen Philosophie.' Lecture, Philipps-Universität Marburg, 1924. *Nachschrift.* Transcript by Werner Bröcker. Typescript by Herbert Marcuse. Dilthey-Forschungsstelle, Institut für Philosophie, Ruhr-Universität Bochum, Bochum, Germany.
– *Die Grundbegriffe der Metaphysik: Welt–Endlichkeit–Einsamkeit.* 1929–30. Vol. 29/ 30 of *Gesamtausgabe,* 1983. Translated by William McNeill and Nicolas Walker as *The Fundamental Concepts of Metaphysics.* Bloomington: Indiana University Press, 1995.
– *Die Grundbegriffe der Phänomenologie.* 1927. Vol. 24 of *Gesamtausgabe,* 1975. Translated by Albert Hofstadter as *The Basic Problems of Phenomenology.* Bloomington: Indiana University Press, 1982.
– *Grundfragen der Philosophie: Ausgewählte 'Probleme' der 'Logik.'* 1937–8. Vol. 45 of *Gesamtausgabe,* 1984.
– *Grundprobleme der Phänomenologie.* 1919–20. Vol. 58 of *Gesamtausgabe,* 1993.
– *Heraklit.* 1943–4. Vol. 55 of *Gesamtausgabe,* 1987.
– *Heraklit.* With Eugen Fink. Frankfurt am Main: Klostermann, 1970. Translated by Charles H. Seibart as *Heraclitus Seminar 1966/67.* Tuscaloosa: University of Alabama Press, 1970.
– *Hölderlins* Germanien *und* Der Rhein. 1934–5. Vol. 39 of *Gesamtausgabe,* 1980.
– *Hölderlins Hymne 'Der Ister.'* 1942. Vol. 53 of *Gesamtausgabe,* 1984.
– *Holzwege.* Frankfurt am Main: Klostermann, 1980.
– Letter to Carl Schmitt, 22 August 1933. 'Heidegger and Schmitt: A Letter.' *Telos* 72 (Summer 1987): 132.
– 'Hönigswald aus der Schule des Neukantianismus.' 25 June 1933. In *Reden und andere Zeugnisse,* no. 65, 132–3.
– 'Kurze Anti-Versailles-Kundgebung.' 26 June 1933. In *Reden und andere Zeugnisse,* no. 66, 134.
– *Logik als Frage nach dem Wesen der Sprache.* 1934. Vol. 38 of *Gesamtausgabe,* 1998.
– 'Martin Heidegger: A Philosopher and Politics.' Interview with Max Müller. In Neske and Kettering, *Martin Heidegger and National Socialism,* 180.
– *Metaphysische Anfangsgründe der Logik im Ausgang von Leibniz.* 1928. Vol. 26 of *Gesamtausgabe,* 1978. Translated by Michael Heim as *The Metaphysical Foundations of Logic.* Bloomington: Indiana University Press, 1984.
– *Nietzsche.* 2 Vols. Pfullingen: Neske, 1961. Translated by David Farrell Krell, Joan Stambaugh, and Frank A. Capuzzi as *Nietzsche,* 4 vols. San Franscisco: Harper, 1991.
– *Nietzsche: Der Wille zur Macht als Kunst.* 1936–37. Vol. 43 of *Gesamtausgabe,* 1985.

– *Ontologie* (*Hermeneutik der Faktizität*). 1923. Vol. 63 of *Gesamtausgabe*, 1988.
– *Parmenides.* 1942–3. Vol. 54 of *Gesamtausgabe*, 1992. Translated by André Schu-
   wer and Richard Rojcewicz as *Parmenides.* Bloomington: Indiana University
   Press, 1992.
– *Phänomenologische Interpretation von Kants* Kritik der reinen Vernunft. 1927–8.
   Vol. 25 of *Gesamtausgabe*, 1977.
– *Phänomenologische Interpretationen zu Aristoteles: Einführung in die Phänomenolo-
   gische Forschung.* 1921–2. Vol. 61 of *Gesamtausgabe*, 1985.
– *Platon: Sophistes.* 1924–1925. Vol. 19 of *Gesamtausgabe*, 1992.
– 'Platons Lehre von der Wahrheit.' In *Wegmarken*, 201–36. Translated by John
   Barlow as 'Plato's Doctrine of Truth,' in William Barrett and Henry D. Aiken,
   eds., *Philosophy in the Twentieth Century,* vol. 3, 251–70. New York: Random
   House, 1962.
– *Prolegomena zur Geschichte des Zeitbegriffs.* Vol. 20 of *Gesamtausgabe*, 1979.
– *Reden und Andere Zeugnisse eines Lebensweges: 1910–1976.* Vol. 16 of *Gesamtaus-
   gabe*, 2000.
– 'Der Ruf zum Arbeitsdienst.' 23 January 1934. In *Reden und andere Zeugnisse,*
   no. 125, 238–9.
– *Schelling: Vom Wesen der Menschlichen Freiheit* (*1809*). 1936. Vol. 42 of *Gesamtaus-
   gabe*, 1988. Translated by Joan Stambaugh as *Schelling's Treatise on the Essence of
   Human Freedom.* Athens: Ohio University Press, 1985.
– *Sein und Wahrheit.* 1933–4. Vol. 36/37 of *Gesamtausgabe*, 2001.
– *Sein und Zeit.* Tübingen: Niemeyer, 1972. Translated by John Macquarrie and
   Edward Robinson as *Being and Time.* New York: Harper and Row, 1962; and by
   Joan Stambaugh as *Being and Time.* Albany: SUNY Press, 1996.
– 'Die Selbstbehauptung der deutschen Universität.' 27 May 1933. In *Reden und
   andere Zeugnisse,* no. 51, 107–17.
– *Die Selbstbehauptung der Deutschen Universität: Das Rektorat 1933/34 – Tatsachen
   und Gedanken.* Frankfurt am Main: Klostermann, 1983. Translated, with an
   introduction, by Karsten Harries as 'The Self-Assertion of the German Univer-
   sity: The Rectorate 1933/34: Facts and Thoughts.' *Review of Metaphysics* 38
   (March 1985): 467–502.
– *Seminare.* Vol. 15 of *Gesamtausgabe*, 1986.
– 'Die Sprache.' In *Unterwegs zur Sprache*, 9–33.
– 'Der Spruch des Anaximander.' 1946. In *Holzwege*, 321–73. Translated by David
   Farell Krell and Frank A. Capuzzi as 'The Anaximander Fragment,' in *Early
   Greek Thinking*, 13–58. San Francisco: Harper and Row, 1984.
– *Über den Anfang.* 1941. Vol. 70 of *Gesamtausgabe*, 2005.
– 'Überwindung der Metaphysik.' In *Vorträge und Aufsätze*, 67–96.

- 'Das unverbrauchte Alemannentum.' 23 January 1934. In *Reden und andere Zeugnisse*, no. 126, 240.
- *Unterwegs zur Sprache*. Pfullingen: Neske, 1975.
- 'Der Ursprung des Kunstwerkes.' In *Holzwege*, 1–72. Translated by Albert Hofstadter as 'The Origin of the Work of Art,' in *Basic Writings*, 139–212.
- 'Vom Ursprung des Kunstwerkes: Erste Ausarbeitung.' In *Heidegger Studies* 5 (1989): 5–22.
- *Vom Wesen der menschlichen Freiheit: Einleitung in die Philosophie*. 1930. Vol. 31 of *Gesamtausgabe*, 1982. Translated by Ted Sadler as *The Essence of Human Freedom: An Introduction to Philosophy*. London: Continuum, 2002.
- 'Vom Wesen der Wahrheit.' In *Wegmarken*, 175–99. Translated by John Sallis as 'On the Essence of Truth,' in *Basic Writings*, 111–38.
- *Vom Wesen der Wahrheit: Zu Platons Höhlengleichnis und Theätet*. 1931–2. Vol. 34 of *Gesamtausgabe*, 1988.
- 'Vom Wesen des Grundes.' In *Wegmarken*, 123–73.
- 'Vom Wesen und Begriff der *Phusis*: Aristoteles, *Physik* B, 1.' In *Wegmarken*, 237–99. Translated by Thomas Sheehan as 'On the Being and Conception of *Phusis* in Aristotle's *Physics* B, 1,' *Man and World* 9 (1976): 219–70. Page references are to the marginal pagination, 309–371, of Sheehan, referring to *Wegmarken*, 1st ed.
- *Vorträge und Aufsätze*. Pfullingen: Neske, 1978.
- 'Warum bleiben wir in der Provinz.' 1934. In *Nachlese zu Heidegger: Dokumente zu sein Leben und Denken*, edited by Guido Schneeberger, 216–18. Bern: private edition, 1962.
- 'Was ist Metaphysik?' In *Wegmarken*, 103–21. Translated by David Farrell Krell as 'What Is Metaphysics?' in *Basic Writings*, 89–110.
- *Wegmarken*. 1967. 2nd ed. Frankfurt am Main: Klostermann, 1978.
- 'Wer ist Nietzsches Zarathustra?' In *Vorträge und Aufsätze*, 97–122.
- 'Die Zeit des Weltbildes.' In *Holzwege*, 73–110. Translated by William Lovitt as 'The Age of the World Picture,' in Martin Heidegger, *The Question Concerning Technology and Other Essays*, 115–54. New York: Harper, 1977.
- *Zollikiner Seminare*. Edited by Medard Boss. Fankfurt am Main: Klostermann, 1987.
- *Zu Ernst Jünger*. 1934–54. Vol. 90 of *Gesamtausgabe*, 2004.
- 'Zum Semesterbeginn.' 3 November 1933. In *Reden und andere Zeugnisse*, no. 101, 184–5.
- *Zur Bestimmung der Philosophie*. 1919. Vol. 56/57 of *Gesamtausgabe*, 1987.
- 'Zur Einrichtung der Dozentenschule.' 29 August 1934. In *Reden und andere Zeugnisse*, no. 156, 308–14.

– 'Zur Eröffnung der Schulungskurse für die Notstandsarbeiter der Stadt an der Universität.' 22 January 1934. In *Reden und andere Zeugnisse*, no. 124, 232–7.

– 'Zur Seinsfrage.' In *Wegmarken*, 379–420.

– '25 Jahre nach unserem Abiturium.' 26–7 May 1934. In *Reden und andere Zeugnisse*, no. 154, 279–84.

Heidegger, M., and Elisabeth Blochmann. *Briefwechsel: 1918–1969*. Edited by Joachim W. Storck. Marbach am Neckar: Deutsche Schillergesellschaft, 1990.

Heidegger, M., and Karl Jaspers. *Briefwechsel: 1920–1963*. Edited by Walter Biemel und Hans Saner. Frankfurt am Main: Klostermann; Munich: Piper, 1990.

Heidegger, M., and Imma von Bodmershof. *Briefwechsel: 1959–1976*. Edited by Bruno Pieger. Stuttgart: Klett-Cotta, 2000.

Heider, Fritz. *The Life of a Psychologist: An Autobiography*. Lawrence: University of Kansas Press, 1984.

Heinz, Marion, and Theodore Kisiel. 'Heideggers Beziehungen zum Nietzsche – Archiv im Dritten Reich.' In *Annäherung an Martin Heidegger: Festschrift für Hugo Ott zum 65. Geburtstag*, edited by Hermann Schäfer, 103–36. Frankfurt am Main: Campus, 1996.

Held, Klaus. 'Fundamental Moods and Heidegger's Critique of Contemporary Culture.' In Sallis, *Reading Heidegger*, 286–303.

Heller, Ágnes. 'Parmenides and the Battle of Stalingrad.' *Graduate Faculty Philosophy Journal* 19, no. 2 (1997): 247–62.

Hellwig, Antje. *Untersuchungen zur Theorie der Rhetorik bei Platon und Aristoteles*. Göttingen: Vandenhoeck & Ruprecht, 1973.

Herf, Jeffrey. *Reactionary Modernism: Technology, Culture, and Politics in Weimar and the Third Reich*. Cambridge: Cambridge University Press, 1986.

Heyse, Hans. 'Die Aufgabe der Philosophie in der deutschen Universität.' In *Volk und Hochschule im Umbruch*, edited by A. Schürmann. Berlin: Stalling, 1937.

Hirst, Paul. 'Carl Schmitt's Decisionism.' *Telos* 72 (Summer 1987): 15–26.

Hobbes, Thomas. *Leviathan, or the Matter, Forme and Power of a Commonwealth Ecclesiaticall and Civil*. Vol. 3 of *English Works*. Edited by William Molesworth. London: John Bohn, 1939. Reprint, Aalen: Scientia, 1966. Page references to the 1966 edition.

Hodge, Joanna. *Heidegger and Ethics*. New York: Routledge, 1995.

Holenstein, Elmar. *Phänomenologie der Assoziation: Zu Struktur und Funktion eines Grundprinzips der Passiven Genesis bei E. Husserl*. The Hague: Nijhoff, 1972.

Honore, Bernard. *Sens de la Formation. Sens de l'être. En chemin avec Heidegger*. Paris: L'Harmattan, 1990.

Hume, David. *A Treatise on Human Nature*. Oxford: Clarendon, 1964.

Husserl, Edmund. *The Crisis of European Sciences and Transcendental Phenomenology*. Translated by David Carr. Evanston, IL: Northwestern University Press, 1970.

Originally published as *Die Krisis der europäischen Wissenschaften und die transcendentale Phänomenologie*, edited by Walter Biemel. The Hague: Martinus Nijhoff, 1962.

- 'Erneuerung als individualethisches Problem.' 1924. In *Aufsätze und Vorträge*, edited by Thomas Nenon and Hans Rainer Sepp, 20–42. Husserliana XXVII. Dordrecht: Kluwer, 1989.
- 'Formale Typen der Kultur in der Menschenheitsentwicklung.' 1922–3. In *Aufsätze und Vorträge*, edited by Thomas Nenon and Hans Rainer Sepp, 59–94. Husserliana XXVII. Dordrecht: Kluwer, 1989.
- *Ideen zu einer reinen Phänomenologie und phänomenologischen Philosophie*. Vol. 1. Edited by Walter Biemel. Husserliana III. The Hague: Martinus Nijhoff, 1950.
- *Ideen zu einer reinen Phänomenologie und phänomenologischen Philosophie*. Vol. 3. Edited by Marly Biemel. Husserliana V. The Hague: Martinus Nijhoff, 1952.
- *Logical Investigations*. 2 vols. Translated by J.N. Findlay. London: Routledge and Kegan Paul, 1970.
- *Logische Untersuchungen*. 2nd ed. 2 vols. 1913–21. Tübingen: Max Niemeyer, 1968.
- *Philosophie der Arithmetik: Psychologische und logische Untersuchungen*. Edited by Lother Eley. Husserliana XII. The Hague: Martinus Nijhoff, 1970.

Iggers, Georg, G. *The German Conception of History: The National Tradition of Historical Thought from Herder to the Present*. Middleton, CT: Wesleyan University Press, 1968.

Jaensch, E.R. 'Zur Neugestaltung des deutschen Studententums und der Hochschule.' *Zeitschrift für angewandte Psychologie und Charakterkunde*. Suppl. no. 74. Leipzig: Barth, 1937.

Jelden, Helmut. 'Vom Raumgefühl im deutschen Menschen.' *Zeitschrift für Geopolitik* 16.1, no. 5 (1940): 201–7.

Johnstone, Christopher Lyle. 'An Aristotelian Trilogy: Ethics, Rhetoric, Politics, and the Search for Moral Truth.' *Philosophy and Rhetoric* 13, no. 1 (1980): 1–24.

Jung, C.G. 'Die Erdbedingtheit der Psyche.' *Der Leuchter: Weltanschauung und Lebensgestaltung* 8 (1927): 83–137.

Jung, Edgar J. *Die Herrschaft der Minderwertigen*. Berlin: Deutsche Rundschau, 1930.

Jünger, Ernst. *An der Zeitmauer*. Stuttgart: Klett, 1959.

- 'Der Arbeiter: Herrschaft und Gestalt.' 1932. In *Essays II: Der Arbeiter, Maxima-Minima, An der Zeitmauer*, 11–317. Vol. 8 of *Sämtliche Werke*. Stuttgart: Klett, 1981.
- 'Totale Mobilmachung.' In *Blätter und Steine*, 122–52. Leipzig: Tauchnitz, 1942.
- 'Über die Linie.' 1950. In *Essays I: Betrachtungen zur Zeit*, 39–279. Vol. 7 of *Sämtliche Werke*. Stuttgart: Klett, 1981.

– 'Über den Schmerz.' 1934. In *Essays I: Betrachtungen zur Zeit*, 145–91. Vol. 7 of *Sämtliche Werke*. Stuttgart: Klett, 1971.

Kahn, Charles H. *Anaximander and the Origins of Greek Cosmology*. Indianapolis: Hackett, 1994.

Kant, Immanuel. *Critique of Pure Reason*. Translated by Norman Kemp Smith. New York: St Martin's, 1965.

– *Kritik der Urtheilskraft*. Leipzig: Verlag der Dürr'schen Buchhandlung, 1897. Translated by J.H. Barnard as *The Critique of Judgement*. New York: Hofner, 1951.

Kapferer, Norbert. 'Diese Art von Philosophiedozenten ist unser Ruin: Zwei Gutachten Martin Heideggers aus den Jahren 1929/30.' www.nzz.ch/2001/09/08/li/page-article 7m1Yl.html

Kassner, Rudolf. *Das Physiognomische Weltbild*. Munich: Delphin-Verlag, 1933.

– *Zahl und Gesicht*. Leipzig: Insel, 1919.

Kervégan, Jean-François. *Hegel, Carl Schmitt: Le Politique entre speculation et positivité*. Paris: Presses Universitaires de France, 1992.

Kirk, G.S., trans., *Heraclitus. The Cosmic Fragments*. Cambridge: Cambridge University Press, 1954.

Kisiel, Theodore. *The Genesis of Heidegger's Being and Time*. Berkeley: University of California Press, 1993.

– 'Heidegger (1920–21) on Becoming a Christian: A Conceptual Picture Show.' In Kisiel and van Buren, *Reading Heidegger from the Start*, 175–94.

– 'Heidegger's Apology: Biography as Philosophy and Ideology.' In Rockmore and Margolis, *Heidegger Case*, 11–51.

Kisiel, Theodore, and John van Buren, eds. *Reading Heidegger from the Start*. Albany: SUNY Press, 1994.

Klaasen, Klaus. 'Die sozial-philosophischen Grundlagen des Nationalsozialismus.' *Deutsches Volkstum* 13, no. 2 (June 1932): 481–8.

Klages, Ludwig. *Mensch und Erde*. 1913. Jena: Eugen Diedericks, 1929.

Klemperer, Klaus von. *Germany's New Conservatism*. Princeton, NJ: Princeton University Press, 1968.

Köchler, Hans. 'Zur Frage der systematischen Wertung von Heideggers nationalsozialistischem Engagement.' In Margreiter and Leidlmair, *Heidegger*, 205–14.

Kockelmans, Joseph J. *Heidegger and Science*. Washington, DC: University Press of America, 1985.

– *Heidegger on Art and Artworks*. Dordrecht: Martinus Nijhoff, 1985.

Köhler, Wolfgang. *Gestalt Psychology*. 1929. New York: Liveright, 1947.

– *The Selected Papers of Wolfgang Köhler*. Edited by Mary Henle. New York: Liveright, 1971.

Koffka, K. *Principles of Gestalt Psychology*. 1935. Reprint, New York: Harcourt, Brace; London: Kegan Paul, 1963.

Koonz, Claudia. *The Nazi Conscience.* Cambridge, MA: Harvard University Press, 2003.

Kosman, Aryeh. 'The Activity of Being in Aristotle's *Metaphysics.*' In Scaltsas et al., *Unity, Identity, and Explanation,* 195–214.

Krämer, Hans Joachim. *Arete bei Platon und Aristoteles. Zum Wesen und Geschichte der platonischen Ontologie.* Heidelberg: Carl Winter, 1959.

Krell, David Farrell. *Daimon Life: Heidegger and Life-Philosophy.* Bloomington: Indiana University Press, 1992.

Krieck, Ernst. 'Allgemeinbildung und Technische Hochschule.' *Volk im Werden* 1, no. 3 (1933): 50–3.

– *Dichtung und Erziehung.* Leipzig: Armanen, 1933.

– 'Die Erneuerung der Universität.' Address on the acceptance of the rectorate, 23 May 1933. In *Frankfurter Akademische Reden* 5. Frankfurt am Main: Bechhold, 1933. Reprinted in Palmier, *Les Écrits politiques de Heidegger,* 315–31.

– 'Führertum und Hochschulreform.' *Volk im Werden* 2 (February 1937): 57–63.

– *Völkischer Gesamtstaat und nationale Erziehung.* Heidelberg: Bündischer Verlag, 1933.

– *Völkischpolitische Anthropologie.* 3 vols. Leipzig: Armanen, 1936–8.

– 'Wissenschaft als Gestalterin unseres völkischen Weges.' *Volk und Heimat: Monatsblatt des Landesverbandes für nationale Volkserziehung* 12, no. 8 (August 1936): 225–32.

– *Wissenschaft Weltanschauung Hochschulreform.* Leipzig: Armanen, 1934.

Lacoue-Labarthe, Philippe. *Heidegger, Art, and Politics: The Fiction of the Political.* Translated by Chris Turner. Oxford: Blackwell, 1990.

Lacoue-Labarthe, Philippe, and Jean-Luc Nancy. 'The Nazi Myth.' Translated by Brian Holmes. *Critical Inquiry* 16 (Winter 1990): 291–312.

Landow, George P. *Hypertext. The Convergence of Contemporary Critical Theory and Technology.* Baltimore: Johns Hopkins University Press, 1992.

Lane, Barbara Miller, and Leila Rupp. *Nazi Ideology before 1933: A Documentation.* Austin: University of Texas Press, 1978.

Langan, Thomas. *Merleau-Ponty's Critique of Reason.* New Haven, CT: Yale University Press, 1966.

Lee, Theresa Man Ling. *Politics and Truth: Political Theory and Postmodern Challenge.* New York: SUNY Press, 1997.

Leighton, Stephen R. 'Aristotle and the Emotions.' In Rorty, *Essays on Aristotle's Rhetoric,* 206–37.

Leopold, John A. *Alfred Hugenberg: The Radical Campaign against the Weimar Republic.* New Haven, CT: Yale University Press, 1977.

Lewin, Kurt. *A Dynamic Theory of Personality: Selected Papers.* Translated by Donald K. Adams and Karl E. Zener. London: McGraw-Hill, 1935.

Locke, John. *An Essay concerning Human Understanding. Works,* vols. 1–2: London, C.J. Rivington, 1823. Reprint, Aalen: Scientia, 1963.

– *Two Treatises of Civil Government.* 1690. London: Everyman's Library, 1966.

Löwith, Karl. *Martin Heidegger and European Nihilism.* Translated by Gary Steiner. New York: Columbia University Press, 1995.

Ludwig, Karl-Heinz. *Technik und Ingenieure im Dritten Reich.* Düsseldorf: Dröste, 1979.

Lutzhöft, Hans-Jürgen. *Der Nordische Gedanke in Deutschland 1920–1940.* Stuttgart: Klett, 1971.

Lyon, Marot L. 'Emotion and Embodiment: The Respiratory Mediation of Somatic and Social Processes.' In *Biocultural Approaches to the Emotions,* edited by Alexander Laban Hinton, 182–212. Cambridge: Cambridge University Press, 1999.

Lyotard, Jean-François. *The Postmodern Condition: A Report on Knowledge.* Translated by Geoff Bennington and Brian Massumi. Minneapolis: University of Minnesota Press, 1991.

Machiavelli, Niccolò. *The Prince.* Translated and edited by Robert M. Adams. New York: Norton, 1977.

Marassi, Massimo. 'The Hermeneutics of Rhetoric in Heidegger.' *Philosophy and Rhetoric* 19, no. 2 (1986): 79–98.

Margreiter, Reinhold, and Karl Leidlmair, eds. *Heidegger: Technik-Ethik-Politik.* Würzburg: Könighausen and Neumann. 1991.

Marx, Karl. *Economic and Philosophic Manuscripts of 1844.* Translated by Martin Milligan. Edited by Dirk J. Struik. New York: International Publishers, 1964.

Maschke, Günter. *Der Tod des Carl Schmitt: Apologie und Polemik.* Vienna: Karolinger, 1987.

Mauer, Reinhardt. 'Das eigentlich Anstößige in Heideggers Technikphilosophie.' In Margreiter and Leidlmair, *Heidegger,* 25–36.

McNeill, William. *The Glance of the Eye: Heidegger, Aristotle, and the Ends of Theory.* Albany: SUNY Press, 1999.

– '*Heimat*: Heidegger on the Threshold.' In Risser, *Heidegger toward the Turn,* 319–49.

– 'Spirit's Living Hand.' In D. Wood, *Of Derrida, Heidegger, and Spirit,* 103–17.

– 'The Time of *Contributions to Philosophy.*' In Scott et al., *Companion,* 129–49.

Merleau-Ponty, Maurice. *The Phenomenology of Perception.* Translated by Colin Smith. London: Routledge, 1962.

– *The Primacy of Perception.* Edited with an introduction by James M. Edie. Evanston: Northwestern University Press, 1964.

Mirvish, Adrian Michael. 'Merleau-Ponty and the Nature of Philosophy.' *Philosophy and Phenomenological Research* 43, no. 4 (June 1983): 449–76.

Mohler, Armin. *Die Konservative Revolution in Deutschland 1918–1932.* Darmstadt: Wissenschaftliche Buchgesellschaft, 1989.

Mongis, Henri. *Heidegger et la critique de la notion de valeur. La Destruction de la foundation metaphysique.* The Hague: Martinus Nijhoff, 1976.

Morris, Christopher W. *An Essay on the Modern State.* Cambridge: Cambridge University Press, 1998.

Mosse, George L. *The Crisis of German Ideology: Intellectual Origins of the Third Reich.* New York: Grosset & Dunlap, 1964.

– *Toward the Final Solution: A History of European Racism.* New York: Howard Fertig, 1978.

Murphy, David Thomas. *The Heroic Earth: Geopolitical Thought in Weimar Germany, 1918–1933.* Kent, OH: Kent State University Press, 1997.

Nadler, Josef. *Das Stammhafte Gefüge des Deutschen Volkes.* Munich: Josef Roesel, 1934.

Naumann, Friedrich. *Mitteleuropa.* Berlin: Georg Reimer, 1915.

Neaman, Elliot Y. *A Dubious Past: Ernst Jünger and the Politics of Literature after Nazism.* Berkeley: University of California Press, 1999.

Neske, G., and E. Kettering, eds. *Martin Heidegger and National Socialism.* New York: Paragon, 1990.

Nicosia, Francis R. *The Third Reich and the Palestine Question.* Austin: University of Texas Press, 1985.

Niekisch, Ernst. *Hitler: Ein deutsches Verhängnis.* Berlin: Widerstandsverlag, 1932.

Nietzsche, Friedrich. *On the Advantage and Disadvantage of History for Life.* Translated by Peter Preuss. Indianapolis: Hackett, 1980. Originally published as 'Vom Nutzen und Nachteil der Historie für das Leben,' *Unzeitgemässe Betrachtungen I–III. Werke,* vol. 3/1. 1874. Berlin: de Gruyter, 1972.

– *Der Wille zur Macht.* Stuttgart: Kröner, 1964.

Noakes, J., and G. Pridham, eds. *Nazism 1919–1945: A History in Documents and Eyewitness Accounts.* Vol. 1, *The Nazi Party, State and Society, 1919–1939.* New York: Schocken Books, 1984.

Nussbaum, Martha Craven. 'Aristotle on Emotions and Rational Persuasion.' In Rorty, *Essays on Aristotle's Rhetoric,* 303–23.

Oakeshott, Michael. *On Human Conduct.* Oxford: Clarendon, 1975.

Offe, Hans. 'Geopolitik und Naturrecht.' *Zeitschrift für Geopolitik* 14.1, no. 3 (1937): 239–46.

Okrent, Mark B. 'The Truth of Being and the History of Philosophy.' In Dreyfus and Hall, *Heidegger,* 143–58.

Ott, Hugo. *Martin Heidegger: A Political Life.* Translated by Allen Blunden. New York: Basic Books, 1993.

Øverenget, Einar. *Seeing the Self: Heidegger on Subjectivity.* Dordrecht: Kluwer, 1998.

Paine, Thomas. *The Rights of Man*. Edited by Henry Collins. Harmondsworth: Penguin, 1971.

Palmier, Jean-Michel. *Les Écrits politiques de Heidegger*. Paris: L'Herne, 1968.

Pangle, Thomas L. *The Spirit of American Republicanism: The Moral Vision of the American Founders and the Philosophy of Locke*. Chicago: University of Chicago Press, 1988.

Papenfuss, Dietrich, and Otto Pöggler, eds. *Zur Philosophischen Aktualität Heideggers*. Symposium of the Alexander von Humboldt Foundation, Bonn-Bad Godesberg, 24–8 April 1989. Vol. 1, *Philosophie und Politik*. Frankfurt am Main: Klostermann, 1991.

Perelman, Chaim. 'Rhetoric and Politics.' *Philosophy and Rhetoric* 17, no. 3 (1984): 129–34.

Petzet, Heinrich Wiegand. *Encounters and Dialogues with Martin Heidegger: 1929–1976*. Translated by Parvis Emad and Kenneth Maly. Introduction by Parvis Emad. Chicago: University of Chicago Press, 1993.

Philipse, Hermann. *Heidegger's Philosophy of Being: A Critical Interpretation*. Princeton, NJ: Princeton University Press, 1998.

Piccone, Paul. Editor's note to Heidegger, 'Heidegger and Schmitt.' *Telos* 72 (Summer 1987): 132.

Piccone, Paul, Paul Gottfried, and Gary Ulmen. 'Ostracizing Carl Schmitt: Letters to *The New York Review of Books*.' *Telos* 109 (Fall 1996): 87–91.

Plamenatz, John. 'In Search of Machiavellian *Virtù*.' In *The Political Calculus*, edited by Anthony Parel, 157–78. Toronto: University of Toronto Press, 1972.

Plato. *Phaedrus*. In *Euthyhro, Apology, Crito, Phaedo, Phaedrus*. Translated by Harold North Fowler. Loeb Classical Library. Cambridge, MA: Harvard University Press, 1953.

– *Politeia*. Vol. 5 of *Sämtliche Werke*. Translated by Friedrich Schleiermacher, supplemented by Franz Susemihl. Edited by Karlheinz Hülser. Frankfurt am Main: Insel, 1991.

– *Republic*. Translated by Paul Story. In *Collected Dialogues*, edited by Edith Hamilton and Huntington Cairns, 575–844. Princeton, NJ: Bollingen, 1963.

– *Theaetetus and Sophist*. Translated by Harold North Fowler. Loeb Classical Library. Cambridge, MA: Harvard University Press, 1952.

Pöggeler, Otto. *Philosophie und Nationalsozialismus – Am Beispiel Heideggers*. Opladen: Westdeutscher Verlag, 1990.

– *Philosophie und Politik bei Heidegger*. Freiburg im Breisgau: Karl Alber, 1972.

Polt, Richard. *Heidegger: An Introduction*. Ithaca, NY: Cornell University Press, 1999.

– 'Metaphysical Liberalism in Heidegger's *Beiträge zur Philosophie*.' *Political Theory* 25, no. 5 (1997): 620–79.

Polt, Richard, and Gregory Fried, eds. *A Companion to Heidegger's* Introduction to Metaphysics. New Haven, CT: Yale University Press, 2001.

Pye, Christopher. 'The Sovereign, the Theater, and the Kingdome of Darknesse: Hobbes and the Spectacle of Power.' *Representations* 8 (Fall 1984): 85–106.

Radloff, Bernhard. 'Foucault's Genealogy of Modernity and the Logic of *Erlebnis.*' *Existentia* 15 (2005): 273–93.

– '*Das Gestell* and *L'Écriture.* The Discourse of Expropriation in Heidegger and Derrida.' *Heidegger Studies* 5 (1989): 23–46.

– 'The Total Mobilization of Art: Derrida's Deconstruction of Heidegger's "The Origin of the Work of Art."' *Existentia* 14 (2004): 231–60.

– 'The Value of Availability in Literary Studies.' *Philosophy Today* 36, no. 2 (Summer 1992): 146–60.

Raschke, Martin. 'Bemerkungen zum deutschen Tanz.' *Europäische Revue* 12 (June 1936): 417–19.

Reeve, C.D.C. 'Philosophy, Politics and Rhetoric in Aristotle.' In Rorty, *Essays on Aristotle's* Rhetoric, 191–205.

– *Practices of Reason. Aristotle's* Nicomachean Ethics. Oxford: Clarendon, 1992.

Reichsnaturschutzgesetz. In *Reichsgesetzblatt.* Berlin, 1 July 1935. Pt 1, no. 68: 821–5.

Renneberg, Monika, and Mark Walker, eds. *Science, Technology and National Socialism.* Cambridge: Cambridge University Press, 1994.

Rickey, Christopher. *Revolutionary Saints: Heidegger, National Socialism and Antinomian Politics.* University Park: Pennsylvania State University Press, 2002.

Rigg, Bryan Mark. *Hitler's Jewish Soldiers.* Lawrence: University of Kansas Press, 2002.

Risser, James, ed. *Heidegger toward the Turn: Essays on the Work of the 1930s.* Albany: SUNY Press, 1999.

Rivera, Joseph de, ed. *Field Theory in Human Science: Contributions of Lewin's Berlin Group.* New York: Gardner, 1976.

Rockmore, Tom. *On Heidegger's Nazism and Philosophy.* Berkeley: University of California Press, 1992.

Rockmore, Tom, and Joseph Margolis. *The Heidegger Case: On Philosophy and Politics.* Philadelphia: Temple University Press, 1992.

Rorty, Emelie Oksenberg, ed. *Essays on Aristotle's* Rhetoric. Berkeley: University of California Press, 1996.

Rosenberg, Alfred. *Der Mythos des 20. Jahrhunderts.* Munich: Hoheneichen, 1939.

Rother, Ralf. *Wie die Entscheidung Lesen? Zu Platon, Heidegger und Carl Schmitt.* Vienna: Turia und Kant, 1993.

Ruttke, Dr. 'Recht und Recht im deutschen Hochschulwesen.' In *Recht und Rechtwahrer.* Berlin: Kohlhammer, 1936.

Ryan, Alan. 'Hobbes's Political Philosophy.' In *The Cambridge Companion to Hob-*

bes, edited by Tom Sorell, 208–45. Cambridge: Cambridge University Press, 1996.

Sagan, Carl. *Pale Blue Dot: A Vision of the Human Future in Space*. New York: Random House, 1994.

Sallis, John, ed. *Reading Heidegger: Commemorations*. Bloomington: Indiana University Press, 1993.

– 'Flight of Spirit.' In Wood, *Of Derrida, Heidegger, and Spirit*, 118–32.

Scaltsas, T., D. Charles, and M.L. Gill, eds. *Unity, Identity, and Explanation in Aristotle's* Metaphysics. Oxford: Clarendon, 1994.

Schalow, Frank. *The Renewal of the Heidegger-Kant Dialogue: Action, Thought and Responsibility*. Albany: SUNY Press, 1992.

– 'A Question Concerning Heidegger's Involvement in National Socialism.' *Journal of the British Society for Phenomenology* 24, no. 2 (May 1993): 121–39.

– 'At the Crossroads of Freedom: Ethics without Values.' In Polt and Fried, *A Companion*, 250–62.

Schelling, Friedrich W. *Philosophische Untersuchungen über das Wesen der menschlichen Freiheit und die damit zusammenhängenden Gegenstände*. 1809. In *Werke*, vol. 4, edited by Manfred Schröter, 223–308. Munich: Beck'ische Verlagsbuchhandlung, 1965.

Schlösser, Rainer. *Das Volk und seine Bühne: Bemerkungen zum Aufbau des deutschen Theaters*. Berlin: Georg Müller, 1935.

Schmidt-Rohr, Georg. 'Die Sprache als politische Grösse im Kraftfeld der Staaten.' *Zeitschrift für Geopolitik* 10, no. 4 (1933): 247–53.

Schmitt, Carl. *Der Begriff des Politischen*. Hamburg: Hanseatische Verlagsanstalt, 1933.

– *Ex Captivitate Salus: Erfahrungen der Zeit 1945/47*. Cologne: Grever, 1950.

– *The Concept of the Political*. 1932. Translated by George Schwab. Commentary by Leo Strauss. New Brunswick, NJ: Rutger's University Press, 1976.

– 'Landschaft und Geschichte.' *Zeitschrift für Geopolitik* 11.2, no. 9 (1934): 580–5.

– *Der Leviathan in der Staatslehre des Thomas Hobbes*. 1938. Cologne: Hohenheim, 1982.

– *Der Nomos der Erde im Volkerrecht des Jus Publicum Europaecum*. 1950. Berlin: Duncker & Humblot, 1974.

– *Politische Romantik*. Munich: Duncker & Humblot, 1925.

– *Politische Theologie*. Berlin: Duncker & Humblot, 1934.

– *Römischer Katholizismus und politische Form*. Munich: Theatiner, 1925.

– *Theorie des Partisanen. Zwischenbetrachung zum Begriff des Politischen*. Berlin: Duncker & Humblot, 1963.

– *Staat, Bewegung, Volk*. Hamburg: Hanseatische Verlagsanstalt, 1933.

– *Über die drei Arten des rechtswissenschaftlichen Denkens*. Hamburg: Hanseatische Verlagsanstalt, 1934.

– *Verfassungslehre.* 1928. Berlin: Duncker & Humblot, 1965.

Schmitz, Mathias. *Die Freund-Feind-Theorie Carl Schmitts: Entwurf und Entfaltung.* Cologne: Westdeutscher Verlag, 1965.

Schnapper, Dominique. 'Beyond the Opposition: Civic Nation versus Ethnic Nation.' In *Rethinking Nationalism*, edited by Jocelyne Couture, Kai Nelson, and Michel Seymour. Calgary: University of Calgary Press, 1998.

Schneeberger, Guido. *Nachlese zu Heidegger: Dokumente zu seine Leben und Denken.* Bern: private edition, 1962.

Schoenbohm, Susan. 'Heidegger's Interpretation of *Phusis* in *Introduction to Metaphysics.*' In Polt and Fried, *A Companion*, 143–60.

Schoenichen, Walther. *Naturschutz als völkische und internationale Kulturaufgabe.* Jena: Gustav Fischer, 1942.

– *Naturschutz im Dritten Reich: Einführung im Wesen und Grundlagen zeitgemäßer Naturschutz-Arbeit.* Berlin: Hugo Bermühler, 1934.

Schrag, Calvin O. *Experience and Being: Prolegomena to a Future Ontology.* Evanston, IL: Northwestern University Press, 1969.

Schultze-Naumberg, Paul. *Kunst und Rasse.* Munich: Lehmanns, 1935.

– 'Rassengebundene Kunst.' In *Volk und Wissen,* vol. 13. Erfurt: Kurt Stenger, n.d.

Schürmann, Reiner. *Heidegger on Being and Acting: From Principles to Anarchy.* Translated by Christine-Marie Gros, in collaboration with the author. Bloomington: Indiana University Press, 1987.

– 'The Ontological Difference and Political Philosophy.' *Philosophy and Phenomenological Research* 40, no. 1 (September 1979): 99–122.

– 'Political Thinking in Heidegger.' *Social Research* vol. 45.1 (Spring 1978): 191–221.

– 'Riveted to a Monstrous Site: On Heidegger's *Beiträge zur Philosophie.*' In Rockmore and Margolis, *Heidegger Case,* 313–30.

– 'Symbolic Difference.' *Graduate Faculty Philosophy Journal* 19, no. 2 (1997): 9–38.

– 'Symbolic Praxis.' *Graduate Faculty Philosophy Journal* 19, no. 2 (1997): 39–65.

Schütrumpf, Eckart. *Die Bedeutung des Wortes* ethos *in der Poetik des Aristoteles.* Munich: Beck'sche Verlagsbuchhandlung, 1970.

Schwab, George. *The Challenge of the Exception: An Introduction to the Political Ideas of Carl Schmitt between 1921 and 1936.* Berlin: Duncker & Humblot, 1970.

Schwan, Alexander. *Politische Philosophie im Denken Heideggers.* Opladen: Westdeutsche Verlag, 1989.

– 'Zeitkritik und Politik bei Heideggers Spätphilosophie.' In *Heideggers Praktische Philosophie,* edited by Annemarie Gethmann-Siefert and Otto Pöggler. Frankfurt am Main: Suhrkamp, 1988.

Schwarz, Hans Peter. *Der konservative Anarchist: Politik und Zeitkritik Ernst Jüngers.* Freiburg im Breisgau: Rombach, 1962.

Scott, Charles E., Susan M. Schoenbohm, Daniela Vallega-Neu, and Alejandro Vallega., eds. *Companion to Heidegger's* Contributions to Philosophy. Bloomington: Indiana University Press, 2001.

Sikka, Sonya. 'The Philosophical Bases of Heidegger's Politics: A Response to Wolin.' *Journal of the British Society for Phenomenology* 25, no. 3 (1994): 241–62.

Sluga, Hans. *Heidegger's Crisis: Philosophy and Politics in Nazi Germany.* Cambridge, MA: Harvard University Press, 1993.

Smith, Barry, ed. *Foundations of Gestalt Theory.* Vienna: Philosophia, 1988.

Smith, Roger. *Inhibition: History and Meaning in the Sciences of Mind and Brain.* Berkeley: University of California Press, 1992.

Sontheimer, Kurt. *Antidemokratisches Denken in der Weimarer Republik.* Munich: Nymphenburger, 1964.

Sorell, Walter. *Mary Wigman. Ein Vermächtnis.* Wilhelmshaven: Florian Noetzel, 1986.

Spengler, Oswald. *The Decline of the West.* 1928. 2 vols. Translated by Charles Francis Atkinson. New York: Knopf, 1980.

Spinosa, Charles. 'Derrida and Heidegger: Iterability and *Ereignis.*' In Dreyfus and Hall, *Heidegger,* 270–97.

Spotts, Frederic. *Hitler and the Power of Aesthetics.* Woodstock, NY: Overlook, 2003.

Stambaugh, Joan. *The Finitude of Being.* Albany: SUNY Press, 1992.

Steinweis, Alan E. *Art, Ideology, and Economics in Nazi Germany: The Reich Chambers of Music, Theatre, and the Visual Arts.* Chapel Hill: University of North Carolina Press, 1993.

Stephenson, R.H. *Goethe's Conception of Knowledge and Science.* Edinburgh: Edinburgh University Press, 1995.

Stobbe, Stefan G. 'Die Bildersprache des "Deutschen Volkstums": Eine Studie zur national-völkischen Metaphorik.' PhD dissertation, Philipps-Universität, Marburg an der Lahn, 1988.

Stodte, Hermann. *Die Wegbereiter des Nationalsozialismus.* Lübeck, 1935.

Stumpfl, Robert. *Unser Kampf um ein deutsches Nationaltheater.* Berlin: Junker und Dünnhaupt, 1935.

Szaz, Thomas. *The Theology of Medicine: The Political-Philosophical Foundations of Medical Ethics.* Baton Rouge: Louisiana State University Press, 1977.

Talmon, J.L. *The Origins of Totalitarian Democracy.* New York: Praeger, 1965.

Taminiaux, Jacques. *Heidegger and the Project of Fundamental Ontology.* Translated and edited by Michael Gendre. New York: SUNY Press, 1991.

– 'Heidegger on Values.' In Risser, *Heidegger Toward the Turn,* 225–39.

– 'The Origin of "The Origin of the Work of Art."' In Sallis, *Reading Heidegger,* 392–404.

Tertulian, Nicolas. 'The History of Being and Political Revolution: Reflections on a Posthumous Work of Heidegger.' In Rockmore and Margolis, *Heidegger Case*, 208–30.

Tertullian, Q.S. *De Spectaculis.* Translated by T.R. Glover. London: Heinemann, 1931.

Tiemersma, D. 'Merleau-Ponty's Philosophy as Field Theory: Its Origin, Categories and Relevance.' *Man and World* 20 (1987): 419–36.

Thiele, Paul Leslie. 'Heidegger on Freedom: Political not Metaphysical.' *The American Political Science Review* 88, no. 2 (June 1994): 278–91.

– *Timely Meditations: Martin Heidegger and Postmodern Politics.* Princeton, NJ: Princeton University Press, 1995.

Tocqueville, Alexis de. *Democracy in America.* 2 vols. Translated by Henry Reeve. New York: Random House, 1990.

Uexküll, Jakob von. *Theoretische Biologie.* 2nd ed. Berlin: Julius Springer, 1928.

– *Umwelt und Innenwelt der Tiere.* 2nd expanded and revised ed. Berlin: Julius Springer, 1921.

Ulman. G.L. 'Return of the *Foe.*' *Telos* 72 (Summer 1987): 187–93.

– 'Toward a New World Order: Introduction to Schmitt.' *Telos* 109 (Fall 1996): 3–28.

Vallega-Neu, Daniella. *Heidegger's* Contributions to Philosophy: *An Introduction.* Bloomington: Indiana University Press, 2003.

van Buren, John. 'Martin Heidegger, Martin Luther.' In Kisiel and van Buren, *Reading Heidegger from the Start,* 159–74.

– 'The Young Heidegger, Aristotle, Ethics.' In Dallery et al., *Ethics and Danger,* 169–86.

– *The Young Heidegger: Rumor of the Hidden King.* Bloomington: Indiana University Press, 1994.

van den Bruck, Moeller. *Das Dritte Reich.* 1922. Hamburg: Hanseatische Verlagsanstalt, 1931. Translated by E.M. Lorimer as *Germany's Third Empire.* 1934. New York: Howard Fertig, 1971.

van Eynde, Laurent. *La libre Raison du phénomène: Essai sur la 'Naturphilosophie' de Goethe.* Paris: Vrin, 1998.

Vetter, Helmuth. 'Anmerkungen zum Begriff des Volkes bei Heidegger.' In Margreiter and Leidlmair, *Heidegger,* 239–48.

Vietta, Egon. *Der Tanz: Eine Kleine Metaphysik.* Frankfurt am Main: Societäts-Verlag, 1938.

Volpi, Franco. '*Being and Time:* A "Translation" of the *Nicomachean Ethics?*' Translated by John Protevi. In Kisiel and van Buren, *Reading Heidegger from the Start,* 195–212.

Vondung, Klaus. *Magie und Manipulation: Ideologischer Kult und Politische Religion des Nationalsozialismus.* Göttingen: Vandenhoeck & Ruprecht, 1971.

von Ehrenfels, Christian. 'Gestalt Level and Gestalt Purity.' In B. Smith, *Foundations of Gestalt Theory,* 118–20.

– 'On "Gestalt Qualities."' 1890. In B. Smith, *Foundations of Gestalt Theory,* 82–117.

– 'On Gestalt Qualities.' 1932. In B. Smith, *Foundations of Gestalt Theory,* 121–3.

von Herrmann, Friedrich-Wilhelm. '*Contributions to Philosophy* and Enowning-Historical Thinking.' In Scott et al., *Companion,* 105–26.

– 'Das Ereignis und die Fragen nach dem Wesen der Technik, Politik und Kunst.' In *Kunst-Politik-Technik,* edited by Christoph Jamme and Karsten Harries. Munich: Wilhelm Fink, 1992.

– *Heideggers Philosophie der Kunst.* Frankfurt am Main: Klostermann, 1980.

von Hofmannsthal, Hugo. 'Das Schrifttum als geistiger Raum der Nation.' In *Prosa,* 390–413. Vol. 4 of *Gesammelte Werke.* Frankfurt am Main: Fischer, 1955.

von Schirach, Baldur. *Die Hitler-Jugend. Idee und Gestalt.* Leipzig: Koehler & Umelang, 1934.

von See, Klaus. *Barbar Germane Arier: Die Suche nach der Identität der Deutschen.* Heidelberg: C. Winter, 1994.

Vowinkel, Kurt. 'Der zweite Reichsbauerntag in Goslar.' *Zeitschrift für Geopolitik* 11.2, no. 12 (1934): 758–64.

– 'Zum Begriff Lebensraum.' *Zeitschrift für Geopolitik* 16.2, nos. 8–9 (1939): 638–9.

Waldenfels, Bernhard. 'The Despised Doxa: Husserl and the Continuing Crisis of Western Reason.' *Research in Phenomenology* 12·(1982): 21–38.

Ward, James F. *Heidegger's Political Thinking.* Amherst: University of Massachusetts Press, 1995.

Weinreich, Max. *Hitler's Professors.* New York: Yivo, 1946.

Wertheimer, M. 'Untersuchungen zur Lehre von der Gestalt, II.' *Psychologische Forschungen* 4 (1923): 301–89.

Whitney, Charles. *Francis Bacon and Modernity.* New Haven, CT: Yale University Press, 1986.

Wigman, Mary. *Deutsche Tanzkunst.* Dresden: Carl Reissner, 1935.

– 'Der Tänzer und sein Instrument.' *Der Kreis: Zeitschrift für künstlerische Kultur* 9, no. 12 (December 1932): 673–6.

Winfield, Richard Dean. *Freedom and Modernity.* New York: SUNY Press, 1991.

Winner, Langdon. *Autonomous Technology.* Cambridge, MA: MIT Press, 1977.

Wolin, Richard. *The Politics of Being: The Political Thought of Martin Heidegger.* New York: Columbia University Press, 1990.

Wood, David, ed. *Of Derrida, Heidegger, and Spirit.* Evanston, IL: Northwestern University Press, 1993.

Wood, Neal. *The Politics of Locke's Philosophy.* Berkeley: University of California Press, 1983.

Woods, Roger. *The Conservative Revolution in the Weimar Republic.* New York: St Martin's, 1996.

Wörner, Markus H. *Das Ethische in der* Rhetorik *des Aristoteles.* Munich: Karl Alber, 1990.

Young, Julian. *Heidegger, Philosophy, Nazism.* Cambridge: Cambridge University Press, 1997.

Zeller, Eduard. *Die Philosophie der Greichen in ihrer Geschichtlichen Entwicklung.* Vol. 1, pt 2, *Allgemeine Einleitung und Vorsokratische Philosophie.* 1920. Reprint, Hildesheim: Georg Ohms, 1963.

Ziegler, Leopold. *Der europäische Geist.* Darmstadt: Otto Reichl, 1929.

– *Fünfundzwanzig Sätze vom Deutschen Staat.* Darmstadt: Otto Reichl, 1931.

Zimmerman, Michael E. *Heidegger's Confrontation with Modernity: Technology, Politics, and Art.* Bloomington: Indiana University Press, 1990.

– 'Ontological Aestheticism: Heidegger, Jünger, and National Socialism.' In Rockmore and Margolis, *Heidegger Case,* 52–89.

– 'The Ontological Decline of the West.' In Polt and Fried, *A Companion,* 185–204.

Index

abandonment of beings (*Seinsverlassenheit*), 5, 34, 46, 50–9, 93, 172, 213, 221–9, 240, 313, 317, 320, 354, 367, 388–9, 404, 425; and metaphysics, 51, 213; and representation, 38, 45, 298, 386; and technology, essence of, 50, 297–303; and Volk, 302–3

aletheia (unconcealment), 37, 45–6, 57, 60, 86, 91, 107, 111, 148, 151, 187, 194, 198, 205, 211, 218, 220–1, 231–6, 243, 246–8, 252, 254, 276, 281, 283, 343–53, 354B5, 362–7, 387, 393–5; and artwork, secs. 7.3.1, 7.3.4; and differentiation of being, 291–5; and founding, sec. 7.1.4; and freedom, 399–410; and the image, truth of, sec. 7.2.3; and *lethe*, 11, 151, 293, 317; and rhetoric, 67–79; and *polemos*, 286–90; and sheltering unconcealment, secs. 7.1.2, 7.2.2; and *veritas*, 411–27. *See also* truth; *veritas*

Antigone (Sophocles), 153, 213, 215, 231–51

anxiety, 74, 79, 84, 150–3, 181, 219, 240, 299–301, 405

arche: and *dunamis*, 102–3; and limit (*peras*), 43, 106, 287; in metaphysics, 51, 100, 249, 293, 349–50, 365; and movement of unfolding, 24, 27, 43, 65, 92, sec. 7.3.3.1; and *phusis*, sec. 7.3.3.7; and *polemos*, 286–7; and style, 365–6; and Volk; 100, 108–10

arete, 67, 103, 414

Aristoteles, Metaphysik Theta 1–3 (Heidegger), 32, 65, 99, 102–9, 337

Aristotle, 11, 13, 22, 27, 30, 32, 43, 47, 49, 51, 88, 151, 166, 170–1, 192, 226, 246, 265, 314, 334–7, 340, 345–58, 361, 365–6, 371, 377, 381, 393, 422; and Heidegger's interpretation of Volk and science, secs. 3.1.1, 3.1.2; *Metaphysics*, 102–4; *Nicomachean Ethics*, 64, 67, 70; *Rhetoric*, 63–72, 109; and rhetoric, sec. 2.1; and *phusis*, sec. 7.3.3; *Physics*, 30, 43, 205, 345–6, 357, 365, 381, 393

artwork, secs. 7.2, 7.3; and community, 62, 289, 317–19, 334–5, sec. 7.2.1; and earth and world, 11, 205, 319, 334, sec. 7.3.4; and gestalt, 9–11, 16, 30–1, 44, 314, 319, 328, 337,